Karl F. Morrison

THE MIMETIC
TRADITION OF REFORM
IN THE WEST

PRINCETON UNIVERSITY PRESS
PRINCETON, NEW JERSEY

For

A.D.M.   S.C.M.   J.C.B.   D.B.F.   M.B.F.

Mirst gesehen als eime kindelîne,
daz sîn schônez bilde in eime glase gesach
unde greif dar nâch sîn selbes schîne
sô vil biz daz ez den spiegel gar zerbrach;
dô wart al sîn wunne win leitlîch ungemach.

Heinrich von Morungen (in F. Vogt, ed., *Des Minnesangs Frühling,* 5th ed. [Leipzig: Hirzel, 1930]: XVIII, 145, p. 164. On Heinrich's French prototype, see L. Vinge, *The Narcissus Theme in Western European Literature up to the Early 19th Century.* [Lund: Gleerups, 1967], pp. 67 f.)

Contents

Contents

Preface

EVERY TRADITION contains mechanisms of change. The survival and vitality of a tradition depend on its ability to adapt to new conditions and, as time goes on, to embrace widely divergent, indeed contradictory, teachings and ways of life. A tradition that merely repeats its dogmas, regardless of the ever-changing world around it, is dead.

The present essay is about one adaptive mechanism in the Western religious and philosophical tradition. To adapt is to mediate between past and future, not to attempt a fundamental break with the past. To adapt is to harmonize experience that is over and done with, growing more and more distant and alien, with experience that extends, alters, and, in some sense, completes the past. As it encounters new conditions, a tradition finds itself reaching toward the wholeness of life that it had always promised. It repeats, or imitates, the old ways. But, to keep them alive, it must also reform them.

In the Western tradition, reform was clearly understood to be part of imitation. If we contrast imitation with originality, it is only because we have stopped thinking that good imitation must be continual invention, as it was, for example, when Bach imitated Vivaldi. From antiquity until the nineteenth century, however, a distinction was drawn between bad imitation, which *did* amount to sterile repetition of old forms (the sort of repetition, as the Roman poet, Horace, wrote, that even cows could do), and good imitation, which cut through to the very heart of the creative process. As an adaptive mechanism, good imitation made it possible to think of mediation between outdated experience (or forms of art) and new demands and opportunities. This was so because good imitation did not concern itself with fixed styles in art or fossilized dogmas in religion or philosophy but with principles and ways of thinking by which people developed formal styles and dogmas. It concerned itself with theory. Therefore, because of its demand for continual invention, the concept of good imitation contained a hard core of criticism. In the arts of thought and expression, the West embraced self-critical imitation as a means of change for the better.

Clearly, these assumptions exclude two familiar stylistic definitions of mimesis: classicism (the imitation of ancient styles) and naturalism (the imitation of the visual world). Illustrations from poetry and painting may clarify the distinction within the Western tradition between imitation in style and in art.

One might expect Sir Philip Sidney, who embodied so many values of Renaissance culture, to deliver a staunch argument for classicism. And yet, in his *Apologie for Poetrie,* he did just the opposite. His main contention was that, in England, poets no longer served the purpose of their art: namely, moral edification. Four elements, he wrote, converged when any poem was written: artificer, art, imitation, and the actual writing, or "exercise." Poets abused both art and imitation because they worked retrospectively, practicing what was already known, instead of what might yet be known. By their mere repetitiveness, they had become "poet-apes, not poets." They confused art with particular works of art. The key to correct understanding was imitation. True poets, Sidney explained, did not follow "artificial rules or imitative patterns." They did not repeat what was already evident. Borrowing "nothing of what is, hath been, or shall be, [they] range, only reined with learned discretion, into the divine consideration of what may and should be." Sidney identified the stages of the process that ensued, a reciprocal process in which the poets "make to imitate" and their readers answer by imitating the sublime goodness toward which the poets had moved them. Poetic imitation had nothing to do with the perpetuation of individual style; it was a manifestation of divine fury and an opening of sacred mysteries.[1]

Pursuing the vital distinction between art and works of art, Sidney perceived that, in art, questions, not answers, were eternal. Even the most refined philosophical formulations, and the most inspired spiritual utterances, were inadequate to explain the great issues of life. In the twentieth century, we are used to thinking in terms of "problems." Problems, by definition, have solutions. Any particular work of art can be thought of as a solved problem. But eternal questions are insoluble enigmas. This emphasis on enigma spilled over from philosophy into theories about art. It was possible to think of poetry (not individual poems) as more than a tactical solution to a technical problem. One

---

[1] J. Charlton Collins, ed., *Sidney's Apologie for Poetrie* (Oxford, 1929), pp. 11, 22, 50, 61f. For antecedents of Sidney's metaphor, poet-apes, see Ernst Robert Curtius, *European Literature and the Latin Middle Ages,* trans. Willard R. Trask (New York, 1963), pp. 538–540. See also Robert Lowell's comments on another mimetic art, translation. Lowell contrasted those who advocate free "poetic translation" (including himself) with "strict metrical translators," who "are taxidermists, not poets, and their poems are likely to be stuffed birds." *Imitations* (New York, 1978), pp. ixf.

could think of it also as an exercise in deeper intellectual strategies, strategies of thinking about representation that operated in many arts. For all representational arts demanded recognition, an association of ideas; all were instruments of delight and instruction. The long career of painting illustrates the same conclusion.

A very old and continuously held theory of art has steadfastly rated the depictive functions of painting lower than the evocative. This theory was held even during periods of extreme visual realism in painting and sculpture, and its history illustrates that, as in poetry, both classicism and naturalism are red herrings for a cultural definition of mimesis. It fails to distinguish the solved problems in individual works of art from the insoluble enigmas of art. Let us consider classicism.

Whether in the Roman imitation of Greek art, or in the Renaissance imitations of Hellenistic or Roman remains, artists relished the delight of forgery, but they—and philosophers who reflected on art—were also aware of objectives that carried imitation beyond counterfeiting. They knew perfectly well that imitation was a means of change. In antiquity, as in the Renaissance, it was usual "with copies after earlier prototypes" for artists to "update the style [and] also [to] introduce certain revealing alterations."[2] What distinguished true from servile imitation was precisely that it went beyond virtuosity in lowly skills of manual labor to intellectual, or spiritual, understanding.

The perfection made visible in a masterpiece was the universal source of harmony, a truth in which the good and the beautiful were identical. Copyists who precisely reproduced exemplary works were always rated "servile" imitators, hardly rising above cattle, except in manual dexterity. The true artist imitated masterpieces for the same reason as he imitated nature: to surpass them. It was not the masterpiece that artists imitated but the rules (or standards) of order expressed in the work, rules by which the masterpiece itself was to be criticized and its defects exposed. Art, like nature, always strove for perfection, and always fell short of it. Every failure generated new attempts, new paradoxes.

Likewise, in the eighteenth century, Sir Joshua Reynolds and Johann Winckelmann praised imitation of ancient art for specifically moral reasons. Through imitation, they held, modern artists indirectly established contact with and conveyed the universal virtues that Greeks and Romans had directly visualized and encapsulated in their works, those virtues that, expressed visibly in art, had elevated classi-

[2] A. Heimann, review, *Burlington Magazine* 119 (1977):779.

cal antiquity above the self-destructive anarchy of barbarism. Of course, Reynolds and Winckelmann were repeating ideas known in antiquity itself and often invoked during the Renaissance. Classicism, therefore, does not exhaust the concept of mimesis.

The same can be said of naturalism. Let us take an example that time has removed from the heat of the moment. Edward Gibbon enjoyed the story about a Greek priest who commissioned pictures from Titian and then declined to accept them because of their three-dimensionality. In his "ignorance and bigotry," the scandalized priest is supposed to have exclaimed that Titian's figures were "as bad as a group of statues." For his part, Gibbon saw nothing but "the last degeneracy of taste and genius" in the icons that "monkish artists" painted in what he regarded as a flat (i.e., two-dimensional) style.[3] And yet, the entire rationale of icon painting, from John of Damascus (ca. 700 - ca. 754) to the present day, has been grounded in an intricately developed strategy of mimesis, one that, in fact, drew ultimately on the same currents of ancient philosophy as did the aesthetic doctrines of Titian and his contemporaries.

Taking the history of Western art as a whole, one could advance an even more fundamental argument. One could hold that mimesis had nothing to do with the classicism or naturalism of a given picture. Mimesis was in the operations of the beholder's mind, even in the thinking of the artist as beholder, and not in the picture at all. The mind imposes meaning on the picture before it[4]; it may invest the painting with representational values that others cannot detect. Many styles have served the same exercise by which the mind invents an equivalence between a painting and an absent (and perhaps nonexistent) subject. Thus Plato looked to the stiff, hieratic art of Egypt whose style, he thought, had deliberately been kept the same for ten thousand years

[3] Edward Gibbon, *Decline and Fall of the Roman Empire* (New York, n.d.), vol. 3, chap. 49, n. 14.

[4] This amounts to saying that, in art, recognition is a mimetic act, and perhaps the essential one. As an example of successful mimesis in this sense, see Paulinus of Nola's comment on a portrait of himself, *ep.* 30.6, to Severus (*CSEL* 29:266f): "Hic etiam, si tantus amor est visibilia quoque captare solatia, poteris per magistras animi tui lineas vel inperitis aut ignorantibus nos dictare pictoribus, memoriam illis tuam, in qua nos habes pictos, velut imitanda de conspicuis adsidentium vultibus ora proponens. Sed si forte ad intellectum verbi tui inscitior manus artis erraverit, dissimiles pinget aliis, tibi tamen nos semper animo consideranti et conplectenti, quoslibet vultus sub nostro nomine inperitia sua pinxerit, tamen tua conscientia nos erimus." For an example of blocked mimesis (i.e., failure to recognize a subject) in painting, see the citation of Pope Gregory the Great, Chapter 3, note 198.

and judged it superior to the novelty-ridden art of Athens as a representation of enduring forms of virtue. Thus the Venerable Bede described paintings in a figurative style of the seventh century—if not precisely in the geometric patterns of Celtic art—and said that they gave the viewer the illusion of seeing the faces of Christ and the saints. (In the mid-ninth century, with a similarly figurative style in mind, Paschasius Radbertus wrote of painters who knew their work so well that they could represent, without a caption or a voice, faces that spoke.) Thus Cézanne stoutly argued that he had followed the artist's true course, the concrete study of nature, and Jackson Pollock insisted that all of his paintings were representational, drawing from nature. Perhaps it is true that continuity runs throughout the periods of art history and that it lies in the conceptual enigmas of art, rather than in the stylistic solutions to technical problems in individual works of art. The sculptor, Caro, thinks so: "In every period the artist has to find a way through to a visual truth that works for him in the time he lives. . . . Abstract art copes with most of the same problems as figurative art and will succeed or fail for the same reasons."[5]

I suggest, then, that the common point of departure in poetry, painting, and (as will be seen) historical writing is not problems with clear, technical solutions but enigmas that can only be resolved in irony and paradox. My theme, generally, is as follows. The word "mimesis" has normally been regarded as a term of style in art: in drama, literature, and painting. As a term, it has been equated with the fictional representation of the world as we actually see and experience it. How vividly does a novel represent the daily realities of life? How completely does a painting fool us into thinking that we see a real person instead of an arrangement of colors on a canvas? These are the kinds of questions about technique that the definition of mimesis as a term of style would answer.

I maintain, however, that as a strategy of art, mimesis was quite distinguishable from the technique and logical problems of style in particular works of art. Essentially, that strategy was a way of thinking

[5] Plato *Laws* 2. 656–657. Bede, *Vitae sanctorum abbatum monasterii*, chap. 6. Paschasius Radbertus in E. Dümmler, ed., "Radberts *Epitaphium Arsenii*," in *Abhandlungen der königlichen Akademie der Wissenschaften zu Berlin* (Berlin, 1899–1900), p. 39. Cézanne, especially the letter to Émile Bernard, 12 May 1904 (no. 168), in *Paul Cézanne, Correspondence*, ed. J. Rewald (Paris, 1937), p. 261. Pollock, quoted in E. H. Johnson, *Modern Art and the Object: A Century of Changing Attitudes* (New York, 1976), p. 115. Anthony Caro, leaflet for *The Artist's Eye*, a special exhibition at the National Gallery, London, 1 June–29 July 1977.

about relationships in nature, in art, and between them. Where other strategies taught an atomized world, mimesis posited a unified one, in which apparently contradictory and discordant elements were resolved into an ultimate harmony. Thus, other strategies could assume that a universal friction of contraries ruled nature, but mimesis assumed that it was governed by universal likeness, mediating and reconciling differences.

In nature, mimesis was the strategy of reproduction that mediated such asymmetries as those between parent and child, between actual and potential states of existence (for example, between an acorn and an oak tree), and between the archetypal world in God's mind and its image, the actual world of human experience.

In art, as in nature, mimesis was identified as a strategy of reproduction, mediating asymmetries between thought and word, design and painting, ancient text and contemporary interpretation. In manual as well as in intellectual arts, it incorporated a number of tactics for the refinement of technique; it entailed an imperative of self-criticism. Thus, many individual endeavors in Western culture acquired a common impulse endlessly to "restore" or "renew" their own traditions from within.

Finally, mimesis was regarded as a reproductive strategy not only in nature and in art but in the space between them. Individual arts existed to achieve specific functions. Philosophers and theologians were able to take a broader view. They could see that mimesis operated on several levels that might coincide. It mediated between an actual object and its natural antecedents, between the object and the picture of it formed in the mind, between the picture in the artist's mind and the representation of it that he made, between the representation—a drama or a painting, for example—and the image formed in the mind of the audience, and, finally, in the critical dialogue between artist and audience. Philosophers and theologians understood mimesis as a subject of theory. Those who thought about art in abstract, but comprehensive, terms realized that art imitated nature not only to copy it but also to rival and correct it. They grasped that the most important level on which mimesis operated was (as Sidney wrote) between things, or men, as they are and as they ought to be. There, as in individual arts, it was a strategy of correction. When we study theories of mimesis that take account of reproduction on this level, we come close to seeing a spark leap between the poles of nature and art—the creative spark that ignites the evolution of social values.

* * *

My task, then, is to indicate that, as in art, so also in social doctrines the common mimetic strategy for mediating asymmetries was adapted to many diverse and even hostile styles of thought. In this particular area between nature and art, the strategy characterized the thought of such disparate nineteenth-century figures as Pope Pius IX and the early sociologist Wilhelm Dilthey. Indeed, it was precisely Dilthey's reworking of mimetic ideas and imagery that laid him open to the charge of deliberate mystification. The barest mention of these names is enough to make the essential point that the history of mimesis cannot be reduced to formulae developed in ancient philosophy but rather that it must take account of a repertoire of possibilities that widened throughout the centuries. Thus, the history of mimesis cannot be understood as a single, linear progression. It displays, instead, an interweaving and ramification of options, some apparent from an early time, others introduced along the way. The history of mimesis is a pluralistic "history of versions." It was right that assumptions about mimesis were not confined to literature or painting but that they also took root in historical doctrines of great diversity, for they informed all areas of work and hope and the deepest, most varied, motivations of man's creative life.

Let me now attempt to draw several lines together and anticipate how the concept of mimesis might appear to the eyes of a historian, rather than a philosopher or an art critic. For my purposes, the history of the concept is its structure; classical antiquity is the foundation.

Ancient writers recognized mimesis as an animal instinct. They saw that it was the essential device by which younger animals learned to follow in the steps of their elders, and they took pleasure in the ways that man could play on that instinct, training nightingales, bears, and apes to perform mimic tricks for his amusement. As an ardent naturalist, Aristotle traced man's superiority to the fact that he was "the most imitative animal in the world," learning and delighting to learn by imitation from childhood throughout life (*Poetics* 4.1448b). Aristotle had more than an inkling of the parallel between genetic and cultural development. When he wrote his often-quoted sentence that art imitates nature, he did not mean simply that plays or statues represent the visible world. He did not have the product in mind so much as the oscillation in the beholder's mind between the intellectual pattern and the physical object. Thus, as he went on to say, art imitates nature by always striving toward better forms, forms that will correct the shortcomings of past attempts. Being conscious and deliberate where nature is blind, art can rival and correct nature itself in this selective process of trial and error. In culture, the transition between pattern and object was also a mediation between nature and art, over which man had control and through which he created culture as a second nature. The result might be to pass from less to more refined forms, as had occurred in the development of tragedy. Aristotle's distinction between the repetitive mimesis in the cycles of physical nature and the inventive mimesis in man's mental world was never lost, even during the long centuries when his writings were all but unknown in Western Europe.

But how, and when, did it become possible to think mimetically about history in the first place? The idea of all history as a work in progress, moving from alienation to wholeness as the image grew in likeness to its archetype, originated with early Christian writers. By regarding history as a branch of theoretical (or speculative) knowledge, they were able to apply varieties of mimetic strategy to the transformation of mankind as a whole, as well as to the redundant movements in the physical universe. Through their teachings, the programmatic strategy of mimesis persisted from Augustine to Marx, serving as a primary means by which the West understood and continually reformed itself.

In time, however, pseudo-Aristotelianisms appeared, clouding the meaning and function of mimesis. They located it in the work of art, rather than in the modeling process between the design and the work: that is, in artistic style rather than in aesthetic mediation between nature and art. These misinterpretations of Aristotle, confusing art with works of art, first appeared in the Renaissance, and they have managed to persist even though they have long been recognized as misrepresentations of Aristotle's own doctrines and, equally important, of the general understandings that Aristotle expressed and that he shared, for example, with Plato. Limiting mimesis to classicism or to naturalism came about through the same sort of misreadings as the Renaissance idea of dramatic unities, and at about the same time. Attached to the methods of classicism and naturalism, the term "mimesis" lost its connotations of rivalry and continual invention. The word denoted little more than "naive" or "servile" imitation; but the mimetic strategy continued, and, in some areas of speculation, continued to develop, particularly in modern theories of social change, including those of Marx.

Thus mimesis began as an animal instinct; it was later rationalized as a concept; it finally became an adaptive strategy in Western cultural traditions. But it was by no means a clear-cut formula. As an adaptive strategy, mimesis united antitheses; it was self-critical, and even self-contradictory. Like ignorance and wisdom, iconoclasm and imagery combined in the two mimetic arts that, working within tradition over the ages, continually changed the actual world as they reconstituted themselves: philosophy and theology. "Truly noble," as Plato wrote, "is the power of the art of contradiction."[6]

This is what one might see if one looked at the concept of mimesis historically. But examining the concept as it passed through so many distant ages and alien societies requires that the past be accepted on its own terms. This is easier said than done. It is not usual nowadays for historians to think in terms of the coincidence of opposites, the unity of subject and object, the subordination of material evidence to theories of beauty, or the tautology of image and archetype in the actual fabric of history. But all these have their place in the historical career of mimesis. To think about mimesis historically, therefore, one needs to temper canons of formal criticism that have become well established since the Enlightenment. One needs to recover some objective awareness of the Dionysian impulses in Western culture. For the strategy of mimesis used paradox to elucidate enigmas of wholeness. Under the double influence of English pragmatism and French rationalism, many schools of thought since the Enlightenment have developed a settled hostility toward paradox. Such has been the dominance of Apollinianism in historical inquiry, whose proper qualities are generally held to be not paradox but certitude and precision.

The Apollinian approach demands from such subjects more than they can give. A substantial portion of Western culture insists that life is fundamentally incongruous. Irony and satire, comedy and tragedy, the exaltation of mystery, and the cult of the absurd are all believable because they reflect the improbabilities, reversals of odds, and capriciousness of human experience. Perhaps the disharmonies in the *oeuvres* of great philosophers—so puzzling and embarrassing to their disciples—show that, when all is said and done, ambiguity in the very nature of things tends to intrude self-contradiction even into the most compelling systems of thought. A deep unity requires us to understand good and evil, justice and injustice, wisdom and foolishness, the sacred and the profane as asymmetrical coordinates. Incongruities of a vastly more complex sort haunt processes of transformation in nature, art,

[6] *Republic* 5. 454a.

and knowledge, not to mention the character of any given person. It is exactly because incongruity is the norm in life that the impulse to find similarity in dissimilar things has been so relentless and potent in magic, religion, philosophy, science, and the arts.

Enigmas resolved in asymmetrical paradoxes are fundamental and lasting concerns in all the visual arts and the arts of verbal discourse, and they are woven into the very fabric of some particular strategies that many of those arts have in common. Mimesis is one such strategy, and we cannot escape the fact of enigma resolved in paradox if we study mimesis historically, as a basic principle in the adaptive evolution of Western culture. It is a principle that both vindicated and experienced historical development through all the visual and the literary arts, including the severe and radical method of criticism that, with prophetic insight, Pascal called "the art of revolution."[7]

I recommend that any reader who wishes a broader orientation to the neglect of mimesis as a theme in historiography turn to the Appendix.

[7] *Pensées,* no. 294. On the convergence of Apollinian and Dionysian strains in the mimetic tradition, see below, Appendix, after note 8.

Acknowledgments

WRITING THIS BOOK has not been a solitary task. At every stage of composition, others familiar with the idea of mimesis in various contexts have allowed me to benefit from their knowledge and experience. There was no question that, within limits, the course of Western culture could be described from the perspective of mimesis as a central theme continuing through the ages, or that one could gain fresh understanding of dominant principles in works of some individual authors if one used the concept of mimesis as an Archimedean point of analysis. But how could one visualize the sense of unity in diversity that would emerge? Some of those who helped me think about this question were close to Augustine's position. The Father wrote: "The Truth by which holy souls are enlightened is one; but, since the souls are many, there can be said to be many truths in them, just as many images of one face may appear in mirrors." Others took another position, one closer to that of Friedrich Schleiermacher. They held that truth was not only reflected but in some way created by an endlessly ramifying mutual reflex of parts and whole in society, as in a hall of mirrors. Still others, like Rilke, argued that the individual created such unity as could exist for him in a relay from one mind to another, "a ballgame for gods," "a game of mirrors," in which each catches the image and holds it just long enough to measure how much strength he needs to flash it on.[1]

The language of mimesis could be used to describe transcendent, immanent, or existential unity. Indeed, it was so used not only by writers at different stages in Western culture but also by contemporaries. This pluralism was a principal lesson that my companions in this work taught me.

They differed in age, background, and interest: it was natural that their perspectives on the subject of mimesis should also vary. The aggregate of their comments was all the richer because they represented generations born between the late nineteenth and the mid-twentieth

[1] On Augustine and Schleiermacher, see below, Chapter 3, note 18; Chapter 14, note 24. Rainer Maria Rilke, "Da stehen wir mit Spiegeln," in *Späte Gedichte* (Leipzig, 1935), p. 88.

century and European as well as American educations. Of course, their range of interests was also of practical value.

A historian of modern Europe and a psychologist (John and Theta Wolf) were midwives when the idea for this book was born, and they have nurtured it to the present time. A historian of the Irish Church and nation and a specialist in children's learning disabilities (Emmet and Dianne Larkin) also grieved and rejoiced with me over the years and argued until I at last recognized the deeply enigmatic nature of what I had too long believed to be a logical problem. On occasion, I have benefited from the advice of church historians (Peter Ahr, Joan Connell, Rosamond McKitterick, John T. McNeill, Martin Marty, and Theofanis Stavrou), students of medieval spirituality and dissent (Bernard Bachrach, Robert Lerner, and Bernard McGinn), philosophers of history (F. Edward Cranz, Leonard Krieger, Arnaldo Momigliano and Thomas Munson), historians of the visual arts (Thomas Hines and Irving Lavin), a novelist (Richard Stern), a photographer (James Ballard), an expert in pastoral theology (Seaver Willey), and a social worker (Mary Rall). With a generosity characteristic of his family, William H. McNeill commented on what turned out to be an early draft, thanks partly to his advice. Frances Hughes let me read Augustine in her studio. Any book reflects the thinking of its intended audience. I hope that the following pages may, in some measure, be true to the varieties of experience and the breadth of understanding scarcely hinted at by this list of names.

The word mimesis sums up a fundamental trait of human nature: the stimulus and response of teaching. In one way or another, all the persons just mentioned are engaged in teaching, and, for this reason, they found mimesis a subject of common interest. Indeed, explaining ideas to students played an important part in the development of the present book. The challenges and encouragement met in the classroom have been more helpful than can be told. I am grateful to have explored the territory of mimesis with students, including, especially, Stewart Jay Brown, who worked for one year as my research assistant and debating partner.

During the year 1976/1977, I held a visiting membership in the Institute for Advanced Study. Discussing the career of mimesis there with F. Edward Cranz and Irving Lavin led me to rethink the scope and direction of this study, and, in effect, to begin anew. Without the hospitality of the Institute, the subvention of the National Endowment of the Humanities, and the advice of Professors Cranz and Lavin, the following portrayal of the career of mimesis would never have taken shape.

Finally, I record once more a deep obligation to the Princeton University Press. In its present form, my essay has greatly profited from suggestions received from anonymous readers of several revisions over a space of time and from the kind and always discerning counsel of Miriam Brokaw.

In his *Apologie for Poetrie,* Sir Philip Sidney argued that, being "captived to the truth of a foolish world," historians could not teach with the power and freedom of poets. I hope that this essay may justify the interplay of ideas that gave rise to it, at least by indicating an area where the ventures of poetry and history joined with others in an existential mirror game such as Rilke envisioned.

Apart from those who have helped me think through the argument of this book, there have been others who generously assisted me in practical matters.

It is a privilege to acknowledge support and encouragement kindly provided by Robert McC. Adams and William Kruskal, successive Deans of the Social Sciences Division at the University of Chicago, and John T. Wilson, former president of the University.

As already mentioned, the Institute for Advanced Study and the National Endowment for the Humanities sustained this work in 1976 and 1977.

In different forms, some conclusions set forth in two of the following chapters have already been published. I am grateful to the American Philosophical Society and to the Centro Italiano di Studi sull' Alto Medioevo for publishing the original studies, and to the Centro, particularly, for the honor and happiness of discussing my ideas about Hincmar of Rheims with colleagues at its *Settimana* in 1979. The articles in question are: " 'From Form into Form': Mimesis and Personality in Augustine's Historical Thought," *Proceedings of the American Philosophical Society* 124 (1980): 276–294, and " '*Unum ex Multis*': Hincmar of Rheims' Medical and Aesthetic Rationales for Unification," *Nascita dell'Europa ed Europa Carolingia: Un'Equazione da Verificare, Settimane di Studio del' Centro Italiano di Studi sull'Alto Medioevo* 27, vol. 2 (1981): 583–712. Sections that are reproduced here have been re-used by kind permission of the original publishers. I should perhaps reiterate that the articles differ in content, length, and organization from the corresponding chapters in this book.

Acknowledgments

An invitation to participate in a series of lectures at Northern Illinois University gave an occasion for organizing my thoughts on the place of mimesis in the liberal arts tradition. I am grateful to the originators and orchestrators of the series, Professors Thomas Blomquist and David Wagner.

John and Anne Coyne helped me in a number of ways, not least by a gift of books.

I gladly acknowledge the assistance given by a number of libraries, including, above all, the Joseph Regenstein Library at the University of Chicago. Other libraries also proved to be more than hospitable to a wandering scholar: in Chicago, the Newberry Library; in Evanston, the libraries of Northwestern University, Garrett-Evangelical Theological Seminary, and Seabury-Western Seminary; in Princeton, the libraries of the Institute for Advanced Study, Princeton University, and the Princeton Theological Seminary.

Preparation of the manuscript in its various transformations engaged a number of people. I am especially obliged to those who typed and retyped copy from noncalligraphic pages: Nancy Berg, Elizabeth Bitoy, Cynthia Cook, Rosemary Garrison, Elizabeth Horton, Sandra Lafferty, Gladys Morrison, Jean Pasdeloup, Margaret Van Sant, Marnie Veghte, and Carol Widrig.

Warm thanks are also due to Gail Filion and Catherine Dammeyer Thatcher, who prepared the terminal manuscript for the printer, and to Martin Secker and Brian Hyland, who assisted me in compiling the index.

Abbreviations

Corp. Christ., ser. lat.	*Corpus Christianorum, series latina*
CSEL	*Corpus Scriptorum Ecclesiasticorum Latinorum*
Mansi	J. D. Mansi, *Sanctorum Conciliorum Nova et Amplissima Collectio*
MGH	*Monumenta Germaniae Historica*
MGH, Cap. Reg. Fr.	*Capitularia Regum Francorum*
MGH, Epp.	*Epistolae*
MGH, Epp. K. A.	*Epistolae Karolini Aevi*
MGH, SS.	*Scriptores*
MGH, SS. Rer. Mer.	*Scriptores Rerum Merovingicarum*
PL	J. Migne, *Patrologiae Cursus Completus, series latina*
WA	*Luthers Werke, kritische Gesammtausgabe* (Weimar)

I

Forming the Mimetic Tradition

PHILOSOPHERS and theologians recognized mimesis as a universal strategy in the arts of mind and hand, but they were especially eager to understand its power for moral education. Their most intense and urgent study focused on the asymmetry between the soul as it was and the model of what it ought to be. They were convinced that understanding the strategy of imitation would give them mastery of such tactics as were needed to perfect the soul by making it conform with its model.

The power to shape the human soul remained a subject of passionate concern across the centuries. Yet, theories about the appropriate modeling process varied. Moral education, Aristotle wrote, employed pleasure to direct the mind toward good action and pain to divert it from bad. Like Plato, he considered moral education of men and women to be analogous with training animals. Deliberately inflicted as punishment, pain was a kind of cure for vice (cf. *Nic. Eth.* II.3.1104b). The object was to internalize patterns of conduct—what ought, and ought not, to be done. Aristotle was concerned with models that existed in the world and with a modeling process that worked through habituation. However, internalizing models by pleasure and pain was more complex in Christianity, where the analogy with animal training did not hold. "Be not conformed to this world," wrote St. Paul, "but be ye transformed by the renewing of your mind" (Rom. 12:2). As though he were an athlete training for a race, the Christian internalized the model of Christ, enduring grief, persecution, and death (Phil. 3:10–13, 21). "Be ye imitators of me, even as I also am of Christ," the Apostle urged the faithful, sharing in the sufferings of Christ, being made conformable with His death, and pressing ever on toward the victor's crown: the resurrection of the dead, when Christ would transform the human body of His follower into the likeness of His own glorious body (1 Cor. 9:24–27). But this internalization was only possible because a change had already occurred. The Spirit had revealed to the soul things that its animal nature could not grasp, renewing it "in knowledge after the image of him that created him" (Col. 3:10; 1 Cor. 2:13–14). It remained for the Church Fathers to discover how this call to alienation from the world could be made into a program both for personal renewal of soul and body, and for social reform.

In the following chapters, I will describe how the mimetic tradition gradually took shape. It arose in a complex repertoire of strategy that

Plato and Aristotle roughly sketched out. It ramified in teachings of Neoplatonists and Hellenistic Jews, including St. Paul. It crystallized in doctrines of the Church Fathers, who armed mimetic strategy for the moral education of man with tactics of pleasure and pain very different from the ones that Aristotle had defined as "the right education."

Chapter 1

Basic Patterns of Mimetic Action
in Greek Thought

THE ORIGINS of mimesis as a strategy of change for the better can be traced to Greek philosophy. To be sure, writers attached a wide variety of meanings to the word "mimesis." Despite wide variations of meaning, a few lines of reasoning stand out clearly in the texts of the two philosophers, Plato and Aristotle, who laid the foundations of formal thought about the term.

Both Plato and Aristotle insisted on the ultimate unity of the cosmos. They could not accept the idea that discord, or chaos, ruled the world. They taught the mutual attraction—instead of the mutual repellence—of things. Thus, while other writers did think that the world was formed by strife, or by the random clash of atoms, Plato and Aristotle described it as a harmonious composition. What other writers considered antitheses, Plato and Aristotle judged to be asymmetrical terms or orders mediated by mimetic strategies.

Plato explored the asymmetry between nature and art, which he interpreted as a segment of a wider tension between the transcendent order of eternal archetypes and the natural order of material things. He argued that wider tension was mediated by an innate attraction of like for like that he called love. Aristotle, too, understood nature and art as asymmetrical. He departed from Plato in thinking that they were parallel orders and that they were alike governed by an asymmetry within nature itself: not Plato's tension between archetype and image but another between potential and actual modes of existence. This tension was mediated by growth.

Aristotle's fascination with the tension between potential and actual regarding what he judged to be man's characteristic faculty—reason— led him to explore yet another area of asymmetry mediated by growth: that, within art, between a work and the concept of the work formed by the mind. He studied this area by analyzing the didactic interaction between an author (or performer) and his audience. Investigating lines of inquiry as they emerged, he developed a concept of all the arts as one vast educational program motivated by a common mimetic exchange of stimulus and response. In a sense, the arts comprised a second nature, replicating the mediated asymmetries of the physical world. Above them all was philosophy, mediating between nature and art.

Broadly speaking, then, there were three areas in which Plato and Aristotle imagined mimetic mediation to be at work: within nature, within art, and between nature and art. In the present chapter, I shall attempt to describe the bare bones of these mediated asymmetries, as Plato and Aristotle understood them, with the object of sketching out a repertoire of different kinds of mimesis. To complete an outline of the basic repertoire, I shall also examine a particular application of the strategy by Neoplatonic philosophers centuries later, in the heydey of the Roman Empire.

Plato

The Sophists taught that imitation was an act that linked the separate domains of nature and art. While Plato rejected the dichotomy of nature and art, he taught a doctrine far more inclusive and menacing than any dreamed of by his Sophist opponents. The propositions and conclusions of the dichotomy, Plato wrote, were equally untrue. The Sophists had originally distinguished between nature and art, and, with them in mind, Plato argued as follows. The dichotomy posited that the material elements in the world—earth, air, fire, and water—came first, before form, and that they *were* nature. By change and by magnetic sympathies, without any intervention of mind, art, or God, they formed the physical universe, including the seasons. Sometime later, according to the Sophists, soul was formed, and art emerged from human experience; art was mortal, whether in the branches that quite imperfectly imitated nature (as in painting), or those that used nature (as in medicine), or those that were independent of and opposed to nature (as in law and government). This argument, Plato held, put first things last. Soul was the primary element in the world. It was life, the origin of all movement and change, and hence of all the processes of generation and decay inherent in the cosmos. This being so, law and art, "the creation of mind according to right reason," existed in and by nature.[1] They therefore belonged to the primoridal unity of soul, which was immaterial, immortal, and simple.

It was easy, Plato acknowledged, to understand how men reached the misleading dichotomy of nature and art. Though soul was prior to and more excellent than matter, the world consisted of body as well as soul. Alongside the unity of soul, there existed another that was material, mortal, and complex. The world therefore displayed two "paradigms," the one divine and the other human.[2] Very few had the inner eye of the philosopher that was needed to see, or to know, the invisible things of this divine order.

Plato's discussion of the asymmetry between nature and art therefore led him to the grander asymmetry between the transcendent order of Ideas and the natural order of the material world, and, consequently, to the concept of the human mind on which his doctrines of mimetic mediation depended.

The key to Plato's doctrine was a specific kind of movement: reversion. The concept of the two paradigms contained Plato's celebrated program for the purification of the soul by a movement of egress and return. Before they descended from heaven to live in the body, all souls saw the eternal Forms, and images of the Forms were left in their minds. Once the soul came into the world, both the images and knowledge of the divine paradigm faded.[3] Knowledge was virtue; and, in this highest sense, virtue, as the recollection of the divine paradigm, could neither be taught nor constructed by exercising the reason. It was an instinct given by God and not necessarily accompanied by reason—a "conversion" that transformed the soul from darkness into light.[4] By this gift of "divine" or "philosophical madness,"[5] the virtuous soul could cast off its estrangement from its heavenly origins and pass up the hierarchy of arts, through human institutions and laws, to perceive "the single science, the science of beauty everywhere." It was this vision that enabled the philosopher to examine the arts of language and mathematics, painting, music, and politics, and to grasp that they imitated a common, eternal truth or beauty, and, moreover, that through the arts, man imitated the divine creative act through which soul called things into existence.[6] Still, in all their discoveries,

---

[1] *Laws* 10. 889–896, 967. Cf. *Timaeus* 34. On the extremely elusive meaning of "mimesis" in Plato, see E. A. Havelock, *Preface to Plato* (Cambridge, Mass., 1963), pp. 20–35, esp. p. 33, n. 37.

[2] *Theatetus* 176.   [3] *Phaedrus* 249–250.

[4] *Meno* 99–100. *Republic* 6. 508; 7. 518–525.   [5] *Phaedrus* 244. 249. 265.

[6] *Cratylus* 440. *Sophist* 265f.

their growth and decay, the arts did not frame a new order. Instead, like the philosopher's mind, they pointed backward to a lost knowledge that, by mimesis, they served to restore.[7]

Thus, Plato described the soul's corrective movement in four stages: egress, aversion from the eternal paradigm (or Forms), (re-)conversion to the paradigm, and a passage by mimetic recollection back to it. This concept of egress and return led him to reject the functional argument that virtue was gained by habit alone.[8] At the same time, he understood that those who lacked the divine gift of virtue had no inkling of the invisible unity behind the human paradigm. They realized that the arts were useful, and that, both as subjects taught and as creative processes, they imitated other things, but they were blind to the real mimetic character of the human paradigm and hence to the unity of nature and art. For the same reason, the unity running through music and gymnastic was beyond the grasp of the citizens in Plato's ideal city who did not go on to the mathematical subjects and, finally, to dialectic.

The doctrine of mimesis had surprising results for the arts. According to the human paradigm, man's creative imitation of a pre-existent design formed a work of art; it informed the work with the design. But according to the divine paradigm, all mimesis in the material order was transcended by the soul's mimetic reversion to the Ideas.

The unity of the arts consisted in their common descent from soul; only the philosopher could perceive their unity. As he examined the arts and what they created in the human order, it was the philosopher's business to judge three things: (1) what was being imitated, (2) whether the imitation were true, and (3) whether the imitation were technically good in its particular medium—words, melodies, or rhythms.[9] This conception had unexpected results of lasting consequence, for Plato's doctrine of unity led him to prescribe that Homer and the poets be revered with divine honors and then expelled from his ideal city together with "the sister arts of imitation."[10]

How was it possible that Plato's theory of correction in the arts led to iconoclasm, and, indeed, to iconoclasm as an expression of supreme beauty? In the *Republic*, of course, he gives the immediate reason: the poets imitate what the ignorant mob thinks good, rather than the truth of things, and, like flute players and others slated for exile, they incite men to imitate perversions of the good.[11] Like Aristotle after him, he

---

[7] *Symposium* 207f.   [8] Cf. *Republic* 10. 619.   [9] *Laws* 2. 669.
[10] *Republic* 10. 601.   [11] *Republic* 10. 601–606; 3. 394–399.

distinguished between bad imitation, that corrupted the soul, and good imitation, that corrected it. There was a deeper reason. For, while other authors, including Aristotle, built their rationales of unity on logical consistency, Plato constructed his on an ordering principle beyond reason.

The main element in the puzzle is the strategy of imitation. Crucial as this doctrine was to the mediated asymmetry of divine and human paradigms, its keystone was an enigma. According to Plato, images—including those of the visible world as well as those made by human arts—were unreal realities.[12] Much depended on winnowing out the real in them from the unreal, the eternal from the transitory. But who could judge? Man was caught in the unreal reality of the material world, of his body, and of images in his mind. He was beset by a second Platonic enigma: the true lie, an ineradicable ignorance in the soul.[13] Even the philosopher, searching through the images of this world for the invisible vision of truth, saw "through a glass darkly."[14] If the soul can know anything at all, it gains access to knowledge only after death.[15] The universal truth is disclosed through the philosopher's conversion in the ecstasy of divine madness; it is incommunicable. It also convinces the visionary that all his knowledge is as nothing when compared with eternal archetypes of truth and beauty. The ignorant sage is at one with the inarticulate ruler, who, grasping the priority of soul and contemplating the mind of nature, brings law and institutions into accord with eternal harmonies and yet "is not able to give a reason of such things as have a reason." Even irradiated and dark with the superabundant light of their great vision,[16] both were limited by the vast difference between what truly was and what they could know and say of it.

Plato envisaged a range of thought in which the tactical, or historical, aspect of style receded and mimesis functioned, not only through signs or analogues but also through timeless symbols recognized by the initiate. In his doctrine of the soul's egress from and return to unity, Plato set up the unstable equilibrium characteristic of any encounter between the asymmetries of ideal and actual. In its instability, it ended

---

[12] *Sophist* 240.   [13] *Republic* 2. 382.   [14] *Phaedrus* 250.
[15] *Phaedo* 66f. Cf. *Apology* 21, 23.
[16] *Sophist* 254. Concerning the place of intuition in Plato's doctrine of analogy, see D. Burrell, *Analogy and Philosophical Language* (New Haven, 1973), pp. 45–48, 75f. For an argument that Plato's concept of rhetoric was aimed against the magical notions of Gorgias, see J. de Romilly, *Magic and Rhetoric in Ancient Greece* (Cambridge, Mass., 1975), pp. 16–22, 30f., 36. Cf. *Phaedrus* 271.

with iconoclasm as a symbolic form of art. This appears to have been true not only of the representational arts (including poetry) banished from the ideal Republic but also of literature as a whole. For in the *Phaedrus* (275–276), Plato embellishes his story about the god Teuth, the inventor of writing, with a grim prophecy. Through writing, he says, men study someone else's recollections of things, instead of their own memories. Consequently, they will give each other, not truth, but its semblance, and they will gain the appearance of wisdom without the reality. What they will lose is "the living word of knowledge," or "the intelligent word graven in the soul of the learner."[17] Passing over into political theory by way of mystical theology, Plato indicated to later generations how his enigmas and mimetic iconoclasm in the service of the Good could be made the center of collective life, and at what risk.

Aristotle

Arguing and agreeing with Plato, Aristotle laid open a vital aspect of our problem, for, in his scattered discussions, he revealed that no single concept of mimesis was adequate to cover all mimetic transformations. The extraordinary power of his intellect to distinguish and divide and his conviction of unity in the world worked together to this end. Aristotle recognized the arts as tactics, beneath the level of theory—as undeliberative applications of higher levels of knowledge. They composed a hierarchy of excellence, and the kinds of mimetic strategies that corresponded with them varied accordingly. At the same time, however, all tactics and strategies were linked through their common relationship to the source of form and being; it is therefore important to devote special attention both to the varieties of mimesis distinguished by Aristotle and to the manner in which he combined them, building a unified conception of the world as it moved through a continual process of egress, transformation, and return.

To identify the varieties of mimesis discussed by Aristotle, I shall need first to sketch the wider context in which he employed them.

One theme unites Aristotle's versions of mimesis: the theme of correction. Even in the humblest manual art—bridle making, for example—matter had to be reshaped according to a planned form. On a far grander level, Aristotle was fascinated by corrective processes that he saw at work in nature. His biologist's eye detected a continual move-

---

[17] Cf. James 1:21, "the ingrafted word."

ment from less to more perfect forms of life, and, as he surveyed the entire range of human knowledge, he found that corrective mimesis unified all the manual and intellectual arts in a vast, interlocking system of thought that paralleled the hierarchy of action in nature.

Aristotle affirmed the dichotomy of nature and art that Plato had rejected. His sentence "art imitates nature" is one of the most durable, and elusive, maxims in Western thought.[18] Whereas the sentence has often been taken to justify naturalism in the plastic and literary arts, this simple interpretation ignores two complicating factors. First, Aristotle was aiming at a general definition of the arts, including the mechanical ones. Second, he added another clause to his maxim: art not only imitates nature but also completes the deficiencies of nature.[19] By striving toward a general definition that included functions both of imitation and of correction, he respected the integrity of each art and yet permitted a doctrine of architectonic unity among the arts.[20]

Aristotle defined all his philosophical terms with regard to their ends. Thus, the parallel orders of nature and art expressed the wider asymmetry of actual and potential in nature as a whole, in every individual thing within nature, and in the artificial second nature composed by the human mind. The end was the purpose, the completion, or the final cause of any action. He considered nature as a cycle of movements—specifically, of generation and decay—through which one kind of end, the generic form, was realized in individuals by growth. The whole of nature moved from God, its prime mover, and toward God, its universal, final cause. Such was the pattern of egress and return in the world. Clearly, the arts too were defined by their origins and goals in the need of man for sufficiency: that is, for wholeness. At the highest level, the circularity of the arts duplicated the cosmic egress and return, insofar as it led the soul back to God.

This fundamental similarity between nature and art brought Aris-

---

[18] *Physics* 2. 2. 194a. What is imitated? Aristotle recognized that "nature" had many meanings. He narrowed them down to two: (1) the material of which something was composed, and (2) a form into which something grows (as a child grows into the nature of a man) (*Physics* 2. 1. 193a–b). Aristotle's primary emphasis fell on this second meaning. "Nature" was the object of growth, or the purpose for the sake of which something was done. To imitate nature, therefore, was to conceive a work in terms of its function (ibid., 2. 2. 194b).

[19] *Physics* 2. 8. 199a; *Politics* 7. 17. 1337a.

[20] Since "no word is by nature," all language and all the literary arts can only be analogues of nature. On this aspect of Aristotle's thought and on the historical aspects of his philological studies, see R. Pfeiffer, *History of Classical Scholarship from the Beginnings to the End of the Hellenistic Age* (Oxford, 1968), pp. 75f, 79–81.

totle to three conclusions bearing on the theme of correction. A distinction between tactics of operation and the general strategy of correction is vital.

The first conclusion is the most complex. Aristotle argued that art imitated nature because both were purposive. Moreover, the ends that they served were prescribed to them. Art was like nature in not deliberating about the end that it achieved.[21] In both, the end came first, and the tactic for realizing it—the art, or generative process—followed.

Of course, there were differences. In nature, there was no division between matter and function, whereas, in art, the tactical function had to be defined and matter appropriate to it selected. "Making" in art was a conscious act informed by experience; "coming to be" in nature was an involuntary, necessary movement,[22] although, Aristotle insisted that "the relation of the later to the earlier terms of the series [of stages by which the end is reached] is the same in both."

Further, art imitated nature in having goals that it achieved, even though they were not the same goals.[23] A rudder was made to serve the helmsman's needs; it had no natural archetype. Among the representational arts, portraits and tragedies were as free of nature as analogues could be. In portraiture, artists always tried to improve on their models without losing a few, basic and characteristic features.[24] In tragedy, the poet rendered an imitation of action and not necessarily of characters, but he departed from the particular facts of human experience; he depicted what might be, instead of what really had been in all the contingencies and incomplete actions of actual life. Indeed, some actual events were too improbable to represent on the stage. A tragedian was therefore "a poet by virtue of the imitative element in his work"; but his entire effort in holding "the mirror up to nature" was to write something about as far from nature as grand opera—a drama that

---

[21] *Physics* 2. 8. 199b.   [22] *Physics* 2. 8. 199a. Cf. ibid., 2. 2. 194b.

[23] On this aspect of Aristotle's argument and its Platonic antecedent, see W. Jaeger, *Aristotle: Fundamentals of the History of His Development,* trans. R. Robinson, 2d ed. (London, 1962), pp. 74f, 90. See also the important discussion by H. Koller, *Die Mimesis in der Antike. Nachamung. Darstellung. Ausdruck* (Bern, 1954. Diss. Bernenses, ser. 1, fasc. 5), esp. pp. 9–11, 21, 63f, 116–118. Koller argues that the sense of copying was attached to the term "mimesis" by Plato, when he departed from a usage that had long been established in music, poetry, and drama. According to Koller, Aristotle retained the older senses of "enact" or "portray." Consequently, Koller holds, it confuses the issue to assume that the word had the same meaning for the two philosophers.

[24] *Physics* 2. 2. 194b. *Poetics* 15. 1454b; 25. 1461b.

possessed "the organic unity of a living creature" abstracted into a convincing illusion of unified action and adorned with choral music and dance.[25] A third mimetic art, dance, also represented something other than the visible world.

The nature, or function, that was imitated therefore could be the practical function of a rudder. It could be the pleasure of instruction that patterns in the minds of portraitists and tragedians once expressed could stir up in the imaginations of audiences, or the movements and harmonies that audiences called for from dancers and musicians. Aristotle left a wide range of speculation open when he wrote that a poet, painter, or other maker of likenesses must represent things under any of three possible aspects: "(1) as they were, or are, or (2) as they are said or thought to be or have been, or (3) as they ought to be."[26]

In his second conclusion, Aristotle argued that art imitated nature because they were both imperfect. The process of generation and decay was the means by which nature strove after the better forms.[27] But, like any artist, nature could not always achieve what she intended[28]; tactics fell short of strategy. Here, too, there were differences. Both art and nature made mistakes; both failed.[29] But imitation in art was a voluntary and not merely a repetitive way in which man corrected his own deficiencies as well as nature's. Art could advance, while nature remained constant in its strivings. The artist drew on collective experience as well as on his own knowledge, and he took models for imitation both from abstract principles and from existing works made by earlier practitioners of his art. The result could be cumulative advancement of artistic proficiency, as where, for example, tragedy passed historically from lower to more perfect forms.

Finally, art imitated nature by correcting natural deficiencies. In this instance, however, the difference between the two was enormous. For, while it was true that art did not deliberate, artists and critics did. The doctrine that art imitated nature to correct it therefore led Aristotle to consider how art advanced by reflecting on its own past, and, even more, how far originality in art could leave nature aside, or even work counter to it.

To carry the distinction between tactics and strategy further, a word must be said about how an artist planned his work. Aristotle recognized a division of labor between people who had needs and artists

[25] The mirror metaphor occurs in Shakespeare's *Hamlet* II. i. 24. See *Poetics* 6. 1450a; 9. 1451b; 23. 1459a; 25. 1461b; 26. 1461b–1462b.

[26] *Poetics* 24. 1460b.   [27] *De Gen. et Corr.* 2. 10. 336b.

[28] *Politics* 1. 6. 1255b.   [29] *Physics* 2. 8. 199a–199b.

who satisfied them. The helmsman may ask for a rudder that performs in a certain way; audiences have their prescriptive expectations. But other people—artists—design and make the rudders or plays or dances. How does mimesis figure when, given a need or purpose, an artist devises a work (for example, a rudder or a play) to satisfy it? The answer, generic mimesis, lies in Aristotle's doctrine of abstraction. In thought, the craftsman (or the scientist) passed from the individual sense perception to a congeries of perceptions that, persisting in the soul, constituted memory. A number of memories composed a higher order of classification: experience. From the manifold of experience, the artisan or the man of science abstracted strategy, the universal principles that he applied in his work.[30] These stages corresponded with Aristotle's first three degrees of wisdom. Art, or making, was the lowest degree of wisdom in the hierarchy, and scientific knowledge— the power of logical demonstration—was the second.[31] Experience as well as innate ability was needed to go beyond to the third level, that of practical wisdom. Young men could become geometers and mathematicians. Knowing the universals but not having a cumulative experience of particulars, they lacked the practical wisdom (or prudence) needed to become philosophers or physicists.[32] At this third level of wisdom, the corrective strategy of mimesis came into play when one acted prescriptively, conforming particular instances to universal principles as one did, for example, in medicine or politics.

It is clear that there could be bad art as well as good art, although distinctions of "bad" and "good" had no meaning with regard to nature. The artist, not blind nature, set the object of imitation. How far could the tactics of art detach themselves from the strategy of mimesis written into the laws of nature? How far could art go in being autonomous, free from nature?

Aristotle's comments on the art of accumulating wealth cast much light on these questions and on the importance of mimesis as a corrective action. Was amassing wealth a liberal art? Aristotle answered that it was, if it were pursued according to nature, but that, otherwise, it was not. The difficulty hinged not on the art so much as on how it was practiced. Aristotle distinguished between natural and unnatural mimesis. There was no question that the art of acquisition did not belong among the servile, mechanical arts performed by slaves at the command of their masters. It clearly belonged among the occupations pursued by free men who stood above bodily toil, occupations like philos-

---

[30] *Post. An.* 11. 19. 100a.   [31] *Nic. Eth.* 6. 3. 1139b.   [32] *Nic. Eth.* 6. 8. 1142a.

ophy and politics that included theory. Furthermore, it was a natural art that included such enterprises as hunting, waging war, and acquiring slaves.[33] The problem was that gaining wealth was one sub-branch of the art of acquisition that could be pursued unnaturally as well as naturally. Was it liberal in either case?

The key to Aristotle's distinction between "natural" and "unnatural" was purpose, and it was to this distinction that Marx assigned extraordinary importance in his theory of values. What function did the art of getting wealth achieve? Aristotle concluded that its primary or natural function—its Marxian use-value—was to enable men to live well. The resources needed for that purpose were limited. Acquiring them was honorable. But Aristotle also observed that most men were not content to satisfy their moderate needs. Their object was not to live well but to live; they accumulated surpluses beyond their needs; their desires ran to excess and they made every effort to exchange their surpluses for unlimited profit.

This secondary function of the art—which Marx called its exchange-value—was declared by Aristotle to be unnatural and dishonorable. For him, coinage summed up this deviation from nature. Money itself was entirely artificial, "a mere sham, a thing not natural, but only conventional." By altering the medium of exchange, men could make money worthless, whatever the natural state of affairs. In any event, a man rich in coin could be deprived of everything that he needed to live, as Midas starved in the midst of his gold. Of all economic enterprises, usury was the most thoroughly divorced from nature (and rightly the most hated), since money was bred from money—not from natural objects, such as fruits or animals—and the offspring resembled the parent in its self-contained, artificial estrangement from the means of life.[34]

Aristotle's comments therefore indicate that functional mimesis could be identical with nature, as in hunting, war, and slave gathering; that it could accord with nature, as in satisfying needs; or that it could be unnatural, as in exchange. Bad mimesis was unnatural and corrupting; good mimesis was natural and corrective.

Thus Aristotle clearly did not argue that all human works were equally natural or that they equally compensated for nature's defects. When he called some modes of music and acquisition unnatural, he

---

[33] *Politics* 1. 7. 1255b. Marx discusses Aristotle's theory of values in *Capital,* chap. 1, sec. 1–3.

[34] *Politics* 1. 9. 1257a–1258b.

applied limits beyond which human originality should not go in violating the corrective strategies of nature. Apart from the functional argument that art imitated nature in its purposiveness, he had in mind other varieties of mimesis that came into play as human works were made and perfected and, finally, as they were judged according to a comprehensive scale of knowledge.

Such was the context in which Aristotle deployed his theories of mimesis. A provisional summary may be helpful.

The traces of a repertoire of mimetic strategies have begun to appear. When he considered how things came to be in nature and in art, Aristotle regarded all transformation as mimetic, since it reflected an end. He defined several kinds of mimesis, differing according to the materials that were transformed.

First, in the cosmos, the process of generation and decay in nature imitates the source of being. God made the process uninterrupted and perpetual, Aristotle argued, so that it might be "the closest approximation to eternal being."[35] Within the totality of nature, individual processes of growth (such as when an acorn grew into an oak tree) were likewise movements in which the end was realized by imitation. This latter kind of change can be called mimesis by augmentation.[36]

Second, in the constructive arts, Aristotle recognized: (a) mimesis by transformation of matter, as in making a statue, (b) mimesis by subtraction, as in carving out a form that one sees already suggested in the shape of a stone, and (c) mimesis by composition, as in bringing together many elements to build a house according to the architect's plan.[37]

Third, he drew an important distinction between natural mimesis, which corrected defects, and unnatural mimesis, which multiplied them.

But my account of the repertoire is still incomplete. I have neither exhausted the possible varieties of mimesis nor described how the numerous varieties were combined in the same system of thought. Apart from the asymmetries between nature and art and between actual and potential within nature, Aristotle defined a third area of asymmetry—that within art: the relation between a work of art and the understanding of that work in the mind of its audience. Here, too, in man's artificial second nature, mimesis as growth was a strategy of corrective mediation.

[35] *De Gen. et Corr.* 2. 10. 336b.   [36] Cf. *Physics* 1. 190b.
[37] On the above three varieties, see *Physics* 1. 190b.

From the previous discussion, it is clear that when Aristotle discussed the varieties of mimesis, he emphasized understanding a work, rather than making it. In his discussions of dramatic poetry and the dance, he was not so much concerned with the objective resemblance of image to archetype (which occupied his thoughts about sculpture) as he was with the mimetic response of the audience. He understood that responsive mimesis could flow from audience to performer and thus shape works of art. This might work for good or ill. Critics goaded dramatists into unremitting expansion of their art. The dancer moved as his spectators wished; they made him what he was. So too, musicians chose perverted modes and unnaturally colored melodies for audiences of depraved taste and more ethical modes for the free and educated.[38] When he turned to drama, however, Aristotle was primarily concerned with the impact of theater upon its audience. The aim was catharsis—an inward purification. By way of mimesis in the mind of the beholder, rather than in the act of making, he came to something fundamental in human nature, and, indeed, basic to the question of unity among the arts. For the key to his discussion of cathartic, or responsive, mimesis is reason, which Aristotle considered the essential characteristic of man and his most intimate likeness to God. Leaving tactics aside, the balance of my discussion will follow this trail, through corrective strategy to unity.

The contours of unity began to appear when Aristotle turned to the medium in which poetry really performed its corrective functions: the minds of audiences. The didactic functions of imitation in the community were primary. Indeed, Aristotle's concept of mimesis in the literary and performing arts hinged on the way in which he thought about education. More than any other animals, he wrote, man learned from infancy on by imitation, and, throughout his life, he delighted in learning from works that imitated and conveyed the meanings of things.[39] Responsive mimesis was a powerful device of moral instruction. Visual arts possessed in slight measure what the aural arts had most fully: the power to engage the feelings of man and to move them in sympathy with the characters that they represented. For this reason, indecent pictures should be banished (except where religious practices sanctioned them), together with immoral speeches in plays. Flute playing could be discarded as contributing nothing to sound knowledge. Finally, young children should be told only such stories as foreshadowed their adult occupations, and they should also be shielded

---

[38] *Politics* 8. 6. 1341b; 8. 7. 1342a.   [39] *Poetics* 4. 1448b.

from dramatic productions and paintings that their moral characters were not yet well enough formed to resist.[40] These comments recall the celebrated iconoclasm with which Plato swept perverse mimetic arts out of his ideal city. They also indicate how, in correction, Aristotle found a common denominator for all his varieties of mimesis in a general pattern of egress and return.

The arts might appear to be nonimitative when their functions were detached from models in the visible and tactile world of nature; they might appear to be separate and autonomous when they observed their individual genres. But, in their educative functions, they pointed beyond themselves, as, through drawing, one learned to judge the beauty of human form.[41] There were many arts, each serving its own good, but they were clustered into families, the subordinate ones serving the higher, as bridle making served horse riding and as bronze casting served statuary.[42] Politics subsumed all arts and all their ends; it was the good for man.[43] Inasmuch as they expressed the inherited wisdom and ethical standards of a particular city or people, the arts thus comprised a modal unity to which citizens were disciplined through the force of law, the mind being blank and written on by habit.[44]

There was an even wider, more complex and basic unity beyond politics, for, in a precise way, the movement of thought by which man exercised his arts reproduced the imitative chain of cause and effect, the generative order in which nature itself continually strove for perfection. Aristotle described the universe as a great causal unity on the biological pattern. Its cohesive bond was the movement of generation. Since, Aristotle argued, nothing moved by itself, the entire process was a sequence in which each being received and conveyed motion. Each was both effect and cause, both pattern and copy. As cause, each transmitted its likeness to its effect. However, the premise of unity excluded indefinite regress, and the mimetic chain of causality had its beginning and end in God, the Unmoved Mover and Final Cause. Such was also the circular pattern of egress and return in the hierarchy of knowledge.

Specific intellectual arts were subsumed into generic arts (and sciences); no genus having its own essential properties could be interchanged with another, any more than arithmetic could be used to prove

---

[40] *Politics* 7. 17. 1336a–b; 8. 5. 1340a; 8. 6. 1341a–b.   [41] *Politics* 8. 3. 1338a–b.
[42] *Nic. Eth.* 1. 1–2. 1094a–b. *Politics* 1. 8. 1256a.   [43] *Nic. Eth.* 1. 2. 1094b.
[44] Cf. *Nic. Eth.* 2. 1. 1103a–b.

geometrical premises.[45] The genera too were arranged in order, passing upward from those subject to chance to those increasingly less so, from those in which the body was most used (or abused) to those in which the mind played the greater, or the entire, role, and finally through sciences in which the use of the mind required progressively greater exactitude and more complete unity between facts as they are and facts as they are known by the reason.[46] Both the carpenter and the geometer considered the right angle. The difference between them was that the carpenter had an eye to practical application, while the geometer asked what (or what sort of thing) it was. And this distinction between the pragmatic and the theoretical explained why the geometer "is a spectator of truth" and why his art was the higher in the order of knowledge.[47]

Reason dominated this scheme in which the arts replicated the order of life, moving from less to more perfect forms, even as logic itself reproduced "the circular process of coming-to-be in nature."[48] This premise carried Aristotle's doctrine that human knowledge replicated the natural order far beyond the tactical arts, to a point, in fact, where strategic knowledge was detached even from politics, the art of arts. The two highest degrees of wisdom dealt with abstract, theoretical knowledge: they were philosophic and intuitive wisdom. Through them, the wise man went beyond the skills of making, beyond the knowledge of universals, and beyond even the ability to apply them to particular cases.

Only the philosopher contemplated timeless actuality, rather than the things that imitated it in this world of time.[49] He gained the knowledge of the true that was prior to the first principles. At the practical level of wisdom, knowledge lost its last vestiges of art; it became an exercise in virtue, perfected in these last two stages. Finally, one contemplated the ultimate good, the good-in-itself. The lower degrees of knowledge corresponded with the areas of natural and moral philosophy—the observation and analysis of phenomena and of man in his dealings with other men—while the higher ones constituted metaphysical philosophy—speculation concerning ultimate causes and principles. At these upper levels, imitation of the natural order through the act of knowing culminated in imitation of God, the universal end. By definition, the ultimate Good was self-sufficient. It neither had needs

---

[45] See, for example, *Post. An.* 1. 7. 75a–b, 1. 28. 87a–b.
[46] *Politics* 1. 11. 1258b. *Post. An.* 1. 27. 87a.   [47] *Nic. Eth.* 1. 7. 1098a.
[48] *Post. An.* 2. 12. 95b.   [49] Jaeger, *Aristotle,* p. 90.

nor was needed; it existed in and for itself alone. By imitating it, a man left his labors of making and action and gave himself over to the supreme happiness of life according to reason, life that was supremely noble. It was a vision of truth beyond tactics and strategy, in which the arts, and even virtuous acts of justice, courage, liberality, and temperance, were trivial and demeaning; it was a vision of unity which disclosed that the highest form of life, being neither needy nor needed, was useless.[50]

In one of his most profound comments about the arts, Aristotle wrote that the craftsman loved what he made because he loved existence. It was an instance of self-love, "for what [the craftsman] is in potentiality, he manifests in activity."[51] The long struggle for virtue through the grades of wisdom from the least perfect toward the noble and the good was also an exercise in self-love, or rather, of the divine element, reason, that was in man and that the philosophic few—"those who are truly fortunate"—recognized as man.[52] To love was to imitate and be like the beloved, and, at the highest level, to be like the self-contemplating God.

Thus far, we have seen that five major varieties of mimesis appear in Aristotle's writings. All of them are strategies of correction within mediated asymmetries. All can be described as strategies of reversion inasmuch as they cast transformation in the light of egress from and return to a primordial model.

1. Cosmic mimesis. This appears, first, in the likeness between eternal being and nature's continual round of "coming-to-be." It appears, second, in the mimesis by addition that occurs as individuals mature, or grow, into their generic forms, a process that slowly manifests potential likenesses between offspring and parents.

2. Functional mimesis. Everything made by man is mimetic because it answers to a preconceived need or end and because it reflects a pattern in the mind of the artist, shipwright, sculptor, or architect. In the constructive arts, there are a number of subvarieties of mimesis: by transformation of matter, by subtraction, and by composition. But function was an inadequate scale of value, since, in practice, arts could be followed honorably, according to nature, or dishonorably, contrary to it or divorced from it. Most sweepingly, everything that was func-

---

[50] *Nic. Eth.* 9. 8. 1169a; 10. 7–8. 1177a–1179a. For the argument that Aristotle was driven to analogy as a way to unify "irreducibly pluralistic" scientific knowledge, see Burrell, *Analogy*, pp. 70–73, 86f.
[51] *Nic. Eth.* 9. 7. 1168a.   [52] *Nic. Eth.* 9. 8. 1169; 10. 9. 1179b.

tional, or useful, fell short of the intuitive mimesis that characterized a supremely happy life.

3. Generic mimesis. Aristotle classified the arts, and especially the genres of poetry. He could do so because he recognized that, through time, each art developed stylized forms—*genres*—that could be relied on to achieve its function. The conventions of the art became self-reflexive. Major innovations occurred, as men stretched the possibilities of their art and critics unreasonably expected poets to surpass all the best achievements of their predecessors.[53] Even so, artists could not step outside the requirements of poetry or probability (as defined by the conventions of their art and common opinion) without being judged to have been "guilty of absurdity as well as a fault of art."[54]

4. Responsive mimesis. One distinction of the literary and performing arts, as opposed to the mechanical ones, was that they evoked mimesis in the minds of audiences. A rudder had a user but no audience. A tragedy succeeded in the degree to which an audience found it convincing, followed the poet in "seeing everything with the vividness of an eyewitness," and felt the emotions portrayed.[55] This gave representational arts their didactic power, especially arts that addressed the senses of sight and hearing. The more a work left to the audience's imagination, the higher it stood on the scale of abstract knowledge. Thus, music, which addressed the hearing, stood higher than painting or sculpture, which engaged the mind through sight. (Even in tragedy, spectacle—the visual aspect of performance—was "the least artistic of all the parts and [had] least to do with the art of poetry." Indeed, Aristotle argued, the effects of tragedy could be achieved without actors or spectacle.)[56]

Further, there were gradations among the verbal arts, according to the degree of abstraction. Thus, the historian was not a poet because he had to describe a plethora of disconnected events. His materials gave him no narrative line. By contrast, the poet made up his plot, and the more he reduced the manifold of actual life to universal principles, the greater was his art. On this ground, the mimetic art of tragedy was higher than that of comedy, which portrayed individual events; it was higher than that of epic poetry, which described an interlacing of many characters and actions.

For my purposes, it is important to emphasize that responsive mimesis—purification or catharsis—required knowledge on the part of

[53] *Poetics* 18. 1456a.   [54] *Poetics* 26. 1462a; 25. 1461b.
[55] *Poetics* 17. 1455a.   [56] *Poetics* 6. 1450b.

the viewer and that this knowledge had to be accompanied by a suspension of disbelief. If tragedy were to strike an audience with pity and fear, as Aristotle taught it should, it had to move within the scope of the audience's experience. But the audience also needed to be so caught up in the action as to forget the difference between the reality portrayed and its portrayal. It had to imagine that it was witnessing the tragic actions themselves. The action had to be plausible, believable. Belief—or at least a measure of credulity—was part of the act of recognition, or knowing, and thus it was essential to the corrective result. It made possible the identification between object and viewer by which the mind became what it thought. But the suspension of disbelief by the audience presupposed an act of divination by the artist.

Finally, responsive mimesis could alter artistic norms, as it did when critics goaded playwrights to surpass their predecessors and audiences determined the performances of dancers and musicians.

5. Intuitive mimesis. All the previous kinds of mimesis depended both upon an artist's ability to unify his work according to its function and on the capacity of others to respond by divining the unity in it. Those abilities, in turn, depended on insight as much as on technical mastery. How could the maker reach the common ground of response? In dramatic poetry, it required of the poet an uncanny gift, or a touch of madness.[57] In philosophy, it required of the investigator extraordinary talents and a direct vision of the source of wholeness. Aristotle insisted that explanatory passages in epics or dramas were not mimetic if the author interrupted the dramatic action to address the audience directly[58] and that, given their nonimitative discourse, philosophers were not poets if they merely set their ideas down in verse instead of prose. His doctrine of intuitive mimesis, however, left no doubt that the writings of philosophers could be regarded as signs pointing toward the inexpressible unity within which all tactical artistic mimesis and all strategic knowing took place. And, indeed, philosophers could write mimetically if they expressed their doctrines in a dramatic form, as Plato did in the Socratic dialogues, employing the nameless "art which imitates by language alone, without harmony, in prose or in verse."[59]

Underlying these varieties of mimesis by reversion (which encompassed being and knowledge as a structure of belief), however, there was a deep contradiction, an element in the dimension of faith that

[57] *Poetics* 17. 1455a.   [58] *Poetics* 19. 1456b; 24. 1460a.   [59] *Poetics* 1. 1447b.

rendered the arts not at all mimetic. Like metaphor, imitation required separateness, similarity in dissimilars.[60] But, according to Aristotle, "a whole and its parts are supposed to be identical."[61] Mimesis played within the hermeneutic circle, in which the whole and the parts were interpreted in terms of one another; but more than a tautology was involved. For this consideration occasionally swept Aristotle quite beyond any kind of functional unity of dissimilar arts to a heuristic doctrine of absolute unity and, in fact, to one of exceptional rigor. In one line of thought about corrective movement, he argued that God was Reason, and that Reason was the divine element in man, an immortal element in a body and soul that composed a mortal unity. Very ambiguously, he wrote that the human soul contained two intellects. The first, the passive, was mortal and belonged to the individual person; the second, the active, was a deathless mind that quickened and enlightened the passive intellect and impelled it to action. Exactly what Aristotle meant by this has been the subject of long controversy. Beyond any doubt, however, he held that God was both above the world and within it and that God was the source of the immortal element in man. His cloudy references to the two intellects made it possible to argue that he had envisioned a world in which the arts were not the man-made reflection of the hierarchy of nature but the means by which God himself working in men created the world of culture. They also contained the germ of a further idea that a dialectical exchange, like that between an artist and his public, existed between God and the world and that, indeed, God became in the processes of nature.

Instead of finding a crisp, general definition of mimesis, I have run into a bewildering thicket of opinions, some of which lacked the minimal clarity that any definition requires. My first conclusion, therefore, is that a history of mimesis in classical Greece must be pluralistic. It cannot narrow its focus to one or two representative "types" because the facts were not that tidy, nor were the possibilities for development correspondingly limited.

My second conclusion is that mimesis was not categorical, even for the writers who thought about it most seriously. It was an act of transition and mediation in asymmetrical relations. It mediated asymmetries between transcendent and natural orders, between actual and potential within nature, between a work of art and its audience within art, between nature and art, and between the divine, archetypal reason

---

[60] *Poetics* 22. 1459a.   [61] *Rhetoric* 2. 24. 1401a.

and its human image. It was an exercise in reproduction by stimulus and response. The strategy of mimesis could be employed in perverse, destructive ways, but rightly directed, it led from less to more perfect stages of knowledge. It could be accomplished in many ways: differently in every act, more intricately in generic arts than in specific ones, more perfectly in liberal arts than in manual ones.

My third conclusion, then, is that any theory of corrective mimesis was a modular construction. The elements that any given writer used and how he pieced them together depended on whether he had a conception of ultimate unity, and, if so, what that vision was at the moment of writing. This is, of course, why Plato's early doctrines of form (and transformation) differ from his later ones. But, being modular, early compositions shared elements with later ones, providing continuity; sophisticated theories shared elements with simple opinions, permitting common values; and hostile schools of thought employed identical modes differently, engendering affinity, exchange, and mutual growth.

Both Aristotle and Plato considered the diverse varieties of mimesis, rightly directed, to be movements of corrective reversion—of egress from and return to a primordial model. But from there their views diverged. Plato advanced a model of imitation as a process of recollection, restoration, or recovery. Aristotle set forth a model of imitation as an initial process in nature—generation—ceaselessly repeated. The same model of generation and growth applied to the potentialities of the human mind, although in view of man's rational capacities, the process was refined through habit, of which education was a particular mode.

The elements of a third reversionary model already existed in their day, one that, like generation, expressed the enduring order that the mind was capable of replicating but that did not involve correction. The components of this third model were diverse. They came *inter alia* from the corpuscular theories of materialist philosophers, from the numerical proportions of Pythagoras, from Plato's description of the world as a fabric pieced together by the Demiurge, and from Aristotle's scheme of celestial spheres. However, the conclusive pieces in the composition belonged to a later time. There were astronomical observations, particularly those made toward the end of the Hellenistic age. The followers of Hipparchus (ob. 126 B.C.), including Ptolemy (fl. A.D. 141), coined a metaphor to describe the imitative character of celestial movements continually repeating themselves. They compared the universe with a machine. By this they did not mean that the cosmos was soulless, or that its parts moved by themselves, but rather that it was a mechanism inhabited by spirits that men could model to scale in wood and metal.[62] The Roman architect Vitruvius (fl. 25 B.C.) repeated an image already worn when he wrote that "all machinery is derived from nature and is founded on the teaching and instruction of the revolution of the firmament."[63]

This third reversionary model of imitation—by repetition—expressed the eternal harmonies of order that informed moral beauty. Although mimesis by repetition did not progress, it was applied to moral correction. For, as Plato wrote, it was "by learning the harmonies and revolutions of the universe" that the person who thought was assimilated to things about which he thought. Thus he resumed his original nature and, having assimilated the eternal verities, he attained "to that perfect life which the gods have set before mankind."[64] Indeed, authors throughout this period, and for centuries after, valued the (for them) cognate arts of music and astronomy because they were tools for studying the cosmic order as a visible sign of the invisible virtue with which the human soul could be made to conform.

To say that the end of the arts was to evoke virtue implanted in the soul was also to say that there should be agreement between man's thought and action. Morals exist in practice. Therefore, several important consequences for action followed from all these efforts to define the unity of the arts within the more general concept of mediated form. Plato reproved the Sophists for teaching that the gods, as they really were in nature, were not such as the laws (that is, art) portrayed.[65] But he himself taught a theology quite at variance with the legends of his people, and he would have expelled Homer and Hesiod and the mythographers from his ideal city for what he judged to be their lying fictions about the gods. Aristotle's god, pure act and self-thinking thought, is as far removed from the gods of legend and public ritual as Plato's "Father and Maker of the cosmos" is remote from human knowledge and ineffable.

In searching for unity under the aspect of form, therefore, men also sought universal values. In advancing doctrines of corrective mimesis,

[62] E. J. Dijksterhuis, *The Mechanization of the World Picture,* trans. C. Dikshoorn (Oxford, 1961), pp. 12, 65f.

[63] *De Architectura* 10. 1. 4. "Omnis autem est machinatio rerum natura procreata ac praeceptrice et magistra mundi versatione instituta." Vitruvius continues to say that, by imitating examples taken from nature, men perfected the resources of life, enlarging the store of useful things by gradual advancement in methods.

[64] *Timaeus* 90. [65] *Laws* 10. 889–890.

25

S074671

they found that those values were at odds with the specific values of their own cities and cultures. Correspondingly the arts did have a unity beyond the external or functional. Their inner unity, however, was disclosed by an occult knowledge accessible to the few, and, moreover, to the fewest of the few who reached the maturity of years in study and contemplation. From their viewpoint, the truth hidden in the arts could contradict social truth, just as authentic theology negated legend. In troubled times, the duality of exoteric and esoteric truth came easily to men who were excluded from active politics. Endangered by the violent ebb and flow of factions, they yet wished to define some cohesive bond in their private and collective lives, even if the effort led them to seek unity of being through belief in ironic enigmas, like Plato's, and even if it brought them to pity the world around them for its values.

Neoplatonists

The concepts of egress and corrective return did enter common knowledge, at least among the educated; but they never lost their covert quality. This was especially true when they entered into the canonical teachings of philosophical sects, as, for example, in the Neoplatonist tradition, which began with the Alexandrine, Ammonius Saccas (ca. 160–242), and reached its fullest development in the Athenian, Proclus (410–485). Through its rejection of all specific values in favor of universal ones, its translation of the world into orders of mystical perfection, and its practice of occult arts for the purification of the soul, this school carried its ancient heritage to a vastly intricate embellishment. According to the Neoplatonist tradition, the arts were valued for what they could contribute to the interpretation of oracular texts, to theurgy and astrology. However, in the ascent of the soul, one must leave "the masses of people who flock together in herds,"[66] abandon the images formed by verbal and mathematical arts, and pass toward the intuition of unity in the madness and self-abandonment of ecstatic love. This fervid vision of unity had a profound effect on the Latin West, first through the influence of Plotinus (204/5–270) and his disciple Porphyry (233–ca. 304) on St. Augustine, and, later, through the texts of Dionysius Areopatigica, which secured central importance in Western theology from the ninth century on.

[66] *Comm. Alcib.,* col. 517f.

26

As synthesizers, the Neoplatonists combined old and diverse elements in new ways. For them, nature was a hierarchy of spiritual perfection, and, within that hierarchy, their primary concern was with the asymmetry between God and the human soul. As they meditated on patterns of natural reproduction, they contributed three new subvarieties of mimetic strategy for the perfection of the soul. These formulae—diminution, dialectical transference, and transposition—proved to be exceptionally important in later thought.

Before he set out to march into Persia in the Emperor Gordian's army, Plotinus had been converted to philosophy, largely by reading Plato's dialogue, *Parmenides*. He found there what struck him as a reasoned statement of the unity of things. As he understood Plato's treatise, he imagined that the cosmos existed primarily by a strategy of mimesis by diminution. Thus, this became the first of his three new modes. All living creatures were parts of a great whole because, like beams of light, they poured out from the same origin in diminishing stages of brightness and purity as they receded from the source. Like Plato, he called this source the One.

Each level in the order of diminishing perfection that issued from the One moved in two mimetic ways. Under the twofold impulse of contemplation and generation, they yearned upward for the higher orders from which they emanated, and they strained downward to reproduce that intelligible order in lower orders, and even in the world of the senses. Each link in the chain of Being gave life to the next beneath it; each received imperfectly the spiritual image of the next link above it; each yearned for, and imitated, the forms of being over it.

Plotinus thus introduced a second kind of mimesis. While he described the entire procession of things from the One in terms of diminution, he grasped the interplay between levels in the hierarchy as a kind of mimetic exchange, or transference. From Aristotle's mimesis of immanent causality, Plotinus took his concept of each order yearning downward to reproduce itself, as, for example, souls cast reflections of themselves in matter, narcissistically attracted by their own brilliant images in the mirror of what is without form or measure or being. From Plato's mimesis of transcendent form, Plotinus took his concept of the soul straining upward toward the state of pure thought, or intellect, in which "the being which is active in the life of the soul is, in some way, reflected back upon it, like the image in a mirror when its polished and brilliant surface is motionless."[67]

[67] *Enneads* 1. 4. 10.

Man held a unique place in Plotinus's scheme of the world, located on the horizon between being and non-being. The identification of being and intelligibility made the analogues of being and knowledge interchangeable in his discussions of man. Thus, the third new mimetic formula—transposition—pertained only to the human capacity to change places within the cosmic hierarchy by passing through degrees of knowledge.

Ceaselessly contemplating itself and always remaining at rest in what Aristotle had described as the "activity of immobility" character-istic of pure Reason, the One would have appeared an unlikely model for human life at its fullest, but that is exactly where Plotinus's argu-ment led. He had taken up Plato's definition of man as a soul using a body. He had also adopted Plato's concept of the soul as a microcosm, as a reduplication of the cosmic order. Like the universe, man's soul was a structured hierarchy of spiritual orders, ranging from the vegetal to the intelligent, each attracted to its immediate superior. The entire structure of the soul culminated, as in the cosmos, in an abstract, un-conscious, impassive Intellect. If the soul were not impeded by matter, the whole of man's true being was drawn in harmony with its own na-ture and the general force of all nature to return into union with the Divine.

How then did the human soul recalibrate its asymmetry with the Divine, achieving transposition by mimesis? The answer is that it dis-solved its limitations by ascetically stripping itself of finite reason, of temperament and emotion, and of concern with material things and ties to finite historical situations. It transcended everything that con-fined it to space and time. It became one with the source of all life.

It has breathed life into them all, whatever is nourished by earth and sea, all the creatures of the air, the divine stars in the sky; it is the maker of the sun; itself formed and ordered this vast heaven and conducts all that rhythmic mo-tion; and it is a principle distinct from all these to which it gives law and move-ment and life, and it must of necessity be more honorable than they, for they gather or dissolve as soul brings them life or abandons them, but soul, since it never can abandon itself, is of eternal being.[68]

Through imitation of the Divine, the soul "is itself what it loves."[69] By its essential union with the One, the principle of Being, each human

---

[68] *Enneads* 5. 1. 2 (in *The Enneads,* trans. Stephen MacKenna, B. S. Page ed. [New York, 1957], p. 370).
[69] *Enneads* 6. 8. 18.

soul contained within itself the seeds and forms of all things; the quest of life was to articulate that universal force and energy, to live in the blinding perception that finite man and infinite God were solitaries in motion toward unity.

In his divinization of the cosmos, Plotinus left no room for conditions of physical existence. He repeated Plato's statement that time was the image of eternity; but it was not an image from which Plotinus tried to learn. His cosmos was entirely nonhistorical. His fundamental devaluation of the specific, concrete, and nonuniversal led him to isolate the individual man, as intellect, from associations of this world, from the passionate commitments of the moment—from the particular historical situation in which any individual person lived. Life in society was nothing but a play. Plotinus had accompanied an imperial army in Persia. He must have heard chilling reports of the barbarian invasions that threatened to bring the Roman world down around his ears. But even with regard to these greatest of all human disasters, he was able to write that "murders, death in all its shapes, the capture and sacking of towns, all must be considered as so much stage-show, so many shiftings of scenes, the horror and outcry of a play." They are like children's games; one dies, one returns. Such things afflict the outer appearance, the "phantasm of the man," but not "the true man, the inner soul."[70]

Summary

To recapitulate what I have said about Greek philosophy's contribution to the career of mimesis:

1. Mimesis was recognized as a reproductive strategy in nature and as the dominant strategy in the unconscious, but continual and creative, process of generation.

2. The arts, culminating in philosophy, were thought to constitute a second nature for man, in which mimesis was used, consciously and deliberately, as a strategy of creative reproduction.

3. Mimesis was also a strategy of reproduction in the area between the parallel orders of nature and art—that is, in thought.

a) It was generally agreed that, to be whole, all works of art needed a beginning, a middle, and an end. This was especially true of compo-

[70] *Enneads* 3. 2. 15 (ed. cit., pp. 172f).

sitions that, like drama or music, required concentrated attention as their patterns unfolded over a space of time so that they could not be taken in at a glance, as could a painting or a statue.

b) When they thought about art, philosophers employed the strategy of mimesis to describe how an artist passed from beginning to end in the process of composition, and, equally important, how, in its own mind's eye, the audience recapitulated the process toward wholeness that the artist revealed.

c) Inasmuch as they explained deliberate, creative action, mimetic doctrines belonged to wider theories about thinking. Thus, mimesis was a subject of epistemology. It belonged to a vision of psychological (or spiritual) wholeness based on analogies with theories of artistic composition.

d) Arguing from analogues in art, mimetic principles of composition were specifically applied to the formation of the mind, man's rational faculty. They were used to explain the entire subject of education, which ancient writers frequently compared with the work of a sculptor carving an image out of a rough block of stone.

e) Applied to the soul, man's spiritual faculty, the compositional strategy of mimesis was given a characteristic pattern of movement that corresponded with the sequence of beginning, middle, and end. The soul went forth from an origin, which was true nature; it passed by imitation through stages of development; it advanced by ever increasing likeness toward an end. This model of egress, formation, and return was the basic framework of many theories of human destiny. I call it mimesis by reversion. Eventually, the pattern of egress, mimetic reformation, and return to wholeness was subsumed into the Christian doctrine of man's creation in the image and likeness of God, his fall into the deformity of sin, his reformation through progressive conformity with Christ, and his restoration to unity with God, man's proper origin and end.

f) Mimesis was a strategy of mind, a way of thinking. It postulated an ideal, or model, imitated by the mind and soul. However, the ideal was capable of being used as a social norm. Those who failed to conform with the ideal might be considered either gods—by participation in divinity—or animals in human form. Plato provided one instance of how the norm could function when he excluded marriage between Greeks and barbarians. So did Aristotle, when he categorized barbarians as suited by nature to be slaves, "human tools," and as beasts of the desert.

It was characteristic of Greek philosophy before its assimilation to Christianity that development of mimetic strategies did not extend beyond abstract categories of being and knowing into categories of history. Such an extension did occur, however, when other peoples received Greek doctrines.

Although many kinds of asymmetry had been imagined, and corresponding strategies of mimesis had been defined as mediating them, the sphere of history was not yet thought to be ruled by asymmetrical relationships. This possibility became conceivable when one culture confronted another. Allowing for the eclipse of natural science, the problems of unity and corrective strategy widened notably when it was a matter, not of transmitting, but of assimilating the liberal arts and doctrines about them as "alien wisdom," tactics that were couched, perhaps, in a foreign language.[71]

For, when one tradition confronted another, it became apparent that mimesis was more than an impulse in nature, or in art, or between those spheres. It was at this point that mimesis as mediation of asymmetries could be plainly identified as an act of historical transformation by which men consciously changed their own tradition and advanced it from one stage to another.

---

[71] For an excellent discussion of the assimilation of Greek culture throughout the ancient Mediterranean world, see A. Momigliano, *Alien Wisdom: The Limits of Hellenization* (Cambridge, 1975).

Chapter 2

Assimilation of Mimetic Doctrines
with Old Testament Theology

IT IS ONE of the great ironies of history that the Hebrews contributed its central metaphor to the mimetic tradition as that tradition was passed on by the Church. God created man in His own image and likeness. This grand conception of asymmetry set down by early editors of Genesis was later woven into the patterns of spiritual transformation expressed by Plato and Aristotle. Nothing could have been further from the minds of the editors of Genesis than to imply the metaphysical unity, the natural affinity, embedded in the mimetic pattern of egress and return. Though extraordinarily profound in its spiritual insights and its human values, Hebrew religious thought of the Old Testament period is fundamentally pragmatic, not speculative or abstract. Correspondingly, the goal of life was, not happiness achieved by the soul reforming itself according to some eternal model, but redemption performed by an external power—that is, by God. Asymmetry might be thought to exist between God and man, but it was certainly not mediated.

I shall now describe how what were and might have remained two entirely antithetic patterns for restoring the soul into wholeness were combined by Philo of Alexandria and the Apostle Paul in ways that proved to be decisive for Western culture. Plato, Aristotle, and the Neoplatonists worked within one, quite varied, tradition. Philo and Paul felt keenly the promise and the dangers of assimilating the foreign wisdom of the Greeks.

Philo of Alexandria

Philo had the delicate task of harmonizing the postulated truths of Greek philosophy with the revealed truths of the Scriptures. His frame of inference was set by a large and authentic tradition of Midrashic writings; he knew all too well that the philosophical arts belonged to a people in whose country the Jews, ancient and modern, abandoned their traditions and forgot their own language, Hebrew. He knew that those liberal arts belonged to a people, indeed, who persisted in referring to the Jews as enemies of the human race.[1]

Philo therefore sensed that assimilation had its limits. The arts were foreign; they belonged to the Gentiles. In his childhood, Moses was taught arithmetic, geometry, and harmony by Egyptians, astronomy by the Egyptians and Assyrians, and "all the other branches of encyclical education" by the Greeks.[2] But the arts were foreign in a second way, too: they were not innate, as knowledge was; they had to be acquired.[3] Innate knowledge was the higher, since it pointed the mind toward the unseen realities of life. However, the intellectual discipline of the arts was essential to the mind's progress beyond the rudiments of childhood education to philosophy and, ultimately, to wisdom.[4] The arts stood in much the same relationship to knowledge as the senses did to the mind and as the bondservant did to her mistress.[5] While the Gentiles grasped that a hierarchy of this sort existed, they lacked the enlightenment that would have guided them away from sophistry and toward authentic wisdom.[6] By election, God gave the Jews the power of beholding Him.[7]

Philo's contribution to the career of mimesis was embedded in his theory of the Logos as mediator between God and the existing world. All the varieties of mimesis set forth by Plato and Aristotle hinged on mediating the asymmetry between archetype and image. Philo's theology of the Logos drew many of those varieties into a relatively unified system of thought, one that prepared the way for Christian doctrines about mediation and mimesis in the work of Christ.

Above all, Philo wove the idea of mimesis in nature into his theory

---

[1] See *Life of Moses* 1. 6. *Special Laws* 2. 167. On the ritual separatism from the Gentiles, which Philo approved in Moses' career, see *Life of Moses* 1. 15. With regard to language, it is worth noticing that Philo considered the translation of the Septuagint to have been achieved through a miracle that brought the minds of the translators into harmony "with the most pure spirit of Moses" (*Life of Moses* 2. 5–7).

[2] *Life of Moses* 1. 5.   [3] *On Mating for the Sake of Knowledge* 22f.

[4] *On Mating for the Sake of Knowledge* 79.

[5] *On Mating for the Sake of Knowledge* 79. 142–144. H. A. Wolfson, *Philo: Foundations of Religious Philosophy in Judaism, Christianity, and Islam*, 2 vols. (Cambridge, Mass., 1947) 1: 81.

[6] *On the Creation* 14.   [7] *Migration of Abraham* 10–11.

of the Logos. His entire theory posited three interlocking natures that bore varying degrees of likeness to each other: the Logos, the existing world, and man. They formed a desending hierarchy of perfection.

By the two higher natures, Philo explained the formation of the world. God proceeded to create the world as an architect would design a city. He formed a plan in His mind, an intellectual model, and then He made the visible world, copying the model. Philo identified the model—the world perceptible only by the intellect—as the Logos, or Reason of God,[8] and he also referred to it as the nature that has no connection with time.[9] This archetype-nature corresponded roughly with Plato's world of Forms or Ideas; it contained the intellectual models of all genera visible to the intellect.[10] The material world therefore constituted a second nature—that in time—twice removed from the image in God's mind. But the two natures did not exist separately from each other, as Plato had them do, for the Reason of God, the model, was actually in the physical world.[11]

When Philo argued that the arts and sciences were rooted in nature, and that the theoretical structure of each art was built on nature,[12] he therefore presupposed these two areas of likeness. The first lay between the perfect and invisible model and ideas in God's mind, the timeless and changeless archetype. The second lay between the Logos and the material world of time and change, where laws were immortal and the genera endured, while individuals came and went, and the act of begetting young forever copied the original creative act. In this reproductive process of continual creation, nature itself worked "as a faultless art."[13] Human arts also occupied this second area of likeness between divine and human natures.

Functional and generic varieties of mimesis that, as we saw, were applied chiefly to the arts and artistic genres also found places in Philo's teaching. The arts derived immediately from nature—the faultless art—and, through the mediacy of nature, from God,[14] just as virtues did through the mediacy of the Logos.[15] There were generic

---

[8] *On the Creation* 4–6. J. Jervell, *Imago Dei. Gen. 1, 26 f, in Spätjudentum, in der Gnosis und in den paulinischen Briefen* (Göttingen, 1960), pp. 52–60.
[9] *Migration of Abraham* 25.   [10] *On the Creation* 4, 7.
[11] *On the Creation* 23. Wolfson, *Philo*, 1: 229–240.
[12] *Who is Heir of Divine Things* 115. *Migration of Abraham* 30.
[13] Cf. *Who is Heir of Divine Things* 172. *On the Creation* 13, 19, 24.
[14] *On the Creation* 22.
[15] *Migration of Abraham* 8. *On the Posterity of Cain* 129.

arts as well as generic virtues that were inexhaustible[16] and that transcended any individual expression or interpretation of a given art. As Philo read the texts before him and experienced the world, he recognized that some arts declined and that entirely new ones occasionally emerged.[17] How was that possible, if the material world were, as he held, a perfect copy of its archetype?[18] The doctrine of Providence gave him part of the answer: namely, that God renewed and enlarged his gifts to man in a precise if hidden sequence.[19] Immanence provided his conclusive answer: namely, that the arts existed and were pursued by people whose minds the divine Logos had inseminated according to the eternal model.[20] In this sense, all the arts, whenever practiced, replicated the higher likeness of the archetype. It could be argued that there was never an entirely new discovery in the arts, but, rather, that all art was the recollection or germination by stages through time of the pre-existent model outside of time.[21]

The third degree of likeness in Philo's doctrine of imitation was his concept of man as the image of God.[22] Man was capable of passing beyond the visible world to the invisible because, among all creatures, he alone possessed intellect and thereby carried the "likeness of that one mind [the Logos] which is in the universe as its primitive model."[23] The "man" actually made in God's image was "an idea or genus . . . imperishable by nature."[24] But, as a composite creature of the material elements, man was also a microcosm, a small-scale replica of the physical world.[25] And this carnal affinity to the material world endangered man's spiritual affinity to God; it haunted the space between nature and art.

By the process of biological reproduction in matter, each generation of mortals moved a step further from the genus[26]; the image remained, but the likeness faded.[27] Philo's entire concept of the arts centered on the means of restoring likeness to the spiritual image, despite the general deterioration of man in material, genetic descent. The soul had to pass upward from reflection to archetype to original, from the mortal

---

[16] *Change of Names* 79–80. *On the Posterity of Cain* 151f. Cf. *Allegorical Interpretation of the Laws* 2. 13.

[17] Cf. *Life of Moses* 1. 5.   [18] Cf. *On the Creation* 44.

[19] *On the Posterity of Cain* 145.

[20] *Who is Heir of Divine Things* 118–119. Cf. *Migration of Abraham* 15, and Wolfson, *Philo,* 1: 342f.

[21] *On Rewards and Punishments* 2. Wolfson, *Philo,* 1: 412.

[22] *Life of Moses* 2. 12.   [23] *On the Creation* 23.   [24] *On the Creation* 46.

[25] *Who is Heir of Divine Things* 155. *On the Creation* 73f, 147.

[26] *On the Creation* 49, 52.   [27] *On the Creation* 23.

to the imperishable, thus discovering, ascending, and recapitulating the order of perfection in nature.[28]

Properly understood, the arts were the beginning of this return to virtue. A rational, responsive mimesis was in play. Through the different lessons that the arts taught, one came to perceive that all of them derived their principles from philosophy.[29] The arts dealt with the lowest degree of likeness, that of the body, and their value as preparatory studies in virtue was antiscientific. Their lessons and principles were moral ones. From grammar, for example, one learned to despise one's private illusions in the light of dreadful calamities suffered by heroes and demigods; from geometry, one gained a sense of justice; from music, the concord beneath apparent discord; from dialectic, the remedy for the soul's greatest plague, deceit.[30] Those who were able to go beyond the "Egypt" of the body to knowledge (that is, to philosophy) abandoned the arts as scientific enterprises and turned from observation of the material world to introspection.[31] They grasped that, in addition to moral discipline, the arts provided tools for penetrating to invisible realities by way of allegory—not through the simple euhemeristic explanation of myth in human terms known to Plato, or the play with metaphor taught by rhetoricians, but as a way to discover the truth, rather than obfuscating it with myth and metaphor. Philo found the basis of his allegorical analysis of words, numbers, and relations in the Midrashic literature.[32] By the force of reason exercised in allegory, and aided by the insemination of the divine Logos, men could achieve knowledge of the first degrees of likeness. They could detect the abstract genera; they could describe the absolute symmetry of the world in which all opposites (including good and evil) constituted a harmonious integrity.[33] But there was still one degree to achieve, if one's likeness to God was to be perfected by advancing from knowledge to wisdom, for every image deceived, affording only a semblance of its original[34]: one had to pass from the model to the original. How could perceptions of God be had from God, instead of from His traces?[35]

---

[28] *Who is Heir of Divine Things* 316.

[29] *On Mating for the Sake of Knowledge* 11–19; 144–149. Cf. *Migration of Abraham* 8.

[30] *On Mating for the Sake of Knowledge* 11–19.

[31] On astronomy, see *Migration of Abraham* 33. Cf. Plato *Republic* 7. 529–530.

[32] *Republic* 2. 378. H. A. Wolfson, *The Philosophy of the Church Fathers,* 3d ed. (Cambridge, Mass., 1970), 1: 29–35. Wolfson, *Philo,* 1: 115f, 158f.

[33] *Who is Heir of Divine Things* 133–156, 207–213, 220–225.

[34] *On Rewards and Punishments* 5.   [35] *On Rewards and Punishments* 6.

As the incessant wrangling among hosts of philosophical sects illustrated, it could not be done by reason alone. One needed to pass from responsive to intuitive mimesis. Philo praised intellect as the image of God in man; but, at the highest level, he discarded reason as treacherous, as following its own laws.[36] He taught that the leap from image to likeness came by faith.[37] From this vantagepoint, he realized that the logical areas of philosophy, and even the rudiments of the arts, were not essential to progress in virtue.[38] Recapitulating in the mind the order of perfection in nature, "the faultless art," the sage went beyond both art and nature. Philo returned to Plato's enigmas.

Together with the priority of soul, Philo had accepted Plato's duality of Forms and images. The enigma of unreal reality was the pitfall of those who became mired in the physical world and practiced the idolatrous self-worship of mind or senses.[39] And, as in Plato's republic, it was countered by iconoclasm in the Law, when Moses cast "the mischievous arts of the painter and sculptor" out of his "commonwealth."[40] The inacccessibility of truth to reason also led Philo to the enigma of the ignorant sage, the man to whom the end of knowledge consists in certainty "that one knows nothing ... since there is only one wise being, who is also the only God."[41] Even Plato's inarticulate philosopher-king has a counterpart in Philo's portrayal of Moses' speech defect.[42]

Plato had begun from the problem set by the Delphic oracle: Know thyself. The impossibility of self-knowledge led him through the train of images to the Forms disclosed by virtue, the divine gift, or the equivalent gift of prophetic madness. Philo followed the same path to intuition. Adam perceived the inner natures of all animals and named them accordingly. Lacking the same sort of knowledge, he could not name himself.[43] Even at the level of philosophy, the soul, like the heavens, remained inscrutable, and mastering what exceeded the capacity of the mind cost the self-negation of the soul[44]: "Mortal and

---

[36] *Who is Heir of Divine Things* 246.

[37] *On Rewards and Punishments* 5. Wolfson, *Philo,* 1: 151, 156f.

[38] *On the Virtuous Being Also Free* 12. *On the Cherubim* 12. *On the Sacrifices of Abel and Cain* 113–116. Cf. *Migration of Abraham* 13.

[39] *On Mating for the Sake of Knowledge* 118.

[40] *Who is Heir of Divine Things* 169.   [41] *Migration of Abraham* 24.

[42] *Life of Moses* 1. 14.

[43] *Allegorical Interpretation of the Laws* 1. 91–92; 2. 15–18. *On the Creation* 148–150.

[44] *Allegorical Interpretation of the Laws* 1. 29. *On Dreams* 24–35. *Life of Moses* 2. 1.

immortal may not share the same home." When the divine light irradiated the soul, the light of human reason fled, and "ecstasy and divine possession and madness fall upon us."[45] Thus, men attained the vision of God unmediated by images—the wisdom imparted to the prophets.[46] In this way, Moses perceived the principles, identical with those of nature, that he reproduced in the Law.[47] Even more, he became what he saw. He became both "the god and king of the whole nation" and God's living law.[48] Thus, he also became a model, "an excellently wrought picture," mediating between "the darkness where God was" and those happy and pious men who copied him in their souls.[49] In a self-voiding vision, like Moses, man, the image, and his archetypal nature had reached the stage at which "the arts which were previously imitative of the works of nature would appear now to have become the nature themselves"[50]: in essence, the human nature that man had become (in a sense identical with the Logos) was also a flawless art.

Like the Greek doctrines of form that he loved and employed, Philo's conception of form led to a doctrine of wisdom accessible to the fewest of the few, to knowledge that ended in ignorance, reason perfected by inspired madness, art culminating in iconoclasm. There was, however, the difference that Philo's ornate structure of mimetic strategies concerned an existing law and actual historical experience, and, to his mind, demonstrated the superiority of Hebrew knowledge to that of the Gentiles. Philo retained the concept of the mind's egress from and corrective return to the good—the pattern of movement taught, in different ways, by Plato and Aristotle. But he also insisted that without the privilege of divine election, the mind's return to the good was arrested. Practitioners of the arts forgot about the unity of knowledge altogether and lapsed into their separate specialisms, squeezing disjointed segments of learning into their little souls.[51] Through impiety and unholiness, still others, professed philosophers, denied the ultimate truths, even the existence of God, or lapsed into polytheism. They were capable of self-worship, claiming that the human mind, or the senses, had been the origin of all the arts and of philosophy. God banished all such from the holy congregation. Their souls were dead, while "the scholars and disciples of Moses" lived a deathless life.[52]

---

[45] *Who is Heir of Divine Things* 264f.   [46] *Migration of Abraham* 15.
[47] *Life of Moses* 2. 2. Cf. ibid., 3. 3–4, on the Tabernacle.
[48] *Life of Moses* 1. 28. Cf. ibid., 2. 1.   [49] *Life of Moses* 1. 28.
[50] *Migration of Abraham* 30.
[51] *On Mating for the Sake of Knowledge* 77, 152. See also ibid., 150.
[52] *Special Laws* 1. 327–345.

Philo thus added a historical mimesis to the metaphysical varieties of mimesis that he inherited from Greek philosophy. In recapitulating the hierarchy of perfection in nature, one also recapitulated the historical experience, the tradition, of God's chosen people. This entire tradition became actual in each of Moses' spiritual imitators.

By the privilege of its election, Israel avoided the error into which all other peoples fell by worshipping and serving created things. As a monument of its sublime knowledge, it also possessed the Mosaic Code that, being stamped with the seal of nature herself, had influenced all peoples, barbarians and Greeks alike. Indeed, Philo argued, every nation should abandon its own code and adopt the laws of Moses.[53] The Gentiles correctly taught that the end of man was virtue: to live according to nature. But they misread the axiom. They did not perceive that virtue, the law of nature, was honoring God and laboring continually in His service.[54] They had no idea that the harmony between words and actions, reproducing the celestial harmony at which they aimed, came by adhering literally to the Mosaic prescripts, including of course those regarding the Sabbath and circumcision.[55] It was only right that, seeing immediately the source and goal of wisdom, Israel should offer thanks and intercession to God on behalf of the entire world.[56]

But the vision of God antedated the Code. Despite his brilliant education in the "encyclical studies" and his exalted position at the Egyptian court, Moses himself had left the Gentile learning aside as spurious and had gone to pursue the education of his kinsmen.[57] Even among Jews, however, the place of the arts in the true order of knowledge was grasped only by those "initiated into the hidden light of the sacred Scriptures."[58] Inspired piety was the essence of true philosophy.

Thus, Philo's praise of piety and righteousness[59] had antecedents and parallels in Greek thought, but it was tied to the literal observance of the Mosaic Code. His concept of prophetic intuition mediating between nature and art as the highest form of knowledge accessible to

---

[53] *Life of Moses* 2. 3.

[54] *On the Posterity of Cain* 185. Wolfson, *Philo*, 2. 182–187.

[55] *Migration of Abraham* 16, 23. *Life of Moses* 2. 8.

[56] *Special Laws* 2. 167. *Life of Moses* 1. 27.   [57] *Life of Moses* 1. 7.

[58] *On Dreams* 26. *Migration of Abraham* 8. On the procession of virtues from God and the vision of God as the original and goal of happiness, see H. Hegermann, *Die Vorstellung vom Schöpfungsmittler im Hellenistischen Judentum und Urchristentum* (Berlin, 1961. *Texte und Untersuchungen,* 82), pp. 17, 26.

[59] *On Rewards and Punishments* 9.

man also had ample philosophical precedents; but it was inseparable from the scriptural prophecies concerning the historical destinies of Israel, prophecies that, being fulfilled gradually through time, testified to the truth of the Hebrews' election.[60] Moses as "king" and lawgiver had a manifest forefather in Plato's philosopher-king. But Philo's Moses also acted as a priest, instituting the priesthood of Aaron and setting aside the Levites to the divine service; the institutions that he established still existed, still adhered to his laws, and still performed their delegated functions on behalf of the entire world. Finally, Moses was a moral exemplar whose deeds were worthy of emulation. And this view placed a categorical obligation on the faithful unprecedented in Greek philosophy: to imitate an angry paragon who killed in the name of virtue, defied and overthrew evil rulers, and executed thousands of his own idolatrous people. Those were some lessons that Philo brought from his Hebrew inheritance to the alien wisdom of the arts. Together with his practice of allegory and doctrines of the Logos and of man as the image of God, they passed on unacknowledged to his Christian successors.

Philo's great achievement lay in employing mimetic strategies to reconcile the revealed truth of the Old Testament with the philosophical content of the arts, and indeed in demonstrating to his satisfaction that the Scriptures were the highest application of mimetic strategies fragmentarily disclosed in the arts. The doctrines of creation, election, and revelation—and therefore the intrusion of God into the natural order—were very difficult elements to reconcile with Greek doctrines of form. Philo, however, found an ingenious solution when he determined that God's creation of the world was not concluded on the sixth day but rather that nature—the Logos—was the flawless art by which it continued, according to eternal laws of generation. By imitating the divine creative act, man participated in it. From this point, Philo went on to locate human arts in the general creative scheme of responsive mimesis, according to which man, having been made in the image of God, lost his original resemblance through sin, regained his divine likeness, and thus approached forms in the mind of God through the mediacy of the Logos. Knowledge advanced by faith; it was crowned by intuition that transcended it.

Thus, Philo preserved Plato's doctrines that mimesis was a reproductive strategy in nature, in art, in the mind, and between nature and art, and, moreover, that, rightly practiced as an intellectual strategy, it

[60] Cf. *Life of Moses* 3. 39.

was esoteric. He retained the pattern of the soul's corrective movement: egress from the forms, aversion from (or forgetting) them, (re-) conversion to them, and, finally, return to and assimilation with them. By applying this pattern to the historical experience of the Jews, Philo's doctrines prepared the way for Christian Platonists who applied the model of egress and return to the broad sweep of history: mankind's creation in the image and likeness of God, deformity through sin, recovery of image-likeness through imitation of Christ, and ultimate assimilation in the life of God. Other apsects of Philo's thought had extreme importance in the development of Christian theology. He achieved his hypostatic union of art and nature in the Logos, by means of allegorical demonstration; he compounded this esoteric method by grafting Plato's ironic enigmas onto scriptural theology in such a way as to assure that, as a guide to historical change, the mimetic tradition could continue to teach both art and iconoclasm, both reason and the divine madness of prophecy, both the sanctions of community and the terrible judgment against the community by the elect.

Paul

Hebrew theology made two distinct contributions to the development of mimesis. The first was the conception of man as the image of God, together with the understanding, so emphatic in the Old Testament, that man could not be abstracted into the two categories, body and soul. Rather, he was the image of God in his integrity. The second was the doctrine that human experience was moving toward an apocalyptic end. Through this latter doctrine, the ancient Hebrews prepared the materials for a dimension of mimesis undreamed of by the Greek philosophers. Like Plato, Aristotle, and Plotinus, they taught that things had unity because they moved toward the same end. But the Hebrew doctrine of ends, as cast by the prophets, involved a community living under an eschatological shadow. The end that gave direction and meaning to individual human experience was the common destruction of the existing world and the reconstitution of a new heaven and a new earth. Mankind advanced toward that transformation through the aggregate of experience—by augmentation, instead of by reversion. In this sense, mankind imitated the future. The combination of the unities of being and knowledge in Greek philosophy with Hebrew eschatology would appear to have been highly implausible. But Philo illustrated that what was implausible was not necessarily impossible, while Paul took up explicitly the two ideas of movement toward wholeness: the soul's triumph by reversion from and to God, and mankind's collective passage, by augmentation, toward its final end.

Greek philosophers had defined three areas in which mimetic strategies performed their reproductive work: in nature, in art, and in the realm where the human mind mediated between nature and art. Philo considered all three areas. Paul, on the other hand, concentrated on the third, almost to the complete exclusion of the first two. It had always been clear that the formation of moral thinking took place in an interplay between the nature that man was born with and the artificial second nature that he made for himself in social traditions and practices: moral formation occurred through mediation between nature and art. That was the area to which Paul gave himself, and there he located the mediating figure of Christ.

Far more directly than Philo, Paul conveyed mimetic doctrines into the mainstream of Western culture. Indeed, his theology resolves itself into the choice of a model: whether to be "conformed to this world" (Rom. 12:2), or to be conformed with the image of Christ (Rom. 8:29). But how did man find himself confronted with such a choice? What modeling process led to conformity with Christ? To answer these questions, Paul employed the reversionary scheme of spiritual egress and corrective return, one of his legacies from Greek metaphysics. But, in the unsystematic way characteristic of his genius, working out the answers took him far afield, into the areas of cosmology, epistemology, and ethics.[61] The world, the glass through which man sees darkly the

[61] On the scriptural context of Paul's mimetic doctrines, see K. L. Schmidt, "Homo imago Dei im Alten und Neuen Testament," *Eranos-Jahrbuch* 15 (1947), esp. pp. 187–194. A specific discussion of Paul's doctrine can be found in E. Lohse, "Imago Dei bei Paulus," in *Libertas Christiana. Festschrift für Friedrich Delekat,* ed. W. Matthias and E. Wolf (Munich, 1957). *Beiträge zur Evangelischen Theologie,* Bd 26), pp. 122–135. Lohse describes mimesis in Paul as being limited to doctrines concerning redemption and eschatology rather than creation, and he emphasizes the identity between Christ and the redeemed soul that comes at the end of the mimetic (or redemptive) process of transformation (see pp. 129f, 133f; comparisons between Philo and Paul at pp. 128, 131f). A much fuller examination of Paul's doctrines occurs in Jervell, *Imago Dei,* pp. 171–336. While he emphasizes the slender evidence for mimetic doctrines that exists in Paul's letters (p. 171) and the difficulty in interpreting key passages (e.g., p. 214, on Christ as the image of the invisible God), Jervell still establishes a number of important conclusions, among them: (1) that the authority of Paul's own apostolate depended upon the transformation effected through visions, which made him a *typos* to be imitated by the community, as Paul himself imitated Christ (pp. 173–175, 195); (2) the doctrine of baptism

invisible things of God, is like the wisdom of God, the cosmic Christ; for He is the informing order of the cosmos: "All things are held together in Him." The thought of man in a state of grace is constantly re-formed in the image of its creator through likeness to Christ in His death and resurrection; the spiritual man has the mind of Christ. This re-formation also reaches into ethics, the sphere of human relationships; for, since God was in Christ reconciling the world to Himself, men who are in Christ by likeness live, and yet it is not they, but God in Christ, that lives in them.

Mimesis by reversion played a large role in Paul's concept of estrangement and reconciliation. Transcendent reason, a leitmotif of mimetic thought, appears in Paul under the aspect of harmony or, to use his word, peace. Paul's first assumption was that a primordial peace had been disrupted in two ways. First, estrangement had come about between the cosmos and God, perhaps through the very act of creation. The whole creation, Paul wrote, groans and travails in pain yearning for the return to unity that will come with the end of the world. Second, estrangement had divided man from God, through death attending Adam's disobedience and through sin prescribed by the Law. While the Law belonged to the Jews, Gentiles were bound under its moral injunctions because of the law of nature written in their hearts. Consequently, all men had sinned and fallen short of the glory of God; all the world was guilty before Him.

Man's egress (or alienation) from God and his return to (or reconciliation with) Him were matters of knowledge that led to recognition and, finally, to obedience. Without the essential knowledge, man remained mired in a confusion of categories in which he could not distinguish the will of the Spirit from the desires of the flesh, the law of faith from the law of sin, the appearance of the Law from the reality that it veiled. This knowledge was not for every person: it was for those whom God foreknew, predestined, called, justified, and glorified, and it led them to the recognition of the wisdom of God, which is foolishness to the world: that is, to the recognition of Jesus who for believers is made wisdom, righteousness, sanctification, and redemption. In this state of enlightenment, man realized that the externals of this world were indifferent, that nothing was unclean of itself, but that cleanness

---

as a means of mimetic transformation (pp. 208, 231–234); and (3) the position that, whether in the relationship of God to Christ, or of Christ to the believer, the image and the archetype were somehow identical, since the archetype was always personally present in the copy (pp. 247f).

or uncleanness, righteousness or sinfulness, was determined by the testimony of the human spirit that, among the elect, bore witness in and with the Spirit.

Knowledge—recognition—obedience—reconciliation with God. None of this was possible without grace. God withdrew knowledge from the Jews; He withheld it from the idolatrous Gentiles; He confided it to Abraham and those of the spiritual circumcision. For only the Spirit of God can know the things of God, and, thus, men's perceptions of God are actually the Spirit regarding God in and through men, in effect God seeing Himself. Human participation in this vision is confirmed sacramentally by baptism, through which men are baptized into the likeness of Christ's death and resurrection, and by the Eucharist, in which they show forth the Lord's death. For Paul, it was authenticated by the invisible visions of the holiness of God, by the unutterable words that were communicated to him on the road to Damascus and again when he was seized up to the third heaven, and by many other revelations of which his infirmity, the thorn in his flesh, was an ever-present reminder.

But these reversions to primordial mysteries, this recognition of Christ through unitive contemplation, imposed on the knower moral ambiguities and antipathies from which the unpredestined were immune. Knowledge of the reality veiled by appearance—even the visible signs of the Law—placed man in the awareness that he was righteous by virtue of Christ's righteousness and condemned by his own sinfulness, reconciled with God in Christ but an enemy of God in his willfulness, governed both by the law of sin and by the law of faith, dead and yet alive, sorrowful and always rejoicing, poor and yet possessing all things, a deceiver yet true.

The end of man's election was that the glory of God be revealed in the faithful, but this glorification was in that hope by which Abraham hoped against hope and received the promise through faith. Paul is full of the metaphors that mystics later used to describe their unitive contemplation—metaphors of the potter, of the spiritual marriage, of the ingrafted branches, of light, and, of course, of the bread that men become because they partake of it. He comes again and again to the triumphant unity of the believer with God in Christ, and of believers with one another in their communion of the body of Christ, a unity by which the faithful become one with Christ of, through, and to whom are all things, so that all things are theirs, and that will be proclaimed at the end of all things when Christ, who is their life shall appear, and they shall also appear with Him in glory. And this will also consummate the return of the estranged creation to unity with its Creator: "For the created universe awaits with eager expectation for God's sons to be revealed" (Rom. 8:19).

However, mimesis by reversion was not the only mimetic strategy at work in Paul's mind. It answered to the metaphysics of transcendence but not to the theology of sin and atonement.

Hebrew prohibitions against visible representations of God militated against the mirror metaphor. In very principle, a mimetic world order governed by transcendent reason and recapitulated in the lives of individual human beings ran counter to the Hebraic understanding of a world without inherent order governed by God's will. This world of nonhuman, material existence was basically separate from the personal bond of sin, atonement, and reconciliation that was summed up in sacrifice and that defined the existence of man before God. Paul had united these two antithetic concepts: transcendence and sacrifice. He did not smooth away the difficulties. Indeed, some of Paul's own statements appear to submerge the sacrificial victim in the transcendent, as, for example, in this powerful imagery: "Where the Spirit of the Lord is, there is liberty. And because for us there is no veil over the face, we reflect as in a mirror the glory of the Lord; thus we are transfigured into his likeness, from glory into glory, according to the Lord, who is Spirit" (2. Cor. 3:17–18; the mirror metaphor is repeated in James 1:23). Paul here draws a correspondence between seeing the glory of God and resembling that glory, the same type of correspondence that appears in 1 John 3:21: "Beloved, now are we the sons of God, and it doth not yet appear what we shall be; but we know that, when he shall appear, we shall be like him; for we shall see him as he is." And it was even possible to go one step more and to draw a correspondence between seeing the glory and being the glory, a position that had no need of sacrifice.

In some passages, Philo appears to have taken the latter step. There were, however, four basic tensions in Paul's thought that prevented him from doing so and that introduced mimesis by augmentation into his thought, side-by-side with mimesis by reversion. The most essential of these was the tension between God and nature. According to Paul, God and His creation, nature—including man—were not a continuum. The world was not begotten but made. God ruled the world; He was not the world. Even life eternal was a creature of God, rather than an inherent quality of the soul, and the resurrection of the dead expressed not the force of nature in the Divine Spark within man but God's power. This distinction led to a fundamental premise: that simultaneous estrangement and reconciliation between man and God were possible. Grace stood independently of nature.

The second and third tensions arose from the Judaic insistence that man was both body and soul. As creations of God, matter and spirit alike had potentialities for good. Man's alienation from and return to God must therefore include his physical as well as his spiritual being. The doctrines of the incarnation of God in Christ and the resurrection of the flesh followed from this. But, since both teachings ran contrary to logic and experience, they set up a second area of potential conflict between faith and reason.

Furthermore, since faith required a conscious and deliberate choice, early Christian doctrine delved into the field of moral psychology. Emphasis on the totality of physical and spiritual life meant that a Christian could not merely withdraw into spiritual exercises, contemplation of the image of God in his own soul. Right belief and purity of heart had to be expressed in conduct, in the way in which one dealt with one's fellow men. The great imperative of the Last Judgment placed the responsibilities of belief and conduct on a scale more exalted than that of self-respect. Personal life would go on after death and even after the world itself had ended. At the last trump, when the dead awakened, each person would be arraigned before the judgment seat of his Creator. The eternal destiny of each depended upon how a person had exercised his will in faith. Christian doctrine therefore set up a third area of tension between the psychological forces that motivated choice, either for good or evil: not the blatant antithesis of soul (= good) and body (= evil), but the more subtle one between the spirit of faith and the desires of the flesh, between man's artificial (or regenerate) nature and his animal (or genetic) one.

These three areas of tension—between God and nature, faith and reason, and man's primary and redeemed natures—were gathered up in the fourth, most comprehensive, area: namely, in that of history. Christianity had inherited its emphasis on the historical dimension from the Hebrews. Under the influence of prophetic traditions, Jesus and Paul recast this emphasis into an eschatology, or, more properly, into a historical teleology. Man's return to God took place in time; it was collective as well as personal, augmentative as well as reversionary. Existence in time was ambiguous, for it had meaning in the light of what was to come, the ultimate end of all things, an end that had not yet come in its fullness but that was also already present in hope and in foreshadowings. The core of this teleology was the fulfillment of a promise, of God's promise to Abraham as renewed and expanded in

Christ. But it ramified through the inherent ambiguity of revelation, which both conceals and discloses and which made of the world a mirror of the future through which one could see but darkly. In this realm of already and not yet, salvation was accomplished but not fulfilled in the soul that was at one with Christ; the formation of Christ in the soul and the formation of the body of Christ in the Church were present but not complete; the victory over darkness was already won but not yet accomplished. All the last things—the complete revelation of God, the second coming of Christ, the establishment of the kingdom of the saints, the resurrection of the dead, the eternal beatitude of the soul, the Last Judgment—all are now and are yet to come.

And this collective passage—in which past, present, and future were identical, though unrealized, and in which they made sense, not because of what they were, but because of the promised goal of all human experience—this passage to God was institutionalized in the community, and especially in the sacraments of baptism and the Eucharist. The two sacraments were neither symbolic nor magical; they were the acts through which the tension existed simultaneously with its fulfillment. They were the heart of the worshipping community, as it grew through time.

Let me recapitulate so as to emphasize one point. On balance, Paul had little to say about mimetic mediation in nature or in art, but he was passionately concerned with the area between nature and art: the area of moral reproduction. There, Paul's mimetic strategies formed two clusters, each centering on one of Christ's two natures.

The first centered on the cosmic Christ, which later Christians identified with the Logos. When he wrote about Christ as "the image of the invisible God and the first-born of every creature" (Col. 1:15), Paul envisaged two imitative strategies. The first was mimesis by reversion, the pattern of egress and return that had a long ancestry in Greek philosophy. All things were made by and for Christ and consisted in Him. The world turned toward reconciliation with God in Him, still groaning as it waited to be delivered from bondage into freedom (Col. 1:15–29; 2 Cor. 5:18–19; Rom. 8:21–22). The second mimetic strategy was augmentative; for, incarnate, the cosmic Christ was also the head of the Church. By the blood of the cross, He reconciled to Himself all things on heaven and on earth; being formed in the ever-growing company of His saints, He manifested in them the mystery hidden from the beginning of the world (Gal. 4:10; Col. 1:20–26).

A second set of mimetic strategies centered on the human nature of Christ. Paul employed these to elucidate modes of transformation. The first mode was inversion. Paul recognized evil inversion, by which, for example, men changed the truth of God into a lie and fell into idolatry, worshipping the creature instead of the creator (Rom. 1:25–32). But he preached other kinds of inversion as well. He preached the inversion by which God chose the foolish and weak things of this world to confound the wise and mighty and by which the cross, which was a stumbling block to the Jews and foolishness to the Greeks, became, to the saved, the power of God (1 Cor. 1:18–27). He attached mimetic inversion especially to the ritual of baptism, through which death changed into life: "For if we have been planted together in the likeness of his death, we shall also be in the likeness of his resurrection" (Rom. 6:5).

Further, Paul conceived of a mode of transformation by subversion. This he also associated with Christ's humanity. Each stage of transformation took shape within the previous one and eventually overturned it. In this way, Paul affirmed a latent, historical continuity between Synagogue and Church. Though the Jews did not realize it, the prescripts of the Law were shadows of things to come, embodied in Christ (Col. 2:16). As Moses veiled his face to hide a passing splendor, so a veil lay over the minds of the Jews when they heard the Law. But Christ lifted the veil, and those who converted to Him, "beholding as in a glass the glory of the Lord are changed into His image, from glory into glory" (2 Cor. 3:13–18).

Naturally, the two sets of mimetic strategies were related in the Apostle's mind. But how could they be integrated into one system? They coincided most plainly in Paul's idea of the Church being formed across the years by the aggregate of individual conversions (or transformations). However, exactly at that point, his paradoxical approach to the concepts of God, humanity, and personal identity betrayed an inner tension that Greek philosophy had not generated. The "gospel of the kingdom" went beyond understanding, and this amply explains why, in their different ways, Jesus and St. Paul made their ultimate appeal not to the reason common to all men but to the most intensely personal of all elements: to faith, to the will enlightened by love. It was not clear how the personal wholeness of being and knowledge so achieved could be harmonized with the institutional unity of the believing community. Unknown to Paul, Philo had already explored possible solutions, some of which gained new currency in the writings of the Church Fathers.

Mimesis as a Strategy of Historical Progress: The Patristic Stage of the Classical Tradition

ANCIENT WRITERS identified three areas in which mimetic strategies operated: in nature, by way of involuntary reproductive processes; in art, by way of deliberate, critical techniques; and between nature and art, through methods devised by philosophers for narrowing the discrepancy between human nature in all its capacity for the good and man as he actually was, forced into the mold of culture, as though into an artificial second nature. The Church Fathers were mainly concerned with the imbalance between man as he ought to be and man as he was. Therefore, their arguments about mimesis centered on the mutual reflex between nature and art. Their comments about nature and art, as separate areas, were peripheral to the great issue of mimetic mediation between the archetype of humanity and its flawed image in actual men.

Ancient writers had devoted much attention to mimesis as a strategy for the formation of man's moral character. This emphasis on morality was later of great benefit to Christians. However, with the Church Fathers, mimetic doctrines became more than just the abstruse teachings of individual thinkers about ethics and morality. The novelty was not that those ideas were set forth in a comprehensive system of thought but rather that, as parts of such a system, they were institutionalized in the Church. They were taught through sermons and treatises, enacted through sacraments, and imposed by judicial sanctions. After the conversion of Constantine, they were also enforced by the sword.

The result was that mimetic doctrines about morality were no longer simply components in abstract systems of thought; they entered into the common dynamism of a culture. Their implications correspondingly widened. Cicero and Philo had employed an old figure of speech when they wrote of men who were human only in physical appearance but who were wild animals in mind and heart. Their judgments carried the weight of moral censure, and, in quite different ways, their arguments were deepened by the widespread (but not universal) assumption that religion, more than anything else, elevated man above brute animals, since worship of the gods sustained law and morality.[1] Before Constantine, the early Fathers wrote in similar terms, denying the humanity of heretics and unbelievers and envisioning social consequences within an individual church, or even within a wider communion of churches—consequences such as deposition from ecclesiastical office or excommunication. But when the Fathers after Constantine wrote in this vein, they knew that the "madness" of heretics and unbelievers could also be punished in the civil courts by debarment from office, confiscation of property, torture, and death.[2]

[1] Philo *Life of Moses* 1. 9. Cicero *De republica* 1. 17. *De officiis* 3. 6. 32. Michel Despland, *La Religion en Occident* (Montreal, 1979. *Héritage et project,* no. 23), pp. 25–30, 55f., 210, and passim.

[2] The key scriptural texts were 1 Cor. 2:14–15, where Paul asserted that the animal man could not know the things of the Spirit of God, and 2 Peter 2:12, where false teachers are described as "natural brute beasts, made to be taken and destroyed." The earliest texts come from the Greek world, and one may cite as examples: *Didascaliae apostolorum* [19] 7. 2. 19, ed. Erik Tidner (Berlin, 1963. *Texte und Untersuchungen,* Bd 75), p. 32; and Clement of Alexandria *Exhortation to the Greeks* 1 (Loeb Classics, pp. 8–10). Irenaeus of Lyon *Against Heresies* 5. 8. 2–4 (*Sources chrétiennes,* no. 153, pp. 96–106). Eusebius of Caesarea retained Aristotle's equation between barbarians and wild animals, and he also equated them with demons. Constantine the Great's conquest and conversion of barbarians transformed "them from a lawless and beast-like life to one rational and lawful." See *In Praise of Constantine* 6. 18; 7. 8, 12. (*In Praise of Constantine: A Historical Study and New Translation of Eusebius' Tricennial Orations,* trans. H. A. Drake [Berkeley, 1975. *University of California Publications: Classical Studies,* vol. 15], pp. 94, 96f.). The equation between non-Christians and animals continued among the Greek Fathers, but since my present concern is with the Latins, the following examples will suffice: Cyprian *De ecclesiae catholicae unitate* 9, 10 (Maurice Bévenot ed. [Oxford, 1971], pp. 72, 74); Augustine *De Trinitate* 12. 11. 16–17 (*Corp. Christ., ser. lat.* 50: 370, *City of God,* 19. 12 (*CSEL* 40, pt. 2: 391f), on Cacus, a semi-man, and below n. 162); Ambrose *De fide* 2. 1. 15 (*CSEL* 78: 62), identifying madness with animality (see below nn. 169, 183, 217); Jerome *Comm. in Isaiam* 1. 1. 3. (*Corp. Christ., ser. lat.* 73: 9); Boethius *Consolation of Philosophy* 4, pros. 3 (*CSEL* 67: 86f.). Civil punishments for religious nonconformity are to be found in contemporary imperial laws concerning Jews, pagans, and heretics, and in such explicit appeals to imperial authority as those made by Ambrose against the restoration of the synagogue at Callinicum and by Augustine against the Donatists (see *ep.* 185).

The equation of Christian culture (as patterns of conduct growing out of orthodox belief) with humanity had a long life. It served as a touchstone by which later Europeans identified themselves. It was a rationale for action against non-Christians, such as "the ferocious dragon," the Turk, and the Aztecs, who, in the eyes of their Spanish conquerors, had the outward appearance of men, though they were destitute of humanity. During the Reformation, it also enabled Europeans to take up arms against one another in good conscience, assured that they were fighting not men but brute animals.[3]

At first glance, "men without humanity"[4] might appear to be an isolated, polemical turn of phrase. Indeed, it was little more than that in the hands of some writers. However, writers of wider ability saw it as an idea that fit into a broad and intricate context. They were able to use it as an instrument of cultural identity precisely because they understood how it functioned in the elaborate theological structure that Paul had summed up in his distinction between the animal man, who received not the things of God's spirit, and the spiritual man, who judged all things and yet was judged by none (1 Cor. 2:14–15). Moreover, the Fathers were able to employ the idea of men without humanity for purposes of cultural identity because of their sense that Christians were made, not born. Becoming human was therefore linked to the specific process of becoming Christian, a modeling process in the area between nature and art by which the soul was conformed with Christ, the image of the invisible God. Through this linkage with conversion, mimetic strategies passed over from doctrines concerning the reformation of the soul into doctrines concerning the renovation of the world: that is, from speculative philosophy (or theology) into interpretations of history.

In the following pages, I shall consider how Christian writers widened the use of mimetic strategies to explain not only the moral formation of individual men and women (as ancient writers had done) but also the great, collective formation of history.

In some regions, the equation of Christianity with humanity is not a thing of the distant past. It occurs, for example, in two accounts of life in different parts of Italy that were written in the 1930s and 1940s: Carlo Levi, *Christ Stopped at Eboli,* trans. Frances Frenaye (New York, 1964), pp. 1f., and Ignazio Silone *The Seed Beneath the Snow,* trans. Frances Frenaye (New York, 1942), p. 43.

[3] Cf. Despland, *Religion,* pp. 159 (on the twelfth century), 178.

[4] Augustine wrote of *"homines inhumani"* in *Contra Faustum* 22. 46 (*CSEL* 25: 638).

Orientations Toward a New Concept of History

Philo and Paul considered mimesis a strategy for personal conversion, as had the Greek philosophers before them. But they went beyond Greek precedents, establishing the basis for understanding the entire course of history as a mimetic process. The essential fact was their concept that historical progress was made up of many kinds of movement. Events might well follow a straight course from the creation to the apocalyptic appearance of a new heaven and a new earth. Within this broad, rectilinear transit from beginning to end, other movements occurred, following the circular path of mimesis. Among them, personal conversion was the most essential. But, apart from suggestive experiments with mimesis by augmentation, Philo and Paul were not able to define with any completeness how the pattern of egress and return, which the reformation of the soul followed, could be used to illuminate the re-creation of the entire world.

This was an innovation of the Church Fathers, and they themselves recognized its novelty. When they spoke on theological doctrine, the Fathers steadfastly proclaimed that they were treading in the footsteps of their predecessors. By contrast, when writers of the fourth and fifth centuries interpreted history, they declared that they were doing something unprecedented. Of course, Christians claimed a special revelation that enabled them to detect God's action in human affairs more clearly than either Jews or Gentiles, but beyond this, believers during the patristic age were conscious of writing about subjects, in genres, and from perspectives that even earlier Christians had ignored.[5]

Mimetic strategies were crucial in the construction of the Fathers' self-consciously new way of thinking about the past. Paul had permanently associated these strategies with doctrines of Christ's divinity and manhood. In the present chapter, I shall illustrate how two Latin Fathers, Augustine of Hippo and Gregory the Great, appropriated these doctrines into wide views of human experience. Augustine, Gregory, and every other writer applied mimetic strategies in personal, even idiosyncratic, fashions. However, the deliberate break with earlier methods of historical writing to which all of them contributed did have some general characteristics. Before entering into details con-

---

[5] See Eusebius of Caesarea *Historia Ecclesiastica,* preface; Jerome *De viris illustribus,* preface (*PL* 23: 634).

cerning Augustine and Gregory, it may be helpful to identify these common features.

Through the practice of scriptural exegesis, historical analysis came to be regarded as a branch of speculative (or theoretical) knowledge. The historical, or literal, level of interpretation led to anagogical, mystical, and moral levels, all connected by a delicate web of association by metaphor and analogy.[6] The emphasis therefore shifted from knowing events to knowing how to understand them, from narrative to psychology. But the psychology was of a special kind; it was speculative, not empirical, epistemology, a version of a most abstract philosophical inquiry that Aristotle had called "thinking about thinking."

Many of these ideas were set forth by the Alexandrine "school" of theologians and, particularly, by Origen (ca. 185–ca. 254). But, at that time, they had not yet been woven into a coherent method of historical interpretation, even by Christians. Shortly after Origen's day, a pagan rhetorician, Lucian of Samosata, took a stance that would have denied Christian exegetes the name "historian." Looking backward six hundred years to Thucydides as his ideal historian, Lucian ridiculed authors who padded their accounts with metaphors and analogy instead of hard data. They composed, he said, "poetry without the wings." He derided historical writers who fell into the trap of interpreting, rather than narrating, events: in Lucian's eyes, they wrote philosophy instead of history. Finally, he insisted that a historian should construct his account as a narrative chain, one link joining up with the next in a linear series; no worthwhile historian, he thought, would arrange his evidence as though it were a skein of parallel strands instead of a chain.[7]

However, once the Fathers had made historical writing a branch of theoretical knowledge, they cast aside all of Lucian's criteria. For Lucian, events were over and done with, although, rightly described, they could serve later generations as useful guides to action. For the Fathers, events had meaning in reference to the future. They belonged to a prophetic order, and the object of studying them was to decode what they signified concerning the eventual fulfillment of that order. The Fathers therefore regarded historical events not as complete in themselves but rather as preparatory, and they were convinced that Scrip-

---

[6] See, e.g., John Cassian *Conferences* 14. 8 (*Sources chrétiennes,* no. 54, pp. 189–192).

[7] Lucian of Samosata, *On the Best Way to Write History,* chs. 8, 51, 55, 59 (*The Works of Lucian of Samosata,* H. W. Fowler and F. G. Fowler, trans. [Oxford, 1905], 2: 113, 132f., 135).

ture contained the key to the fulfillment that events signified and anticipated.

As they considered the broad sweep of events from the creation of the world toward the final transformation of heaven and earth, they perceived a compositional wholeness taking shape before their eyes. When complete, the entire history of the world would be seen as a perfect whole, like a picture or a garment. Now, however, it could only be seen in part, as one sees a painting in progress or a robe still emerging on a loom. All the same, different kinds of mediation between nature and art were evident. The complex interplay of different movements passing through stages of corrective augmentation toward wholeness was clear. There was the straight parade of events from man's creation onward, a dramatic passage through fall and redemption toward a final reconciliation that was yet to come. This straight transit, however, turned out to be a circular passage of egress and return, a passage that was impelled by the mimetic asymmetry of image and archetype mediated in the conversion of the individual soul. Thus, all men and their powers proceeded from God. Through sin, the image and likeness of God in their souls was deformed or lost. Through imitation of Christ, the man, it was morally reformed. Through conformity with Christ, the Logos, each redeemed person, and all the redeemed collectively, were transformed beyond humanity into the image of the invisible God, the universal source and goal.

By their teaching that the damages of sin were gradually being corrected, the Fathers therefore brought about a strategic fusion of the various kinds of mimesis that Paul had identified with the two natures of Christ. Drawing on centuries of thought about ethics, they built up a manifold strategy for the formation of the mind that employed many tactics, including philosophical reasoning, the liberal arts, and social organs of coercion and terror. In the following pages, I shall consider this concept of all history as a corrective passage from estrangement toward wholeness, taking my first examples from the writings of Augustine.

Augustine

To Augustine's mind, all human experience—past, present, and future—made up an interim.[8] It was a special kind of interim: not a gap

---

[8] On the conception of history as an interim, see *City of God* 19. 26 (*CSEL* 40, pt. 2, p. 421).

between two events but the kind of transition that elapses between the time when an artist conceives a plan in his mind and the moment when he completes the work of art that conforms with that mental picture. As the passage from Creation to Last Judgment, the interim was far from random; it included all the stages of transition that completed, in the physical world, a design that existed full-blown in the mind of God.

Augustine therefore approached historical writing from a perspective directly opposed to Lucian's, one in which the mediated asymmetry of image and archetype was crucial. For him, events were less important in themselves than for what they illustrated concerning transition toward the ultimate goal, the corrective passage from man's deformation through sin to his reformation through grace. What then did they tell about the course and processes of corrective moral transi-

---

My discussion of Augustine is a substantially revised version of an earlier essay, "Mimesis and Personality in Augustine's Historical Thought," *Proceedings of the American Philosophical Society* 124 (1980): 276–294. Some pertinent bibliographical citations, provided for the sake of orientation in that article (p. 276, n. 1) are not reproduced here.

For metaphors describing history as a work of art in progress, see *City of God* 11. 18 (poem), 23 (painting) (*CSEL* 40, pt. 1, pp. 537f, 545); *Conf.* 11. 28 (song) (*CSEL* 33: 308); *Serm.* 53, ch. 6, and *En. in Ps. 147*, 23 (a garment on the loom) (*PL* 38: 336; *Corp. Christ., ser. lat.* 40: 2159).

Sculpture gave Augustine a specific metaphorical linkage with history as an educational process. Ancient writers employed the metaphor of sculpture to describe the formation of the soul by study. Thus, Cicero compared the soul with a statue carved by nature in the rough. The soul's task was to complete the effigy, carving out its own humanity by applying the arts and philosophy. See *De finibus* 4. 13. 34. Regarding Christian doctrine as *paideia* and philosophy, the Fathers also employed this figure of speech. See Werner Jaeger, *Early Christianity and Greek Paideia* (Oxford, 1969), p. 87 (on Origen), and Max L. W. Laistner, *Christianity and Pagan Culture in the Later Roman Empire* (Ithaca, 1951), p. 96 (on John Chrysostom). Augustine's cross-reference with history is indicated by his comparison of the soul with a statue, deformed and waiting to be recarved. Only God, the artist who first made it, could reshape it in this world by the process of conversion, or, in the next, at the resurrection of the flesh, when the body would be reformed as a sculptor melts down an old statue and recasts the metal into a new and more beautiful one. See *Enchiridion* 23 (89) (*Corp. Christ., ser. lat.* 46: 97). *City of God* 22. 19 (*CSEL* 40, pt. 2, p. 629). Cf. *En. in Ps.* 6. 5 (*Corp. Christ., ser. lat.* 38: 30): "Cum autem nos convertimus, id est mutatione veteris vitae resculpsimus spiritum nostrum. . . ." Here, too, the emphasis is on God as the ultimate sculptor, for Augustine concluded: "Sana me ergo, inquit [psalmista], non propter meritum meum, sed propter misericordiam tuam." Teaching the same lesson, Augustine employed the metaphor of old coins submitted for remintage (*Tr. in Joan.* 11. 9). Cf. *Tr. in Joan.* 11. 1. 2 (*Corp. Christ., ser. lat.* 36: 355f, 358).

tion? According to Augustine, events must be read for their significance. But the character of history as a creative process was somehow concealed. Its main features eluded everyone except Christians, and even Christian exegetes found them difficult to identify and interpret. How for example, could one pry open the letter of the Old Testament text and disclose secrets prefiguring the future and "referring to Christ and His Church, which is the city of God"?[9]

Augustine found himself in a quandary. Individual salvation and the welfare of the whole Church depended on right understanding of the Scriptures. And yet, such knowledge came by contemplating a wisdom that eye had not seen, nor ear heard, and that had never risen in the heart of man. Carnal and animal men could not see the things of God. How, then, did wisdom arise in the hearts of the saints—for example, in the heart of John the Evangelist? Was he not a man? Augustine answered, "God does not call us to be men" but rather "gods and sons of the Most High." The experience of John revealed that saints are transformed into something better than men. It also made plain that a man's first step toward beginning to be an angel, a messenger of God, was to acknowledge that he was a man, that he was nothing. Without this act of humility, he would never rise to greater heights of virtue. Indeed, he might even lose what he was, as had heretics and schismatics who, exalting themselves, divided the Church of God.[10]

From this doctrine that God did not "call us to be men," a few guidelines can be derived that will aid in the subsequent discussion. Significance—basically a mimetic relationship between separate events—is possible because there is a patterned unity of human experience, a pattern grounded in the common origin of mankind and in the eschatological goal of history. But not every event signifies something. Stringed instruments are composed of parts; the whole produces music, even though not all parts are struck. Thus, in prophetic history, some things are told that signify nothing in themselves but that are included for the sake of elucidating things that signify.[11] Even so, the significance of an event may not be readily apparent; it may not be detected for many centuries; it may never be detected by any except those whose minds God enlightens with grace. There is a great pattern in God's mind for the corrective reformation of human nature. This

[9] *City of God* 16. 2 (*CSEL* 40, pt. 2, p. 127).

[10] *Tr. in Joan.* 1. 1. 3–4 (*Corp. Christ., ser. lat.* 36: 2).

[11] *City of God* 16. 2 (*CSEL* 40, pt. 2, p. 127). The same figure of speech occurs in *Contra Faustum* 22. 94 (*CSEL* 25: 701).

pattern is realized in events, as a garment takes shape on a loom or a song is sung or a painting is completed. Events mirror the grand design; recognition of their significance also mirrors the original pattern, but this mental image is twice removed from the reality, and it is, moreover, limited and colored by the mind that contains it. From my very brief discussion thus far we can therefore anticipate that Augustine's assertion of ultimate unity went along with a self-critical, even iconoclastic, idea of significance, even more surely iconoclastic than Plato's because the perfection of knowledge through time was itself the means for a radical destruction and re-creation of the world.

In the following sections, I shall consider how Augustine's argument was composed of various tactics for correction, drawn from philosophy, the liberal arts, and government, and I shall also describe mimetic strategies for mediating the asymmetry of image and archetype, strategies that, according to the Father, these tactics served. As will become apparent, it was natural that Augustine, the teacher, constructed his paradigm for the advancement of knowledge from these three elements. Each corresponds with one of the three ways in which man normally learns. Augustine related philosophy (appropriated into theological reasoning) to the eye. But, as a rhetorician, he knew that physical vision was directed and interpreted by the mind: an accomplished orator could evoke mental images by the use of words, and, through vivid illustrations, he could conjure up events before "the eye of the audience, almost as if they were transacted in front of them."[12] Consequently, Augustine insisted that vision was a complex act that brought into play the eye of the mind as well as, and even more than, the eye of the body. Not only rhetoric but all the liberal arts were taught chiefly by verbal instruction, without visual aids. They corresponded with the second means of learning: the ear.[13] And finally, one learns through bodily discipline, as well as through the eye and the ear.[14] Augustine's advocacy of political coercion corresponds with kinesthesia, and so too on the level of personal devotion does his approval of ascetic mortification of the flesh. Taken together, the three kinds of tactics denote a universal program of corrective moral education, and, as it happened, the seedbed of a culture.

[12] Quintilian *Institutes* 9. 1. 27, referring to Cicero *De oratore*, chap. 52–53, and *Institutes* 9. 2. 40.

[13] On an earlier period, cf. Stanley F. Bonner, *Education in Ancient Rome: From the Elder Cato to the Younger Pliny* (Berkeley, 1977), pp. 129–131.

[14] On the use of corporal punishment in schools, see Bonner, *Education in Ancient Rome*, pp. 117, 142–145.

Techniques of Philosophy: Thinking about Thinking

General Propositions. The keystone of Augustine's theory of history was his theory of mind. Thus, my starting point must be psychology: thought about the very processes of thinking. Augustine's assumptions about the individual mind—that its operations were mimetic, and that, if properly used, mimesis was a mediating strategy of correction and advancement in thinking—were basic to his further assumptions about the progressive conversion of the world. Still, these two ideas about the mind were by no means new or peculiar either to Augustine or to Christian doctrine.

As we saw, Aristotle identified imitation as essential to learning, and he wrote that man was superior to lower animals exactly because he was, by nature, the most imitative creature in the world, ever learning, and delighting to learn, from works of imitation. In this way, he held, primitive wordplay evolved into the increasingly diverse and refined genres of poetry.[15] With these comments, Aristotle alluded to a specific kind of imitation—one that I have called responsive mimesis—a kind that Aristotle also identified in the response of audiences to tragic drama. Because "reason, above all else, *is* man,"[16] the imitative response was rational, critical, and purposive; it fed upon the rivalry between ancients and moderns; thus, it became a strategy for advance. Repetitive without being redundant, it sustained both continuity and change. Of course, this was true of many activities other than poetry, as Aristotle recognized when he discussed the career of philosophy. Common experience taught that change through imitation was a timeless and general feature of education.

Quite naturally, this feature found a place in Augustine's sweeping characterization of the entire human race as one collective person and the conversion of the world as a single process of moral education.[17] His starting point, like Aristotle's, was the individual mind; his elaboration, unlike Aristotle's, was theological.

The operations of the mind were mimetic. Even Satan and his off-

[15] *Poetics* 1448b. See above, Chapter 1 at note 29.

[16] *Nic. Eth.* 1178a. Compare Augustine's comment that a man would rather loose his treasure than his eyes and his eyes rather than his mind. "For a mind without the eyes of the flesh is human, but the eyes of the flesh without a mind are bestial. Who indeed, would not rather be a man, even though blind in the flesh, than a beast that can see?" *De Trinitate* 14. 14. 19 (*Corp. Christ., ser. lat.* 50A: 448).

[17] *City of God* 10. 14 (*CSEL* 40, pt. 1, p. 470). On the general problem of historicity and personality in Augustine (especially with reference to the *Confessions*), see Karl J. Weintraub, *The Value of the Individual: Self and Circumstances in Autobiography* (Chicago, 1978), pp. 44–48.

spring were creatures of God, and their wicked pride perversely imitated Him. Thus, Augustine began from the premise that all minds were reflections of the same archetype, "an eternal pattern (*ratio*)." The way to find out what the mind really was, and how it worked, was not to launch an inductive study, examining many minds and abstracting generic and specific categories from common traits or similarities. Instead, one should work deductively by introspection, looking into one's own mind for characteristics that others, by parallel acts of introspection, would recognize in themselves, characteristics that did not vary with conditions but that persisted as "inviolable truth, from which to define perfectly, as far as we can, not of what sort the mind of any one particular man may be, but of what sort it ought to be according the eternal patterns (*rationibus*)."[18] The desire to "gaze upon inviolable truth" and to deduce from it knowledge about particular instances was a mimetic operation of a high order.

But even the most ordinary operations of the mind were mimetic. The entire process of thought, as Augustine conceived it, was made up of a series of imitations in a field of asymmetries between the mind and objects of thought. We see because the image of something outside us is impressed upon our senses. We remember because a similitude of that image has passed into the memory. We think because the will composes an inner vision from the deposit of remembered similitudes. We speak, using words that reflect our thought. But even this first stage of a complex process is only possible because of a prior mimetic reality. Man is the image of God in the operations of his mind. Even the soul immersed in carnal images moves by triune—if misdirected—operations; it is an image of the triune God, driven by perverse desire for likeness to God.[19]

We can go further. At every stage of thought, mimesis occurs by

[18] *De Trinitate* 9. 6. 9 (*Corp. Christ., ser. lat.* 50: 301, 324). Following the same thought, Augustine applied the metaphor of the mirror to the souls of saints. *En. in Ps. 11.* 2 (*Corp. Christ., ser. lat.* 38: 82): "Veritas una est, qua illustrantur animae sanctae; sed quoniam multae sunt animae, in ipsis multae veritates dici possunt, sicut ab una facie multae in speculis imagines apparent." On the use of the same metaphor (with different meanings) by John Scotus Eriugena, Thomas Aquinas, and Meister Eckhart, see Chapter 6, note 17; Chapter 8, note 44; Chapter 9, note 16. See also Schleiermacher's metaphor of a hall of mirrors, Chapter 14, note 24. On Satan and his sons as perverse imitators of God, see *City of God* 19. 12 (*CSEL* 40, pt. 2, p. 393).

[19] *De Trinitate* 11. 2. 2; 11. 2. 5; 11. 5. 9; 11. 7. 12; 12. 11. 16; 12. 15. 25 (*Corp. Christ., ser. lat.* 50: 334f., 338f., 344f., 348f., 370f., 379f.). On the soul's process of "invention" by introspection, see ibid. 10. 7. 10 (50: 323f.).

mediation between asymmetrical terms. At the beginning, body and soul mingle by the mediation of sensory faculties. At the moment of perception, the sensory image is formed when will links the object perceived with the faculty of perception. The will also mediates between memory (the storehouse of carnal images) and the inner vision at the moment that mental images are formed. At the highest level, it is through the mediation of Christ that man stretches beyond rational knowledge of temporal things to wisdom, the cognizance of eternal things.[20] We can, therefore, extract two habitual features of Augustine's thought about thinking: (1) that mimetic acts occurred by mediation between two poles, and (2) that, in thinking, as in sculpture or painting, wholeness was achieved through a complex series of mimetic acts.

In thought, as in the visual arts, mimesis, by mediating asymmetries, could be a strategy of advancement by correction. Augustine alluded to this strategy at the beginning of his treatise *On the Trinity*. He had undertaken the treatise, he said, as a task "not so much of discoursing with authority on things I already know, as of learning those things by discoursing with piety about them."[21] To discourse, for Augustine, was to reason by analogy, and I shall consider analogy as a key to the corrective effects of mimetic operations rightly performed.[22] Later, I shall return to analogy as a specific mode of scriptural interpretation, rather than as a general way of thinking.

Believing that plays on mythological subjects had eroded the moral fiber of Roman society and thus greatly contributed to political decay, Augustine was not one to underestimate the power of analogy to form the mind by responsive mimesis. In the theater, audiences drew analogies between themselves and the characters that they saw portrayed. One of Augustine's severest objections to the theater of his day was precisely that audiences—especially the young—identified themselves

---

[20] In addition to the passages cited in note 19, see *De Trinitate* 13. 19–20, 24–25; 14. 12. 15; 14. 16–17, 22–23 (*Corp. Christ., ser. lat.* 50A: 415–418, 443, 451–455).

[21] *De Trinitate* 1. 5. 8 (*Corp. Christ., ser. lat.* 50: 37).

[22] On the place of analogy in the formal structure of Augustine's thought, see the innovative study by J. Mader, *Die logische Struktur des personalen Denkens. Aus der Methode der Gotteserkenntnis bei Aurelius Augustinus* (Vienna, 1965). Mader's discussion of imago, and particularly of man as the image of God, is relevant to comments above: "Der Mensch ist somit konkret Bild Gottes nur, insoferne er sich selbst als Bild versteht und vollzieht, in den Weisen seines Daseinsvollzuges jenem Prinzip folgt und es verwirklicht, das in der Dreieinigkeit des absoluten Geistes als wirklich von Augustinus erkannt wird: das dialogisch-heterothetitische Leben" (pp. 134f.). For a definition of "heterothesis," see pp. 62f.

with the lascivious and demonic roles enacted before them and that they modeled their actual behavior on theatrical pretense.[23] Furthermore, as a rhetorician, Augustine mastered an art that, like the theater, swayed emotions in the degree to which audiences could be persuaded of a kinship between themselves and other people in quite alien circumstances. Thus, the Father easily accepted analogy as a stimulus of responsive mimesis when he considered the formation of the soul.

Lucian, too, had evoked a kind of responsive mimesis when he wrote that the historian should do nothing more than reflect events, as though he were a mirror. But Augustine conceived of a responsive mimesis that changed the mind of the knower even as it reproduced past events before his mind's eye. "Knowledge (*notitia*)," Augustine wrote, "is a kind of life in the reason of the knower."[24] Knowing mimetically could not be static, anymore than life itself. Consequently, the Father's idea that the inward act of thinking mimetically transformed the individual mind led him to place, at the core of his historical thought, the very analogical methods that Lucian had condemned.

Augustine built up his argument by the use of rhetorical devices, especially metaphor. His historical discussions were exercises in interpretation rather than narration; thus, they were designed as philosophical (or theological) inquiries. Finally, because Augustine read events typologically, regarding them as so many expressions of the same primordial truth, he aimed at establishing their parallelisms, the points at which they mutually reflected one another, far more than he wished to set forth their chronological sequence. To be sure, Augustine recognized chronological sequence, but the historical and the prophetic orders ran by different clocks. Temporal relations did not fetter the prophetic order, and, in his relentless quest for significance in events,

---

[23] Concerning the impact of theater on Augustine himself, see *Conf.* 3. 3 (*CSEL* 33: 44–48); *City of God* 2. 27 (*CSEL* 40, pt. 1, pp. 104–106). Augustine was particularly fond of a scene from Terence's comedy, *The Eunuch*, in which a boy alleges that he was induced by a painting to imitate Jupiter in fornication, an example that involved many levels of imitation: (1) the imitation of human crimes by poets in their legends of the gods, (2) the imitation of legend by painting, (3) the imitation of life by the play, (4) the imitation of the scene in the painting by the boy in the play, and (5) the imitation (which Augustine feared) of the action in the play by spectators. See *ep.* 91. 4 (*CSEL* 34, pt. 2, pp. 429f), *Conf.* 1. 16 *(CSEL* 33: 23), *City of God* 2. 7; 8. 26 (*CSEL* 40, pt. 1, pp. 68f, 402–404). On Augustine's recognition of the theater's moral impact, see Robert J. O'Connell, *Art and the Christian Intelligence in St. Augustine* (Cambridge, Mass., 1978), p. 125.

[24] *De Trinitate* 9. 4. 4 (*Corp. Christ., ser. lat.* 50: 297).

the Father discussed them as a skein of parallel instances far more often than he did as links in a chain. Reasoning by analogy, then, was a step toward mimetic action: that is, toward mediating the asymmetry of archetype and image. This was equally true of the soul and of history.

The techniques of reasoning by analogy that Augustine employed were far from random. They followed from a coherent system of inference that he had pieced together from various elements in late antiquity. From his education in rhetoric, he gained the use of metaphor as a device for associating dissimilar things or ideas. Augustine thus distinguished between the outer man (the physical body and the senses) and the inner man (the faculties of mind). He employed metaphor as a means for associating data learned through one of the senses (e.g., vision) with data learned through the others, and, thus, for constituting what he called "carnal images," standards of judgment such as length, breadth, depth, height, space, and time—measures by which men evaluated and worked upon the world around them. Whereas "carnal images" came through "the eye of the body," a second altogether different kind of standard was accessible to "the eye of the mind." Plato taught the existence of an ideal standard, transcending the relative proportions of physical things, a standard essential to all the arts and their productions.[25] In his Platonic inheritance, Augustine received the conviction that there was such a transcendent norm reflected in the material world. There was, he wrote, a *"ratio dimensionum atque figurarum"* by which we gauge actual bodies; there were *"rationes incorporeales et sempiternae"* by which the human reason judged.[26] Drawing on an exegetical lineage dating back to Philo of Alexandria, he was also able to identify the Logos, the Word of God, as the repository of the transcendent *ratio*, or *rationes;* for, he wrote, "all things visible and invisible are laid up in the Only Begotten, ordained in their respective *genera.*"[27]

Augustine discarded strictures such as Lucian's against mixing poetry with history because he considered rhetoric a discipline that gave man power to organize his perceptions of the physical world. He put aside strictures against mixing philosophy with history because he assumed that the material world—and human arts—actually reflected a transcendent order. Finally, he violated the premise that histories should be composed in chains, not bundles, because of a third stan-

---

[25] *Statesman* 284.   [26] *De Trinitate* 12. 2. 2 (*Corp. Christ., ser. lat.* 50: 357).
[27] *Tr. in Joan.* 110. 6 (*Corp. Christ., ser. lat.* 36: 626f.).

dard of analogy accessible, not to the eye of the body, nor to the eye of the mind, but to that of faith.

Paul referred to the "analogy of faith," the measure given by God to each person (Rom. 12:13). Augustine followed him in imposing this divine gift upon other standards of measurement, and, moreover, in setting it above them inasmuch as eternal life surpassed material and intellectual existence. Augustine wrote: "As long as we are pilgrims, absent from the Lord, a rational action ought to be subject to such rational contemplation, as may be granted through faith to the person who takes it; for so it will be through sight, when 'we shall be like him for we shall see him as he is'."[28] In the common, yet most individual, analogy of faith, Augustine's exercises in typological "bundles" flourished; all the saved manifested the same archetype: "For whom he did foreknow, he also did predestinate to be conformed to the image of his Son, that he might be the firstborn of many brethren" (Rom. 8:29).

Augustine's three-tier distinction between the carnal, intellectual, and spiritual levels of analogical inference elucidates a contrast that he drew between painting and words as stimuli of responsive mimesis. Discussing the Old Testament account of how Judah seduced his daughter-in-law, Augustine observed that, if he saw a painting of a lascivious subject, he would immediately censure it. (This level corresponds with carnal images.) If he read the text of Scripture according to the letter, he would, with a fuller understanding of the event, fit it into a scheme of moral exemplarism, among the evil acts unworthy of emulation. (This level corresponds with rational understanding.) But, if he read the account in the spiritual sense of the prophetic order, he would perceive that, unknown to Judah, what he did signified a great good accomplished in the person and work of Christ.[29] (This level corresponds with spiritual wisdom.)

Augustine realized that each level of analogical inference moved by different kinds of association. Moreover, different sequences were at play in the psychology of the individual person. For example, perception by the mind was instantaneous, "a swift flash of light," while perception through the ears was drawn out, occupying stages of time.[30] Thus, even as one listened to the notes of a song, each occupying a duration of time, one could also perceive through the mind "a measure (*numerositas*) standing without time in some secret and high silence."[31]

[28] *Contra Faustum* 22. 27 (*CSEL* 25: 621).
[29] *Contra Faustum* 22. 83 (*CSEL* 25: 685f.).
[30] *De catechizandis rudibus* 2. 3 (*Corp. Christ., ser. lat.* 46: 122).
[31] *De Trinitate* 12. 14. 23 (*Corp. Christ., ser. lat.* 50, pt. 1, p. 377).

According to this theory, the sense of hearing and the tempo of performed music followed one sequence, thought and the principle of
harmony, another.

Augustine's belief that God, and God's archetypal creations, existed
"above time" enabled him to read history in corresponding ways.[32]
History could be broken down into its components, each of which
emerged and endured in time, as did the notes of a song. But, considered as a work of art, history was the sum of all its parts. Subsumed
into the whole, the individual components co-existed as did the head
and the arm of a statue, even though each of them took shape at a different time. Again, as a work of art, history was the sum not only of
co-existing parts but also of the design that it incorporated more or less
completely.

In history, as in psychology, time afforded only one sequence, and
not necessarily the most instructive one, for Augustine's purposes. God
moved all temporal things without any movement that time could
measure. Likewise, He knew all time with a knowledge that time could
not measure.[33] In its constant effort to rise above carnal images and beyond its own intellectual finitude to spiritual truth, the enlightened
soul strove to grasp the atemporal sequences according to which God
had built the concept and design of the world. These included particular manifestations of "incorporeal and eternal *rationes*," the order of
nature, graded according to dignity and power,[34] and the moral order,
the order of justice, calibrated according to degrees of goodness.[35]
These orders negated the dimension of time and rendered all events
and lives mutually illuminating testimonies to "the mystery (*sacra-
mentum*) of the inner man imparted by Christ."[36]

Augustine's system of analogy mediating on three tiers of asymmetrical relations corresponded with the ancient division of philosophy
into physics, logic, and ethics. Physics inquired into the operations of
nature, logic into those of the reason, and ethics into moral conduct.
Ancient philosophers had taught that the blessed life could be attained
by exploring this three-fold way;[37] and it is not surprising that Augustine's basic structure of carnal, intellectual, and spiritual levels of analogical inference matched the ancient divisions, or that, together, they

[32] *Conf.* 11. 30; 12. 12–13 (*CSEL* 33: 309, 319f.).

[33] *City of God* 11. 21 (*CSEL* 40, pt. 1, p. 541).

[34] *De catechizandis rudibus* 3. 6 (*Corp. Christ., ser. lat.,* 46: 125).

[35] *City of God* 11. 16 (*CSEL* 40, pt. 1, pp. 535f.).

[36] *De Trinitate* 4. 3. 6 (*Corp. Christ., ser. lat.* 50: 168f.).

[37] *City of God* 11. 25 (*CSEL* 40, pt. 1, pp. 549f.).

belonged to what Augustine called "catholic instruction (*disciplina*)."[38]

The Father was well aware that passing through this kind of educational program fundamentally altered one's perception of reality, including particularly the sense of historical reality. The moral conclusions to which his analogies led were incomprehensible to many; although he preached them openly, his doctrines remained esoteric.[39] The greater part of mankind never escaped carnal images: the lessons of intellectual and spiritual analogies were hidden from them. Only the few could achieve a clear intellectual perception of the eternal verities: subject to forgetfulness, even they had continually to rethink what they had already learned. Finally, spiritual wisdom belonged to the fewest of the few: it had not been revealed to pagans and Jews; it had been deformed by heretics and schismatics; it was indifferently received by those who were Christians in name only, and who would, at the Last Judgment, be winnowed out as chaff from the wheat.[40] Hidden though they might be from the many, however, Christian doc-

---

[38] *De utilitate credendi* 36 (*CSEL* 25: 47). The three-tier structure described in the text differs from the three tiers that Augustine himself considered in his great exposition of Genesis. There, Augustine identified corporeal, spiritual, and intellective sight. He elucidated them by distinguishing three ways of "seeing" the text "Thou shalt love thy neighbor as thyself": (1) with the eyes, when one reads the letters themselves, (2) "through the spirit of men, by which the neighbor is thought of even when absent"; and (3) "through scrutiny (*contuitus*) of the mind," by which love is seen. In Augustine's scheme, love represents a large category of things that can be known though never perceived through the physical eyes. According to this classification, the term "spiritual vision" denotes a way of using carnal images to think of absent things, something quite different from what I have used the term to denote. As I employ the term, it refers to a kind of vision that Augustine specifically excluded from the exposition on Genesis, one that comes by a gift of the Holy Spirit and of which prophecy and the understanding of prophecy are examples. See *De Gen. ad lit.* 12. 6, 8–9 (*CSEL* 28: 386f., 390f.).

[39] Cf. *De Trinitate* 15. 17. 27, where Augustine concluded a discussion with the sentence: "Anyone who does not discern this must seek understanding from the Lord, not an explanation from us; for we can not say anything more clearly." Of course, Scripture itself intimated doctrines that were not unfolded openly but that were "to be understood by those who could understand it." See *De Trinitate* 2. 10. 17 (*Corp. Christ., ser. lat.* 50A: 502; 50: 103). Augustine described the nub of his quandary when he wrote: "Proinde quia liquidus purusque intellectus de illa substantia, quae corpus non est ac per hoc ad carnis sensum non pertinet, verbis carne editis exprimi non potest, eligit doctrina sapientiae per quaslibet corporeas imagines et similitudines utcumque cogitanda insinuare divina quam ab officio talia docendi cessare. . . ." See *Contra Faustum* 22. 54 (*CSEL* 25: 649f.).

[40] *De Trinitate* 12. 11. 16; 12. 14. 23 (*Corp. Christ., ser. lat.* 50: 370f., 377). *De utilitate credendi* 16 (*CSEL* 25: 20f.). *De catechizandis rudibus* 25. 48; 27. 54 (*Corp. Christ., ser. lat.,* 46, 171f., 176f.).

trines elucidated the great design that was being progressively realized in human events; they comprised the educational process by which men and women responded to their vocation to be, not human beings, but "gods and sons of the Most High."

A Specific Application: The Tractates *on John.* Appropriately, Augustine's ideas about the mimetic operations of the mind and their corrective effects found magnificent expression in a long series of treatises that began as a course of sermons on the Gospel of John. His use of philosophical tactics to describe the mediated asymmetry of God and man was especially appropriate to the subject, for Augustine judged the Gospel of John more sublime than the other Gospels because it taught the theology of the Logos, a sublimity of vision represented by John's symbol, an eagle, or the eye of an eagle.[41]

The Father's three-tier structure of analogy—on the carnal, intellectual, and spiritual levels—gave him the tools of analysis. The deep coherence and truth of Christian doctrine, he argued, was accessible to the eye of faith, which saw the design in life that the eyes of the body and mind could glimpse but dimly.

Under the pressure of running controversies, the central question for the Father as he interpreted the Gospel of John to his congregation was personality. How could he teach his people, as they gathered before him in the cold basilica, that the incommunicable wholeness of a person survived in a higher unity of persons? He presented the matter of personality to them under two aspects: first, in regard to the Trinity (especially the relationship of the Father to the Son), and, second, in regard to the unity between Christ and the believer. These two aspects were central to Augustine's instruction. On both counts, he tried to teach his flock—his "little children"—by means of the mimetic scheme of spiritual life, since he understood personality in terms of exemplary form and derived likeness.[42]

---

[41] *Tr. in Joan.* 15. 1; 36. 1. 5 (*Corp. Christ., ser. lat.* 36: 150, 323, 327).

[42] Augustine knew, and used, the metaphor of the mirror of the mind (*Tr. in Joan.* 14. 7 [*Corp. Christ., ser. lat.* 36: 146]). He frequently paired the great mimetic verses of the New Testament: "Now we see through a glass, in a riddle; but then, face to face. Now I know in part; but then shall I know even as also I am known" (1 Cor. 13:12). And: "Beloved, now are we the sons of God; and it doth not yet appear what we shall be. But we know that, when He shall be manifested, we shall be like Him; for we shall see Him as He is" (1 John 3:2). Although, for Augustine, the connection between seeing and being remained a strong one, his use of the mirror metaphor was extremely rare, and he built his development of mimesis correspondingly on allusion and analogy rather than on explicit metaphors. There were good reasons for this with regard to both aspects of his teaching on personality. As

Augustine's concept of divine personality put these terms to the test. A good bit of caution was required because he touched on controversial issues. Looking into the faces of his people, he knew that he had to fight two heresies that had taken root in their city, if not actually among them: he had to win them away from the Arians, who denied Christ's consubstantiality with the Father, and the Sabellians, who denied the personal separateness of the Father from the Son.

This was a particularly difficult task, since both extremes found their key doctrines in John. Augustine constantly repeated the opening verses of the Gospel to show that his enemies on both sides had forgotten that the Word was God and that "the Word was made flesh and dwelt among us." Against the Arians, he taught that Christ, the divine Word, was not a pale, derivative reflection of God's original thought. Christ emptied himself and took on the form of a servant without losing the form of God. Certainly, in the form of a servant, He was less

---

for man, the mirror metaphor conveyed a physical truth—the eye cannot see itself—that was not appropriate to spiritual reality. Philo of Alexandria had used this analogue to argue that, just as the eye could not see itself, the soul could not know itself. Augustine too was sometimes prepared to argue that the soul was a great deep and that one could not fathom the mysteries of one's own soul, much less know the souls of others (*En. in Ps.* 41. 13 [*Corp. Christ., ser. lat.* 38: 470f.]; *Conf.* 4. 14 [*CSEL* 33: 69f.]). In his *Tractates on John*, however, he took the opposite line: though we cannot see our own faces, he argued, the intellect can understand itself, and we can see our own consciences, our true selves, within (*Tr.* 47. 3; 74. 5. Cf. *Tr.* 90. 1 [*Corp. Christ., ser. lat.* 36: 405, 515, 551]). As for Christ, Augustine observed in another work, commenting on Christ's character as the image and the eternal brightness of the Father, there was an ineffable difference between the image produced by a mirror and the image co-eternal with the archetype, and this disjunction between metaphor and reality, as well as the unresolved tension between lifeless image and living original, made the mirror metaphor inadequate for Augustine's purposes (see *De Verbo Domini, serm.* 117. 5. 8 [*PL* 38: 665f.]).

For a very informative discussion of the themes in this section that I have not treated in great detail, see A. H. Armstrong, "St. Augustine and Christian Platonism," in *Augustine: A Collection of Critical Essays,* ed. R. A. Markus (Garden City, N.Y., 1972). Another essay is the same anthology pursues a method of analysis rather different from that followed by Armstrong and from the one represented in the present chapter. In his article, "On Augustine's Concept of a Person," A. C. Lloyd identifies similarities between Augustine's formal thought about personality and Aristotle's. To achieve that purpose, he dismisses "the elements of homily and of Scripture which pervade the analogies" between the Trinity and the soul (in the treatise *De Trinitate*) and he also discounts Neoplatonic metaphysics as not germane to the problem (pp. 191, 196). For a description of how mimesis entered into Augustine's understanding of personality, one needs to take account of precisely those analogies and that metaphysical basis. On all stages of Augustine's career, see P.R.L. Brown, *Augustine of Hippo: A Biography* (London, 1967).

than the Father and less than the Holy Spirit. But the Word was, and remained, God. Likewise, in the form of a servant, Christ was less than Himself in his divine character because "the unlost form of God is greater than the assumed form of a servant."[43] The Sabellians also missed the point of the Gospel. A profound truth lay in the verse "I and the Father are one." But it was not what the Sabellians taught. Through charity, the Father and the Son were inseparable in their works.[44] They had the same nature, in which seeing, hearing, being and capacity, begetting and being begotten, loving and knowing were identical.[45] What they have is therefore the same as what they are: they are the life that they have.[46] All this points to an equality that is conterminous with identity. Christ's personality consisted precisely in that He combined the form of man with the form of God. The other two persons of the Trinity lacked the human character. Christ alone participated in human weakness.[47] He alone could be said to be both visible and invisible, both here and with the Father, both absent and present. He alone had died and also lived forever.[48] Thus, the Word, the Image, was not inferior to the Father, and He was also one with the Father in the sense that "the Father, sending the Son, sent his other self."[49] Likewise, the Holy Spirit differed from the Father and the Son in functions and in character but composed, with them, one God.[50] The Spirit was co-eternal and co-equal with the Father and the Son, since it was "the substantial and consubstantial love of both" Father and Son and "the substance of the will of both."[51] The Son was Son only in relation to the Father. The Father was Father only in relation to the Son. But the Holy Spirit was the spirit of both, not begotten, but proceeding from both and infusing into the hearts of the elect the love that was God, the love without which human souls were accounted dead.[52]

The pairing of personal separateness with an unseen unity of per-

---

[43] *Tr.* 78. 1–2 (*Corp. Christ., ser. lat.* 36: 523f.).

[44] *Tr.* 20. 3. 6 (*Corp. Christ., ser. lat.* 36: 204, 206).

[45] *Tr.* 18. 9; 20. 8. 9; 99. 5–9; 106. 5 (*Corp. Christ., ser. lat.* 36: 185f., 207f., 585–587, 612).

[46] *Tr.* 48. 6; 54. 7; 70. 1 (*Corp. Christ., ser. lat.* 36: 415f., 462, 502).

[47] *Tr.* 60. 2 (*Corp. Christ., ser. lat.* 36: 478f.).

[48] *Tr.* 36. 9; 50. 4; 53. 1; 76. 3–4; 77 passim (*Corp. Christ., ser. lat.* 36: 329f., 434f., 452, 518–519, 520–522).

[49] *Tr.* 14. 11 (*Corp. Christ., ser. lat.* 36: 149).

[50] *Tr.* 105. 3 (*Corp. Christ., ser. lat.* 36: 604).

[51] *Tr.* 105. 3 (*Corp. Christ., ser. lat.* 36: 604); *Tr.* 111. 1 (*Corp. Christ., ser. lat.* 36: 628).

[52] *Tr.* 9. 8; 99. 5–9 (*Corp. Christ., ser. lat.* 36: 95, 585–587.

sons took on even greater complexity when Augustine turned from the Trinity to the relation of believers to Christ. On the one hand, he could teach that Christ "took us into himself as our head," and therefore that we all became one man. We were made Christ, our maker and brother,[53] and (with appropriately odd syntax) we are also He and He is we.[54] On the other hand, seeing, knowing, and being are clearly not one in man; he is not the life that he has; and in his mortal finitude and sinfulness, he cannot say, with Christ's sense of equality, "I and God are one."[55] Augustine used the ambiguities of mimesis to resolve this complexity as he developed his instruction in the stages—from predestination to vocation to justification to glorification—by which predestinate man became conformed with the image of the Only Begotten, and so became one with Him.[56]

As Augustine lectured to his congregation on the problem of form and likeness in the theology of the Word, he attributed high importance to one premise: thought and Word were equal and identical in the Godhead, just as were seeing and being. All of Augustine's powerful discussion of man ruled out unity of that sort in human nature. He took for granted the duality of the inner and the outer man and, correspondingly, of inner and outward sight. He further distinguished inner vision into intellectual (open to man's natural faculties) and spiritual (opened to man by divine illumination). In the *Tractates*, Augustine was primarily concerned with the vision opened by grace to the eye of faith or, as he also put it, to the eyes of the heart. He repeatedly contrasted the eyes of the flesh with those of the heart. As the body is an intolerable burden on the soul,[57] men must crush and annihilate carnal thought, for the pictures that man makes in his mind out of carnal images—length, breadth, shape, thickness, color, finite space, and time—obscure the inner sight that carnal man cannot bear: that is,

---

[53] *Tr.* 12. 9; 52. 1 (*Corp. Christ., ser. lat.* 36: 126 ["In uno estote, unum estote, unus estote."], 446).

[54] *Tr.* 21. 7–8 (*Corp. Christ., ser. lat.* 36: 216f.). *Tr.* 108. 5 (*Corp. Christ., ser. lat.* 36: 618): "quoniam in me, etiam ipsi sunt ego." *Tr.* 111. 6 (*Corp. Christ., ser. lat.* 36: 632f.): "Aliter enim est in nobis tamquam in templo suo, aliter autem quia et nos ipse sumus, cum secundum id quod ut caput nostrum esset, homo factus est, corpus eius sumus." *Serm.* 134. 8 (*PL* 38: 742): "Iam vero si nos ipsos adtendamus, si corpus eius cogitemus, quia et nos ipse est. . . . Ergo et nos ipse, quia ipse caput nostrum, quia totus Christus caput et corpus."

[55] *Tr.* 48. 10 (*Corp. Christ., ser. lat.* 36: 418).

[56] *Tr.* 26. 15; 105. 7 (on Rom. 8:28–30) (*Corp. Christ., ser. lat.* 36: 607).

[57] Wisdom 9: 15. *Tr.* 23. 5; 35. 9; 75. 4; 96. 4 (*Corp. Christ., ser. lat.* 36: 234, 323, 516, 571).

they cloud the invisible vision of God.[58] Within the soul, memory is the seeing faculty, and mind (*mens,* or thought), the vision.[59] But, in order to see, the eyes of the heart must be enlightened, just as the carnal eyes need light from an external source—from a lamp or from the sun. Christ is the bread that feeds man's inner hunger; to the eyes of the mind, Augustine wrote, Christ is the light of the inner world.[60]

As lights, the eyes—carnal, mental, or spiritual—are enlightened rather than enlightening; their vision is derived.[61] Whereas Augustine taught that the difference between man and beast is, not man's possession of a soul, but his understanding, the fulfillment of human capacity requires something more: namely, that the soul's understanding be irradiated by the higher light that is God.[62] While Augustine taught that man is a rational soul having a body, he accounted that soul to be dead if it is not beatified by the substance of God, if God has not become the life of the soul.[63] It was this enlightenment, withheld from heretics, that decoded Scripture's mystical language, disclosed the inner meaning of Jesus' deeds (which metaphorically were also words), and unlocked the sacraments as visible words.[64] It was this understanding that transformed a sound into a word by enabling the mind to apprehend it as such and to see the link between a name and the thing named: supremely, it revealed the identity of Christ as the means by which the Name of God became manifest.[65]

Augustine frequently referred to words as signs, and to the duality of thought and word by way of illustrating the relation between the Father and the Son, His Word.[66] It was also his way of pointing up the distance between the ideal and the actual, the exemplars of all things that were in the divine Word and the actual world modeled on them,[67] the Creator in the soul and the soul transfigured into His image. To know was to love; to love was to imitate, to move toward, to become one with the exemplar. Every instance of love was unique; all knowledge of God was fragmentary, proportional to the knower. Certainly,

[58] *Tr.* 44. 4; 54. 4, 8; 74. 5; 75. 2; 102. 4; 106. 6; 111. 2 (*Corp. Christ., ser. lat.* 36: 383, 460f., 463, 515f., 596f., 612, 629f.).

[59] *Tr.* 23. 11; 35. 3 (*Corp. Christ., ser. lat.* 36: 240, 319).

[60] *Tr.* 26. 11, 12; 34. 3; 35. 6 (*Corp. Christ., ser. lat.* 36: 264–266, 312, 320f.).

[61] *Tr.* 14. 1; 19. 11; 35. 4; 36. 5 (*Corp. Christ., ser. lat.* 36: 141, 194, 319, 326f.).

[62] *Tr.* 15. 19; 17. 8 (*Corp. Christ., ser. lat.* 36: 157, 175).

[63] *Tr.* 19. 15; 23. 5–6; 47. 8 (*Corp. Christ., ser. lat.* 36: 199, 234–236, 408).

[64] *Tr.* 10. 2; 12. 11; 80. 3 (*Corp. Christ., ser. lat.* 36: 101, 126, 529).

[65] *Tr.* 104. 1; 106. 4 (*Corp. Christ., ser. lat.* 36: 601, 610f.).

[66] See, e.g., *Tr.* 14. 7 (*Corp. Christ., ser. lat.* 36: 145f.).

[67] *Tr.* 37. 8 (*Corp. Christ., ser. lat.* 36: 336).

there were general limits to the *imitatio Christi*. Martyrs could imitate Christ in dying but not in redeeming, in having human flesh but not in freedom from sin, in rising from the dead but not in choosing the time of their deaths, or in laying down and resuming their lives at will, or in slaying death in themselves, or in working out their own salvation, or in being the life that they had.[68] For they lived this life, which is not yet life.[69] True imitation of Christ—and of His types, Job and Abraham—meant replicating His humility and obedience. "Let man first imitate [Christ's] patience, so that he may attain His power."[70]

Know thyself. This was basic to all knowledge.[71] Self-knowledge found its fulfillment through humility in knowledge of God, in recognizing the Creator in the soul, in His own image.[72] Seeing, knowing, and loving mingled in Augustine's thought. And yet, he wrote, we cannot see, or know, or love God unless He is in us, unless He gives Himself to us.[73] To know God in the soul was to love Him and to perfect the understanding that made one fully man.[74] Without grace, even self-knowledge was deformed and love, misdirected, not toward God, but toward a conception that one put together for oneself.[75] Augustine never became insensitive to idolatry or to the ease with which the mind could let its own fantasies masquerade as truth.

Those whose inner eyes saw the figments of their own imaginations imitated the devil. Like the evil spirit, they believed in God but did not love Him.[76] They did not love Him because they were not predestined to see Him. God loved them as His creatures. He loved them even when He hated them for the defects that He had not created.[77] But they did not see the radiance of this love, any more than the blind man could see the light of the sun shining full upon him.[78]

Even the elect were in partial ignorance. "We believe in order that

---

[68] *Tr.* 84. 2 (*Corp. Christ., ser. lat.* 36: 537).

[69] *Tr.* 22. 3 (*Corp. Christ., ser. lat.* 36: 224).

[70] *Tr.* 41. 9; 42. 4–5; 43. 1 (*Corp. Christ., ser. lat.* 36: 363, 367f., 373).

[71] *Tr.* 25. 16 (*Corp. Christ., ser. lat.* 36: 257).

[72] *Tr.* 23. 10 (*Corp. Christ., ser. lat.* 36: 239).

[73] *Tr.* 74. 5 (*Corp. Christ., ser. lat.* 36: 515).

[74] *Tr.* 88. 4 (*Corp. Christ., ser. lat.* 36: 548).

[75] *Tr.* 74. 1 (*Corp. Christ., ser. lat.* 36: 513). *Tr.* 40. 4 (*Corp. Christ., ser. lat.* 36: 351): "Nolite ita cogitare, ne in corde vestro idola fabricetis." Cf. *Tr.* 100. 2–3 (*Corp. Christ., ser. lat.* 36: 589f.).

[76] *Tr.* 83. 3 (*Corp. Christ., ser. lat.* 36: 536).

[77] *Tr.* 110. 6 (*Corp. Christ., ser. lat.* 36: 626).

[78] *Tr.* 35. 3–4 (*Corp. Christ., ser. lat.* 36: 319).

we may know."[79] We love in faith now, for, even though by grace we glimpse the invisible vision of God in this life, we shall not truly love Him in contemplative sight until the resurrection.[80] As the Apostle Thomas saw and touched Christ, "the Man, and confessed the God whom he neither saw nor touched,"[81] we too are tied to existing and passing signs, such as words, deeds, and sacraments, as long as we are in the body. As the Church, we know two states of life: one in faith, the other in sight; the first in earthly exile and the second in contemplation. Like its individual members, the Church lives both in the active and in the contemplative state, and the interplay of the one with the other is both a sign of imperfection and a means of perfectibility in this world, as we progress in knowledge of the truth that we already see through a glass darkly.[82]

Augustine's three levels of outer and inner sight found a ready paradigm in the fact that both Judas and Peter were among the Apostles and partook of communion with Christ, though Peter partook unto life and Judas unto death.[83] It was well and good to contrast those who were united by love with those who were knit together by the poisonous depravity of human life, to set the lovers of minds against the lovers of bodies, to teach that the love of God was prior to the love of neighbor, which it also instructed and informed.[84] But who was the neighbor? Who actually saw with eyes of faith? Augustine's answer rules out externals and allows for the imperfection of the inner eye. His answer is impersonal, abstract. The outer eye is often misled by false glory, deceptive righteousness, specious good.[85] In fact, the hearts of other men are inscrutable, and we are obliged to suspend judgment upon them "until the Lord come and illumine the hidden things of darkness, and disclose the thought of the heart." We must not love individual human beings in the carnal images that we form according to shape and size, color and weight, and outer signs of righteousness. We must love justice, goodness, and truth in them, and hate the opposite vices.[86] For, in the same way, "What did [Christ] love in us except

[79] *Tr.* 40. 9 (*Corp. Christ., ser. lat.* 36: 355): "Credimus enim ut cognoscamus non cognoscimus ut credamus."

[80] *Tr.* 75. 4 (*Corp. Christ., ser. lat.* 36: 516f.).

[81] *Tr.* 121. 5 (*Corp. Christ., ser. lat.* 36: 667f.).

[82] *Tr.* 124. 5 (*Corp. Christ., ser. lat.* 36: 683–686).

[83] *Tr.* 50. 10; 112. 2 (*Corp. Christ., ser. lat.* 36: 437, 634).

[84] *Tr.* 32. 3; 65. 1; 87. 1 (*Corp. Christ., ser. lat.* 36: 301, 491, 543).

[85] *Tr.* 100. 2 (*Corp. Christ., ser. lat.* 36: 551–553).

[86] *Tr.* 90. 2–3 (*Corp. Christ., ser. lat.* 36: 551–553).

God?"[87] Thus, transcending the vision both of flesh and of mind, we may in faith love or hate a person whom we never knew, and even love unknowingly a person whom we cast off and with whom we refuse to break bread or live in common.[88]

The Church—the congregation of the elect—holds a central place in Augustine's mimetic theology. At any moment, the knowledge of the Church—both the congregation that Augustine saw listening to his words and the hidden community advancing through all time—was partial. It was always proportionate to the sum of the faith of its members. In this hidden, increasing aggregate communion of love, which will be disclosed at the end of time, the Father wrote, we become members one of another through concorporation with Christ. Because of God's own unity, the enlightening grace and the invisible vision of God that it opened were one for all the elect. Their capacities varied; their knowledge varied. And yet, beyond carnal images, in universal abstraction, they beheld the same beauty of righteousness, the same beauty of wisdom, the same beauty of holiness. They became one in the enduring permanence of truth.[89] They became what they saw and loved and imitated. Thus, there was a diversity of gifts among them, a variety in the analogy of faith, but, in love's oneness, there was also a community of glory.[90] Because the Church speaks all tongues, each member speaks with all tongues,[91] for, through the communion of love, which is God, many separate hearts and souls have become one heart and one soul.[92] Through seeing, knowing, loving, imitating, they have been made not only Christians but Christ, in such a way that Christ can say, "When one of the least of mine learns, I learn,"[93] and again, "In Me, they are also I."

This principle of analogies of faith within an ultimate unity had implications for the doctrine of sacrifice, which Augustine set forth in the *City of God.* He recalled that Christ was the High Priest who entered into the holy place not by the blood of goats and calves but by His own blood (Hebr. 9:12), and that the ever-enlarging body of the faithful

---

[87] *Tr.* 65. 2 (*Corp. Christ., ser. lat.* 36: 492).

[88] *Tr.* 90. 2–3 (*Corp. Christ., ser. lat.* 36: 551–553).

[89] *Tr.* 36. 10; 40. 4 (*Corp. Christ., ser. lat.* 36: 330, 352).

[90] *Tr.* 67. 2 (*Corp. Christ., ser. lat.* 36: 495f.).

[91] *Tr.* 32. 7 (*Corp. Christ., ser. lat.* 36: 303f.).

[92] *Tr.* 39. 5 (*Corp. Christ., ser. lat.* 36: 348).

[93] *Tr.* 21. 7; 108. 5 (*Corp. Christ., ser. lat.* 36: 216f., 618). For Augustine's metaphor of one face reflected in many mirrors, see above note 18.

was the temple of the Holy Spirit. God thus inhabits each believer individually. He is fully and completely present in each. The soul, inflamed with the fire of God's love and endowed with His beauty, lost the form of earthly desire and was transformed in the image of enduring loveliness. The Body of Christ grows through this transfiguration in every believer. "The entire community of saints is therefore offered to God as our sacrifice through the great High Priest, who offered Himself to God in His passion for us, that we might be members of this glorious head. . . ." United with its Mediator, Priest, and Sacrifice, one body in Christ, the increasing Church was therefore offered at the altar in the oblation that she made to God.[94]

Augustine's answers to Sabellianism and Arianism, the two heresies toward which he directed the tractates on John, were studies in ambiguity; they ran counter to the elementary principles of logic. The principles of identity, contradiction, and the excluded middle assumed that one thing could not simultaneously be another and that what was true could not also be false. But these two logical monstrosities were built into the heuristic circularity of Augustine's arguments.

As he instructed his people on the Gospel of John, Augustine recognized that unity came through knowledge, a highly individual act that enhanced an already-present likeness of the knower to the known. But, regarding sacred doctrine, he detected some inescapable ambiguities. First, knowledge always implied ignorance: the mind, like the moon, had two sides, one bright, the other dark, each defining the other. Second, knowledge came about through a heuristic circle. The tautology of knowing is most apparent in Augustine's statement that what God loves in man is Himself. At the human level it appears in his assumption that knowledge is possible (1) because the knower is like the known, and (2) in proportion to the degree of that likeness. This meant that a person actually knew the picture in his own mind, whether it were a picture that, like Lucifer, he had made for himself, or one that he had composed according to an informing vision given to him by God. Augustine recognized the self-deceptive powers of the mind closed in on itself: the soul that knew only itself could not rise, and, in its finitude, it could fall away from itself as well as from God, sinking "to those things that are not what itself is, to which it is superior . . . by

[94] *City of God* 10. 3, 6. Cf. ibid., 10. 16f., 31 (*CSEL* 40, pt. 1, pp. 449f., 456. Cf. *CSEL* 40, pt. 1, pp. 475–477, 502f.). Augustine also thought of the whole kingdom of the ancient Hebrews as a collective person: that is, as one great prophet foretelling the advent of Christ. See *Contra Faustum* 13. 15; 22. 24 (*CSEL* 25: 395, 619).

loves that it cannot conquer and errors from which it sees no way to return."[95]

Augustine's tractates on John have a dramatic force and complexity because they illustrate how, by his three-tier structure of analogy, he tried to break out of the circle. At every stage of argument, he used what was known to point beyond to what was unknown. To employ this strategy of split references for instructional purposes, he assembled a large arsenal of metaphor and allegory and appropriated tactics of philosophical reasoning. I shall now turn to a second set of tactics by which he sought escape from his heuristic circle: tactics provided by the liberal arts.

The Liberal Arts

Augustine's analysis of psychology combined the ironies of Plato with the enigmas of Paul. The same intricate pairing characterized his thought on another tactical level: the liberal arts as tools for the formation of the soul.

Augustine applied the distinction between tactics and strategy in the most celebrated portion of his argument in *On Christian Doctrine.* There he described the liberal studies as analogous to the spoils of the Egyptians. As the Israelites on the exodus from slavery to freedom carried off the Egyptians' gold, silver, and raiment, so, he argued, had Christians rightly appropriated valuable elements of pagan learning. To be sure, the arts were foreign. They grew up outside the Church (where there is no salvation) and belonged to an inimical and benighted way of life.[96] Still, their principles—number and the process of

---

[95] *De Trinitate* 14. 14. 18 (*Corp. Christ., ser. lat.* 50: 446).

[96] *De doctrina christiana* 2. 139–142 (*CSEL* 80: 73f.). Augustine's doctrine of the liberal arts has been repeatedly studied. For considerations of particular aspects of his thought, see G. H. Allard, "Arts libéraux et langage chez Saint Augustin," and P. H. Baker, "Liberal Arts as a Philosophical Liberation: St. Augustine's *De Magistro,*" both in *Actes du Quatrième Congrès International de Philosophie Médiévale: Arts libéraux et philosophie au moyen âge* (Montréal-Paris, 1969), pp. 481–492, 469–479. On the trivium, see H. I. Marrou, *Saint Augustin et la fin de la culture antique* (Paris, 1938), pp. 239f., and on the quadrivium, see pp. 251f. See also E. Kevane, *Augustine the Educator: A Study in the Fundamentals of Christian Formation* (Westminster, Md., 1964), pp. 176–180. On the various meanings of "arts" in Augustine, see O'Connell, *Art and the Christian Intelligence,* pp. 29–32.

To say that Augustine regarded the arts as tactics is also to draw connections with his doctrine of signs. For the background of Augustine's theory of signs and a general and thorough sifting of the unresolved ambiguities in it, see D. Jackson, "The Theory of Signs in St. Augustine's *De doctrina christiana,*" and R. A. Markus, "St. Augustine on Signs," both in *Augustine: A Collection of Critical Essays,* ed. R.

inference—imperfectly reflected, or resembled, the order that God established in nature, between Himself, immutable Being, and mutable things.[97] From those universal mines of gold and silver, open to all men, the pagans dug up their treasures.[98] All the good knowledge that they conveyed was already present in the Scriptures; the rest—the errors—had to be condemned.[99] But because they could be converted to serve the truths of the Church, the arts might be employed as com-

---

A. Markus (Garden City, N.Y., 1972). Markus begins with an analysis of the theory as it appears in *De magistro,* and continues with a discussion of *De doctrina christiana* (pp. 73f.). In the former part of his discussion, he very clearly elucidates the circular nature of Augustine's argument: while visible (or sensory) things are signs of the invisible, they are also understood in the light of the invisible. To recognize them as signs, Markus continues, the observer must already know the thing that they signify. This prior knowledge is what makes it possible for the thoughts of one mind to pass, through the medium of words, into another mind, re-enacting "the speaker's expressive activity embodied in the [*verbum mentis*]" (p. 82). This re-enactment, which I am calling responsive mimesis, was the means by which the Word of God generated its unspoken words in the soul (pp. 84f.). On the process of transfer, see especially Jackson, pp. 108–111, and, on texts in which Augustine argued that before the Fall men knew God directly, without signs, which appeared as a consequence of sin, see Jackson, p. 113.

Obviously, the arts need not bear Christian signification, and some, like the practical arts of coinage, need bear no signification beyond themselves. See *De doctrina christiana* 2. 3. 4 (*CSEL* 80: 34): even brute animals communicate by signs. On a higher level, cf. Augustine's ambiguous apostrophe to the arts in the *City of God* 22. 24 (*CSEL* 40, pt. 2, pp. 643–646). Here he writes in great detail on the profusion and inexhaustible inventiveness of the arts and yet concludes that the ingenuity of the human mind, rather than the way of truth, presently adorned life. R. A. Markus argues convincingly that, except for superficial remnants, Augustine gradually expunged Neoplatonism from his thought about secular life and government. *Saeculum: History and Society in the Theology of St. Augustine* (Cambridge, 1970), pp. 78f., 81f., 94, 101f. This change of mind would certainly illuminate Augustine's view that the earthly city pointed to nothing beyond itself (cf. *City of God* 15. 2). On the latter passage, see F. Edward Cranz, *"De Civitate Dei,* XV 2, and Augustine's Idea of Christian Society," in Markus, ed., *Augustine: A Collection of Critical Essays.* I would place more emphasis than Cranz on the fact that Augustine uses the verb *demonstrare,* instead of *significare,* in this passage, thus thoroughly discounting whatever representative or significatory functions might have been ascribed to temporal institutions. In this very informative article, Cranz opposes the interpretation of Augustine's comments as expressing Neoplatonic exemplarism. He argues that Augustine was thinking, rather, in terms of prophetic (or historical) analogies that were not shared by the society of the unredeemed. On the Church as a sign and on signification in history and prophecy, see Markus, *Saeculum,* pp. 182–186, 189f.

[97] *De doctrina christiana* 2. 101–103, 129–132, 136–137 (*CSEL* 80: 62f., 70f., 72f.).
[98] *De doctrina christiana* 2. 145 (*CSEL* 80: 75f.).
[99] *De doctrina christiana* 2. 151 (*CSEL* 80: 78).

ponents in a Christian method of analysis, teaching, and disputation—one that used the arts against the pagan culture that had given them life.[100] Like silver and gold, they could be abused in the worship of demons or converted to the "obedience of Christ."

Rightly understood, the arts could lead one from corporeal to incorporeal things. As disciplines, they enabled the wise man to recover truths that had slipped from memory.[101] However, the very propositions that the arts served outside the Church were false.[102] Just after his baptism, Augustine was able to write that the arts belonged to the hierarchy of true knowledge, beginning with simple animation and culminating in a seventh step, the contemplation of God. As the common possession of good and wicked men alike, the arts stood only at the third level, above the two degrees that man had in common with animals. They stood below the point at which the soul, gradually detaching itself from the body, begins its movement, through purification, to reunion with God.[103] In *On Christian Doctrine,* Augustine recast this hierarchy as steps of knowledge beginning with the fear of God and culminating in wisdom. At the third step, contrition, the soul turns to an intense study of the Scriptures, and it is there that the arts, with their "two-faced *ratio,"* partly true and partly false, may be brought in to assist it.[104] But, at the higher levels, the soul surpasses the types and shadows of sacred doctrine itself.

Augustine's argument against cultural assimilation parallels a stance portrayed by Cicero in *De oratore,* where he discussed the liberal arts as an importation from Greece. In both cases, the arts belong to an alien wisdom, against which "our authors" or "our customs" must be defended. The burden of Augustine's comments on teaching sacred doctrine are to the effect that rhetoric is not a subject that requires special instruction but that, like grammar, eloquence can be learned by association and habit, particularly by reading and rereading the Scriptures and works by estimable Christian writers.[105] This position

---

[100] *De doctrina christiana* 2. 147 (*CSEL* 80: 76).

[101] *Retractationes* 1. 5. 6 (*CSEL* 36: 27). *De Trinitate* 12. 14. 23 (*Corp. Christ., ser. lat.* 50, pt. 1, p. 377). Cf. Augustine's allegation that pursuit of the liberal arts brought scarcely any profit to this present life: *De utilitate credendi* 16 (*CSEL* 25: 21).

[102] *De doctrina christiana* 2. 117 (*CSEL* 80: 67).

[103] *De quantitate animae* 33 (72), 35–36 (79–80) (*PL* 32: 1074f., 1079f.).

[104] *De doctrina christiana* 2. 16–25 (*CSEL* 80: 37–40). On the "two-faced *ratio,"* see *Solil.* 2. 10. 18. Cf. *De ordine* 2. 11. 34 (*PL* 32: 893; *Corp. Christ., ser. lat.* 29: 126f.).

[105] *De doctrina christiana* 4. 6–12 (*CSEL* 80: 119–121).

also resembles the view, which Cicero states without approving it, that forensic rhetoric is not an art at all but a skill learned through habit, by association with great figures in the profession and by familiarity with major legal texts. Augustine refers explicitly to *De oratore* in *On Christian Doctrine,* and, given a common resentment of assimilation, his orator quite naturally bears a family likeness to the adversary position in Cicero.

Augustine also argued, as Cicero did in another way, that the orator needed only a superficial knowledge of the arts. In view of their ancillary role, the arts were not expected to display much refinement. Some rudimentary knowledge of zoology and botany and music would save an interpreter from unfortunate errors.[106] The demands of etymology were largely satisfied by interpretive glossaries of names and untranslatable words in the Scriptures. The needs of the exegete with regard to number symbolism could be satisfied by corresponding handlists, which, Augustine wrote, existed but were hard to get.[107]

Such similarities of attitude between Augustine and Cicero, however, conceal a profound difference of principle. Cicero regarded the arts as tools for the formation of humanity; Augustine considered them tactics serving a higher vocation—God's calling of men to be, not men, but "gods and sons of the Most High." As Augustine constructs his argument for "unlearned learning," he comes to a point where the arts have no place at all. Without grammarians, and expressing themselves in common speech, the writers of Scripture made abundant use of tropes.[108] Without following the rules of rhetoric, the prophet Amos and the Apostle Paul achieved heights of eloquence[109]—not that of the pagan rhetors and poets but "our eloquence," which admitted obscurity, barbarisms, solecisms, and uneducated usages.[110] Despite their fastidiousness, the pagans had appropriated some features of this style.[111] The purpose of rhetoric was not artificial refinement in the

---

[106] *De doctrina christiana* 2. 57–67 (*CSEL* 80: 49–53).

[107] On the superficial degree of knowledge expected with regard to manual and gymnastic arts, see *De doctrina christiana* 2. 62–65, 115–116, 141–143 (*CSEL* 80: 51f., 66f., 74f.).

[108] *De doctrina christiana* 3. 87–89; 4. 31–33 (*CSEL* 80: 103, 124f.). Augustine specified *exempla,* allegory, enigma, parable, and catachresis.

[109] *De doctrina christiana* 4. 31–48 (*CSEL* 80: 125–130).

[110] *De doctrina christiana* 2. 43–45; 4. 25–27, 64–66 (*CSEL* 80: 45f., 123f., 134f.). Cf. *Tr. in Joan.* 2. 14, where Augustine justifies mistranslation if it clarifies the meaning of Scripture: "Let us say so, then, and not fear the rod of the grammarians so long as we reach the solid and certain truth" (*Corp. Christ., ser. lat.* 36: 18).

[111] *De doctrina christiana* 2. 46–49; 4. 28–30 (*CSEL* 80: 46f., 124).

manipulation of words. Rather, it was instilling love of good habits and aversion to evil[112] through words, discharging the universal function of signs: that is, conveying the movement in one soul to another. To those grown perfect in faith, hope, and charity, no erudition, no books—not even Scriptures—were necessary, except for teaching others.[113] To them, and to others not so far advanced in contemplation, the strange eloquence of the Scriptures was open because the divine mind that inspired the writers of Scripture with eloquent wisdom was the same wisdom that enlightened the eye of the exegete's heart when he looked into the heart of Scripture.[114]

Without faith (proportionate as it was), no one could perceive that the uncouth style of the Scriptures concealed an eloquence other than that of rhetoric. Such had been Augustine's own disbelief, put to flight by the mystic illumination in the garden.[115] "Faith is the gift of Him who has apportioned to each his share." The elaborate structure of analogies on which Augustine's entire thought turned—and, specifically, the higher theological truths regarding man and the Logos— were closed if the eye of the mind were not cleared by his heavenly gift. How could men love and imitate examples that they never knew? Augustine's severe doctrine of election runs beneath his argument that the analogues of faith are true, whether recognized or not, just as the sun shines on a blind man without infusing his eyes with light.[116]

What were the implications of all this for a man whose chief labor and joy was to detect significance in the Scripture? The question for him was: "How do the arts assist in the task of decoding the signs of Scripture?" Augustine answered this question by working out the split references and analogies that ran between known and unknown: he thereby framed a solution to the dilemma of matching Platonic mimesis with Pauline. Indirectly, he had already resolved the dilemma on a number of occasions before 396, and certainly before the final revision of *On Christian Doctrine* in 427. This part of his solution can be summarized with reference to the four senses of scriptural exegesis.[117]

[112] *De doctrina christiana* 4. 142–144 (*CSEL* 80: 162f.).

[113] *De doctrina christiana* 1. 93 (*CSEL* 80: 32).

[114] *De doctrina christiana* 3. 103–105, 133–134; 4. 17–20, 59–60 (*CSEL* 80: 107f., 117, 121f., 132f.). The ultimate iconoclasm to which Augustine's concept of the arts led is eloquently described by O'Connell, *Art and the Christian Intelligence,* pp. 89f. Father O'Connell provides a detailed and imaginative reconstruction of the general aesthetic that, in his view, informed the Father's judgment.

[115] *Conf.* 3. 5; 8. 12 (*CSEL* 33: 50, 194f.).

[116] *De doctrina christiana* 1. 20–21 (*CSEL* 80: 13).

[117] *De utilitate credendi* 3, 5–8 (*CSEL* 25: 5f., 7–12).

1. *History.* At its simplest level—what has been written or done, or written as though it had been done—history provided raw information from which Augustine drew his unusual sensitivity to the variation of customs from one society to another, and to changes of cultural systems.[118] Sacred history was unlike secular, however; it needed to be read spiritually as well as literally.[119] As signs, events in sacred history had to be read with a higher understanding of analogies than the pagans, or even the Jews, possessed. One had to realize that historical change was the unfolding of a pre-existent beauty, like the singing of a psalm.[120] Augustine explained what he meant in terms of poetry and painting. God foresaw evil, he wrote, and He also knew how He would use evil men and angels to heighten the beauty of His work. Just as a writer employs antitheses in a poem to enhance the grace of his composition, so God arranged contrasts in time, pairing evil off against good, life against death, sin against redemption, to increase the beauty of history. He worked with the pageant of mankind as though it were a poem or a painting in which the black areas of sin were deployed for the beauty and grandeur of the whole.[121] Before his conversion, Augustine himself failed to see this broad pattern, and thought the less of Old Testament writers for blending history and prophecy.[122]

2. *Causality.* The most substantial benefits of all came from the light that the arts shed on the causes of things. The arts disclosed the underlying *ratio* of the world, they provided the analogical means of discerning true from false, and they pointed the mind to mathematical proportions—the very weight, measure, and number by which God created the world—relations that existed quite independently of the world.[123] The arts conveyed "some truths concerning the worship of one God,"[124] including on the high level of Platonic philosophy the doctrine of the Logos as the universal creative agent, the life and light of men. But unless, by illumination, the "intellectual life" turns to the Creator, it flows formlessly[125]; God hid the entire causal doctrine of the Incarnation, death, and resurrection of the Logos from the wise

---

[118] See, e. g., *Conf.* 3. 7–8 (*CSEL* 33: 53–58). Markus, *Saeculum,* pp. 5f., 102.

[119] *De doctrina christiana* 3. 20–21 (*CSEL* 80: 84).

[120] *Conf.* 11. 26–28. *De Gen. ad lit.* 1. 8. 14 (*CSEL* 33: 303–308; *CSEL* 28, pt. 1, p. 11).

[121] *City of God* 11. 18, 23 (*CSEL* 40, pt. 1, pp. 537f., 545).

[122] *Conf.* 3. 7 (*CSEL* 33: 53–56).

[123] *De Gen. ad lit.* 4. 3. 7–10. *De ordine* 2. 19. 50. *Solil.* 2. 19. 33 (*CSEL* 28, pt. 1, pp. 102f.; *Corp. Christ., ser. lat.* 29: 134f.; *PL* 32: 901).

[124] *De doctrina christiana* 2. 145 (*CSEL* 80: 75f.).

[125] *De Gen. ad lit.* 1. 9. 17 (*CSEL* 28, pt. 1, pp. 12f.).

and revealed it to babes.[126] Thus, the causal systems of the pagans lacked the essential element in human life: how man, far from God in the region of unlikeness, could be changed into Him.[127]

3–4. *Analogy and Allegory.* Pre-Christian literatures naturally reached their limits with regard to these modes of exegesis. There was little in the arts to assist in demonstrating that the Old and New Testaments were not mutually antagonistic and in expounding the figurative interpretation of the Scriptures. Pre-Christian writings devoted especially little to allegory, which was justified by the assumption that the Holy Spirit had informed the letter of Scripture with a deep, hidden meaning: only sacred texts could be read spiritually. Augustine's principal charge against the pagan practitioners of the arts was that they had no spiritual vision. Even when they tried to escape from the senses, they were still submerged in sensual impressions and images, failing utterly when they attempted to discern the "ineffable mysteries of truth."[128] Leaving aside Manichaean experiments, Augustine apparently learned the method of allegory not from his education in the arts but from hearing the sermons of Ambrose.

Analogy was a rather different case, not in its limited application to the Old and New Testaments but rather in the method of which that was but one application. At the most basic level, all reasoning and learning proceeded by comparing likeness and unlikeness. Augustine took account of this universal fact in his description of the mental vision, sorting through images of previous experiences, actual and vicarious, and collating them with present ones. He also recognized that the arts—detecting and expressing a universal *ratio*—proceeded in the same fashion, by contrast and comparison. Manifestly, one of the arts, dialectic, followed the analogic process in its task of comparing, dividing, and generalizing. Even more fundamentally, among the verbal arts, analogy was a major tool of grammar. It also permeated the numerical arts, as proportion, or *corrationalitas*.[129] As such, it played in his mind whenever he considered the degrees of harmony or justice ranging over the celestial movements, the aesthetic contrast of good with evil in history, the productive cycle of a tree, the coordinate parts of an animal's body, or music.

Thus, the entire structure of Augustine's appraisal of the arts was of

---

[126] *Conf.* 7. 9 (*CSEL* 33: 155).   [127] *Conf.* 7. 10 (*CSEL* 33: 157).

[128] Cf. *De utilitate credendi* 1 (*CSEL* 25: 1). On this passage, and on the necessity of considering analogy and allegory together, see H. de Lubac, *Exégèse médiévale* (Paris, 1959), 1: 180f.

[129] *De musica* 6. 17. 57 (*Bibliothèque augustinienne*, ser. 1, vol. 4, p. 474).

a piece with his general conception of thought. They both rested on a logic of similarity tested by analogy. This is apparent in his concept of a *ratio* coordinating the three tiers of carnal, intellectual, and spiritual knowledge, a *ratio* that made it possible, by deciphering signs, to move from what one could see in part to an uncircumscribed whole.

In summary, Augustine was not driven compulsively to read significance into everything in sight. Some, perhaps many, events and human institutions signified nothing. This was true of the arts in particular and of social customs in general, which involved mimesis of the sort that society uses to perpetuate itself. So regarded, the arts belonged to a doctrinally neutral complex of knowledge, custom, and usages that men had invented to safeguard the needs and the integrity of social life. With profit, if also with caution, they could be used by Christians in their external lives.

Among these applications, Augustine included weights and measures, currency denominations, the forms of letters, historical accounts, the useful mechanical arts, and the sciences of disputation and number.[130] As they did not pretend to represent a higher reality, they did not impinge on the truth disclosed to and by the Christian exegete. But Augustine argued in this way regarding the tactics of genre and style because he had other aspects of unity and more complex strategies of corrective mimesis in mind.

His deeper mimetic conceptions fell into two clusters: the one formed around the nucleus of Neoplatonic metaphysics, and the other, around a second nucleus of Pauline eschatology. Different as they were, these two clusters had a distinct trait in common: they explained transition, the process by which something becomes what it is not. Therefore, they explained how apparent contradictions in the visible world and in human experience actually testified to a higher, informing unity accessible to the eye of the mind. Both Neoplatonic and Pauline doctrines were aesthetic because they taught an inner wholeness (or form), proportion, and beauty in the structure of the world and the mind. But they were also aesthetic because they taught how form was given. They described the invisible form being realized in the visible world and the soul participating in, and becoming, what it saw as it passed through the carnal, intellectual, and spiritual levels of knowledge.

Thus far, Augustine's two conceptions of unity repeated arguments going back to the very origins of the arts. Part of this classical heritage

---

[130] *De doctrina christiana* 2. 100, 101, 140, 144 (*CSEL* 80: 62f., 74, 75).

was that the object of education was to awaken the innate virtue in man, a virtue that was composed of "justice, moderation, and holiness of life."[131] The novelty in Augustine's thought was not that he regarded the arts as a corrective aid to holiness—the blessed life—and embedded them in an aesthetic matrix redolent of mystical philosophy: he had the most venerable pre-Christian precedents for that. Instead, Augustine's innovation was in realigning that aesthetic. He centered his theory of Beauty on the crucifixion. He was able to do so because he considered the historical order to be as much a divine institution, outside nature and the world, as musical proportions. At the crucifixion, the types and symbols of all previous human experience were fulfilled, and it became possible for "all the treasures of wisdom and knowledge" hidden in the Logos to be mediated by the Logos as man to men.[132]

We found that Paul conceived of two sets of mimetic strategies, each corresponding with one of Christ's natures. Cosmic (or global) strategies of reversion and augmentation corresponded with Christ as the principle of creation and the head of the Church. Historical strategies of inversion and subversion corresponded with His human nature, and Paul employed them to elucidate the passage from death into life by individual conversion, the transition from synagogue to Church, and the reversal of worldly values by the Gospel of Christ crucified.

Augustine too followed this general pattern of thought. But the changed position of the Church in the world enabled him both to refine his understanding of the strategies of inversion and subversion and to associate with them tactics undreamed of by Paul. In the ancient world, terror—the fear of the schoolmaster's rod—was an integral part of education. Augustine's doctrines of history illustrated how, in one man's mind, social organs of coercion and terror joined philosophical reasoning and the liberal arts as corrective tactics for the education of mankind.

Tactics of Terror and Strategies of Historical Mimesis

Human beings learn primarily in three ways: through sight and hearing, and through discipline of the body. Augustine's comments on philosophy and the liberal arts concerned mainly how the mind could transform sensory data into knowledge. But kinesthesia, symbolized by the schoolmaster's rod, persistently recurs in his writings, and it was

[131] Plato *Protagoras* 324–325.
[132] Cf. *Conf.* 10. 43; 11. 2 (*CSEL* 33: 278–280, 281–283).

natural that bodily, as well as mental, discipline, figured in his concept of the soul's mimetic passage through the carnal, intellectual, and spiritual levels of knowledge.

Quite early in his career, Augustine summarized the effects that the progressive Christian education of mankind had had. Men and women, he wrote, had learned to revere nothing sensual as God. They had learned to practice long fasts, to choose chastity in contempt of marriage and offspring, to endure the agonies of cross and fire, to divest themselves of their inheritance for the benefit of the poor—in short, to scorn the world and embrace ascetic self-mortification, even to the point of craving death. He imagined whole peoples approving and loving these signs of spiritual progress and fecundity, although few could perform such works well and wisely.[133]

Ascetic discipline belonged to the kinesthetic element of Christian education. It hardened souls for the continual warfare between the believing world and the hostile world;[134] but it normally began as the result of fear. Augustine recognized terror as the corrective part of education, used by fathers to correct their sons, or by schoolmasters to improve their disciples. He recalled being beaten by his schoolmasters. He had prayed that God would stop the torments, but they continued. God did not listen. Though they wished him no evil, Augustine's parents laughed at his great fears and at his suffering. Augustine also remembered that his mother had hoped that God would be a father to him, in some fashion replacing Patricius, his natural father. In the long process of his conversion, God, like his parents, did not lighten Augustine's physical suffering and spiritual anguish but rather laughed and, as it were, broke his bones with the rod of discipline for his spiritual correction.

His own experience disposed the Father to think that a "most salubrious terror" generally launched a person's conversion; for, in this instance too, fear and pain were useful preliminaries to teaching.[135] On

---

[133] *De utilitate credendi* 35 (*CSEL* 25: 44f.). On Augustine's theories of development (or progress), see, in general, Jeremy Y. du Q. Adams, *The Populus of Augustine and Jerome: A Study in the Patristic Sense of Community* (New Haven, 1971), pp. 199f. See also Theodor E. Mommsen, "St. Augustine and the Christian Idea of Progress: The Background of The City of God," in *Medieval and Renaissance Studies,* ed. E. F. Rice (Ithaca, 1959), pp. 271, 297f., and "Orosius and Augustine," in ibid., pp. 336f.

[134] *En. in Ps.* 45. 4–5, 7 (*Corp. Christ., ser. lat.* 38: 519f., 522). Ibid. 71. 16 (*Corp. Christ., ser. lat.* 39: 982). *Tr. in Joan.* 110. 2; 111. 1 (*Corp. Christ., ser. lat.* 36: 623, 628).

[135] *Conf.* 1. 9, 11; 6. 6, 14 (*CSEL* 33: 13f., 16, 122, 138). *City of God* 22. 22 (*CSEL*

the grand scale of history, the Church could act rigorously against its own, following the example of Moses, who commanded that three thousand of his people—worshippers of the Golden Calf—be put to the sword, "not in cruelty, but in great love" for the offenders as well as for those who refused to follow them in idolatry. The Apostle Paul also acted not in cruelty but in love "when he delivered a man up for the destruction of the flesh, so that the spirit might be saved in the day of the Lord Jesus."[136] Christ Himself employed chastisement and fear as tactics of instruction, notably when, on the way to Damascus, He first struck Paul to the earth, blinding, and later teaching him.[137] In Augustine's own day, the Church, following these examples, invoked imperial persecution of the schismatic Donatists, with love for the persecuted and prayers that this extreme measure would produce their repentance and conversion, even if it also issued in their bodily deaths.[138]

Plainly, Augustine regarded terror as one tactic by which the conversion—or education—of mankind was legitimately advanced. My task is not to analyse the rationale for persecution that Augustine set down and that became a classical point of reference in later centuries but rather to describe deep mimetic strategies that, in Augustine's view, the tactic of terror served. The strategies in question are the same two that Paul had associated with Christ's human nature: mimesis by inversion, which God taught to man most spectacularly by His chastisement of the Jews, and mimesis by subversion, illustrated by the reversal that put the sword of persecution into the hands of the once-persecuted Church. As we shall see, these strategies were far broader than any particular tactic. For Augustine, the use of terror accentuated them and provided objective evidence of the transformations that more hidden tactics were achieving in human hearts.

40, pt. 2: 636), approving corporal punishment of children on Scriptural grounds. *De catechizandis rudibus* 5.9 (*Corp. Christ., ser. lat.* 46: 129). *Ep.* 185, 2. 7; 6. 21 (*CSEL* 57: 6, 20). Augustine frequently employed metaphors from medicine and surgery to describe the pain that might have to be endured if the soul were to be cured of sin. These analogues had a long life, especially as Augustine set them forth in his defense of persecution as a means of recalling Donatists to the Church (*ep.* 185). For bibliographical references, and Hincmar of Rheims' use of the Father's words and ideas, see below Chapter 5, note 43.

[136] *Contra Faustum* 22. 79 (*CSEL* 25: 680f.).

[137] *Ep.* 185, 6. 22 (*CSEL* 57: 21).

[138] *Ep.* 185, 2. 11; 3. 14; 8. 32–34 (*CSEL* 57: 9f, 13, 29–31). See Augustine's opinion that the visible sword was no longer used in the Church, having been superseded by deposition and excommunication. *De fide et operibus* 2. 3 (*CSEL* 41: 37).

Paul affirmed that the truth foreshadowed in the Law had been embodied in Christ. Following him, Augustine argued that the Jews exemplified mimesis that had outlived its legitimacy and that, once good, had been inverted into evil. When it was given, the Law foreshadowed the revelations of Christ. But the Jews could not see that, with Christ's advent, the Truth that the Law prefigured had come: they held firmly to partial revelations and defective ceremonies of the past. Convinced that they served God, the Jews killed both Christ and the Apostles who preached Him,[139] and, persisting in an outdated mimesis, they ceased to imitate Christ, as they had done by anticipation, and became imitators of Satan. Through Christ, Augustine wrote, believers became sons of Abraham by imitating his deeds and virtues, not by carnal procreation. The Jews, however, became the children of the devil by imitating his disobedience and pride, as manifested in the impieties of the Amorites and the Hittites. They took as parents, not those who gave them birth, but those whose customs they followed down the road to condemnation.[140]

Under the Old Dispensation, the Law had been given to teach piety by means of the "threats and terrors of punishment" set forth in it.[141] Under the New Dispensation, God's punishment of the Jews stood forth as a terrible admonition to the entire world, perhaps yet more instructive in its concrete, historical effects than the promises of eternal punishment, which some mistakenly believed were meant to terrify, without being literally true.[142]

The wretchedness of the Jews certified the operations of Pauline mimesis by inversion. Augustine's discussion of lying illustrates more closely how he understood this strategy.

The Father's basic assumption was that the literal contradictions between prescripts of the Old and New Testaments actually testified to the same truth, imperfectly foreshadowed among the Hebrews and disclosed in the Church. One Christian sect, the Priscillianist, argued that the Scriptures throughout sanctioned the use of falsehood to throw the hostile world off the scent of authentic doctrine. They invoked as authorities various specific statements by Christ as relayed in

---

[139] *Ep.* 185, 5. 20 (*CSEL* 57: 18). *Tr. in Joan.* 93. 3 (*Corp. Christ., ser. lat.* 36: 559f.).

[140] *Tr. in Joan.* 42. 10. 15 (*Corp. Christ., ser. lat.* 36: 369f., 372f.).

[141] *De utilitate credendi* 9 (*CSEL* 25: 12).

[142] On the Jews, see *City of God* 18. 46 (*CSEL* 40, pt. 2, pp. 346f.); *Tr. in Joan* 16. 3 (*Corp. Christ., ser. lat.* 36: 165–167). On the discount that some placed on threats of eternal punishment, see *Enchiridion* 39. 112 (*Corp. Christ., ser. lat.* 46: 109f.).

the Gospels and His parables and, especially, the use of figurative speech and metaphor in the Old Testament. Indeed, they argued, there were instances in which patriarchs lied to their own advantage, as when Jacob deceived his father.

Augustine's rebuttal is important, and, as an essay in meaning, it forecast the process of inversion framed by Hegel and reshaped by Marx. The metaphor of God as the creative light was central to Augustine's response. In history, as in man's innermost self, the light was never fully revealed. Even when it blinded the mind's eye with its splendor, it remained partly, indeed largely, hidden. There is something of Marx's time-bound truth growing false with age in Augustine's conception of pagan thought and cult, which changed the truth of God into a lie and passed as truth until unmasked and destroyed by Christian doctrine. The more intricate part of his teaching, however, concerned movement in the other direction, the ambiguity of a falsehood that proved to be true.

Of course, Augustine does not argue that good and evil are equivalent, or, as Marx did, that truth was a circumstantial matter, and that, with changing times, what was true became false and an earlier falsehood became true. What Augustine does say is this. In its own time, an act may be false and deceptive. Such was Jacob's fraud against Esau. But, he continued, a quite unknown significance may hide beneath the surface. Jacob's deception had its analogic fulfillment in a revelation of Christ (Luke 13:28–30), and it was, therefore, true because it signified what was true. The Priscillianists erred on the side of literalism, regarding prefigurations as lies because they were sometimes like lies,[143] and in their historical settings, they were lies.

Thus, Augustine contrasted the level of the act apparent to deceiver and deceived with the higher level of the unseen historical order, the poetic structure that was already complete in God's eye, but that, to men, appeared to be composed slowly, by the accretion of life to life and with apparent contradictions that time disclosed as consistent.

Terror served the second historical strategy, mimesis by subversion, as it did the strategy of inversion. Paul employed this strategy to ex-

---

[143] *Contra mendacium* 10.24–12.26 (*PL* 40: 533–537). See also Augustine's interpretation of Judah's crime in (unwittingly) mating with his daughter-in-law, in *Contra Faustum* 22. 83 (*CSEL* 25: 686). Judah took Tamar out of lust; he had no idea of the lofty truth that his action prefigured anything concerning the redemption of mankind: "Ita factum Iudae secundum illius libidinem malum fuit, sed illo nesciente magnum bonum significavit; a se ipso quippe malum fecit, sed non a se ipso bonum significavit."

plain how the Church took form within the Synagogue and, in due course, superseded it, and how souls of the elect were transferred from glory to glory. Augustine too found it useful in explaining the paradoxical mingling of continuity and change in history. Terror became an issue when Augustine was forced to defend the request that he and other bishops had made for imperial intervention against the Donatists. Such a request had no apostolic sanction, for the Apostles never beseeched the kings of the earth to persecute their enemies. But in the apostolic age, Augustine observed, kings were still raging against the Lord and His anointed. No emperor had yet believed in Christ and served Him by defending piety against the impious. Among the ancient Hebrews, kings had served God through their coercive powers. Now, with the conversion of emperors to Christianity, their example could be followed once more. Times had changed; a new order had come into season.[144]

Augustine's thought about coercion paralleled his doctrines concerning the liberal arts. In both cases, he distinguished means from ends. The use of force was not an end in itself. It was neutral, a tool waiting to be used for good or ill. There were many parallels. Pagans had used virginity, sacrifice, and works of mercy without gaining any spiritual benefit, because they did not perform those acts for the glory of God. Schismatics and heretics performed the Eucharist and sought martyrdom, but, estranged from God in their misbelief, they kept the outward forms of the Church without its inward reality. Instead of blessing, they consumed damnation with the consecrated elements of the Eucharist; instead of the crown of martyrdom, they found a death that was hard to distinguish from suicide.[145]

Correspondingly, persecution could be used unrighteously or righteously. In its early stages, progress in the education of mankind had been won through the predictions of the prophets against evil kings and perverse priests, by Christ's humanity and teaching, by the Apostles' weary travels, and by "the insults, crosses, bloodshed and deaths of martyrs."[146] In the new age, employing persecution in the spirit of love, the Church rendered it a work of mercy, correcting disbelievers by terror in order to restore them to wholeness.[147]

Inversion (the recognition that what had been considered true or false at an earlier time had actually been the opposite) and subversion

[144] *Ep.* 185, 5. 19–20 (*CSEL* 57: 17f.).

[145] *Ep.* 185, 2. 8–9; 3. 12; 11. 48–49 (*CSEL* 57: 7–9, 11, 41–43).

[146] *De utilitate credendi* 35 (*CSEL* 25: 45). Augustine also mentions the exemplary lives of saints and timely miracles as contributing to progress.

[147] *Ep.* 185, 2. 7; 3. 13; 6. 23; 7. 26; 8. 34 (*CSEL* 57: 6f., 12, 21f., 25, 31).

(the overturning of beliefs or institutions from within) were clearly related. For Augustine, as for Paul, the experience of the Jews illustrated both strategies at work. Quite naturally, then, Augustine elucidated both inversion and subversion with the same metaphor, that of biological procreation. The Jews became sons of the Devil, imitating him when their law and ceremonies had been inverted into empty shadows. Christians subverted the Jews, becoming the sons of God through imitation of Christ. I have already alluded to one instance in which Augustine employed the metaphor of procreation by mimesis and I must now consider its wider import for the strategy of subversion.

As I previously stated, Philo employed the same metaphor. He used it to describe a scholar's impregnation of his own soul by "mating" with the liberal arts. True to Aristotle, Philo also regarded generation as the means by which the genera sustained themselves, extensions of God's original creative act. Finally, and here Augustine was in accord with him, Philo appropriated the Stoic conception of *logoi spermatikoi,* the principles of specific growth and development derived from the Logos and realizing themselves in individual beings by the endless process of generation and decay. Insofar as not all had yet appeared, the visible world could "be said to be pregnant with causes of beings still to come."[148]

Augustine's concern with historical regeneration led him, however, to an entirely different usage. He understood three unions in much the same light: (1) spirit and flesh, (2) husband and wife, and (3) Christ and the Church. In each case, the first was prior to the second, "according to the beauty of order."[149] The union of spirit and flesh concerns us only in that Augustine equated husband with spirit and wife with flesh, and applied the equation to Christ and the Church.[150]

[148] See E. Gilson, *The Christian Philosophy of St. Augustine* (New York, 1967), p. 206. Cf. J. C. Plumpe, *Mater Ecclesia: An Inquiry into the Concept of the Church as Mother in Early Christianity* (Washington, D.C., 1943), esp. p. 127.

[149] *De continentia* 9. 23 (*PL* 40: 364). *De doctrina christiana* 1. 51–53 (*CSEL* 80: 21f.).

[150] *Tr. in Joan.* 2. 12–16 (*Corp. Christ., ser. lat.* 36: 17–19). Cf. *De doctrina christiana* 1. 33; 2. 12 (*CSEL* 80: 16, 37). This metaphor contrasts with another that illustrates yet a further way in which Augustine understood the unity of believers with Christ: namely, grafting. The grafting metaphor, of course, emphasizes the unification of organically separate and unlike elements; it was so used by St. Paul in Romans 11:17–24. It can also connote growth without procreation. Cf. Augustine's discussion of the tree of life that, by extension of its branches, has spread over all the world. *Ep.* 185, 8. 32; 10. 44; 11. 50 (*CSEL* 57: 29, 38f., 44). However, Augustine was capable of combining the metaphor of grafting with that of procreation by imitation, as he did in the passage in *Tr. in Joan.* 42. 10, 15, cited above note 140.

From the *Canticle of Canticles* and the letters of Paul, Christians had long since described the Church as the spouse of Christ and as the mother of the faithful. Drawing on these already venerable images, Augustine unfolded a pattern of genetic reproduction that varied from Aristotle's or Philo's in that the begotten forms—though not the generic ones—changed. It would certainly be anachronistic to define this formula as "evolutionary." At the same time, Augustine does describe the movement as a genetic one, characterized by a sequence of mutations, advancing toward the formation of a new species.

Adverting to the *ménage à trois* of Abraham, Sarah, and Hagar, Augustine wrote that the sons of God were begotten of the Bridegroom's seed, whether in the womb of the Church or in that of the handmaid. Some who were born of the lawful wife fell away; others, born "outside," were admitted to the promise. But the Church had given birth to Abel and Enoch, Noah and Abraham, Moses and the prophets, "the apostles and martyrs, and all good Christians . . . even to the end." In addition, there were stages in procreation. Between Adam and Moses, both covenants were hidden. After Moses, the Old Covenant was revealed, with the New hidden within it. Christ came in the flesh, revealing the New Covenant.[151] At every stage, children were begotten, having natural or spiritual vision. And still the process continued, as men were born of God according to His Word, all composing the spiritual Israel, offspring of the fathers in whose seed was Christ.[152]

In a yet more exalted vision, Augustine perceived that, since Christ himself had been born under the Old Dispensation, the Church was not only both Virgin and Spouse but also His Mother. So, too, was every soul, travailing until He was formed in its womb.[153] Even now, he wrote, the Church was pregnant with the blessed life, "travailing in birth with groaning" until she bring forth the "male child" of contemplation.[154]

Surveying the long interplay of contemplation and action through which the Church constituted the rule of faith,[155] and the even longer sequence of ages that revealed the divine order underlying events, Augustine concluded that the formation of the body of Christ was a steady, genetic progression of knowledge in which each state super-

---

[151] *Tr. in Joan.* 2. 12–16 (*Corp. Christ., ser. lat.* 36: 17–19).

[152] *De doctrina christiana* 3. 110–113 (*CSEL* 80: 109–111) and references in the next note.

[153] *De virginitate* 2, 5 (*PL* 40: 397, 399).

[154] *Tr. in Joan.* 101. 5 (*Corp. Christ., ser. lat.* 36: 593).

[155] *De doctrina christiana* 3. 3–4 (*CSEL* 80: 79f.).

seded the one before by realizing its latent promise and containing the seeds of the next state. In this way, the knowledge of signs possessed by the Jews anticipated that vouchsafed to the Christians, just as the liberal arts, wrenched out of the Gentiles' world of counterfeit signs, gave Christians the tools with which to destroy that world.

Like the individual soul, but in a rather more complex fashion, the Church progressed in concentric tiers from carnal to spiritual vision, from the carnal images known to the Hebrews, to the mediated images accessible to man's mind and heart under the new dispensation, toward the completed and unmediated spiritual vision of the next world.

Since the revelations of God in time would only end with time, every stage in the Church's history fulfilled the typologies of previous ones. The discrepancy remained between what was and what was known. The Scriptures still displayed plural meanings. Consistency within the doctrine of salvation left no alternative to embracing contradictions, summed up in the paradox that the foolishness of God was wiser than the wisdom of men.[156] As the Church advanced through its earthly pilgrimage, new understandings of the signs in Scripture would be framed, all foreseen and prepared by the Holy Spirit,[157] but all were provisional. Contemplating the diverse senses imposed on the Scriptures, Augustine could only pray that God would reveal the "one true, certain, and good sense" intended among the many proposed.[158] For, in this world, the Church, like its individual members, saw through the mirror of an enigma. It walked more by faith than by sight,[159] it cried out in travail with the birth of the life that would supersede its own. Whenever one spoke of the ineffable God, one only wished to speak, and never said what one wished.[160] The Church itself was an analogue; and, in its dim vision through other signs, there lay a typological area of conflict. It was more than the conflict against Satan, more than that of the spirit against the flesh, more even than that against heresies which, Augustine the controversialist knew, were necessary "that they which are approved may be manifest among you" (I. Cor. 11:19). For

[156] *De doctrina christiana* 1. 13–14; 1. 22–23; 1. 28–29 (*CSEL* 80: 11, 13f., 15).

[157] *De doctrina christiana* 3. 84–85 (*CSEL* 80: 102). On Augustine's idea that later councils could amend mistakes of earlier ones because of intervening experience, see Fritz Hoffmann, "Die Bedeutung der Konzilien für die kirchliche Lehrentwicklung nach dem heiligen Augustinus," in *Kirche und Ueberlieferung,* ed. Johannes Betz and Heinrich Fries (Freiburg-i.-B., 1960. *Festschrift J. R. Geiselmann*), pp. 81–89.

[158] *Conf.* 12. 31f. (*CSEL* 33: 343f.).

[159] *De doctrina christiana* 1. 66; 2. 19–20 (*CSEL* 80: 25, 38).

[160] *De doctrina christiana* 1. 13–14 (*CSEL* 80: 11).

Amos, Paul, and Christ himself were examples of how, as conformity with God increased in their minds and consciences, some of the elect had opposed the visible community of faith.[161]

Under the threats of eternal punishment, the Church in its season as persecutor was subject to ceaseless scrutiny, criticism, and correction, as it was gradually formed, through mimetic strategies, into its perfect state.

Summary

Augustine represents a decisive moment in the career of mimesis: the moment when mimetic strategies passed from esoteric philosophical schools into the mainstream of Western culture. These strategies became tools by which an entire society explained its origins, justified its actions, and envisioned its future.

As set forth in Augustine's writings, mimetic strategies possess an extraordinary strength by virtue of their completeness. They addressed the most fundamental processes by which man learns (that is, by which the mind is formed): seeing, hearing, and feeling. Consequently, Augustine was able to conceive of a universal program of education, guided in all its aspects by the same principles.

Certainly, mimesis was a universal principle for Augustine in far more than the pedagogical sense. The entire world was a structure of mediated asymmetries. At least in part this was true because he believed that God had created all things according to weight, number, and measure; the universe was a vast, planned work of art. Thus, Augustine could define the origin, composition, and direction of the physical world, as well as of the historical one, in terms of mimetic relationships—in terms that described the mediated asymmetry of image and archetype in any kind of composition, for example in poetry, sculpture, and painting.

However, mimesis in the physical world amounted to redundancy: the repetition of natural cycles and movements. Mimesis in the historical world was repetitive but not redundant; it could be corrective. I have been particularly concerned with the chain of corrective mimetic strategies that Augustine described as leading from fundamental operations of the mind to grand processes of history. He was able to connect psychology with history because he regarded all human experience as a movement of conversion in which the re-creation or reformation of the individual mind was the basic unit. The sum of in-

---

[161] Cf. *De doctrina christiana* 4. 61–62 (*CSEL* 80: 133f.).

dividual conversions made up the corrective "education" of mankind.

To be sure, because mimesis was ingrained in all human nature, Augustine allowed for bad imitation as well as for good. In the blindness, or wickedness, of their minds, unbelievers and merely nominal Christians were impelled "by a perverse desire for the likeness of God." Despite all tactics of reasoning, education, and social coercion, the informing "reason of wisdom" could be overwhelmed and shunted aside by "the sensuous movement of the soul, which is common to us with beasts"; in such a state, one learned by experience of temporal and changeable things, by carnal senses, rather than through love of wisdom. Thus, by misdirection, the soul could be dehumanized, transformed from likeness to God into likeness to brute animals.[162]

Augustine argued that the results of bad imitation were particularly apparent in the case of the Jews, who could not perceive the spiritual reality hidden in the carnal foreshadowings of the Old Testament and whose spiritual blindness led to destruction. But God had allowed for perverse imitation in His masterplan, just as painters included black patches, or poets, antitheses, for the beauty of the composition.

As he worked out the mimetic strategies linking the innermost secrets of the mind with the vast panorama of humanity in the process of correction, Augustine employed some elements from the repertoire of thought that he had inherited from pre-Christian antiquity; but he transformed them and invented others to meet the demands of Christian doctrine. Among the received strategies for mediating the essential asymmetries of human existence, responsive mimesis was fundamental. Aristotle had identified this as an inborn trait of human nature. Assuming critical reason as man's characteristic faculty, he had also considered responsive mimesis as a means of progressive and cumulative development in various creative activities, such as poetry and philosophy. Augustine shared these premises. However, his own theological convictions led him beyond the levels of sensory and rational (or intellectual) perception that Aristotle had considered. Augustine argued that the mind was capable of progressive imitation on a spiritual level that transcended and completed the other two, and consequently his idea of responsive mimesis lent itself to a three-tier method of reasoning by analogy: analogies of "carnal images," of "incorporeal and eternal patterns (*rationes*)," and of divine truths disclosed by faith.

---

[162] *De Trinitate* 12. 11–12, 15 (*Corp. Christ., ser. lat.* 50: 370–373, 379f.). Cf. *Tr. in Joan.* 42. 5 (*Corp. Christ., ser. lat.* 36: 367). The Jews gloried in their descent from Abraham, but Jesus rebuked them as "a generation of vipers—not by any means of men, but of vipers. He saw the shape of men, but he recognized the venom."

How could the mind pass beyond itself? Between the foolishness of man and the wisdom of God, there was one point of transition: the wisdom of man. If man were to be redeemed, Augustine wrote, it was necessary "both that man be imitated and that our hope not be placed in man." To satisfy this paradox, the "eternal, unchangeable wisdom" of God became man.[163] By imitating the Word-made-flesh, man passed from physical and rational analogies to the spiritual, moving toward that point where analogies would no more be needed, where man would no longer see through mediatory analogies, "a mirror in an enigma," but immediately face-to-face.

Augustine's *Tractates* on John provided us with an example of how he applied his three-fold concept of responsive mimesis to mediate asymmetries between God and man. The three tiers of analogy gave Augustine a way of analyzing individual conversion, but they hardly satisfied the need for a coherent picture of all history. To this greater purpose, he applied two other ancient mimetic strategies for correction. One was mimesis by reversion, which Plato set forth with regard to the soul and which Neoplatonists developed to explain the cosmic egress from, and return to, God. The second strategy was mimesis by augmentation, which Aristotle and others had employed to describe organic growth. Augustine thought conversion to be the dominant theme of history—the aggregate conversion of the world. Consequently, mimesis by reversion and augmentation entered his thought (as they had St. Paul's) to elucidate the operations of the Logos in the physical world and in the Church as another cosmos, "the believing world." But they had been fundamentally changed by the theology of sin, rebirth, and resurrection.

On the highest metaphysical level, the basic formulae of responsive mimesis remained Plato's mimesis by reversion. Plato had used his doctrine of innate ideas and recollection to explain how the individual soul imitated and moved toward assimilation with its archetype, and Neoplatonists had adapted this theory to the entire cosmos. Augustine's counterpart was the doctrine that man retained the image of God, in which he had been made, but that he had lost his original likeness to God, which was renewed by grace. The same difference was at the heart of Augustine's departure from the concept of mimesis by intuition, which originated in Plato and Aristotle, and reappeared, much altered, in Augustine's descriptions of the mystic raptures of Moses and St. Paul.

---

[163] *De utilitate credendi* 33 (*CSEL* 25: 42).

Thus, Plato's asymmetrical structure of two worlds, the sensual and the intelligible, persisted in Augustine's thought. So, accordingly, did the enigmas with which he defined the structure from the human perspective. But Augustine's Pauline concept of a progressive historical order meant that the enigmatic ironies of mimesis had to be played out in time and human action. Certainly, Plato's two paradigms are similar to Augustine's concept of a "two-faced *ratio*" in the arts. Augustine went far beyond Plato when he welded the arts into an apparatus of social criticism. To see invisible things meant perceiving the unreal reality of images.

For Augustine, as for Plato, the comparison of the ideal with the actual rendered iconoclasm a symbolic form of art. No words or other analogues were adequate to contain the reality of God. One honored Him with silence; the imitative arts—painting, sculpture, poetry, theatrical productions—mired the soul in sensual representation, and they should be excluded from Christian life. Music too fell under suspicion. Through the centrality of the crucifixion, aesthetic iconoclasm moved toward the veneration of the ugly. The beauty of the Church, Augustine wrote, is as that of a tree. One delights in its leaves, and fruit, and restful shade. But the root is Christ crucified in whom there is no beauty. He was spat upon, humiliated, beaten, crucified, wounded, and despised. The Church is beautiful; but the more deformed her Spouse, the dearer and sweeter He became to her.[164]

When he turned beyond metaphysics to eschatology, Augustine therefore framed a new variety of mimesis by reversion, a historical formula. I have called this corrective formula mimesis by inversion, because Augustine used it to explain how ugliness could be inverted into beauty and falsehood into truth, always maintaining a basic, unalterable identity at the heart of things.

As Paul did before him, Augustine associated this strategy with Christ's humanity—the Incarnation—rather than with His divinity. In particular, he employed it to explain the paradox of continuity and change that, in his mind, legitimated Gentiles as the seed and heirs of Abraham.

But this strategy also addressed the partial and obscure version of truth available in the Church. Explaining inversion by the metaphor of the creative light that simultaneously hid and revealed itself, Augus-

---

[164] *Serm.* 44. 1–3 (*PL* 38: 258–260). This also bears on the qualification with which Augustine approved Plato's expulsion of the poets from his ideal city. See *City of God* 2. 14 (*CSEL* 40, pt. 1, p. 78).

tine transposed the counterpoint between imagery and iconoclasm into an resolved tension between community and conscience.

Still, inversion could not exhaust the strange interplay of continuity and change that Augustine sensed in the long course of history. Consequently, the Father developed a second mimetic formula that Paul had associated with Christ's humanity, mimesis by subversion. He used the metaphor of genetic reproduction to describe the latency of the covenants in the stages that preceded their revelations and the travail of the Church to bring the blessed life to birth. This art, by which later, higher forms of likeness subverted earlier, inferior ones, posited ignorance at every stage, and accordingly, the total dependence of the Church upon her Spouse. In part, it explains why Augustine recast Plato's enigma of the ignorant sage as he did. Without the arts, the Scriptures had all the wisdom in the arts. How could it be that Christ chose Peter, a fisherman, to be an apostle? Why didn't He choose an orator, a master of eloquence, or a senator who wouldn't talk with a man like Peter even when he bought fish from him, or, more grandly, an emperor? God had chosen the weak of the world to confound the strong and the foolish to confound the wise. An orator, or senator, or emperor, could glory in himself; a fisherman could boast only of Christ and lay before the world a double lesson: understand the words that are written and preached so that you may believe; believe so that you may understand the Word of God.[165] The arts and all Christian knowledge were directed toward the first object; they were completed and destroyed, as all analogues and enigmas must be, by the second. In this powerful and enduring fashion, Augustine gave historical depth to the concept, present from the beginning, that life achieved its unity from a hidden and holy truth, detected by men through reason, manifested by poetic intuition or prophetic madness, and attained, if ever, by stages of conflict.

At the beginning of this chapter, a contrast was drawn between canons of historical writing set down by Lucian of Samosata, a non-Christian writer of the third century, and the canons stated and followed by the Church Fathers. Consciously and deliberately, the Fathers departed from the classical—indeed archaizing—standards that Lucian advocated. They did so in large measure because they considered history a branch of theoretical knowledge, a philosophical enterprise, rather than a faithful and impartial record of events.

Augustine's writings illustrate the scope of that departure. His life

---

[165] *Serm.* 43. 5–7 (*PL* 36: 256–258).

also illustrates the further proposition that, given the full range of his mimetic strategies, the Father thought of the historian's task in a way quite different from Lucian. Lucian argued that the historian should purge himself of poetic and philosophical pretensions and simply act as the faithful mirror of events.[166] Because he regarded historical consciousness as an instrument of change for the better, Augustine considered the historical writer to be an exegete who detected hidden meaning, a teacher who proclaimed it, a polemicist who confounded its enemies. The Christian was one with God. The Christian historian was not a mirror of events but an instrument by which God's eternal design for the correction of human nature was accomplished. He contributed to the mediation of the asymmetry between God and man.

Thus the historical writer promoted corrective change through his works: by critical judgments and controversies, by invocation of civil force (if occasion arose) for the constraint of erring consciences, by his own martyrdom (if need be) in conflict with the hostile world. The iconoclastic impulse for such works came from a deeper source. Searching for models of life, the historical writer turned aside from knowledge gained by experience of natural and transitory things to a beauty beyond style, a justice beyond institutions, and a wisdom beyond human understanding and glimpsed by the fewest of the few. He himself was being transformed from likeness into ever more complete likeness to that beauty, justice, and wisdom by an inaccessible, yet most inward, creative light. This mimetic transition from form into more perfect form, which impelled him to act in militant contempt of the world, also advanced the progressive re-creation of the world itself toward the final stage, when analogies would yield to direct sight and the mysteries of God "need no more be given tongue by us in words of faith and sounding syllables, and we may imbibe them in that silence with most pure and burning contemplation."[167]

Gregory the Great

Evidently, the redemption of man occurred in the area between nature and art; when they spoke about nature, or about the arts of hand and mind, the Fathers never imagined that they were dealing with autonomous realms that had meaning apart from sacred history.

---

[166] See above note 7.
[167] *De catechizandis rudibus* 25. 47 (*Corp. Christ., ser. lat.* 46: 171).

My discussion thus far has indicated some general conclusions. (1) Mimesis between nature and art was regarded as a universal trait of mind that could be directed for good or ill—for the formation or deformation of human nature. (2) An individual writer's total concept of mimesis was generally made up of several paradigms. (3) Those paradigms, being logically independent of each other, could be broken apart and recombined, according to the judgment of a given writer. (4) Since mimetic doctrines of progress taught a mediated, asymmetrical tension between ideal and actual, they also held up imperatives of self-criticism and social estrangement: that is, the use of mimesis for the corrective reformation of human nature entailed conflict and pain. (5) Consciousness of progressive strategies of mimesis was limited to the fewest of the few. Division consequently separated the initiate from the others and, within the body of the initiate, the wise from the simple.

One vital aspect of the career of mimesis in the patristic era is that the poetic doctrine of mimesis, with its inherent critical bias, had left the shady arbors of philosophers and dilettanti. It had entered the tradition of a community, the Church, that for centuries dominated European life. Embedded in the theology of Christ as Logos and as man, it prescribed imperatives for individual and collective reform. Again and again, the institutions of European culture were to encounter the practical effects of the tension between the unifying imagery of mimesis and its iconoclasm.

Augustine supremely represents the intellectual achievement of this stage in the career of mimesis as a device of humanization. Pope Gregory the Great (ca. 540–604, reigned 590–604) represents yet more plainly than Augustine the role that mimetic doctrines of mediated asymmetry had assumed in European society. As Pope, Gregory taught, judged, and governed. Though menaced by enemies at home, his opinions and his actions were reckoned with throughout the Mediterranean world, even by those who eventually ignored them. As an exemplary theologian and administrator, Gregory exerted massive influence during the centuries after his death not only because his pontificate had manifestly been a turning point in the history of Europe but also because it was thought to epitomize concord of theory and life in Christian society.[168]

---

[168] Gregory himself conceived of an invisible society of faith, generally conterminous with the empire, that deserved to engage the official actions of individual Christian rulers in their realms. See his reference to a *"christianae reipublicae societas"* in a letter to the Ostrogothic Queen Theodelinda and to the *"christianae*

Gregory's letters and treatises, therefore, provide a glimpse into the motivations of a man who consciously employed mimetic doctrines in government and who found institutional homes for them through his contributions to the monastic ethos, to the law of the Church, and to the general formation of political theory. As to basic structure, his ideas followed the pattern taught by Augustine. He retained the Augustinian pattern of education, with its coordinates of psychology, formal disciplines (the arts), and physical coercion. In each of the three areas, Gregory, like Augustine before him, confronted the paradox that to employ mimetic strategies for the perfection of humanity was also to embrace divisions, conflict, and pain.

The tensions of mediated asymmetry appear most fundamentally in Gregory's concept of the human mind. Reason set men apart from brute animals and bound them to God, "the cause of causes, the life of the living, and the reason of rational creatures."[169] It was both the locus of man's image-relation to God and the means by which its likeness could be restored. "A man had to be sought out who might be offered for man, so that, for a rational sinner a rational victim might be slain. . . . Not by power, but by reason," Christ the sinless victim defeated Satan.[170] And yet, even for exalted men such as Moses and Jeremiah, the sublimest levels of knowledge must remain inferential, partly because man's vision was impaired by the corruptibility of his flesh,[171] partly because finite man could see God only through finite images and not through the uncircumscribed light of eternity.[172]

Augustine had maintained that man could perceive God directly, although never uninterruptedly in this life and never completely even in the next. Gregory withdrew provisional finality from knowledge. "How therefore are we illuminated by approaching [Him] if we can not see the light by which we are illuminated? But, if by approaching Himself we see the light by which we are illuminated, how is it asserted to be inaccessible?"[173] Gregory found this quandary in apparently contradictory texts of Scripture; he resolved it with a doctrine of proportion, an analogy of knowledge completed by faith.

Even the saints in eternal joy, reformed to the likeness of God, are

reipublicae regimen" assumed by the Emperor Maurice. *Reg.* 6. 61; 9. 67 (*MGH, Epp.* 1: 436, and 2, pt. 3, p. 88).

[169] *Moralia in Job* 30. 4. 17 (*PL* 76: 533).

[170] *Moralia in Job* 17. 30. 46 (*PL* 76: 32).

[171] *Moralia in Job* 27. 8. 12 (*PL* 76: 405).

[172] *Moralia in Job* 18. 54. 88 (*PL* 76: 92).

[173] *Moralia in Job* 18. 54. 92 (*PL* 76: 94).

both like and unlike Him. Seeing the eternity of God, it is as though they were eternal, and, when they receive the gift of His vision, they imitate the beatitude that they see. They are like God because they are blessed, each in his own measure; and they are not like the Creator because they are creatures. They have a certain likeness to God because they have no end; and yet they do not have an uncircumscribed equality with Him because they are circumscribed.[174] The same principles apply on earth to the contemplative state. Men see eternity according to their capacities, and they participate in what they see by imitating it as far as they are able.[175] Still, contemplation, as well as the active life, was in bondage on earth; the liberty of the mind was but imitated, since the final inner peace was seen in an enigma.[176]

The doctrine of proportion, or analogy, by which Gregory resolved the quandary of how one could be enlightened by an inaccessible light, led him to indefinite progression. The soul's transformation advanced "through intervals of time." It suffered under the thick darkness of temptation; it rose up, reformed to the light of grace, as though a morning star.[177] But the exaltation passed.

The Holy Spirit was a great artificer, informing and changing the human mind as soon as it touched it.[178] But, even under inspiration, earthly sharing in eternity was an imitation twice removed from the eternal itself. Heaven mingled with hell in the individual person "when the mind which already contemplates the light of the homeland above also bears the darkness of hidden temptation, because of the warfare of the flesh."[179] The soul was in constant anguish, tasting inner sweetness, aflame with love, striving to rise above itself, and yet always falling back broken "into the darkness of its infirmity."[180] In a terrible conflict, the soul struggled against its estranged self, seeking freedom. "For it is a rough yoke, indeed, and a weight of harsh bondage, to be subject to temporal [affairs], to canvas earthly things, to take hold of those that slip away, to wish to stay amidst things that do not stay, to

---

[174] *Moralia in Job* 7. 28. 36 (*PL* 75: 786).

[175] *Moralia in Job* 18. 54. 93 (*PL* 76: 96).

[176] *Homil. in Ezech.* 1. 4. 13 (*PL* 76: 811f.).

[177] *Moralia in Job* 10. 15–18. 31–34 (*PL* 75: 935–940). See G. B. Ladner, "Gregory the Great and Gregory VII: A Comparison of their Concepts of Renewal, with a Note on the Computer Methods Used [by D. W. Packard]," *Viator* 4 (1973): 5.

[178] *Homil. in Ev.* 30. 8 (*PL* 76: 1226).

[179] *Moralia in Job* 10. 10. 17 (*PL* 75: 931).

[180] *Moralia in Job* 5. 33. 58 (*PL* 75: 711).

seek after things that are passing, but still to be unwilling to pass away with them as they go."[181]

And what of those who lacked the informing wisdom of the Holy Spirit? Gregory knew the phenomenon of "sinful imitation."[182] He believed that, left to himself, a man could fall into the idolatry of self-worship. Mad with pride, he could be turned by his insanity into an irrational animal; he could loose his human being.[183] Gregory followed well-established conventions, employed also by Augustine, when he referred to Gentiles, Jews, heretics, and schismatics as "insane," and thus defective in the rationality that characterized human being.

Such lamentable instances of destructive imitation as these were more than examples of ignorance or perversity, for man endured blessings and temptations as a vessel was formed in its maker's hands.[184] God's invisible hand was at work in individual lives and in the great *tableau vivant* that they collectively formed. Gregory repeated Augustine's metaphor of history as a painting, complete in God's mind. His version is the more severe. The beauty of the whole was evident, he argued, in the agonies of the impious in hell and the eternal happiness meted out to the good. For God well ordained that contrast, as a painter adds black to enhance the beauty of an adjacent white or red.[185] So too in the historical accounts of Scripture, Truth deployed the virtues and vices as musicians temper the harmony of chords, so that, when one chord is touched, it strikes resonances with others widely separated from it, thus establishing the general order of the whole.[186]

Authentic knowledge of God had not been given to those many Gentiles devoted to the studies of the world's wise men, who lived respectably and yet, convinced that philosophy was sufficient, did not seek the mediator between God and men. It was given to the Jews, and, for that reason, the lives of the prophets served as models for later men.[187] But, Gregory wrote, the Jews could not fathom the spiritual

---

[181] *Moralia in Job* 30. 15. 50 (*PL* 76: 552).

[182] *Cura Pastoralis* 1. 2 (*PL* 77: 16), the people's imitation of unworthy prelates.

[183] *Cura Pastoralis* 1. 4 (*PL* 77: 18), on Nebuchadnezzar.

[184] *Moralia in Job* 34. 5–7. 10–13 (*PL* 76: 724f.).

[185] *Moralia in Job* 33. 14. 29 (*PL* 76: 691). See also *Moralia in Job* 20. 40. 77 (*PL* 76: 184f.). For another painting simile, see *Moralia in Job* 29. 8. 19 (*PL* 76: 487).

[186] *Moralia in Job* 1. 8. 11 (*PL* 75: 532).

[187] *Moralia in Job* 23. 19. 34 (*PL* 76: 271f.).

truth shrouded by the deep mists of Old Testament allegory.[188] Prophecies were of no avail to them, since the function of prophecy is not to predict what is to come but to disclose what, though hidden, already is.[189] (If its message is not understood, it is not a prophecy for those deaf to its meaning.)[190] Though they held to the letter of the Law and gloried in the divine inspiration of Moses and the prophets, the Jews did not recognize the Word, the Lord of knowledge (*dominus scientiarum*) whom Isaiah and Jeremiah foretold.[191] The eschatological reflex between past and future eluded them. The Church had a fuller, but still partial, revelation, through strategies disclosed by Christ's Incarnation: the mimetic processes of inversion and subversion.

Passages in the Old Testament that seemed absurd or contemptible according to the letter of the text were inverted into sacred mysteries under the light of revelation embodied in Christ.[192] Augustine's (not Plato's) concept of the "true lie" recurs in Gregory's argument that deception or crime described in the Old Testament inverts into good under the new dispensation. The principle of inversion allowed him to interpret David's adultery with Bathsheba as testifying to Christ's marriage with faithful Israel, and the death of Uriah as exemplifying the destiny of Jews who obdurately held to their misunderstanding of the Scripture.[193]

Eschatology therefore brought Gregory to hold that, through the labile equilibrium of contemplation and action, what was taken for knowledge of truth could alter by inversion from one thing to another, from falsehood into truth (or vice versa), or by the related strategy of subversion as indicated by the Church's abandonment of the Synagogue's signs and symbols.[194] Such changes had not ceased, and the consequences were plain for the Church, still in its earthly pilgrimage,

---

[188] *Moralia in Job* 18. 38–39. 59–60 (*PL* 76: 71f.).

[189] *Homil. in Ezech.* 1. 1. 1 (*PL* 76: 787).

[190] *Moralia in Job* 11. 20. 31 (*PL* 75: 968).

[191] *Exposit. in I. Reg.* 1. 91. 94 (*Corp. Christ., ser. lat.* 144: 107–111). Gregory's authorship of this commentary was once contested, but the work is now accepted as genuine. See the literature cited by D. Hoffmann, *Die geistige Auslegung der Schrift bei Gregor dem Grossen* (Münsterschwarzach, 1968. Münsterschwarzacher Studien, Bd 6), p. 8, n. 32.

[192] Cf. *Moralia in Job* 2. 3. 3 (*PL* 75: 556f.). *Moralia in Job* 18. 40. 61 (*PL* 76: 72f.).

[193] *Moralia in Job* 3. 28. 55 (*PL* 75: 625–627).

[194] Cf. the inversion of the true law of God into the sacrifice of Satan by the wicked: *Cura Pastoralis* 3. 24 (*PL* 77: 94). On the need to combine the active and contemplative states, see *Moralia in Job* 6. 36–37. 55–61 (*PL* 75: 759–765).

still to be raised at the Last Judgment to perfect beauty through likeness to its Creator.[195]

The progression of the Church's wisdom was cumulative, as it moved by subversion through stages of greater and greater likeness to Christ, its risen head. While the story retained its integrity as it unfolded, the episodes were distinguished by characteristic degrees of knowledge. Prophets, Apostles, and Fathers formed a sequence of witnesses, all opening the secret meanings of the Scriptures to common knowledge, adding testimony to testimony.[196] And so

Moses was more learned in knowledge of Omnipotent God than Abraham; the prophets more than Moses; The Apostles, more than the prophets. . . . The man, therefore, who remembers to meditate in the Law is proven to understand more than all who teach him and more than the elders, for he shows that he has received more divine knowledge than Moses. But how are we to show that the holy Apostles were more learned than the prophets? Truth says with certainty, "Many kings and prophets have wished to see what you see, and to hear what you hear, but they have not." They knew more of divine knowledge than the prophets, therefore, since they saw physically what they [the prophets] had only heard in spirit. . . . For the more closely the world is led to its end, the more widely is the approach to eternal knowledge opened to us.[197]

Gregory's assumptions about psychology cast some light on his judgment on the liberal arts. The liberal arts were important because they assisted in the reflexive action between past and future that an interpreter practiced as he examined the Scriptures to disclose the Last Things. Gregory alluded to this interplay when he contended that secular learning was of great benefit in private life, and, moreover, that those ignorant of it could not penetrate the depths of Holy Writ.[198]

The words in Scripture, he wrote, were like colors in a painting. The words represented meanings, just as colors represented things. Anyone who read the words without being able to decode them was in a state of ignorance like that of a man who saw a painting without recognizing its subject.[199] The arts of worldly knowledge were essential to the

[195] *Moralia in Job* 9. 11. 18 (*PL* 75: 869).

[196] *Moralia in Job* 27. 8. 12–14 (*PL* 76: 405f.). *Exposit. in I. Reg.* 4. 171–173 (*Corp. Christ., ser. lat.* 144: 387f.). On the succession of ages in the Church through enlarged understanding, conversion, and reform, see C. Dagens, *Saint Grégoire le Grand. Culture et expérience chrétienne* (Paris, 1977. *Études augustininennes*), pp. 227f., 323f., 347.

[197] *Homil. in Ezech.* 2. 4. 10–12 (*PL* 76: 979–981).

[198] *Exposit. in I. Reg.* 5. 85 (*Corp. Christ., ser. lat.* 144: 472f.). See P. Riché, *Education et culture dans l'Occident barbare, VIe-VIIIe siècles* (Paris, 1962), pp. 197f.

[199] *Exposit. super Cantica Canticorum, proem.* 4 (*Corp. Christ., ser. lat.* 144: 5).

task of getting beyond the signs to the realities. Certainly, Gregory wrote, mastering the liberal arts required one to descend from the mountaintop of Christian simplicity to the plain of the Philistines. But one had to make the trip to sharpen the tools of understanding and speaking. Thus, Moses informed his untrained mind with all the knowledge of the Egyptians as a prologue to his study and proclamation of divine law. Isaiah excelled the other prophets because he was "nobly taught and urbane." And the Apostle Paul studied earthly things at the feet of Gamaliel before, swept up to the third heaven, he learned the heavenly.[200] More than book learning was involved, however, for, since the soul replicated the same principles of harmony as the cosmos, it expressed their common archetypal reason. As it was conformed with its model by the discipline of the arts and enlightened by grace, it gained the wholeness that it had lost. It became free and calm. Thus, it prepared itself for the contemplative unity of image and archetype that Gregory compared with a person beholding his image in still waters.[201]

Some scholars would think it injudicious to choose Gregory as exemplifying late-classical thought, particularly with regard to the liberal arts. What is their evidence? On one occasion, the Pope rebuked a bishop for teaching grammar: that is, for profaning his lips with the name and abominable acts of Jupiter.[202] He prefaced one of his own scriptural commentaries with a defiant assertion that he had disdained to observe the "art of speaking," even at the cost of committing grammatical howlers, since the words of the heavenly oracle should not be bound by the rules of Donatus.[203] In hagiography, he praised St. Benedict for fleeing the study of secular letters, "knowingly ignorant and wisely untaught,"[204] and the illiterate priest, Sanctulus of Nursia, for a wise ignorance that overshadowed "our ignorant knowledge."[205] The evidence consists of one letter in the more than eight hundred that survive, two sentences in volumes of scriptural exegesis, and two hagiographical pen-portraits. On these passages, and on an exegetical method that modern scholars find inelegant, hangs the conventional judgment that "the converging currents of barbarism and classical

---

[200] *Exposit. in I. Reg.* 5. 84 (*Corp. Christ., ser. lat.* 144: 472).

[201] *Homil. in Ezech.* 1. 11. 26 (*PL* 76: 917).

[202] *Reg.* 11. 34 to Desiderius of Vienne (*MGH, Epp.,* 2, pt. 3, p. 303).

[203] *Moralia in Job,* preface, ch. 5 (*PL* 75: 516).

[204] *Dial.* 2, preface: ". . . scienter nescius et sapienter indoctus." In U. Moricca, ed., *Gregorii Magni Dialogi* (Rome, 1924), p. 72.

[205] *Dial.* 3. 37 (ed. cit., p. 224).

decadence meet in him."[206] How can one avoid the conclusion that, by reacting "violently" against classical culture, Gregory exemplified how thoroughly "the tradition had been emptied of all its contents by the prevailing decadence?"[207]

And yet, my review has indicated that these few passages, interpreted as hostile to the arts, actually express ancient characteristics of the arts tradition. Plato banished the poets from his ideal city, recognized the inspiration in the garbled syntax of oracles, and portrayed the ignorant sage in Socrates. The enigmas of which these were elements endured from his day on, through Philo, the Neoplatonists, and the Alexandrine theologians of the second and third centuries, and so into Latin thought.[208]

In his personal reflections, and in his official acts as Pope, Gregory was true to this tradition. Clearly, he did not include the liberal arts in

---

[206] F. B. Artz, *The Mind of the Middle Ages, A.D. 200-1500,* 2d ed. (New York, 1954), pp. 192f. Gregory is mentioned only as the biographer of St. Benedict in James Bowen, *A History of Western Education* (New York, 1972), 1: 331.

[207] H. I. Marrou, *A History of Education in Antiquity,* trans. G. Lamb (New York, 1956), p. 348. A concise, balanced statement of Gregory's position, without reference to its conceptual basis, occurs in Riché, *Education et culture,* pp. 187–200.

[208] Cf. Spörl's argument that Gregory was an excellent Latinist and that his attitude toward culture derived from the tradition of Roman morality. Gregory, Spörl wrote, was "cut out of the same wood as a Cato and Seneca." See J. Spörl, "Gregor der Grosse und die Antike," in *Christliche Verwirklichung. Festschrift Romano Guardini,* ed. K. Schmidthus (Rothenfels a. M., 1935. *Schildgenossen,* Beiheft 1), pp. 202f., 210. Dagens expressed his verdict more pungently: "Faire de Grégoire un adversaire de la culture profane serait donc un nonsens." See "Grégoire le Grand et la culture: de la *terrena sapientia* à la *docta ignorantia,*" *Studia Patristica* 11, pt. 2 (1967. *Texte und Untersuchungen* 108), p. 21. Dagens found no basic contradiction in Gregory's thought between the externality of secular studies and the internal sacred doctrine. He set forth the same argument in an article bearing the same title in *Revue des études augustiniennes* 14 (1968): 17–26. The sentence noted above is repeated, in a wider context, by Dagens in *Saint Grégoire le Grand,* p. 50; there he provides a very helpful review of the ambiguities in Gregory's posthumous reputation (pp. 15f.). On Gregory's "detachment" from classical culture, see Dagens, *Saint Grégoire le Grand,* pp. 31–35, 38–40, 436; on the paradoxical terms, *docta ignorantia* and *sapiens stultitia,* see pp. 45–50; on the degree to which Gregory relied on Augustine, see pp. 271–273. See also G. B. Ladner, "Gregory the Great and Gregory VII," p. 1, and J. Leclerq, *The Love of Learning and the Desire for God: A Study of Monastic Culture,* trans. C. Misrahi (New York, 1960), p. 32. On Gregory's extraordinary posthumous influence, see two studies by R. Wasselynck, *L'Influence des Moralia in Job de s. Grégoire le Grand sur la théologie morale entre le VIIe et le XIIe siècle* (Lille, 1965. Diss. Lille, 1952), and "L'Influence de l'exégèse de s. Grégoire le Grand sur les commentaires bibliques médiévaux," *Recherches de théologie ancienne et médiévale* 32 (1965): 157–204.

the "false wisdom of this world" that Christ destroyed by appearing in the flesh.[209] They were tactics, well or ill used; they had no intrinsic meaning of their own that could impair Christian doctrine. Still, their rules did belong to the sphere of "external discipline."[210] As such, they were essential in decoding the signs of Scripture, but neither they, nor any sign, could stand beside the source of wisdom. Had Moses been taught in all the wisdom of the Egyptians? He was tongue-tied when he heard the Lord speaking. Was Isaiah "nobly taught"? After he saw the Lord sitting high and lifted up on a throne and the Seraphim crying out one to another, he fell silent, since he was a man of unclean lips. And so it was also with Abraham, Jeremiah, and Ezekiel, who, in the presence of the wisdom, justice, and beauty of God, recognized how abject human analogues were by comparison.[211] But then, by comparison with the life that God was, men did not exist.[212]

Thus far, we have seen that Gregory understood the arts as elements in a tactical effort to apply eschatology, resolving a dilemma between what we know and what we are. In regard to cosmic order, no knowledge was adequate to bridge the gap between, on the one hand, man's finite existence and his capacity for knowledge and, on the other, the unity that he sought. But Gregory related the arts to a historical unity as well as to a cosmic one, and here, too, can be detected a ground for his conservative appraisal of the arts. For, in the collective experience of the Old and the New Israels, knowledge advanced according to the pace set by the divine artificer, modifying, or even reversing, earlier perceptions of truth. The community of faith advanced in likeness to the truth, while its goal remained immutable.

Gregory portrayed the soul struggling against itself as it moved through stages of renewal.[213] The church also follows this mimetic paradigm, experiencing through imitation the inversion and subversion of previous modes of knowledge. Comments by Gregory that have been regarded as hostile to the arts actually concerned the entire range of knowledge into which they had been integrated. Like life, all knowledge was derived, provisional, and analogous, advancing by stages, each completing and superseding earlier ones and preparing for the next.

---

[209] *Moralia in Job* 33. 10. 19 (*PL* 76: 684).

[210] *Moralia in Job, prefatio.* 5 (*PL* 75: 516).

[211] *Moralia in Job* 35. 2. 3 (*PL* 76: 751f.). Cf. *Moralia in Job* 18. 50. 82 (*PL* 76: 87f.).

[212] *Moralia in Job* 18. 50. 81 (*PL* 76: 86f.).

[213] *Moralia in Job* 5. 33. 58 (*PL* 75: 711). *Moralia in Job* 30. 15. 50 (*PL* 76: 552).

None of the Latin Fathers was more concerned than Gregory with the moral application of doctrine, and my final remarks must address this aspect of his thought. Quite naturally, his concepts of the human mind and of the arts as tactics for its formation entered into his judgments as Pope. But consistency of theory and administrative action is especially clear in his pronouncements concerning terror as an instrument of education. His contemplative thought began with fear of the Lord. Agonizing in anticipation of the Last Judgment, he wrote that the soul must lacerate itself with the wounds of terror, continually punishing its own transgressions.[214] Compunction was an inner counterpart to flagellation; together they comprised a method of teaching by which the soul could pass from the slavery of fear into the grace of liberty, from fear into the love of God.[215]

No doubt Gregory imbibed these convictions from the monastic discipline, to which he converted as a young man and which he continued to observe while Pope. The *Rule* of St. Benedict describes the monastery as a "school for the Lord's service," an institution where the purpose of life—the correction of faults—could be accomplished better than anywhere else. The entire object of the *Rule* was to set down guidelines by which "the life of conversion" could be advanced, and its author, like Gregory, began with fear of the Lord. He held up before his readers the danger that God would, as an angry father, disinherit them, or that, as an awesome master, He would bind them over into slavery because they refused to follow Him into glory. Before the monks lay a choice between the pains of hell and the joys of eternal life.

Always insisting on the need for moderation and prudence, the author of the *Rule* prescribed a curriculum for the mortification of body and will. As one instructional device among many, he placed corporal punishment in the hands of the abbot, as a means for correcting the obdurate, for training men in the supreme virtue of humility, and thus also for ruling them. The abbot was a spiritual physician, applying progressively severe remedies for the disease of sin, as a case required. If the ointments and poultices of rebuke failed, he should resort to the cautery of physical punishment. If the case were incurable, he had to amputate the rotten member with the blade of excommunication in order to save the rest of his flock from infection. As we shall see, these

---

[214] *Moralia in Job* 7. 6. 6 (*PL* 75: 769f.). *Cura Pastoralis* 2. 2; 4. 1 (*PL* 77: 27f., 125f.).

[215] *Moralia in Job* 22. 20. 48 (*PL* 76: 242f.). *Cura Pastoralis* 3. 13 (*PL* 77: 70).

figures of speech had implications of terror and pain that were not entirely metaphorical.[216]

Gregory's commitment to the monastic life enabled him to make a similar connection between terror and government in general. He was convinced that government ran counter to human nature in its original condition. By nature, he wrote, all men were equal. God made them superior to the beasts but not to other men. They were to be feared by brute animals, not by one another. And yet, in the state of sin, men refused to fear God's judgments. Therefore, to restrain sin, at least as far as could be done by human judgments, it was necessary that men be separated into orders, and that rulers be feared by subjects. Rulers should use terror to seek justice for their subjects. But, insofar as they exacted fear from sinful men, they acted as though they governed animals, and, to be sure, subjects were ruled by fear inasmuch as they actually were animals.[217]

Normally, Gregory was concerned specifically with Christian government, rather than with general principles of power. In the hands of Christian rulers, he taught, terror was more than the restraint of men whom sin had transformed into animals. It was, as in monasteries, an instrument of humanization. Of course Gregory recognized that there were some, in monasteries and outside them, who despised physical torture; when extreme measures failed to convert such men, they could only be left to the tortures of God's own, more severe punishment.[218] But the idea that coercion might fail did not remove it from Christian discipline. Gregory admonished a bishop of Sardinia to seek the conversion of idolaters "with burning zeal." If they were slaves, the bishop should have them beaten and tortured until they came to a better view; if they were free and contemptuously disregarded words recalling them from danger of death, they should be placed in close confinement, to the end that torture of the body might restore them to wholeness of mind.[219] As Pope, Gregory himself was inspired by the example of his predecessor, the Apostle Peter, who humbly welcomed Cornelius when the centurion venerated him but struck Ananias and Saphira dead with a word when they disobeyed and tried to deceive him.[220] All bishops, even the most exalted, were obliged to destroy the

[216] See the prologue of the *Rule* and chapters 2, 3, 5, 7, 23, 28, 55, 70, 71, 73.
[217] *Cura Pastoralis* 2. 6 (*PL* 77: 34f.).
[218] *Moralia in Job* 26. 30. 56 (*PL* 76: 383).
[219] *Reg.* 9. 204 (*MGH, Epp.* 2, pt. 3, p. 192).
[220] *Cura Pastoralis* 2. 6 (*PL* 77: 36).

pride of the subjects, to use every means that "the hand of correction" could grasp for the purpose of overthrowing obstinate wickedness.[221]

Within the structure of Christian society, those means included the collaboration of secular rulers. Gregory rejoiced when the Visigothic king, Reccared, repressed the Arian heresy and imposed legal sanctions "against the perfidy of the Jews." By the very act of rejoicing, the Pope claimed to become a participant in the King's achievements.[222] He urged Frankish rulers to promote and guarantee canonical trial and punishment of simoniac bishops, to prohibit the ownership of Christian slaves by Jews, and zealously to defend the Church against its internal, as well as its external, enemies.[223] Praising the Emperor Maurice as the "guardian of ecclesiastical peace," he also urged him to "apply the medicine of correction to the insane minds" of the Donatists, the very sect against which Augustine too, long before, had invoked imperial coercion.[224]

These few examples are enough to indicate that Gregory regarded terror as a device of government in general, and as an educative device of Christian government in particular. It was one means by which sinful men could be brought into conformity with Christ. He insisted that a prudent ruler must apply both tenderness and pain. But the ruler himself would suffer a cruel sentence from God if he were delinquent in treating the wound of sin.[225] It was hard to determine when devices of tenderness should be abandoned and tactics of pain imposed.

Gregory believed that organs of government could promote conversion of mankind, but he did not confuse the ends of conversion with the means of governmental institutions. An ancient hostility toward secular government sprang to life in Gregory's assertion that the Church was healthier under persecution, when men were elected bishops knowing that they would be the first of their flock to be martyred. The same distance between the Church and temporal government, and perhaps the vision of martyrdom, motivated him when he declared that he would never consent to an impious usage, even at the point of imperial swords.[226]

Employed to teach holy mimesis, the device of terror also had sub-

---

[221] *Cura Pastoralis* 3. 34 (*PL* 77: 118).

[222] *Reg.* 9. 228 (*MGH, Epp.* 2, pt. 3, pp. 222f.).

[223] *Reg.* 9. 213, 215; 11. 46–48 (*MGH, Epp.* 2, pt. 3, pp. 198–203, 318–321).

[224] *Reg.* 6. 61; 7. 6 (*MGH, Epp.* 1: 437, 449).

[225] *Cura Pastoralis* 2. 6 (*PL* 77: 36).

[226] *Cura Pastoralis* 1. 8 (*PL* 77: 21). *Reg.* 5. 37 (*MGH, Epp.* 1: 323).

versive implications for ecclesiastical authority. On the one hand, Gregory insisted on the wholeness and authority of the Church,[227] and he imposed the duty of obedience upon subjects, setting them an example of submissiveness in his dealings with murderous rulers.[228] Was not humility the imitation of Christ?[229] On the other hand, there was another, balancing side, for Gregory recognized that Moses and the prophets had received their revelation in, but not through, time. They received it from God, not by following the commonly accepted "examples of the people."[230] God first spoke to Moses, not in Egypt, but in the isolation of a desert mountain, and later in the seclusion of the Tabernacle. And it was the nature of man's imperfect vision of perfect things always to have a secret, divisive character.[231] So Christ, himself, declining to become king, fled what all sought, and He sought what they fled.[232] Gregory had to look no further than Moses and Isaiah or the other prophets closest to his heart, Ezekiel and Jeremiah, to demonstrate the source of their higher wisdom. In pointing to the prophets, however, he also indicated the results of their knowledge: they stood alone, estranged, imprisoned, or hunted down, because, applying their erudition, they cursed the idolatrous arts and institutions of their own communities.

This line of moral application conveyed its own imitative norms, at odds with obedience unto death. For remembering that Christ said, "I came not to send peace, but the sword," Gregory acknowledged that the peace of this world was to be both loved and despised: loved for its tranquility and despised because that very benefit could detract men from eternal peace and bring them into unwholesome concord with the wicked.[233] It was no surprise, therefore, that strife existed in the historical order, where action intersected with contemplation, or that it was an integral part of eschatological progression. For God chose the foolish things of the earth and informed them with inner wisdom to confound men wise in the external things of earth. Inwardly seized up above themselves, looking down, as from a mountain on the plains of life, they saw how contemptible earthly glories were, and they were

---

[227] *Moralia in Job* 28. 10. 22–24 (*PL* 76: 461f.).

[228] Cf. *Cura Pastoralis* 1. 1 (*PL* 77: 14f.), God permits evil rulers to govern.

[229] *Moralia in Job* 35. 14. 28–32 (*PL* 76: 765–768). See also *Cura Pastoralis* 3. 12 (*PL* 77: 66f., 80).

[230] *Moralia in Job* 30. 17. 56 (*PL* 77: 554f.).

[231] *Moralia in Job* 23. 20. 37–39 (*PL* 76: 273f.). *Cura Pastoralis* 2. 6, repeated partially in *Reg.* 1. 9. 25; 1. 21 (*PL* 77: 36–38; *MGH, Epp.* 2, pt. 3, pp. 34–36).

[232] *Moralia in Job* 30. 24. 69 (*PL* 76: 562).

[233] *Cura Pastoralis* 3. 22 (*PL* 77: 91f.).

merciless toward any powers arrayed against truth. So Moses returned from the desert to defy Pharaoh, and Nathan and other prophets fearlessly denounced kings face to face. So Peter withstood priests and princes who beat him and forbade him to preach; and so, too, the protomartyr Stephen raised up the authority of his voice against the force of his persecutors in the Synagogue.[234]

Gregory had to look no further than the heretics of his day to grasp how these examples might be misconstrued and abused. It was well and good to teach that those weak in understanding should venerate, but not imitate, such models of life's freedom,[235] and that the learned should conceal from the multitude secrets too high for them rightly to grasp. But what of those strong in wisdom who, like Moses, veiled their enlightenment from the people?[236] Furthermore, given God's propensity to elect the simple, how could the foolish of this world be expected to revere, without imitating, examples of dissent?

Gregory's insistence that holy men and women must cross-pollinate the active and contemplative lives hid a seditious principle, which the Pope had every reason to understand from his own experience. Judging contemporary lives by patterns set in the Scriptures, he no doubt sensed the coincidence between the estrangement and persecution of the prophets and the dramatic conversion that led him to reject the delights, wealth, inherited status, and secular power of his early life, and to embrace the austerities of monasticism. The same transvaluation of values prompted his mature judgment on non-Christian learning.

Still, we have seen that resistance to external authority was a subordinate component of the liberal arts tradition from its origins. Following Augustine, and quite against his own instinct for administrative obedience, Gregory gave it a foundation in the historical order. Indeed, he portrayed it as an impelling movement within the broad progression of ages and, within loosely conceived institutional limits, a moral obligation of the enlightened conscience. Such was one reconciliation of originality with the tradition of mediated asymmetry.

Historians generally depict Gregory as a first-class administrator and a second-rate theologian. It is true that the fire of creative genius is sometimes hard to find in the dark and convoluted forest of his allegory. But the great and enduring popularity of Gregory's writings—especially of the *Moralia*—show that generations of men and women

---

[234] *Moralia in Job* 7. 35. 51–54 (*PL* 75: 795–798).

[235] *Dial.* 1. 1 (ed. cit., p. 19, and see next note).

[236] *Cura Pastoralis* 3. 39 (*PL* 77: 124).

found much that was unique and precious in his works. Early in the fifteenth century, Coluccio Salutati, still dominant among Florentine humanists, expressed his admiration for the *Moralia,* the "divine work" that Gregory wrote on Job. "What," he asked, "is more mysterious, and what more poetical than the book and history of Job?" Gregory disclosed that it contained "as many sacraments as words, and, through his explication, he opened a profundity in the book that raised many above themselves, and drove them almost mad, in ecstasy."[237]

The status as classics achieved by the *Moralia* and other writings by Gregory was due in no small degree both to the comprehensive unity of knowledge that they expressed and to the standards for moral practice deriving from that unity. It was also due to the presence in Gregory's works of mimetic doctrines that earlier generations read back into the Scriptures as well as into the literatures of Greece and Rome. Coluccio alluded to that quality in recommending Augustine's *On Christian Doctrine* as an exegetical guide, since "all holy Scripture overflows in mystic senses and abounds everywhere in various sacraments, which is the special property of poets."[238]

Summary

As they reflected upon the mediated asymmetry between nature and art, the Latin Fathers constructed mimetic theories of social change. For the future, the decisive facts were that these theories were actually incorporated into organs of ecclesiastical and secular government and that they consequently found permanent shelters where they survived the dismemberment of the society that gave them birth. In retrospect, this institutionalization is a landmark in the social history of Europe, but, from the perspective of the Fathers themselves, it signified a Christian innovation in thought: the employment of history as a branch of theoretical knowledge. The Fathers detected a pattern in human experience as a whole that had been hidden from Gentiles and Jews. In searching out the broad contours of that implicit design, they used and reshaped some mimetic strategies that had long been features of the classical tradition; to meet new conceptual needs, they invented

---

[237] *Ep.* 8. 11, to Giovanni Conversano da Ravenna (1392?), in *Epistolario di Coluccio Salutati,* ed. F. Novati (Rome, 1893), 2: 416. *Ep.* 14. 24, to Giovanni Dominici (1400), in ibid., vol. 4, p. 236.

[238] *Ep.* 14. 24, in ibid., vol. 4, p. 239.

others. The old and the new were embodied in institutions as signs and agents of spiritual enlightenment under the watchword "correction."

What needed to be remedied was sin. Correction, therefore, was interpreted with reference to the two natures of Christ, and each of them sustained mimetic strategies of correction—the Logos, those of reversion and augmentation, and the man, those of inversion and subversion.

The novel and enduring result of the Fathers' work was the fusion that they effected between the two Christological sets of mimetic strategies mediating the asymmetry between God as archetype and man as image. They first concluded that, as the historical order appointed by God was enacted, an apparent evil might be inverted into good and an apparent truth inverted into a lie. They concluded, secondly, that, as the elect moved toward the final beauty of likeness to the Creator through corrective strategies, each age destroyed its predecessors by fulfilling them and bore the hidden seeds of its own supplanter.

In God's mind, the Fathers reasoned, history itself was an aesthetic unity, like a poem or a painting. The motif of historical correction was an analogy with the process by which a work of art passes from idea to rough sketch to finished object. The eschatological oneness of past, present, and future placed the arts, and all human knowledge, in a broad and unfolding pattern for the eventual perfection of sacred doctrine, and hence of moral beauty among men. The arts were essential to life in the secular world. Though given over to false opinions, the Gentiles retained the image of God, deformed and effaced as it might be in them. Through the imperfect vision of truth that the Gentiles consequently had, the arts also testified to the ultimate, ineffable source of all wisdom, and Christians could use them—in the mystical property of numbers, or etymology, or allegorical speculation—to correct ignorance and error by disclosing evermore completely the occult content of Scripture. But, like scriptural revelation itself, all tactics, including the arts, belonged to a dispensation that was passing and that was already past, one that would be completed and destroyed at the end of time by the transfiguration of the world, which would also be the end of knowledge mediated by shadows and enigmas and unified by belief, and the beginning of unmediated knowledge of truth, as it is.

Powerful mystical beliefs informed the Fathers' conceptions of mediated asymmetries in human experience. When he wrote that the body of each redeemed person became the flesh of the Crucified, Pope Leo I tersely captured their implications. All the redeemed composed one body, Christ, and what they did in and through the love that united them was the work of God. Thus, through the ages, the image of God in collective man was gradually perfected. Leo perceived that beyond the unity of the Church there was the wider unity of human nature, through which all men were one with Christ, though only believers participated in His divinity. Augustine too understood the course of history as a process of education in which the human race could be regarded as one person, a movement by which its humanity, animalized by sin, was restored. Both Fathers identified the humanizing advance of mankind with the redemption of the elect so closely that they did not extend their model of progression beyond the community of faith to material culture as a whole. They had, however, framed doctrines of rebirth through imitation and suffering that, long after, were generalized and applied to all history. As we shall see, doctrines of emanation, which entered Western thought from the twelfth century on, were basic to this application.[239]

These models of corrective change and the metaphors that signified them continued to inform Western thought into modern times, not least in doctrines of reform and revolution. Perhaps the most pervasive souvenir of ancient and patristic thought was the view that, despite his moral freedom, man could only reproduce a higher, ideal order as he knew it in his time, through the cryptic irony of enigmas, incompletely and provisionally and often in strife. By the end of the sixth century, this way of thinking about corrective reformation of the world had been formalized in theology and institutionalized in the militant ethos of monasticism, in texts of Church laws, and in ideals of Christian kingship.

[239] Leo I, *Serm.* 12. 1, 2; 63. 6, 7 (*Sources chrétiennes, serm.* 82, vol. 200, pp. 150–156; *serm.* 50, vol. 74, pp. 82–84.) Augustine, *City of God* 10. 14 (*CSEL* 40, pt. 1, p. 470).

II

Changes in the Mimetic Strategy During
the Reconstitution of Europe

IN THE PRESENT SECTION, I will discuss how the concept of mimesis outlived the society that had given it birth and how it became a major adaptive strategy in the new societies that reconstructed Western Europe after the fall of Rome.

The Fathers—represented for us by Augustine and Gregory the Great—had not written for a monastic culture, but their teachings lodged firmly in the literature and spiritual discipline of monasteries. Thus, mimetic doctrines concerning the transformations of the soul and of the world found an institutional shelter from the destruction that eventually befell so much of ancient learning. Moreover, they found a shelter in a peculiarly militant ethos. Monks called and regarded themselves as soldiers of Christ, engaged in ferocious warfare against Satan and spiritual powers, against the world and the flesh. No quarter was asked, and none was to be given. Attitudes called for actions. Spiritual warfare entailed a stern abandonment of the family; in this case, Jerome wrote, to be cruel was a kind of piety (*ep.* 14). It required mortification of the flesh and suppression of the will. It might demand persecution of unbelievers and heretics. Such actions were tactics for the reformation of the soul and the conversion of the world. From this belligerent monastic ethos, doctrines of mimesis continued to engage minds and hearts after the fall of Rome. They became integral components of thought about society as a whole in the eighth and ninth centuries.

I shall begin, therefore, by suggesting how the Carolingians translated the strategy of mimesis into the vernacular of a culture quite foreign to the one in which it had arisen.

The Carolingian age was the early dawn of a civilization. By the eleventh and twelfth centuries, the reconstituted social order had begun to feel its strength. As its endeavors surged ever more broadly and deeply beyond the intense but restricted limits of monastic discipline, it turned once again to the philosophical basis of the mimetic tradition.

At this moment of burgeoning doubt, Aristotle entered the scene. In the concluding chapters of this section, I shall try to suggest a range of solutions to enduring problems that different writers extracted from their common heritage, greatly enlarged as it had been by its Aristotelian components. It will be my particular concern to describe how the newly discovered materials gave unexpected importance to the paradigm of organic growth known to St. Paul and the Fathers but relatively undeveloped by them—mimesis by augmentation. Having begun with Carolingian representatives of monastic culture, I shall end by suggesting how the ventures of mysticism and humanism disseminated this idea, with its potential for social conflict, through the culture of late medieval Europe.

A few preliminary words of orientation to the Carolingian era may be in order. In many ways, the largely monastic culture of the Carolingian age was rough-hewn. Scholars knew, with astonishing thoroughness, theological and legal texts from the patristic era. And yet, despite this remarkable knowledge, they confused genuine material with forged: while they argued from precedent, the precedents in their texts were occasionally historical fictions. Despite the greatest efforts of which the age was capable, errors in manuscript copying and defective textual traditions confused the reading of authentic documents. Moreover, learned men were at hand to prepare forged texts and whole collections of texts in support of their own conceptions of government. Counterfeit sources like the *Donation of Constantine* and the collections of Ansegisus, Benedictus Levita, and Pseudo-Isidore quickly became classics in the field of legal thought. But they also compounded ambiguities and contradictions already present in genuine texts and thus put enormous stumbling blocks in the way of thinkers who wanted to frame smooth schemes of procedure on the basis of precedent.

In addition to confusion in the authenticity of legal precedents, failure to develop philosophical speculation limited Carolingian scholars. Independently, some men in the ninth century hit upon the principles that, in the twelfth century, blossomed into the dispute between the realists and the nominalists. But Carolingian scholars did not develop any schools of speculation. Except for small fragments, they did not know the philosophical writings of the ancient world, and among the Germanic peoples there was no tradition of abstract formal thought that they could widen into a speculative system.

Finally, the actual experience of Carolingian thinkers was limited to the society in which they lived. From a few texts, they knew something about the mores of Roman society in the age of the Fathers, but they did not understand that their own society was not simply a continuation of the form and spirit of late Roman life. Because they assumed an identity between the mores of past and present—and also because their historical evidence was scanty—they had no way of grasping the elaborate mechanism that had made Rome a state instead of a league of tribes.

The assimilation of mimetic principles into Carolingian culture was encouraged by two great events. The first was the Frankish defense of religious images against Byzantine iconoclasm, which received full statement at the Synod of Frankfurt in 794. The second was the reception of the treatises by (Pseudo-) Dionysius Areopagitica as a gift from the Byzantine Emperor to Louis the Pious in 827, and their subsequent translations into Latin, initiated at the great monastery of St. Denis. These contacts with the Greek world obviously brought the questions of mimesis forcibly before the Carolingian kings, their clergy, and their monastic communities. Still, the basic principles were readily accessible in the theological writings of the Fathers, in canons of synods and councils, and in other patristic texts, such as the decretals of fifth- and sixth-century popes that were accepted as canonical authorities; assimilation had begun at least by the mid-eighth century.

Mimetic themes that had begun in Paul's Christology and that had widened into keys to historical interpretation among the Fathers recur throughout the texts of the Carolingian era. The Fathers had bent tactics of speculative psychology, formal disciplines (especially the liberal arts), and terror to the service of mimetic strategies. These tactics also entered Carolingian thought, but in a different key. Frankish prelates were political and military leaders, as well as officers of the Church. In their reflections, they were working out principles of actual government over villages and provinces, the rationales for power over men that they themselves exercised. Under the Roman Empire, the Fathers lacked the union of civil and ecclesiastical power that prelates in Western Europe subsequently wielded. True to their Roman imperial origins, Byzantine prelates never took the reins both of civil and of ecclesiastical government into their hands. Gregory the Great plainly indicated the powerful effects that strategies of mimesis could have on the social order if they were spread by tactics of education and terror, though he lacked the opportunity and the administrative mechanisms to disseminate them on every social level. Within the limited territories under their control, Germanic bishops had that opportunity; their authority reached to each monastic cell, to individual households in every parish. As occasion offered, Carolingian prelates were able to employ organs both of secular and of ecclesiastical coercion to mold an entire society according to ideas of mimetic progress that the Fathers had applied to the soul and the Church and only in a fragmentary way to the secular world. Before their kings, they held as a primary responsibility of the royal office the coercion of wrongdoers and unbelievers by force and terror.

In the following chapters, I shall consider two Carolingian experiments in applied mimesis. Both were performed by men devoted to the monastic life: Paschasius Radbertus (ca. 790–ca. 859), a monk and abbot of the monastery of Corbie, and Archbishop Hincmar of Rheims (ca. 806–882), one of the most learned and powerful men of his age, a monk at St. Denis when the treatises of Dionysius Areopagitica were first received in Gaul and translated and, while Archbishop, abbot of the monastery of St. Remi in Rheims.

"Christ in Us, Moving Toward the Father": Paschasius Radbertus's View of History

PASCHASIUS RADBERTUS (ca. 790–ca. 859) is best known as a writer on the Eucharist and as an early advocate of the cult of the Virgin Mary. His concept of history has not been studied, much less appraised as a factor that might cast some light on habits of thinking in the Carolingian age and, perhaps also, on the place that those habits gained in the general course of European history. There are reasons why his ideas about history should have been ignored. His two works of a historical nature, the *Vita Adalhardi* and the *Epitaphium Arsenii,* are memoirs of two brothers, Adalhard and Wala, who succeeded each other as abbots of Corbie and to whom Radbertus was bound by deep affection. These writings are apologetic and panegyrical;[1] Radbertus's flagrant subjectivity raises doubts about his accuracy.

---

[1] Lorenz Weinrich puts the case crisply: "Radbert, der Schüler Adalhards und langjährige Begleiter Walas, ist kein Historiker. Wenn er als Theologe 'historische' Bücher schreibt, dann nur, um das Andenken an die beiden verehrten Äbte leuchtend zu erhalten." *Wala, Graf, Mönch und Rebell. Die Biographie eines Karolingers* (Lübeck, 1963. *Historische Studien,* Heft 386), p. 7. A valuable discussion of the *Epitaphium Arsenii* follows this remark. For similar judgments on Radbertus's theological preoccupations and subjectivity, see Ernst Dümmler, ed., *Radbert's Epitaphium Arsenii, Abhandlungen der königlichen Akademie der Wissenschaften zu Berlin* (phil.-hist. Kl., 1899–1900), p. 9; Henri Peltier, *Pascase Radbert, abbé de Corbie* (Amiens, 1938), passim; these views are repeated in Peltier's *Adalhard abbé de Corbie* (Amiens, 1969. *Mémoires de la Société des antiquaires de Picardie,* t. 52), pp. 25f, 38, 129; Albert Ripberger, ed., *Der Pseudo-Hieronymus-Brief IX, "Cogitis Me": Ein erster marianischer Traktat des Mittelalters von Paschasius Radbert* (Freiburg, 1962. *Spicilegium Friburgense* 9), p. 4; Allen Cabaniss, *Charlemagne's Cousins: Contemporary Lives of Adalhard and Wala* (Syracuse, N. Y., 1967), esp. pp. 15f. Apart from some useful observations on Radbertus's idea of progress in the history of

I am here not concerned with Radbertus's truthfulness, however, but rather with the guiding ideas according to which he developed a coherent view of human experience. What reasoning lay behind his conception of all the redeemed as one person, engaged in a single movement—Christ, in us, advancing from this world to the Father?[2]

The fact that this metaphor occurs in *On the Body and Blood of the Lord,* a treatise on the Eucharist, witnesses to the fact that Radbertus's view of history was subordinate to his theology of salvation. As we saw, Augustine regarded only man's covenanting with God to be mystically significant; the experience of those who did not belong to the covenant—Old Testament non-Israelites, and reprobate since the Incarnation—were insignificant and therefore unhistorical. Much later, Thomas Aquinas followed Augustine in asserting that, to be figurative, the experience of a people had to refer to Christ. Consequently, he wrote, the wars and deeds of the ancient Jews could be expounded in a mystical sense, while those of the Assyrians and Romans could not be, although they were "far more brilliant in the eyes of men" (*S.T.* Ia IIae. Q. 104. A. 3 *ad* 2.).

Between Augustine and Thomas, Radbertus shared their historical convictions. He placed his striking figure of speech—Christ in us moving toward the Father—at the conclusion of a rich and intricate discourse. This metaphor graphically expresses Christ's mediation of the asymmetry between man and God, and he intended it to epitomize for the reader all that he had written concerning the mediated union of believers with God in Christ by means of the sacraments, of penance, and of regular moral discipline. Throughout the treatise, Radbertus strove to explain St. Paul's doctrine that all believers composed the body of Christ (Rom. 12:5; 1 Cor. 12:27), and, conversely, that Christ could be magnified in the body of each believer—indeed, that it was not the believer who lived but Christ who lived in him (Phil. 1:20; Gal. 2:20). Radbertus devoted much attention to the logic of Pauline me-

---

doctrine (p. 141), Gérard Mathon concentrated on knowledge of classical texts and rhetorical practices and omitted history from his account of humanism in "Pascase Radbert et l' évolution de l'humanisme carolingien. Recherches sur la signification des Préfaces des livres I et III de l' *Expositio in Mattaeum,*" *Corbie, Abbaye royale, volume du XIIIe cénténaire* (Lille, 1963), pp. 135–55. The predominance of theology in studies on Radbertus is indicated by the bibliography in Bedae Paulus, ed., *Pascasius Radbertus: De corpore et sanguine Domini* (Turholt, 1969. *Corpus Christianorum, continuatio mediaevalis* 16), pp. liii–lvii.

[2] *De corpore et sanguine Domini* 22 (Paulus, ed., pp. 129f).

diation and to the mechanisms of rite and discipline by which that logic could be realized in individual lives.

Prior to these formal concerns, however, there were aesthetic assumptions about the mediated asymmetry of image and archetype, assumptions that appear consistently in the treatises that Radbertus composed on various occasions for highly diverse audiences throughout his career. As a theologian, Radbertus vehemently argued that Christ was perfect God and perfect man. When he spoke of Christ moving toward the Father, he therefore had separate kinds of movement in mind, corresponding to the divine and human natures of the incarnate Word.

The first kind of movement, described in metaphysical terms, was the egress and return of the Logos from and to the Father. While it also included the procession of the created world from God (in the Logos) and its return toward Him, this movement was ahistorical, or even antihistorical. It characterized the timeless metaphysical asymmetry between God and creation, mediated by the Word.

The second kind of movement, described in theological terms, was more complex. Like the metaphysical components of Radbertus's thought, the theological components described circular movement: first, Christ's going forth from the Father, when He became incarnate, and His return to the Father through His death, resurrection, and ascension; and, second, man's egress from God, his turning aside (or defection from God through sin) and his (re-) conversion to God through grace and faith.[3] This elaborate set of movements was historical; it produced the changing degrees of asymmetry between God and the individual soul and between God and the Church, mediated by Christ, the Word-made-flesh.

Radbertus knew how dim and perilous mediation of the historical asymmetries could be. The conversion from alienation to wholeness was only begun here; it was to be consummated in the eternal city,

---

[3] Radbertus was guided by the Platonic idea that the soul is moved by love toward its exemplar, and especially toward God, its origin. See *De charitate* c. 13. 3 (*PL* 120: 1486). On Christ's egress from and return to God, see *Expos. in Ps. 44.* 2 (*PL* 120: 1015). On the idea that His egress into the Incarnation (by self-emptying and taking on the form of a servant) did not impair his egress as Logos, see *Expos. in Matt.* 2. 2; 8. 18 (*PL* 120: 132, 618). On the egress of the human soul from, and return to, the bosom of God, see *Expos. in Lament.* 2, Gimel (*PL* 120: 1112). On the threefold movement of egress, aversion (by sin), and conversion, see *Expos. in Lament.* 5 (*PL* 120: 1254). On the natural tendency of things to return to their origins (divine words, issuing from perfection, cannot pass away; human words, issuing *de nihilo,* return to nonbeing), see *Expos. in Matt.* 11. 24 (*PL* 120: 826).

when the saints would be separated from those who frequented churches, received the Eucharist, prophesied, spoke in tongues, delved knowingly into mysteries, and worked signal acts of faith, and who, doing all these things without the love of Christ, had deceptively transfigured themselves, like Satan, into angels of light.[4]

To be sure, some general characteristics of conversion, or change of heart, could be defined. The "whole man" desired God in many ways,[5] with his physical senses as well as with his mind and soul. However, not all men in fact went beyond the senses, and, declining from reason into brutal ferocity, they were, not men, but beasts or evil spirits in human forms.[6] Given man's animal nature, the return to God had to start at the level of the senses—that is, with externals. But, if men were to surpass the animals, they had to pass from externals to an interior vision, seeing invisible things by faith and thus becoming, not animal, but spiritual.[7]

The eye represented "the inclination of the heart" (*intentio cordis* or *mentis*),[8] and, in this metaphorical sense, Radbertus employed the eye to describe the stages of the moral ascent that was possible for man. He identified the eyes of the flesh, which were opened in Adam, those of the mind, by which the mind, if enlightened, could be one with God, and the two eyes of the Church, moral and mystical. Radbertus reserved his greatest praise for the mystical eye, filled with the love of Christ, despoiled of self, and poured back into unity with God.[9] The passage from the externals of the physical world to contemplative union with God was a return, a conversion, to man's original dignity.[10]

---

[4] *De charitate* 13. 1 (*PL* 120: 1484).   [5] *De charitate* 5 (*PL* 120: 1469).

[6] *Expos. in Lament.* 4 (*PL* 120: 1205f.). *De Passione SS. Rufini et Valerii* (*PL* 120: 1498, 1501). In this spirit, Radbertus applied to the Jews Christ's rebuke of the Pharisees and Saducees as a "generation of vipers." He went on to describe how the Church, "cum Christo in terra gradiens, omnia serpentum genera suis conculcat pedibus et repellit incredulos." See *Expos. in Matt.* 2. 3 (*PL* 120: 157). On Augustine's parallel exegesis, see Chapter 3, note 162.

[7] *Expos. in Matt.* 2. 3; 11. 25 (*PL* 120: 181, 838).

[8] *Expos. in Lament.* 4. Phe, and *Expos. in Matt.* 4. 6 (*PL* 120: 1226, 305). On Hincmar of Rheims' use of the same metaphor in his mimetic doctrines, see Chapter 5, at notes 25 and 29.

[9] *Expos. in Matt.* 3. 5, and *Expos. in Lament.* 3. Ain (*PL* 120: 222f., 118f.). Radbertus wrote of an "oculus intelligentiae" in *De charitate* 14. 1 (*PL* 120: 1487). On the inward blindness of those who do not believe rightly, see *Expos. in Matt.*, preface, and 4. 7 (*PL* 120: 44, 316).

[10] *Expos. in Lament.* 4. Beth, and cf. ibid., 2. Daleth (*PL* 120: 1203, 1112). In *Expos. in Lament.* 1. Heth (*PL* 120: 1078), Radbertus described this movement as a turning back, a response to God recalling the believer from behind.

Radbertus understood it in artistic terms, as a modeling process by which the soul was reshaped according to the pattern in which man had been made, a creative process that gradually reduced the asymmetry between image and archetype.[11]

But conversion included more than a personal change of heart. It also included collective expansion of the Church and the growth of sacred doctrine. Manifestly, the Church, the Body of Christ, enlarged as the ages ran on, and there were those not yet in Christ who would come to Him so that all His members might be complete.[12] Christ had said, "Thou art Peter, and upon this rock I shall build my Church," meaning not Peter only, or all the Apostles, but every faithful person insofar as he was an imitator of Christ, a light illuminated by the Light.[13] From the beginning, the Church spread by conversion, as it continued to do in Radbertus's own day.[14]

The Church was not complete, nor were the people of God perfect in virtue and knowledge, for they were not yet blessed and immaculate. Even though, through the sacraments, they had been buried and raised with Christ, they were *in via,* walking by faith instead of sight, daily slipping into sin, ardently wrestling to disclose the truth that was still wrapped in figures and obscurities.[15]

While Radbertus's metaphysics therefore led him to a timeless unity, his moral theology of conversion led him to a gradually achieved, and multiple, process of unification. What unified the entire structure was the mediated asymmetry, at every level, between archetype and image. Quite naturally, Radbertus described this mutual reflex in mimetic terms, some of which Plato had first employed, and which, having found a place in the books of the New Testament, gained central importance in patristic theology. Thus, in its eternal egress and return, the Logos acted as the image of the invisible God and the figure of His substance.[16] The procession and return of crea-

---

[11] *Expos. in Matt.* 5. 9 (*PL* 120: 380): "Quia qui posuit cum formaret ex nihilo deposuit ut imponat iterum manum et reformet eam de perditione . . . et ad imaginem primae creationis reformaret." *Expos. in Matt.* 4. 6 (*PL* 120: 293): "de die in diem interior [homo] reformatur."

[12] *Expos. in Matt.* 3. 4, and 4. 6; *Expos. in Lament.* 3. Aleph (*PL* 120: 192, 283, 1141).

[13] *Expos. in Matt.* 8. 16 (PL 120: 561).

[14] On the conversion of the Danes, see *Expos. in Matt.* 9. 24 (*PL* 120: 805). Cf. *Expos. in Ps. 44.* 2 (*PL* 120: 1029f.).

[15] *Expos. in Matt.* 11. 26; *De spe* 3. 1 (*PL* 120: 871, 1440f.). *De corpore et sanguine Domini* 9 (Paulus, ed., pp. 52f.).

[16] *De corpore et sanguine Domini* 4 (Paulus, ed., p. 29).

tures was explained as the natural reflex of visible things to the invisible orders on which they were patterned and which ruled them.[17] Finally, the two miraculous components—Christ's mission in the historical world and the redemption of the believer—joined in one mimetic act: the slow, progressive reformation of the soul according to the image and likeness of God in which it had originally been created but which sin had deformed.

I will now examine in greater detail the mimetic strategy at work in conversion, a subject that leads, eventually, to Radbertus's ascetic spirituality. True to his Augustinian heritage, Radbertus argued that mimesis was a mode of procreation;[18] by imitating their respective exemplars, evil men became sons of the devil and good men, sons of God.[19] But what figure of speech could describe the inherent likeness that made the act of imitation possible? With regard to right mimesis, Radbertus employed Christian versions of Neoplatonic images—the seal set into the soul as the image of the Father[20] and the carved image duplicated on coins.[21] These metaphors captured the mimetic asymmetry between image and archetype, but the individuality and the gradual progress of mediation eluded them. Thus, Radbertus also employed metaphors of the soul as both a statue being carved by the Holy Spirit[22] and as a painting in process of composition.

Radbertus followed ancient precedents in thinking that composition in painting or literature, or educating the soul, deployed the same methods. In three separate contexts, he repeated a story that Cicero had told about the Greek artist, Zeuxis. The people of Croton, Cicero wrote, commissioned Zeuxis to paint a picture of Helen of Troy. Instead of selecting one living model, he combined features of five different women, achieving a "form of beauty" in which all participated but which none fully represented. In two instances, Radbertus compared Zeuxis's method with his own writings—once, in an exposition on the Gospel of Matthew that drew together elements from earlier commentators, and, again, in a literary portrait of Abbot Wala of Corbie.[23]

---

[17] On the special case of the soul's reflex upon Christ, see below, following note 34.

[18] On Augustine's doctrines concerning the following points, see Chapter 3.

[19] *Expos. in Matt.* 3. 3; *Expos. in Lament.* 2. Mem (*PL* 120: 158, 1130). Cf. *Epitaphium Arsenii* 1, intro. 2; 1. 11. 4 (Dümmler, ed., pp. 19, 38), on the shaping by imitation of *"paternos vultus"* in Wala's disciples.

[20] *De charitate* 13. 2; *Vita Adalhardi* 18 (*PL* 120: 1485, 1518). Cf. *Epitaphium Arsenii* 1. 7. 12 (Dümmler, ed., p. 31).

[21] *Expos. in Matt.* 10. 22; 11. 25 (*PL* 120: 751, 855f.).

[22] *"Cogitis me"* 107 (Ripberger, ed., p. 109).

[23] *Expos. in Matt.* prologue (*PL* 120: 34f.). *Epitaphium Arsenii* 1, intro. 1 (Dümmler, ed., p. 18). Cf. *Epitaphium Arsenii* 1. 2. 5 (Dümmler, ed., p. 23).

Both times, Radbertus quite deliberately compared his mode of literary compositions with Zeuxis's search for the universal form (or ideal) of beauty through its fragmentary reflections, a line of argument justified by the proposition that, like beauty, truth was one in itself and was disclosed in parts to individual philosophers and theologians.[24]

The telling point is that Radbertus also employed Cicero's account to describe how St. Adalhard of Corbie reformed the image of Christ in himself.[25] Radbertus told how Adalhard imitated the humility of one saint, the gentleness of another, the abstemiousness of a third. He took his model of patience from one, and that of clemency from yet another. From these fragmentary reflections of virtues, he formed a single image of Christ, the source of virtue; he composed himself as "one man, perfect [and] full of God."[26] Evidently, Radbertus liked the story of Zeuxis because it addressed the paradox of stability and change in human experience and also because it underscored the importance of individual judgment. Like Adalhard, each saint reformed his soul by imitating the universal exemplar, Christ; and each, forming his soul as a distinctive composition, became imitable, a model for those who were to follow.[27] The image of Christ was universal; the conversion process, particular. By imitation, each, according to his own measure, has been "conviscerated" with Christ, re-created in the form of His blessed immortality, reformed according to the image of His glory, and transmuted according to the form of the incorruptible God.[28]

The danger of self-deception beset this emphasis on individual judgment in the reformation of the soul. Radbertus was amply warned by examples of spiritual blindness among Jews and heretics captivated by illusions of their own fabrication. He attempted to avoid the danger

[24] *Expos. in Matt.* prologue (*PL* 120: 34).

[25] *Vita Adalhardi* 21 (*PL* 120: 1519).

[26] *Vita Adalhardi* 19, 21 (*PL* 120: 1518f.). The same idea of composition is implied in the *Epitaphium Arsenii* 1, intro. 10 (Dümmler, ed., p. 20), where Wala is said to have displayed, in his own acts, the uprightness of many illustrious men.

[27] Cf. *Epitaphium Arsenii* 1. 15. 1, and 1. 16. 4–5, 7 (Dümmler, ed., pp. 43, 46f.). Cf. also *Vita Adalhardi* 4, 38 (*PL* 120: 1509, 1529). Radbertus's use of the term "imago sanctitatis" to describe a counterfeit or sham contrasts with his references to Adalhard as "species sanctitatis, forma virtutum" and "speculum sanctitatis," and with Hincmar's application of the term to St. Remigius. See *Expos. in Lament.* 4. Aleph (*PL* 120: 1199) and Hincmar of Rheims, *Vita Sancti Remigii* 3 (*MGH, SS. Rer. Mer.* 3: 264).

[28] On "conviscceration," see *De corpore et sanguine Domini* 19 (Paulus, ed., p. 101). *De charitate* 2 (*PL* 120: 1464). Cf. *Expos. in Matt.* 2. 3 (*PL* 120: 175). On transformation, see *De corpore et sanguine Domini* 1, 20 (Paulus, ed., pp. 19, 106f.), and *De charitate* 8 (*PL* 120: 1473f.).

in his own doctrines of conversion by teaching that the soul was shaped not only by personal insight and judgment but also by the hand of Christ.[29] Radbertus's doctrine of mimesis did not teach an unbridgeable gap between archetype and image but an asymmetry between them in which a dialectical mediation took place. Man, the image, was in the archetype; Christ, the archetype, was in His image. The dialectical mediation was part and parcel of Radbertus's doctrine that believers were "concorporated" with Christ[30] and that Christ moved in them toward the Father.

While it bridled self-delusion, this device also introduced a harsh element of criticism into Radbertus's mimetic strategy for progress in virtue, one that derived from patristic doctrines of terror as an educational tactic. Radbertus taught that the soul was progressively reformed, not only by a person's own judgment but also by the hand of Christ.[31] What results did this idea have? Like a potter, Christ formed some souls as vessels in the midst of life, as He did when He took up Matthew, the despicable taxgatherer, and reshaped him into an Apostle.[32] But such a transformation was arduous. If a vessel of honor is to be formed, the gold must pass through the purifying fire; it must be beaten into shape and burnished with a file.[33] To recast a vessel of dishonor, the potter must break it and begin anew.[34]

The result of Radbertus's idea of moral conversion was therefore a passionate and severe asceticism. The mutual reflex between Christ and the soul occurred through an interplay of contemplation and action.[35] As his comment on mystic sight indicates, Radbertus was particularly drawn to the contemplative state, and, for this reason, he cherished the conviction that monasticism was a version of the angelic life.[36] Over and over, he praised his friends and predecessors, the

[29] *Epitaphium Arsenii* 1. 9. 7 (Dümmler, ed., p. 35).

[30] *Expos. in Lament.* 2. Mem, and *Expos. in Matt.* 2. 3; 11. 25 (*PL* 120: 1129f, 168, 864).

[31] *Epitaphium Arsenii* 1. 9. 7 (Dümmler, ed., p. 35).

[32] *Expos. in Lament.* 4. Beth (*PL* 120: 1203f.). *Expos. in Matt.* 5. 9 (*PL* 120: 370). Cf. the instance of the Apostle Thomas, *Expos. in Matt.* 6. 10 (*PL* 120: 406): "Siquidem hominis carnem palpat sed Deum et Dominum exclamat. Propterea igitur Thomas jure 'abyssus' interpretatur qui de tanta deformitate sua pervenit ad tantam profunditatem mysterii."

[33] *Vita Adalhardi* 31 (*PL* 120: 1525).

[34] *Expos. in Lament.* 4. Beth (*PL* 120: 1204).

[35] *Epitaphium Arsenii* 1. 10. 9 (Dümmler, ed., pp. 37f.). Cf. *Expos. in Matt.* 11. 25 (*PL* 120: 851).

[36] *Vita Adalhardi* 13 (*PL* 120: 1515). Cf. *Expos. in Matt.* 2. 3 (*PL* 120: 153): "imitari angelicam vitam," on John the Baptist.

Abbots Adalhard and Wala of Corbie, for the grace of contemplation that, like the Apostle John on Patmos, they had received in captivity.[37] As the constant companion of the two men, Radbertus also had a mystical spirituality of his own that shines through his reference to the soul inflamed with love and inebriated with the light of divine visitations.[38] The Virgin Mary exemplified the height of contemplation available to those who were in the Spirit, while they lived in the flesh.[39] Tortured with love and afire with yearning, suffering the passion of Christ in her mind, she became more than a martyr since, in love that was stronger than death, she had made the death of Christ her own.[40]

Such exalted contemplative states happened well along in the modeling process. They had to be prepared for by long and painful discipline; progress in virtue entailed conflict. For Adalhard and Wala, the mutual reflex between Christ and the soul in the active state included works of charity to the poor and sick, rejection of family and status, and self-abasement through poverty, vigils, weeping often heightened by self-flagellation, and fasts so austere and protracted that the flesh hardly stuck to the bones.[41] For the Virgin, it included perfect humility and a sorrow that, like her love, exceeded all others.[42]

Plainly, Radbertus avoided self-delusion by embracing a highly critical strategy of mimetic conversion. Its effects were not purely theoretical, since virtue was proven and perfected in action. Radbertus's own writings illustrate that a person who applied the mutual reflex of the strategy could find himself in militant hostility toward the historical world in which he lived and, particularly, toward civil society, the institutional Church, and himself. He thus insisted that the redeemed should strive to be alien from their time and dead to the world.[43] The

---

[37] *Vita Adalhardi* 8, 27, 28, 39, 70 (*PL* 120: 1512, 1522, 1529, 1543); chapters 39 and 70 place Adalhard in the company of angels while in this life. *Epitaphium Arsenii* 2. 11. 2; 2. 12. 2 (Dümmler, ed., pp. 77, 79).

[38] See, e.g., *De charitate* 14. 1 (*PL* 120: 1488), and *De corpore et sanguine Domini* 10, 21 (Paulus, ed., pp. 71, 112, 117). Cf. Radbertus's characterization of Adalhard, who, while mortally ill, "nec minus amore Christi febricitans elanguebat." *Vita Adalhardi* 78 (*PL* 120: 1547).

[39] "*Cogitis me*" 85 (Ripberger, ed., p. 98).

[40] Ibid., chap. 81–83 (pp. 95–97), and chap. 90 (p. 101).

[41] *Vita Adalhardi* 13 (*PL* 120: 1515). *Epitaphium Arsenii* 1. 10. 9 (Dümmler, ed., pp. 37f). *Vita Adalhardi* 13, 23, 25 (*PL* 120: 1515, 1520, 1521).

[42] "*Cogitis me*" 90 (Ripberger, ed., p. 101).

[43] *Epitaphium Arsenii* 1. 29. 4 (Dümmler, ed., p. 59). Cf. *Expos. in Matt.* 3. 4 (*PL* 120: 184), on Christ's retreat into the desert: "Per desertum quippe a mundi pressuris et tumultibus remotior vita significatur, ut omnes discant quietem appetere et soli Deo vacare etiamsi inter homines videantur versari."

world did not love them; it persecuted them because they were not of the world. The Church must therefore stand as a queen behind Christ, her Spouse, as He fought against the world.[44] Time and again, beginning with the moment when the Virgin conceived, Christianity had withstood the traditions of the world and overcame them. Whether by the teachings of Christ, or the resistance of the martyrs, whether by the vows of monks and nuns, the message of redemption overrode the ties of family, the force of traditional learning (including the liberal arts), and the commands of secular rulers.[45]

It was true that Christ commanded his followers to render tribute to Caesar, but the whole man was owed to God.[46] To His imitators, Christ also exemplified contempt for secular status.[47] And rightly, for did not the ruin of Pompey and Caesar prove the smallness, vanity, and grief of worldly pomp?[48] Radbertus contrasted the glittering paraphernalia of secular rulers—"the wretched power of the world and vain presumption of men"—with the royal symbols of Christ's passion—the rod, the scarlet robe, and the crown of thorns—with which He triumphed forever.[49] Most threatening of all, Radbertus repeated the familiar distinction between the rightful king, who ruled with due regard for truth, mercy, and justice, and the tyrant, who ruled without regard for virtues.[50] Bearing some such distinction in mind, he recalled Wala's conflicts with Louis the Pious, comparing the Abbot with "saints and prophets who manfully withstood kings and fought for justice to the death."[51] Both Adalhard and Wala had converted to the

---

[44] *Expos. in Matt.* 2. 2, and *Expos. in Ps. 44.* 3 (*PL* 120: 144f, 1042).

[45] *De nativitate Mariae.* 8 (*PL* 30: 312). *Expos. in Lament.* 5; *Expos. in Matt.* 3. 5, and 7. 15; and *De Passione SS. Rufini et Valerii* (*PL* 120: 1242, 263, 530f., 1502f.). On the superiority of Christ's wisdom to the liberal arts (especially rhetoric), see *Expos. in Matt.* 9. 21 (*PL* 120: 720). On the liberal arts not serving the principal moral good, see *De charitate* 13. 3 (*PL* 120: 1486). See also *Expos. in Matt.* 8, preface; *Expos. in Lament.* 2, preface; and *De Passione SS. Rufini et Valerii* (*PL* 120: 555f., 1103, 1499). Radbertus did have a qualified respect for moral insights of pagan philosophers, and he argued that heretics corrupted them as well as the content of Scripture. See *Expos. in Matt.* 8. 16; *Expos. in Lament.* 4. Sade (*PL* 120: 570, 1228).

[46] *Expos. in Matt.* 10. 22 (*PL* 120: 751f.).

[47] *Expos. in Matt.* 5. 8 (*PL* 120: 346): "Discant igitur ex hoc loco imitatores Christi altiora saeculi contemnere...."

[48] *De Passione SS. Rufini et Valerii* (*PL* 120: 1504f.).

[49] *Expos. in Matt.* 12. 27 (*PL* 120: 943).

[50] *Expos. in Ps. 44.* 2 (*PL* 120: 1032).

[51] *Epitaphium Arsenii* 2. 15. 3 (Dümmler, ed., p. 82). Cf. Radbertus's reference to Louis the Pious's public penance in *Vita Adalhardi* 51 (*PL* 120: 1534f.).

monastic life in recoil against decisions or policies of their kings, and, in the monastic ethos represented by Radbertus, they found the militant hostility toward the world that made it possible for Wala's friends to regard him as a man of peace and wisdom, but for others, observing his political actions, to denounce him as a man of discord.[52]

Radbertus's mimetic strategy for the mutual reflex of the soul with Christ also led him to a severely critical view of the institutional Church. The evangelical form of life, represented by John the Baptist, was most rarely found, he wrote; but everyone pursued honors, preaching poverty and seeking power.[53] Ironically Radbertus's duties as a ruler over men forced him to interrupt his massive exposition on the Gospel of Matthew,[54] but this discrepancy between his own theory and circumstances did not prevent him from rebuking his contemporary prelates and religious for immersing themselves in every kind of secular concern. There were, he wrote, many lovers of the world in ecclesiastical orders, and by their preoccupation with temporal acts and vices, the Church had been cast down and stripped of her beauty, having none to help her with doctrine or good works.[55] There were signs on every hand. As evils multiplied, so did admonitory miracles.[56] In the monstrous evils of the barbarians, and in the cruel civil wars, the depredations, seditions, and crimes that daily increased around him, Radbertus could see more than a divine chastisement visited generally upon his people.[57] He could see God drawing His bow against the delinquent Church, His enemy, slaying what was beautiful in the tabernacle, and, it might be, permitting her members to be torn apart and savaged.[58]

Finally, Radbertus's strategy for the soul's mimetic transformation through mutual reflex with Christ estranged him from himself. To save the soul, one had to lose it, voluntarily dying to the self as well as to the world.[59] I have already referred to the austerities for which Radbertus praised Adalhard and Wala and in which Radbertus may have joined his friends. These practices were justified by the idea that the Christian

---

[52] *Epitaphium Arsenii* 1. 1. 3–4 (Dümmler, ed., p. 22).

[53] *Expos. in Matt.* 2. 3 (*PL* 120: 153).

[54] *Expos. in Matt.* 5. prologue (*PL* 120: 333).

[55] *Expos. in Lament.* 4. Aleph (*PL* 120: 1199). *Expos. in Lament.* 1. Vau; 2. (*PL* 120: 1074f., 1109).

[56] *Epitaphium Arsenii* 2. 1. 5 (Dümmler, ed., p. 61).

[57] *Expos. in Lament.* 4. Lamei (*PL* 120: 1221). *De corpore et sanguine Domini,* prologue (Paulus, ed., p. 4).

[58] *Expos. in Lament.* 2. Daleth (*PL* 120: 1112f.).

[59] *Expos. in Matt.* 8. 16 (*PL* 120: 571).

131

life was a kind of gladiatorial show in which the faithful struggled against the whole world and the princes of darkness and against every spiritual wickedness, and in which each person, inwardly divided, joined combat with himself.[60] Mortification of the flesh was part of this bitter conflict against the self, for killing the senses was part of dying to the world.[61]

Adalhard and Wala went beyond physical mortification, of which they were past masters. Radbertus praised them especially for their relentless moral self-criticism. Wala, he wrote, judged no one more severely than himself.[62] Adalhard judged no one more cruelly than himself and, indeed, punished himself for the deeds of others.[63] Radbertus described the object of this intense and continual scrutiny: it was to direct the mind, to form habits of thought that would enable the soul to obtain what was perfect. In other words, it was to advance the mimetic transformation of the soul according to the image of Christ.[64]

Above all, under monastic discipline one could imitate Christ, "the exemplar of perfect imitation," more beautiful than any other man in His sufferings, wounds, and crucifixion.[65] One could hope, by imitating Christ, to bear His mortification in one's own body and to enter into that self-negating wholeness of which St. Paul exclaimed, "I am crucified with Christ; nevertheless, I live; yet not I, but Christ liveth in me."[66] What matter that moral strife engendered pain and sadness? The Scriptures promised that laughter and joy in this world would turn into lamentation and sorrow in the next and that those who grieved here would be blessed hereafter.[67] What matter if Wala's severity overflowed into the use of coercion and terror against the monks subject to him and that others therefore rebuked him for not being sufficiently conformed with Christ? It was the fate of righteous men to be reproved by the self-indulgent.[68] What matter if Radbertus himself

---

[60] *Expos. in Matt.* 3. 4 (*PL* 120: 184): "verum etiam idem in seipso divisus homo contra se dimicat ac certat."

[61] *Vita Adalhardi* 26 (*PL* 120: 1522).

[62] *Epitaphium Arsenii* 1. 4. 5; 1. 9. 5; 1. 25. 1–3 (Dümmler, ed., pp. 26, 35, 54f.).

[63] *Vita Adalhardi* 54, 76 (*PL* 120: 1535f., 1546).

[64] *Vita Adalhardi* 68 (*PL* 120: 1538).   [65] *Expos. in Ps. 44.* 2 (*PL* 120: 1017).

[66] *Epitaphium Arsenii* 1. 11. 11 (Dümmler, ed., p. 40). Cf. *Vita Adalhardi* 82 (*PL* 120: 1548f.). Adalhard died at the ninth hour: "Tum idem quando et Christus in cruce emisit spiritum, ut daretur indicium quod cujus crucem in vita tulerat, quemque secutus fuerat ejus et in mortis articulo sequeretur vestigia, donec perveniret ad eum quem quaesierat, quem optarat, quem et diu de toto corde desiderarat." Cf. *Vita Adalhardi* 11 (*PL* 120: 1514f.).

[67] *Expos. in Lament.*, preface (*PL* 120: 1062).

[68] *Epitaphium Arsenii* 1. 23–24 (Dümmler, ed., pp. 53f.).

appeared to be a "cruel doctor" in denouncing the wrongs of his day?[69] He was imitating the example of the blessed Adalhard, who, in judging himself cruelly, was also "the cruelest persecutor" of vices in others.[70]

Corbie derived part of its corporate heritage from Celtic monasticism. It is tempting to see a residue of that heritage in the peculiar blend of austere asceticism and contemplative exaltation in Radbertus's doctrines. Many Carolingian writers whose spiritual pedigrees afforded them no direct linkage with Celtic Christianity emphasized, as Radbertus did, a severely penitential life as a way of restoring unity between God and the soul, but they lacked the mystical passion that Radbertus expressed. Hincmar of Rheims was such a writer.

Radbertus's devotion to the monastic life grew out of a vehement need for moral wholeness. A similar need has been clinically observed in recent times among people who, like Radbertus, having been separated from their parents at an early age, moved through life haunted by guilt and self-hatred and driven by hope of eventual forgiveness and reconciliation. Radbertus expressed his need and response theologically. To his mind, man was born into guilt and alienation from God, the wounds of sin could be healed by ascetic discipline, and, formed according to the pattern of Christ, life could move by stages toward the restoration of wholeness. Radbertus's compelling need reinforced very ancient strands in his intellectual heritage. Emotion and reason combined in the *idée fixe* of wholeness in virtue as the end for which man was made but which lay beyond his grasp in this world.

Radbertus's concept of history combined metaphysical unities with strategies for moral change. It was possible to describe the broad course of events as the passage of one person: "Christ, in us, moving from this world to the Father." But this general transition was made up of many kinds of movement. The one that integrated the entire corporate passage was conversion, the act by which the soul, misshapen by sin, was reformed according to the image of God, in which it had originally been made. The Body of Christ was composed by vast numbers of individual conversions, each mimetic, drawn to the same archetype of goodness and truth as all the others, but also distinctive and incommunicable. The reformation of the soul was a progressive act of mutual reflex between the soul and Christ. The modeling process could not be completed in this world, and the dialectical mediation

[69] *Expos. in Matt.* 4. 7 (*PL* 120: 318).   [70] *Vita Adalhardi* 59 (*PL* 120: 1539).

between archetype and image retained a tension that overflowed into contempt of the world, of the fallen Church, and of the self. This contempt entailed relentless scrutiny and criticism.

True to precedents of the Fathers, Radbertus acknowledged the tactical cruelty called for by his mimetic strategy. Although he recognized that it had been divisive in his own experience and in that of his exemplars, Adalhard and Wala, he embraced the mimetic strategy of moral conversion with all its pain as the means of integrating the soul and building up the Body of Christ.

Such was Radbertus's need for moral wholeness that he could not be satisfied until the mimetic asymmetry between archetype and image was fully mediated. Duplication of the one in the other had to be elevated into identity. The mimetic circle had to be closed. Thus, unlike some other theologians of his day and, indeed, those within his own monastery, he insisted that the elements of the Eucharist became the historical body and blood of Christ, the same that was born of the Virgin and nailed to the Cross. Thus the sacrament was both a figural and an actual enactment. Not the priest but Christ was the actual officiant at the altar; not bread and wine but Christ's flesh and blood were consumed; Christ administered Himself to His members, that is, to Himself. By this line of reasoning, Radbertus brought the wholeness that he required within his intellectual grasp. He assured himself that Christ was truly sanctified in the faithful, and that, by a real unity of flesh and bone, He moved in them to the Father.[71]

Metaphysical unity was assured; historical asymmetry remained. In the historical world of moral struggle, the wholeness and beauty that Radbertus sought were spiritual and incomplete, always being formed through penitential exercises that gave monasteries their claim to be schools of virtue.[72] As long as the present world endured, the interior man was to be reformed to wholeness (*ad integrum*) by self-accusation, penitence, and weeping.[73] The wholeness of the Church was enhanced by the "happy desolation" and anguish that drove her to humility and led her through patience to hope. By grief and tears, her beauty was daily renewed.[74]

---

[71] See Jean-Paul Bouhot, *Ratramne de Corbie. Histoire littéraire et controverses doctrinales* (Paris, 1976), esp. pp. 115–140, on the debate between Radbertus and Ratramnus.

[72] *Epitaphium Arsenii* 1. 9. 1 (Dümmler, ed., p. 34). *Expos. in Ps. 44.* 3 (*PL* 120: 1046f., 1050).

[73] *Expos. in Lament.* 1. Beth; 3. Nun (*PL* 120: 1067, 1176).

[74] *Expos. in Lament.* 1. Beth (*PL* 120: 1067).

In a dark moment, Radbertus envisaged God laying the axe to the roots of the Church because the thinking of his day was fruitless.[75] However, the ideas that he expressed about the course of history did bring in an abundant harvest. Corbie was among the first centers of the reforms associated with the "Carolingian Renaissance." Radbertus's beliefs yield powerful evidence of the impulses behind the insistence on ecclesiastical correction and reform not only in Corbie but generally in Carolingian culture, and to be sure, through the monastic ethos in later times. It remained for other generations to puzzle out what consequences the mimetic strategy of moral progress through criticism and suffering might have if it were systematically applied by militant minorities to the values and institutions of this world.

[75] *Expos. in Lament.* 4. Lamei (*PL* 120: 1221): "Iam securis ad radices arborum posita est, quia infructuosa est mens nostra."

Chapter 5

Mimetic Principles of Church Government: Hincmar of Rheims

RADBERTUS'S high spirituality led him to the practical issue of how an individual Christian, committed to principles of mimetic transformation, should conduct himself in the world. The same corrective principles could be applied to church government. The writings of Archbishop Hincmar of Rheims (ca. 804–882) give ample evidence of the conclusions that one man, who was long and directly active in government at the highest level, drew from such application. Radbertus and Hincmar had in common devotion to monastic discipline and reverence for the writings of Augustine and Gregory the Great. Further, they shared many important doctrinal commitments, notably with regard to the Eucharist and the veneration of the Virgin Mary. Like Radbertus, Hincmar found in these ascetic disciplines and theological doctrines an assurance of wholeness in the soul and in the community of Christians that answered an evident and profound psychological need.

Lacking the metaphysical sensitivities of Radbertus, and perhaps also his mystical exaltation, Hincmar concentrated his own attention on corrective rationales for government, especially for that by bishops. The basic core of his thought remained the two mimetic patterns—reversion and augmentation—that had appeared imprecisely in the teachings of St. Paul, that had combined in the theology of Augustine, and that had persisted in the common heritage of Christian doctrine, notably in the monastic ethos. These strategies centered on Christ as Logos. Traces of the two mimetic strategies of inversion and subversion, which Paul and Augustine had associated with Christ's humanity, also appear in Hincmar's ideas of the Church's self-critical changes in doctrine and discipline. However, it was characteristic of ninth-century theology that inversion and subversion were not regarded as distinctive strategies and they they were combined with reversion and augmentation, notably with the latter. The strategy of augmentation itself came to be identified with Christ's humanity, as doctrines evolved that taught the steady building up of Christ's body in the flesh of believers through "concorporation" or "convisceration." The strategy of reversion continued to be attached to Christ as Logos. With regard to the unfolding shape of the Church, mimesis by augmentation carried the greater weight, as it had for St. Paul himself, and under its influence, Hincmar developed an important doctrine of consensus as a source of political norms.[1]

Hincmar of Rheims never tired of proclaiming the unity of the Church, and yet that idea was radically ambiguous for him. Difficult questions arose. If God wished all men to be saved, as Scripture affirmed, why did He not give the same knowledge of truth to the whole world at the same time, and why, over the course of centuries, did perplexing irregularities occur in the vocation of the Jews? Even within the Church, evil took place, raising the quandary that, while Jesus suffered for all, all were not redeemed by the mystery of His Passion, and some, indeed, were spiritually destroyed by the sacraments.

Ambiguity was inescapable, since the Church lived a double life, part being exalted in heaven and part still engaged in its earthly pilgrimage. Thus, Hincmar adopted an Augustinian metaphor that emphasized the promised but not yet achieved unity of the Church. He likened this unity to a garment taking shape on the loom—in particular the tunic of Christ.

His interpretation of this symbol was important. The tunic's four equal parts, he wrote, represented the dissemination of the Church, in concord, throughout the four quarters of the earth. Its wholeness represented the unanimity produced by the bond of charity; the fact that it was woven from top to bottom illustrated the superiority of charity to knowledge.[2] And yet, the tunic was faith,[3] not the clear and unme-

---

[1] A fuller version of this chapter will appear under the title, " '*Unum ex multis*': Hincmar of Rheims' Medical and Aesthetic Rationales for Unification," in *Nascita dell'Europa ed Europa Carolingia: Un'equazione da verificare* (Spoleto, 1981. *Settimane di studio del Centro italiano di studi sull' alto medioevo* 27, vol. 2 (1981): 583–712.

[2] *De praedestinatione, diss. post.* 38, *epilogi*, ch. 1. *De regis persona* 25 (*PL* 125: 418f., 850). See also Yves Marie-Joseph Congar, "Structures et régime de l'Eglise d' après Hincmar de Reims," *Communio: Commentarii Internationalii de Ecclesia et*

diated vision of God that heaven afforded. The Pauline and Augustinian dichotomy—faith in this world, sight in the next—operated in Hincmar's statement that the tunic was woven together by the labors of the Fathers, including the comparatively recent Bede and perhaps the even more recent Alcuin and Paulinus of Aquileia.[4] While the unity of faith was preserved, spiritual understanding changed. Charity being superior to knowledge, some doctrines remained as they were when they were instituted, while others shifted over time or were entirely abolished. Likewise, canons varied according to the needs of the time, although the same spirit inspired them.[5] The whole Church over the centuries, and regional churches at any particular time, were diverse in customs while one in faith.[6]

As faith, the tunic belonged to a heaven and earth that were both transitory and permanent, to an existence that would pass away in its figural aspects and abide forever in its true essence.[7] One result of this ambiguity was that Hincmar accepted uncertainty and conflict; it was part of the corrective modeling process that the Church experienced through the ages. As they explored the inner recesses of belief, the Fathers differed among themselves and changed their minds. Controversy with heretics had been, and remained, he wrote, a major impulse for the review and clarification of doctrine. In the course of dispute, solutions to very different questions were discovered, and enduring doctrines—on the Trinity, on penance, on baptism, and on the natures of Christ—were perfected. But, if Satan were the author of discord, how could Hincmar rejoice in the idea that "truth, often stirred up, flashes with a more brilliant light?"[8] A double—and therefore problematic—vision was needed to fathom the ambiguities of faith.

To cultivate that vision, Hincmar drew from his patristic learning a wide filiation of ideas all of which emphasize the process of correction.

Theologia (1968) 1: 7. The reference to the tunic, in *De regis persona,* is taken from Pseudo-Cyprian's *De XII. Abusivis saeculi,* 11, a crucial text for Hincmar in its emphasis on penitential correction, and hence on change. J. W. Wallace-Hadrill's essay, "History in the Mind of Archbishop Hincmar," in R.H.C. Davis and J. M. Wallace-Hadrill, eds., *The Writing of History in the Middle Ages: Essays Presented to Richard William Southern* (Oxford, 1981), pp. 43–70, appeared after this book had gone to press.

[3] *Ep.* 1 (*PL* 126: 13).

[4] *De praedestinatione, diss. post.* 22, 34 (*PL* 125: 205, 351–353). *Ep. ad Carolum Calvum de praedestinatione* (*PL* 125: 54).

[5] *LV Cap.* 20 (*PL* 126: 353f.).   [6] *Ep.* 18 (*PL* 126: 108).

[7] *De divortio, responsio* 6 (*PL* 125: 663f.).

[8] *Ep.* 23 (*PL* 126: 154).

To speak of correction is to presuppose a model, or standard, from which one has departed. In this sense, Hincmar accepted the arts as important—if not essential—tools in the mimetic work of salvation, reversing the primal fall into idolatry and thus into pluralism. Correction had been the leitmotiv of the Carolingian "Renaissance" during Hincmar's childhood and youth in the reigns of Charlemagne and Louis the Pious. Mimesis entered ideas of correction that Hincmar kept from his early years, but it also caused problems.

In the first place, mimesis entered Hincmar's thought simply because he presupposed models of authenticity for any regulatory work. The model might be either the "norm" of the monastic rule or that set down in papal decrees, both of which Hincmar considered divinely inspired.[9] "Form" was the word he most often used to describe the governing standard; frequently it appears to imply nothing more than a procedural routine or protocol. Thus, Hincmar laid down the "legal and regular form" for the election of bishops and the "form" according to which degrees of pre-eminence were established within the episcopal order.[10] But to a man convinced that God's creative act—prescribing measure and order—continued through the canons,[11] "form" implied much more than external observance. The externals of any sacramental act might conceivably be performed without effect. Suppose that a person left the baptismal font unregenerate, just as he had entered it. The ritual acts would then be all a game. In marriage too, it was possible for observance to be all simulation and no truth. In either case, "the mere form," or "image," was received "without the power of santification."[12] This, Hincmar vehemently argued, was true of clerical ordinations performed by his predecessor and rival Ebo, after being deposed and briefly reinstated in Rheims.

Thus, when Hincmar employed terms such as "the form of royal power," or "the form of bishops," and when he wrote about the "form of Peter" set up "for all rulers of the Church" to follow in their judgments, he implied something beyond strict adherence to the letter of the law.[13] For him, as for us, "form" could mean "mold." When he used the term, he implied a creative act by which a given man—king

[9] See, e.g., *epp.* 31, 45 (*PL* 126: 221, 266).

[10] *Epp.* 19, 48 (*PL* 126: 117, 268f.). *LV Cap.* 13 (*PL* 126: 326), one of Hincmar's most frequent patristic citations.

[11] *LV Cap.* 10 (*PL* 126: 321).   [12] *Ep.* 22 (*PL* 126: 145).

[13] *De una et non trina Deitate* (*PL* 125: 508). *Ad episcopos admonitio altera pro Carolomanno rege* 4 (*PL* 125: 1009). *Ep.* 27, to Hadrian II (*PL* 126: 183). *Ep.* 8: Charles the Bald to Hadrian II (*PL* 124: 894).

or bishop—was shaped by being pressed into a pre-existent form, and by which he, in turn, became a "form," or "exemplar," to his people.[14]

The greatest difficulty came in distinguishing partial, or probable, forms from true forms,[15] and thus in gauging degrees of analogy. The three main tests were truth, authority, and reason. A fourth, custom, was subordinate to these.[16] Clearly, reason was pivotal to all the others; it was the mental faculty by which evidence was sifted and decisions reached and by which analogies were drawn and appraised in law or theology. Throughout Hincmar's writings, the four terms constantly reappear in pairs, of which *ratio* is the common denominator— *ratio veritatis, ratio et auctoritas,* and so forth.[17] Beneath all his bitter charges against his nephew, Bishop Hincmar of Laon, ran the conviction that the Bishop "had acted contrary to reason," rebelling "unreasonably" against his king and his archbishop.[18] Hincmar of Rheims charged that, in so doing, he had paid no attention to the *ratio* in canonical texts and that he had attempted to evade or pervert them by compiling his own rules of action, "frivolous, useless things, lacking in reason."[19]

A second way, then, by which mimesis entered Hincmar's thought about correction was by way of *ratio.* Again and again, he emphasized that reason was man's distinctive faculty, since human persons, made in the image of God, were defined as "individual subsistences of a rational nature."[20] To support this notion, he emphasized the fact that

[14] For the phrase, "forma cui imprimatur," see *De fide Carolo regi servanda* (*PL* 125: 966); *Libellus expostulationis* 5 (*PL* 126: 573); Charles the Bald to Hadrian II, *ep.* 8 (*PL* 124: 889). For the bishop as "forma gregi," see *De ecclesiis et capellis,* in Wilhelm Gundlach, "Zwei Schriften des Erzbischofs Hinkmar von Reims," *Zeitschrift für Kirchengeschichte* 10 (1890): 126.

[15] *PL* 126: 555f.   [16] *PL* 126: 546. *De presbyteris criminosis* 9 (*PL* 125: 1096).

[17] *PL* 125: 399, ch. 35. *LV Cap.* 8 (*PL* 126: 315): "contra rationem et veritatem." *LV Cap.* 25 (*PL* 126: 387f): *ratio* and *veritas* are preferable to *consuetudo. Epp.* 15, 20, and *LV Cap.* 47: letter to Hincmar of Laon (*PL* 126: 97, 121, 462, 501). *De divortio, responsio* 12: "contra legem vel rationem"; *Pro ecclesiae libertatum defensione, exposit. prima:* "ratio est et non obstitit auctoritati . . ." (*PL* 125: 699, 1051). On the general problem, see Hans Liebeschütz, "Wesen und Grenzen des karolingischen Rationalismus," *Archiv für Kulturgeschichte* (1951) 35: 17–44, esp. pp. 28, 43, and Pierre Riché, " 'Auctoritas,' 'ratio,' et 'divina pagina' dans la culture théologique à l'époque carolingienne," in *Nascita dell'Europa ed Europa Carolingia: Un' equazione da verificare* (Spoleto, 1981. *Settimane di studio del Centro italiano di studi sull' alto medioevo* 27, vol. 2 (1981): 719–758.

[18] *LV Cap.* 30, 46 (*PL* 126: 409, 459; *PL* 126: 504, 509f.).

[19] *LV Cap.* 43, 47 (*PL* 126: 422, 463).

[20] Hincmar employed Boethius's definition in *De una et non trina Deitate* (*PL* 125: 585f.). He also applied the Augustinian argument that the triune structure of

God had placed all irrational creatures under Adam's rule.[21] But how was *ratio* mimetic? If we are too Cartesian, or humanistic, in understanding the word, we will overlook something basic and perhaps surprising. *Ratio* has many meanings. One can rightly emphasize it as serving philosophy. According to my sense, however, it opposes the human limits of philosophy, and this sense is borne out by Hincmar's quite consistent disparagement of philosophy and philosophers, a *typos* that he derived from the Fathers and to which I shall return.

The sense of a "right and perfect reason" beyond human nature kept Hincmar from embracing the strict legal formalism to which his canonistic studies might have led him, for he was convinced that the "right and perfect reason" was virtue, a goal in God that men perceived imperfectly in this life but toward which the good were called to struggle, ascending by imitation progressively "from virtue into virtue" until they attained the beatific vision of God.[22] Without rational perception of that super-human goal, struggle, persecution, and martyrdom contributed nothing to salvation. Hincmar stood squarely on patristic conventions when he argued that, directed to wrong spiritual goals, human intellect fell into the madness of heretics and schismatics.[23] Deprived of the exemplary *ratio* that was identical with divine

---

the human mind carried the image of God (*PL* 125: 541). I would argue that this rather than a theocratic meaning was implied when, writing in the name of Charles the Bald, Hincmar had the king assert *"in imagine tamen Dei ambulantem esse nos hominem."* He then invoked Charles's succession to the royal office as a second line of argument (*PL* 124: 881). Cf. Hans Hubert Anton, *Fürstenspiegel und Herrscherethos in der Karolingerzeit* (Bonn, 1968), p. 340. All men are of the same substance: *De una et non trina Deitate* (*PL* 125: 524).

[21] *Vita Remigii* 4 (*MGH, SS. Rer. Mer.* 3: 266).

[22] *De una et non trina Deitate* (*PL* 125: 579). Cf. *De cavendis vitiis, praefatio* (*PL* 125: 857): "quotidie magis ac magis de virtute in virtutem proficiendo custodietis." *Vita Remigii* 31 (*MGH, SS. Rer. Mer.* 3: 328): "Videamus etiam, quomodo hic beatus pater et pastor noster, benedictionibus sibi a legislatore Deo datis, ipsius auxilio in seculi huius convalle lacrimarum ascensiones in corde suo disposuit et de virtute in virtutem gratia Dei provectus excrevit, usquequo eum quem semper desideravit spiritu facie ad faciem videre promeruit." I contend that this sense of moral ascent stood between Hincmar and what Devisse has called "le reproche qui peut le plus justement être fait à Hincmar, celui de formalisme juridique," and that Devisse himself acknowledged as much when he wrote that, for Hincmar, law was an instrument of social instruction, not an end in itself. Jean Devisse, *Hincmar, Archevêque de Rheims (845–882)*, 3 vols. (Geneva, 1975–1976), 2: 617, 1133.

[23] *PL* 126: 551. Cf. Gottschalk of Orbais's self-delusive anticipation of martyrdom, see *De una et non trina Deitate* (*PL* 125: 613). On the persecution that Hincmar claimed to have endured from his nephew, see *PL* 126: 547f. On patristic ante-

(or Christian) virtue, pagans were "monsters," and violent, lawless men were hardly more than "brute and irrational beasts."[24]

Significant as they were in themselves, Hincmar's comments on form and reason had their place in a wider framework. Here, problems begin to appear. When he thought about knowledge as a whole, Hincmar conceived of three discrete structures, corresponding with the three levels that, as I previously mentioned, comprised Augustine's system of analogy. Hincmar identified the structures in terms of vision: the eyes of the body, the eyes of the mind, and the eyes of God. Occasionally, he could argue that the three coincided, but he also recognized vast discrepancies among them. By contrast with the total and immutable wisdom of God, man's knowledge labored under its own fragmentary, shifting character. Change operated only in the structures of human knowledge, and, even there, further discrepancies set the physical apart from the intellectual vision and the intellectual, unenlightened by grace, apart from the eyes of faith.[25]

The importance of form and *ratio* in this overall concept was that they could mediate the asymmetry between the three varieties of human knowledge (the eyes of body, mind, and faith), on the one hand, and divine wisdom on the other. A complex act was required to bridge the gap. It combined two sorts of mediation by mimesis: ordinary human communication and a second, higher kind of communica-

---

cedents for the distinction between men and animals, see Chapter 3, following note 2. On Radbertus's similar view, see Chapter 4, notes 6–7.

[24] *Vita Remigii, (MGH, SS. Rer. Mer.* 3: 262, and *De Coercendo raptu viduarum* 4. (*PL* 125: 1019f.). Cf. *De divortio, responsio* 5 (*PL* 125: 658). See also ep. 2, to Nicholas I, regarding Rothad of Soissons (*PL* 126: 31): "De eo autem quod benignitas animi vestri pensans non belluinum, sed humanum hominis animum scripsit . . . sciat dignatio vestra, non illum esse huiusmodi temperantiae." The Archbishop also wrote of Hincmar of Laon in similar terms, comparing him, in his impaired *ratio,* with a rhinoceros and a unicorn (see note 47). The Bishop of Laon alleged that his uncle had planned to capture him, urging Charles the Bald to bring "tales homines strenuos et peritos, sicut opus est ad talem bestiam capiendam." *LV Cap.* 23, 24 (*PL* 126: 602, 604). See also ep. 11 (*PL* 126: 88): ". . . quia veteres constitutiones jam quasi pro vili apud quosdam habentur, his novis decretis carnales et animales homines territi, quiddam reverentius contra ecclesiam indignitati meae commissam agerent."

[25] See *De una et non trina Deitate* (*PL* 125: 565), on distinguishing between the eyes of the mind and those of the body. *De divortio, responsio* 6 (*PL* 125: 660): the eyes of faith see what the eyes of the body cannot (cf. *os corporis/os cordis, LV Cap.* 47 [*PL* 126: 464]). See *De divortio, responsio* 12 (*PL* 125: 699f.); ep. 22, and *LV Cap.* 52 (*PL* 126: 141, 489), all of which refer to the disparity between human judgments and those *coram divinis oculis.* On Augustine's three levels of analogy, see Chapter 3, following note 21.

tion by which—through sacraments—divinity was mediated to man. Hincmar explicitly described this act in regard to baptism. He drew its aspects together when he explained the mimetic act of the Holy Spirit in the soul, but he also emphasized that, without the faith of the baptisand, the ritual was profitless. The baptisand must, by faith, act as God's fellowworker if the cycle were to be complete by which he became incorporate in the Mediator of God and men.[26] The same emphasis on the recipient led Hincmar to conclude that the Eucharist was poison to the wicked and salvation to the good, and that, before the eyes of God, other sacraments and sacramental actions might have effects very different from what they appeared to have in the eyes of men.[27] This emphasis on individual faith also entered his general theory of knowledge, as, for example, when he wrote about Gottschalk of Orbais. How, with all his learning, could Gottschalk have fallen into wrong doctrines about the Trinity? As a monk, he had sung every day, boy and man, a vesper hymn that could have kept him from error, and yet his heart did not perceive its meaning, for wisdom could not enter his wicked soul.[28]

Where thought led, action followed. The "eye," Hincmar wrote, was action; agreeing with Radbertus, he thought that the "eye" was the turning of the heart (*inclinatio cordis*). Alluding to the assertion in the Gospel of Matthew that the eye was the light of the heart, Hincmar wrote that if one's "eye" were single, then one's whole action would be full of light. But, if the intention of the heart were dark, no words could express the darkness in actions that it caused.[29] At least in theology, knowledge reflected the mind of the knower—his light or darkness—rather than the nature of the thing known. And yet, reason might guide human structures of knowledge "from virtue into virtue,"

---

[26] *Ep.* 18 (*PL* 126: 105f.), quoting 1. Cor. 3:9.

[27] *Ep.* 16; *ep.* 19, ch. 10; *ep.* 33, ch. 4 (*PL* 126: 99f.; 116; 247). *De divortio, responsiones* 6, 10, 13, 15 (*PL* 125: 671f., 685, 710f., 720). See *Annales Bertiniani* (866), in *Annales de Saint-Bertin,* F. Grat et al., ed., (Paris, 1964), p. 129, concerning the ordination of Wulfhad of Bourges, in which, Hincmar wrote, the new Archbishop "pro ordinatione episcopali maledictione indutus est sicut vestimento." Cf. *Cap. Pistensia* (862) (*MGH, Cap. Reg. Fr.* 2: no. 272, ch. 4, p. 310: ". . . qui participatione nominis Christi christiani vocantur, hoc, quod humano ore dicimur, in divinis oculis esse valemus."

[28] *De una et non trina Deitate* (*PL* 125: 578).

[29] *De divortio, praef.* (*MGH, Epp.,* 8, *K. A.* 6, p. 77). Hincmar has adapted Matt. 6:21–23 to read *cor/cordis* instead of *corpus/corporis.* The equation between *oculus simplex* and *recta intentio* also appears in *Pro libertate ecclesiae defensione, exposit.* 1. (*PL* 125: 1037f.).

toward a final balance with what the eyes of God could see. There was no escape from the discipline of humility if one remained true to the faith, no abandonment of relentless self-criticism always correcting the slow and hazardous process of mediating asymmetries.

Bearing these considerations in mind, we can understand that Hincmar's mimetic concept of unity in human affairs was really a concept of corrective mediation. Employing the arts in the Church's corrective work came easily to Hincmar. He delighted in the glint of sunlight on gold, especially on flashing sequins.[30] He knew how greatly moved men and women could be by visual pomp.[31] His eye was keen to illusory or real discolorations, and metaphors of painting and the other arts crept unobtrusively into his discourse.[32] If he was not able to join his contemporary, the brilliant John Scotus Eriugena, in conceiving of theology as poetry, at least he could see that, by deploying his textual citations, he worked as an artist did, painting black under white to make his point clear by contrast.[33] Some sense of poetic license did enter into his observation that the divine word was like a pearl that could be drilled at any point. Thus, he wrote that, even if he interpreted a text of Scripture in a way quite different from the intent of its author, the theologian would not be a "craftsman of falsehood" (*fabricator mendacii*), so long as he remained true to the understanding of his elders.[34]

Artistic analogies suited Hincmar's idea that the episcopal office existed to correct. This was so partly because of his own troubled pontificate. His title was frequently in hazard; resort to analogy was part of his defense. Almost from the beginning of his pontificate, clerics ordained by Hincmar's predecessor, Ebo, challenged his legitimacy as

---

[30] *Pro ecclesiae libertatum defensione* (*PL* 125: 1049). *De regis persona, praefatio* (*PL* 125: 833).

[31] *De cavendis vitiis* (*PL* 125: 906).

[32] *Ep.* 30, 33 (*PL* 126: 208). *De praedestinatione, diss. post.* 16 (*PL* 125: 147). On metaphors—for example, suffering as like a refiner's fire—see *ep.* 11 (*PL* 126: 77f.); and letter to Hincmar of Laon, *PL* 126: 552. Cf. also his use of the verb *depingere* in *ep.* 11 (*PL* 126: 78); letter to Hincmar of Laon, *PL* 126: 511; *LV Cap.* 53 (*PL* 126: 492).

[33] On John Scotus, see Peter Dronke, "*Theologia veluti quaedam Poetria*: Quelques observations sur la fonction des images poétiques chez Jean Scot," *Colloques Internationaux du C.N.R.S.,* no. 561 (Paris, 1977), p. 243. Hincmar's reference occurs in *De praedestinatione, diss. post.* 27 (*PL* 125: 282).

[34] The citation occurs in *ep.* 25 (to Hildegar of Meaux) and *De divortio, responsio* 6 (*PL* 126: 165; *PL* 125: 667). A variant is in *De praedestinatione, diss. post.* 5 (*PL* 125: 87).

bishop of Rheims, taking their case to the papal court. The tortured litigation stretched over sixteen years; before his life ended, Hincmar had been threatened with excommunication by three popes in this and other matters.[35] The integrity of his episcopal ordination had been challenged. Rome, to which he always looked as the oracle of Christian unity, threatened to repudiate him. During the dispute over predestination (in the 850s), some of his episcopal breathren accused him of teaching doctrines that ran contrary to the faith.[36] Given his education and temperament, it was natural that, through all the attacks upon him, he found symbolic reassurance in the power of the arts to correct discord and establish harmony.

Broadly speaking, he found analogues for the bishop's corrective functions in three arts: the gradual achievement of unity, as in building according to a blueprint through architecture; re-integration, as in restoration to health through medicine; and organic amplification of something toward its inherent potentiality, as in the expansion of the mind through verbal instruction.

The first analogue has as a dominant metaphor God the builder. For nearly seventeen years, Hincmar superintended the reconstruction of the cathedral that his ill-starred predecessor, Ebo, had begun. He devoted a massive proportion of his see's resources to the fabric and adornment of this building with lavish ornaments of gold and windows of glass. None of his extant letters deal with the cathedral; Hincmar's only surviving reference to it occurs as a brief entry in the *Annales Bertiniani,* recording the consecration of "the mother church of this province" to the Virgin in the presence of Charles the Bald and a large company of bishops.[37] And yet, this protracted and costly work illuminates the mentality behind the persistent references in *Annales* to precious ornaments, furniture, and vessels[38]; it casts into sharp relief Hincmar's contempt for the young man who despaired of being remembered among the good and burned the temple of Diana at

[35] The seriousness of Hincmar's danger is quite apparent in the letter of Leo IV to all bishops of Gaul (*MGH, Epp.* 5, *K. A.* 3, no. 36, p. 605), and in Hincmar's letter to Nicholas I in *ep.* 2 (*PL* 126: 39).

[36] Jaroslav Pelikan, *The Christian Tradition: A History of the Development of Doctrine,* vol. 3, *The Growth of Medieval Theology (600–1300)* (Chicago, 1978), p. 85.

[37] *Annales Bertiniani* (862), ed. cit., p. 94. On Hincmar's cathedral, see Devisse, *Hincmar, Archevêque* 2: 914–917.

[38] *Annales Bertiniani* (868, 869, 876, 877), ed. cit., pp. 144–148, 151, 155, 201, 204f., 216, 218f.

Ephesus, so as to be remembered at least among the evil.[39] By constructing the new cathedral with all its splendor, Hincmar proclaimed the legitimacy of his own title, but he also expressed connotations that played in his mind when he wrote that Christ founded the episcopal order to build and not to destroy.[40] He struck an analogy between the bishop and God, that "masterful and skilled mason" who determines where each living stone will fit in His city, Jerusalem, as clear and light as pure gold and glass.[41]

Amidst his trials, Hincmar could take some comfort in the thought that, as builder, he imitated God, gradually perfecting His city through time.[42]

But other mimetic paradigms also came to mind that likewise witnessed to the corrective powers of art.

The model of Christ as "the true physician"[43] was perhaps even closer to Hincmar's heart than that of God the builder. Wounded and poisoned by Satan, the serpent, man looked to Christ for the healing balm, the antidote, of grace.[44] Architecture and medicine overlapped. Both aimed at wholeness: the first worked toward realizing the integrity of a design, the second toward re-integration, the recovery of a

---

[39] De praedestinatione, diss. post. 22 (PL 125: 195f.); cf. De una et non trina Deitate (PL 125: 195f.), and LV Cap. 5 (PL 126: 302f.).

[40] See Hincmar's reference in a letter to the clergy and people of Laon, ". . . a quo [Christo] et per quem in aedificationem et non in destructionem sacer ordo episcopalis accepit exordium" (PL 126: 514). Compare his letter to Charles the Bald on predestination (PL 125: 50).

[41] De praedestinatione, diss. post. 19, 20, a reference to Rev 21: 18, 21. (PL 125: 171, 181).

[42] For other references to God as a maker, see the following: 1) De una et non trina Deitate (PL 125: 574), (quoting Ambrose's phrase, "maker of the world-machine"); 2) De praedestinatione, diss. post. 38, epilogi, ch. 3, (PL 125: 438), (quoting Prosper of Aquitaine—God as an artifex, free from the order of time); and 3) ep. 21 (PL 126: 124), (Synod of Douzy—as opifex hominis). On the parallel between Christ and Beseleel in the Libri Carolini, see Gert Haendler, Epochen karolingischer Theologie. Eine Untersuchung über die karolingischen Gutachten zum byzantinischen Bilderstreit (Berlin, 1958. Theologische Arbeiten, Bd. 10), p. 85.

[43] De praedestinatione, diss. post. 26 (PL 125: 269). On the patristic background of this usage, see Gervais Dumeige, "Le Christ médecin dans la littérature chrétienne des premiers siècles," Rivista di archeologia cristiana 40 (1972): 115–141. On Augustine's use of the metaphor, see Rudolf Arbesmann, "Christ the medicus humilis in Saint Augustine," Augustinus Magister 2 (Paris, 1955): 623–629, and Jean Courtés, "Saint Augustin et la médicine," Augustinus Magister 1 (Paris, 1955): 43–51.

[44] Vita Remigii 8 (MGH, SS. Rer. Mer. 3: 284f.). LV Cap. 39 (PL 126: 437). Cf. De praedestinatione, diss. post. 25 (PL 126: 231).

damaged wholeness. There had always been a close connection between the monastic life and the practice of medicine. This might be sufficient to explain the very detailed attention with which Hincmar recorded various illnesses of Carolingian rulers, their families, and others in the historical composition the *Annales Bertiniani*.[45] But there were also more personal reasons. Periodically Hincmar himself was confined by illness. Toward the end of his life, his active and acute mind rebelled, yearning to be released from the "prison" of his "infirm and senile body."[46]

Quite understandably, then, metaphors of healing, like those of visual arts, entered Hincmar's vocabulary.[47] He frequently employed them to describe the penitential sanctions imposed by bishops to restore unity in the Body of Christ.[48] To some prelates of great holiness, such as St. Remigius, God gave the power to heal the physical bodies of the faithful and even to raise the dead.[49] Hincmar also knew of physical cures that had been performed even by less exalted priests through the use of consecrated salt and oil[50] and by exorcism. Their prior curative task, however, was spiritual. While they, like all men, were enfeebled by sin, priests were spiritual physicians. God's good

---

[45] *Annales Bertiniani* (864, 865, 870, 875, 876, 877, 878, 879, 880), ed. cit., pp. 105, 125, 175, 197, 209f., 211, 216f., 218, 222, 234, 242.

[46] *Ep.* 20, c. 10 (*PL* 126: 120f.). Cf. *ep.* 2 to Nicholas I; *ep.* 11 to Nicholas I; *LV Cap.* 4, 39; *Libellus expostulationis* 24, 30; *ep.* 38 to Anastasius (*PL* 126: 39; 89; 300, 436f.; 606, 618; 257.) See also *De divortio, responsio* 3 (*PL* 125: 645). A letter by Hincmar's confrère, Pardulus of Laon concerns a gastric disorder from which the Archbishop was suffering. The letter is published in John J. Contreni, "The Study and Practice of Medicine in Northern France during the Reign of Charles the Bald," John Sommerfeldt and E. Rozanne Elder ed., *Studies in Medieval Culture*, VI and VII (Kalamazoo, 1976), p. 537. For further evidence of Pardulus's medical knowledge, see John J. Contreni, *The Cathedral School of Laon from 850 to 930: Its Manuscripts and Masters* (Munich, 1978. *Münchener Beiträge zur Mediävistik und Renaissance-Forschung*), p. 89.

[47] Hincmar's familiarity with the natural sciences are worthy of additional study. Compare his references to the *libri physicorum* or *physica lectio* in *De divortio, responsio* 12, and *De verbis psalmi: Herodii domus dux est eorum* (*PL* 125: 694, 959). His references to animals normally come via patristic quotations—e.g., hedgehogs (*PL* 126: 557, 562), the rhinoceros (*LV Cap.* 36 [*PL* 126: 457f.]); the unicorn (*PL* 126: 602, 604f.), and birds (*Vita Remigii* 5 [*MGH, SS. Rer. Mer.* 3: 266–268]).

[48] Cf. *Ep.* 55 (*PL* 126: 278).

[49] *Vita Remigii* 31 (*MGH, SS. Rer. Mer.* 3: 332).

[50] *De divortio, responsio* 15 (*PL* 125: 717, curing sexual impotence, and 725, using consecrated oil and salt to exorcise demons who inhabited the senses, or who sought to have sexual intercourse with human beings, or who afflicted men and women with ulcers).

will gave them the office of healing sinners, applying severe medication, or amputating a rotten member, as the case required.[51] The exorbitant cost of medicine should not deter a patient, nor, if medication failed, should the excruciating pain of the knife stay the physician's hand.[52]

I have now considered two mimetic paradigms of episcopal correction. Hincmar illustrated a progressively constructed unity of design with reference to the visual arts, especially architecture. He illustrated the restoration of a lost integrity with reference to the art of medicine. There remained the organic expansion of unity, and this he referred to the verbal arts.

The paradigm of Christ, the Word of God teaching His followers with words shimmered before Hincmar's mind—the Word sent by the Father to propagate the faith, preaching, calling to repentance, and bearing witness even as He underwent the death of the Cross.[53] But as he considered the verbal propagation of faith, Hincmar also reached for two other paradigms. The one was St. Peter, pontiff and martyr. Pressed onto all bishops, the "form of Peter" conveyed the character of equity as set forth in the written judgments of individual bishops and in the decrees of synods and councils, texts that had been disseminated in the West through churches established by Peter and his successors.[54] The other was the Virgin. The function of the bishop as nourisher (*nutritor*) was crucial to Hincmar, but the word "regeneration" had a force that was not included in "nourishment" and that was not exhausted even by the concept of the bishop as husband and father and of his church as wife and mother.[55] The Archbishop could certainly recall that when He nourished those regenerated by his blood, Christ Himself acted as a mother does, feeding a child with her milk.[56] But the Virgin was the exemplar par excellence of the propagation of the

[51] *MGH, Epp.,* 8, *K. A.,* 6, no. 125, p. 60. *De divortio, responsio* 5, *quaestio* 7 (*PL* 125: 655; 772).

[52] *De praedestinatione, diss. post.* 24 (*PL* 125: 220). *Libellus expostulationis* 35 (*PL* 126: 630). This passage from Ambrose's commentary on Ps. 118 also occurs in *De regis persona* 19 (*PL* 125: 846).

[53] See the general discussion of Hincmar's theology in Johann Heinrich Schrörs, *Hinkmar, Erzbishof von Reims. Sein Leben und seine Schriften* (Freiburg-i.-B., 1884), pp. 150–164. Detailed studies of Hincmar's theology are very rare. As a welcome exception, see L. D. David, "Hincmar of Rheims as a Theologian of the Trinity," *Traditio* 27 (1971): 455–468.

[54] Charles the Bald, *ep.* 8 (*PL* 124: 894). Hincmar, *ep.* 27 (*PL* 126: 183).

[55] See, e.g., *LV Cap.* 51 (*PL* 126: 488 and passim). Cf. *LV Cap.* 44 (*PL* 126: 454).

[56] *De praedestinatione, diss. post.* 35 (*PL* 125: 375).

Word. Together with the Apostles, the predecessors of bishops, the Virgin had been crowned with tongues of flame by the Holy Spirit at Pentecost; and like her, bishops were "thrones of God," bearing within themselves the presence of Divinity, the "flame of fire" that engendered Christ.[57] Thus, in a deep sense, Hincmar could accept the idea, forged by Gregory the Great, of the penitent fleeing to the mind of his pastor, as to his mother's bosom.[58]

The ultimate object of spiritual birth and growth was to enter into the "treasures of wisdom and knowledge," but the journey began with "the men who wrote the rules for the art of grammar" and the "doctors of orthography," and it progressed to "those who treat of sacred Scripture."[59] Mastery of the verbal arts included study of etymologies and of such rhetorical devices as metonymy, irony, and antiphrasis.[60] It required the ability to clarify doubtful readings by various specialized techniques, including the collation of texts.[61] Above all, it demanded a clarity of understanding that permitted an author to set down his words in a rational order: that is, to compose them in a unified, coherent way.[62] If illiterates were ordained as bishops, unable to fathom the wholeness of Scripture and the marvellous harmony of the canons, the Church's vigor would perish, and miseries of every kind, including famine, plague, and sterility would befall their unhappy people.[63]

Accordingly, Hincmar valued his own mastery of the verbal arts, provided for instruction in literacy through the rural parishes of his

[57] On the Virgin at Pentecost, see *De divortio, quaestio* 3, *responsio* (*PL* 125: 749). On bishops as thrones of God and as seats of the flame of fire, see *De divortio, quaestio* 6, and *De fide Carolo servanda* 17 (*PL* 125: 758; 971). On the Holy Spirit as fire, see *ep.* 33. 4 (*PL* 126: 248). On the Holy Spirit as a "Holy Flame" engendering Christ in the womb of the Virgin, see Hincmar's verses, inscribed at her image on the main altar of Rheims cathedral, and his *Carmen de Virgine Maria.* Flodoard, *Historia Remensis Ecclesiae* 3. 5 (*MGH, SS.* 13: 479, and *MGH, Poetae Latini Medii Aevi* 3, p. 409 no. ii, p. 410 1. 7.

[58] *De divortio, responsio* 1 (*PL* 125: 635). On other evidence for the veneration of the Virgin in the ninth century, see Haendler, *Epochen,* p. 134.

[59] *PL* 126: 508. On the rudiments of grammar, see ibid., col. 555.

[60] *De una et non trina Deitate* (*PL* 125: 564. See also *PL* 126: 546).

[61] On Hincmar's classical allusions and general facility in the verbal arts, see Devisse, *Hincmar, Archevêque* 2: 1056ff., 1067f., which contains a valuable discussion of Hincmar's library.

[62] Compare the charge that Hincmar of Laon, lacking right understanding, had compiled his authorities *sine ratione. LV Cap.* 43 (*PL* 126: 448f.). Cf. *De praedestinatione, diss. post.* 22 (*PL* 125: 195f.).

[63] Cf. *Libellus expostulationis* 11 (*PL* 126: 578). *De praedestinatione, diss. post.* 36 (*PL* 125: 382, 387).

diocese, and, from time to time, undertook the personal supervision of training in letters.[64] Great mysteries in the fecundity of the word were to be plumbed through the literary arts, for, as the Trinity had made the flesh of Christ in the Virgin's womb, so by words, priests made the body of Christ at the altar. And God Himself, the paradigm of bishops, had deployed good and evil in the whole course of history as a poet adorns a most lovely song with antitheses.[65] Great prizes were to be won through the use of words in praying, catechizing, exhorting, and calling to repentance. Through the power of words, Hincmar's predecessor, St. Remigius, had converted Clovis and all the Franks and, in baptism, brought them forth from "the immaculate womb of the Church."[66]

It was common among Carolingian writers, as among the Fathers, to argue that the verbal arts were inadequate to true knowledge and that they were even harmful without formation of the moral character through Christian doctrine.[67] Hincmar, too, considered the "wisdom of this world" to be "hostile to God."[68] The delusions of worldly wisdom had reached their most noxious virulence among heretics and philosophers, those organs of the Devil who stood arrayed against the teachers of orthodoxy, "the organs of Christ, who reign with Him in heaven and shine with miracles on earth."[69] Men who confided only in human shrewdness were a real and present danger; they should not only be repressed but utterly ground out.[70] Even in theology, earthly

---

[64] Devisse, *Hincmar, Archevêque* 2: 1084ff. *LV Cap.* 39 (*PL* 126: 437): ". . . litteris per me et per quoscunque potui erudivi. . . ."

[65] Synod of Quierzy to Louis the German (858), 15 (*MGH, Cap. Reg. Fr.,* 2, no. 297, p. 439). *De praedestinatione, diss. post.* c. 12 (*PL* 125: 115). Prosper of Aquitaine, Hincmar's source, was consciously using Augustine's metaphor. See Chapter 3, note 8.

[66] *Vita Remigii* 5 (*MGH, SS. Rer. Mer.* 3: 267).

[67] Einhard, *ep.* 57 (*MGH, Epp.* 5, *K. A.* 3, p. 138). Cf. Hincmar's *De praedestinatione* 31 (*PL* 125: 296).

[68] *De ordine palatii* 31 (*MGH, Fontes Iuris in usum scholarum,* p. 86).

[69] *De divortio, responsio* 15; *quaestio* 7, *responsio* (*PL* 125: 720, 768).

[70] *De ordine palatii* 31 (*MGH, Fontes Iuris in usum scholarum,* p. 86). Hincmar was prepared to pay tribute to Charles the Bald as a philosopher-king (*PL* 125: 931). See Pierre Riché, "Charles le Chauve et la culture de son temps," *Colloques Internationaux du C.N.R.S.,* no. 561 (Paris, 1977), p. 38, and passim. At the same time, his attitude toward philosophy could be distinctly hostile. He portrayed St. Remigius overwhelming an Arian who confided in his own dialectical powers (*Vita Remigii* 21 [*MGH, SS. Rer. Mer.* 3: 313f.]), and, even if the treatise is not his, the sentiment expressed in *De diversa animae ratione* conforms with his outlook: "vera ratio et prophetica auctoritas" gives the laugh to the "ratiocinatio philosophorum."

wisdom was ignorance. The humbling truth was that no one could claim to be sole master of the Scriptures or canons so long as he had to learn about them from other men and not immediately from God. It was in the simplicity of their faith that the Apostles, uneducated fishermen, had instructed orators and subjected emperors to themselves.[71]

Idolatry was the great peril that Hincmar saw in the visual and medical arts, as well as in the verbal ones. When he converted the Franks to Christianity, St. Remigius tore them away from visible idols just as the Prophet Jeremiah had recalled his people from the service of graven images;[72] but there were still plenty of idolaters about. In fact, a member of the Carolingian dynasty, Pippin II of Aquitaine drove this fact home by falling into apostasy, absconding to the Northmen, and keeping their rituals.[73] With regard to the visual arts, the strictures of the second commandment therefore retained a quite literal interpretation. This was also true of the medical art—or rather, of magic, its perverted counterpart—for, according to Hincmar's reading of the canons, enchantment could not take place without idolatry.[74] In the verbal arts, the danger lay in the ease with which men made idols out of their own words and interpretations, an ease that warranted thinking of idolatry as the mother of heresy.[75]

There were varieties of idolatry on every hand—in deviant sexual acts[76] and, above all, in avarice whether for wealth or for position. In all its variations, idolatry occurred because the eyes—whether of the body or the mind—did not see the reality veiled within appearances. To be sure, grace could reduce this discrepancy. Thus, when he touched the risen Christ, the Apostle Thomas saw one thing and believed another; he saw a man and confessed God.[77] Still, the discrepancy remained, deluding and enticing, as it had when Satan tempted Adam and Eve from unity—the worship of one God—into the plural-

---

Chap. 8 (*PL* 125: 946). See *De una et non trina Deitate* (*PL* 125: 481); *De praedestinatione, diss. post.* 30 (*PL* 125: 295).

[71] *LV Cap.* 24 (*PL* 126: 379). *De una et non trina Deitate* (*PL* 125: 564).

[72] Cf. *Vita Remigii* 1 (*MGH, SS. Rer. Mer.* 3: 262).

[73] *Annales Bertiniani* (864), ed. cit., pp. 105, 113. J. M. Wallace-Hadrill, *Early Medieval History* (New York, 1976), pp. 226f.

[74] *De divortio, responsio* 16 (*PL* 125: 728).

[75] *De praedestinatione, diss. post.* 16 (*PL* 125: 142). *LV Cap.* 36 (*PL* 126: 429). *De una et non trina Deitate* (*PL* 125: 479f.).

[76] *De divortio, responsio* 12 (*PL* 125: 693f, 698). *LV Cap.* 47, 51, and *Libellus expostulationis* 30 (*PL* 126: 465, 485–488; 618).

[77] *De divortio, responsio* 6 (*PL* 125: 672).

ity of self-worship with the lying promise, "Ye shall be as gods."[78] The Archbishop judged that, like the parents of the human race, Hincmar of Laon and Gottschalk had lapsed into idolatry. They had not properly subordinated the analogues of art to the higher analogues of faith.

How could one avoid idolatry? Hincmar drew the answer from his monastic roots.[79] The ascetic virtue of humility counteracted the divisiveness of self-worship; it promoted unity. Hincmar incessantly admonished kings and other bishops to humility and obedience. It is easy to regard these austere rebukes as self-serving tactics. However, another interpretation—not necessarily excluding self-interest—is also plausible. Hincmar grew to adulthood as a monk; he practiced monastic austerities while archbishop.[80] He served as abbot of St. Remi, and considered monks his "brothers and sons." He resorted to the *Rule* of St. Benedict in an attempt to edify Pope Nicholas I. There is no reason to suspect hypocrisy in his statement that humility was the virtue that safeguarded all the others.[81]

Hincmar recognized humility as an antidote to divisiveness when he invoked St. Benedict's provision that the abbot should forbid artisan monks to ply crafts in which they took pride. The same idea led him to quote Augustine's opinion that man should hate his own work, as sin, in order to come to God. In church order, as well as in private spirituality, this ascetic self-denial served the ultimate goal of unification; for it was through humility and holy obedience that believers could be one in Him who prayed "that all may be one, as thou, Father, art in me and I in thee, that they may be one in us."[82]

From the patristic texts before him, including St. Benedict's *Rule,*

---

[78] *De una et non trina Deitate* (*PL* 125: 479f.).

[79] Schrörs, *Hinkmar,* pp. 11f.: "Jedenfalls aber ist das Ringen des alten Ordensgeistes gegen weltliche Erschlaffung nicht ohne Einfluss auf seine Charakterbildung geblieben, da die seltene Willensstärke, der nie erkaltende Eifer für kirchliche Zucht und Ordnung und der ernst-asketische Zug, der von den Jünglingsjahren an durch das ganze Leben des Mannes geht, auf eine frühe Schule von Erfahrungen und Prüfungen hindeuten."

[80] As witnessed by the letter of Pardulus cited in note 46.

[81] *PL* 125: 503. *PL* 126: 77, 266. Cf. Schrörs, *Hinkmar,* p. 69, on the Emperor Lothar I's assumption of the monastic habit before his death. One of the most serious charges made by Pope Leo IV against Hincmar was that he had violated his monastic vows when he became archbishop, and, years later, Hincmar found it still necessary to answer this allegation (obliquely) when writing to Pope Nicholas I. See *ep.* 11 (*PL* 126: 81f.).

[82] *PL* 125: 503. *De praedestinatione, diss. post.* 23 (*PL* 125: 215). *LV Cap.* 16 (*PL* 126: 337). John 17:21.

Hincmar realized that coercion and humility were related. Terror was a corrective device, a duty of all rulers, and, as a pedagogical device, a specific obligation of bishops. Hincmar's three paradigms of the bishop, drawn from architecture, medicine, and the verbal arts, all implied the forceful shaping of materials but none more than the model of the bishop as spiritual physician. As monk and abbot, Hincmar knew the Benedictine *Rule*'s description of abbots as spiritual physicians, and he must also have known from practical experience that physical as well as mental pain were inseparable from this model. Paschasius Radbertus recalled a monk who was thought to have lost his senses because he wanted to leave the monastery. By favors, threats, and blows, Wala, his abbot, had so disciplined his brethren that they would not let the defector lapse. They kept him in close confinement and knew that he had been cured when, smitten with fear and drenched with tears, he threw himself penitently at Wala's feet.

Doubtless, Hincmar had austere precedents such as this in his own background, and, as we shall see, he was not writing pure metaphors when he drew analogies between physical punishment and the practice of spiritual therapy. "No one strikes the madman harder than the physician who seeks to cure him." If a patient cannot be restored to health by a gentle medication, the physician could often succeed with a bitter potion. If medication failed, one might go to the extreme of cauterization or amputation. Hincmar readily used these analogies from the Benedictine *Rule,* together with others, to describe the magisterial office of the bishop. God Himself instituted the requisite severity when He said, "Those whom I love, I rebuke and chasten" (Rev. 3:19). "For whom the Lord loveth he chasteneth, and scourgeth every son whom He receiveth" (Heb. 12:6). The bishop was held to this precept because of his spiritual powers. Hincmar followed Augustine and Gregory the Great in arguing that it was far worse to kill others spiritually than to destroy them physically. At the Last Judgment, he wrote, the bishop would be punished for the heavier crime of spiritual murder if he had been slack in his duties of rebuke and chastisement.[83]

For Hincmar, as for the Fathers who inspired him, physical pain and spiritual compunction were two parts of the same enterprise. His discussions of idolatry provide specific examples of his thought and action. Augustine reminded him that, among the ancient Hebrews, "idol-

[83] See the references in notes 51 and 52. The citations in this paragraph occur in Synod at St. Macra, *Mansi* 17: 539, and *LV Cap.,* preface, ch. 42–43 (*PL* 126: 291; 440, 451f.). For the reference to Paschasius Radbertus, see Chapter 4, note 68.

atry was punished by the sword," by burning, slaughter, and captivity.[84] From other sources, he learned that idolatry in enchantment was to be punished by beating and torture and, in sexual offences, by "great affliction of the flesh and contrition of the spirit." The idolatry of Pippin II of Aquitaine expressed itself in armed rebellion; and it was as "a traitor to his land (*patria*) and to Christianity" that he was subdued through military action and kept under heavy guard until his death.[85] The educative force of penance entered more clearly into the actions that, after synodal judgments, Hincmar took against "idolatry" in the cases of Gottschalk of Orbais and Hincmar of Laon. Idolatry and madness were hard to distinguish; in invective, the words were interchangeable. The Archbishop followed to the letter his prescription for the violent restraint of madmen when he treated the "insanity" of Gottschalk of Orbais, which arose through heresy, and that of Hincmar of Laon, which arose through disobedience. He imprisoned Gottschalk for life, under conditions that appear to have unhinged his captive's mind. He secured the deposition and imprisonment of his nephew. Perhaps by fiat of the King, Charles the Bald, whose orders he had defied, the former bishop was blinded in captivity, and the papal order that restored him to his diocese shortly before his death could not restore his sight.

One could both practice and teach humility through pain. Coercion amounted to persecution when the unrighteous imposed it on the godly; and persecution was the gateway to martyrdom. Hincmar believed that, in their fierce conflict, his nephew persecuted him, and that, by enduring, he died for Christ in spirit, as John the Baptist had done in body. The Archbishop argued with grim irony that he was imitating Christ Himself, "who came to die even for His enemies, and yet said that He was going to lay down His life for friends, so as to demonstrate to us that when, by loving, we can gain advantage from our enemies, even those who persecute [us] are friends." Before Hincmar's mind, there shimmered other venerable examples, including the apostles of Gaul, Dionysius the Areopagite, who was martyred by the Romans, and Remigius, who endured suffering and still did not die a martyr, a predecessor in whose character and pontificate Hincmar found many lustrous parallels with his own.

But, pre-eminently, suffering in humility found a paradigm that we

---

[84] *Libellus expostulationis* 30 (PL 126: 617).

[85] *Annales Bertiniani* (864), ed. cit., p. 113. After an earlier rebellion, before his apostasy to the Normans, Pippin had been punished by being tonsured and remanded to a monastery.

have already encountered in Hincmar's devotional life: the Virgin Mary—more than a martyr, as Radbertus had written, because of what she suffered inwardly at the Crucifixion.[86] Like Radbertus, Hincmar cherished a special devotion to the Virgin. For him, the Virgin's humility was the nodal point at which history became one, for there, the Old Testament fused with the New. Moreover, in a striking way, the Virgin exemplified Christ's own saving humility. She adored Christ as her Lord and King,[87] but, from her royal Son, she learned to be humble and to preserve the other virtues under the shelter of humility. She did not learn from Him how to construct the heavens, or to create angels, or to perform the signal wonders of divinity. But she did learn the lesson that He taught, saying, "Learn of me, for I am meek and lowly of heart" (Matt. 11:27), and that He enacted when He performed the work of redemption, becoming obedient to the death of the Cross.[88] Hincmar made the Virgin the central figure in the relief that adorned his tomb, thus testifying to the importance that the ascetic virtues of humility and obedience had in his concept of unification.

The three rationales of unification—in architecture, medicine, and the verbal arts—have led me to the theological bedrock on which Hincmar rested his mimetic analogies: the Incarnation. The corrective functions that I have mentioned—building, healing, and procreating—were all devoted to building up the body of Christ. This progressively expanding body was unified primarily through the "mystery of action" in the sacraments, in which the priest imitated visibly the invisible operation of the Holy Spirit (in baptism) or of Christ, the true Pontiff (in the Eucharist). To Hincmar's mind, one fact kept the ritual actions of priests (and, more broadly, all the workings of the human mind) from being idolatrous: through those actions, believers escaped the deceptive area of likeness and analogy accessible to their limited intellects and passed over into an area of identity with Christ, the Wis-

---

[86] *LV Cap.* 39 (*PL* 126:437f.). Hincmar accepted the letter *"Cogitis me"* as an authentic work of St. Jerome and had it sumptuously copied and bound for the altar of his cathedral. See above, notes 56–58.

[87] Albert Ripberger, ed., *Der Pseudo-Hieronymus-Brief IX, "Cogitis me": Ein erster marianischer Traktat des Mittelalters von Paschasius Radbert* (Freiburg, 1962. *Spicilegium Friburgense* 9) ch. 87, p. 99.

[88] Ibid., ch. 104, p. 108. Cf. Hincmar, ep. 45 (*PL* 126: 266): "... cum charitatis concordia, quae est omnium virtutum mater et cum humilitate quae est custos ipsarum virtutum, atque cum vera obedientia, quae scala est qua ad caelum pertingitur." *LV Cap.* 13 (*PL* 126: 327): Christ was obedient to the Father, even to the death of the cross. Thus, "Christus humilis hominem obedientem reduxit ad vitam."

dom of God. Christ became *totus in singulis, totus in omnibus* (whole in individuals, whole in the sum of all men). But this passage from analogy to identity was possible because, through their humility, believers participated in the flesh of Christ.

This insistence was yet another point of agreement with Radbertus. Hincmar's emphasis on wholeness in each of the two aspects of the Incarnation—mediation of divinity to man and of carnality to Christ—underlies his program of correction by the episcopal functions of healing, participation, and, most comprehensively, by imitation.

My argument thus far can be summed up as follows. I have now reviewed three mimetic functions of bishops—building, healing, and propagating—and have related those functions to the Incarnation. All of the functions served progressive correction. In the light of this apparent, and passionate, commitment to change, it would be difficult to conclude, as some have done, that, for Hincmar, dogma and Church order were permanently closed structures, in which there could be no further development.

The fact that Hincmar's thought focused as it did on the Incarnation was decisive. For my purposes, the important feature of his theology of the Incarnation was that it encompassed theories of change, and, explicitly, of correction. Whatever the precise subject—the Incarnation itself, the sacraments, or the rebirth of the soul—the theme was movement from an imperfect order of being to a perfect one. It was a movement of a precise kind. It took place by mediation between the asymmetrical poles of divinity and humanity, a mediation that did not cease when Christ was born of the Virgin but that went on continually through the sacraments of the Church, for through them, Hincmar taught, Christ was incorporate not merely in His own flesh but also in every believer and in the entire Church.

One major adjustment had to be made in Hincmar's mimetic apparatus, then, if it were to be applied to all humanity—the "one man" that, like Radbertus (and other followers of St. Augustine), Hincmar thought was forming in Christian society.[89] A new faculty, a collective reason (*ratio*), was needed, one by which the whole could perform the critical functions of reason on a universal scale and thereby react upon its individual members as they did upon it. To Hincmar's mind, consensus was that faculty. But we must remember that reason was equivalent to spiritual power or virtue and that the soul moved toward it by

---

[89] *De praedestinatione, diss. post.* 29 (*PL* 125: 289).

stages of perfection, "from virtue to virtue." Consensus was a compound made up of individual minds. Like its components, it moved through stages of incompleteness toward an archetype that was both present in part and absent in its completeness. Like that of its components, its virtue was perfected in weakness, that is, in faith.

Thus, while the faith remained one and inviolable, consensus was susceptible to change. In this world, canon law belonged among the works of knowledge, which were inferior to charity in weaving the tunic of Christ. The canons were made by human minds, individually and collectively, using the critical arts of philology and exegesis. They expressed consensus that, while divinely inspired, was empirically determined and therefore bound to specific times and situations. Hincmar asserted unity in faith, charity, and "true understanding" that transcended particular circumstances.

Imitation established that unity. Later generations imitated the wisdom of earlier, but, even more, they imitated their faith. Mimesis operated particularly in the area of faith, where human reason could provide no self-sufficient proofs. For, by informing their doctrines and canons with the faith of "imitable" bishops, such as Gregory the Great, modern prelates became their heirs, born to them as sons to fathers and, like them, imitators of Christ.[90]

Canon law was not perfect, and Hincmar's own experience of consensus as criticism of criticism provided many examples of how retrograde its actual movement could be. Therefore consensus, the collective *ratio*, also labored under ambiguities, as it advanced by analogical inference, applying its mimetic strategies of adaptation, self-criticism, and correction. Learned bishops at the synods of Valence and Langres had embraced doctrines about predestination that Hincmar condemned; bishops had consented to the restoration of his deposed predecessor, Archbishop Ebo, to Rheims; bishops in synod had approved the divorce of King Lothar II of Lotharingia. Not stopping at what Hincmar considered misapplication of the canons, the bishops of Gaul

---

[90] *PL* 126: 223; *PL* 124: 887 (imitable bishops: the first reference is to destructive examples set by wicked bishops; the second, is to the good example of Gregory the Great). *Vita Remigii* 15 (*MGH, SS. Rer. Mer.* 3: 279 (insufficiency of rational proofs). *PL* 125: 965, 967; *PL* 126: 291, 328 (imitation of faith). *MGH, Cap. Reg. Fr.* 2: 528 (imitating the wisdom of earlier men). Psalm 44:17 ("pro patribus tuis nati sunt tibi filii") was one of Hincmar's favorite passages with regard to the apostolic succession of bishops. See, e.g., Synod of Quierzy to Louis the German (858) *MGH, Cap. Reg. Fr.*, 2, no. 297, ch. 15, p. 441.

had strained themselves to write new canons approving the "spiritual adultery" by which a prelate might hold two sees.[91] Such things were not unexpected, Hincmar wrote, in his "most pestilential time,"[92] when everyone did what was right in his own eyes. Through the Flood, God had destroyed the entire world for its wicked consensus, and it was possible that, in the events of recent years, there might lie hidden another terrible judgment upon the sons of men.[93] In these apocalyptic tones, Hincmar's doctrine of consensus retained the ascetic, self-critical element of humility that is apparent in his aesthetic and spiritual thought.

Quite obviously, consensus was a fundamental juristic concept in Hincmar's picture of Church government. It was an act of will that enabled licit marriages to be performed, bishops to be elected and consecrated, and every sort of administrative act to be executed. The motif of correction, however, has carried us beyond formal jurisprudence to the inmost, nonrational dimension of faith. When Hincmar taught that universal consensus could deceive, he plainly indicated that, as a means of correction, consensus was a theological notion with legal consequences, rather than being first and foremost a legal concept. Its detachment from juristic formalism becomes yet more obvious in regard to enforcement.

To be sure, Hincmar's ecclesiology gave him a magnificent order of hierarchic adjudication, in which the greater blessed and judged the less. Beginning with the diocesan court, he passed upward to the provincial synod over which a metropolitan presided, and thence to a general synod that combined provinces, and, finally, to the apostolic see, which had the power to reconsider and to sustain or annul judgments of provincial and general synods. Beyond the Pope, there was the wider community. The Holy Spirit had descended upon the Apostles, the faithful, and the Virgin, at Pentecost, bestowing its gifts on over 120 followers of Christ. Consequently, St. Peter, the prince of the

---

[91] *Ep.* 31, ch. 16 (*PL* 126: 226). This was an instance in which Hincmar changed his mind abruptly and perhaps "avec beaucoup d'hypocrisie." See Devisse, *Hincmar, Archevêque* 2: 790, n. 514.

[92] *De divortio, quaestio* 1, *responsio* (*PL* 125: 746).

[93] *PL* 126: 52, 115, 244, 249, 433, 537, 630f., quoting Innocent I, decretal 56. Hincmar apparently did not realize that, by invoking this principle, he negated the principle of catholicity, which he had invoked against the "new predestinarians" (*PL* 125: 350–352). The principle of catholicity—that universality is a sign of authentic faith and practice—was also used against the Byzantine iconodules by the *Libri Carolini* (4. 28), in a passage known to Hincmar (*LV Cap.* 20 [*PL* 126: 360f.]).

Apostles, rightly submitted to cross-examination by the brethren, and, following his example, prelates should humbly answer accusations against them before those who hold inferior authority.[94] The theological principle of general inspiration pervades this structure. But it leaves juristic questions unresolved.

In fact, Hincmar's juristic notions are elegantly clear with regard to diocesan and provincial adjudication but prodigiously vague with regard to higher levels. At the highest, the Pope may review decrees of synods and councils, but are there circumstances in which, betraying his sacred ministry by violence, neglect of the canons, or heresy, he, like any other bishop, could come under judgment of a synod? What juristic recourse was there when a self-proclaimed universal council issued canons contrary to the teachings of orthodox doctors and a pope assented to its decrees?

Neither was an abstract query. "Not by the rules, but by force," Pope Nicholas I had commanded that Rothad be reinstated as bishop of Soissons, though he "had been canonically deposed by bishops of five provinces." Casting aside canonical order, Nicholas "restored him by his own power," without the "advice or consent of the bishops who had deposed him." Pope Hadrian II had provided another lamentable example of malfeasance when he assented to the decrees issued by the Council of Constantinople (869–870) on the veneration of sacred images.[95] And yet, neither in these instances nor in any other of his many serious disputes with popes did Hincmar invoke juristic sanctions. Hincmar the theologian insisted that popes were subject to correction by the force of consensus, but Hincmar the canonist supplied no mechanism by which that could be done, even in cases of heresy.

When he turned to the problems of synodal judgments, Hincmar likewise encountered questions that could be answered in terms of faith but not in those of law. The descent of the Holy Spirit on the Apostles, collectively and individually, imparted a wisdom to the episcopal order as a whole that was superior to the wisdom of any single bishop. And yet, assemblies of bishops erred; their acts required emendation by other synods. How could any synod know that it had spoken by the Holy Spirit and not by its own imperfect wisdom? Hincmar answered that it would do so if it built with the living stones of orthodox judgments, conforming its decrees with the meaning, doc-

---

[94] *De divortio, quaestiones* 1–3 *responsiones* (*PL* 125: 746–751).
[95] *Annales Bertiniani* (865, 872), ed. cit., pp. 118, 187.

trine, and very words of the Fathers. Even so, he was aware of a wide discrepancy between the mediated knowledge that men could transmit from one to another and the immediate perception of truth, open to the eyes of God and to those, like Paul and Dionysius the Areopagite, who had been rapt up to the third heaven. Even in synods, consensus was bound to the changefulness of this world.

Hincmar applied the strategy of mimesis by augmentation to Church government, with far-reaching implications. Faithful to patristic doctrines and to the monastic ethos of his day, his mental world was a sacramental dynamic, a structure of mediated asymmetries, rather than one of stable forms. Throughout his life, he continued to preach the message of correction that, in his youth, he had learned at St. Denis and at the court of Louis the Pious. Therefore, he represents a mentality institutionalized by monastic life that persisted in his homeland and that passed with many changes into the movements associated with the names of Gorze and Cluny. Given his opposition to papal centralization, Hincmar was certainly not a forefather of the Gregorian reform. But, as Marx recognized when he denied that he was a Marxist, great ideas may be applied in many ways. In 1049, a Lotharingian, Pope Leo IX, inaugurated the Gregorian program before Hincmar's altar to the Virgin in the cathedral of Rheims, lifting the relics of St. Remigius to his shoulders, and an interlacing of theology and canon law resembling Hincmar's played in his mind.

There was, however, one great difference between the idea of correction, represented by Hincmar, and the various programs of ecclesiastical reform that followed it. Later advocates of reform deplored the corruption of recent times and aimed to recover an ancient purity. This pattern of loss and recovery is absent from Hincmar, and it is perhaps a telling difference between reform—or renewal—and correction, understood as a permanent and continuing state of life.

The idea of continual correction relates Hincmar's mentality to a wider spectrum in European intellectual history, one that transcends the monastic doctrine of reform. From their predecessors in the Merovingian age and under the first Carolingians, Hincmar and his contemporaries—bishops and abbots—inherited secular functions that were quite unprecedented as territorial princes, as captains of men, as dominant members of a military, landed aristocracy. Trying to elucidate their own novel position, they began weaving the idealist structure of self-criticism and mediated oppositions into a program for transforming the entire social world by inquiry, education, and terror.

Their major legacy lay in the questions that they opened and left unresolved. Providing adequate answers was the work of centuries; and the practical results of the doctrine of corrective process that I have described are still to be read on the map of Europe and, indeed, throughout the world in the diaspora of Europeans and their culture.

Chapter 6

Summary and Anticipation: The Transit of Jesus

LIKE PLATO'S ideal Republic, the Church was a vast and intricate educational organ, and it contributed to the formation of European culture through many tactics. Through its formal disciplines—the liberal arts culminating in theology—it preserved the literature and remade the traditions of the ancient world. Through its penitential discipline, it enforced, and so taught, a moral system. Through its legislation and worldly power, it adapted social systems according to its program for the rebirth of man. Such were the means of change.

But, through the work of ninth-century theologians, Europe was defining itself in more ways than by the development of institutions. What gave the course of history its direction was not fixed institutions but the goal toward which it was moving and the process by which it moved. Europe was defined by the modeling process of regeneration, which encompassed transient institutions and ultimate purpose.

Like the Fathers, Carolingian writers were not primarily concerned with transformations in nature or with those in art. Their major concern was with the area of thought and belief between nature and art. Thus, in the hybrid language inherited from the Fathers, Carolingian writers found that the formative process of genetic reproduction (as between father and son) was interchangeable with the corrective process of artistic reproduction (as between archetype and copy). They found different aspects of a common mimetic strategy in both; and they were able to see it as the dominant strategy in the progressive regeneration of mankind.

The Neoplatonic concept of egress and return and the Augustinian doctrine of mediated asymmetry between God as archetype and man as image remained clear beneath the surface of Carolingian interpretations of history. Radbertus epitomized the composite result in his depiction of history as Christ moving in the redeemed toward the Father. This amalgam of ancient and modern ideas consisted both of metaphysical and of historical elements. Radbertus and Hincmar of Rheims dealt more richly with the moral concerns of this world than they did with metaphysical contexts. Their propositions, emphases, and conclusions were shaped by conventions of the Latin West, but, even as they wrote, a third scholar was at work whose thinking had been pervaded by doctrines of the Greek Fathers and whose understanding of the transit of Jesus through the process of regeneration differed markedly from theirs. That man was John Scotus Eriugena (ca. 810-ca. 877).

Greek theology took shape outside the intellectual world that, in the West, had crystallized around such disputed topics as predestination and free will. It was also unaffected by the development of theories about Church government and by the growing library of canon law that the ascent of the papacy had stimulated. These disputes and movements forced Western theologians to scrutinize man's historical circumstances and their spiritual meaning. Detached from such needs, the Greek Fathers remained chiefly in the realm of metaphysics. They moved within the intellectual systems of pre-Christian antiquity. They were able to think of redemption as a purging of defects within the natural order, rather than as a drama of crime and punishment played out in the quite different historical order in which Western theologians generally placed it. Evidently, John Scotus or any other theologian who attempted to reconcile Greek authorities with Latin (instead of merely patching them together as, for example, Hincmar did) must reason differently from one whose orientation was homogeneously Western. Such, for example, was the case much later when Thomas Aquinas reconciled Aristotle with Augustine.

In the Carolingian age, John Scotus was singular in the degree to which he relied on Greek theologians and, consequently, to which he anticipated developments in mimetic doctrines that followed the discovery of Greek philosophy by the West, beginning in the twelfth century. Through works by such authors as Gregory of Nyssa and two men whose works he translated, (Pseudo-) Dionysius the Areopagite and Maximus the Confessor, he placed himself in an intellectual lineage that ran back to Plotinus and ultimately to Plato. Though he spent most of his mature years in the Gaul of Radbertus and Hincmar, John Scotus came from the British Isles. He never received high office but remained a pre-eminent master of the liberal arts. Thus, the formation of his thinking and the conditions under which, as a scholar, he applied ideas to life set him apart from such Frankish prelates as the two whom I have discussed. For whatever reasons, John Scotus was by no means typical of his age, but the distinctive conclusions that he reached concerning the regenerative pattern of egress and return provide a point of reference from which we can both summarize prevalent ideas in the ninth century and anticipate ideas associated with the introduction of Greek learning three hundred years later.

Like Radbertus and Hincmar, John Scotus thought that two imitative strategies—mimesis by reversion and mimesis by augmentation—propelled the cycle of egress and return. Like them, he also insisted that both strategies operated through the mediation of Christ and that, because of the mimetic union of Christ with the world through His humanity, the creature's return to God was also a transit of Christ to the Father. However, as he tested those propositions, John Scotus frequently recognized discrepancies between Greek and Latin authorities. Ironically, the harmonizations of patristic views that he devised set him at odds with his own contemporaries and led to synodal condemnations of his views on predestination.

More was at issue than differences on individual points of doctrines. The cardinal points of Christian theology were the two natures of Christ. A salient feature of the career of mimesis in Western culture was that each nature acted as the nucleus of a set of imitative strategies. Metaphysical strategies—for example, those explaining the world's egress from God and return to Him—clustered around Christ as Logos. Historical strategies—for example, those explaining the growth of the Church—clustered around Christ as man. Any theologian employed both sets of strategies to organize his thoughts, just as he affirmed the two natures of Christ. Still, emphases varied, and overwhelming preoccupation with Christ as Logos—and therefore with nature—was at the heart of John Scotus's distinctive teachings.

Mimesis by reversion had at first been associated with Christ as Logos, together with mimesis by augmentation. Mimesis by inversion and subversion had been associated with His humanity. However, these last two strategies had ceased to figure as separate categories of thought. They had been merged into the two other strategies. Notably, they had been combined with the strategy of augmentation through the "concorporation" or "convisceration" of believers in the body of Christ. In the carnality of His saints, the humanity of Christ was manifested with ever increasing variety and richness.

When Radbertus and Hincmar wrote about mimesis by reversion, they stressed the carnality of Christ. Through the corruption of the will by sin, the flesh, too, had been corrupted. Thus, human nature, they reasoned, had been deformed. It stood in need of radical reformation such as Augustine had compared with the melting down of an old statue to recast its material into a new and more beautiful form. They insisted that this re-creation could be performed only through the carnality of Christ, in which the faithful participated indirectly by analogues of belief and directly by the sacraments.

For John Scotus, carnality and humanity were quite different things, and his conception of sin and the corrective process of imitation that it required varied accordingly. "Man," he argued, was "a certain intellectual idea (*notio*) eternally made in the divine Mind." In that idea, created in the image of God, all men were made. But humanity remained incorruptible only in the Word, having been contaminated by sin in actual human beings.[1] Thus, the earthly, mortal body and its sensory faculties did not belong to authentic humanity either as defaced in man or as incorrupt in Christ. Animality, rather than sensualism, was a spiritual energy in the soul. John Scotus argued that the physical body was added to man after the fall, and, consequently, that man could be regarded as having two natures, the one original and immaterial, and the second, a later physical accretion, added after man had sinned. From this assumption, he could proceed to argue that sin was not a flaw in human nature itself but that it was instead something superimposed on an incorruptible human nature, as grime can obscure the brightness of a mirror without damaging its surface. Sin was not a deformation so much as a defilement. Correcting the damages of sin, therefore, did not require a radical re-creation of human nature but a cleansing from "the accretions that render[ed] it unlike its Creator," a purification that could "restore it to its first, unblemished state."[2] Restoration occurred not through carnality but through the incorrupt humanity that Christ raised "above all the angels and celestial powers."[3]

Focusing as they did on the physical existence of Christ, Radbertus and Hincmar argued that mimesis by reversion was not open to all. Doctrines of predestination convinced them that only grace could disclose the mystery of the Word-made-flesh to men and that this revelation had been withheld from many. Only the elect could choose to return to God by the imitation of Christ.

---

[1] *Periphyseon* 4. 7, 9 (*PL* 122: 740, 777). *Periphyseon* (or *De divisione naturae*) was composed between 862 and 866, just after John Scotus had completed his translation of Dionysius the Areopagite and while he was at work on a translation of Maximus the Confessor.

[2] *Periphyseon* 5. 2 (*PL* 122: 862, 864).   [3] *Periphyseon* 5. 20 (*PL* 122: 895).

John Scotus's concept of humanity in the Logos, however, allowed him to argue that the way of reversion was open to all. Instead of opposition between God and nature, Scotus imagined the divine as among the divisions of nature and nature as "not only the created cosmos (*universitas*), but also its creatrix." Therefore the way of reversion was accessible in this world. Saints could die to the world, rising above everything, even themselves, and "crossing over" into God by contemplation while still in the body.[4] The Word by which the soul was purged of its accretions was always open to the sight of human nature.[5] To be sure, there were restrictions. By free choice alone, man could abdicate the rational powers that led to the Creator and embrace the irrational movements of the soul characteristic of brute animals, but only when grace intervened could he freely choose to become spiritual.[6] And yet, at the resurrection, Christ would restore all human nature to the state that He had fulfilled in Himself, and the whole world

[4] *Periphyseon* 5. 21 (*PL* 122: 897). *Periphyseon* 3.1 (*PL* 122: 620f.).

[5] *Periphyseon* 5. 2 (*PL* 122: 864).

[6] *Periphyseon* 4. 5 (*PL* 122: 755). John Scotus retained the concept of animality as a state of mind that permitted writers to conceive of "men without humanity," as the Fathers and pagan philosophers before them had done. His exegesis on the five barley loaves mentioned in John 6 illustrates his position. *Comm. in Joan.* 6. 2. 41–79, in *Commentaire sur l'Évangile de Jean,* ed. Édouard Jeauneau (Paris, 1972. *Sources chrétiennes* 180, 332–336): " 'Qui habet quinque panes ordeaceos.' Quinque panes ordeacei sunt quinque mosaicae legis libri, qui ordeacei non inmerito dicuntur, quia carnales homines illis pascebantur. Ordeum quippe iumentorum est proprie alimentum, non hominum. Carnalis populus adhuc sub littera degens, et vetustatem primi hominis—de quo scriptum est, 'Homo cum in honore esset, non intellexit, comparatus est iumentis insipientibus, et similis factus est illis' [Ps. 48:13]—non deserens, in numero iumentorum brutorum conputabatur ac, per hoc, sola littera, quasi quodam ordeaceo pane mixto cum palea, non autem spirituali medulla ipsius litterae vescebatur.... Quinarius quoque numerus hordeaceum panum quinque corporeos sensus insinuare non incongrue intelligitur. Quanto siquidem quis fidelium in his, quae per quinquepertitum corporis sensum accipiuntur, delectatur, tanto inter bruta animalia ordeo vescentia conputabitur. Dum vero eos, sensus dico, actionis et scientiae incrementum deserens, spirituali esca vescitur, non iam inter bruta, sed inter rationabilia animalia reputetur." John Scotus continues to say that, while carnal men could not scale the height of spiritual understanding, even those who could had to begin by detecting the meaning in sensory things, a stage that would later be superseded. *Comm, in Joan.* 6. 6. 85–96, in *Commentaire,* ed. cit., pp. 364–366. John's insistence that spiritual knowledge had to begin with sensory things ties in with his rejection of the Manichee doctrine that the world accessible to the senses had been made not by God but by the Devil. See Édouard Jeauneau, ed., *Homélie sur le prologue de Jean* (Paris, 1969. *Sources chrétiennes* 151, 18: 288–290).

would die and cross over into God.[7] To be sure, the universal return of men to God, each according to his own capacity, did not mean that all would enjoy eternal blessedness or that those who did would partake of it in the same degree.[8]

The idea that the return to God was universal indicates how widely John Scotus's view of mimesis by reversion differed from the thinking of Radbertus and Hincmar; it also provides a scale of his divergence with regard to mimesis by augmentation. Here, too, his preoccupation with the Logos was the crux of the matter. For Radbertus and Hincmar, the strategy of mimesis by augmentation explained a historical movement: the growth of the Body of Christ, "one Man" made up of the elect, participating in His flesh and blood by the sacraments. For John Scotus, it encompassed mankind and, indeed, the entire world. God made man an epitome of all creation, visible and invisible; man was the cosmic mean unifying the extremes of spirit and body. In a sense, all things were created and lived in man, and, after proceding from him into the existing world, they would eventually return to him and, through him, to God.[9] When, in eternal procession, the Logos went out from the Father and assumed human nature, He thereby assumed the whole world subsisting in it, and His redemption of human nature saved both the visible and the invisible worlds through humanity in the Logos.[10]

Radbertus and Hincmar contended that the augmentation of the Body of Christ occurred through the reformation of the image of Christ in the individual soul. But, just as he widened the movement of return from a historical to a cosmic event, John Scotus also widened augmentation from an event that regenerated created natures into one that transformed creation into God.[11] Creatures became theophanies, or manifestations, of God because God was made in them. The incarnate Christ was a theophany.[12] Intellectual natures, including man's, were made theophanies by knowing God on the general principle that

---

[7] *Periphyseon* 5. 20, 21 (*PL* 122: 895, 898).

[8] *Periphyseon* 5. 27, 36, 38–40 (*PL* 122: 921f., 981, 992–1022).

[9] *Periphyseon* 3. 37; 4. 8; 5. 20 (*PL* 122: 733f.; 744; 895).

[10] *Periphyseon* 5. 24, 25 (*PL* 122: 911, 913).

[11] *Periphyseon* 1. 10. I. P. Sheldon-Williams, ed., *Iohannis Scotti Eriugenae Periphyseon* (*De Divisione Naturae*), (Dublin, 1968. *Scriptores Latini Hiberniae* 7), 1: 58.

[12] *Periphyseon* 5. 24 (*PL* 122: 911f.). Cf. *Comm. in Joan.* 1. 25. 85f., in *Commentaire,* ed. cit., p. 124: "Theophaniae autem sunt omnes creaturae visibiles et invisibiles, per quas deus—et in quibus—sepe apparuit, et apparet, et appariturus est."

the act of knowing made the known part of the knower.[13] However, John Scotus's cosmic vision was more specific. By an act of cosmic emanation, there was a procession, or movement, of God through all things from the highest intellectual nature to the lowest worm, a creative movement by which all things participated in divine being. Thus, "the only-begotten Word of God both makes everything and is made in everything."[14] God and creation, John Scotus wrote, were one and the same thing, one in the process of making and being made, for "the Maker of all, made in all, begins to be eternal."[15] "Whole He makes the universe (*universitas*); whole He becomes in the universe, whole in the whole of the universe, whole in its parts, because He is both whole and part, and neither whole nor part."[16]

Here the realm between nature and art has grown indistinct. In some passages, Scotus appears to have lost sight of it entirely by identifying God with the world, including intellectual natures. Still, the phrase "and neither whole nor part" (that is, in any sense that the human mind could grasp) indicates an avoidance of pantheism. While John Scotus's critics and admirers alike frequently overlooked the distinctions that he consistently made, his concept of God's transcendence did not allow him to identify God completely with the world. For example, he insisted that, even in theophanic union with God, creatures retained their individuality. During this life, John Scotus wrote, Jesus was found in His theophanies, reflected in the minds of those who understood him as though they were mirrors.[17] At the resurrection, souls would be like many individual lamps in a chandelier, each shining with its own flame; what would appear to be a single light would really be the sum of many parts.[18]

All the same, despite his nice distinctions, serious moral perplexities followed from John Scotus's theory that God was made in His crea-

---

[13] *Periphyseon* 1. 7, 9, 10, 64, in Sheldon-Williams ed. cit., pp. 46, 52, 54, 188. *Periphyseon* 4. 9; 5. 7–8, 25 (*PL* 122: 780; 875f., 911).

[14] *Periphyseon* 3. 9, 16, 17; 4. 1 (*PL* 122: 646, 668, 678, 743).

[15] *Periphyseon* 3. 1, 17 (*PL* 122: 621, 678).

[16] *Periphyseon* 4. 5 (*PL* 122: 759).

[17] *Periphyseon* 5. 38 (*PL* 122: 1010). John Scotus was repeating an analogy employed by Augustine (see Chapter 3, note 18), taken up into the *Glossa Ordinaria* on the Scriptures and adopted by other writers, including Thomas Aquinas and Meister Eckhart (see Chapter 8, note 44, and Chapter 9, note 16). On Schleiermacher's similar analogy of a hall of mirrors, see Chapter 14, note 24.

[18] *Periphyseon* 1. 46, in Sheldon-Williams ed. cit., p. 140. See also *Periphyseon* 5. 12 (*PL* 122: 883).

tures and that, through the cycle of egress from God, explication, and return, the world was turning into God.[19] John Scotus recalled Augustine's analogy between the moral world and a painting in which the artist added dark colors for the beauty of the whole. He agreed that no beauty was produced except by the conjunction of likes and unlike, nor any good rightly praised without the contrast of an evil.[20] But God Himself is both like and unlike and the cause and maker of contraries, including the contrariety of evil and goodness. All things subsist in Him. Is God, "the founder of all good things," therefore made in evil creatures as well as in good?[21]

John Scotus's assertion that God and creation were one thing led not only to moral perplexities but it also required him to think in a distinctive way about mimetic regeneration in the space between nature and art. Other scholars of his time, including Radbertus and Hincmar, thought that the mimetic correction of sin was a modeling process that changed, or perfected, the human image but left the divine archetype intact. John Scotus, however, was able to write of the divine Word as the "principal exemplar of all things, visible and invisible," and also to assert that God began to be eternal in His creatures and that, within Himself, He was "infinitely multiplied" through the ramifications of genera and species.[22]

For John Scotus, creating, being, and knowing were related acts. Thus, he was able to write in similar terms about God's growth in knowledge. Maintaining that God's ignorance was ineffable understanding, John Scotus was still able to teach that God did not know events that He had foreknown and predestined until they actually appeared in due course. He did not know the wicked and irrational movements in human minds that He would punish at the Last Judgment, since they were not among the patterns (*rationes*) of all things that He had created in the Logos. Most important, He did not know what He Himself was, except through the succession of His theoph-

---

[19] On the three kinds of movement, straight, spiral, and circular, see *Periphyseon* 1. 74, quoting Dionysius the Areopagite, *De Divinis Nominibus* 9. 8-9, Sheldon-Williams ed. cit., pp. 99f. On God as the beginning, middle, and end, and the circuit, course, and reversion of all things, see *Periphyseon* 3. 1, 17 (*PL* 122: 621f., 675).

[20] *Periphyseon* 5. 35, 36 (*PL* 122: 953, 988). On Augustine, see Chapter 3, note 8.

[21] *Periphyseon* 1. 21, 66, in Sheldon-Williams ed. cit., pp. 96, 192; ordainer of evils, *Periphyseon* 5. 36 (*PL* 122: 982f.); primary exemplar, not cause of any sin or evil, *Periphyseon* 5. 35 (*PL* 122: 959); maker of like and unlike *Periphyseon* 3. 6 (*PL* 122: 637).

[22] *Periphyseon* 3. 9, 17 (*PL* 122: 642, 677f.).

anies, just as the human intellect, His image, could not know what it was except as it appeared in acts of reason.[23]

Instead of a polarity between archetype and image in which only the image was susceptible to change, John Scotus therefore conceived of a dialectical exchange between archetype and image in which both were made and gained in self-knowledge.[24] This was his great contribution to the idea of mediated asymmetry between God and man. Through his concept of God becoming and comprehending what He was in His creatures, John Scotus showed that it was possible to think that the ravages of sin were corrected by a dialectical participation of archetype and image in one another.

However, this was not the whole story. Humanity was the means, not the end, of the world's transformation into God. God was immanent in the world in several regards, but, as the end of the cosmic return, He remained above the hierarchy of creation. Opposites coincided; creation was a work in which God, the artist, was both an integral part of the composition and transcendently beyond it.

"And, Lord, what is this, your transit, except an ascent through infinite degrees of your contemplation? For, in the intellects of those who seek and find, you always make yourself the transition." The transit of Jesus, which is God made in His theophanies, describes an infinite progression because of the divine transcendence. All of His theophanies fail to reveal Him as He is, transcending nature. The seekers find Him in intellectual theophanies, but, not finding Him as He is, beyond the intellect, move ever onward.[25]

[23] *Periphyseon* 2. 23, 28 (*PL* 122: 577, 593–596).

[24] See, e.g., *Periphyseon* 3. 9 (*PL* 122: 646).

[25] *Periphyseon* 5. 38 (*PL* 122: 1010). Cf. *Comm. in Joan.* 1. 32. 36–44, in *Commentaire,* ed. cit., p. 182: "Itaque in suis fidelibus Christus cotidie moritur et ab eis crucifigitur, dum carnales de eo cogitationes, seu spirituales adhuc tamen imperfectas, interimunt, semper in altum ascendentes, donec ad veram eius notitiam perveniant; infinitus enim infinite, etiam in purgatissimis mentibus, formatur." *Comm. in Joan.* 3. 5. 66–69, in *Commentaire,* ed. cit., p. 228: "Nemo ascendit in Christo ad patrem, nisi qui ex spiritu nascitur, ut conformis fiat imaginis filii dei hoc est, ut Christus in illo formetur et unum cum Christo sit."

A considerable difference set John Scotus's idea that God was made in His theophanies from the more limited idea of transit expressed by St. Ambrose: "Et quia de calciamento pedum tractatum sumpsimus, cui alii nisi verbo dei incarnato convenit dici: 'Crura eius columnae marmoreae fundatae super bases aureas'? Solus enim Christus inambulat animis et graditur in mente sanctorum, in quibus velut aureis basibus fundamentisque praetiosis solidata vestigia verbi caelestis haesereunt." *De fide* 3. 10. 74 (*CSEL* 78: 136). Plainly, Ambrose and John Scotus shared with Radbertus the notion that sacramental unity was a fundamental aspect of the transit of Jesus.

Therefore, by his preoccupation with Christ as Logos, John Scotus worked out an idea of correction through dialectical exchange; he envisioned that progression as infinite. Holding to a less metaphysically complex idea of mimesis because of his emphasis on the carnality of Christ, Hincmar of Rheims had framed doctrines of government—particularly a theory of consensus—that also promised continual advance through corrective imitation within the institutions of Christian society. John Scotus had no administrative responsibilities comparable with those of the Archbishop; he had no practical stimulus to apply his theology to politics; he had, moreover, no discernible interest in history.[26] And yet, the time did come when men applied the corrective model of indefinite dialectical progression to human society. It came after the space of centuries, when Western scholars returned to the writings of Scotus and his Greek antecedents. Then, as before, institutions were at hand to make social order conform with theory through arts, laws, and force of arms. "Revolution" was one word that John Scotus learned from the poetic vocabulary of theology; detached from ideas of reversion, the variety of mimesis by augmentation that he explored eventually returned to life in the "poetry of revolution."[27]

[26] The absence of historical argumentation from the *Periphyseon,* his major work, is sufficient to illustrate how little Scotus permitted his metaphysics to be contaminated by history. A few references in his commentary on John and in his homily on the prologue to that Gospel make his attitude explicit. In a cursory fashion, he listed the seven ages of the world, but, to his mind, only the *simplex Christianus* would remain bogged down in the historical accounts of Scripture. To be sure, history was a branch of speculative thought, but it was certainly the lowest, rather like a deep valley, far below the lofty peak of theology. Using another, cosmological metaphor, John Scotus compared history with the earth at the middle of the world, ethics with the abyss surrounding the earth like waters, physics with air, and theology with the fiery empyrean. *Comm. in Joan.* 4. 2. 42–61; 6. 6. 34–42, in *Commentaire,* ed. cit., pp. 288–290, 360. *Hom.* 14, in *Homélie,* ed. cit., pp. 268–272.

[27] John Scotus used *revolutio* as the equivalent of "transmigratio" in discussing the transformation of Christ in Galilee, the type of the "transmutation of human nature into its original glory" by which believers would "pass over into Christ." *Comm. in Joan.* 4. 1. 71–82, in *Commentaire,* ed. cit., pp. 282–284. On John Scotus's conception of theology as a poetic enterprise, see Chapter 5, n. 33. On Marx's idea of "the poetry of revolution," see Chapter 15, at note 53.

Chapter 7

Strategic Reorientations

CHRISTIAN THEOLOGIANS described all human experience as a passage from deformity of sin to conformity with Christ, the image of the invisible God. They believed that mankind advanced from one stage to the next by various mimetic strategies that mediated the asymmetry of archetype and image. With the conversion of Europe, conformity became a political device as well as a spiritual goal. Institutions and tools of government, both ecclesiastical and secular, were applied to advance the reformation of man by force when it could not be secured by persuasion.

However, the conformity enforced by institutions was not identical with that taught by Scripture and tradition. Prophets, apostles, and martyrs had defied established institutions. Christ Himself embraced the poor even as he rebuked the priesthood and refused a worldly kingdom. Seeing His own death draw near, He commanded His followers to sell their cloaks and buy swords. Indeed, such examples as these inspired mimetic enterprises of dissent, but generally such quests to imitate the life of the primitive Church called forth no broad or lasting reorientation of basic strategies in Christian thought. Existing in practice more than in theory, and lacking the preservative of institutionalization, they normally centered about individual leaders and dissipated once the leaders were gone.

A major reorientation of mimetic strategies did occur beginning almost imperceptibly in the eleventh century, one that sharply distinguished between political and spiritual conformity and that eventually prepared for doctrines of revolution as a means of historical progress. Transforming mimesis as a strategy for spiritual conversion into one of political revolution was the work of centuries. It began among those preoccupied with conversion: theologians and mystics. From them, it spread, still in the vernacular of religion, throughout the orders of society. In the slow, evasive ways by which tradition begins as one thing and ends as several others, it finally took root in minds that, while hostile to formal religion, used the heritage of Christian culture against it. The Fathers had similarly used the arts of pre-Christian Greece and Rome against the predominant culture of their day. The duty of an enlightened, militant minority to reform the social world was one of the most persistent characteristics of the mimetic tradition.

In the present chapter, I shall only begin to trace this long course of development. The first step must be to sketch its background, especially the reception of Aristotelian doctrines that answered the collective needs of the eleventh and twelfth centuries and that launched the tradition into directions that it followed throughout the next two hundred years.

Were the cosmic mimesis of the Logos and the penitential *imitatio Christi* paths to truth? In the elaborate system of Christian mimesis, the great danger was idolatry—worshipping the creature instead of the Creator, mistaking the transient image for the enduring reality. Inveighing against the ignorant wisdom of this world, the ascetic, reformer, and cardinal, Peter Damian (ca. 1007–1072), taught that God chose the foolish things to confound the wise and saw this election represented allegorically by the golden calf that Moses cast down, melted, and ground into dust.

For the calf is described as having been gold, since the rite of idolatry is seen as instituted by wise men, and gold is the emblem of wisdom. . . . Of the wise, the Apostle, indeed, says: "For when they came to know God, they glorified him not as God, nor did they give thanks, but they became vain in their imaginations, and their foolish heart was darkened. For in anything that they were wise, they were made fools, and they changed the glory of the incorruptible God into the likeness of an image of corruptible man, and of birds, and of four-footed beasts, and of crawling things [Rom. 1:21–23]." And so, through this vanity of mad wisdom, poets, philosophers, magi, diviners of the stars, and those trained in the skill of all liberal disciplines are wont to adore the emblematic likenesses of demons.[1]

The world of formal learning did not bear this reproach alone. It was more than a rhetorical flourish when Pope Gregory VII (d. 1085) accused the Emperor Henry IV (d. 1106) of idolatry for his simony and disobedience and deposed him; when Gregory's enemies charged that

---

[1] *Sermo* 6 (*PL* 144: 535f.).

the Pope himself was idolatrous in distorting the Scriptures to serve his own interpretations and withdrew their obedience from him; when one candidate in a disputed papal election denounced his opponent as an idol set up by bloody hands under cover of darkness and proclaimed him an antipope; and when religious enthusiasts damned the sacraments with the same sentence and revolted against the Church of hierarchy, law, and property. In each case, the profane was judged to have usurped the place of the sacred by denying that, as something profane, it was an image of a higher reality: that is, by making itself its own archetype. It had crossed the boundary between image and counterfeit. Satan tempted Eve with an invitation to the idolatry of disobedience: "Ye shall be as gods."

There remained the terrifying doubt that faith did not discover an underlying truth, that there was no substance of things hoped for or evidence of things not seen. An obscure German monk heard the Tempter whisper in his ears: "Why wear yourself out in such vain toil? Where is the hope that you kept until now in Scripture? Could you not demonstate from your own encounters, most foolish of all mortals, that both the testimony of Scripture and the imagination of men are without reason or rule? Do you now know from experience that the telling of the divine books is proven to be one thing and the life and practices of men quite another?"[2] Was there an underlying unity, a stable, universal truth in sacred knowledge?

The austere reformer and mystic, St. Bernard (1091–1153), sensed the danger of this question in the thought of his philosophical prey, Abelard (1079–1142), for he saw that Abelard's theology made religious faith a matter of opinion. Deny that theology stood on a "solid and unshakable foundation of truth," admit ambiguities in understanding the truth revealed in the Incarnation and Resurrection, doubt everything—and faith loses its substance. It becomes private opinion, "a phantasy of empty conjectures." Abelard's relentless logic exposed irreconcilable disharmony among the doctors of the Church. It postulated no necessary unity or consensus, and hence it challenged belief in a tradition that was ever old and ever new, always and everywhere the same. In this skepticism toward the unity of truth, St. Bernard grasped the loss of certitude that tormented the German monk and that had beset even the exalted spirituality of the Archbishop of Canterbury, St.

---

[2] Othloh of St. Emmeram, *Liber de temptationibus suis et scriptis* (*PL* 146: 32).

Anselm (1033–1109): "And so, O Lord, Thou art not simply that than which a greater cannot be thought; rather Thou art something greater than can be thought. . . . Thou art wholly present everywhere, and I do not see Thee. In Thee I move and in Thee I have my being, and I cannot come near to Thee. Thou art within me and about me and I feel Thee not."[3]

Into the void created by these questions came theories of change framed, or inspired, by Aristotle. Some authors seized upon the newly discovered doctrines. A few combined them with John Scotus's teachings. But their conclusions sounded the alarm of heresy. By giving themselves over enthusiastically to pre-Christian texts and to exegeses by Jewish and Islamic writers, authors risked throwing overboard the theology both of Creation and Redemption, including doctrines about Christ's humanity. Similarly, the newly received theories of casuality had nothing to do with the Creation or the Incarnation. They taught that the world came into being not by a free and gratuitous call of life out of chaos but by the necessary unfolding of the substance of God, or by God's transformation of pre-existing matter, or by the filtering of divine power down from God through a hierarchy of secondary causes. The great Arabic commentator on Aristotle, Averroës, informed Latin writers that it was merely using a figure of speech to say that the world began. The world, he argued, could never have begun historically; otherwise, the cosmos would have been disfigured by a vacuum before it appeared. Likewise, neither time nor motion ever began or would end. Sin and salvation, the key elements in doctrines of the Incarnation, had no necessary place in a world ruled by these genetic, mechanistic, or (it might be) pantheistic reflexes.

The strategic reorientation that began in the twelfth century went even further. Aristotle and his commentators provided new ways of thinking about the asymmetry between image and archetype. In the mimetic tradition, the world had always been depicted as a composition made by God. Aristotelianisms made it possible to think of the artist not as standing apart from the composition and shaping it from the outside but as an integral part of the composition. Thus, one could think of God actually becoming in the continual movement of creation. Drawing mainly on patristic authorities, John Scotus had been able to teach similar doctrines and still retain the ideas of the world as

---

[3] *Proslogion* 15, 16 in *A Scholastic Miscellany: Anselm to Ockham,* trans. E. R. Fairweather (Philadelphia, 1956), p. 84.

a hierarchy and of God as transcendent above the hierarchy even while, by divine procession, He made and was made in all things. Equipped with non-Christian texts, writers from the twelfth century onward were able, if they chose, to abandon the doctrine of God as a changeless creator above the apex of the hierarchy of life. Such was the first great shift in the strategy of mimesis by augmentation: the transcendent hierarchy of life was flattened into an organic unity, and the principle of change itself became, in some sense, subject to change.

A second major shift followed from the flattening of hierarchies. As a way of thinking about composition, mimesis had been from the beginning a doctrine of relationships. While the hierarchy stood, these relationships moved vertically toward a common transcendent source. Once the transcendent hierarchy was flattened into organic unity, a vastly more complex explanation was needed. The biological unities embedded in Aristotelian doctrines provided a scheme. They took for granted that an organism was made up of component parts related to each other in many different ways. The end, or object, that gave the organism its direction and meaning was immanent, within the organism itself, rather than transcendent outside and above it. Mediation involved more than the one-to-one relation of image to archetype. It involved the interaction of many relationships on each other. A change in the relation between any two components had implications for the whole. The great subject of study came to be a genetic relation of relations, the mutual reflex of the whole and its parts in the mediating process of growth.

Of course, these two major changes in thought about mediation between archetype and image had important implications for historical thought as well as for concepts of nature. Clearly, if the end of the historical movement or institution were thought to be immanent, the object of change need not be to return to a primiodial, changeless heavenly source but rather to realize some good that was organically unfolding in this world.

However, not all writers who employed the strategy of augmentation accepted these two new options. Thus, the reorientation of mimetic strategies took a wide variety of directions. I shall begin by discussing the thought of Thomas Aquinas, a writer who embraced doctrines of Aristotle and his commentators and yet continued to imagine the world as a hierarchic order and to teach that mankind's advancement resulted from a permanent asymmetry between God as archetype and man as His image. Still, Thomas did combine the older concept of mediation as transcendent change with that of mediation of genetic growth. I shall then go beyond this particular case to general reorientations in mysticism and humanism, where the new options prevailed and where, gradually detaching itself from reversion, the concept of mimesis by augmentation received fresh and powerful expressions.

Thomas Aquinas's Recapitulation
Theory of Tradition

FROM CLASSICAL ANTIQUITY onward, transmitters of the mimetic tradition imagined two currents of knowledge: one consisted of formal disciplines and objective data, open to all; the other comprised esoteric operations of belief, disclosed to the few. Among Christians, it was taught that sacred doctrine was available to all, but understood by few, among whom there was a further distinction between the simple and the wise. The esoteric strand was conveyed "from faith to faith" within a militant minority, into whose hands was given the plan, the impulse, and the responsibility for the transformation of the world.

This view persisted in the thought of Thomas Aquinas. There are many resonances between his doctrines and those of earlier writers, including Augustine and Hincmar. However, Thomas's profound study of Aristotle and his commentators led him to explore the mimetic operations of belief in ways that infused new possibilities into old ideas. There were, primarily, two points of innovation: his emphasis on the integrity of individual experience, and his Christology—above all his interpretation of Christ's nature as Logos in the light of casuality. Since Thomas died before he completed the last part of his *Summa Theologiae,* where he planned to set forth his Christology in a systematic way, one finds the implications of his thought most fully developed in works that he wrote as an exegete and preacher, rather than in those that he wrote as a philosopher.

True to Aristotle, Thomas rejected the Platonic contention that the real man was an immaterial category, the abstract Humanity of all existing men, and that men of flesh and blood were human only by derivation from that ideal.[1] To the contrary, he argued, humanity was real-

---

[1] *Comm. in lib. Dionys. de div. nom.,* prologue (*Opera* 15: 259). Cf. *Lect. in Joan.* 1.1.4 (*Opera* 10: 289). All references to *Opera* are from the Parma edition.

ized in the carnality and temperaments of individual men and women. True to Aristotle, he wrote: "Humanity can not be without the man."[2] Certainly, "Just as the different members of a body are parts of the person of one man, so also all men are parts and, after a fashion, members of human nature. For this reason, Porphyry says that, by participation of the species, many men are one man."[3] But man was the image of God in the freedom of his will, and this, in itself, prevented the individual from being absorbed into the anonymity of the species.[4]

The common traits of human nature, particularly intellect, made it possible for men to teach other men, but, in every case, the act of knowing issued from the choice and engaged the faculties of the individual person. This insistence that tradition took place essentially in individual experience, led Thomas to the further conclusions that each

---

[2] F.J.A. de Grijs, *Goddelijk Mensontwerp. Een Thematische Studie Over het Beeld Gods in de Mens Volgens het Scriptum van Thomas van Aquine* (Antwerp, 1967) 2: 391. Klaus Kremer, "Wer ist das eigentlich—der Mensch? Zur Frage nach dem Menschen bei Thomas von Aquin," *Trierer Theologische Zeitschrift* 84 (1975): 77–79.

[3] *Comm. in Rom.* 5. 3 (*Opera* 13: 51–52): "Est enim considerandum quod sicut diversa corporis membra partes sunt personae unius hominis: ita omnes homines sunt partes, et quasi quaedam membra humanae naturae. Unde et Porphyrius dicit quod participatione speciei plures homines sunt unus homo." *Summa Theologiae* Ia IIae. Q.81. A.1. On Adam as the "head" of all mankind and on Christ as the second Adam, see Yves M. J. Congar, "L'historicité de l'homme selon Thomas d'Aquin," *Doctor Communis* 22 (1969): 301f., and " 'Traditio' and 'Sacra Doctrina' bei Thomas von Aquin," in *Kirche und Ueberlieferung,* ed. Johannes Betz and Heinrich Fries (Freiburg-i.-B., 1960. Festschrift Josef Rupert Geiselmann), pp. 179, 205–206.

[4] William Hoye, *Actualitas Ominum Actuum: Man's Beatific Vision of God as Apprehended by Thomas Aquinas* (Meisenheim-am-Glan, 1975. Monographien zur philosophischen Forschung, Bd 116), pp. 198, 205, 221–227. Thomas's doctrine that God saved individuals, not the species, also entered into this teaching. See Walter Mostert, *Menschwerdung. Eine historische und dogmatische Untersuchung über das Motiv der Inkarnation des Gottessohnes bei Thomas von Aquin* (Tübingen, 1978. Beiträge zur historischen Theologie, Bd 57), pp. 40, 45, 156–157. Cf. *Summa contra Gentiles* 3. 113: "Si igitur homo haberet directionem in suis actibus solum secundum congruentiam speciei, non esset in ipso agere vel non agere, sed oporteret quod sequeretur inclinationem naturalem toti speciei communem ut contingit in omnibus irrationalibus creaturis. Manifestum est igitur quod rationalis creaturae actus directionem habet, non solum secundum speciem, sed etiam secundum individuum." See Giovanni Baget Bozzo, "San Thommaso e la teologia della Storia," *Renovatio: Rivista di teologia e cultura* 2 (1967): 117: The great object of historical process is man's assimilation to God. "La via di assimilazione si realizza concretamente sotta i nostri occhi e noi la connosciamo soltanto attraverso l'azione dei giusti." (See also p. 113).

of the saved recapitulated the entire tradition of faith, and that the body of Christ was the aggregate of all such recapitulations.

Thomas began with the experience of knowing, and, like Augustine and many others, he defined three tiers of knowledge. Thomas's order was: knowing by participation through the intellect, in the light of reason; knowing by participation through the will, in the light of faith; and knowing by participation, through love, in the light of glory. Thomas also identified each avenue of knowledge with a mode of life: intellect, with the life of the flesh (*vita carnis,* or *vita mortalis*), which all men shared; faith, with the life of grace (*vita gratiae,* or *vita spiritualis*), which restored the elect in the world as to their minds, but not as to their bodies; and, finally, love, with the life of glory (*vita gloriae,* or *vita aeterna*), the fruition of Christ, "our glory," partly in the world and fully in the next.[5] For Thomas, thus, tradition was not a matter of custom or history so much as it was a state of mind. Thomas certainly recognized collective exoteric tradition that passed from mind to mind across the years, changing as it moved. But he also conceived of an esoteric tradition of faith that was not the mediated handing on of a torch from generation to generation, but an immediate relationship between each believer and Christ. Thus, through his experience, tradition could be, and was, fully present to each believer regardless of where he stood in the sequence of years.

Christ was the universal object of faith in every stage of sacred history: the "day of the law of nature" (before the Covenant with Abraham), the "day" of faith (divided into two parts, the "day of the written law," the Old Testament, and that "of the law of grace," the New Testament), and finally the "day of glory."[6] Before the Incarnation, Christ came to Abraham, not in the flesh, to be sure, but in the mind; and the mystery of Christ's passion was imitated beforehand under the prefigurative types and shadows of Old Testament ceremonies. Assuredly, past, present, and future became simultaneous in the regen-

---

[5] On the *vita mortalis* (or *carnis*), see *Comm. in 1. Cor.* 15. 3 (*Opera* 13: 282), and *Comm. in Gal.* 2. 6 (*Opera* 13: 400). On the *vita spiritualis* (or *gratiae*), see *Comm. in 1 Cor.* 15.3 (*Opera* 13: 282f.), and *Comm. in Gal.* 2. 6 (*Opera* 13: 400). On the *vita aeterna* (or *gloriae*), see *Comm. in 1. Cor.* 15. 7 *Opera* 13: 291). On the equation, knowledge = being = life, see *Lect. in Joan.* 5. 4. 5 (*Opera* 10: 391): "Sic ergo vitam a Christo qui est Dei sapientia participamus inquantum anima nostra ab ipso sapientiam percipit. Haec autem vita intellectualis perficitur in vera cognitione divinae sapientiae quae est vita aeterna."

[6] *Lect. in Joan.* 2. 1. 1., and 4. 5. 1 (*Opera* 10: 330, 374). Aquinas equates Christ with "the day" or with the sun of justice, *Lect in Joan.* 9. 1. 4, and 9. 1. 6; (*Opera* 10: 465).

erative experience of modern Christians not only by faith but also through the works of Scriptural commentators. By unlocking the literal and spiritual meanings of Scripture, they realized in their own minds and in those of their readers the unity of faith and hope running through all stages of sacred history, the one glory in which all the just would be subsumed, and in which, through Christ, "the glory of the Lord," they already participated imperfectly in this world.[7]

Like the redemptive experiences of patriarchs, apostles, and saints, the branches of wisdom converged at the Cross. This, Thomas wrote, was signified by the tablet that Pontius Pilate ordered affixed to the Cross, proclaiming Jesus as king in three languages. Unwittingly, Pilate disclosed a mystery. For Hebrew signified "theological philosophy, because knowledge of divine things was conveyed to the Jews." Greek signified natural philosophy, "for the Greeks toiled over speculation about natural things." Latin too expressed a hidden meaning, "because moral science flourished most of all among the Romans." The placard was written in these three languages, Thomas concluded, "so that all methods of understanding might thus be reduced to captivity in the service of Christ."[8]

This vision of Christ dominating all branches of formal thought involved historical elements. But it was hostile to tradition as mediated, collective wisdom. For the kingship of Christ was certainly hidden to the Jews, Greeks, and Romans. And, Thomas wrote, even the Christian who would contemplate the mysteries of Christ must leave himself, and fleshly custom, behind.[9] The blindness of the Jews, the errors of the Greek, and the ignorance of the Romans to Christ's dominance illustrated that the structure of redemptive knowing fell outside the experience of unbelievers. Through His works of creation, Thomas wrote, God revealed His wisdom, power, and excellence to all men, but He did not manifest Himself to the world or to worldly men. Again and again, Thomas returned to the Christian's duty to preach to the unbelieving world, to seek the conversion of his neighbor, especially in hard times when the perversity of the evil increased. Still, Thomas

---

[7] *Lect. in Joan.* 8. 5. 5 (*Opera* 10: 454). *Summa Theologiae* Ia IIae. Q.102. A.5, and Q.103. A.2. *Summa Theologiae* I. Q.1. A.10. Ia IIae. Q.103. A.3. See *Lect. in Joan.* 4. 4. 4 (*Opera* 10: 373), on the single glory of the just in the Old and New Testaments. See *Comm. in 2. Cor.* 3. 3 (*Opera* 13: 316), and cf. *Lect. in Joan.* 1. 8. 1 (*Opera* 10: 307), on the Apostles seeing the *claritas* that Thomas identified with glory, "per praesentiam corporalem."

[8] *Lect. in Joan.* 14. 6. 4.; 19. 4. 2.; 20. 1. 3 (*Opera* 10: 558; 618; 624).

[9] Ibid.

held, it was not the responsibility of Christians to expose sacred teachings to the derision of the infidel. Instead, it was right to hide truth in parables and figures, according to the words, "Give not that which is holy to dogs."[10]

Thus far, I have noted that the experience of redemptive knowledge was an event consisting of three phases or tiers, and that this structure replicated, in the experience of the individual, the entire redemptive history of the elect. I may now go a step further. My description indicates that Thomas's structure of the experience of knowing was dynamic. The various kinds of imitation that Thomas believed impelled it forward must now be identified. The essential fact was that Thomas preserved the asymmetry between man as image and God as archetype. Despite infusions of Aristotelian views, this Platonic asymmetry persisted, incapable of being brought into equilibrium and reconcilable only by mediation. I therefore turn to his doctrine of Christ, a double exemplarism according to which the incarnate Word was the exemplar of humanity and the Logos, the universal exemplar of creation, of justification, and of unity. Doctrines of causality taught by Aristotle and, especially, by his commentators colored Thomas's teachings on the Logos.

As man, Christ was the exemplar of humanity. The model of life that Christ set forth in the Gospels indicated an austere side of the event of regenerative knowing. Where there was likeness, there was also unlikeness, and Thomas's doctrines reveal that a call to hatred came of insisting that the faithful imitate Christ, who, having loved His disciples, loved them to the end and laid down His life for them. Where likeness predominated, the consequences were positive. By participation in Christ, who was God by essence, Christians became God, and, since God was love, it was only right that the insignia of Christ's soldiers were insignia of love. "Likeness," Thomas wrote, "is the cause of love." But the association of love with the conversion of others, in Thomas's mind, indicates a severe militance.[11]

If similarity were the cause of love, then dissimilarity was the cause

[10] *Comm. in lib. Boeth. de Trin.* Q.3. A.1 (*Opera* 17: 367). Thomas insisted that God did not manifest Himself to the world or to worldly men. *Lect. in Joan.* 14. 6. 4 (*Opera* 10: 558). *Summa Theologiae* I. Q.1. *Comm. in lib. Dionys. de div. nom.*, prologue (*Opera* 15: 259). On the need of preaching, most of all in evil times when converts are oppressed, see *Lect. in Joan.* 8. 8. 1 (*Opera* 10: 459).

[11] See below, notes 12–13, 15. *Lect. in Joan.* 7. 1. 6, and 17. 3. 6 (*Opera* 10: 426, 596), quoting Ecclesiasticus 13: 19, "Omne animal diligit sibi simile, et odio habet dissimile." *Lect. in Joan.* 15. 4. 3 (*Opera* 10: 571): "Hic ponit causam quare apostoli habentur odio a mundo, quae est dissimilitudo."

of hatred.[12] Thomas explained that the Apostles were hated by the world because they were unlike it. Enmity still ran between the world and the saints because the world was in death, while they were in life; because they endeavored to correct it, rebuking its deeds; and because they sought modes of life—poverty, mourning, hunger, and bitterness—that displeased the world.[13] The saints were universally hated by the world, as Christ had been, and from that hatred came persecution.[14] For their part, it was by contempt of the world that Christians became worthy to receive the grace of the Holy Ghost. Chiefly by contempt, the world was overcome; and it was faith that disclosed the invisible things for which the world was to be despised.[15]

The Church might suffer persecution; but it might also punish. Augustine had justified persecution of the Donatists, calling also for human clemency, and Thomas likewise insisted that the iniquity in wicked men should be persecuted, even while mercy was shown to the common human nature in them.[16] It would be as good to kill a sinner as to kill a wild beast, since, by virtue of his reason, an evil man was worse than a beast and could do ten thousand times more harm.[17]

A physician did not hesitate to cut off a less noble member to save one that was more noble or to preserve the entire body. Likewise, in human affairs, the body was more noble than external things, and the soul more noble than the body. It was right to impose punishments on material goods, or on the body, for the sake of the soul. Thus, it was right for the children of Sodom to be killed with their parents for the good of their souls. They did not deserve to die, but it was better that they not live to be punished yet more cruelly for piling sin on top of sin as they imitated the malice of their forebears.[18] Taking up the same theme in another context, Thomas observed that wise children dissociated themselves from their parents. "We ought," Thomas wrote, "to

---

[12] *Lect. in Joan.* 15. 4. 2 (*Opera* 10: 570–571): "Sic ergo quia in amore amicitiae similitudo causa est amoris, dissimilitudo causa odii; inde est quod mundus odio habet quod suum non est et sibi dissimile et diligit, idest dilectione amicitiae, quod suum est." On the importance of fear and terror as a stimulus of spiritual advance in Thomas's views, see André Guindon, *La pédagogie de la crainte dans l'histoire du salut selon Thomas d'Aquin* (Montreal, 1975. Recherches 15. Théologie), pp. 151, 361, 407.

[13] *Lect. in Joan.* 7. 1. 6 (*Opera* 10: 426).

[14] *Lect. in Joan.* 7. 1. 6, and 15. 4. 1 (*Opera* 10: 426, 570).

[15] *Summa Theologiae* Ia IIae. Q.106. A.1. *Comm. in Hebr.* 11. 7 (*Opera* 13: 769).

[16] *Comm. in Gal.* 6. 2 (*Opera* 13: 439–440).

[17] *Summa Theologiae* IIa IIae. Q.64. AA.2–3. *Sententia libri ethicorum* 7. 6 (*Opera* 21:208).

[18] *Lect. in Joan.* 8. 9. 1 (*Opera* 10: 463).

support, love, and revere parents as far as nature is concerned, but to hate them for the ways in which they turn us from God." Light has no communion with darkness, and those who are powerfully drawn to their parents are well advised to root out this carnal affection, making themselves orphans so that God could adopt them as His sons.[19]

The saints willingly sought and endured the hatred of the world and its persecution, embraced affliction, poverty, and sorrow, and denied carnal affections. Christ, their exemplar, had suffered anguish and wept, mystically teaching that those who rose from their sins ought to persist in continual mourning all their days. By this same example, they were assured that, going forth weeping and casting their seed, they would come again rejoicing, bearing their sheaves with them.[20]

How was mimesis a strategy of progress in this regard? Unlikeness was the reason for conflict against heretics and unbelievers and, within the Church, for fraternal correction, for clarification of doctrine by dispute, and for the rebuke of bishops who abused their office and who declined to adhere to Christ, the "unfailing exemplar of holiness."[21] Thus, Thomas's doctrine of the imitation of Christ, as exemplar of humanity,[22] encased a strategy for moral advancement by criticism, chatisement, and reform. Insofar as these acts enlarged the faith of individual believers, they also advanced the formation of the body of Christ.

Christ's humanity was but one instrument of salvation. When Thomas thought about humanity, its weakness came vividly to mind. Christ, the *exemplum humanitatis*,[23] endured hunger, thirst, and weariness.[24] Sorrowing and perturbed at heart, He suffered, groaned inwardly, wept,[25] and died. If Christ had taught the Apostles "on the basis of His humanity, according to Himself (*ex ejus humanitate secundum se*), He would have lied; for 'God is true; but every man, a liar.' "[26] Not Christ as man, but Christ as Logos, was the Son of God, the first-born of all creation.

Both natures were necessary for salavation; but the Logos was the exemplary cause of life. Therefore, man did not live by conformity with the humanity of Christ, but by conformity with the Word, "since

---

[19] *Lect. in Joan.* 14. 5. 1, and 19. 4. 10 (*Opera* 10: 554, 620).

[20] *Lect. in Joan.* 11. 6. 1, and 12. 4. 8 (*Opera* 10: 498, 513).

[21] *Comm. in I. Cor.* 11. 1 (*Opera* 13: 234).

[22] *Lect. in Joan.* 13. 2. 4 (*Opera* 10: 529).   [23] Ibid.

[24] *Lect. in Joan.* 4. 1. 8 (*Opera* 10: 361).

[25] *Lect. in Joan.* 2. 1. 4; 11. 6. 1; 13. 4. 1; 16. 2. 2 (*Opera* 10: 332; 498; 534; 578).

[26] *Lect. in Joan.* 5. 6. 3 (*Opera* 10: 396).

the life of the soul came by the Word alone." The resurrection of souls will come about through the Word; but the resurrection of bodies will occur when the bodies of the faithful are conformed with the body of Christ through the life of glory. Thus, the resurrection of bodies takes place through the Word-made-flesh.[27]

The magnitude of the asymmetry between man and his divine archetype becomes apparent as Thomas unfolds his doctrines on the causality of the Logos. In his lectures on John, Thomas adverts to the Word's "infallible and all-sufficient" exemplarism from three aspects, other than the moral exemplarism given by the incarnate Christ. In the first place, the Word is the exemplar of creation.[28] The Word was the model of the cosmos, elevated above it, and the Word was also the fountainhead from which all things emanated. As exemplar, the Word was, finally, the bearer of the grace that the act of creation was, the grace by which the world was informed and drawn back to the source of its being.

In the second place, the Word was the exemplary cause of justification.[29] For Thomas, this point of overlap with Christ as "exemplar of humanity" meant that the process of salvation could be understood in the mimetic terms of St. Paul: through baptism we are configured with the death of Christ, and thus are buried with Him.[30] At the resurrection, through Christ's exemplary causality, our souls are conformed, not with Christ's humanity, but with the Word, and our bodies, with the body of Christ, through glory.[31] And "the intellect of man is said to be glorified when it, thus deified and transcending all material things, is raised to the cognition of God, for through this it is made a participant of His glory: 'We, however, with face uncovered, mirroring the glory of the Lord are transformed into the same image' (II Cor. 3:10)."[32] Indeed, we are deified—transformed into God—since the splendor of God is nothing else than His substance.[33]

In the third place, the Word is cause and exemplar of unity,[34] and all lines come together at this point. Having participated in the being of

---

[27] *Lect. in Joan.* 5. 5. 2 (*Opera* 10: 394).

[28] *Lect. in Joan.* 13. 3. 3 (*Opera* 10: 532). See also ibid., 1. 5. 1 (*Opera* 10: 301): "Sicut in artificio manifestatur ars artificis, ita totus mundus nihil aliud est quam quaedam repraesentatio divinae sapientiae in mente Patris conceptae."

[29] *Lect. in Joan.* 5. 5. 2 (*Opera* 10: 394).

[30] *Lect. in Joan.* 3. 1. 2 (*Opera* 10: 345).

[31] *Lect. in Joan.* 5. 5. 2 (*Opera* 10: 394).

[32] *Lect. in Joan.* 13. 6. (*Opera* 10: 539–540).

[33] *Lect. in Joan.* 1. 11 (*Opera* 10: 312).

[34] *Lect. in Joan.* 17. 5. 2 (*Opera* 10: 597).

God, men had virtual likeness to God but not, as did the Word, an identical one with Him. Thomas meticulously held to the proposition that, whatever union there might be between God and man, and while God addressed men as "gods" (e.g., Exod. 7:1; Ps. 81:9): "It is one thing to be called gods, and another to be God. Whence the Word is said absolutely to be God, since it is God according to its nature, and not by participation as are men and angels."[35] "For the love by which the Son loves the disciples is a certain likeness of this love by which the Father loves the Son. For since to love someone is to wish him good, the Father loves the Son according to the divine nature inasmuch as He wishes for Him His own infinite good, which He has, by communicating to Him exactly the same nature that He has ... He also loves Him according to human nature. . . . And according to neither of these did the Son love the disciples, for neither did He love them that they might be God by nature, nor that they might be united with God in person; but He loved them after a certain likeness to these ways, namely that they might be gods by participation of grace. 'I have said, ye are gods' (Ps. 81:61). 'Through whom He hath given us great and precious promises, that through this we may be made sharers of the divine nature' (II Pet. 1:4). And, again, that they might be assumed into unity of feeling, since 'he who adheres to God is one spirit' (I Cor. 6:17). 'They whom He did foreknow to be conforming images of His son that He might be the firstborn among many brethren' (Rom. 8:29)."[36]

All forms existed through the Word, since it was the universal exemplar, the *ars plena rationum viventium,* the wisdom in which are the *rationes omnium agendorum,* the Light that manifested all things that were manifested.[37]

If the Light were sufficient to make all things plain, what need was there of testimonies like those of John the Baptist? And what about John the Evangelist, who even in this life mounted up like an eagle and contemplated the Word of God in the bosom of the Father? Did the visionaries become the Light that they saw? Was it possible that the asymmetry between man and his divine archetype had indeed been resolved?

At this point, likeness could shade into identity.[38] Going beyond

---

[35] *Lect. in Joan.* 1. 1. 3 (*Opera* 10: 288).

[36] *Lect. in Joan.* 15. 2. 1 (*Opera* 10: 565). See also ibid., 1. 8. 1–2 (*Opera* 10: 307).

[37] *Lect. in Joan.* 1. 4 (*Opera* 10: 297).

[38] Cf. Hoye, *Actualitas Omnium Actuum,* p. 135: "There comes a point in one's study of St. Thomas Aquinas when one seriously wonders how Thomas can possi-

metaphysics, the theology of faith renders the possibility all the clearer when it holds that God is actually present in the mind of the believer. More than resemblance was at issue—more than the theory that "every thing that proceeds from something has the likeness of Him from whom it proceeds. Wherefore, all who truly know according to their respective levels in the procession from God have various knowledge of Him."[39] The fact was that human knowledge of God derived from the Word; the knowledge of the Word was the font and root from which all the knowledge of the faithful derived.[40] The intellectual light itself—the Logos, "the true Light which lighteth every man that cometh into the world" (John 1:9)—was shed forth in all human souls; and it "is nothing else than a participated likeness of the uncreated Light in which are contained the external exemplars."[41] Even more, all cognition was caused by participation of the divine Word[42]; for the human mind was to the divine Light as the air was to the light of the sun: "although the air is capable of receiving the light of the sun, yet, considered in itself, it is dark. Thus, the 'Light'—that is the life that is the light of men—'shines in darkness'—that is, in created souls and minds."[43]

There was one Truth, one Light, and all lesser truths reflected its brilliance. In the firmament of lights, Christ was the sun; the Virgin, the moon; and the saints, the stars, arranged in due order.[44] God gave the riches of glory abundantly to all the saints, but most amply to Apostles, and, after them, to teachers, by whom others are instructed

---

bly avoid pantheism or panentheism." See also ibid., p. 116. Hoye's solution is at p. 143.

[39] *Lect. in Joan.* 7. 3. 7 (*Opera* 10: 433).

[40] *Lect. in Joan.* 17. 6. 2 (*Opera* 10: 601).

[41] *Summa Theologiae* I. Q.84, A.5.

[42] *Lect. in Joan.* 6. 2. 1 (*Opera* 10: 405).

[43] *Lect. in Joan.* 1. 3 (*Opera* 10: 295).

[44] *Comm. in 1. Cor.* 15. 6 (*Opera* 13: 288). See also, *Lect. in Joan.* 1. 8. 3 (*Opera* 10: 308). *Lect. in Joan.* 1. 10. 3 (*Opera* 10: 311): "Dicendum est, quod ipse est per suam essentiam veritas increata, quae aeterna est, et non facta, sed a Patre est genita; sed per ipsum factae sunt omnes veritates creatae, quae sunt quaedam participationes et refulgentiae primae veritatis, quae in animabus sanctis relucent." See also his use of Augustine's metaphor of one face reflected in many mirrors, a metaphor that he appears not to have used except in quotation from the Father, perhaps because it evoked Averroistic connotations. *Summa Theologiae* I. Q.16. A.6 *Quaest. disp. de veritate* 1. 4. On the use of this metaphor by Augustine, John Scotus Eriugena, and Meister Eckhart, see Chapter 3, note 18, Chapter 7, note 17, and Chapter 9, note 16. On Schleiermacher's related metaphor of a hall of mirrors, see Chapter 14, note 24.

and called to the faith. The greatest doctors had an increment of glory beyond what all have in common; "wherefore, according to Daniel 12:3, the taught are likened to the brightness of the firmament, but teachers to the stars: 'And they that be taught shall shine as the brightness of the firmament, and they that instruct many in righteousness, as the stars for ever and ever.' "[45] At the resurrection, each would shine in his own magnitude of glory, according to the degree of his love.[46] Here and now, where the righteousness of God was revealed from faith to faith, their manifestations of Christ, the one light in every age, already constituted a single great constellation.[47]

Was the consequence that—in Christ or in the saints—the Holy Spirit suppressed the individual soul and reduced it to a mindless tool of divine power? Or was it possible that, by some process of emanation, all men were simply concrete expressions of one divine being? Thomas's insistence on the mimetic distance between divine archetype and human image kept him from accepting either of these possibilities, and it also safeguarded his doctrine of free will. For, although the individual will was not its own cause or end, the integrity of its freedom was basic to the place of humanity as a means by which divine knowledge passed to men through other men. Indeed, it belonged to the wider generative process by which God "employs secondary causes so that the beauty of order may be preserved in the universe and also that [God] may communicate to creatures the dignity of causality."[48] Was it not because of impairment to the freedom of the will that children and the insane were forbidden to receive the Eucharistic Body of Christ?[49]

Thomas, therefore, had more than one reason to argue that "God performs all our works in us."[50] And yet he preserved the freedom of

---

[45] *Comm. in Eph.* 1. 6.(*Opera* 13: 453). Interestingly, Thomas omits prophets from the hierarchy of apostles, prophets, teachers, and miracle workers in 1 Cor. 12:28–29.

[46] *Comm. in Hebr* 11. 8 (*Opera* 13: 771).   [47] See above, notes 44, 49.

[48] *Summa Theologiae* I. Q.23. A.8. See above n. 37.

[49] *Lect. in Joan.* 6. 7. 2 (*Opera* 10: 419).

[50] *Lect. in Joan.* 1. 5; 6. 3. 7; 15. 3. 2 (*Opera* 10: 300; 409; 568). *Comm. in Rom.* 4. 1 (*Opera* 13: 41). Hoye, *Actualitas Omnium Actuum,* pp. 100–105. See also *Lect. in Joan.* 15. 1. 5 (*Opera* 10: 564): "Opera enim nostra aut sunt virtute naturae, aut ex gratia divina. Si virtute naturae, cum omnes motus naturae sint ab ipso Verbo Dei, nulla natura ad aliquid faciendum moveri potest sine ipso. Si vero virtute gratiae, cum ipse sit auctor gratiae . . . manifestum est quod nullum opus meritorium sine ipso fieri potest [Thomas here quotes 2. Cor. 3:5]. Si ergo nec etiam cogitare possumus nisi ex Deo, multo minus nec alia."

the will; asymmetry remained, mediated but unresolved, between God, as archetype, and man, as image. Thomas dismissed the idea that the regenerate Christian became an involuntary tool of the Holy Spirit. Likewise, he rejected the pantheistic (or panentheistic) options that these cosmological arguments opened. Since the cause "becomes" in the effect by likeness, one could say that God, having imparted His likeness to all things, was moved toward a goal by all things, or that He proceeded to all things. Thomas avoided both dangers by holding that one could speak metaphorically in this way—as Dionysius the Areopagite had done—but not properly.[51] Perhaps he conceived of the logical possibility that John Scotus had taught four hundred years before and that Meister Eckhart (or one of his followers) expressed a century later: that God became in His creatures.[52] But similitude by participation, such as ran between creatures and God, was by no means equivalence of nature, such as existed between the Father and the Son.[53] Even without the doctrine (that Eriugena and Eckhart taught) of dialectical reflex between Creator and creatures, the way in which Thomas related whole and parts by regenerative, mimetic likeness led to highly controversial conclusions.

Centering his doctrines on the two natures of Christ, Thomas therefore understood likeness as a principle of cosmic unity; and imitation as a strategy of cosmic change. The same principle and strategy governed man's inner life, the place where tradition occurred. By imitation of sin, man could become a child of the devil; by imitation of faith and its works, a son of Abraham; by imitation of Christ's humility, an adoptive son of God.[54]

Did saints become the Light that they saw? We can now understand why Thomas answered, "Yes and no." God used human testimonies in the same way as He used secondary causes, not because He could not

---

[51] *Comm. in lib. Boeth. de Trin.* Q.5. A.4 (*Opera* 17: 388). He did teach that, by act, each individual manifested a form that was a similitude of the first act (that is, of God). *Comm. in lib. Boeth. de Trin.* Q. 4. A.2. (*Opera* 17: 374).

[52] F. Pfeiffer, ed., *Deutsche Mystiker des vierzehnten Jahrhunderts,* vol. 2, *Meister Eckhart* (Leipzig, 1857), pp. 180–181. Thomas explicitly rejected the idea of "God becoming" when he wrote: "relationes autem de novo dictae de Deo in respectu ad creaturas non important mutationem ex parte Dei sed ex parte creaturae novo modo se habentis ad Deum." *Lect. in Joan.* 1. 7. 1 (*Opera* 10: 305).

[53] *Lect. in Joan.* 17. 3. 1 (*Opera* 10: 595).

[54] On imitation of the devil, see *Summa Theologiae* I. Q.114. A.3. *Lect. in Joan.* 8. 6. 1–2, and 14. 5. 1 (*Opera* 10: 455, 554). On imitation of Abraham, see *Lect. in Joan.* 8. 5. 2 (*Opera* 10: 453). On imitation of Christ, see *Lect. in Joan.* 6. 4. 9, and 10. 6. 6 (*Opera* 10: 412, 488).

produce effects directly, but so as to communicate the dignity of causality to them and thereby to ennoble them. "So that proper order be observed in things, and so that He might ennoble some men, He willed that divine cognition go to men through other men"—and, moreover, so that, by their good works, He might be made glorious among men.[55] Spiritual vision, however, came only through the Holy Spirit, and the Holy Spirit was infused only through the washing of regeneration, whether the "figural regeneration" of the Old Testament or the "true regeneration" of the New. Without this grace, no one could see the Kingdom.[56] With it, one could glimpse the vision of God in this life by a total abstraction from the senses, by voiding the soul of worldly images.[57] Perfect sharing in the divine Light came only in glory; the testifiers in this life, the prophets and visionaries, participated in it by hope, anticipating the day when exemplar and copy met, when "all we, mirroring the glory of the Lord with uncovered face, will be transformed into that same image (namely that which we have lost) from splendor to splendor."[58] What Thomas may have said in the mystical verses of *Adoro Te Devote,* he did say here. Human testimonies to the Light were not sufficient to reveal the Light. Yes: John and all the saints were the Light. No: They were the Light by participation, not by nature. Illuminated and illuminating, they bore witness to others "from faith to faith" manifesting the wisdom, power and glory of God. They acted *ex similitudine* to Christ; but only Christ, the Son of God, was Light by essence[59]; only He, in the event, could make all things plain.

What of the souls, already rapt in the beatific vision, and already transformed into the Light, from glory to glory?

In this life, the vision of God opened by grace renewed the believer inwardly; in Heaven, the vision of God renewed the believer both inwardly and externally, both in soul and in body, and man was joined to God in perfect fruition.[60] When he took this matter up in the *Summa Theologiae,* Thomas was able to write of the "connaturality" of the saints with the divine things that they saw.[61] And yet this celestial vision of God perfected reason, the common denominator of hu-

---

[55] *Lect. in Joan.* 1. 4 (*Opera* 10: 297–298).

[56] *Lect. in Joan.* 3. 1. 4 (*Opera* 10: 345).

[57] *Lect. in Joan.* 1. 11, and 14. 6. 3 (*Opera* 10: 312, 557).

[58] *Lect. in Joan.* 1. 4 (*Opera* 10: 298).

[59] *Lect. in Joan.* 1. 4–5 (*Opera* 10: 297–301).

[60] *Lect. in Joan.* 3. 1. 4, and 17. 6. 1 (*Opera* 10: 345, 600).

[61] *Summa Theologiae* IIa IIae. Q.45. A.2.

manity, and exalted the intellectual life that was possible in this world.[62] It did not, therefore, obliterate man's intellectual finitude. Thus, Thomas could write that in God's house—that is, in glory, which is God—" 'there are many mansions,' which is to say, diverse participations in His blessedness, since he who understands (*cognoscit*) the more, will have the greater place. Diverse participation of divine cognition and fruition are therefore diverse mansions"; for only God enjoys the absolute perfection of blessedness. In the divine vision "he whose heart is the more elevated above earthly things will see God the more, and see Him the more perfectly;" and in the delight of fruition, "he whose heart is then more burning with the love of God will be the more delighted in the divine fruition." Though all the blessed see and enjoy the same object, they see and love it in different modes.[63]

"The vision of the divinity of the Father and the Son *per essentiam* is our ultimate end and the object of faith."[64] The life of the damned is not life, but death eternal, because it passes apart from this beatitude,[65] which each enjoys according to his own capacity and experience.

As exemplar of justification in the actual experience of each believer, the role of the Logos overlapped with the function of Christ as exemplar of humanity (and of holiness). But, under the aspect of eternity, the Logos' role in justification was seen to be part of His universal causality, of a piece with His role as exemplar of creation and unity. Thus, through the varieties of causal mimesis, Thomas aligned cosmology with sacred history. Like the varieties of mimesis that clustered around the incarnate Christ, those that centered on the Logos entailed critical strategies, precisely because the asymmetry of image and archetype remained incapable of resolution. Thomas referred over and over again to the Christological controversies of the patristic age as illustrations of how defective reasoning (or unbelief) had led men— even great and holy men such as Augustine—into error.[66] He deployed the entire range of his logical and exegetical methods as a critical strategy to reveal and avert misunderstandings of the theology of the Word. In this sense, his works were all an extended critique of the propositions, methods, and conclusions of other theologians, including the Fathers.

---

[62] *Lect. in Joan.* 5. 4. 5 (*Opera* 10: 391).

[63] *Lect. in Joan.* 14. 1. 3–4 (*Opera* 10: 544).

[64] *Lect. in Joan.* 6. 4. 11 (*Opera* 10: 412).

[65] *Lect. in Joan.* 5. 5. 3 (*Opera* 10: 394).

[66] *Summa Theologiae* I. Q.35. A.2. IIa IIae. Q.11. A.2. *Lect. in Joan.* 1. 7. 2 (*Opera* 10: 306). See Congar, "Traditio," p. 197.

From the exemplarism of the incarnate Word and that of the Logos, Thomas derived a manifold, but unified, critical strategy for advancing each individual soul, and the entire body of Christ, through the three tiers of knowing. In all its mimetic varieties, that strategy practiced imitation for one purpose: rebirth to newness of life.

What made such ideas about relationship plausible to Thomas? Clearly he was influenced by the biological analogue of pregnancy and birth. Aristotle's embryology set forth the recapitulation theory, at least in the doctrine that the embryo passed through the vegetal, animal, and human stages of development, the last subsuming the other two. Thomas occasionally referred to embryonic formation and childbirth as a paradigm of growth from less to more perfect form, which he considered the dominant movement in nature. Even without the explicit teaching of Aristotle, he would have been able to draw from Scripture the same parallels that he drew between biological generation and spiritual regeneration.[67]

Thomas understood the word "regeneration" in its literal and miraculous sense. Reversing the order of nature,[68] the soul was reconceived and reborn. "The conversion of man is called birth. Job 39:3, 'They bend themselves to the fetus and give birth.' Rev. 12:2, 'She, giving birth, cried out, and was pained to be delivered.' " Christ, being formed in the soul, corresponded to the fetus being formed in the womb. Each individual conception was universal, engendered by the same Spirit; each soul, regenerated through the formation of Christ, was reborn by the same faith, the same baptism. But each conception was also singular; for Christ was imperfectly formed in some hearts, and in some Christ died. And so, according to a man's progress in the faith, Christ's formation advanced. Correspondingly, the formation of Christ was retarded by the individual soul's defective faith.[69]

The end of gestation was birth in travail and suffering, but after her pain the mother rejoiced in her child. Thomas applied this analogue to

---

[67] Thomas refers to Aristotle's *De generatione animalium*, e.g., in *Lect. in Joan.* 1. 6. 5 (*Opera* 10: 304). See *Comm. in Rom.* 5. 3 (*Opera* 13: 51), on such congenital afflictions as leprosy, podagra, a coleric temper, and insanity. Aquinas's statement, "Sicut autem verbum Dei est semen in anima hominis . . . ita Verbum Dei carne indutum est semen missum in mundum, ex quo maxima seges pullulare debebat," refers to vegetal reproduction, but it suggests at least a metaphorical cross-reference to animal insemination. *Lect. in Joan.* 12. 4. 5 (*Opera* 10: 512). A full statement of Aristotle's recapitulation theory—put into the mouth of Statius—occurs in Dante's *Purgatorio* 25. 37–108.

[68] *Lect. in Joan.* 3. 1. 3–4 (*Opera* 10: 344).

[69] *Comm. in Gal.* 4. 6 (*Opera* 13: 421).

the heavenly bodies, groaning in the travail of their constant movement (which Thomas considered a kind of innovation); to the Apostle Paul travailing in the birth of new Christians; to Christ, suffering on the Cross; and, finally to souls repenting in this world for their sins.[70] For our purposes, it is most important that Thomas applied this figure to men, groaning in travail partly because of evils in this world, partly because of the good that they anticipated after death—the glory for which "we suffer the same things in the time of grace as the ancient fathers suffered before Christ."[71] It was fecund pain that brought the already formed fetus forth into the light, and joy in glory, when without experiencing their pains the saints would recall the miseries that they had suffered. For Christ had been fully formed in them: that is, Christ, had appeared, in all His beauty, to others through them.[72]

Gestation and death were alike for Thomas. In a way familiar to twentieth-century anthropologists, he regarded each as a process in which the hidden subject moved toward a summary moment that both revealed and altered it. Thomas argued that there were really two biological births: the first, at the moment of conception in the womb, and the second, at the moment when the infant left the womb. Until it left its mother's body, the child's body was not completely formed, and its soul lacked the use of reason and free will. Thus, it could not receive the sacraments, nor, consequently, could it be reborn through them or rise from the dead.[73] When he turned to death as an analogous moment of transformative relevation, Thomas naturally gave considerable importance to rebirth through the sacraments. Here, again, there were two moments, the first, hidden and the second, open. Through baptism, Thomas wrote, even a great man could enter into the spiritual womb of the Church, being conformed with the death of Christ in such fashion that his heart became not only—as I have said—the womb but also the tomb of the Crucified awaiting resurrection.[74] The Church is the womb containing the believer; the believer's heart is the womb containing Christ; womb and tomb are alike places of gestation, pre-

---

[70] *Lect. in Joan.* 16. 5. 5 (*Opera* 10: 583). *Comm. in Rom.* 8. 4 (*Opera* 13: 82). On Thomas's acceptance of circularity in historical thought as well as in cosmology, see Max Seckler, *Das Heil in der Geschichte. Geschichtstheologisches Denken bei Thomas von Aquin* (Munich, 1964), pp. 29, 35–36.

[71] *Comm. in Rom.* 8. 4 (*Opera* 13: 83).

[72] *Comm. in Gal.* 4. 6., and 4. 8 (*Opera* 13: 421, 424). *Lect. in Joan.* 16. 5. 5 (*Opera* 10: 583).

[73] *Comm. in Sent.* 3. 3. 1. 1a; 4. 6. 1. 1a; 4. 43. 1. 1b. *Summa Theologiae* III. Q.27. A.3, 1.

[74] *Lect. in Joan.* 3. 1. 3, 4, and 20, 6. 2, 4 (*Opera* 10: 344f., 622f.). See below n. 88.

paring for the second moment of birth, that of egress. The process of regeneration only began in this world; it passed through its stages of concealment. A favorite verse assured Thomas that the summary moment of revelation and change—rebirth—lay ahead: "Beloved, now we are the sons of God, and it doth not yet appear what we shall be: but we know that, when He shall appear, we shall be like Him, for we shall see Him as He is" (1 John 3:2).

The biological, and spiritual, phenomenon of gestation and birth corresponds with what I have said concerning the ambiguities in Thomas's concept of tradition. Like the event of knowing, each embryonic formation is unique and follows its own course to death or to life; but each also expresses the same primordial laws of generation and growth. Each is an act of reproduction by which the individual recapitulates the stages of life, and, by advancing from less to more perfect degrees of life, each enlarges the species. Each is transformed, by stages, from partial to more complete form. Each, in the total course of recapitulation, endures pain for the sake of future joy. Thomas's idea that to transmit sacred doctrine was to transmit life—that knowledge and life were identical—established a ready parallel between tradition and birth, between the events of spiritual regeneration and carnal generation, both of which were discontinuous and universal. Being universal, they were also anchronistic, even while they took place in time. Being reproductive, they advanced by mimetic action, repetitious but not redundant.

By the way of summary, I shall consider a concrete example of tradition as esoteric relationship moving in the asymmetry of image and archetype. This example—the experience of the Apostle Thomas—struck resonances in the thought of his namesake from Aquino. The Apostle was a minor figure in the Gospel. Yet, Aquinas gave him a major role in the drama of salvation. At two critical moments, the Apostle Thomas elicited revelations concerning Christ's natures. Aquinas could write his key sentence, about Christ as man—"humanity is the way, not the end"—because the Apostle grieved at his approaching separation from Christ, and said, "Lord, we know not whither thou goest; and how can we know the way?" (John 14:5). Christ answered, "I am the way, the truth and the life."[75] Moreover, Aquinas could assert the resurrection of each body, in all its individuality, because the Apostle had hardheadedly disbelieved the resurrec-

---

[75] *Comm. in Matt.* 28 (*Opera* 10: 277). *Lect. in Joan.* 14. 2. 2–3 (*Opera* 10: 546). Cf. also the verses in *Adoro te devote:* "Plagas, sicut Thomas, non intueor/Deum tamen meum te confiteor."

tion of Christ until he saw the Lord's wounds and thrust his hand into His side. In that moment, Aquinas argued, the Apostle suddenly became "a good theologian," the first to confess Christ, not merely as Lord, or as the son of God, but also as God.[76] Thus, the continuing dialogue between disciple and Master revealed knowledge needed for man's transformation into God.

In particular, the regenerative significance of the wound into which the Apostle set his hand was not lost on Aquinas. Unlike the other wounds of Christ, the gash in His side was inflicted after death: that is, after the Old Testament prophecies had been fulfilled. The water and blood issuing from it superseded the ceremonies of the Old Testament and formed, or consecrated, the Church through the sacraments of the New Covenant, the water, through baptism, and the blood, through the Eucharist. By his spear, the Roman soldier therefore opened the door of eternal life through Christ's side[77]; and the Apostle's hand entered there.

Three points deserve emphasis.

1. The Apostle's confession came at the apex of a three-tier phenomenon of knowledge. The resurrection was hard for Thomas to believe. He had to be convinced by sensory evidence—and not that of one sense only, but of two, sight and touch. Seeing was believing, but Thomas saw one thing (Christ, the man, and his wounds) and believed another (Christ the God).[78] From the levels of sensory evidence and faith, Thomas had advanced to that of glory, beyond what had been vouchsafed to him before the Passion. Christ appeared yet again to him and to six others on the shores of Tiberias. The number of witnesses invited Aquinas to abandon his tripartite division of history in favor of another. It signified "the appearance of the glory that is to come after the seventh age, namely in the eighth, which is the age of the risen, as is written in Isaiah (66:23), 'Month will succeed month, and sabbath, sabbath, and all flesh will come to worship before my face'."[79]

---

[76] *Lect. in Joan.* 20. 6. 3 (*Opera* 10: 634).

[77] *Lect. in Joan.* 19. 5. 4–6 (*Opera* 10: 622). *Comm. in Rom.* 5. 4 (*Opera* 13: 55). *Comm. in Sent.* 4. 18. 1. 1a. For the idea that all five wounds are the *porticus* of spiritual healing, see *Lect. in Joan.* 5. 1. 1 (*Opera* 10: 380). With regard to the analogue of pregnancy, it should also be noted that Thomas drew the conventional parallel between Adam, from whose side Eve (prefiguring the Church) was taken, and Christ, from whose side came "the water and the blood by which the Church is consecrated." *Lect. in Joan.* 19. 5. 4 (*Opera* 10: 622).

[78] *Lect. in Joan.* 20. 6. 4 (*Opera* 10: 634).

[79] *Lect. in Joan.* 21. 1. 2 (*Opera* 10: 635f.).

2. The regeneration of the Apostle through the three tiers of knowledge occurred by means of mimetic action. As an Apostle, Thomas was among those who replicated the filiation of Christ, "the firstborn of many brethren." Christ therefore loved them "after a certain likeness . . . namely, that they might be gods by participation of grace." Beholding the glory of God through His bodily presence, the Apostles became the Light that they saw, enlightened and illuminating in the process of conversion by which the glory of God was manifested among the peoples.[80] The Apostles had been chosen from among the humble—fishermen, tentmakers, and the like—to prove, by the weakness and simplicity of their preaching, that the faith was independent of human power and wisdom.[81] Departing from worldliness and conforming with the image of the invisible God, the Apostles came to hate the world and to be hated and persecuted by it, as was Christ. Thus, out of love for Christ, the Apostle Thomas urged his brethren, "let us also go, that we may die with Him" (John 11:16).[82] The Apostle's life, then, exemplified how the humanity of Christ had served as a means when Christ, speaking as man to man, had instructed the Apostle "by the sweetness of His conversation" and, later, by the wounds of His glorified flesh. Put another way, my second point is that Christ's humanity was the way for the soul's mimetic transformation according to the double exemplarism of Christ as man and as Logos.

3. The transformation was progressive, notably with reference to the community. The Apostle's experience demonstrated how God used the humanity of the saints to manifest His righteousness and glory "from faith to faith," and thereby to enlarge and transform the believing community through likeness. Thomas had been absent from the

---

[80] See above, notes 44, 45, 55.

[81] Shortly after, God provided for the conversion of learned, noble, and powerful men, so that sacred doctrine should not be held in contempt because it had been received by the lowly and foolish and also so that the victory of the faith over the world could be openly displayed. *Lect. in Joan.* 3. 1. 1 (*Opera* 10: 342). *Expos. in lib. Boeth. de Trin.* Q.2. A.3 (*Opera* 17: 362). In a short time, the Apostles—simple fishermen—were made more venerable than all kings and more eloquent than philosopher and rhetors, being companions of the Lord of the entire world. But it was also true that they developed proud ways, since they had been catapulted so quickly into an honor for which they were unprepared. *Lect. in Joan.* 4. 1. 12 (*Opera* 10: 362).

[82] *Lect. in Joan.* 11. 3. 5 (*Opera* 10: 492). Aquinas here takes a comment about Lazarus (John 11:16) and applies it to Christ, using it to elucidate (by anticipation) John 14.

first apparition of the risen Christ to the Apostles, missing the solace of that vision, the blessing of peace, and the descent of the Holy Spirit. "We are instructed by this," Aquinas wrote, "not to be parted from the group (*societas*)." But, he continued, the Apostle had been absent, not by chance, but by divine dispensation. Being absent, he doubted what the others had seen. Doubt afflicted him; but, out of love for the human race, God permitted apostles, prophets, and saints to be afflicted, and even to sin, so that some benefit for mankind could eventually be brought forth. Because the Apostle doubted until he touched his Master's wounds, the wounds of belief were cured in others—"in us." And so, the faith of the elect profited more from Thomas's disbelief than from the belief of the other disciples.[83]

The confession of Thomas, "the good theologian," transformed his own life. Once more timorous, weaker, and less faithful than the others, he became stronger, indeed irreproachable, striding alone through the world.[84] His testimony also transformed the community in the time between the crucifixion and the publication of the Gospel, that interim when Jewish Christians could still keep the ceremonies of the Law, if only they did not believe them necessary to salvation. Later, when Thomas, the other Apostles, and the Evangelists had done their work, the transformation was achieved. Christ was formed in the faithful. Then, the ceremonies of the Old Testament were forbidden as both dead and deadly, because men plainly recognized that the Passion of Christ had subsumed and superseded them.[85] The third point, then, is that the Apostle's mimetically transformed humanity was a means by which the Body of Christ was formed.

[83] *Lect. in Joan.* 20. 5. 1 (*Opera* 10: 632).

[84] *Lect. in Joan.* 11. 3. 5 (*Opera* 10: 492), drawing on an interpretation by John Chrysostom.

[85] *Summa Theologiae* Ia IIae. Q.103. A.4. The sacraments of the New Dispensation were "constructed"—that is, they became efficacious—through the Passion. *Expos. in Matt.* 16 (*Opera* 10: 155). On the life of Christ as taking place in an interim between the Old and New Testaments, see *Lect. in Joan.* 12. 3. 2 (*Opera* 10: 510), where Thomas commented on Christ's entry into Jerusalem: "Sciendum autem, quod facta Christi sunt quasi media inter facta veteris testamenti et novi; et ideo turba tam quae praecedebat quam quae sequebatur, cum laudabat, inquantum facta Christi sunt regula et exemplar eorum quae fiunt in novo testamento et praefigurata a patribus veteris testamenti. Asellus autem, quod est animal rude, significat populum gentium, super quem sedit, ut significaret quod ipse redempturus esset gentes."

All three observations teach the disposition of humanity as a means to its end: the transformation of men into gods. It required an esoteric dialogue with something wholly other. The name "Thomas," Aquinas wrote, means "abyss," and an abyss has two characteristics: depth and darkness. Therefore Thomas was an abyss because of the darkness of his disbelief, which he had on his own, and also because of the depth of mercy, which he had from Christ. The Psalmist wrote, "abyss calleth unto abyss" (KJV Ps. 42:7). Thus, by mercy, the abyss of depth (namely, Christ) calls to the abyss of darkness (namely, Thomas), and, by confession of faith, the abyss of hardheadedness (*obstinatio:* namely, Thomas) calls to the abyss of depth (namely, Christ).[86] This asymmetrical, inward dialogue passed mimetically through the three levels of knowledge that I have identified. We have seen that Aquinas's recapitulation theory permitted him to integrate the Apostle's discontinuous, progressive relationship to Christ with the collective transformation of the elect.

The collective transformation was made up entirely of discontinuous and most inward relations, repeating the Apostle's dialogue of abyss with abyss. For, until tradition ended in the immediate vision of the divine essence, Christ mystically admonished every one of His renascent followers to pass from incredulity to belief, and from belief to glory, as Thomas had done, thrusting a hand into His lance-pierced side[87]; that is, into the wound from which flowed the water that signified the people who were to be renewed by Christ's blood, the water that seemed, in spiritual regeneration, to have the place of a mother's womb.[88]

How can we visualize this deliberately anachronistic concept of tradition, in which all stages were simultaneous, and yet in which there was repetition without redundancy? The metaphor of a torch, relayed from hand to hand, will not do. In the *Paradiso,* the voice of Thomas Aquinas speaks from amidst a fiery light. Twelve historians and theologians from every age of sacred time dance around Dante and Beatrice, as a crown of suns. Thomas identifies them, and when he stops,

---

[86] *Lect. in Joan.* 20. 5. 1 (*Opera* 10: 632).

[87] *Lect. in Joan.* 20. 6. 2 (*Opera* 10: 634).

[88] *Comm. in Sent.* 4. 8. 1. 2b. *Summa Theologiae* III Q.67. A.4. Thomas also drew the connection between sacraments and fertility by way of a symbol for the Holy Ghost: i.e., the dove (*columba*), "quae est animal fecundum." *Lect. in Joan.* 20. 4. 5 (*Opera* 10: 631). See above, notes 67–74.

"Then, like a clock that calls us
At the hour when the bride of God arises
To sing matins to her Bridegroom, that he may love her,
Even as a clock where the one part draws and drives the other,
. . . .
Just so I saw the glorious wheel
Move itself and match voice to voice in timbre
And in sweetness that none can know
Save in that place where joy begets eternal joy."

(Dante Paradiso 10. 139–148)

Chapter 9

Toward a New Theory of Progress
by Augmentation

In Thomas Aquinas's day and during the generations that followed, many movements in thought yielded programmatic visions of the reform of human nature. A number of teachings produced by leaders of these movements differed from Thomas's conclusions about the reformation of man inasmuch as they accentuated the leveling of metaphysical hierarchies and gave predominance to the strategy of mimesis by augmentation. Among the most crucial of them were some doctrines that arose among mystics and that by the fifteenth century had taken root in humanism. They addressed the familiar dramatic transit of egress and return; they retained mimesis as the strategy of movement from alienation to wholeness. But Aristotelian teachings had opened alternatives to an irresoluble asymmetry between God, as archetype, and man, as His image. They opened prospects of organic wholeness, and these doctrines pressed to their outer limits the implications of reading human experience in terms of incremental growth.

The Aristotelian strategy of mimesis by augmentation advanced; the Platonic strategy of mimesis by reversion declined.

At first glance, it could appear strange to couple mysticism, which aimed at the annihilation of self-will, with humanism, which exalted the independence and the creative power of the will. The mystic disparaged worldly wisdom as folly; the humanist exalted it as the common treasure of mankind. The mystic was iconoclastic. He labored to leave the world of sense impressions, to annihilate all mental images including consciousness of self, to return to God in the void, formlessness, and unconsciousness. The humanist cultivated imagery. He strove for verbal symbolism in rhetorical elegance; he developed representational aspects of the arts, such as painting and music; he gave particular attention to the use of memory, or mental images, as a magical device for returning to God by active and conscious contemplation. And yet, the two ventures had much in common. Plato himself had seen an intimate relation between mystery religions and philosophy.

Both acknowledged man's fragility as the basis of human greatness. In ways utterly foreign to Seneca, they elaborated the Stoic's perception: "it is truly great to have the frailty of a man and the security of a God." The Latin Fathers had expressed the views that life was a constant striving to leave behind the imperfections of the human condition, the prison of the body, and to gain the perfection of divine knowledge. The conflict and interdependence of change and identity was at the heart of the anguish described by Gregory the Great when he wrote that man labored under a heavy burden, "seeking after passing objects and yet being unwilling to pass away with what are passing."[1] Thomas Aquinas recognized the same systemic tension when he observed that man was ordained to an end of eternal life that was disproportionate to his natural powers, unaided by grace.[2]

As we have seen repeatedly, this tension between man, the imperfect image and his perfect archetype was thought to be mediated by imitative movement. Without imperfection, without struggle and suffering, without an ultimate goal of wholeness, there could be no passage from lesser to greater perfection. Enhanced by the doctrines of original sin and the Incarnation, man's incessant striving toward perfection, toward freedom, became a sign not merely of the fragility of human life and of the sickness of the human will but also of the hope for eternal glory.

Scholastic philosophers repeated this ancient theme. But mystics and humanists placed it at the center of their thought. For them, human fragility was the very condition of freedom and glory. For mystics, Christ summed up human existence in His poverty, in His abandonment of self to the will of God, and in the agonies of the Crucifixion. Contempt for the world, extinction of self-will, mortification of the flesh all followed from a mystical striving through imitation toward union with Christ, the Suffering Servant. The mystic's progress was itself an agony; even if he did not participate in the burning Passion of Christ and achieve the annihilation of self, the more spiritual he became, the more wretched his life in the world seemed to him and the more keenly he sensed the distance between his sufferings and

---

[1] *Moralia in Job* 30. 15. 50 (*PL* 76: 552). See above Chapter 3 at n. 181.
[2] *Summa Theologiae* Ia IIae. Q.109. A.5. Cf. P.I. Q.91. A.4 (on the creation of man).

Christ's, between the sufferings of existence and the impassibility of true being. "Who am I, Lord?" St. Catherine of Siena asked Jesus, "Who am I? And also tell me who you are." "My daughter," He answered, "you are that which is not, and I am that which is."[3]

The humanists' sense of progress was in some ways more benign than the mystics'. For them both, imperfection of human knowledge led to insatiable striving; for the humanists, this led through a competitive imitation of the ancients to a cumulative refinement in the arts and sciences. And yet, the humanists realized that their striving would never end, that it would never reach its goal, perfection, and that the cost of all progress was therefore frustration. Their concept of progress was tragic. Moreover, apart from the imitation of the ancients, many of them shared the asceticism and religious preoccupations of the mystics in the imitation of Christ. Vittorino da Feltre, for example, flagellated himself each day before mass. Sir Thomas More also practiced self-flagellation and wore a hair shirt, even after he ceased, as a layman, to observe the Carthusian discipline that set the pattern of communal life described in the *Utopia.* Erasmus concluded his *Praise of Folly* by enjoining on men "meekness, patience, contempt of life" (ch. 36), and extolling the "madness" of ecstatic visions in which the soul abandoned itself to foretastes of heavenly bliss (chs. 39, 40). In the experience of spiritual values, mysticism was close to humanism.

By inquiries into the order of nature, scholastic philosophers devoted themselves to externals—whether in the formal rules of logic or in the interpretation of natural phenomena. Nature engulfed man. Mystics and humanists alike rejected this approach. Man and humane values could not be understood in the framework of external relations; they could not be grasped in the quantified abstraction. The way to truth did not lead through the external world. It led through introspection, the soul's self-contemplation.

Mysticism

The transformation of the self into God evoked some startling rhetoric. St. Catherine of Genoa (1447–1510) was careful to distinguish between the exterior self and the interior (or real) self when she wrote of the latter, "My 'I' is God. I know no 'I' other than my God Him-

---

[3] Raymond of Capua, *Life of St. Catherine of Siena* 1. 10. *La Vita della serafica sposa di Gesu' Cristo S. Caterina da Siena,* ed. Bernardino Pecci (Siena, 1707), p. 96.

self. . . . Everything that has existence holds it through communication of God's sovereign essence." She drew back from the extreme consequences of this position by saying that, "My being is God, not through simple participation, but through true transformation and annihilation of personal being."[4] But the identity of the human "I" and the divine "God" through the communication of the divine essence remained, as it had in the vision of Angela of Foligno (1248–1309), two centuries earlier: "In the vast darkness, I did doubtless behold the Holy Trinity. And to me it seemeth that I am fixed in the midst of it."[5]

One of the most powerful and pervasive exponents of this conception was Meister Eckhart (ca. 1260–1327), who exposed its mimetic foundations. In the Dominican Order, Eckhart distinguished himself as an administrator, theologian, and mystic. As a preacher, moreover, Eckhart had wide influence personally through his addresses and, posthumously, through written drafts of his sermons. His thoughts figured prominently in the wave of popular devotion that began to crest in the Low Countries and the Rhineland during the second half of the fourteenth century.

"The eye in which I see God," wrote this spiritual brother of Thomas Aquinas, "is the same eye in which God sees me. My eye and the eye of God is one eye, and one is the vision or seeing, and one the knowing, and one the loving."[6] The metaphor of the mirror had entered the mimetic tradition to describe the likeness of image to archetype. It had respected the inequality between them, even while it stressed their similarities. But, in this sentence (and, indeed, in the entire sermon from which it comes), Meister Eckhart leapt from the similarity between man and God to their identity. Against charges of pantheism, he insisted that he taught only a virtual identity and not a complete one. But, as always, the line between God as all-in-all and God as all was nebulous. What meanings did Eckhart encapsulate in his strange, ambiguous words?

From the age of the Fathers onward, reflections on the nature of God had set the pattern by which men defined human nature. This

---

[4] *Biographia,* ch. 15. P. Umile Bonzi da Genoa. *S. Caterina Fieschi Adorno,* vol. 2 *Edizione critica dei manoscritti Cateriniani* (Genoa, 1962), p. 170.

[5] *The Pool of Divine Consolation of the Blessed Angela of Foligno* trans. Mary G. Steegman, Treatise III, seventh vision (New York, 1966), p. 184.

[6] Serm. 12, on Eccles. 24:30, in *Meister Eckharts Predigten,* ed. J. Quint (Stuttgart, 1958) 1: 201. Also in *Rechtfertigungsschrift,* IX, 19. Augustinus Daniels, *Eine lateinische Rechtfertigungsschrift des Meister Eckhart* (Münster-i.-W., 1923. *Beiträge zur Geschichte der Philosophie des Mittelalters,* Bd 23, Hft 5), p. 42.

was also true in Eckhart's case, but his mimesis by augmentation sharply departed from patristic ideas of reversion to stable archetypes. When he discussed the relationship between the Father and the Word, Eckhart set down in precise detail what he meant by the dyad of image and exemplar. Similarity was, of course, fundamental, a similarity in nature and kind that was expressed and poured out by the exemplar. Following what he understood of Aristotle, Eckhart held that the likeness existed through the species (*per speciem*), rather than through an eternal form (*per ideam*), as he thought Plato had taught. It followed that the image and the exemplar could not be counted as two distinct substances, since the one was in the other, both because together they formed one vicarious mutuality (which Eckhart called an offspring) and because neither should lack anything that was in the other, nor contain anything that was not in the other.[7] The relationship of image to exemplar stood in the intellectual nature, and Eckhart's discussion moved primarily from his equation between knowing and being, which, in his view, sprang from the same principles.[8] In considering the Father and the Word, this equation enabled him to argue that the image and the exemplar were coeval, that the expression or begetting was "a certain formal emanation," that the image was completely in its exemplar, and, vice versa, that the image was unique in itself. Eckhart therefore maintained both identity and similarity with regard to the Father and the Son, "the invisible image of God." Other points of reference were easier to transfer to the human condition: that the image received its being from its exemplar alone and that, as image, it took nothing from the subject in which it was, but rather took its entire being from the object of which it was an image.[9]

It is telling, however, that, when he actually turned to the relationship between God and man, Eckhart appropriated most of this conceptual framework. The intellectual nature was again the key element: for "like is always known by like."[10] How is this likeness—in knowing and being—established? It is already present, since man was made in the image of the whole Trinity, and since the light of God "lighteth every man that cometh into the world." It is perfected by the regen-

---

[7] Serm. 49 in *Die lateinische Werke,* ed. J. Quint (Stuttgart, 1956, *Sermones,* Bd 4, Lieferung 6/7, pp. 424ff.

[8] Knowing was furthermore a precondition of loving. Cf. Serm. 50, ibid., pp. 429f.

[9] *Expositio sancti evangelii secundum Joannem,* in *Die lateinischen Werke,* ed. J. Quint (Berlin, 1936, Bd 3, Lieferung 1). On John 1:1–5, see pp. 19ff.

[10] *Expos. in Joannem* 1:14, ibid., Lieferung 2, p. 107.

eration of men into conformity of nature with Christ, "the image of the Father,"[11] a regeneration by which Christ, the known, and man, the knower, overflowed into, or engendered, a single image in the human soul. Because, in this way, God is in the memory, intellect, and will, "I think, I know, and I love Christ."[12] Through the same introspection, just as reflections of men's faces are formed whenever mirrors are placed before them, men who behold the justice of Christ in their souls are formed, and informed, and transformed into it.[13]

The way in which Eckhart used the principle of formal emanation to define the image/exemplar relation between man and God had wide implications. In fact, the *effectus dei* was common to all genera, illuminating some with life and others with mere being.[14]

Thus understood, the teaching that God was all-in-all led Meister Eckhart to further conclusions about man in time that recall teachings of John Scotus Eriugena. If God was the eternally present, the sum of all acts both in foreknowledge and as they were done, then every life, every act, was an essential part of God. The nice academic concept of virtual identity shrank before other principles. Change was the self-realization of God, and the acts of men were the substance of change. Meister Eckhart concluded that, before there were creatures, God was not God, but what He was in Himself. He became God in the creatures.[15] Even when he defended himself against the charge of pantheism, Eckhart insisted that God was not distant and similar, as an original is to its reflection in a mirror, but that He was most intimate to every person.[16] And, in a sermon from Eckhart's circle, if not actually

---

[11] Ibid.   [12] Serm. 50, Lieferung 6/7, pp. 429f.

[13] *Exposit. in Joannem* 1:14, p. 104.

[14] *Exposit. in Joannem* 1:11 and 1:9, pp. 88f., 78ff.

[15] Serm. 52, *Meister Eckharts Predigten* (Stuttgart, 1971), 2: 492.

[16] *Rechtfertigungsschrift,* 9, 59. Daniels, ed., *Rechtfertigungsschrift,* pp. 63–65. In this section, Eckhart explained what he meant when he affirmed that there was no distinction between the only begotten Son and the soul. It would be untrue, he wrote, to say, "I am God," except in the sense that the believer was a member of God, as Augustine, for example, affirmed when he imagined Christ saying of the faithful, "In me, they are I" (above, Chapter 3, note 54). It was possible, he added, to think of this relationship by analogy with the reflection of one face (=Christ) in many mirror-images (=human souls); but, as indicated above, this analogy failed to convey the intimate and essential unity between the Son and the soul that Eckhart had in mind. On the use of the same analogy by Augustine, John Scotus Eriugena, and Thomas Aquinas, see Chapter 3, note 18; Chapter 6, note 17; Chapter 8, note 44. On Schleiermacher's use of the related analogy of a hall of mirrors, see Chapter 14, note 24.

by him, the speaker argued that the sun and its image in a mirror became one, not two, and that, analogously, God was in the soul with His nature, His being, and His divinity, imparting being to the soul, with the result that God became in all creatures, and God's utterances became God.[17] Under the conviction of the unity of things in their formal efflux from God, and of men in the eternal generation of the Son, mysticism, through emanationism, embraces its opposites: corporality, temporality, and multiplicity.

Perhaps the most influential statement of mimesis by augmentation in Christian mysticism was an anonymous treatise written about the middle of the fourteenth century. The *Theologia Germanica* has passed through nearly two hundred editions and translations since the sixteenth century, more than sixty of them in the eighteenth and nineteenth centuries. Its doctrine powerfully affected the thought of Martin Luther, who discovered and first published it, and its papal condemnation (1612) did nothing to hinder its spread among Lutherans, Calvinists, and the circle called the Cambridge Platonists. The author of the *Theologia Germanica* was a scholar, but, like Meister Eckhart, he or she wrote, not merely for the learned, but for the greater, febrile world of popular devotion.

To an astonishing degree, the cardinal points of Christian theology are missing. By omitting eschatology—the resurrection of the dead, the Last Judgment, and the millennial kingdom of the Saints—the author showed that he had abandoned Christian teleology. By omitting the doctrine of the atonement, he cast aside the concept of Christ as a historical figure who actually lived in the flesh and died; the miracle of the Incarnation; the moral horror of the redemptive sacrifice; the victory over death; the entire structure of thought that promised the believer freedom from "the body of this death" and true life in, with, for, and through Christ.

The drift of the author's thought becomes clear in his comments on the theological points that he does consider: Creation, Fall, and Redemption. Formal theology had taught that these events—like the Last Judgment and the Incarnation—took place in time, once for all. According to the *Theologia Germanica,* they are events without historical situation. They are constantly repeated in individual lives. God requires creatures so that He may have His due praise, and so that—through them as secondary causes—He may achieve perfection. But

---

[17] F. Pfeiffer, ed., *Deutsche Mystiker des vierzehnten Jahrhunderts,* vol. 2 *Meister Eckhart* (Leipzig, 1857), pp. 180f.

the need of praise is constant; perfection is always in process; creation therefore is not the work of an instant but the flow of creatures from God, always becoming nothing in themselves under submission to Him, always flowing back to Him. The eternal return is also at the heart of the author's teaching on the Fall and on Redemption. For the Fall is not Adam's one act of disobedience, but the ever-repeated and ever-new acts by which men assert their separateness from God, flaunting their own wills and selfhoods, defying the universal all-in-allness, or harmony, of God. Likewise, Redemption is not an act of atonement, but rather one of reconciliation by which God takes on manhood, and man becomes God in the experience of every person who voids himself of himself, yielding entirely to God and living no longer his own life but the life of Christ.

This eternal return was Averroistic, and thus augmentative, as is plain when the author wrote, "the will in the creature, which we call a created will, is as truly God's as the eternal will, and is not of the creature" (ch. 41). Recognizing the implications of this doctrine, the author reached an ambiguous position. He taught an emanation of good that left man the power to assert his self-will, but only at the cost of falling away from true love and being, which was the divine movement of eternal creation and reconciliation, the Logos, the life of Christ.

The author of the *Theologia Germanica* understood man as essentially spirit. He had lost sight of the Scriptural figure of man as a union of body and soul, as is most obvious in his indifference to the doctrines of the Incarnation and the resurrection of the flesh. This is a symptom of his whole attitude toward the meaning and value of life as it is lived. One can throw the implications of this attitude into high relief by referring to an earlier and equally influential masterpiece of mystical reflection, Bernard of Clairvaux's *On Loving God.* For Bernard, the flesh was all-important; carnality was the essential link between man and Christ. Through the flesh, man was tied to his own historical situation; through the flesh, Adam fell; through the flesh, all the sons of Adam were congenitally tainted by his sin; through the flesh, Christ atoned for their sins; through the flesh, each man approached Christ for redemption, being raised from the dead and, in the day of Judgment, sent to his reward. For the author of the *Theologia Germanica,* separateness was an evil. For Bernard, it was the condition of everything else, in the reality of events in sacred history, in the experience of the soul, in the personal lives and relationships of God and man.

Bernard kept the sense of God as an immediate presence in the world and the absolute dependence of man upon God for all that he is.

He drew on texts of Christian Neoplatonists to describe the mystic union in terms compatible with those of the *Theologia Germanica*. In its ecstasy, he wrote, the soul of man melts away from itself and takes on the appearance of the Other as a drop of water does in a cup of wine, as iron takes on the color of fire, as air is transfused with the brilliance of light. But Bernard was careful to add that the separate substance—and therefore the fundamental separateness—of men would remain, however transformed, however glorified. The need for Christ crucified did not lead to renunciation of the self; in the progress of the soul toward loving God, the first and most essential stage, subsumed in all the rest, was the love of self.

For mystical writers, such as Meister Eckhart and the author of the *Theologia Germanica,* likeness was an intrinsic aspect of causality. This much they had in common with many writers, including Thomas Aquinas, who retained the metaphysical hierarchy. But it is apparent that mystical speculation, such as we have mentioned, leveled that hierarchy by replacing similarity of cause and effect with identity. The exemplar and the image were reciprocally in one another. In voiding himself of sensible and mental images, man made room for the image of God. Christ, the Son and Logos, was the image of the invisible God. When God engendered His Son in the voided soul of man, Christ and man became the same Son, the same image of the eternal Father. As image, Christ was the efficient, exemplary, and final cause of the new and perfect form of the soul, eternally renewed as the Son was eternally begotten, by God and in God. His causality was a begetting, or a process without interruption that gave all creatures life, created and ordered them according to itself, the divine exemplar, and subsumed them in its own relation to God.

As ideas, the conclusions of mystical writers were startling, and they showed how new and potentially revolutionary norms of human behavior were taking shape even as thinkers looked backward to the precedents and authoritative texts of Christianity. The concept of mimesis by augmentation that we have reviewed prepared the ground for many fundamental, if miscellaneous, ideas, some of which we associate with the nineteenth and twentieth centuries: the divinization of change through the "spirit of the age" or the "spirit of the people"; the extinction of the individual moral personality; the concept of historical process as something made by man; the view of truth not as an abstract, enduring standard but as the existing situation; the tragic struggle between the finite and infinite in the lives of men; the existential anguish in which one person bears the suffering of all mankind and so transcends his finite humanity. But beyond these long-range effects in the realm of ideas, mysticism had an immediate impact on society.

Mysticism was no monopoly of the priesthood. Women and laymen led this tidal wave of spirituality, driven on by strange Platonistic ideologies and by the brute force of emotion. Some of them—such as Catherine of Siena and Rita of Cascia—were said to have received the wounds of Christ. Inevitably, the techniques of mystical revivalism led many to seek not merely private enlightenment but also group experience of spiritual values. Religious confraternities of laymen were organized in individual parishes and dedicated to special devotions (for example, to the sacrament of the Eucharist). New sodalities, including some monastic orders, were established; among them the most notable was the Brethren of the Common Life, an order founded in the Netherlands to serve the mystical discipline of the *devotio moderna.*

These religious groupings embodied the deep earnestness of mysticism, and, as such, they heralded the time when the religious fabric of Europe would be torn apart, not by skepticism, but by faith. Mysticism between the thirteenth and the fifteenth centuries was part of a movement that continued into the sixteenth and seventeenth. To say that this sweep of four hundred years was a golden age of mysticism is also to say that it was a time when external religious authorities were endemically and bitterly challenged. In a world where the established religious authorities were discredited and degraded in the game of politics, mysticism showed the way to a spiritual enlightenment that did not depend on a Church governed by the traditional structure of offices, administered under law, and sustained by property. Leveling the metaphysical hierarchy anticipated leveling the ecclesiastical.

When religious movements broke into social revolutions, the leaders came from universities, not from cloisters or confraternities. They were philosophers and theologians, not mystics. Wycliffe was a doctor of theology at Oxford; Hus, a master of arts, dean of the philosophical faculty, and finally rector of the University of Prague. The leaders of the Conciliar Movement were university men. Calvin studied in three colleges at the University of Paris, and Luther, having followed lectures at the University of Erfurt, earned his doctorate in theology at the University of Wittenberg. Their predecessors and fellow-workers—such as Marsiglio of Padua and Philip Melanchthon—similarly attacked religious issues from the standpoint of philosophy, instead of from that of mysticism. For them, the active and conscious will, the awakened soul, held the center of attention. But when they broke entirely with traditional forms of government and worship in the

Church, when they dispensed with priestly order, hierarchic discipline, the real presence of God in the sacraments, consecrated places of worship, and religious images, they did what radical mystics before them had done. They raised an ensign to which mystical preachers had for generations won popular allegiance. While they could not accept the complete passivity and indifference of mystic self-denial, they followed the mystics in insisting that the direct pararational experience of the holy was decisive for every believer. Neither the formal structure of the Church, nor the weight of tradition, nor any other external authority held greater weight than likeness to God in the believer's own conscience. Luther, the editor of the *Theologia Germanica*, echoed Eckhart as well as Ockham when he wrote that what is, is right because God wills it. His understanding of Isaiah's view of man as a tool in God's hands was pure Eckhart. "Christians are not driven by a free will, but by the Spirit of God (Rom. 8:14). To be driven is not to act, but to be seized as a saw or an ax is driven by a carpenter."[18]

Humanism

Humanism followed mysticism in being a learned enterprise, both esoteric and eclectic, and the gradual recovery of ancient writings placed before the humanist scholar an astonishing array of philosophical and religious texts. These were on the whole the main writings on which the Latin intellectual tradition was based. Wherever they looked, the humanists found familiar resonances, pure and unmediated by suspect authorities. Beginning in the fourteenth century with texts of Latin antiquity, the humanists widened their philosophical scope early in the fifteenth to include Greek texts and, finally, toward the end of the fifteenth century, they turned to Hebrew studies. Together with the mystical and exegetical writings of Latin Christianity, a dazzling variety of Epicurean, Stoic, and Neoplatonic texts, the original writings of Plato and Aristotle, the Gnostic texts of magic that passed under the name of Hermes Trismegistos, the works of Origen, the Old Testament and the Hebrew Cabala—all this and much more was opened to study.

The mimetic tradition had required a twofold response to texts: the first, the exercise of textual criticism, the second, the search for hidden meaning, primarily through the use of myth and allegory. Dominated

---

[18] *De servo arbitrio* (*WA*, 18: 699).

by the concept of the metaphysical unity of wisdom, humanists practiced both interpretive methods. The actual texts were poetic veils covering the divine light, manifold revelations of the One. They revealed their secrets only to students initiated into the disguises that covered sacred mysteries. Under these convictions, the humanists in the intellectual currents with which I am concerned turned, almost as mystagogues, to the recovered treatises.

Two of these, the late humanists, Giovanni Pico della Mirandola (1463–1494) and Nicholas of Cusa (1401–1464), were motivated by theories of mimesis by augmentation. Both imbibed Averroistic doctrines during studies at Padua; both drew upon mystical thought, Pico as he approached the spiritual conversion that for the last two years of his life kept him in Savonarola's orbit, and Cusa, as he pursued directions that he gained in boyhood from the Brethren of the Common Life.

Pico's career was brief, and he is known largely through a biography written by his nephew, Gianfrancesco Pico della Mirandola. Gianfrancesco was a devout follower (and later the biographer) of Savonarola; quite naturally, he emphasized the severe asceticism with which his uncle mortified the flesh after his conversion. The biography was written for an edition of Pico's works (1496), and it underscored the austere cast of later writings, in which Pico laid aside his vast philosophical undertakings and turned to themes of prayer and meditations upon the Scriptures. This ascetic character recommended Pico's philosophical achievements and life as a model to Sir Thomas More, who translated Gianfrancesco's biography into English. More and many others heard the voice of Pico lamenting the human predicament. Man, as image, would not conform with God, its exemplar. Remembering his hair shirt and self-flagellation, the condemnation of his works by one pope and his reconciliation with the next, they also heard Pico declare his way out of the predicament: that, in this world, men should reject earthly ambitions and the sensual appetites that made them brute animals; they should continually strive to become spiritual, conforming the human image with the divine exemplar.[19]

Pico struck a different tone in his writings before 1492. Then, he explored with exhilarated verve the metaphysical leveling that mysticism had achieved. His celebrated eclecticism was one aspect of this cast of mind.

[19] Eugenio Gavin, ed., *De hominis dignitate Heptaplus. De ente et uno* (Florence, 1942), ch. 10, pp. 438, 440.

Pico's *Oration* on the dignity of man showed one direction in which the impulse of mystical humanism moved. He saw ancient writings as a means of penetrating into the causes of things, the ways of nature, the plan of the universe, the purposes of God, and even the mysteries of heaven and earth.[20] It was the characteristic of a narrow intellect, he wrote, to confine itself to one philosophical school. Breadth was required of the true sage. In the first place, one had to know all schools before choosing from among them; and, in the second, each school had some special perception that it did not share with the others. Pico himself gloried in eclecticism. He had gone beyond Latin philosophy to Greek; and beyond formal philosophy to the Gnostic texts of Hermes Trismegistos, the Orphics, the Chaldeans, and the Pythagoreans. He had delved into the writings of the Church Fathers. He had studied the Cabala; he had devoted himself to the mystic science of numerology; though he despised astrology, he had studied magic as a device for the mastery of nature. Logic, magic, natural philosophy, and theology led to the hidden concordance among all religions. All, Pico argued, proved the unity of wisdom, just as the Cabala confirmed Christian doctrine and as his mystical researches had demonstrated the essential harmony of Plato's teachings with Aristotle's. But the ultimate composition of thought, chosen from many sources, depended on private judgment; for, Pico said, "philosophy herself has taught me to depend on my own conscience rather than on the judgments of others."[21]

This eclecticism may have anticipated the argument for toleration that *philosophes* advanced powerfully in the Enlightenment. It did not, however, lead Pico to the philosophical skepticism and religious agnosticism on which the *philosophes* grounded their arguments. Instead, Pico considered his attitude a vindication of religious faith. For our purposes, the salient facts are his contentions: (1) that all systems of belief and cult were proportionately true, partial witnesses to the same universal truth; (2) that the character of each man's life was also established by his relation to that truth; and (3) that each man had the power to take the miscellaneous evidence of philosophies and religions and compose his own relative truth out of their materials.

Pico's thought moved through circles of relativity: the relativity of philosophy and religion to ultimate truth, that of the individual person to literatures of inherited wisdom, and, finally, that of the person,

[20] E. Cassirer et al., *The Renaissance Philosophy of Man* (Chicago, 1948), ch. 21, p. 237f.
[21] Ibid. (adapted), ch. 22, cf. p. 238.

through those literatures, to truth itself. But knowledge, being partial, was only one side of the coin; ignorance was the other. The term that included them both was faith. A circle cannot be hierarchical; and one distinctive feature of Pico's stance is that, while he continued to think of the natural world as a hierarchy, or ladder, of being, he read human existence in terms of a concentric order of knowledge calibrated by faith.

A second aspect of metaphysical leveling, therefore, was Pico's double argument that there was a hierarchy of being in which, however, man had no fixed place. Instead of being a fixed rung on the ladder of life, man could choose his own level. Choice required sacrifice. Cultivating his lowest nature, the vegetal, meant losing the higher natures. Cultivating the highest faculties required "discounting all human concerns, despising the goods of fortune, and disregarding those of the body."[22] It required ascetic devotion to learning, a rejection of the senses as a way to knowledge, as taught by Aristotle and approved both by Thomists and nominalists. Greatly inspired by the Neoplatonism of Hermes Trismegistos, Pico taught a form of occult knowledge that, like the ancient doctrines, led to divinization. For, by neglect of this world and the physical body, man could "frequent the feast of the gods while yet living on earth, and, drunken with the nectar of eternity, be endowed with the gift of immortality though still a mortal animal."[23] "And if, content with the lot of no created things, he retreats into the center of his own unity, his spirit, made one with God, in the solitary darkness of the Father, who is set above all things, will excell them all."[24]

Evidently, Pico still worked within the structure of analogy defined by Augustine (see Chapter 3). The Father had identified three levels of existence to which the soul had access by corresponding modes of knowing: material existence, through analogues of existence (the eye of the flesh); intellectual existence, through analogues of being (the eyes of the mind); and spiritual existence, through analogues of faith (the eye of faith). The last two were primary in Pico's doctrine of mimetic transformation, as they had been in Augustine's.

Christ was essential to Pico's mysticism, but He was not primarily the Crucified, the sacrificial victim, the suffering and dead God, with whom the mystics wished to be united. Pico's mimetic strategies were

[22] Ibid., p. 233.   [23] Ibid., ch. 16, p. 233.
[24] Ibid., ch. 4, p. 225. On Pico's Christology, see C. Trinkaus, *In Our Image and Likeness* (Chicago, 1970) 2: 511, 522. The balance of Trinkaus's discussion is also illuminating.

associated with the Logos rather than with the man. For him, Christ was the Gnostic mediator, the leader whose personal union of divine and human formed the bridge over which man could pass into God, as Christ was formed in the believer. But man must choose and labor to pass from the lower to the higher nature. He must make himself God. As an independent and active power, man stood apart from the chain of life. In a sense, man was free from the fixed order of being, and, only by virtue of this alienation could he work out his private destiny.

With great embellishments, Pico repeated the ancient outline of creativity, the process by which man took the entire world into his soul, reshaped it into patterns, and then projected those patterns onto the world of actual things by re-making them according to the pictures in his mind. But Pico emphasized that man originated this process. Since each person contained the seeds and forms of all life, he was a microcosm, a small-scale model of the universe. At least in part, Pico rejected astrology because it curtailed the freedom of the human will. He agreed that the fate of the cosmos was tied to that of each soul; for he considered the universe to be the sum of all spiritual beings, and a change in one of its parts meant a change in the whole. But it was by deliberate, conscious, and incessant striving toward a higher plane of knowledge that each man could pass into the mystic extinction of self and become God, the creator of the spiritual cosmos. The terrifying grandeur of this conception reached its climax in the sense that by becoming God, the individual did not submerge himself in a nameless and oblivious spiritual death, he asserted himself; by the same acts with which he created the world in his own soul when he became God, he made God. In this way, Pico received and altered the yearning for salvation that had been so much a part of the analogy of faith, an idea that the Apostle Paul bequeathed to Christian theologians (Rom. 12:3; above, Chapter 2).

Such was the exhilarating vision that Pico patched together from Latin, Greek, and Hebrew texts, and that shimmered before his mind's eye when he wrote: "Thereupon Bacchus, the leader of the Muses, by showing in his mysteries, that is, in the visible signs of nature, the invisible things of God to us who practice philosophy, will inebriate us with the fullness of God's house, in which, if we prove faithful, like Moses, all most sacred theology shall come and animate us with a double frenzy. For, raised up to her most exalted vantage-point, we shall measure therefrom all things that are and shall be and have been in indivisible eternity; and, taking on their primaeval beauty, like the seers of Phoebus, we shall become her own winged lovers. And, finally, roused by ineffable love as by a sting, like burning Seraphim rapt from ourselves, full of the divinity, we shall no longer be ourselves but He Himself who made us."[25]

To Pico's mind, then, the analogy of being still existed in the hierarchy of life, but man was free of it. Human life was shaped by knowledge that, being partial, was also ignorance. Ultimate truth lay in the vast sphere of darkness, or ignorance, into which man penetrated by mystic intuition, and where his soul achieved a form analogous to its perception of truth. The analogy of faith referred, not to a hierarchy, but to an expansive concentric order composed of many parts.

Before Pico wrote, Nicholas of Cusa had already achieved a more radical leveling of metaphysics, one that applied to the analogy of being as well as to that of faith.

As a boy in Deventer, Cusa imbibed the mystical insights of his teachers, the Brethren of the Common Life. As a young man, at the University of Padua, he studied law, philosophy, and, especially, mathematics. His career, after he took holy orders and advanced, step by step, to the cardinalate, was extremely varied; it displays many of the less heroic traits of character associated with the ambidextrous politics of the Renaissance papacy. Before he was co-opted into the papal Curia as cardinal, he favored a general council as supreme in the Church; afterwards, he proclaimed the supremacy of the popes. Still, despite his political adroitness, Cusa retained a profound spirituality, which he expressed in one way by directing ecclesiastical reform; and he fused the humanistic enterprises of his early life into unity with it.

There is an apparent disjunction between Cusa's thought about being, which he defined mathematically, and that about faith, which he defined theologically. Let us begin with his concept of being.

Cusa's metaphysics began and ended with the concept of infinity. Man's supreme task was to cross the gap between his own finitude and the infinity that encompassed all the principles of knowledge. But, in this world, man existed within a sphere, not in an ascending hierarchy. The task of judging degrees of excellence was not possible; for mediation did not run from higher to lower, as in the Neoplatonic chain of being. Instead, all genera and species—the entire range—performed the function of mediation equally in the circle between God as the absolute maximum of infinity and God as its absolute minimum.[26] As the

---

[25] Cassirer et al., *Renaissance Philosophy of Man* (adapted), ch. 16, cf. p. 234.

[26] Nicholas of Cusa, *De docta ignorantia* 3. 1. 2 (*Philosophische Bibliothek,* ed. Raymond Klibansky [Hamburg, 1977, Bd 24c] 3: 2–16).

terms of infinity, present in any mathematical progression, He was equally distant from and present in all unity. "He is the center of the earth and of all things that are in the world, and, at the same time, he is the infinite circumference of all things."[27] God is sphere, center, and circumference; He is all in all. The cosmos is spiritual, and the spiritual growth of man in knowledge is the self-evolution of the cosmos, the self-explication of God.

On this point, Cusa's thought approaches Pico's; it recalls John Scotus's and Meister Eckhart's. The universe was composed of a vast number of spiritual beings, each of which had its independent center of life, its own identity. But each of those independent centers in turn responded to the gravitational pull of the same divine center; each, by existing, contributed to the absolute. Through its own self, the individual participated in God, and, in fact, became a constituent and a constituting part of God. For God was the incremental creative process to which all things contributed. Each man was part of that process, which was God actualizing Himself; and thus, insofar as he developed his own nature, man was making God. "In Thee, God, being created coincides with creating. For the likeness (*similitudo*) which seems to be created by me is the truth which created me."[28] In this way, the infinite and the finite, the eternal present and passing time, divinity and humanity all coincided in the unity that reconciled all contradictions, that united the image with the unchangeable truth that it represented.[29]

The apparent discrepancy between Cusa's analogies of being and faith occurs because of his doctrines concerning Christ. The univer-

---

[27] In a new cast, Cusa is repeating the thought of a Pseudo-Hermetic tract that once taken up by Alain of Lille (*Theologiae regulae*, Reg. VII [*PL* 210: 627]) passed into the common mystical vocabulary: God is the "intelligible sphere whose center is everywhere, and whose circumference is nowhere," *De docta ignorantia,* 3. 1 (ed. cit. 3: 6): There is one *terminus* of species, genera, and the universe, a *terminus* that is the center, circumference, and cohesive bond (*conexio*) of all. Ibid., 3. 8 (ed. cit. 3: 60), God is the center and circumference of intellectual nature. Cf. Bonaventura, *Itinerarium mentis ad Deum* 6. 7 (*Opera Omnia* [Quaracchi, 1891], 5: 312). Jean Gerson, *Contra curiositatem studentium*, in ed. P. Glorieux, *Oeuvres complètes* (Paris, 1962), 3: 232; Pascal, *Pensées,* 72. See also Frances A. Yates, *Giordano Bruno and the Hermetic Tradition* (New York, 1969), pp. 247f. The figure was also accepted by Herder in his defense of Spinoza, as a symbol of the endlessness of eternity. *Gott. Einige Gespräche,* 2. Gesp. Bernhard Suphan, ed., *Herders Sämmtliche Werke* (Berlin, 1887), 16: 456.

[28] *De visione Dei,* ch. 15. L. Gabriel, ed., *Nikolaus von Kues, Philosophisch-theologische Schriften* (Vienna, 1967), 3: 162.

[29] *De visione Dei,* 15 and 23, pp. 162, 200ff.

salism that his concept of being implies would seem at odds with his insistence that each person's humanity depended upon his union, by faith, with the Crucified. Indeed, there are passages, composed during the Cardinal's many-faceted intellectual Odyssey, in which creedal differences—among Christian, Saracen, and Jew—were minimized. At such moments, Cusa grounded humanity in the circularity of being. *Humanitas,* he wrote, was the power by which man took the world into himself by the senses, formed mental images, and realized those images in the unshaped matter of the world. It was the form-giving power in the world, the force that subordinated nature to ideas. It was the quality that made man the likeness of the Creator God, and that made him in some sense God. Centuries earlier, the author of the Pseudo-Hermetic treatises had written, "gods are immortal men and men are mortal gods." Nicholas of Cusa repeated these words almost exactly and gave his own interpretation: "Man is God," he wrote, "but not absolutely since he is man. God therefore is human. Man is also the world. But not all things on a contracted scale, because he is man. Man is therefore a microcosm, or the world is human. This realm of humanity therefore encompasses God and the whole world by its human power. Man can therefore be a human god and God, humanly, can be a human angel, a human beast, a human lion or bear or any-thing else. For all things exist, each in its own way, within this power of humanity."[30] Nicholas attributed to *humanitas* the same features as the divine Logos had had in Greek philosophy and in writings of the early Church.

But the connection with the Logos never allowed Cusa to exclude the Crucified definitively from his theories. Only Jesus, the first-born of all creation, both God and man, had been able to rise above human nature to eternal things. Only through His death were the carnal de-sires of human nature extinguished and purged. By their own powers, without Christ, men could do nothing. But, transformed into His na-ture and absorbed in Him, they abandoned their animality, becoming part of His full humanity, which subsumed the entire power of the human species. Certainly, the Cardinal wrote, there was one humanity for all men. But there was a difference between capacity and fulfill-ment. Man attained the vision of eternal things, the immortality, and the incorruptibility that fulfilled his humanity by forsaking the world

---

[30] *De conjecturis* 2. 143 (*Nikolaus von Kues Werke* ed. Paul Wilpert [Berlin, 1967. Quellen und Studien zur Geschichte der Philosophie,* Bd V], 1: 173). *Corpus Hermeti-cum* 12 (13), 1.

of flesh, imitating Christ in daily mortifications, and exultantly following Him by taking up the cross. The fulfillment of humanity required
that each person believe in Christ up to the limit of his own, individual
capacity. Without such faith, small as it might be proportionately, no
one would taste the fruit of redemption.[31]

Pico had admonished his reader to seek knowledge by turning inward, "into the center of his own unity." In this way, Cusa likewise rejected empiricism. The mind must search itself and freely explicate its
own being. Mathematics, Cusa thought, was the only sure device of
this explication. The most abstract of languages, it did not carry the
freight of connotations that confused verbal expressions. The most
comprehensive of mental systems, it brought infinite and finite into an
intellectual balance and relationship that Aristotelian logic denied as
an illicit harmony of opposites. Through mathematics, man created
the divisions of time, by which he perceived the interrelation of events
and the harmony in music and in the movements of the heavenly
bodies. Through mathematics, man established the degrees of value in
achievements, knowledge, and modes of existence. Through mathematics, the mind gave meaning and order to the undifferentiated
knowledge that came to it through the senses. Through mathematics,
the mind moved toward the absolute.

And yet, all knowledge remained indefinite, conjectural. Fond as he
was of paradoxes, Nicholas had no difficulty in concluding that ignorance was the greatest learning, or in holding that faith was the core of
all understanding that encompassed every intelligible thing, disclosing
even the greatest mysteries of God to the simple and hiding them from
the wise.[32]

Even in mathematical abstractions, knowledge dealt only with the
contingent and the limited; as Augustine wrote long before, it was
"learned ignorance," with equal weight on the two terms. No matter
how refined the formulation, no matter how precise the mathematical
measurement, another more elegant formulation, another fractionally
more precise measurement, was possible. The infinite eluded all proportion, but human knowledge remained circumscribed by comparisons and analogues.[33]

There was a way, however, in which the apparent disjunction between the analogues of being and faith could be resolved, and positive

[31] *De docta ignorantia* 3. 3, 6, 8, 11, 12; ed. cit. 3: 20–24, 44–46, 56, 82–84, 86–90.
[32] Ibid., 1. 2; 3. 11. Paul Wilpert ed. (Hamburg, 1964), 1: 12; ed. cit., 3: 76.
[33] Ibid., 1. 1. Ed. cit. 1: 6–8.

knowledge reached. Nicholas described that way in his short treatise, *On the Vision of God.* Mimetic conceptions dominate the whole treatise. Nicholas described God as a "mirror of eternity" (ch. 15), a "living mirror in which all things shine forth" (ch. 12). This was so because God beheld all things in Himself, and also because things that actually existed in the world beheld their exemplars in Him. Nicholas united art and mystical spirituality, seeing and form. He began with the pedagogic device of the icon of God, which gave the impression of looking directly and solely at the individual viewer. Much of Nicholas's argument hangs on equations that he drew with sight, equations that repeat the words of St. Augustine. Seeing equals all the attributes of God. Seeing equals giving of self, and, since it also equals receiving of self, it is equivalent to being seen. Seeing equals motion, presence, and work. Seeing equals causing. Seeing equals God, essence, and existence. Seeing equals speaking: that is, the Word, God's one and only concept. Through this elaborate structure, which owed much to St. Augustine and his followers, including Thomas Aquinas, Nicholas sustained his argument that the omnivoyant icon truly represented God's creation and preservation of the world by beholding each individual creature. In this sense, the Cardinal forecast Berkeley's position that to be was to be perceived.

Nicholas's equations concerning sight were part of a broader argument expressing the Neoplatonic concept of form. The entire treatise was built as an elegant series in which Nicholas considers God in various archetypal roles, beginning with God as absolute sight, and progressing through His increasingly more comprehensive characters: absolute ground of natures, absolute reason, absolute beauty, absolute power, absolute being, absolute freedom, absolute cause, absolute form, and others, ending in the last sentences with the most comprehensive of all—absolute God. In all these points, Nicholas worked out the formal aspects of the argument while he also elucidated its dynamic aspects through the equations of sight. Likeness established dependence and dependence, unity. As absolute sight, God was the pattern and basis of all limited modes of sight, and the same identity between being and acting tied man, as image, to God, as exemplar, in all other respects.

And yet, Nicholas's concept of mimesis went beyond the doctrine of stable, transcendent forms, for, in some ways, the image was the archetype. After considering God as absolute form, Nicholas went on to fill out his portrait of God with other characteristics entirely foreign to Platonic thought. God was absolute necessity and absolute potentiality. These roles implied a lack of finality or of abiding unity in the world of forms, and Nicholas explicitly developed a teleology that described God as an "end without an end" that appeared in matter and in the phenomena of time, and that was all potential being. Nicholas carried his Augustinian model to a new height when he insisted that divine nature did not change, and yet he taught that the divine nature was the very principle of change in a cosmology that described the world as God's continual self-unfolding and self-enfolding. He made God the archetype of necessity and potentiality, and, through the coincidence of opposites anticipated by John Scotus Eriugena, he identified creating with being created, the truth with the images that expressed it. In this non-Augustinian sense, one has to understand Nicholas's Augustinian maxims that God did not follow mutability and that He did not follow the creature (ch. 15).

One more set of archetypal roles sets Nicholas apart from the stable, transcendent forms: namely, those dealing with Christ. Nicholas described Jesus as the absolute mediator and absolute son. But his Christology was not primarily one of atonement. Like John Scotus, Eckhart, and Pico, Nicholas emphasized the Logos rather than the man. Jesus was not identical with the divine Word; He was an "all-perfect" man who was "most closely linked" with the Word, and, in this qualified sense, He was the Word of God humanified, and man deified. Moreover, the death of God did not occur. Christ was never separated from true life, even though He truly submitted to death. He laid aside His vivifying soul and took it up again when He wished; He rose in His own power. (The shadow, or apparition, of the true man, which had appeared in time, disappeared; the true man rose from the dead.)[34] God was the "Idea and exemplar of all men" (ch. 9); one approached this Idea through the mediacy of Jesus. For Nicholas, Jesus had become a cosmic spirit that could not "be lacking to any spirit" (ch. 25). Grace and sin, the bases for the theology of sacrifice, had been eroded in Nicholas's thought. For God beheld all who believed in Him. His Word continually spoke within man, needing only to be heard. It was man's choice whether to yield to the lower powers—the vegetal, or animal, or imaginative, or reasoning faculties—or to listen to the Word speaking in the intellect, the highest power of the soul, and thus to become increasingly like the Word, indeed, to become Christ.

[34] Ibid., 3. 7. Ed. cit., 3: 50.

Nicholas transformed Christ as atoning sacrifice into Christ as cosmic principle, as a model of human conduct, as a teacher of wisdom, but, even more, as "maximal humanity," the total, and growing, union of believers with Christ. And in this transformation, the world created for spiritual redemption also changed into a Gnostic world made for the sake of the intellectual nature, mounting by its own powers into the divine darkness, moving progressively and cumulatively toward the invisible vision in which absolute necessity and absolute impossibility coincided.

To their own minds, Pico and Cusa kept the patristic doctrine that God and man were separate, as archetype and copy, and that they were therefore related and divided by similarity (which implies dissimilarity). But they also exalted a virtual relationship between image and archetype that, given the ambiguities of metaphor, the excesses of rhetoric and the passions of mind sometimes went beyond relationship into complete identity.

The importance of their thought for our account lies in the weight they gave the lives of individual, historical men. The metaphysical hierarchy of being did not figure in their reflections on human capacity. The decisive factor was faith, which subsumed both the knowledge by which man's soul was formed and the vast ignorance in which stood his archetype and goal. To loyal Augustinians, analogues of faith counted for much more than those of being, and they were gauged on the aggregate scale of quantity, not on the qualitative one of hierarchy.

A further characteristic of their thought was the reciprocal action of image and archetype upon each other. This followed from flattening the metaphysical hierarchy. The archetype was in the flux of things, rather than above it. Consequently, the partial truths that individual men realized in their lives enlarged the archetypal truth. The circularity of this interplay is indicated by Pico's argument that, when men became God, they made Him who made them and by Cusa's sentence, "the likeness which seems to be created by me is the truth which created me." The historical man personified the creative force of the cosmos; but he was also engulfed by it.

Finally, the historical life of man was not his physical existence. For the interplay of image and archetype required an ascetic mortification of the flesh, a negation of natural desires and ambitions, and a withdrawal into the concentric order of knowlege, beyond what was accessible to the senses, reason, or intellect, and beyond the imagery of words, into the center, the resplendent darkness of informing silence.

Summary

It is time to summarize what had been achieved before the Reformation dawned. Beginning with the sixth century, Europe entered into a series of social configurations that the received tradition was inadequate to explain. Even to men who lacked modern techniques of historical criticism, and even to those who insisted that truth was always and everywhere the same, it was apparent that contemporary problems could not be solved merely by applying doctrines that belonged to a dead social order. The substance of those controversies over government and faith called for ways to legitimate change. The power of man to bring about licit changes in the established order of things was therefore both one of the most apparent facts and one of the most fundamental problems. It was necessary to find some way to demonstrate that the eternal verities had been upheld, even while institutions and whole systems of thought that they had once sanctioned were overthrown. The importation of ancient Greek texts and of more recent non-Christian commentaries on them enlarged the means by which the Latin West could analyze the problem of legitimating change. Because those texts had nothing to say about Christian dogma, they also introduced running controversies.

Before the twelfth century, Christians taught two major ways in which the world advanced toward perfection.

The first was reversion; this method posited the double act of egress and return set forth in Neoplatonic idealism. The material world and its creatures were reduced copies of divine being. The cosmos was a descending hierarchy, each stage of which reflected the divine perfection less well than the one above it. By yearning for completeness, each moved toward the orders above it; the soul of man could regress through all the intervening stages to God, the origin and goal of the cosmos.

The second way was augmentation, especially in doctrines of continual creation. It was put succinctly by an illustrious forerunner of Christian exegetes, Philo of Alexandria, in his commentary on the account of the six days of Creation given in *Genesis:* "But we pointed out that God, when ceasing or rather causing to cease does not cease making, but begins the creating of other things, since He is not a mere artificer, but also Father of the things that are coming into being."[35] The

---

[35] *Allegorical Interpretation of Genesis 2:3* 1. 18. 7. Loeb. transl., *Philo* 1: 157.

doctrine passed through the Alexandrine theologians to the West, where Augustine argued that God commanded all generative agents to "increase and multiply," ever-replenishing the world. In obeying, they drew out the moment of creation, just as, in a figurative way, the same command was given to apostles, prophets, and teachers in the Church who obeyed with labors through which the Gospel steadily increased and multiplied among men.[36] When transferred from the sphere of metaphysical being to that of historical experience, the doctrine of augmentation described a continual Incarnation. The Fathers adapted it to teach that the Church was the Body of Christ, growing through time as new members were added to it.

The progressive sense of augmentation was complex. For, to explain likeness in this way before the twelfth century, one could not only suppose that God was above the world as its Maker. One had to think also that He was in it as the life that was the life of all creatures and as the spirit of love that transformed the souls of men and compacted them into the Body of Christ. Even so, the archetype that man and the world imitated remained above them and outside of time. Taking into account continual creation, Augustine was able to write that, in the eternal present of His knowledge, God had already made all things that had been, or were, or were still to be.[37] The formation of the Body of Christ through stages of history was also part of the cosmic poem that had ever been complete in its Author's mind.

For the career of mimesis, it was decisive that the Fathers incorporated mimetic strategies in the very heart of their theology: that is, in their doctrines of Christ. Inasmuch as they elucidated cosmic order and the natural cycle of generation and decay, both strategies of reversion and augmentation were applied to Christ as Logos, "the art of the Father," by and in whom all things were made. To imitate Christ as Logos was to live according to reason (*ratio*), the faculty that, above all, marked man as the image of God. However, because sin had deformed human nature, this could not be done without the corrective mediation of Christ as man. Thus, the moral aspects of life had to be reformed by the imitation of Christ in His carnality, as portrayed in the Gospel, and as administered to believers through the sacraments. While strategies of reversion and augmentation tended to be associated with Christ as Logos, those of historical inversion and subversion were attached to Christ as man. Both clusters operated in individ-

---

[36] *Conf.* 13. 24f. (*CSEL*, 33. 375–377).
[37] *City of God* 22. 2. (*CSEL*, 40, pt. 2, p. 585).

ual conversion; for one shared in Christ's divinity by participating in His humanity. Both clusters operated in the history of the world; for the return of Christ to the Father was the growth of His Body, the Church. Except in the Eucharist, the asymmetry of image and archetype could never be resolved, but only ceaselessly mediated. The centrality of these doctrines in Christian theology ingrained mimetic strategies of transformation into the West's common culture, as well as into the esoteric culture of the learned.

By the ninth century, the strategies of inversion and subversion had ceased to be independent categories of thought. They had been absorbed into the strategies of reversion and augmentation.

This was the heritage that Europe received in the twelfth century and that it gradually altered thereafter. Two Aristotelian premises were decisive: causality and the active intellect. Along with these, Aristotle and his commentators also brought other provocative concepts into Western thought, such as the eternity of matter and the indestructibility of the world. As these new and startling doctrines were considered and digested, conveyance of likeness by augmentation through time was seen to correspond with concepts of the organic unity of human experience more adequately than the conveyance of likeness by diminution. But it, too, had to be adapted. Very slowly, writers began to combine doctrines of mimesis with one of Aristotle's non-mimetic theories of change. In describing how things come to be, Aristotle had argued that each of the four elements—earth, air, fire, and water—could change into any of the others, unlike as they were, by a process of conversion or reciprocal transformation.[38] This kind of change differed from mimetic transformation by change of shape, as in a statue, by increment as in growing things, by subtraction, as in realizing a pattern already present in natural materials, or by composition, as in building a house. But intense reflection from the twelfth century onward demonstrated that change by conversion could be used to describe the mimetic relations of God and man extending through time. It was only necessary to reconcile the concepts of God and change to round out a theory of mimesis in the process of augmentation.

The Platonic strategy of mimesis by reversion retreated as the Aristotelian strategy of mimesis by augmentation advanced.

There were two major variants of this new theory. The first variant

---

[38] *De Gen. et Corr.* 2. 4. 331a–b. Cf. *Physics* 1. 190b. Above, Chapter 1, after note 52.

kept creating and being created separate. Thus, it preserved the integrity of the individual and regarded the course of change as fulfilling a predetermined end or capacity. Aristotle's simile of an acorn growing into an oak tree aptly illustrates this concept. But the individual was regarded as part of a wider community that he defined and by which in turn he was defined. In theology, the composite elements summed up in mimesis by growth led to a conception of man as the image of God in two senses. The first isolated him in his particular time and place and capacity for freedom; the second made him universal by the irradiation of his soul with the light of God's countenance. The theory that man was both solitary and universal also figured in the second variant.

The second variant identified creating and being created. According to it, mimesis in augmentation isolated the individual by assigning to each person the freedom to choose his own spiritual nature, without regard for a hierarchy of being. But the doctrine of faith that enveloped that freedom had a contrary effect. It was characteristic of this variant that the emphasis shifted from Christ as man to Christ as Logos, eroding the line between God and His image in the enlightened soul. From Plotinus to Thomas Aquinas, authors had insisted that the deification of man produced a heightened similarity, a transfiguration in which likeness was restored to the image, but diversity remained. Through doctrines of the communication of idioms, fourteenth- and fifteenth-century thought advanced to the point at which it was hard to distinguish similarity from identity. Asymmetry of image and archetype shaded into unity. From the doctrine of God as all-in-all, some preachers and writers moved quite deliberately into pantheism. Others used the language and metaphors of pantheism, even while they maintained that several bands on the spectrum of meaning divided them from that family of heresies. In either case, creating and being created were aspects of the same act; God became in His image. If an author held to the doctrine of the eternity of the world, and had disdained the dogma of the Last Judgment as a vestige of an aboriginal age, he could foresee no end to this reciprocal transformation of God and His image. It could go on indefinitely, infinitely. The transcendent hierarchy was leveled. The strategy of mimesis by augmentation became a study, not in the asymmetry of a fixed transcendent order, but rather in a relation of relations within an expanding concentric order, an interaction of parts by which the whole itself was changed.

The identification of God with man in the process of mimetic augmentation meant that God did not merely set the rhythm of change, as Augustine taught. He was that rhythm, the archetype of transition that destroyed as it created, and that men performed in their struggles and sufferings. The artist was an integral part of the varying relations that made up the total composition. And so it could be said that—in history as well as in nature—God became as phenomena expressed Him.

Mimesis by augmentation was in the ascendant; mimesis by reversion, in decline.

But was there any wholeness such as these theories took for granted? Did not the analogue of faith, as developed by mystics and humanists, preserve erroneous doctrines and arrogant, self-worshipping metaphors drawn from pagan doctrines of being? Augustine had spoken with two voices, the one full of imagery, the other iconoclastic. From the fourteenth century onwards, there were men of great fervor who embraced the iconoclastic Augustine and rejected all mental images and their visible expressions as idolatrous, applying to them Jesus' reproach, "Full well ye reject the commandment of God that ye may keep your own tradition" (Mark 7:9). For what was the value of form devised by men, when Christ Himself, the transcendent sacrifice, was without form or comeliness? "He had no beauty . . . no grace to make us delight in Him. His form, disfigured, lost all the likeness of a man. His beauty changed beyond human resemblance" (Isaiah 53:2).

It was apparent, moreover, that pressed to extremes, the identity of God's spirit with man's did away with one element that was crucial both in Augustine's philosophy of mimesis and in his theology of salvation: that is, it diffused the role of mediation. There was no need of mediation if the archetype and the copy were the same; there was no unique mediator if all believers, or even the entire cosmos, performed mediative functions.

Inspired by these perceptions, Augustinian iconoclasts threw aside sensual images and poetic analogues. They returned to the Scriptures as the only authentic rule of life, and rejected whatever smacked of self-admiring anthropomorphism. They insisted on the distance between man and God, and the need of a mediator to bridge the gulf between them. They embraced the warfare of the militant minority, the people of God, against the world. They denied any spiritual merit in human works. They stigmatized as depraved the creative power that others had described as certifying that man was the image of God: the power of the will. The Reformation, that great conflict of faith against faith, was at hand.

III

Mimesis in the Renewal of the Classical
Tradition: ca. 1500–1900

Chapter 10

Challenges to the Mimetic Tradition

BEGINNING with the Reformation, powerful institutions and articulate and influential cohorts within the intelligentsia began to reject some basic assumptions of the mimetic tradition, which had earlier been questioned only by isolated individuals. Throughout the history of Western culture, strategies of mimesis had been thought to operate in nature, in art, and between nature and art. In the ceaseless renewal of tradition, mimetic mediation between nature and art was dominant. From the patristic age onward, ideas about mimesis in that area had been rooted in theological propositions about Christ as mediator between God and man, and about the mind as mediator between transcendent Truth and the soul. Denials of these two sets of assumptions in the sixteenth century came chiefly from two quarters: first from the theology of reformers (especially Luther and Calvin) and, later, from empiricist philosophies of thought. The mimetic tradition was too deeply ingrained into the fabric of European culture to be eradicated. It pervaded high culture, to be sure. It was also an integral part of popular culture, as the writings of Jacob Boehme, a cobbler, and John Bunyan, a tinker, indicate. The challenges from theologians and philosophers therefore evoked responses and reformulations that drew directly from a widespread social mentality.

In the present chapter, I shall briefly describe some issues on which, in very different ways, Luther, Calvin, and advocates of empirical psychology challenged ideas of mimetic mediation between nature and art during the sixteenth and seventeenth centuries. In the next two chapters, I shall suggest a wide spectrum of religious and secularized mimetic doctrines that these challenges left untouched. Finally, I shall turn to the specific theme of how the challenges and residual doctrines combined into mimetic strategies mediating asymmetry by historical progress, as exemplified by two thoroughly diverse writers in the eighteenth century, David Hume and Johann Gottfried von Herder, and by four German scholars in the nineteenth century.

As a strategy of correction by mediating the asymmetries of nature and art, or archetype and image, mimesis early found a secure footing at the heart of Christian theology. From the Apostle Paul onward, it was embedded in doctrines about Christ, explaining how, as mediator, He remedied the defects of human nature. Differing mimetic strategies were attached to the two natures of Christ. Taken together, teachings about man's innate likeness to Christ as Logos and about his moral conformity with Christ as man justified institutions as well as theological premises. Salvation came by assimilation to Christ's divinity. The first step was participation in Christ's humanity by the *imitatio Christi;* and, as we have seen, doctrines concerning the resurrection, the veneration of the Virgin and saints, the sacraments (especially baptism and the Eucharist), penitential discipline, and the hierarchic Church centered on the humanity of Christ. Institutions designed to translate theory into practice by teaching and constraint had the same center.

How a given person combined mimetic strategies of mediating asymmetry depended on his doctrine of Christ. Throughout the career of mimesis, a persistent division separated those who emphasized the cosmic operations of the Logos from those who gave first place to the ascetic self-denial of Christ, the man. Evidently, any major change in thought about Christ's mediation entailed reappraisal of mimetic strategies.

Luther and Calvin proved to be deniers of mimetic strategies of transformation because they rejected mimetic Christology.

Luther and Calvin

The keystone of mimetic Christologies was the idea of mediated asymmetries. The Logos, the Word of God, mediated between divinity and the actual world. Christ, the Word-made-flesh, mediated between the wisdom of God and the ignorance of man. In each case, archetype and image could be assimilated to each other because their natures combined in the mediator. By participation, they were, not mutually exclusive, but mutually reflective.

Luther rejected the idea of mimetic mediation. For him, Christ as mediator performed a single act: propitiation. The saving effects of mediation came about, not by participation, but by imputation: the imputation of Christ's righteousness to man and of man's sinfulness to

Christ. By this imputation, which took place on the Cross, Christ reconciled God and man, the offended and the offender, satisfying the Law in His own body, by Himself. The other functions that Luther ascribed to Christ as mediator—such as intercession—were encompassed in this one juridical act,[1] which entailed the deliverance, but not the transformation, of the soul.

Luther rejected mimetic mediation because he first denied the asymmetry of archetype and image between God and the soul. Writers who taught mimetic Christologies had argued that Christ's mediation consisted partly in His exemplarism. By imitating Him, souls were assimilated to Him, healed and reformed. Repudiating the idea that human works contributed to salvation, Luther was of a different mind. He invoked the instance of Abraham. Abraham was not saved, he wrote, because Christ set an example and Abraham modeled his actions on it, but rather because Christ redeemed and Abraham believed.[2] When Paul wrote, "I am crucified with Christ," he did not mean that the Crucifixion gave an example of ascetic self-denial for man to imitate. The Apostle spoke of the moment when, once and for all, sin, the devil, and death, were crucified in Christ, not in the believer. Christ did all alone; but, by faith, the Christian was crucified with Christ.[3] Luther's doctrines excluded assimilation to Christ by mimetic action as firmly as it did mimetic transformation.

When they set forth the Crucified as an example to be imitated, Luther argued, the Pope and his followers preached the false doctrine of works. They thereby concealed the knowledge that Christ was made a curse to deliver men from the curse of the Law, with all the works that it prescribed. Instead of conveying the comfort that Luther found in his doctrine of utter dependence, they erected a new law, as full of terrors as the Mosaic Law, and they transformed Christ from a propitiator into an angry, condemning judge.[4] Indeed, hypocrites and idolaters that they were, they used exemplarism to enhance their own powers. For they claimed that by works and hierarchic order they imparted righteousness: that is, they pretended to exercise the divinity and office of Christ.[5] Having limited mediation to juristic satisfaction, Luther ascribed spiritual transformation to the Holy Spirit, not to Christ, and he ruled out almost every trace of Christ's exemplarism.

Luther's concept of mediation as a juristic act thus excluded doc-

---

[1] *Commentary on Galatians* 3: 6, 13, 20 (*WA*, 40, pt. 1, pp. 364, 371f., 450f., 501f.).
[2] Ibid., 3: 9 (*WA*, 40, pt. 1, pp. 389f.).
[3] Ibid., 2: 20 (*WA*, 40, pt. 1, pp. 280f.).   [4] Ibid., 3: 13 (*WA*, 40, pt. 1, p. 434).
[5] Ibid., 3: 10 (*WA*, 40, pt. 1, p. 406).

trines of mimesis as a corrective strategy associated with Christ. Thus, it militated against institutions—such as monasticism, penetential discipline, veneration of the saints, and the Church hierarchy—called forth, and justified, by those doctrines. Naturally, as we shall see later in this chapter, it also excluded the doctrines of the sacraments as acts of mimetic transformation. But all of these effects were facets of a broader consequence: Luther's assault upon tradition.

The various strategies of mimetic change that Luther rejected had enabled men to think of human experience as an unfolding, harmonious work of art, the slow, but continual, realization of a pattern in God's mind. However, Luther contended that the visible Church had for centuries perverted authentic doctrine with "the impious traditions" of the Pope. The Church's appeal to continuity was a sign that it had "only a historical faith concerning Christ, which the devil also and all the wicked have."[6]

Against the "merely historical faith" of the papists, Luther advocated his own doctrine of an inward and incommunicable union with Christ. He demolished the force of tradition by his insistence that "Christ and my conscience must become one body" in such fashion that "Christ and I are made as it were one body in spirit." For it was by this union that imputation occurred, and the believer became partaker, with Christ, in grace, righteousness, and life.[7]

The outcome was the intimate conviction that Christ performed His work of mediation "for me." The authenticity of this feeling outweighed the authority of tradition. It also undercut one further element of earlier mimetic strategies. Just as it involved a rejection of the ascetic exemplarism of Christ crucified, it also entailed a rejection of the cosmic exemplarism of the Logos. We have seen repeatedly that strategies of reversion and augmentation were keyed to the idea that man was the image of God in his finite reason, the Logos being archetypal reason. This premise lay behind the assumption that progress in knowledge about God took place through study, reflection, and debate over the centuries: in other words, that tradition advanced by criticism of criticism that was both rational and mimetic. Thus, Thomas Aquinas taught that each person recapitulated the tradition in his own spiritual growth, and that each recapitulation enlarged the Body of Christ.

Luther also dislodged this major element of mimetic strategies; for

---

[6] Ibid., 2: 20, 21 (*WA*, 40, pt. 1, pp. 285, 304).
[7] Ibid., 2: 20 (*WA*, 40, pt. 1, pp. 282, 284).

him, reason was a "beast" to be killed by faith.[8] Far from being the archetypal characteristic that distinguished men from brute animals and made them like God, it was precisely this faculty that prevented carnal men from discerning the things of the Spirit. Among those spiritually blinded by reason could be counted the "dogs and swine" that opposed Luther's teachings.[9]

Augustine, a guiding star in Luther's intellectual firmament, had taught that the faculties of man's soul—the memory, intellect, and will—constituted the image of the Trinity, distinct in idioms, but one by the communication of idioms. Luther could not accept this interpretation; for, if the image existed in the faculties of mind, Satan, having memory, intellect, and will, must also be the image of God. Certainly, Luther argued, man had been created as the image of God in his wisdom, justice, and knowledge of all things. But, through Adam's sin, this ontological image was lost, just as the original world and Paradise disappeared. The faculties of the soul remained, though enfeebled and depraved. The physical existence of the world became corrupt through the same cosmic disaster, plagued with disease and thorns; the nature of beasts changed into ferocity.[10]

As a whole, mankind had lost the image of God and taken on that of the devil.[11] Ontologically, therefore, all men carried the image (that is, the nature) of Adam, a sinner whose reason was blinded, whose flesh was destroyed, with ardent love of sin, disbelief, and doubt. Through faith, the elect carried the unfinished image of Christ, and, through it, they put on Christ's death and resurrection, His life, grace, and virtue. God's grace opened this second image only to a few, by rebirth.

Luther compounded the ambiguities in his thought when he wrote in terms of a double existence. Falling back on St. Paul's distinction between the animal man and the spiritual man (1 Cor. 2:10–16), he said, "There is then a double life. The first is mine, which is natural or animal; the second is another, that is to say, the life of Christ in me. As touching my natural life, I am dead, and now I live another life."[12] Because the image of Christ is still incomplete, the redeemed state of existence is not yet fully achieved. It is already and not yet present— already in hope, not yet in actuality. And so, in terms of his human

[8] Ibid., 2: 20, 3: 6 (*WA*, 40, pt. 1, pp. 293, 362).
[9] Ibid., 3: 19 (*WA*, 40, pt. 1, p. 475).
[10] *Commentary on Genesis* 1: 26–27; *Genesis* 2: 2–8 (*WA*, 42, pp. 41ff., 56ff.).
[11] *Sermon on Genesis* 1: 24–27 (*WA*, 24, pp. 50ff.).
[12] *Commentary on Galatians* 2: 20 (*WA*, 40, pt. 1, p. 287).

existence, the elect is a sinner under the curse, while he is also, in terms of his second existence, holy and redeemed.

Why Luther departed from the old mimetic doctrine that man participated in God's transcendent image, the Logos, is shown by his interpretation of what St. Paul meant when he said that Christ was in the form of God and yet took on the form of a servant in the Incarnation (Phil. 2:5–8). Here again, Luther explicitly rejected the premise of an exemplary, ideal form. It was wrong, he said, to apply the terms "form of God" and "human form" to divine and human nature. The form of God was not nature, but the operations that expressed righteousness; the form of a servant was the works of service by which, not only the divine Christ, but even a mortal Christian, could be said to take on the likeness of men and be found in human form, dealing with other men as God, through Christ, had dealt with him.[13]

Luther severed the worlds of transcendent nature and human art when he denied exemplarism of Christ both as Logos and as self-giving mediator, or sacrifice. However, he did retain Christ's exemplarism in moral conduct, not for salvation, but for the welfare of the community; and this led to a further difficulty. For it located what was left of mimetic doctrine in the outer context of existence, rather than in the internal one of faith.

"Christ's life and suffering are presented to us in two ways in the Scripture: first, as a gift that we grasp through faith, and second as an example and archetype."[14] Clearly, Christ's sufferings and death belonged to Christ's flesh, in which sin, the devil, and death were crucified. They were not crucified in the believer, but in Christ alone. Christ suffered *for* the believer. The believer did not participate in Christ by likeness, but became part of Christ's actual body, "one loaf" with the propitiator. Being crucified by faith with Christ, he could only acknowledge that sin, the devil, and death were crucified and dead for him (but not in him or through his efforts).[15] Thus, the believer acknowledged the benefits of atonement when he followed Christ's example of suffering and service for others; but his works contributed nothing to Christ's complete and sufficient self-sacrifice, for ultimately, all men with their works and services were the enemies of God.[16]

This doctrine clearly had the greatest importance for Luther's con-

---

[13] *On the Freedom of a Christian,* chs. 26–27 (*WA,* 7, pp. 34ff.).

[14] *Sermon on I. Peter* 4: 1 (*WA,* 12, p. 372). *Sermon on I. John* 3: 5 (*WA,* 20, p. 701).

[15] *Commentary on Galatians* 2: 20 (*WA,* 40, pt. 1, pp. 298ff.).

[16] *Commentary on Exodus* 19: 25 (*WA,* 16, pp. 417f.).

cept of the Church; by restricting mimetic exemplarism to the social context, Luther fundamentally changed the concept of the visible Church from that of inward communion to that of community, held together by external bonds, understood as duties. The difference is apparent in Luther's understanding of the verb "to be" in two key propositions: "The Church is the body of Christ," and the Eucharistic statements, "This is my body.... This is my blood." In both instances, Luther denied that the verb could be understood literally.

The same reasoning lay behind both Luther's doctrine of the Church and his denial of transubstantiation. The fundamental act by which man participated in Christ was faith, answering to God's calling through grace. It was a personal and not a collective act. As Luther said at Worms, the Pope was no judge of things touching the Word of God and the faith. Every Christian must inquire and judge how he ought to live and die according to God's Word and faith; for those two things were private to each man in the whole community.[17] Thus, it followed that the disciple of Christ must consider the whole world as his enemy—not only the wicked, but even his closest and best friends, venerable and holy people in the eyes of the world who, in answer to his faithfulness to Christ, would condemn and persecute him as a heretic, the property of Satan, and the foulest abomination on earth.[18]

Even within the Church, then, the believer was essentially alone, reliant on the dictates of his own conscience. To be sure, Luther always insisted that membership in the Church imposed obligations of love. But the love that impels a believer to share in his neighbor's situation is a lost love, given without regard for gain or loss, without regard for the neighbor's response, and in recognition that it has no bearing on salvation for anyone, least of all for those from whom God has withheld Himself.

To summarize: Luther limited mimesis of Christ to the sphere of moral conduct. He attached to imitation no metaphysical connotations; he denied its transformative effects in the area between nature and art. Following his Christology to its wider conclusions, he excluded mimesis as a corrective strategy either in the soul or in social institutions, including the Church. On all counts, he substituted external community for inward communion, and it was in the external relations of men that he left the imitation of Christ, not as a strategy for correction and progress, but as one of social integration.

Like Luther, Calvin removed both the asymmetry of archetype and

[17] Letter to Count Albrecht of Mansfeld, 3 May 1521 (*WA Briefe,* 2, no. 404, p. 325).
[18] *Sermon on John* 17: 14 (*WA,* 28, p. 158).

image and its mediation by mimesis between nature and art from his teachings about Christ, as mediator. He distinguished three offices of mediation. As prophet, Christ witnessed and proclaimed the divine treasures of knowledge and understanding, revealing what had been hidden and incomprehensible in God. As king, He conferred spiritual riches on the elect, leading them to union with God and breaking the unrighteous with a rod of iron. As priest, He expiated for the sin of man. The curse of sin was transferred to His flesh. By the Cross, He offered Himself as a propitiatory sacrifice. In His risen and glorified body, He stood as man's advocate and intercessor before God's judgment seat, and all human prayers ascended to the Father through Him.

As Luther had done before him, Calvin taught that Christ's mediation took effect, not through mimesis, but by imputation. The event on which all hinged—Christ's propitiatory self-sacrifice—occurred once for all, and the papists gravely erred in the mimetic doctrines by which they argued that their Eucharists daily re-enacted it. The other offices of Christ as mediator were similarly inimitable; and the correction of man's spiritual deformity occurred through the action of the Holy Spirit, rather than through an innate likeness to Christ, the Logos, or assimilation by mimesis to Christ, the man.

Certainly, Calvin discussed theories of being that focused on the Logos, but only to discount them. For men, Calvin wrote, there is no being other than subsistence in the one God.[19] This subsistence, however, is not a replication of divine being. Consequently, one does not either fall away from God or approach Him by imitation (that is, by the assimilation of like to like). Both sin and righteousness come by communication, the first from Adam and the second from Christ. Like Luther, Calvin made his rejection of ideal, transcendent forms plainest in his treatment of the verb "to be" in considering the sentences, "The Church is the body of Christ," and "This is my body. . . . This is my blood." The sentences, he said, were figurative.[20]

This point of view was near the heart of Calvin's attack on tradition as a channel of authentic doctrines about the Church. Rejecting mimetic mediation, no one could justify the offices of the visible Church on the ground that, by replicating and sharing in the hierarchies and liturgies of the heavenly kingdom, they also participated in the beauty, justice, and goodness that was God. No one could defend the veneration of saints through images, relics, and pilgrimages by arguing that "connaturality" enabled the faithful to participate, through the saints,

---

[19] *Institutes,* 1. 1. 35.   [20] Ibid., 4. 18. 1–4; 4. 17. 22.

in the fountainhead of virtue. The principle that one participated in invisible things through their visible representations had been a warrant for hierarchic orders and ceremonial observances from the patristic age onward. But, like Luther before him, Calvin denied this principle when he taught that the Church participated only in the salvation and blessedness brought by Christ, and not in Christ's divine nature. In secular life, statues and paintings could give great pleasure. In religion, however, images forged by human ingenuity, Calvin wrote, were treacherous diversions from the true, spiritual worship of God, whether they were "idolatrous" statues and paintings of saints, or "pompous theatrical" rituals, or laws, customs, and patterns of government that concealed true religion and subverted consciences.

A symptom of Calvin's deeper reasoning on this subject appears in his use of the mirror metaphor. For Thomas Aquinas, God had been an intelligible mirror—for Nicholas of Cusa, a living mirror—of the world in the sense of creative, exemplary cause. The metaphor was also applied to other things—to the world itself and to the human soul—to describe the approach of image to archetype through which mimetic transformation occurred.[21]

Calvin described the mirror as though it were a painting,[22] an important evidence of something unseen and invisible. But it was a matter of the surface, without movement or depth.[23] Calvin did not use the mirror as representing the inherent likeness of archetype to image, or as suggesting the growth of the image toward its invisible archetype. Indeed, he urged his followers to practice introspection as a way to the perception of God; but, for him, self-knowledge led to knowledge of God because it revealed, not the mediation of likeness, or kinship, but the terrifying distance between man's wretchedness and God's maj-

[21] Calvin was reticent about applying the mirror metaphor to God or to the human soul. He wrote that the order of the cosmos was a kind of mirror in which one could contemplate the invisible God. (*Institutes,* 1. 5. 1. See also 1. 5. 11. God represents Himself and His kingdom in the mirror of His works, 1. 14. 21. In creatures, we see, as in mirrors, the vast riches of God's wisdom, justice, goodness and power, 1. 5. 10. God's works represent His glory as in a painting.) Mankind was a clear mirror of God's works (1. 5. 3). The Scriptures are a mirror that reveal the living likeness of the invisible God. (1. 14. 1. See also 2. 2. 11. Man can recognize himself in the faithful mirror of Scriptures; and 2. 3. 2.) The sacraments, as "visible words" (Calvin uses a phrase of Augustine's) are also mirrors in which men contemplate God's grace (4. 14. 6). God manifested Himself in teaching and exhortation, as in a mirror, so as to be known spiritually (4. 1. 5).

[22] Cf. the equivalent metaphor in 1. 5. 10.

[23] On Augustine's use of the metaphors of painting and poem, see above, Chapter 3, note 8.

esty. Thus, Calvin was reluctant to describe God and the soul as mirrors, basically similar beings reflecting and growing into one another. The mirrors of cosmos, Scripture, sacraments, and teaching were manifestations, just as Christ manifested the Father, as in a mirror, according to man's need.[24] Even in this sense, they were mirrors only to the man of faith.

When he turned to the Church as the body of Christ, therefore, Calvin saw communication at work instead of the assimilation of like to like. With Luther, Calvin had a profound sense of the stewardship that Christians should observe toward one another. The love of God, flowing into love of neighbor, required believers to seek the image of God, even in evil men, forgiving their transgressions and embracing them. Among the brethren, responsibilities for one another ran yet deeper, for they imitated Christ in giving themselves for the sake of others, and communicating themselves to those with whom they jointly participated in Christ.[25]

Still, this sharing occurred on the level of existence, without participation in any transcendent being. In the absence of prevenient grace, works had no righteousness. They could not be thought of as just because they participated in transcendent justice. Only the man of God's calling, the man of faith, could become like Christ by following the way of the Cross through his particular duties.[26] Further, the mutuality among believers did not go beyond the external situations of the members of the community. Like Luther, Calvin was haunted by the differences between the true Church and the visible Church. The true Church might lack all outward form, as it did in the days of Elijah,[27] when it appeared to be all but extinct. Even when the visible Church appeared to flourish, the true Church constituted a small part of the vast multitude, known only to God's secret election, and by marks apparent to His elect.[28]

Certain that man's nature had been deformed by sin, the reformers continued to preach the need of correction, but they kept hardly anything of the mimetic strategies of correction between nature and art that the Fathers had so intricately worked out. Luther and Calvin also discarded some of the tactics that the Fathers had used in that task. Of the latter, one was allegory, the analytical method that the Fathers and their successors had employed to construct the analogies that mimesis required. More tolerant of allegory than Calvin, Luther retained it as a

---

[24] 4. 18. 20. [25] 4. 2. 6; 4. 1. 19; 4. 1. 2–3; 3. 7. 5–6; 4. 14. 7; 4. 17. 38–40.
[26] 3. 8. 1. [27] Prefatory letter to Francis I, ch. 6. [28] 4. 1. 2.

mode of ornamentation, a way to beautify a proposition that had been proven and substantiated by other means.[29] However, other tactics of correction remained in full force. Some of them were tactics of the mind. Both Luther and Calvin were deeply read in pre-Christian philosophy; they fostered education in the liberal arts, applying both techniques of philosophical reasoning and ancient pedagogical disciplines to serve their teachings.

(Paradoxically, the mimetic strategies that they rejected were set forth in ancient and patristic texts that they approved. Thus, they had not so much erased those strategies from their systems of thought as they had reduced them to latency. Later, this made it possible for successors of Luther and Calvin to re-integrate mimesis into their views of transformation in human nature.)

Because their theology was scholarly, as was the one they wished to supplant, they also continued to distinguish not only between carnal and spiritual men but also, within the community of faith, between the wise and the simple. It was the duty of the wise to prevent the simple from being misled, as they were, for example, by the Anabaptists, and once they had been misled to correct them. Thus, the reformers continued to invoke, not merely patristic tactics of argument and mental discipline but also those of coercion. Parents, schoolmasters, and magistrates, Luther observed, could never perform their duties rightly without using the tools of rebuke, terror, and corporal punishment. Wild, indomitable beasts were chained to keep them from savaging men; even so, chains, swords, and executioners existed to inhibit or coerce "insane and raging man." God appointed civil laws with penalties of bondage and death to preserve public peace, but especially so that the extension of the Gospel might not be impeded by wicked men.[30] Calvin, too, looked to civil power as an indispensable safeguard of religion and humanity among men. For the ordinance of God established rulers as the ministers of his wrath against the insane and barbarous, and Calvin invoked ferocious acts of two gentle men, Moses and David, as models: "Both men," he wrote, "by executing the vengeance ordained of God, hallowed by cruelty the hands that, by mercy, they would have defiled."[31]

The doctrines of Luther and Calvin actually anticipated developments that mimetic theories later experienced when they were com-

---

[29] *Commentary on Galatians* 4: 24 (*WA*, 40, pt. 1, p. 532).

[30] Ibid., 3: 1, 19, 24 (*WA*, 40, pt. 1, pp. 310, 479f., 528).

[31] *Institutes*, 4. 20. 1, 3, 10.

bined with empirical psychology. For the reformers saw that if, as they taught, there were no common, transcendent being, then such likeness as there was among men had to be sought in the particular circumstances of existence. They grasped that if assimilation of like to like were out of the question, the mediation of likeness must occur through community instead of communion. And finally, they understood that, if archetypes of form were not to be discovered through the generalizing precepts of reason, then perhaps they could be looked for in the isolating acts of will. But these propositions received considerable elaboration before they emerged in historical idealisms of the nineteenth century, including the myth of the state.

Empirical Psychologies

The relocation of mimesis from the sphere between transcendent nature and human arts into that of particularized historical existence passed from its theological stage in the Reformation into a philosophical one toward the end of the sixteenth century. The dismemberment of the mediated asymmetry between nature and art passed from Christology to a matter that theologians had in common with secular philosophers: the theory that the reason mediated transcendent truth to the soul.

Throughout this account, we have seen that many authors believed that mimetic strategies in the outer world of events reflected mimetic strategies in the inner world of thought. In general, the concept of mimesis as a strategy of corrective mediation between nature and art rested on three premises concerning reason: (1) The first was that the visible world reflected an invisible, rational order. It existed as a whole composed of many parts that, left to themselves, would have been mutually antagonistic. An archetypal reason drew the parts into a harmony of beauty and goodness, a vast continuum in which dissimilars were reconciled in a deep and universal similitude. (2) The formal disciplines of speculative knowledge recapitulated the order of nature and, therefore, the invisible order that it manifested. The continuity among things matched the continuum of knowledge. Man was the image of God in his reason. Imprinted in his mind were natural dispositions toward the archetypal virtues of beauty and goodness that informed the world and that were transcendent above it in the divine intellect. Thus, the formal disciplines for studying the material world were rooted in the very principles of cosmic order, and, by applying them, man could pass from the material world to its immaterial order, and beyond, from visible creatures to the invisible things of God. (3) Each person, and each generation, formed a link in the chain of knowledge by recapitulating and criticizing the received tradition. The continuum in things and knowledge also pervaded time. By this mimetic criticism of criticism, progress ensued in the arts and in sacred doctrine, a collective advance made up of the reflections of countless individual persons.

To challenge these assumptions about epistemology was to lay an axe to the roots of the mimetic tradition. At the beginning of the seventeenth century, one founder of British empiricism, Francis Bacon (1561–1626), renewed ancient doubts concerning them and at once established a point of contact with the Protestant reformers' denial that reason mediated truth, much less universal being. "The human understanding," he wrote, "is like a false mirror, which receiving rays irregularly, distorts and discolors the nature of things by mingling its own nature) with it."[32] Man was the victim of insidious preconceptions: "The reflexion also from glasses so usually resembled to the imagery of the mind every man knoweth to receive error and variety both in color, magnitude, and shape, according to the quality of the glass.... I do find therefore in this enchanted glass four Idols or false appearances of several and distinct sorts, every sort comprehending many subdivisions: the first sort, I call idols of the Nation or Tribe, the second, idols of the Palace; the third, idols of the Cave; and the fourth, idols of the Theatre."[33] Words belonged to the last class of idolatry, which Bacon also called idols of the marketplace. They had rendered philosophy and science sterile, for men had forgotten that, while reason governed words, words also shaped understanding. Indeed, words were shaped according to the vulgar understanding and resisted all change to suit the true divisions of nature.[34] Bacon's advice was to give up rhetoric and the mimetic discussion of ideal forms that inhered in it. "Matter rather than forms should be the object of our attention, its configurations and changes of configuration, and simple action and law of ac-

[32] *Instaurationis Magnae*, 2. 1. 41 (*Novum Organum*, aphorism 41) *The Works of Lord Bacon* (London, 1879) 2: 435.

[33] *De augmentis scientiarum*, 5. 4. *The Works of Lord Bacon*, 2: 363f.

[34] *Instaurationis Magnae*, 2. 1. 59 (*Novum Organum* aphorism 59), *The Works of Lord Bacon*, 2: 437.

tion or motion; for forms are figments of the human mind, unless you will call those laws of action forms."[35]

Bacon posed a challenge. John Locke (1632–1704) responded by accepting, on principle, Bacon's empiricist theory of knowledge and yet retaining the three propositions concerning mimesis as a strategy of progress through rational criticism. However, the results of this hybrid doctrine replaced a continuum among things, in knowledge and through time, with radical discontinuities. Locke dismantled the idea of mediated asymmetry between nature and art.

As firmly as any mimeticist, Locke believed that a rational order informed the world: the order of natural law. However, while mimeticists argued that the invisible order that the actual world expressed was prior to, and transcendent above, the world, Locke argued only that it could be demonstrated to be immanent in the world. More one could not say, he argued; for one could not experience anything beyond the actual world. Was there an archetypal order, much less one of virtue? With a scrupulous regard for the limits of human reason, one could justifiably "suspect that either there is no such thing as truth at all, or that mankind hath no sufficient means to attain a certain knowledge of it."[36]

Thus, when Locke repeated the second mimetic principle—that man was the image of God in his reason—he likewise came to anti-mimetic conclusions. God, making man in His image and likeness, made him "an intellectual creature and so capable of dominion." Ministers of the Gospel and Christians generally were transformed into the image of Christ, bright and clear mirrors reflecting His glory.[37] However, Locke did not mean that the mind—even one enlightened by grace—was imprinted with images of archetypal virtues. Locke dismissed the concept of innate ideas and reverted to Aristotle's concept of the mind as a

---

[35] Ibid., 2. 1. 51 (*Novum Organum* aphorism 51). *The Works of Lord Bacon,* 2: 437.

[36] *An Essay Concerning Human Understanding,* I. introduction, 2. ed. Peter H. Nidditch (Oxford, 1975), p. 44.

[37] *Paraphrase* of II Cor. 3:18 and note to 4:6. *A Paraphrase and Notes on the Epistles of St. Paul* . . . (Cambridge, 1832), pp. 201f., 204. *First Treatise of Civil Government,* par. 30 (Peter Laslett ed. *Two Treatises on Government* [Cambridge, 1960], p. 180). Locke may have been influenced by his friends among the Cambridge Platonists in this regard for he several times used one of their favorite images when he described reason as "the candle of the Lord set up by Himself in men's minds, which it is impossible for the breath or power of man wholly to extinguish" (*An Essay Concerning Human Understanding,* 4. 3. 20 [ed. cit., p. 552]. Cf. ibid., I. introduction, 5; 4. 19. 13, 14 [ed. cit., pp. 46, 703f.]).

blank slate. The eternal verities were not in-born dispositions of mind, but conclusions to which any mind would come by a correct process of abstraction.[38] Though Locke used the metaphor of the mirror to describe mental processes, he used it only by way of analogy to indicate the mind's passivity before sensory data.[39] Born in complete ignorance, the mind passively received, as a blank sheet of paper was written on, the experience necessary for its approaches to knowledge.[40]

Even correct use of the reason, however, did not open the vast cosmic panorama that mimetic strategies had promised. Unable to rise above or to go outside itself, the mind remained a prisoner of its own ideas. It could never know things but only the ideas that it composed from diverse sensory experiences.[41] Thus, man lived in a twilight of probability.[42] He had as little knowledge of the immense fabric of the world "as a worm shut up in one drawer of a cabinet hath of the senses or understanding of a man."[43]

Finally, Locke's empirical view of knowledge led him to repeat the third mimetic premise in a new key. The individual mind did indeed recapitulate received tradition, and in a critical fashion. It was not clear, however, that progress would result. Any person's thought was conditioned by habit[44]; but habit, or memory, was itself conditioned by what a particular cultural grouping accepted as probable.[45] Locke recognized that his doctrine of cultural conditioning cast the shadow of determinism over his concept of inherent rational freedom. General consensus was not enough to dispel that shadow. It led to the prevalence of false opinions that confirmed the diversity of religions: "heathen in Japan, Mohammedans in Turkey, Papists in Spain, Protestants in England, and Lutherans in Sweden."[46] In politics, only gross absurdities could ensue if custom were followed "when reason has left it."[47] It was also possible for custom, accruing over the years, to establish institutions that violated the law of Nature.

Absolute monarchy, Locke wrote, was an institution of this sort, empowering some men to use force against others without law. The legitimate ruler or magistrate did not command allegiance in his own right, but rather as "the image, phantom, or representative of the common-

---

[38] *An Essay Concerning Human Understanding*, 4. 11. 14 (ed. cit., p. 639).
[39] Ibid., 2. 1. 25 (ed. cit., p. 118).   [40] Ibid., 2. 1. 2 (ed. cit., p. 104).
[41] Ibid., 2. 23. 29, 32 (ed. cit., pp. 295ff., 362ff., 384ff.).
[42] Ibid., 4. 14. 2 (ed. cit., p. 652).   [43] Ibid., 2. 2. 3 (ed. cit., p. 120).
[44] Ibid., 2. 9. 8–10; 2. 10. 7–10 (ed. cit., pp. 145–147, 152–155).
[45] Ibid., 4. 15. 4, 5 (ed. cit., pp. 655–657).   [46] Ibid., 4. 15. 6 (ed. cit., p. 657).
[47] *Second Treatise of Civil Government*, par. 157 (Laslett ed. cit., p. 390).

wealth . . . and thus he has no will, no power, but that of the law."
When he ceased to act as a representative, he deposed himself.[48] If
custom issued in fundamental violations of the law of nature, such as
absolutism warranted, government was dissolved from within. A state
of war existed between rulers and ruled, "and, in that state, all former
ties are cancelled, all other rights cease, and everyone has a right to
defend himself and to resist the aggressor."[49] Each man acted on his
own behalf.

While Locke retained fundamental propositions of the mimetic tradition, therefore, his concept of thought set them into a context hostile
to mimesis as a corrective strategy between nature and art. Mimetic
theorists had argued that things could be known as they truly were:
that is, in their eternal archetypes. They had also argued that one
could know the connections relating things: that is, by reasoning from
analogies, passing by a complex system of cross-references and figures
of speech from sensory data to intellectual abstractions. Like many
others, Locke concluded that man could know not things, but only his
own perceptions of things. Further, since things could not be known as
they were in themselves, Locke denied that connections among them
were self-evident or, given the unsatisfactory state of methods for analyzing ideas, that connections among perceptions of things could be
discovered.[50] As his mind ranged over the three mimetic propositions,
Locke ended by setting aside the one assumption that mimesis as a
corrective strategy required: that is, mediated continuity—whether
that of the asymmetry between archetypes and images or of that
among things, or of that between one mind and another. His view of
thought as an empirical operation was one of radical discontinuities.
This view of psychology, at least, he shared with other writers of his
age some of whom are not considered empiricist philosophers: for example, Thomas Hobbes (1588–1679).

Like the empiricists, Hobbes rejected the belief that the human
mind was informed by images of an eternal archetypal reason. He
came to this conclusion through his study of language, a study that
also led him to his celebrated judgment that life was "nasty, brutish,
and short." What was the relation between words and things? Did
words convey or shape empirical reality, or both? Hobbes resolved
these questions by saying that words were merely signs of private con-

---

[48] Ibid., par. 151 (Laslett ed. cit., p. 386).

[49] Ibid., parr. 140, 168, 213ff., 226, 232 (Laslett ed. cit., pp. 380, 397f., 426f., 433f.,
437).

[50] *An Essay on Human Understanding*, 4. 3. 22 (ed. cit., p. 553).

cepts, not of things, and that, even in that limited sphere, words contained all the truth there was. Stripped of moral absolutes, except those laid upon him by the state, and denied inherent spiritual reality, the individual became a physiological object. His psychology became a matter of physical relations. Hobbes's universe consisted of matter regulated by laws of motion. Thought was not a means of discovering universals. Instead, it was a highly particularized physiological movement through a given nervous system; it was sparked by sensory experience and kindled by the appetites, in a regular mechanistic fashion. For Hobbes, men and animals alike were automata, isolated in their individual existences. Consequently, the thoughts and words of man were mechanical and material processes that were true only in reference to the particular mechanism that produced them.

Pressing skepticism as far as they could, some empiricist psychologists denied that there was an inherent correspondence between the outside world and the order in which each human mind reconstructed its experiences. Thought was seen as an event, something occasional and accidental, a random possibility that occurred by chance or by physiological (or mechanical) reaction. It had its own reality, isolated from external reality and valid in itself; it disclosed no intrinsic truth about things-in-themselves; it implied no necessary continuity or sequence between propositions or even among thoughts. The physiologist David Hartley (1705–1757) established these principles and upon them erected a doctrine of thought as mechanistic event.

As they demolished the metaphysical unities of being and mind, empiricists framed a concept of the uniqueness and, therefore, the isolation of each individual existence. There were many efforts to qualify their conclusions. Leibniz (1646–1716) most fully applied the typology of mimesis to the task. Enclosed upon itself and turning only its hard, polished surface to other finite beings, each personality, each monad, was "an indestructible mirror of the universe."[51] Nothing could go in or out of it. It could only communicate with other monads indirectly, through the mediation of God.[52] By its appetites, each monad formed for itself representations of the cosmos, valid for itself. These were finite and confused, but by following its architectonic appetites the model imitated God in creating the world. Souls were "living mirrors or images of the universe of created things; spirits are also images of

---

[51] *Monadology*, 77. *Gottfried Wilhelm Leibniz, Philosophische Schriften,* ed. Hans Heinz Holz (Darmstadt, 1965) 1: 474.

[52] Ibid., 7, 51 (pp. 440, 460f.).

the Deity Himself, that is, of the Author of nature." Through knowledge of the system of the universe and imitation of it by way of its own artificial models, each monad was, in its own finite sphere, a little god,[53] self-sufficient, stable, absolute, and enduring.

Leibniz insisted that the unity established by souls, each in its private communication with God, constituted a moral world within the natural world, a moral order that displayed the glory, wisdom, power, and goodness of God.[54] But his doctrine that an "ideal connection" bound things up into an ultimate spiritual unity in the Monad of monads was also a doctrine of incommunicability among monads.

Leibniz reached his conceptions of unity in an effort to refute what he considered the extreme empiricism of John Locke. Because he recognized the brilliance and cogency of Locke's portrayal of the isolated intellect, Leibniz appropriated some of the weapons of his enemy while he also taught that there was a higher unity than that allowed by Locke's fairly atomized intellectual world. For this very reason, his reflections proved to have extraordinary interest and value for Kant, who, in his own rebuttal to Hume, eventually laid the foundations of historical idealism. The point to bear in mind now, however, is that, even at Leibniz's rarefied height of speculation, the effect of new philosophies of the mind was to locate such analogy as there might be in relations among unique individuals—that is, in action—rather than in a transcendent, rational being. Clearly, this idea of discontinuous, unmediated relationships was hostile to the concept of mimesis as a corrective strategy, mediating between nature and art. And yet, antagonism prepared for interchange between mimetic and anti-mimetic schools of thought, partly because of archaic survivals in the broad social context within which advances in the high culture of philosophy took place.

[53] Ibid., 83, (p. 476f.).   [54] Ibid., (p. 478).

Chapter 11

Continuity of Mimetic Strategies in the Sixteenth Century

ALONGSIDE innovations in religious doctrine and emotion, there ran powerful inner continuities. Within social institutions, especially the churches, the mimetic tradition, as formulated by the Fathers and recast in the Middle Ages, continued in two ways: first, in educational curricula centered upon the classical languages and literatures and, second, in the doctrines of the Roman Church, including its Christology. This persistence in the one European institution that could claim to be universal was fundamental. Together with the persistence of mimetic doctrines ingrained into popular culture through centuries of religious devotion, it explains how, despite all countervailing theories, and despite advances in the empirical sciences on the level of high culture, the idealist tradition of mimesis as a mediating strategy between nature and art continued to live in European culture, and how, in the end, what appeared to be its decline was actually its expansion by integrating theories of its critics.

In this chapter, I shall be concerned with the area in which the mimetic counterpoint of rational and occult knowledge had been most fully developed, and through which it persisted into the Enlightenment: that is, mysticism.

There were Augustinianisms, and iconoclasms, outside the Protestant confessions. The powerful current of Neoplatonic spirituality flowed through the texts of Christian antiquity, whether they were read by Luther and Calvin or by their contemporaries, the great Spanish mystics—Ignatius Loyola, Theresa of Ávila, and John of the Cross—or, later, by Pascal and Jacob Boehme.

But the Spanish mystics differed from Luther and Calvin in retaining the exemplarism of Christ as Logos and as ascetic master. Through the Logos, there was an inherent likeness between God and the human soul, and, through that ideal likeness enhanced by grace, the soul could be progressively transformed into God. Becoming more perfectly like God, its archetype, it would be God by participation.[1] Unlike Luther and Calvin, the Spaniards did not reduce the mediation of the incarnate Christ to the single event of the Cross or believe that the benefit of the Passion extended to believers by imputation, instead of by imitation. Thus, they could teach that salvation was a process in which the soul could, through works, perfect the image of God in itself, uniting its own sacrifice with that of the Crucified, "so that it may have the value won for it by our will."[2]

Calvin avoided using the mirror metaphor of God or of the human soul. By a keen instinctive perception, Theresa of Ávila grasped that the protestants had voided the mimetic ontology to which she still held. The Godhead, she wrote, is like a mirror, or the reflective brightness of a diamond that holds everything within itself. Her soul, too, appeared to her completely bright as a mirror—though less sublime than the Godhead—with the image of Christ at the center and in every part. When a soul is in mortal sin, she wrote, the mirror of the soul becomes clouded. Christ cannot be seen, though He is yet in us, giving us our being. But, "with heretics, it is as if the mirror were broken."[3]

Some of the themes that appear in the writings of the three Spanish mystics strongly recall conversionist innovations that we observed in discussing currents in fourteenth- and fifteenth-century thought. Particularly, this is true of the concepts that the individual soul could by its own works express the image of God, and moreover express it in such a way as to enlarge the Body and the sufferings of the Crucified. Earlier, I related this concept to a grand proposition that God became in His creatures, that He became as phenomena expressed Him. The writings of the Spanish mystics were valuable restatements and recastings of this sense of God as the rhythm within historical change. They prepared for startling and decisive developments of that theory in the seventeenth century. But one must look elsewhere for a distinct advance in the theory of mimetic augmentation in the area between nature and art.

[1] John of the Cross, *Dark Night of the Soul* 2. 20. 5, trans. E. Allison Peers (New York, 1959), p. 175.

[2] Teresa of Ávila, *Interior Castle,* seventh mansion, c. 4, trans. E. Allison Peers (New York, 1961), p. 233.

[3] Teresa of Ávila, *Autobiography,* c. 40, trans. E. Allison Peers (New York, 1960), p. 390.

It would be possible to illustrate the concept of mimesis as a multiform strategy of organic growth by referring to a number of seventeenth-century authors, such as Thomas Traherne, Blaise Pascal, and Angelus Silesius. However, one mystical author was particularly decisive in the later history of the transformation that we are describing, and, indeed, he forecast the contours on which the spheres of being and existence were eventually reconciled in historical idealism. That man was Jacob Boehme (1575–1624).

Not long after the first stages of the Reformation, Neoplatonic reactions began to appear in Protestant lands, endeavors in mystical speculation that restored a general order of discourse interrupted by the reformers. Pietism was such a movement in German states, and Boehme, one of its earliest and most widely influential spokesmen.

Like all other mystics, Boehme drew on long precedent. The depth and range of his knowledge are all the more astonishing because he had no great library and no cosmopolitan society to reinforce his own thinking. He was a cobbler, living in the border area between Prussia and Poland. Boehme's thought presents surprising similarities to various positions taken by thinkers associated with the Platonist "school" of Chartres, in the twelfth century, particularly to the views of Gilbert de la Porrée. While it is implausible in the highest degree that Boehme knew the twelfth-century writings directly, it is equally apparent that he was inspired by thinkers who stood, perhaps remotely, in the Chartres tradition and that among them was Nicholas of Cusa.

Boehme's teaching was a strange mixture of discordant elements. True to Lutheran theology, he accepted the Scriptures as a source of revelation, and he likewise held to the cosmic drama of Creation, Fall, Redemption (including Incarnation and Resurrection), and Last Judgment. He followed an allegorical method of Scriptural interpretation that was strongly mystical and anagogical, asserting that the Old Testament was prefigurative of the New, and that both testified to the same truth. He insisted on the freedom of the will and the separation of God from nature; thus, he could not equate God with nature, as Spinoza did, or teach that the being of God was conterminous with the historical world, and that God (as nature) was bound up by the necessity of His own character. And yet, this perfectly orthodox scheme, built around sin and grace, interweaves with thoroughly unscriptural elements, for Boehme was heavily influenced by alchemical teachings of the school of Paracelsus.

Alchemy originated in Greek philosophy of matter, and it preserved, untouched by Christianity, a structure of thought that drew its inspiration, language, and symbols—including that of man as microcosm—from pagan antiquity, and ultimately from Babylon. True to its origins, alchemy postulated a materialist universe. All things were composed of one and the same material base, the *prima materia.* Variations in things occurred because secondary qualities—Aristotle's earth, air, fire, and water—combined in different ways. Men who knew the mechanics of composition, through magic and astrology, could transmute elements—for example, lead into gold—stripping the qualities away from a given thing, down to the *prima materia,* and rebuilding with the qualities necessary to achieve the desired product.

In this subversionist doctrine of composites was embedded the nucleus of the doctrine of thesis and antithesis that passed to Boehme and thence, indirectly, to Fichte and Marx. It was a basic principle of alchemical work that the quality that appeared to dominate in an existing thing was matched by an opposite, hidden quality that could be revealed by fire. Drawing on Neoplatonic learning, Paracelsus added to this materialism an elaborate doctrine of spiritual interaction. Man's life was the sum of cosmic life; for the "dust of the earth" out of which God created man, according to *Genesis,* was composed of all the qualities previously created, and man was moved by this material affinity to the cosmos as well as by the astral spirit that pervaded the entire cosmos.

There are many points of contact between alchemical thought and Boehme's theology: for example, between the three earths that Paracelsus taught—mercurial, vitreous, and combustible—and the three worlds that Boehme saw taking shape through the eternal passage of God from "abyss to abyss" in self-contemplation—the dark fire world, devoid of essence; the spiritual, light angelic world; and "this outward, visible world," in "the form of time." But Boehme's view of the world as a revelation of truth came to him, neither through Scriptural learning nor through alchemical technology, but through visions, through inspirations that struck him while reading the Scriptures, that unlocked to him the whole book of God, in nature and in Scripture.

The intuitive combination of Lutheran Scriptural exegesis and Paracelsian alchemy yielded a world in which there was no division between existence and being, one that unfolded in all its manifestations from one internal element, just as the astral regions also were "nothing else but the out-breathed powers from the inward fiery dark-and-light world, from the great Mind of divine manifestation, and is only a formed model, wherein the great Mind of divine manifestation looks upon itself in a time and plays with itself."[4] The invisible world was hidden in the visible world, as the soul was in the body, working through the visible elements. Beyond the invisible world itself, and animating it, is the Spiritual Word, and this Word, moving through the spiritual world to the visible world, formed all empirical life, including that of animals and vegetables. God was the ground of the Spiritual Word and thus of all essences. Boehme shrank from identifying God with nature itself. God was anterior to and outside nature; the eternal utterance of the Word is incomprehensible to nature.[5]

This distinction was possible because, for Boehme, even the creative forms of God were not the ultimate reality. Like Gilbert de la Porrée in the twelfth century, Boehme separated the forms of God from the higher reality, the nature of God, an *Ungrund* from which God's forms derive and, in them, the three worlds. The *Ungrund,* the divinity behind the divine, was the eye of the abyss, the eternal chaos in which all things existed undifferentiated. From the will in the abyss flowed the first form of God, desire that something be; the second form, the object of the desire; the third form, the anguish or welling forth, produced by the first two, the creative suffering by which what had been undifferentiated first separated and became the senses and mind and then unfolded into the objects accessible to the senses and mind. The triad thesis-antithesis-synthesis, as an eternal creative recurrence, originated in this divine circuminsession and, thus, ultimately in the theological Trinity of God, the utterer, the Son, the uttered Word, and the Spirit, the uttering. Boehme departed from his theological prototype by teaching that the entire natural world and all human institutions (especially laws and governmental offices) were unfoldings of this process, offshoots from the single tree of life, a tree of good and evil.[6]

Boehme foresaw an end to the outward world and thus to the generation of forms in nature by the divine circuminsession, when "the formed Word shall be entirely freed from vanity and gives by its last repentance (*Reue*) the holy spiritual world."[7] But his eschatology varied from the Christian image of the Last Judgment. His view of the ultimate unity of opposition portrayed God as all being, essence, or substance; evil and good; heaven and hell; light and darkness; eternity and time; beginning and end.[8] Evil and good inhered in the spiritual being of the world, "and the one cannot be without the other."[9] Certainly, the two realms of good and evil, separated when they began, became

---

[4] *Magnum Mysterium,* 7. 19 (*Jacob Boehme, Sämtliche Schriften* ed. W.-E. Peuckert [Stuttgart, 1958] 7: 39.
[5] 60. 40–49 (ibid., 8: 633–635).   [6] 29. 4ff (ibid., 7: 247ff.).
[7] 31. 44f (ibid., 7: 287).   [8] 8. 24 (ibid., 7: 44).   [9] 11. 15 (ibid., 7: 69).

invisible and incomprehensible to one another. But, springing from the same eternal root, they really formed one kingdom.[10]

Boehme taught a highly developed doctrine of atonement that varied powerfully from Luther's Christology. Christ crucified was the mediator between man and the God of wrath. Man could inherit the kingdom of God only by sacrificing himself through the self-immolation of Christ, killing sin in the flesh by entering into the death of Christ, by dying to selfhood and, with utter resignation casting himself on the mercy of God. And yet, Boehme's view of nature also led him to say that God dwelled "even in the abyss of the wicked soul" though His love remained hidden to the wicked. The godly man likewise was in a state of tension, reflecting the divine circuminsession, for he must always "have enmity in himself and trample underfoot the monster [of evil] and . . . continually kill it." Through this unceasing enmity, the soul reenacted the divine creativity; it conceived itself through the divine desire in it, generating its being (*ens*); a spirit arose in the *ens* and begot the creature, bestowing an outer sign in the body. Grace had none of the judgmental aspects that Luther gave it. It virtually belonged to the realm of nature,[11] to the world of the incorporated Word; for man had all three divine principles in himself and was free to form himself by recapitulating Christ's birth, death, and resurrection.[12] It belonged to man to choose whether he adhered to Lucifer or to Christ; but both belonged to the same cosmic and divine order, to the same divine All.

For Boehme, this was an order without a purpose. "In God there is no purpose or beginning to will."[13] Together with his argument for the ultimate unity of good and evil in God, Boehme's rejection of a divine plan for the world came very close to the argument that whatever is, is right. Certainly, Boehme's entire theology excluded reason as a divine principle. Desire was the first creative form of God, and there was nothing of reason in the other two forms: the object of desire and begetting anguish. Counsel, Power, Awe, Virtue—these are the names of the *Ungrund*,[14] all of them confounding reason by the very character of the eternal chaos. Will was the whole act of God—will "to manifest his own good, that he himself is."[15] Boehme excluded the last possibility of divine plan or reason or purpose when he denounced it as a "folly of reason to speak of compulsion and inevitable necessity" binding God.[16] After all, reason had been the source of the theological

---

[10] 4. 1, 10 (ibid., 7: 18, 20).   [11] 27. 12–18 (ibid., 7: 216f.).
[12] 26. 58–72 (ibid., 7: 210–212).   [13] 61. 61 (ibid., 8: 651).
[14] 1. 8 (ibid., 7: 6).   [15] 61. 62 (ibid., 8: 651).   [16] 61. 66 (ibid., 8: 652).

disputes, idolatry, the religious desolation, the murderous hatreds by which the visible Church had extinguished all love and truth.[17]

For our purposes, one factor in this continuation of a very ancient mode of inquiry was especially important: that is, the conception of human acts and institutions as parts of nature's mystical unity. We have seen antecedents of Boehme's teaching in doctrines of John Scotus Eriugena and fourteenth- and fifteenth-century mystics. The understanding of the life of God as processual, which was common in seventeenth-century mysticism (and particularly in Boehme's representation of that life in a dialectical relation with itself, and manifesting itself in institutions), was well-grounded in earlier mystical traditions. It had an important place in eighteenth-century thought and in the reconstitution of the mimetic tradition at the end of the eighteenth century.

To a public whose intellectual leaders—including Robert Boyle and Leibniz—still accepted the Scriptures as divine oracles and embraced alchemy as a true way to knowledge and mastery of the universe, the teachings of Boehme, the cobbler from east Prussia, seemed inspired. In the seventeenth century, Boehmist sects were founded, like the Philadelphians in England, disseminating the writings of their great teacher. In *Paradise Lost,* Milton gives signs of having been deeply influenced by Boehme; and Isaac Newton, still a devotee of alchemy, once spent three months in a careful study of Boehme's works. Boehme's influence continued to be felt in eighteenth-century England, especially through the writings of William Law, but his greatest effect was felt in eighteenth-century Germany. There, given new impetus by Ötinger, Baader, and Schlegel, Boehme's theology of the unity of nature as an expression of cosmic, spiritual anguish, and his doctrine of an irrational, all-encompassing, and purposeless will— a will that unfolded itself in stages, necessarily devouring its previous manifestations—entered the reflections of the German idealist philosophers. It was from him and from the sources on which he drew that they learned to think of history in terms of the Great Mystery, a magic will regarding itself in the mirror of its wisdom, drawing forth unities always present but hidden for a time, and impelling a dialectical movement in which "one mysterium follows the other and each mysterium is the mirror and prototype of the next."[18]

I have now identified two major currents in European thought from

---

[17] 27. 49ff; 50. 50; and passim (ibid., 7: 224ff.; 8: 525).
[18] *Sex Punkta Mystica,* Punkt VI, ed. cit. (Stuttgart, 1957) 4: 96.

the Reformation onward. Both dealt with the area of speculative knowledge between nature and art. The first appeared to be bent on destroying the mimetic tradition. On the high level of theology and philosophy, it rejected that tradition's dogma and poetry as souvenirs of cultures that had been either spiritually perverse or ignorant of historical and scientific facts, while rich in fantasy. Ancient writings ceased to be authoritative in areas where knowledge advanced. New concepts of institutional sanctions, Scriptural authority, and the processes of thought were framed, and, for many people, they replaced mimetic paradigms of being, with what Bacon called "laws of action."

The second current ran directly counter to the first. Under the pressure of the Reformation, the "Turkish menace," and religious conflicts within Europe, institutions of government, the texts on which formal education was based, and powerful strains in the common culture (including religious devotion) gave the tradition renewed vigor. Consequently, in the minds of a village parson here, a tinker there, a cobbler in yet another place, the tradition advanced beyond what, in the fifteenth century, it had taught concerning man's power to change himself and the world around him. The combination of rational and occult knowledge from its earliest days had marked the mimetic tradition of mediated asymmetry between nature and art; it persisted in this second current of thought. And with it there also survived the symbolic and magical connotations that, through mimesis, man had bestowed on his self-image.

Chapter 12

Continuity of Mimetic Strategies
in the Enlightenment

For centuries before the outbreak of the Reformation, scholars and artists had looked to antiquity for inspiration and guiding principles. "Antiquity," to be sure, included primitive Christianity as well as pre-Christian Greece and Rome. Almost every age between the fifth and the fifteenth centuries can claim its own "Renaissance." The generations that followed the Reformation were beneficiaries of this long, continuous study. Beginning with the Reformation, however, the return to pre-Christian and Christian Antiquity ceased to be characteristic merely of scholarship and art. Its ramifications widened and unfolded into an age that paradoxically delighted both in its novelty and in its classicism. The new classical age matured in the eighteenth century and yielded a magnificent harvest in the formal thought of the nineteenth.

No tradition can survive without adapting to altered circumstances and, ultimately, without addressing the inmost needs of human life. I have given an account of mimesis in both respects—first, as an inherent response by some specific writers to an evident psychological need for wholeness and, second, as a conscious strategy of adaptation and renewal within the classical tradition.

Throughout the present section, I have been concerned with the indistinct point at which the programmatic level of need and response intersected with the prescriptive level of cultural forms. The theme of the chapters that follow is this: Between the Reformation and the Enlightenment, some theorists took the mimetic program out of its religious matrix and secularized it. Mimesis—particularly mimesis by augmentation—came to be understood as a strategy for the advancement of secular society. Older views persisted, however. There were, in fact, many points of contact between secularized versions of mimesis and older religious versions of mediated asymmetry between nature and art, both through the inescapable weight of literary tradition and through running disputes among contemporaries. For, as we shall see in discussing nineteenth-century doctrines, far from extinguishing earlier theories, secularization increased the repertoire of ways in which the program of need and response could be understood. One point that both old and new views had in common was the insistence, characteristic of the mimetic tradition, that the reformation of the social world was the duty of an enlightened and militant minority.

Perceptions of Decay

How was it possible that mimetic theories took a new lease on life during the Enlightenment and, in fact, gained an extraordinary diversity and refinement of expression?

The answer is rooted in a new sense of tension between the nature of man and the arts of culture. An urgent need for wholeness penetrated all classes, and all areas, of European culture between the sixteenth and the nineteenth centuries. In the early decades of the period, religious wars were no doubt responsible for some measure of a widespread pain of estrangement, as were the effects of industrialization in later decades. At some point, the pain and the outcry against it became habitual. Before I resume this account of the history of ideas, I shall have to take note of this groundswell, from which arose both the cry for wholeness and adaptations of mimesis as a corrective strategy of mediation between nature and art.

The history of ideas in these centuries is an elaborate contrapuntal fugue of many voices. Some passages are joyful, sure, triumphant. In them, the Age of Reason resolves dissonances into its rare but characteristic harmony of freshness and splendor. In other passages, dark and agitated voices prevail, moving through dissonances left unresolved. The sense of alienation was one such voice. It was not the experience but the consciousness of alienation as a social condition and its persistence as a theme in many branches of the literary and visual arts, and in the new sciences of the eighteenth and nineteenth centuries that distinguished this age from others.

The period is thronged with reforms and, even more, with daring projects for reform. Many of them arose specifically from the sense of alienation. A few examples from France will represent an impulse that cut across national lines. Rousseau portrayed man, as citizen, alienated from his own nature by existing patterns of education. Montesquieu obliquely referred to his own country when he wrote that fear, the principle of despotic regimes, divided the sovereign from his subjects, a people corrupted by the severity of their laws and habituated to despotism through the violence of the government. La Rochefoucauld-Liancourt and Pinel confronted the self-alienation of insanity. Fourier wrestled with the alienation of man from man perpetuated by social institutions. The list could be indefinitely extended. Great visions and heroic achievements in education, law, penology, mental therapy, and social theory sprang from the pain of alienation, from the sense that the social order must be changed if man were to experience a wholeness for which he was made.

These ideals and accomplishments expressed old pessimisms and new insights. The age—indeed, the court—of Louis XIV knew many polemics against the nobility of man, whether because his will was tainted or because his showy pomp was at the mercy of blind fortune. Fontenelle, that conscious artifact of the age of Louis XIV, living past the middle of the eighteenth century, reflected that only the illusions of man made it possible for him to endure the finitude and uncertainty of knowledge, the miseries of life, and to escape from them in his creative actions. In England, Robert Burton's (1577–1640) *Anatomy of Melancholy* provided an exhaustive statement of somber religious pessimism that described madness penetrating every aspect of culture because it inhered in human nature.

Such reflections drew heavily on Stoic traditions of contempt for the world and on Christian doctrines of sin as a congenital taint in the soul. As the eighteenth century advanced, mental alienation—insanity—was recognized as a disease that could be treated therapeutically. If madness were a disease, curable in some instances, the idea that madness inhered in human nature was surely wrong. Then, it could be seen to take root in the susceptibilities of individual persons, though it was still regarded as the result of moral flaws. However, this concept of mental alienation opened a new and terrifying prospect. Insofar as man was shaped with the world around him, could it be true, as so many alleged, that the arts, customs, and institutions of society vitiated the mind and deepened, if they did not actually create, the moral defects that gave rise to insanity?

Composed in the shadow of this question, eighteenth-century literature is full of themes already familiar to philosophic and ascetic writings in antiquity and assiduously developed by centuries of Christian thinkers: skepticism of human achievement, the decadence of the world, the vanity of wealth, position, and power. Rousseau's hostility to culture as a spiritual disease tainting the souls of men had many precedents, as it had many offspring, not the least of which was Kant's view concerning the necessity of evil for the advancement of mankind through pride, ambition, and greed. In the German romantic movement, Schiller too saw nothing but sterility and decay in his world—wounds, he said, that culture had inflicted upon humanity.[1] "The world seems what it is—a grave,"[2] a grave not merely for men's earthen bodies but also for the life with which the ancient Greeks had invested the cosmos. Schiller blamed Christianity for introducing terrors of spirit. He blamed science for reducing the cosmos to dead matter. He lamented the lifeless word brooding over the desolate void that was left, meaning nothing.[3]

Contemplation of death was a part of Christian thought that turned to morbidity in many expressions. But the desire for a death unglorified by martyrdom or by the hope of resurrection and fascination with the macabre for its own sake appeared in the pre-romantic and romantic movements of the eighteenth century and steadily fanned out into a wide range of poetic and philosophical writings during the nineteenth century. The possibility of bringing about one's own death, and indeed the desirability of doing that, was part of the melancholia that afflicted Byron, Hölderlin, Kleist, Sénancour, and many others. Suicide was more than a philosophical or literary motif. By 1770, contemporaries were convinced that suicide had become a common phenomenon throughout Europe; by 1878, Thomas Masaryk (1850–1937) concluded, on the basis of statistics, that the inclination to suicide had become endemic, even among very young children, and that the trend had reached its greatest intensity in his own day. Twenty years after Masaryk's study appeared, Émile Durkheim (1858–1917) discovered no abatement of this trend.

Some observers followed Darwin in judging suicide a useful means for purging the unfit from the natural struggle for existence. But others, including Masaryk and Durkheim, traced it as "a social mass phenomenon" to civilization itself. Masaryk, for example, considered suicide, together with the spread of insanity, a product of the uprooted

---

[1] "Über die aesthetische Erziehung des Menschen." Briefe 5–6, in Friedrich Schiller, *Sämtliche Werke* (Munich, 1967) 5: 581, 583. Compare Schiller's attack on egoism with Herder's, below, Chapter 13 after note 46.

[2] "Poësie des Lebens," *Sämtliche Werke* (Munich, 1965) 1: 221.

[3] "Die Götter Griechenlands," *ibid.,* 1: 172f.

migratory population of cities and of educational institutions that had destroyed the unity of the old religious world view and left in its place an incoherent mentality with an over-educated intellect and an under-educated moral will, capable only of weariness with life and disposed to psychosis or to suicide. Durkheim traced suicide to the large network of interlocking associations that, he argued, made up society. If one considered suicide an impersonal, social phenomenon rather than an individual event, one saw that each region and country had its own characteristic suicide rate. That particular rate normally remained uniform year after year, in good times and bad, reflecting the stability of the social order. However, like Masaryk, Durkheim had observed a "tremendous aggravation" of the suicide rate in western Europe during the century before he wrote. He concluded that the cause of this increase was a pathological abnormality in conditions under which European civilization had followed its call to progress in the sciences and industry. It had uprooted institutions of the past without putting anything in their place. It had steadily increased its brilliance, but it had also generated an alarming moral poverty, a morbid state of crisis that could not safely be prolonged. As we shall see, Durkheim urged that the only cure was to reconstruct the associations that made up society.[4]

A second mass phenomenon, drug addiction, coincided with major chemical achievements. The remarkable growth of anaesthesiology set the nineteenth century quite apart from all experience of previous men, for it showed that physical pain was not inevitable. Drug addiction also was a symptom of a wider movement, one that Schopenhauer and his posthumous disciple, Freud, described in saying that all of culture was flight from the pain of existence.

The connection between analgesics and society, including the arts, is immediate. Opium had been known and used in Europe at least since Paracelsus, but in 1783 Warren Hastings could still call it "a pernicious article of luxury, which ought not to be permitted but for the purpose of foreign commerce only." By the first years of the nineteenth century, opium had become so plentiful that it was no longer a luxury. De Quincy (1785–1859) witnessed that, by 1804, opium was the relief of the poor, for whom ale or spirits were too expensive.

---

[4] Thomas Masaryk, *Suicide and the Meaning of Civilization*, trans. W. B. Weist and R. G. Buston (Chicago, 1970). Émile Durkheim, *Suicide: A Study in Sociology*, trans. John A. Spaulding and George Simpson (Glencoe, Ill., 1951).

What the people had, the poets also used. Byron, Coleridge, De Quincey, Rossetti, Poe, Baudelaire, Mallarmé, Verlaine, . . . the list could be greatly extended. Addiction is a frequent motif in Dickens; Conan Doyle described Sherlock Holmes as addicted to morphine and the "aristocratic vice" of cocaine. What did drugs bring to the artist? De Quincey recorded that he took opium to escape physical pain, but even more to evade the misery of being the incommunicable in a transitory world, "blank desolation," "absolute despair," "a settled and abiding darkness."[5] More than alcohol, hemlock, henbane, or chloroform, opium held, he said, an almost divine power over bodily disease and pain and "over the grander and more shadowy world of dreams." It brought "an apocalypse of the world within me,"[6] a world of dreams that made impotent the guilt, ugliness, and sorrow of the world outside.

It was telling that the poppy became a recurrent motif in the ornamental designs of *art nouveau,* with its profound escapism into aesthetic isolation, and that Baudelaire, having "sung the mad pleasures of wine and opium," thirsted for a liquor beyond the drugs of heaven that would grant him "to know nothing, to teach nothing, to will nothing, to feel nothing, to sleep and still to sleep . . . a base and loathesome wish, but sincere."[7] How broadly this aspect of social consensus spread is indicated by the fact that the authors writing on the theme included Tennyson (1807–1892), who captured the artistic despair of his day and translated it into the classical analogy of the *Lotus-Eaters* (1832).

Here is the way of thinking that Goethe, not long before 1832, argued against in *Faust,* and that Kierkegaard had recognized as the eliding reality of the moment, as the self-denial of despair, the sickness unto death, in which one is present and struggles against the self-contradiction of being erased into the past, and through which one must choose to penetrate anew each moment, even by means of madness and horror, to affirm his existence and freedom.

As early as 1770, the German poet Hölderlin sensed the terrible consequences of self-estrangement that historical events had brought to bear. "I cannot imagine a people that could be more mangled than the Germans. You see artisans, but no human beings, thinkers but no human beings, young and old people, but no human beings. Is it not like a battlefield, where hands and arms and all members lie strewn al-

---

[5] *Confessions of an Opium Eater* (London, 1928), pp. 21, 66f., 68, 201.

[6] Ibid., pp. 6ff., 179, 181.

[7] Draft for preface to *Les Fleurs du mal,* in *The Flowers of Evil,* ed. M. and J. Mathews (New York, 1958), p. xvi.

together in pieces, while the spilled blood of life runs away in the sand?"[8]

It is impossible to grasp the impulses of culture between the sixteenth and the nineteenth centuries without taking into account the conscious need for wholeness that pervaded the arts and the new social sciences. From the beginning, philosophers and theologians had distinguished three areas of mimesis: in nature, in art, and between nature and art. Reflections on man in society took place in the third area, and it was there that Christian doctrines about the regeneration of man occurred. From the sixteenth century onward, the sense of disequilibrium between man as he ought to be, by nature, and man as culture made him kept the center of debate in the area between nature and art. I now turn to mimetic doctrines with which man rationalized and attempted to satisfy the need to remove disparities between natural and artificial man, adapting legacies of the classical tradition. A distinction must always be drawn between the rigid forms often called "classicism" and the classical tradition, which continued to flourish, resilient and tenacious, over the centuries while, one after another, the societies that nurtured it rose and passed away. If "classicism" means rigid forms, it means the contrary of everything that made the classical tradition a vital force in European culture. But this line of reasoning would lead to the paradoxical conclusion that mimesis was an anti-classical element that lurked at the heart of the tradition from its very origins. It would also conceal the role that classical rationales for change actually played in movements of religious, political, and social protest between the sixteenth and the nineteenth centuries.

Between Nature and Art: Mimesis and the Spirit of Criticism in the Enlightenment

Thus far, we have seen that the mimetic tradition persisted in mystical spirituality. There, perhaps, it calmed the urgent need for wholeness. But how can one suggest a *longue durée* of mimesis at the heart of the Enlightenment: that is, in the very theories of criticism that turned many of its endeavors toward pre-Christian classicism and against Christian elements in the classical tradition? How did mimesis figure in theories that the Enlightenment used in satisfying the pervasive

---

[8] *Hyperion* 2. ii. 7 in *Hölderlins Werke und Briefe,* ed. F. Beissner and J. Schmidt (Frankfurt-a.-M., 1969) 1: 433.

need for wholeness, in planning the moral regeneration of society? The present chapter contends that men continued to think of mimesis as a strategy of correction in nature, in art, and between nature and art. My primary concern remains with the third area.

Gibbon made a habit of reading Pascal once each year to enhance the clarity of his style. Were there perhaps unknown affinities between the two men, hidden linkages with philosophy and religion, a residue of Gibbon's youthful (and quickly reversed) conversion to Catholicism, that peered out from behind his pride in the "bold and sagacious spirit of criticism" in the eighteenth century? Certainly, residues of Lutheran pietism played in Kant's mind even as he declared: "Our age is in every sense of the word the age of criticism, and everything must submit to it."[9] Anyone who examines the frontispiece in the first volume of the *Encyclopédie* (in the 1752 edition) will grasp a curious fact about this general spirit of criticism, this effort to subject all knowledge to the tests of empirical science.[10] The paradox is that the editors declared their rationalistic program with sacred allegory, an allegory, moreover, that gave prominence to the mimetic arts. The frontispiece depicts a ceremony in the temple of Truth. Symbolism begins with the architecture of the temple, which is in the Ionic order, an allusion to the origin of rational discourse about nature among Ionian philosophers, to whom the *Encyclopédistes* attributed the discovery of geometry, cosmology, and physiology. The central figure represents Truth herself, shrouded with a heavy veil yet emitting a light that scatters the clouds of darkness. At Truth's left side, Reason and Philosophy begin to lift the veil, while Theology, sitting at the feet of Truth, receives light from above.[11] In descending order of theoretical generalization, a series of figures flows down the picture, standing for the historical arts,

[9] E. Gibbon, *Decline and Fall of the Roman Empire,* ch. 20, on the vision of Constantine I. I. Kant, *Critique of Pure Reason,* preface to the first edition, note 1, trans. J.M.D. Meiklejohn (London, 1950), p. 2.

[10] For the story of the *Encyclopédie* as a business venture, and of its early editions, see Robert Darnton, *The Business of the Enlightenment. A Publishing History of the Encyclopédie* (Cambridge, Mass., 1979).

[11] The sequence of subjects that follows is shown as a genealogical tree in the chart inserted in volume I of the indices to the *Encyclopédie.* There, however, three branches are represented as springing from the trunk of "physical beings." The main one, extending upward, is reason, from which philosophy, or science, derives. A second, shooting off to the right, is memory, diverging into sacred, natural, and civil history. (The subject of natural history, defined as uniform nature, is subdivided into celestial, terrestrial, and maritime branches.) The third major branch, to the left, is imagination, which ramifies into poetry and the subdivisions of painting, music, and architecture.

more and less abstract sciences (comprising "natural history"), and ending with a throng of practical crafts and professions. The clutter of figures is less dense in the place of honor at Truth's right. There, Imagination rushes forward to adorn and crown Truth, while the *genres* of poetry and, beneath them, the lesser arts of imitation watch in varying degrees of rapture.

On the one hand, the frontispiece puts originality before us, the discovery of Truth by Reason and Philosophy. Such was the critical program of the *Encyclopédie,* one that convinced many that the editors conspired to overthrow all traditional order, including the monarchy and the Church. (Diderot took the brunt of his hostility in the twenty years of clandestine labor to which suppression and the threat of suppression drove him.) On the other hand, even if it is a *jeu d'esprit,* the frontispiece presents us with imitation: the fulfillment of Truth adorned by Imagination in poetry and the other mimetic arts beneath poetry in order of generalization.

The task of this section will be to unravel this paradox. How could men who were dedicated to replacing a social consensus tainted by superstition with a new consensus based on empirical rationalism still declare their goals in mystic allegory taken over from the tradition that they meant to purge?

A number of adaptive mechanisms have already become apparent. First is the variety of mimetic strategies and of the ways they could be compartmentalized or combined. Second is the pervasive influence of classical languages and literatures in elementary and secondary education; through them, minds were trained from an early age to conceive the world in mimetic terms. Next, between the sixteenth and the eighteenth centuries, religious institutions and mystical practices continued to preach the mimetic order of the spiritual world at every level of society, and the dominant political institutions—whether republics or monarchies—were sanctioned by mimetic ideologies. Then, too, a defense had already been prepared against the advances of the physical sciences, which disproved mimetic concepts of the actual structure of the world, inherited from Plato and Aristotle; for, from the very beginning, even in those same philosophers, mimesis had followed an unscientific and even an anti-scientific, bent. Its literary (and specifically poetic) norms were insulated from the physical sciences. This was a peculiarity of mimesis as a reproductive strategy of the mind in the area between nature and art.[12]

---

[12] For the distinctions of mimesis in nature, in art, and between nature and art see above, Preface and Chapter 1, after note 70.

Indeed, a characteristic of the age was that, at the very moment when the sciences discarded Aristotle as the highest arbiter of knowledge, the arts drew his *Poetics* out of obscurity and enshrined it as a supreme authority. Intense discussion of the *Poetics* during the first half of the sixteenth century established a dominance that it continued to exercise as late as Herder's day (1744–1803) and, later still, in Newman's (1801–1890). (For the sake of our later discussion, however, it is important to register a dissenting voice. David Hume asserted, "The fame of Cicero flourishes at present; but that of Aristotle is utterly decayed.")[13]

As criticism passed in its great arc across the world of knowledge, it encountered mimesis as a major topic on every level of culture. For passing tradition through the refiner's fire was not an end in itself; it served a higher purpose. In the hands of men between the sixteenth and eighteenth centuries, the overriding object of criticism was not to break the traditional world of knowledge apart. It was to reconstitute the elements of that old world, together with modern discoveries, so as to create and proclaim new systems of unity. Constructing systems that dispersed in order to unify knowledge, men turned again and again to the ancient principles of organization. Did mimesis have a place in literature? The recovery of Plato's treatises, the new prominence of Aristotle's *Poetics,* and the discovery of Longinus's *On the Sublime* provided grist for mutually hostile arguments that ran on for three centuries. Did mimesis have a place in religion? Protestant iconoclasm and denial of the cult of the saints made this question unavoidable in thought about art and morality. Did mimesis have a place in political life? Materialism and doctrines of social utility left it none; various idealisms of the nation-state reaffirmed it.

The very concept of criticism proved crucial to the persistence of mimetic strategies. Long before the Reformation, criticism was recognized as part of the strategy of mimesis. As a function of dialectical reasoning, serving the advancement of the community through education, it had been assiduously cultivated by Christian exegetes for centuries. The Reformation and the Enlightenment therefore inherited the concept of criticism as a regenerative device in society, mediating the asymmetry between man as he ought to be and man as he was; that

---

[13] *An Enquiry Concerning Human Understanding,* sec. 1. L. A. Selby-Bigge (3rd ed. by P. H. Nidditch [Oxford, 1975]), p. 7. The standards of judgment that Hume used in this passage are unclear, as indicated by his further comment that, among philosophers, Addison might continue to be read when Locke was forgotten.

is, between man as made by nature and as remade by the artificial second nature of culture.

Although it appealed to ancient formulae and prescriptive elements of the mimetic tradition in its methods and aims, therefore, the purpose of criticism as theory between nature and art was to correct as well as to convey.

Criticism was outside nature as well as above art. The axiom that art imitated nature continued to be repeated, but it gradually became obvious that in the arts criticism was exerting an effect comparable to that of mechanics in the sciences: that is, it tended to create an area independent of nature, or even to violate nature.[14]

Style was regarded as an applied science in this creative work. How did a writer describe an event? How did a painter represent a given scene? The rules of style amounted to a symbolic code understood by the artist and his public. The artist designed a psychological effect by representing particular subjects in prescribed ways, and the border between style and stylization was not always clear. But style was not a matter of general fascination only because it could be used to stimulate an effect.

Along with laws, commerce, agriculture, and morality, the arts were thought to be indices of culture. The premise that the arts need not merely represent things as they were but could raise them above their natural condition had reference to the future as well as to the past. Applied according to the right critical theories, style was a mechanism by which culture as a whole could be elevated, and the primary analyses of style centered on the activity that had always epitomized man's creative powers and in which strategies of mimesis had been most thoroughly rooted: that is, on poetry. Discussions of style, therefore, became conduits by which thought about mimetic strategies in poetry passed into other areas of inquiry. Granted that through its variable rules, art imitated nature,[15] what was the nature that criticism, in its independence, mediated to artists? By the end of the sixteenth century, four broad answers had appeared in literary criticism, and by referring to them the limits within which criticism was thought to use its mimetic functions for the progress of culture may be clarified.

[14] Cf. A. R. Hall, *The Scientific Revolution, 1500–1800. The Formation of the Modern Scientific Attitude,* 2d ed. (Boston, 1966), p. 18.

[15] B. H. Hathaway, *The Age of Criticism: The Late Renaissance in Italy* (Ithaca, 1962), pp. 439f.

1. Nature is magisterial reason, set forth in the prescripts of ancient authors and exemplified in the formal structures of their writings.

One imitated nature by adhering to those prescripts and examples. But authors differed on the warrant for their argument. Some held that ancient authors had taken their principles from an eternal Idea, from an instantaneous perception of an unalterable truth. Others held that poetry, for example, came before rules and that Plato, Aristotle, and the others had drawn the rules out of preceding experience. By defining the rules, however, they established a parallelism between art and nature that could not be broken so long as the rules were observed.[16] But neither of these arguments satisfied authors who thought that they smacked of what Horace had branded servile imitation, like that of cattle. Advocates of free imitation followed other visions of nature.

2. Nature is reason in quest, and it is set forth in the experiments of ancient authors.

A number of critics realized that ancient prescripts meant one thing when they were first devised and another in the sixteenth century. Pressed to logical conclusions, the discrepancy made it possible to argue that, by modern criteria, Homer and Virgil were not poets.[17] Indeed, ancient writers themselves defined imitation as a free adaptation of fairly loose rules, as an artist's own judgment acting in variable situations required. Had not the painter Apelles pieced together his own mental picture of Aphrodite from observations of several human models? Standards of judgment also varied according to national character, the technical capacities of a given language, and the particular stage of historical development.[18] Ancient authors set a model by writing according to the standards of their day, but, since art was continuous, universal criteria of judgment had to be drawn out of the entire career of literature, rather than from one episode.

It was possible, therefore, to reverse the ancient axiom that art imitated nature. For so Julius Caesar Scaliger (1484–1558) held that Virgil was a supreme poet because he did not learn from nature, but rather, by combining experiences, competed with her, creating laws for her to obey.[19]

3. Nature is a super-rational impulse of spirit.

[16] Ibid., pp. 447, 455ff., 458.   [17] Ibid., pp. 150, 194.

[18] Ibid., pp. 62, 457. On seventeenth-century continuations of this argument, see J.W.H. Atkins, *English Literary Criticism: Seventeenth and Eighteenth Centuries* (London, 1951), pp. 19ff.

[19] R. W. Lee, *Ut Pictura Poesis: The Humanistic Theory of Painting* (New York, 1967), p. 11 n. 43.

Arguing for radical originality, some critics who held this position insisted that artists were born, not made, and consequently they denied that there was any art in the sense of rules that consistently applied could achieve the end of poetry.[20] Even though they took dreams, visions, and madness into account as sources of inspiration, most advocates retained classicism. They agreed that enlightenment came to souls disciplined by rules and that ancient artists had most fully combined discipline and furor.[21] Just as novice mystics trained their souls by imitating the ascetic practices of past matters, artists should imitate ancient works in pursuit of the illumination that informed them. But, if it succeeded, mimesis was an act by which the artist freely imitated his own invisible vision.[22]

4. Nature is a process of trial and error.

A fourth cluster of critics combined the historical relativism of classical rules with the psychological uniqueness of free mimesis. They found ancient authors, especially Aristotle, elusive and inconsistent in their definitions of form and imitation. They considered that no artist, however profound his inspiration, achieved a perfect work. One learned from the mistakes of the ancients. The explanation, they said, was that nature herself was imperfect, always striving to create things as they ought to be, and always failing.

Aristotle had written that a maker of likenesses—a poet, a painter, or any other—could imitate things "either as they were or are, or as they are said or thought to be or to have been, or as they ought to be."[23] Sixteenth-century critics gave artists a certain advantage in imitating nature's striving. For, they held, an artist could exceed the realities of nature as long as his work stayed within the realm of probability.[24] The artist reproduced, not fact, but verisimilitude. Consequently, Sir Philip Sidney (1554–1586), following Aristotle, remarked in the *Apologie for Poetrie* that the poet could make a nature better than the one around him or even a nature entirely different from the world of fact.[25] Of course, by this dramatic assertion of poetic freedom, Sidney had no intention of rejecting the classical conventions, metaphors, and meters that filled his entire *oeuvre*. For him, they contributed to verisimilitude. But, in itself, to invoke verisimilitude rather than ancient prescripts was to recognize that every poetic reconstruction of nature was provisional and that it was part of the wider movement in which a

---

[20] Hathaway, *Criticism*, pp. 419, 430, 437.

[21] Ibid., p. 416. On Dryden, see Atkins, *English Literary Criticism*, p. 113.

[22] Cf. Hathaway, *Criticism*, p. 16.   [23] *Poetics*, 1460 b.

[24] Hathaway, *Criticism*, pp. 160–202.   [25] Ibid., pp. 117, 140–160, 326f.

society, in its own way, strove to correct its defects and to realize its ideal forms.

Poetry was ironic; for in attempting to translate a vision into words what it said always differed from what it meant. Repeated over a long space of time, in the works of many poets, each imitating and competing with his predecessors, this irony had a positive side: progress. The cumulative effect of building criticism into the writing of poetry was refinement of the most basic kind. For analyzing the rules of poetry with the view of improvement led inevitably to changing them. The generations that re-invented tragedy, re-cast the epic, and produced the sonnet were fully aware that the writing of poetry was a critical exercise that changed the forms of poetry, and that, by altering style, reshaped the rules of art, and its social world. Like nature, its model, art transcended rules and style, and it could destroy them.

These arguments were framed two centuries before Diderot, and still they point toward a solution of the *Encyclopédie*'s puzzling frontispiece. Remarkably, none of the four describes "nature" as actually existing, tangible objects in the world. In all the positions that we have identified, "nature" is itself a term of art, whether it were the order of reason, set down once and for all by the ancients in their magisterial rules, or the more general rules that unfolded in man's rational quest, or the source of creative inspiration, or the process of self-correction. The four positions therefore illustrate that the criteria of mimesis applied by critics of poetry were not drawn from the observation of sensory things. Empirical aims were violated in a second way. For it is also true that, in the first instance, the criteria did not come from analysis of poems. Rather, the common aesthetic basis of the four definitions derived from philosophical texts, and it was then applied to poetry. The "nature" that poetry was held to imitate existed between nature and art in the theories of the critics. What I have said about poetry was also true of criticism in the other imitative arts (portrayed, in the frontispiece, as music, painting, sculpture, and architecture).

The same attitude prevailed in the eighteenth century, deepened and elaborated by the slow growth of aesthetic theory. It had two dominant characteristics: the conservative philosophical basis of criticism, built as it was with teachings of classical antiquity, and the insistence that one approached originality by way of imitation. Such was the core of David Hume's (1711–1776) distinction between the merely "natural," which was "disagreeable" or "insipid," and "nature drawn with all her graces and ornaments, *la belle nature.*"[26] The general acceptance of these propositions in the eighteenth century can be illustrated by reference to two very diverse areas of inquiry—natural history and art.

The persistence of mimetic strategies in the area between nature and art presupposed resonances in thought about nature and about art.

For many years, Buffon (1707–1788) dominated the institutions of botanical and zoological research in France from his position as director of the Jardin du roi and the royal museum. He owed a great measure of his celebrity and power to the vast and comprehensive treatise on natural history that he enterprisingly turned into a commercial as well as a literary triumph. Despite his unstinting search for specimens in every part of the world, despite his practice of scientific experiments, despite the affront that, as the Sorbonne deemed, his cosmology presented to Christian doctrine, many of the principles on which he built were Aristotelian doctrines that had been fully integrated into scholastic philosophy long before. Buffon discounted advances in science that questioned traditional knowledge and that proclaimed the existence of modern science. For example, he continued to teach that nature consisted of a continuous chain, or hierarchy, of beings derived from a common element, the fixity of species,[27] and, in some species, the spontaneous generation of life. Perhaps he intended to appease the ecclesiastical censors with his rhetorical tributes to the Creator of the world. Whatever the sincerity of those remarks, Buffon built his cosmology not around creationism, but around another principle derived from ancient philosophy: namely, that the existing world, a "universal mechanism," was patterned on an archetypal idea, an ideal expressed in "eternal and necessary laws" of movement.[28] There was a "primitive form of every living being" hidden in nature and, as the individual developed, it gradually perfected the hidden form.[29]

---

[26] "Of Simplicity and Refinement in Writing," in *Essays: Moral, Political, and Literary* (Oxford, 1963), p. 196. On the origins of the concept of *la belle nature* in seventeenth-century Italian thought, especially that of Giovanni Pietro Bellori, see E. Panofsky, *Idea, A Concept in Art Theory,* trans. J.J.S. Peake (Columbia, S.C., 1968), pp. 105ff., 159, 167ff. Lee, *Ut Pictura Poesis,* p. 16. Julius Caesar Scaliger represented a divergent, and important, current in criticism by regarding Virgil, instead of Homer, as the poet par excellence.

[27] *Histoire Naturelle, des animaux,* chs. 1, 5, (*Oeuvres choisies de Buffon* [Paris, n.d.] 1: 116, 157f.). *HN de l'homme, de la nature de l'homme* (ibid., p. 174).

[28] *HN de l'homme, de la nature des animaux* (ibid., pp. 517–519).

[29] *Discours sur le style* (Paris, 1905), p. 17.

What place did man have in this world, imitating its model by endless repetition?

Buffon the scientist answered: "One is forced to place him in the class of animals."[30] Like all animals, he learned through his senses, which were mechanistic[31] and therefore imitated the eternal and necessary laws of motion. Following this line of thought, Buffon determined that, since imitation never created anything new, man as imitator could not create but only produce.[32]

Buffon the philosopher could not let the argument rest there. For, he wrote, man differed from the animals in his reason.[33] All animals learned by imitating the physical responses of their elders. The human child did too, but the imitation was both physical and intellectual. The crucial difference between a dog and a child was that, while the dog moved in blind, unthinking reaction, the child was educated to compare sense perceptions, forming ideas, and to compare ideas, forming reasons.[34] Just as man changed the natural state of animals by domesticating them,[35] he changed and perfected his own state of life by educating the reason in this comparative and constructive task. The well-trained dog and the educated man differed in that the latter, being capable of reflection, was also capable of living in society. In fact, rational imitation was the very basis of society.[36] But there was a stage beyond the level of conformity, or "servile imitation," achieved by most people, a level that entitled man to be regarded as the masterpiece of created nature.[37] Beyond the mechancial "blind imitation" of animals[38] and the rational, "servile imitation" of social man, there was the critical imitation motivating the man of genius.

Imitating nature in his sensual responses, imitating the rules of order gained through the composition of mental images, the genius penetrated beyond existing norms into the common subject of poetry, history, and philosophy: that is, man and nature.[39] The advancement of knowledge and thus of society depended on such efforts. And yet, man

[30] *HN de l'homme, de la nature de l'homme* (*Oeuvres choisies de Buffon*, p. 179).

[31] *HN des animaux,* ch. 1 (ibid., p. 115).   [32] *Discours sur le style* (ibid., p. 17).

[33] *HN de l'homme, de la nature de l'homme* (ibid., pp. 179–184); *HN de la nature des animaux* (ibid., pp. 491–500).

[34] *HN de l'homme, de la nature des animaux* (ibid., pp. 500, 512f.).

[35] *HN, Quadrupèdes, animaux domestiques* (ibid., 2: 1–3).

[36] *HN de l'homme, de la nature des animaux* (ibid., pp. 482, 484, 518f., 517).

[37] *HN des animaux,* ch. 1 (ibid., p. 115); *HN de l'homme, de la nature des animaux* (ibid., pp. 491, 500–503).

[38] *HN de l'homme, de la nature des animaux* (ibid., p. 517).

[39] *Discours sur le style* (ibid., pp. 20–24).

and nature as they were always differed from what men knew about them. Even criticism, prescribing rules about nature to art, stood outside the realm of nature. Advances in human knowledge broke old norms of imitation only to set new ones. Knowledge remained partial and inexact at every stage.[40] For example, nature had no classes, no genera, or species. These categories had been made up by the human mind; nature knew only individuals.[41] The varieties of animals were greater than classificatory systems could represent.[42] Nature's greatest marvel, the power of procreation, was a mystery that man could not fathom.[43] Systems of classification were among the images that men of genius composed. By them, man could not change the being of things, but he could strive to pass from the particular to the general, from the known to the unknown.[44] They were images formed by analogy, which is another way of saying the mind imitating what it knew of nature.

Even at the highest level, therefore, the human spirit could not create anything. Natural things were outside of man; style was the man himself. As to things outside, the human mind only produced, having been impregnated by experience and meditation. "But if, by style, it imitates nature in its sequence and its labor, and if it raises itself to the highest truths and unites itself with them and, by reflection, forms a unified system, it will establish enduring monuments" in the literature by which poets, philosophers, and historians paint their portraits of man and nature.[45]

With texts of classical antiquity in mind, Buffon realized that style could keep works alive long after criticism had discredited their scientific data. He could not fully appreciate the danger hidden in the importance that he gave imitation in the development of style: namely, that one could preserve one's originality while imitating the style of earlier men only on condition that one also shared their ideas. Otherwise, one could derive striking expressions and brilliant images from them but these metaphors would be lifeless and unintelligible because they had been wrenched away from the context of ideas that gave them meaning. Perhaps it was unkind of his enemy, Condorcet, to point this out in a memorial oration on Buffon.[46]

---

[40] *HN des animaux,* ch. 5 (ibid., p. 155); *HN de l'homme, de la nature des animaux* (ibid., p. 526).

[41] *HN de l'homme* (ibid., p. 179).   [42] *HN des animaux,* ch. 5 (ibid., p. 155).

[43] *HN des animaux,* ch. 1 (ibid., p. 116).

[44] *HN, de la nature des animaux* (ibid., p. 461).

[45] *Discours sur le style* (ibid., pp. 17, 26).

[46] *Oeuvres choisies de Buffon,* ibid., 1: 9.

Mimetic strategies were among the elements that Buffon drew from his classical heritage and that blinded him to advances in empirical science. There were reasons for Buffon's preferences, and the history of art also shows that, in the special case of painting, there was a practical reason why canons of criticism were drawn from literary texts rather than from empirical examination of evidence. When Sir Joshua Reynolds (1723–1792) admonished artists to imitate the masters, he referred, as far as Greek sculpture was concerned, to a very slender body of original works, plaster casts, and Roman copies. Nor did artists know what they were imitating. As the dispute whether the Elgin Marbles were classical or Hellenistic works indicates, criteria of authenticity and chronology were grossly inexact, and it was possible for Winckelmann (1717–1768) to accept the Apollo Belvedere as the most perfect example of classical Greek sculpture, though it is now recognized as a Roman copy, heavily restored in the sixteenth century.

In fact, as president of the Royal Academy, Reynolds knew perfectly well that the absence of a public collection placed a severe limit on his advice and not only with regard to ancient art. The first public gallery in London, at Dulwich College, opened in 1815. Before that time, students of art had access to major paintings only through engravings, on the sufferance of private collectors in England, or by the costly means of travel abroad. Indeed, more than twenty years after Reynolds's death, the agreement of Dulwich to lend it a mere six pictures annually permitted the Royal Academy to establish a school of painting. Parallels could be found in every country, in France, for example, where the first major public collection, the Louvre, opened in 1793.

Art and art theory, therefore, had too little evidence for the comparison and analysis that criteria of empirical knowledge required. As a result, criticism fell back on literary and, especially, on philosophical texts. The treatises of Winckelmann, and Lessing's fragmentary rebuttal to them, the *Laokoön,* are exercises in textual criticism that use individual statues to illustrate aesthetic propositions pieced together from ancient writings. When Reynolds delivered his famous *Discourses* on painting it was hotly disputed whether they had been written by an artist, by Reynolds himself, or by a man like Samuel Johnson, who lacked practical experience in painting but had wide literary knowledge.

One of those propositions was that originality came through imitation. "A mere copier of Nature," Reynolds said, "can never produce anything great."[47] Still, nature was to be imitated because it displayed "in each species of things" an invariable idea of beauty: the masters were to be imitated because they developed techniques for reproducing those "general forms of things." They were also to be challenged and rivaled; for "genius is the child of imitation."[48] The art of seeing nature was the art of using models "to supply the natural imperfection of things, and often to gratify the mind by realizing and embodying what never existed in the imagination." Through technical mastery and imaginative fantasy, the artist digested, methodized, and compared his observations, composing his own inner picture.[49]

This was the ideal that lived in the artist's heart. Try as he might, he could never succeed in conveying it; for, invisible to the eye, and inexpressible by the hand, it belonged to an order entirely different from the physical world of nature and the tactile materials in which the artist worked. Even so, the imitative rivalry of great artists over the centuries did elevate the public mind away from natural appetites and to "general and intellectual" beauty and, thus, to virtue. Such had been Raphael's achievement as he worked "always imitating, always original."[50]

Winckelmann was even more emphatic than Reynolds in teaching that "imitation of the ancients is the only way for us to become great and inimitable." The masterpieces of the Greeks displayed more than nature; that is, composite ideals, beauties of nature made up of pictures sketched out in the mind. *Die schöne Natur, la belle nature,* is this ideal beauty pieced together by the artist to raise nature above itself. The ancient Greeks captured these elevated forms with an extraordinary refinement, but, by combining imitation of their statues and techniques with his own discoveries, the modern artist could pass beyond rules. He could become a rule himself, exercising the sovereign freedom of Poussin or Michelangelo.[51] How was this paradoxical freedom through imitation possible?

It was possible, Winckelmann asserted, because there were no final answers in art. Art had its youth as men do, its maturity and decline. But the lack of finality, and thus the chance for originality, existed not

---

[47] Discourse III, *Discourses on Art* ed. S. O. Mitchell (Indianapolis, 1965), p. 27.
[48] Discourse VI, ibid., pp. 74, 91.
[49] Discourses IX, XII, XIII, ibid., pp. 143, 189, 207.
[50] Discourses VI, IX, ibid., pp. 83, 143f.
[51] *Gedanken über die Nachahmung der Griechischen Werke in der Malerei und Bildhauerkunst,* in *Kleine Schriften zur Geschichte der Kunst des Altertums,* ed. H. Uhde-Bernays (Leipzig, 1925), 1:60, 61, 68, 73.

in the organic growth of art so much as in its essence: that is, in the effort to create meaningful, sensual signs of things that were not sensual, to make visible signs as analogues of invisible subjects. "It is only by way of allegory, through pictures, that general concepts can be expressed," and it was through the purifying study of allegory that truth and understanding could be achieved and the prevalent corruption of modern taste be dispelled.[52] The career of the artist as critic therefore led from imitation to the composition of ideals and finally to the use of allegory to inspire, instruct, and purify.

These examples indicate the persistence of mimesis as a strategy of correction in nature, in art, and in the area between nature and art.

In a figurative way, the frontispiece to the *Encyclopédie* expresses the same persistence; and the articles in the *Encyclopédie* support this conclusion. They illustrate, particularly, how the practice of criticism altered the language of mimesis, replacing the transcendent idea with the immanent ideal or type.

The riddle of the frontispiece is summed up in the sentence, "Good imitation is continual invention."[53] But the meaning embedded in this sentence rests on the following assumptions.

1. Nature is not what we can know through the senses. The article on "Nature," permits a number of meanings: the system of the world (the machine of the universe, subsuming all created things), each being (created or not, spiritual or physical), the essence of a given thing, the order and natural course of things (laws of movement), the powers or capacity of a given body, and the impelling principle of all things (providence, God, fate). In poetry, "nature" had three further meanings derived from Aristotle, and slightly altered: all that actually exists in the universe, all that existed before us and that we can know by history, and finally, all that can exist, but that has never, and will never, exist.

2. Nature is imperfect.[54] For example, nature can rarely produce a body as handsome as Antinous's, though that can regularly be done in art.[55]

---

[52] Ibid., pp. 100, 103.

[53] "Imitation" (1765 ed., 8: 568), by L. de Jaucourt, 1704–1776, a collaborator of Buffon. He studied theology at Geneva, natural science at Cambridge, and medicine at Leiden.

[54] "Critique" (1754 ed., 4: 493B), by Jean-François Marmontel (1723–1799), a poet, playwright, journalist and historian, who replaced Bougainville in the Académie française.

[55] Jaucourt, "Nature—La belle nature" (1765 ed.) 11: 44 A.

3. Though imperfect, nature, imitating nothing, is always true, while art risks being false in the degree to which its imitations diverge from nature.[56]

Divergence is inevitable; art and nature differ in kind. For the arts create things that are stable, while nature ceaselessly varies every position, every action.[57]

4. The risk of falsehood occurs in part because works of art are fictions that themselves rest on a fiction. The prior fiction is *la belle nature,* the intellectual model according to which imitation ought to correct nature.[58]

La belle nature imitates nature, not as it is, but as it could be, and as it can be conceived by the mind. From the beauties of nature, the artist derived the ideal beauty, which provided him grandeur and nobility. In nature, he found the human element of his work. He could imitate what he saw there; he could be a copyist, a portraitist, limiting himself to one subject. (Though his meaning has been disputed, Lessing also appears to have granted portraiture a lower place than other kinds of painting, since "it is the ideal of a particular man, not the ideal of Man.")[59] In the ideal, however, the artist found the divine element, which ought to enter his work, elevating his soul to universal Beauty. With experiments in all the arts, the Greeks had defined *la belle nature,* a second nature. Imitating their achievements was a short way to learn to imitate the first nature, of which the second was an analogue, a real beauty idealized and, thus, perfected.[60]

The risk was compounded by the fact that human knowledge must always be fragmentary. Man composed his intellectual model out of what he knew. Yet nature was hidden by a continual, though partial eclipse, and knowledge of its immense disk grew but slowly, age by age.[61]

5. A double imitation was in play, and a double correction. Art imitated and corrected itself, as it imitated and corrected nature.

Criticism was the tool of this twofold effort. Though the arts differed in media and in objects, they all fell under the same principle of

[56] Diderot, "Imitation" (1765 ed.) 8: 567.

[57] Marmontel, "Critique" (1754 ed.) 4: 493 B.

[58] Diderot, "Beau" (1751 ed.) 2:177f.

[59] *Laokoön,* ch. 2, in *Werke* (Munich, 1969) 2: 16. Reynolds too regarded portraiture as an inferior enterprise, since, rather than painting man-in-general (as "history-painters" did), the portraitist painted "a particular man, and consequently a defective model" (Discourse IV, ibid., p. 53).

[60] Jaucourt, "Nature—La belle nature" (1765 ed.) 11: 43f.

[61] Marmontel, "Critique" (1754 ed.) 4: 491 B.

growth. In the liberal and mechanical arts, as well as in natural history, the inventor was like an adventurer lucky enough to be blown into harbor by a gale. The critic was like an experienced pilot, guiding himself deliberately into harbor by his art. However, the art itself was a series of tentative steps and fortunate discoveries, made as one groped along with quaking steps. The critic's task was to observe facts, determining their relations and rectifying false observations, to interrogate nature, not to put words in her mouth.[62]

6. The critic as interrogator was a copyist, a portraitist, a historian. He was also a poet in putting together his evidence, and deploying it according to his best judgment. His imitative work involved both history and poetry.[63] Even in the sciences, the historical function required study of ancient texts.[64] Did not Buffon owe his early reputation as a scientist to demonstrating that Archimedes could indeed have destroyed a Greek fleet with a burning glass? The copyist's sort of imitation weighed yet more heavily in literature and the other mimetic arts. But it was through imitation of their ancient models that men became original, as, long before, Plato imitated Homer and Virgil imitated many worthy predecessors.[65]

Yet, standards changed. Expressions that were good in one writer might damage his admirer in another time and place. In all the arts, ancient models had to be applied according to expectations unknown to the ancients.[66]

7. The object of the artist as critic mediating between nature and art, therefore, was not to proclaim final answers, but to explore and test the possibilities of art. And yet not all men exercised the "methodological doubt" that superior criticism required. There was ignorant criticism, which never doubted because it had negligible powers of comparison, and subordinate criticism, which lacked the ability to form transcendent models and so to advance beyond servile imitation of existing productions. The dominance of superior criticism was far from inevitable. The fate of ancient literature after the fall of Rome illustrated disruption. Ancient texts required at least a semi-educated reader. When that public was lost by a profound change of *moeurs,* the func-

---

[62] Ibid.

[63] Diderot, "Imitation" (1765 ed.) 8: 567. Cf. Jaucourt, "Nature—La belle nature" (1765 ed.) 11: 43f.

[64] Marmontel, "Critique" (1754 ed.) 4: 490f.

[65] Jaucourt, "Imitation" (1765 ed.) 8: 568.

[66] Jaucourt, "Imitation," and Voltaire, "Histoire" (1765 ed.) 8: 225 B, 568f.

tions of superior criticism ceased, only to be recovered by slow and painstaking steps.[67]

8. The further task of the artist as critic, then, was to draw society with him as his art advanced from the intellectual model on which existing works were patterned to another, better one.

In all the imitative arts, copying was sterile; progress turned on critically sound decisions by which the artist chose elements out of the hodge-podge of nature and framed them so as to deceive, delight, and instruct the soul. The type and rule of his compositions lay in the artist's knowledge of man and his affects, rather than any primordial design in nature.

Of the arts, two had no models at all in nature. They happened also to be the most firmly grounded in imitation of ancient models: architecture—where the Greeks established proportions that appeared destined to be eternal models of art—and rhetoric. The ancients established norms in these two arts because they discovered the psychological effects of art, "the relation of objects with the organ of sentiment" and, particularly in rhetoric, "the influence of mind on mind, the action of soul on soul."[68]

The practice of criticism might be disruptive in any area, but it could be especially so in these two arts, as they reached into the archetypal depths of proportion and justice. Was not criticism in architecture capable of revolting against *"bisarrerie* of usage, tyranny of habit, which sterility and sloth had raised up as inviolable law"? Grounded in rhetoric, the practice of literary criticism extended to the analysis of history and morality. Literary criticism had much to say about the inalienable rights, duty, and interest of man as citizen: that is, about the foundation on which laws and morality stood. How pregnant with consequence was Marmontel's insistence that the literary critic withstand prejudice, that he judge not only how each man followed "the morals (*moeurs*) of his own age and the laws of his own country, but also the laws and morals of all countries and all ages, according to the invariable principles of natural equity." Marmontel could not foresee how intellectual models extracted from rhetoric and poetry would be applied, or what results would follow from his insistence that the critic draw the public to a model beyond the beauties of nature and the productions of art and educate it to the height of judgment at which the

[67] Marmontel, "Critique" (1754 ed.), 4: 496f.
[68] Marmontel, "Art" *Suppl.* (1776 ed.) 1: 586.

public itself would become "the most faithful mirror which the arts can consult."[69] It must have given him some pause to recall these opinions as he spoke in the National Assembly, and later when he was silent under the Terror.

9. Imitation was a psychological function that could be turned to good or evil purposes. An enlightened political order could use the fine arts, as Marmontel wished, to penetrate every level of society and thus to enhance the general happiness of mankind.

The classical period of Greece and the apogee of the Etruscans were "the golden age of liberty" and during this period the fine arts served their rightful purpose most completely: the formation of public morality and the support of philosophical and religious teaching. Thereafter, in the Hellenistic age, the arts declined together with liberty. The Romans deflected the arts from the service of the common good. Using them to adorn tyranny, they corrupted the very principles of art. Although those principles were renewed in the Renaissance, and although eighteenth-century man surpassed the Greeks in his mechanical powers and perhaps also in his study of man and nature, the fine arts remained what they had been for the Hellenistic period on: captives to the rich. "The great had artists as they had cooks, and the arts that earlier provided health-giving cures for the soul were incapable of giving more than rouge and perfumes."[70]

Far from having abandoned critical strategies of mimesis, therefore, the *Encyclopédistes* incorporated them into their program for purifying social consensus. Between the sixteenth century and the eighteenth, new ways in which the strategies of mimesis were understood had been introduced. Aristotle's two axioms are the theme; everything else is variation. The first axiom was that men (and all animals) learned by imitation. By the eighteenth century, this principle extended, more thoroughly than Aristotle ever intended, to all areas of human knowledge. The second axiom was that art was grounded in imitation of nature. This principle distinguished human creativity, which ebbed and

---

[69] Marmontel, "Critique" (1754 ed.) 4: 492f., 494 B, 495 B.

[70] "Art—Beaux-arts," *Suppl.* (1776 ed.) 1: 594, a translated passage from *Allgemeine Theorie der schönen Künste* (1771–1774), by Johann Georg Sulzer (1720–1779), a Swiss theologian and, from 1747, professor at the University of Berlin. In another excerpt, Sulzer ridiculed artists who imitated the works of previous artists, or obeyed the dictates of fashion; but this censure corresponds with the contempt, noted above, for servile imitation. "Nature—La belle nature," *Suppl.* (1777 ed.) 4: 20. On the career of the arts from Greek genius to modern decadence, see also Jaucourt, "Nature—La belle nature" (1765 ed.) 11: 44.

flowed, from the steady repetition that could be observed in nature, particularly in animal behavior, for example, in the "political order" and the "architecture" of bees. It hinged on man's distinctive rational powers, on his freedom to learn from past errors, to calculate advantage as he formed new visions of the future, and, finally, to correct or rival nature.

Writers between Luther and Goethe elaborated these Aristotelian themes in highly original ways. Perhaps their most important departure was incorporating critical strategies into all the arts and sciences. By this device, mimesis became a means of progressive transformation, and it was possible for the *Encyclopédistes* to teach that imitation should be a continual invention. They recognized that imitation could be unoriginal and servile copying of individual exemplars. Some of them set portraiture in this category. What they aimed at was a free imitation based on comparison of individuals that yielded a high degree of generalization, an act of analysis and synthesis that enlarged the possibilities of art. By contrast with portraiture, three paramount examples of painting by abstraction and synthesis were known from literature, and one could still be seen: Apelles's *Aphrodite,* Zeuxis' *Helen,* and Raphael's *Galatea,* in which the beauties of individual women were combined into one intellectual or ideal model.

Clearly, then, theories of mimesis persisted in critical thought of the Enlightenment about corrective movement in nature, in art, and, above all, in the area between nature and art. However, it is also true that theories of progress hostile to imitation had also taken root. In part, they followed from advances in historical knowledge that discredited both aesthetic theories that men had built upon them from the Renaissance onward and the ways of thinking by which those theories had been constructed.

The eighteenth century was punctuated by a series of jolts as Europe was forced to discard its preconceptions of Greek art. A vast body of knowledge still waited to be discovered through archaeology and through the study of ancient vase-paintings. Even so, Villoison's publication of the Venetian scholia (1788) opened the highest representative of classical poetry, Homer, to historical criticism. The publication of engravings that depicted pre-classical and classical Greek architecture as it actually was aroused disbelief shading into revulsion from what was deemed the barbarism of the Doric order. Of all Greek arts, excluding literature, sculpture was the best known. And yet, one of the greatest jolts came with the slow realization that the Elgin Marbles

279

were not late, or crude, or meretricious, but that the vivacity of the animal and human figures expressed aesthetic values of classical Athens. Men gradually realized that ideal and immoble serenity had been read back into the past by Europeans of the post-Renaissance era, the product of self-delusive ignorance. The nineteenth century had to discard further standards of judgment, and consequently to acknowledge the errors on which they stood, when it discovered that Homer had described historical events instead of composing from a free poetic imagination and that the Greeks had not desired the stark purity of unadorned marble but rather had polychromed their buildings and statues.

Was it possible that ancient works were inimitable, not because they expressed eternal values in ways that were beyond the powers of later men, but because they lived, and could live, only within a specific social order that had perished? If that were so, many assumptions about the imitation of nature by art would have to be discarded. Indeed, with the growth of historical sciences, the concept of nature itself took on new ramifications beyond those accessible to sixteenth-century writers. Some of the new propositions were anti-mimetic.

1. Nature is history: things as they were. The goal of textual and historical criticism was to establish the archetypes, the authentic forms, in which the Scriptures, Roman Law, and classical writings had been composed. These efforts extended also to the post-classical monuments and institutions of Germanic peoples. The imitative effects of criticism on this level are apparent in drama, architecture, and painting, and, no less, in political arguments based on "common law," or on the "fundamental law" or constitution of a given people.

From the sixteenth century on, however, this view implied an anti-mimetic stance. Bodin and the students of the English common law had rejected the universal applicability of Roman models. Montesquieu and Vico rejected universal archetypes and argued decisively for the self-explication of national characters. In the fine arts, the debate between the ancients and moderns ignited a range of arguments against classicism. Most damaging of all, the advancing discovery of Greece, through textual criticism and archaeology, proved that classicism itself was a modern conception, a tissue of theories based on ignorance of the ancient world as it really had been. With great irony, Lessing argued that classicism in drama actually disrupted authentic classical tragedy, which had persisted from Sophocles to Shakespeare. In 1864, Fustel de Coulanges merely stated epigrammatically what

Montaigne had argued in the sixteenth century, and what many in the eighteenth century had demonstrated. Fustel wrote that the Greeks and Romans were foreign to the existing world, "absolutely inimitable." "Nothing in modern times resembles them, nothing in the future can resemble them. It is almost always ourselves that we see in them."[71]

2. Nature is "eternal and necessary laws": things as they are. As endeavors to discover ordering principles, the arts and sciences attempted to penetrate what was visible and tangible. What composed the system of the world or of a particular being or essence? What were the laws of motion, the coordinated powers of a body, or the providence, God, or fate that established the harmonious unity of opposites? Imitation of ancient literary styles, statues, and architecture might be a short cut to those eternal laws. But it was necessary to test one's models. Some ancient writings corrupted the style. The good varied according to time, place, and circumstance. And the maturation of a profound discovery never ended, though it occupied men over long generations.

When they coincided with scientific thought, these reserves also provided anti-mimetic propositions of two kinds. The first derived from psychology. How did one explain human creativity in all its variations? One could argue that creativity came about because there was no universal access to nature. The mentality of each human being was shaped by his unique experiences. He perceived, not nature, but his own ideas of nature. Or one could argue that true creativity, as distinct from routine production, came about through genius, through some exception to rules, a freedom from dominant social norms that could not be explained or reproduced. A second anti-mimetic proposition derived in part from science: namely, that nature was lifeless matter. It moved mechanically, an unfeeling, valueless, and unthinking force, alien and dangerous to man. By his arts, man did not imitate physical nature so much as create his own nature. Art was autonomous: it became possible to reverse Aristotle's axiom and to say that nature imitated art. However, it is important not to overemphasize the novelty of this reversal. When Kant taught that the mind prescribed laws to nature and that nature could be called beautiful because men judged it as art,[72] he was recasting an argument that had been drawn out of ancient texts in the sixteenth century.

---

[71] *The Ancient City* trans W. Small (Garden City, New York, 1956), pp. 11f.
[72] Cf. *Critique of Judgment*, sect. 45.

3. Nature is an intellectual model for the future: things as they ought to be. Insofar as eighteenth-century culture remained literary and classicist, it is not surprising that nature continued to be regarded as invisible and imperfect and that art also kept its familiar role as a second nature, an essay in analogy. Yet the ancient definitions had changed by being placed in a novel setting. As critical analysis developed, men took for granted that decomposition was a necessary prologue to making. They recognized that decomposition of the object had to be radical if man were to make something original. Where were analogues to be found for a truly original work? Insofar as they were possible, analogues lay, not in the stable forms of metaphysical being or theological faith, but rather in human labor or experience. What were the limits of decomposition? Since all labor and experience were social, it extended to society as a whole. The conviction that the arts had grown decadent in the eighteenth century was an implied judgment against the existing social and political order. Aristotle's definition of art as what ought to be gained unprecedented meaning; for, in discourse about freedom, art had become the instrument of political ideology.

In my discussion of earlier centuries, I identified several kinds of mimesis that mediated the asymmetry of ideal and actual, and I emphasized that they were capable of being combined in different ways or limited to particular areas of inquiry while they were excluded from others.

Any concept of human life, I indicated, could include one or a bundle of these paradigms of change. Mimesis by augmentation had special importance for the concept of historical progress, partly because of the ease with which it could be enriched with the paradigm of growth and so appeal convincingly to the imagination as a "natural" explanation of things. Because it derived from ancient doctrines of cosmic mimesis, and still carried their traces, the augmentative idea of change in the political world was the most comprehensive of all, and its inclusiveness passed into concepts that it inspired for the regeneration of the social world by a militant, enlightened minority.

To approach this further stage in our account of mimesis as a strategy of corrective mediation between nature and art, I note one aspect of the frontispiece for the *Encyclopédie* that I have not explained. Why is the picture cast as a sacred allegory, complete with goddess and temple? There is some connection with the ancient, and the sixteenth-century, identification of nature as a super-rational impulse of spirit, acting as a poetic *furor,* of art as prior to rules and possibly destructive of them. I have referred to the persistence of mimesis in religion, particularly in mystical thought of the sixteenth century, and the element of natural religion has silently intruded itself into my comments on artistic inspiration, genius, and *la belle nature*. Properly, Aristotle has figured very large in our account; the mystical heritage of Plato and the Church Fathers was also woven into the "typical" or the "ideal," bound though they were to time and place and, thus, sentenced to obsolescence. Indeed, the definition of the ideal marked a further stage in what Plato described as the struggle between philosophy and poetry, a running feud that broke open again in the age of Thomas Aquinas and that humanists and mystics resolved in the fourteenth and fifteenth centuries. Changes in the concept of mimesis as a strategy of correction between the sixteenth and the eighteenth centuries sprang from a recurrence of this conflict, and new reintegrations of mimetic with iconoclastic elements.

Chapter 13

Mimesis by Augmentation in Two Theories of Historical Development

AT A DISTANCE, it might appear that the spirit of criticism moved over a world divided between enlightened rationalists and illuminated obscurantists. However, the actual state of affairs has proven to be both more complex and more interesting. As I have shown, the mimetic strategy of mediation between nature and art persisted in highly diverse currents of thought between the Reformation and the Enlightenment, and it was the substance of critical theories by which men translated thought into action.

Mimesis remained, as it had been from the beginning of the classical tradition, a strategy of progress from fragmentation toward unity. In the doctrines of ancient philosophers and Christian theologians, unity had been defined with reference to metaphysical being. In the doctrines with which I am here concerned, it was defined with reference to historical experience. However, in the hands of empiricist historians, the program of mimetic progress retained tensions that had also characterized its metaphysical forerunners.

Paradoxes in the critical spirit found an articulate observer in Henry St. John Bolingbroke (1678–1751). Repeatedly ill-fated in political intrigues at home, Bolingbroke improved his periodic exiles in France with amours and philosophy. Devoted to British empirical philosophy as developed by Bacon and Locke, he found much that was congenial in teachings of the *philosophes*.

He grasped that the critical method of empiricism had a Trojan horse inside its gates, the great problem of knowledge itself: generalization. All knowledge was grounded in nature, but nature was composed of individuals. Nature provided men, but not man-in-general, specific actions, but not general morality. Where nature could not lead, men followed "her mimic, art." "Thus knowledge, particular by nature, becomes in some degree general by art." How should one mediate between particular facts and general theories? The further man departed from nature, the more readily he fell into error, enmeshed in complex ideas that had no basis in fact.[1] Metaphysicians and theologians had driven themselves headlong into fallacies of their own making, and Bolingbroke swept the whole lot of them away—Plato and Aristotle, Descartes and Leibniz, and the entire succession of Neoplatonists. Their systems were like portraits painted without models: "being taken from imaginary, not real existence, the picture will be the picture of nobody, and the system, the system of nothing."[2]

Without imitation of a subject, art degenerated into artifice.[3] But there was always room for greater likeness between the subject and its representation. The triumph of the empirical sciences was to demonstrate human ignorance. The greater their discoveries, the more profound and extensive the ignorance proved to be, and the more fallacious any effort to generalize by analogy beyond particular experiments. Science grew as did principles of the "law of nature and civil jurisprudence," by slow, incremental experience. The endless ignorance of expanding sciences was preferable to the philosophers' ignorance of nature. The wisest course was to ignore their elaborate discussions of archetypes outside and inside the mind. Scientific criticism had discredited theories of enduring archetypes, just as historical criticism had demonstrated, to Bolingbroke's satisfaction, that the Old Testament had no right to be called the Word of God. Metaphysics and theology were nothing more than diverting romances, together with their allegories, their false analogies between man's life and God's.[4]

But the imitative mediation that was needed to form general theories allowed old metaphysics to enter new empiricism. Bolingbroke knew that generalization was not a matter of tailoring evidence to suit theories. It was a process by which the mind patterned complex ideas. Equally, by composing ideas, the mind learned to decompose them and build others, as evidence multiplied and reflection deep-

---

[1] "Essay Concerning the Nature, Extent and Reality of Human Knowledge," sec. 5. *The Works of Lord Bolingbroke* (Philadelphia, 1841), pp. 118f.

[2] Ibid., sec. 4, p. 107.   [3] Ibid., sec. 5, sec. 7, pp. 131, 157f.

[4] Ibid., sec. 3, pp. 86–88; sec. 4, pp. 106, 123, 104, 109; 102, 107; sec. 7, 161. "A Letter Occasioned by one of Archbishop Tillotson's Sermons," ibid., p. 32, cf. also pp. 16f., 34f., 39.

ened.[5] Bolingbroke realized that this skill in mediating between facts and theories was rare.

While he approved the free imitation of the subject in art and, by analogy, in the formation of general scientific theories, Bolingbroke denounced the servile imitation of most thought. The "illiterate, unthinking crowd of mankind" were educated to speak by rote, furnishing their minds "with the fancies of other men," instead of compounding, decomposing, and reconstituting ideas for themselves. Yet more alarming, Bolingbroke saw that, while the fictions of metaphysics and theology had been exploded in the physical sciences, they persisted "in all that relates to spiritual nature: and modern philosophers, like tyrants driven out of one province, have made themselves amends, as it were, by exercising a more arbitrary power in another." Most serious of all, these hypothetical generalizations intruded into the thought of empiricists. Bolingbroke wrote that even Locke, the most eminent of them, had (unavoidably) used figurative style in attacking figurative style, and had yielded himself to the enemy's embrace when he assumed the existence of a spiritual nature and discussed the formation of archetypal ideas by abstraction and intuition.[6]

Blinded by his ardor for experimental, concrete knowledge, Bolingbroke could only censure this co-existence of opposites, even in Locke's mind. He liked clean distinctions. Progress, he thought, demanded the total victory of new empiricism over the old "unnatural method of studying nature."[7] Without recognizing it, however, he identified something more intricate than the warfare of science against superstition, something that he himself implied when he described art as nature's mimic. He exemplified the tenacity of old mimetic doctrines in new iconoclasms when he assumed that general theories could reflect uniformities in nature, thus disclosing a means by which mimetic ideas invaded ways of thinking empirically about history.

It was by no means exceptional that mimetic doctrines should be employed in historical thought, as they were in so many other areas of inquiry and expression. One may, however, usefully illustrate the scope of historical interpretations in which the mimetic program found a place. Bolingbroke's own idea that each national tradition developed an organic integrity as it grew, was one example of this historical point of view. For the sake of contrast, however, I shall describe how the mi-

[5] "Essay," sec. 2, p. 82; sec. 3, p. 111.

[6] Ibid., sec. 4, p. 111; sec. 5, p. 147; sec. 9, p. 202; sec. 5, pp. 129f., 125f., sec. 8, pp. 172f.

[7] Ibid., sec. 3, p. 87.

metic strategy of augmentation was taken up and employed by two men who were intellectual antitheses of each other, David Hume (1711–1776) and Johann Gottfried von Herder (1744–1803).

Hume

Descartes had recognized his own deference to inherited opinions (including those of Augustine and Aquinas) even as he sought to free himself from the history of philosophy. Locke had resorted to the Aristotelian tradition in theology, represented by Hooker, while he struggled to establish moral principles secured by the pure objectivity of mathematical axioms. So, too, David Hume found himself pulled by contrary demands. In a famous passage, Hume explained how he felt caught between the skeptical demands of his epistemology, which isolated him as "some strange, uncouth monster," and the ties of habit and experience, which made it possible for him to enjoy the company of his friends and to enter into "the common affairs of life." His skepticism denied universals and coherent entities, even personal identity. His reflections on society demanded universals, supremely that of human nature. Hume recognized, moreover, that if the mind strictly followed his skeptical principles it would end by subverting itself and all human understanding in science and philosophy. To avert these "fatal consequences," even epistemology had to compromise with earlier metaphysical reasoning. Hume saw no alternative to embracing this "manifest contradiction."[8]

Incongruous theological survivals opened the systems of Descartes and Locke to mimetic conceptions. In a parallel way, Hume's retention of a universal term, "human nature," inconsistent as it was with his denial of certain knowledge, actually had two surprising results. It gave unexpected scope to argument by inference and analogy; and it provided the impetus for a new doctrine of mimesis. Both the argument and the impetus became dominant when Hume wrote his history of England. This might well appear improbable.

And yet, the question of form was capable of being dealt with very differently by the same author in different lines of inquiry. Even when an author entirely rejected the metaphysical basis of the mimetic tradition in one area, components of the tradition could reappear, dismembered and reappraised, in another area where the need for general

---

[8] *A Treatise on Human Nature*, 1. 4, ed. A. D. Lindsay (New York, 1951) 1: 249f.

models were acknowledged. An apparent disjunction of this sort obtained between Hume's epistemology and his moral theory, both in itself and in its effects on his historical writings.

Throughout this account, I have noted that many writers believed that historical change originated in human states of mind. The world of action reflected that of thought. Thus, mimetic strategies at work in the mind were projected into, and shaped, the great course of human events. Writers employed analogy to affirm the coherence between the inner processes of thought and the outer movements of history. Although Hume severely criticized contemporary scientists and theologians for their analogical methods and conclusions, he also made analogy central to his epistemology. Against his adversaries, Hume insisted that thought was an empirical act. However, once one accepted inference by analogy—empirical or not—one also retained mimetic strategies for establishing analogues.

There were intimidating results. Hume argued that reasoning by analogy hinged on empirical knowledge of causal relationships. However, reasoning from experience proceeded "upon the supposition that the future will be conformable to the past." Did all reasoning from experience, and the acts that it prompted, move in a vicious circle? Hume recognized this circularity as a danger in his epistemology, but he considered it a virtue in history.[9]

When he argued that only "quantity and number"—that is, mathematical or geometric knowledge—were capable of abstract demonstration, Hume did not exclude other kinds of knowledge from serious reflection. To be sure, matters of "fact and existence"—including all moral thought and causal analysis—could not be demonstrated as mathematical facts could be. They were enmeshed in the categories of space and time, which appeared so obvious and incontestable and yet which, as logical tools, were "full of absurdity and contradition."[10] When it described objects in terms of sensory qualities, the mind read into them characteristics (such as hot and cold, rough and smooth, and colors) that had nothing to do with the objects themselves, but rather with the veiled analogues under which it perceived them. Finally, all analysis of fact and existence also rested on analogy, and more exactly on experience, which made it possible to "infer the existence of one object from that of another," or to "expect from any cause the same effects which we have observed to result from similiar causes."[11] Hume

[9] *Enquiry Concerning Human Understanding*, 4. 2, ed. L. A. Selby-Bigge (3rd ed. by P. H. Nidditch, Oxford, 1975), p. 35.
[10] Ibid., 2. 2 (p. 156). [11] Ibid., 9; 12. 1–3 (pp. 104–108; 149–165).

was prepared to argue that this area of moral and causal reasoning was not dominated by the (rational) understanding, but, instead, by taste and sentiment. Still this, not abstract science, was the area of his major effort, and his recourse to experience and analogy led him to recast the doctrine of mimesis in a new context.

From these propositions, Hume went on to use mimesis in explaining how a body of knowledge could grow and change and yet keep its characteristic features. By contrast with Plato's mimesis of reversion, therefore, Hume taught a mimesis of augmentation, in which an original core unfolded and enlarged, each concentric circle of growth reflecting the center.

He reasoned about imitation on three levels. The first was the most indistinct and general. Hume argued that thought paralleled nature. As it put its conceptions together, the human mind instinctively followed a path that corresponded by "a pre-established harmony" with the course of powers and forces in nature. Neither the degree of correspondence nor the "power and forces" could be known.[12]

The second level of imitation was that of individual thought. Sensory impressions reproduced the external world for the mind, but, on this higher level, the mind performed elaborate mimetic functions as it copied sensory impressions and, gazing into the "faithful mirror" of past sentiments and affections, divided and composed them into ideas of varying complexity.[13] The task was an exercise in ascertaining degrees of analogy between discrete events, or ideas, and Hume identified three kinds of likeness that might be established. He wrote of (1) connection by resemblance, as between a portrait and the sitter, or between religious cult and the object of faith, (2) connection by contiguity, in time or place, and (3) connection by causation. None was capable of logical demonstration. Each could be accepted, however, because one believed in the connection or likeness; and one believed in it because of custom, "the great guide of human life."[14]

The third level on which imitation figured in Hume's thought was social practice. When he wrote that custom directed the imagination in its composition of ideas, Hume partly meant personal habit. But he also recognized that even belief, the inmost mental habit, was a social function. Hardly any individual action was complete in itself; it needed a response; "the actions of others [were] required to make it answer fully the intention of the agent." This broad, common under-

[12] Ibid., 5. 2 (pp. 54f.).   [13] Ibid., 2 (pp. 18, 19f.); 5. 2 (p. 49).
[14] Ibid., 3; 5. 1; 5. 2 (pp. 23f., 44, 50ff.).

standing rendered experience useful, by providing analogues with present experience, lessons in how to adjust means to ends, and models for any productive effort aimed toward the future.[15] No eternal ideal was at issue, but rather social norms that varied by historical period and country. Such was "the great force of custom and education which mould the human mind from its infancy and form it into a fixed and established pattern." Through believing acceptance of the imitative patterns of culture, even Hume's enlightened contemporaries betrayed their long-past "ignorant and barbarous ancestors' " superstitious bent of mind, for, as the body of collective experience enlarged, its entire thrust was to transfer even the distinct past to the future.[16] While his epistemology threatened to extinguish the self and universal ideas, Hume's moral theory restored both. His argument regarding the origin of morals is that they derive from general norms of social utility and benevolence, and not from the expedience of the moment or self-love.

Hume's mimetic ideas embraced both the uniformity of human nature and the relativism of custom. Attacking the age-old equation of reason with divinity, and the corresponding premise that reason was man's dominant faculty, Hume held firmly to his conception that reason was the "slave of the passions."[17] In considering utility and benevolence as general motivations, he was not attempting to reestablish universal and absolute forms like the Platonic ideas. Thus, although he taught that the mind operated mimetically, he struck at the roots of mimetic epistemology as transmitted through various Platonisms. The purpose of moral speculation was to move men to avoid the deformity of vice and to embrace the beauty of virtue. This, he argued, could not be achieved through reason, which discovered truth and procured "only the cool assent of the understanding," but through the "particular fabric and constitution of the human species," a sentiment that took possession of the heart and animated men to embrace and maintain what is honorable, fair, noble, and generous. Much reasoning often preceded the acceptance of virtue, but the acceptance itself came from "some internal sense of feeling which nature has made universal in the whole species."[18]

Hume's comments on justice illustrate his argument. For Plato, justice had been the ordering principle in cosmos, mind, and state, and it

[15] Ibid., 8. 1; 5. 1 (pp. 89; 40ff.).   [16] Ibid., 8. 1; 10. 2; 6 (pp. 86, 119, 58).

[17] *A Treatise on Human Nature*, 2. 3. 3 (ed. cit., 2: 127).

[18] "An Enquiry Concerning the Principles of Morals," I.1., L. A. Selby-Bigge, ed., *Enquiries Concerning Human Understanding and Concerning the Principles of Morals*, 3rd ed by P. H. Nidditch (Oxford, 1975), p. 173.

informed them with the intelligible beauty of the eternal, universal, and ineffable Ideas. For Hume, justice was a "cautious jealous virtue" that would have no place either in a primitive golden age or in some future state in which, through common friendship and generosity, the "divisions and barriers of property and obligation" would have no place. The existence of property, however, was essential to the advancement of art and industry and to the welfare of the whole community.[19] Consequently, public utility called forth justice. To demonstrate that utility was prior to justice, Hume provided a number of illustrations in which the rules of equity or the ordinary rules of justice would rightly be suspended or ignored: in case of shipwreck or siege, to save lives, in the case of punishment inflicted on a condemned criminal, in a conflict between a civilized nation with barbarians who observed no rules of war, as in the struggle between the English and and "barbarous Indians," when it was necessary to "throw off all restraints of justice and even of humanity in dealing with them." It followed that government, too, existed because it was useful to mankind in preserving peace and order, but both the forms of government and the norms of justice varied. The laws, "which extend, restrain, modify and alter the rules of natural justice," also change according to "the constitution of government, the manners, the climate, the religion, the commerce, [and] the situation of each society."[20] It also followed, therefore, that norms of justice varied from one constitution to another according to standards of public utility. Courage was the predominant virtue in primitive nations, replaced by other excellences in societies that had experienced higher social virtues; tyrannicide was once approved and subsequently considered improper; luxury, condemned among the ancients, had become recognized as fostering industry, civility, and the arts, and thus was laudable or innocent; laws concerning degrees of affinity in marriage varied among peoples; and, with advances in perceptions of the true interests of mankind, we "adjust anew the boundaries of moral good and evil."[21]

Hume was saying that public utility, and justice as its derivative, were variable, but that human nature, which determines utility, was constant. Justice and property promoted public utility and supported civil society, but they were not derived, like hunger, love of life, and other passions, from "a simple, original instinct in the human breast,

---

[19] Ibid., 3. 1 (p. 185); 3. 2 (pp. 194f.).
[20] Ibid., 3. 1 (pp. 191f.); 4. 1 (pp. 205f.); 3. 2 (p. 196).
[21] Ibid., 2. 2 (pp. 180f.).

which nature had implanted for like salutary purposes." Questions of property involved a vast range of legal technicalities that a hundred volumes of laws and a thousand volumes of commentators had not sufficiently exhausted. These complicated and artificial matters fell in the sphere of reason. "Have we original, innate ideas of praetors and chancellors and juries? Who sees not that all these institutions arise merely from the necessities of human society? All birds of the same species, in every age and country, build their nests alike. In this we see the force of instinct. Men, in different times and places, frame their houses differently. Here we perceive the influence of reason and custom. A like inference may be drawn from comparing the instinct of generation and the institution of property."[22]

While he dismissed innate ideas as well as the Platonic Ideas, therefore, Hume appealed to another universal when he invoked the "human species" and instincts that motivated all men. A trace of the mimetic relation between exemplar and copy appears in his doctrine of mental images. It was, of course, experience that chiefly formed the associations of ideas,[23] but in Hume's theory of morals that experience was not the act of viewing shadows flitting through the theater of the mind. His principal argument against the position that morals originate in self-love rested on the conviction that each person viewed with sympathy the experiences of other human beings. A person in solitude loses "all enjoyment, except either of the sensual or speculative kind; and that because the movements of his heart are not forwarded by correspondent movements in his fellow-creatures."[24] Personal judgments of morals depend on "images of human happiness or misery" and "images of vice and virtue" that he gains as spectator touched by pain or pleasure at the happiness or misery that other men bring to society through their actions. This association of ideas occurs in the individual mind, but it is also a collective endeavor, analogous with "general language [that] being formed for general use, must be moulded on more general views, and must affix the epithets of praise or blame, in conformity to sentiments which arise from the general interests of the community."[25] In another sense, images also occur in society, as well as in the individual mind. For, "by our continual and earnest pursuit of a character, a name, a reputation, in the world, we bring our own deportment and conduct frequently in review, and consider how they appear in the eyes of those who approach and regard us. This constant

[22] Ibid., 3. 2 (pp. 201f.).   [23] Ibid., 5. 1 (pp. 217f.).   [24] Ibid., 5. 2 (p. 220).
[25] Ibid., 6. 2 (pp. 224f., 228f.).

habit of surveying ourselves, as it were, in reflection, keeps alive all the sentiments of right and wrong, and begets, in noble natures, a certain reverence for themselves as well as others, which is the surest guardian of every virtue."[26]

The tension between Hume's subjective epistemology and his acceptance of universals in moral theory—whether instincts or social norms—becomes even more apparent when the argument moves to a higher level. Beyond sentiments stands humanity. "The humanity of one man is the humanity of every one; and the same object touches this passion in all human creatures. But the sentiments which arise from humanity are not only the same in all human creatures and produce the same approbation or censure, but they also comprehend all human creatures; . . . And every quality or action, of every human being, must by this means, be ranked under some class or denomination, expressive of general censure or applause."[27] Subjectivity and social norms merge from this point of view; for universal humanity makes it possible for any person, in moral doubt, "to enter into his own breast" for the answer. This is presumably the scientific method of inquiry that Hume had adopted: the method of fact and observation, rather than *a priori* argumentation that "may be more perfect in itself, but suits less the imperfections of human nature and is a common source of illusion and mistake."[28] But following the trail of subjectivism led him to the honest self-doubt of skepticism. In his view, Hobbes was "as positive and dogmatical as if human reason, and his reason in particular, could attain a thorough conviction in these subjects." The result was that "Hobbes's politics are fitted only to promote tyranny, and his ethics to encourage licentiousness."[29] Hume was aware "that nothing can be more unphilosophical than to be positive or dogmatical on any subject; and that, even if excessive skepticism could be maintained, it would not be more destructive to all just reasoning and inquiry." And yet, considering his own moral theories, he fell "back into diffidence and skepticism and suspected that an hypothesis so obvious, had it been a true one, would long ere now have been received by the unanimous suffrage and consent of mankind."[30] If subjectivism led to skepticism, the universals led beyond even humanity to "something mysterious and inexplicable . . . a manner, a grace, an ease, a gentleness, an I-know-not-what . . . that must be trusted entirely to the blind but sure testimony of taste and sentiment,

---

[26] Ibid., 9. 1 (p. 276).   [27] Ibid., 9. 1 (p. 273).   [28] Ibid., 1. 1 (p. 174).
[29] *The History of England* (Philadelphia, 1859) 2: 465.   [30] Ibid., pp. 358f.

and must be considered as part of ethics left by nature to baffle all the pride of philosophy and make her sensible of her narrow boundaries and slender acquisitions."[31]

In working out an uneasy compromise between psychological subjectivity and social exemplarism, and particularly in discussing the variations in norms of utility (and so of justice), Hume discounted some mysteries whose force depended entirely on socially ingrained belief. He referred to various religious practices: "A fowl on Thursday is lawful food; on Friday abominable. Eggs in this house and in this diocese are permitted during Lent; a hundred paces farther, to eat them is a damnable sin. This earth or building, yesterday, was profane; today, by the muttering of certain words, it has become holy and sacred." Was it not possible, he asked, that a comparable superstition entered into all the sentiments of justice, "and that, if a man expose its object, or what we call property, to the same scrutiny of sense and science, he will not, by the most accurate inquiry, find any foundation for the difference made by moral sentiment?" For example, "I may lawfully nourish myself from this tree; but the fruit of another of the same species, ten paces off, it is criminal for me to touch. Had I worn this apparel an hour ago, I had merited the severest punishment. But a man, by pronouncing a few magical syllables, has now rendered it fit for my use and service." The difference between superstition and justice is that "the former is frivolous, useless, and burdensome; the latter is absolutely requisite to the well-being of mankind and existence of society. When we abstract from the circumstance, . . . it must be confessed that all regards to right and property seem entirely without foundation, as much as the grossest and most vulgar superstition. Were the interests of society nowise concerned, it is as unintelligible why another's articulating certain sounds, implying consent, should change the nature of my actions with regard to a particular object, as why the reciting of a liturgy by a priest, in a certain habit and posture, should dedicate a heap of brick and timber, and render it, thenceforth and forever sacred."[32]

Hume was able to turn aside the affinity between superstition and justice with the argument that to weaken the obligations of justice, or diminish "the more sacred attention to property," would undermine "human society, or even human nature." This affirmation of faith was all that kept him from abandoning the world of the universals and following his skepticism to its necessary political conclusion, a conclusion

[31] Ibid., pp. 345f.   [32] Ibid., pp. 270f.

that, as he knew, had already been reached along a different road by revolutionaries in seventeenth-century England.

In his *History of England,* Hume's Tory convictions decided the contest even more plainly in favor of universal models. The pluralism, perhaps even the nominalism, that informed his comments on political constitutions in the *Inquiry Concerning the Principles of Morals* has vanished. The critical edge of Hume's social mimesis appears glitteringly well-sharpened, undulled by the rust of relativism. In the *Inquiry,* Hume called the Indians "barbarous," and he made it clear that ancient cultures, particularly those of Athens and Rome, were early stages beyond which his own had greatly advanced. His remarks on non-European peoples, such as the Turks and the Muscovites, and on other European nations in the *History* also betray a failure to accept alien cultures on their own terms: that is, to accept their conceptions of public utility and justice as independently valid. Hume measured them against the ideals of personal freedom and representative government that the British constitution exemplified, and he condemned them. It is only right to add that Hume's contempt for other cultures as undeveloped by comparison with eighteenth-century Britain, and his attitude that the English had had to lay their humanity aside in suppressing the "barbarous" Indians, are of a piece with his attitude toward earlier periods in European culture; he was able to condemn scholastic philosophers as "monkies in human shape."[33]

As an historical exposition, the *History of England* is fascinating in its combination of variable circumstances with persistent ideals. Through his friendship with Adam Smith and other associations, Hume was fully alert to the influence of wealth on political forms. The feudal order was fixed on property as land. As long as commerce languished and political institutions rendered their poverty perpetual, the feudal parliament did not include the commons; later parliaments did, because of changes in the economic structure. As the fortunes of the military landed aristocracy declined, and those of the commercial classes rose, there appeared "a new plan of liberty founded on the privileges of the commons."[34] By the time of James I, Elizabeth's alienations of royal lands and the "increase of commerce had thrown the balance of property into the hands of the commons," who considered that the royal prerogatives, so freely used under Elizabeth and James, had "almost annihilated the constitution," and who "were re-

[33] *The Natural History of Religion* ed. A. Wayne Clover (Oxford, 1976), p. 94.
[34] *The History of England* 2: 130

solved to secure liberty by firmer barriers than their ancestors had hitherto provided for it." In the parliaments of 1610 and 1621, they challenged the royal prerogatives. In the Revolutions of 1649 and 1688, they achieved "the most entire system of liberty that ever was known amongst mankind."[35]

Hume disapproved Tudor absolutism, just as he disapproved of what he considered the barbarous taste and stylistic crudity of Tudor *moeurs,* exemplified in Shakespeare. Yet he did not condemn earlier governmental forms in England as he did those of other cultures.

Hume was able to survey the great panorama of "liberty and oppression, order and anarchy, stability and revolution"[36] from the ancient Britons to the Glorious Revolution and to discern a stability of principle. Honor and fidelity, the election of kings, and rights of subjects were present from the beginning. So too was aversion to the view that "any man trained up to honor and inured to arms was ever to be governed without his own consent by the absolute will of another or that the administration of justice was ever to be exercised by the private opinion of any one magistrate without the concurrence of some other persons whose interest might induce them to check his arbitrary and iniquitous decisions." The king was regarded as the "head of the community and the chief fountain of law and justice."[37] Throughout the English constitution persisted, not as forms of government, but as principles of liberty, imperfectly understood, inaccurate, and all but suppressed by royal absolutism. But whenever "the privileges of the nation have at any period been overpowered by violent irruptions of foreign force or domestic usurpation, the generous spirit of the people has ever seized the first opportunity of reestablishing the ancient government and constitution." In 1621, James had "with so rash and indiscreet a hand, torn off that sacred veil which had hitherto covered the English constitution, and which threw an obscurity upon it so advantageous to royal prerogative."[38] The revolutions that followed were explications of the principles of liberty.

The Platonic Ideas, which Hume expelled from his epistemology and tentatively received back into his moral thought, returned unabashedly in his view of British history. It is quite apparent, however, that those universals he recognized were not tied to any specific political forms. Their persistence through the centuries, through the changing patterns of government, through stages of increasingly clear compre-

---

[35] Ibid., p. 648.   [36] Ibid., 1: 225.   [37] Ibid., p. 228, 230.
[38] Ibid., 2: 177f.

hension and complete realization, is a paradigm of the moral progress that Hume described. The constitution passed through epochs of elucidation; patterns of administrative order succeeded one another. The principles of liberty persisted in the fugitive images of the mind, in the progressively changing norms of the human species, in the prevailing interests—or is it superstition?—of society. The ideals endure, not in eternity, but under the aspect of history.

In epistemology and in historical thought, Hume represented two divergent movements in seventeenth- and eighteenth-century thought: on the one hand toward isolation of the individual, and on the other toward the envelopment of the individual by the mass. Oddly, these are the same divergent tendencies that characterized mysticism from the fourteenth century onwards and that led to the divinization of change. More than analogy is at issue. It is very well known that Hume's epistemology aroused Kant to reformulate idealism and that Kant's work, in turn, was fundamental to the historical idealism of Hegel. It is equally important, but less frequently emphasized, that Hume's concept of the English constitution as containing principles of freedom—"the spirit of the constitution"—that were gradually disclosed and realized through collective experience overlapped in some telling ways with Hegel's philosophy of the Absolute Spirit's self-explication through progressively complete stages of freedom.

Herder

Far more than Hume, Herder prepared for some directions that historical philosophy took in the nineteenth century. Despite all his strengths, Hume did not develop a fully articulated theory of historical development as Herder did, and we can begin to grasp the impact that Herder (rather than Hume) had on later historical writers by beginning with his idea of Christ.

From St. Paul onward, Christology had kept doctrines of imitation as a manifold corrective strategy at the heart of European culture. Various individual strategies of mimesis attached themselves to the two natures of Christ. How they figured in particular systems of thought depended on whether individual writers emphasized Christ's divine or His human nature, and on how they understood His role as mediator. These variations in emphasis had important consequences for the ways in which writers patterned human experience, dominated, as all agreed, by the theme of redemption from sin.

Hume was repelled by formal religion. He discarded Christology with the whole cargo of dogma and cult. A celebrated Lutheran pastor and preacher, Herder retained Christology, and mimesis as a corrective strategy between nature and art, as the key to history, though he drained them of their supernatural content. "Mankind," he wrote, "is a fallen race." Christ was the savior of the world, and history the process by which the seeds of divinity that Christ awakened in man grew and advanced the human race in an endless course toward happiness.[39]

One striking characteristic of Herder's theology, however, is the almost complete distinction that he drew between doctrines about Christ and those about change through imitation. In this regard, he was true to Luther's revolt against exemplarism (Chapter 10). Christ, Herder wrote, was "the most intimate expositor of divinity and its all-efficient organ for the restoration of mankind to the God-like dignity that descended to it."[40] But Herder did not consider Christ a mediator in the supernatural roles of Logos or ascetic exemplar. Herder reasoned that mediation occurred through other agents, and in his teachings corrective mimesis found other, transitory exemplars. I shall now examine this distinction between the work of Christ and progress through imitation.

Herder consciously developed his Christology in opposition to two camps: dogmatists, heirs of patristic and scholastic theology, and deists, advocates of natural religion. Like Augustine, he formulated his theories most plainly in reflections on the Gospel of John, and his quarrels with the dogmatists can be clarified by contrasting his stance with what I have said about the Father.

The most apparent difference concerns method. Augustine's whole concern was with the text and inner meaning of Scripture as a self-contained and self-explanatory whole. Herder quoted verses from the Gospel of John, but new sciences of historical criticism permitted him to recognize that the Gospel was not complete in its own terms. He argued that, in early times, the truth that it set forth had not been vouchsafed only to the Hebrews and codified, as prophetic anticipations, in the Old Testament. Its deep truth had been generally perceived. The pre-history of the Gospel included the entire Near East. The ideas of many peoples and generations—Persian, Greek, and Jew-

---

[39] "Von Gottes Sohn, der Welt Heiland. Nach Johannes Evangelium," 1. 38, 34; 5. 1 *Herders sämmtliche Werke* [cited hereafter as *S.W.*], ed. Bernhard Suphan (Berlin, 1880), 19: 296, 303, 350).

[40] Ibid., 1. 34 (p. 296).

ish—converged in it. Furthermore, the Gospel had been written, not in a vacuum, but rather for specific, polemical objectives, which shaped its theme and message. Thus, the Church's confession that Christ was the Son of God came about by a long and intricate conflation of ideas imported into Palestine from lands to the east, west, and south. Combined with the misery of the age, the same ideas had generated other doctrines—strange idols and fantasies—that the Gospel of John was designed to refute, clarifying and authenticating what had been implicit in all previous ages.[41]

Herder's historical criticism freed him from the duty of internal, allegorical interpretation of the Scripture under which Augustine had toiled. He retained the Father's insistence that the Gospel of John had a singular place in the redemption of the world. But, in this regard too, he abandoned patristic norms. For Augustine, John's distinctive characteristic was that he portrayed the divinity of Christ. Herder wrote that, while some had said that John "theologized" the Son of God, it would be nearer the truth to say that he had "anthropologized" the divinity that is recognizable by man, revealing its counsel and love to men so that they could join in its work on earth. Christ "was only the Son of God in [His] love for men." John preached a Gospel of friendship and brotherhood; those who heeded it in action participated in the work and purpose of Jesus.[42]

In this sense, the Gospel of John was "dogmatic-historical," rather than merely historical, as were the three synoptic gospels, and it was also necessary in world history because it, uniquely, gave the key to mankind's progress from sin to reconciliation.[43] However, it was by no means dogmatic in the sense, or with the consequences, that the Fathers had intended. Augustine deliberately invoked tactics of philosophy, the liberal arts, and coercion in the service of his doctrine, and this continued to be true in magisterial churches, including those established by Luther and Calvin. Herder repudiated these tactics. The Gospel preached by John was hostile to the "mythologies" perpetrated by the Church Fathers, to the elaborated structures of doctrine and law piled up by scholastics and canonists, to the external trappings of cult, and to any bloodshed, oppression, or conquest, most particularly in the name of religion.[44]

---

[41] Ibid., 1. 8. 15–17 (pp. 279, 282f., 283f.).

[42] Ibid., 1. 40; 5. 2 (pp. 250, 304). "Nachahmung Jesu" *S.W.* (Berlin 1889) 29: 436.

[43] "Von Gottes Sohn," 1. 18 (*S.W.* 19: 285).

[44] Ibid., 1. 33–34, 36–37; 5. 12, 31–32 (pp. 299f., 302, 350, 365, 366).

Christ, the savior of the world, evaded ecclesiastical and political dogmatism because he was "the active organ of divinity in mankind."[45] Just as the pre-history of the Gospel included more than the people of Israel, so too, the unfolding of the effects of the Gospel embraced not only a small company of the elect, as Augustine had taught, but the entire world. The crown of Christ's short life on earth was the awakening of an imperishable and heavenly friendship that encompassed all peoples, each modulating the message of the Gospel according to its own purpose.[46] Together with his doctrines of election and predestination, Augustine's Christology and his teachings on salvation had focused on the person. Herder utterly rejected personalism in favor of collectivism. The enemy of human friendship and brotherhood, he wrote, is egoism. Christ solemnly prohibited egoism among His followers. Following His command, the earliest Christians created an enduring order for the happiness and welfare of mankind; but, recognizing egoism as their enemy, they labored self-effacingly, without any wish to be remembered in this world.[47] All alike "sons of God," each individual and every people was subordinate to the divine purpose: the liberation of the human race. For all time, Christ set an example by sacrificing Himself to this ultimate goal. The Son of God called Himself the son of man, for "to Him the divine in man was nothing other than the purest, most comprehensive humanity." He manifested, not the Word, but the Father in Him, not transcendent personality, but the God immanent in man.[48]

A final difference between Herder and the dogmatists concerned duration. Augustine and, later, the scholastic theologians had envisioned the progressive movement of the elect toward the moment when the world and time would end. Herder contemplated a process that would extend indefinitely toward the realization of mankind as "a happy brotherhood, of divine origin"; for, in Christ, earth and heaven had already become one.[49]

Herder's revulsion from ecclesiastical and political dogmatism did not drive him to the opposite extreme of natural theology. Against the deists' insistence on self-evident truths, deduced from nature as it could be observed through the senses, Herder accepted Scriptural revelation. Against the deists' contention that the Gospel accounts were myth, Herder insisted that the Gospel of John was indeed written by

---

[45] Ibid., 1. 39 (p. 303).   [46] 4. 14; 5. 46 (pp. 339, 374).
[47] Ibid., 5. 24, 30 (pp. 362, 365).   [48] Ibid., 5. 46, 11 (pp. 374, 337).
[49] Ibid., 1. 30; 4. 11 (pp. 303, 337).

the Apostle John, an eyewitness of the events that he described, and, moreover, that Christ was actually a man of flesh and blood, whose body, wounded and dead, lay in the tomb, and who, raised in the flesh, ascended into heaven. Against the deists' reliance for confirmation of faith on individual feeling of oneness with the Spirit of the universe (for example, in perception of the sublime), Herder invoked the historical evidence of the development of a community of pure friendship established by Christ.[50]

Herder's message consisted of two propositions: (1) God was pefect humanity; (2) mankind was God in the process of becoming. By rejecting dogmatism and retaining Christology, however, Herder created a difficulty in linking these ideas. What relation was there between the human Christ who lived and died centuries ago and the present? After His death, how did Christ continue to function as "the all-efficient organ for the restoration of mankind"? How did the work of Christ—awakening divinity in man—persist, if not by supernatural imitation of Christ as Logos and as man?

Advocates of natural religion dismissed these issues when they judged the Gospels as myths and fables and Christ as an ethical master of a bygone age. But it was precisely from these opponents that Herder gained a solution to his quandary. The solution came by way of the idea of spirit. There was also a point of contact with the theology of Luther, who ascribed to the Holy Spirit transformative mediation that earlier writers had attributed to Christ (Chapter 10). In the event, therefore, Herder incorporated ideas of mediation and mimetic transformation into theories of history as the reflection of spirit.

For Hume, the "spirit of the constitution" had been the underlying principles according to which social relations within a given natural environment were organized into a system. Though this "spirit" proceeded from human nature (or reason) operating within geographical constraints, it was something artificial. In that regard, it was like Montesquieu's "spirit of the laws" or "general will." Herder considered nature to be identical with spirit, and this identity made it possible for him to put man's search for meaning in political and social experience within a framework very different from Montesquieu's or Rousseau's. Spirit, or order, was not something prescribed to nature; it was nature manifesting itself in the visible world; it was history. Consequently, Herder was able to consider the spirit prior to institutions and, hence, to conceive of a cultural unity in which the works of the mind had pri-

[50] Ibid., 4. 27, 35; 5. 29 (pp. 343, 346, 364).

ority and patterns of trade and government were lesser manifestations. He sought the spirit of a people in the ballads and folksongs of lower social ranks, rather than in high politics. He exalted instinct, or feeling, over reason, since he believed that man's passions were impulses of a universal power that, though unconscious of itself, drove man toward the best.[51] It followed that he considered religion to be "the highest humanity of man."[52]

There were in Herder two conflicting moods. Herder had an oppressive sense of the transience of things that led him to doubt the value of any creative effort. In moments of hopelessness, he wrote passages reminiscent of Augustine's despair of beautiful things that pass away and of Beowulf's laments for the evanescence of strength and fame. The whole course of man's life is change; the entire human race is in metamorphosis. Men are but shadows; their ideas are dreams of shadows that appear and vanish.[53] Nations rise and are destroyed; the more brutal conquer the more refined, as Rome broke Greece. Despots reign; sages die. The lessons of human experience are no more permanent than lines traced in the waves of the sea. One year runs on into the next; destroyers create works that will be destroyed.[54]

But this was only one of Herder's moods. Beneath the ceaseless flux of things, Herder detected an unfolding organic growth, an unresolved harmonic progression. It lacked, perhaps, a final cause in time and space; it lacked predetermined direction; and still it gave meaning and pattern to human experience.

His doubts concerning progress and meaning were answered by a doctrine of the ultimate unity of things. Within the flowing river of life, which could never return to its source, there was one living, organic power; one universal plan of nature that formed each crystal, each snowflake, and informed the continuity and progress of the human species.[55] Herder pressed Aristotle's immanent teleology into service when he argued that each thing contained the form that growth would give it. According to the law of nature, everything held within itself the principles of truth, goodness, and beauty, the symmetry and balance for which it was made and according to which it would mold itself

---

[51] *Ideen zur Philosophie der Geschichte der Menschheit,* 15. pref., ii. (*S.W.* [Berlin, 1906] 14: 215 [317]).

[52] 4. vi. 6 (*S.W.* [Berlin, 1887] 13: 161 [255]).

[53] 7. i (*S.W.* 13: 253 [75]). 8. ii. 5 (*S.W.* 13: 309 [157]).

[54] 15. pref. (*S.W.* 14: 205f [302–303]).

[55] 15. iv (*S.W.* 14: 238 [348].) 15. v. 12 (*S.W.* 14: 249f [364]).

in body and in mind.[56] Aristotle's distinction between primary and secondary substances, in which the actually existing individual was more real than the abstract category, also appears in Herder's argument. It appears, however, tinged with Leibniz's theory that each organism encapsulates the entire species. For Herder understood each individual person as a particular manifestation of the energy and capacity of the human race.[57] In the same way, he considered each nation as bearing within itself its own character, or principle of growth, which was unique and incommunicable, though, taken together, through the course of history individuals and nations constituted an incremental whole. The earth was made to bear fruit in all its varieties, to hear from the instrument of mankind every possible note that has been or will be struck.[58]

There were four points on which Herder felt apprehensive. For each one, he also framed a positive counterpoint. The first was that all things appeared to flow unremittingly toward extinction. Against this, Herder described the ultimate unity of nature. With regard to man, he understood that unity in terms of reason and justice. Reason detected the relations of things and described them in such a way as to balance opposing forces in a dynamic and enduring equilibrium or symmetry. Justice was reason in its moral aspect, which applied the formula of equilibrium on which the harmony of all creation depended. Moreover, reason conformed to the internal powers of nature. It was an attribute of God and a common property through which all men were sharers in the same World Soul. Despite the appearance and the fact of change, men were not isolated in their distinctive cultures. Despite the incomparability and incommunicability of each national character, reason and justice established a community out of time in which every thinking, feeling mind was the brother of every other one. In it met the hearts and minds of all people in all ages.[59] Mankind, taken in all its manifestations, was a permanent natural system.[60]

Herder's second apprehension followed from the tendency of human achievements to perish. He was oppressed by the ceaseless and apparently pointless rise and fall of nations and, in that formless sequence, by the prevalence of the powerful over the good. His counter-

---

[56] 7. iv; 15. iii. pref. and 1 (*S. W.*, 13: 273f [104–106]; 14: 225–227 [330–333]).
[57] 15. iii. 1 (*S. W.* 14: 227 [332–334]).
[58] 8. i; 8. v. 2, 3 (*S. W.* 13: 298 [142], 335–342 [197–206]).
[59] 15. iii. 5 (*S. W.* 14: 229–234 [336–343]).
[60] 15. iii. pref. (*S. W.* 14: 226 [332]).

weight to this point was tradition, which he called the organ of reason. Those achievements of a culture that accord with reason, justice, and wisdom survive. Those that are foolish perish, for madness and folly destroy themselves, and they may also destroy the earth.[61] God understood that men were prone to err; but He implanted in mistakes the capacity for detection. In time, they were recognized as errors and discarded. No truth, once discovered, was ever lost. It might be despised or obscured when it was found out, but it belonged to the human species, which in changed circumstances would recover it and acknowledge its necessary forces.[62]

Herder's third point of concern was the apparent lack of advancement in human events or morality. In his pessimistic mood, he described the bloody career of post-Roman Christianity as a distinct argument against any theory of indefinite progress. It was true that each nation achieved only what was possible for it. According to the spirit of its time, each man and nation became exactly, and only, what it was capable of becoming. But, even in the worst of times, reason and its organ, tradition, gave grounds for tracing a slow movement toward higher levels of achievement and morality. Within the husk of the Middle Ages, the seed of the modern world germinated, and, in its ripeness, it burst through and discarded its shell.[63] While it was so that man had advanced in past ages at the cost of vast destruction, as the achievement of Virgil cost rivers of Roman blood and the destruction of kingdoms and nations without number, it was also true that, since the savagery of the Middle Ages had been overcome, men had learned to use without destroying, and to work for the common benefit of all in the amiable and peaceful spirit of industry, agriculture, trade, and knowledge. Even the recalcitrant were beginning to acknowledge the demands of humanity and its eternal laws.[64]

Herder's fourth point of apprehension confirmed the other three. It was his denial of final causes. Yet there was an exception. His entire argument set humanity as the final cause of nature and history, even as he traced the structure of all brains, whether the earthworm's or man's, to the same prototype. His comments on reason and justice, on tradition, and on progress point to this conclusion. Despite many differences with Kant, he concurred on this with views that he had heard in Kant's lectures at Königsberg. Nature calculated for the welfare of

---

[61] 15. v. 7, 12 (*S.W.* 14: 247 [360], 249 [364]).

[62] 15. iv (*S.W.* 14: 241–243 [352–356]).

[63] 14. vi; 15. v. 7 (*S.W.* 14: 202 [296], 247 [360]). 19. ii. 6 (*S.W.* 14: 416 [227]).

[64] 14. vi (*S.W.* 14: 201 [295]). 15. ii. 2 (*S.W.* 14: 219 [322]).

man, not for that of rulers and states. Through the law of nature, other species remained what they had been in the beginning, while God gave change and direction only to man: that is, the capacity to become what he was capable of becoming. This was what it meant to be the image of God, a deity on earth, having within himself the principle of self-motion by which he advanced.[65] Progress came through conflict. For just as God gave only man the capacity for change, He gave to him alone the dialectical confrontation with himself and with the world through which he could transcend himself. In this conception there is something of the humanistic *magus,* as Herder encountered that figure in his teacher, Hamann, or in the tradition illuminated by Giordano Bruno and, more remotely, Nicholas of Cusa. Humanity manifested and reinforced itself in government, in the arts, and in all the sciences; the true philosophy of man lay in tracing its course through them. "The further he advanced, the more his humanity was formed; and this must be formed, or he must groan for ages beneath the burden of his mistakes."[66] God had given the outcome of this metamorphosis—the unfolding of God's image—into man's own hands, but He had placed all His sacred, eternal laws of nature at man's service.[67] In the total view, man had completed only the preliminary stages of his development.

It was telling that Herder returned to the tradition-bound metaphors of mimesis in discussing humanity as the final end of creation. In addition to that of man as the image of God, Herder employed the metaphor of the mirror of the mind. As he recognized, Leibniz preceded him in teaching that the mind was the mirror of the cosmos, a statement that, to Herder, meant that the powers of the universe were latent in the human mind, awaiting only the correct organization to impell them into action, and so to transcend not only the former stage of humanity but also time and space.[68] In dilating on this theme, Herder borrowed more and more from the Neoplatonic tradition as it had passed to him through mystical and theological authors. The organic metaphor of the plant, the mirror metaphor, the description of man as *homo duplex,* belonging to and linking the two orders of creation, the animal and the rational—all were found in Plotinus. So, too, occurred the ultimate spiritual unity of the world, the supreme collectivism, in which the individual is subsumed in the All. For Herder, there were no

---

[65] 15. v. 10 (*S.W.* 14: 248 [362]). 15. i (*S.W.* 14: 213 [314]).
[66] 5. i–iv (*S.W.* 14: 167–189 [265–299]). 4. vi (*S.W.* 14: 154–165 [244–260]).
[67] 15. i (*S.W.* 14: 213 [314]).   [68] 5. v (*S.W.,* 13: 193f. [305–307]).

great figures who changed the course of history. Even Jesus, he said, who preached the most genuine humanity, and thereby brought about an unexpected revolution in ways and concepts, was the son of man, and the principles of his doctrine, as well as the stages of His career, were the natural consequences of His historical situation.[69] The individual was a part of the whole, subsumed in the nation, mankind, and finally the World Soul. The idealization of personality was rejected. Herder's conception of man as the final end of creation coincided with his doctrines of national character, reason, tradition, and argumentative progress in the union of man with God, to which he applied a formula, mystic and mimetic, that Augustine used to describe the union of Christ with His elect:

> To the lowest creature
> My sense feels and tastes and stretches:
> All beings are in harmony
> With me, yes, I am they[70]

Many elements in Herder's thought coincided with attitudes of his friend Goethe. Both understood man as having to strive against the flux of things and to labor for the common advancement of humanity. Both found that the futility and the imperative labor were mediated by God as the eternally active creative force in and under the events of the world. Both framed their doctrines of man according to aesthetic theories of poetry and conceived the advancement of man as the self-explication of the image of God, a work defined by an immanent teleology. In his last years, as his friendship with Goethe and others, including Hamann, became embittered, his religious orthodoxy was vociferously denied, and criticism of his historical theories sharpened, the balance in Herder's own mind between individual isolation and traditional collectivism shifted toward the former. In the history of thought, however, Herder's great contributions lay on the other side.

By his fusion of Aristotelian with Neoplatonic conventions, Herder had introduced theories of ethnic integrity that were of paramount importance to nationalist doctrines in the nineteenth century. He had described culture as a system limited by the possibilities of historical situation, and cultural change as a process of mimetic augmentation that moved by the dialectical negation of one stage by the next, and even by the gestation of the future stage within the one that it was to negate. His theory that culture expressed the spirit of a people led him to look

---

[69] 17. pref. (*S.W.* 14: 290f. [52]).

[70] "Die Schöpfung," cf. "Das Ich," l. 82ff. (*S.W.* [Berlin, 1889] 29: 444, 137).

for its authentic expressions not in the works and institutions of high culture, but in the primitive literatures and songs of the lowest social orders. For writers who came after Herder, this sense that the language and bonds of collective unity existed most authentically at the bottom of society combined with a metaphor that Herder did not draw from Aristotelian or Neoplatonic conventions. They were able to match their own mechanistic figures of thought and speech to Herder's sense that, in the world of nature, as in "the Nature-world of History," all things work together, ever acting reciprocally on one another.[71]

It was possible to reconcile mimesis with the new conceptions, but more was needed than the mysticism and spiritualization that Herder provided. It was necessary, not that space and time be transcended, as Herder said, but that they be idealized. This was the decisive work of Kant.

By the middle of the eighteenth century, it was clear that the analytic methods of philosophy must find a new course if the intelligibility of abstract speculation were to retain any practical relevance to life. Immanuel Kant (1724–1804) found such a course but in a system of thought that crowned developments that began with Descartes and codified an idealism that proved to be a central element in the metaphysical doctrine of revolution: "world-destroying thought," as Heine called it.

Though Kant himself had no fully developed philosophy of history, his new idealism had two aspects that proved to be normative in that field. The first was his concept of the autonomous man, constituting his own god, drawing *a priori* forms of judgment from within himself, prescribing laws to nature, and assuming moral judgment as a categorical imperative that had universal validity. This isolation and universalization of the self were essential in the moral ethos of the next century. But Kant made a second contribution to its reformed idealism: the division of Being from Reality was part of an entirely new ideality. The central ideas for Kant were those by which the mind organized its world: namely, time and space. Reality belonged to whatever the autonomous will set into an intelligible pattern according to those ideas. The real was what a historically situated person willed to reconstruct for himself.

The ideality of time and space was part of the concept of the autonomously willing man, but it also meant that there was no absolute

[71] Cf. 14. vi (*S. W.*, 14: 199 [393]).

world of forms, or even of morality, as far as practice is concerned. It is clear what happens to the dialectical conflict between ideal and actual in Kant's thought. Neither individual nor social man was seen as tied to eternal archetypes. The dialectical conflict therefore occurs in time because man has the power and the moral obligation to shape his own character. As ideas in the mind by which man constituted the world of phenomena, space and time gave this revived concept a metaphysical unity that was universal but not absolute. So much for the ideal and the actual. But what happens to the third term of mimesis, the mediator? Kant's doctrine of organism, in which everything was reciprocally a means and an end, gives the answer. Man, the final end of creation, carried within himself the means for achieving the immanent teleology of the world, and that teleology moved in an evolutionary course from one stage to the next, sometimes by peaceful means, sometimes violently, as reason made its phenomenal world and its god. Even the nature in which man lived and constructed his social world was itself constituted when man prescribed laws to it. The historical was the real; in process, the end transformed itself into a means purposively but without final purpose, as each manifestation of humanity subverted and superseded the one before it and prepared the way for the one that would come after and surpass it.

In 1792, Kant began the publication of a work that many considered an attack upon sacred history and that eventually led King Frederick William II of Prussia to demand that Kant promise never again to write or lecture on religious subjects. According to the argument that Kant set forth, the career of Christ was the focal event of historical idealism. In *Religion within the Bounds of Pure Reason,* he argued that man was originally good but that he had become radically evil. Still conscious of the moral law, man departed from it to the fullest, and this aversion could be corrected only by a revolution in thought. Deliberately not invoking dogmatic and historical connotations in the same "Jesus" and "Christ," Kant referred to the "Son of God." The Son of God, he wrote, personified humanity in its moral completeness. His suffering and death for His enemies demonstrated plainly that He was the Ideal and Exemplar of the Good. In Him, opposites coincided: the Ideal was the historical. In His followers, too, belief coincided with practice as, through their actions, the Ideal gradually unfolded and ramified, always seeking its widest extent, always being tested, proven, and adapted by the aspirations and sufferings of men, bound by dependence on the Archetype in the shifting contingencies of their lives. Such were some of the ideas that Herder may have heard when he attended Kant's lectures at Königsberg and that, despite his reaction against Kant, he adapted to suit his own historical interpretations.

To summarize: In the sixteenth and seventeenth centuries, some Protestant reformers denied theological premises in the mimetic tradition, and, later, empiricist philosophers rejected other propositions, especially those concerning human knowledge. At the same time, various religious currents—some of them within Protestant churches—retained and developed mimesis in the context of mystical theology. Steeped as they were in the classical literatures, ardent secularists of the Enlightenment habitually employed the language and strategies of the mimetic tradition, even as they repudiated Christian elements in their culture. David Hume, for example, had no use for formal Christianity, but he esteemed Cicero, who set forth doctrines of mimesis in education and society, and whose idea of moral exemplarism in culture have important parallels in Hume's own teachings about ethics and history.

Men continued to accept as legitimate the fundamental problem of mediating asymmetry between archetype (or ideal) and image. Ancient texts continued to inspire answers. There were, therefore, many channels by which mimetic doctrines passed into the classicizing world of the seventeenth and eighteenth centuries. Individual authors were capable of combining mimetic and anti-mimetic propositions in one and the same system of thought. Thus, by the end of the eighteenth century, the assimilative mechanisms of tradition had done their work. Mimetic theories of historical progress had taken root and flowered in England and in Lutheran Germany, precisely the areas where the onslaughts of Protestantism and empiricism had begun. During the Romantic era, the reconstitutions of mimetic strategy for mediating asymmetries between nature and art took many forms, and some of the most fecund of them appeared in one city: Berlin.

Then, as in the patristic era, mimesis by augmentation was thought to advance by two substrategies: subversion and inversion. The writers now to be discussed accordingly gave particular attention to this interlacing of strategies.

Chapter 14

Four Lutheran Reconstitutions of Mimesis
As an Historical Strategy

WHAT PRACTICAL IMPLICATIONS could be drawn from what Heine called Kant's "world-destroying thought"? How could the reconstitution of mimetic strategy be achieved according to the pluralistic definitions that he laid down and that Herder had intuitively explored?

During the eighteenth and nineteenth centuries, major revisions of mimetic doctrines took place in German Protestant universities. The mimetic strategy that began in Plato and passed through the many-colored prism of Christianity was transformed by Hegel and his followers into historical dialectic, and inverted by Marx into dialectical materialism. As Engels wrote in an introduction to *Socialism: Utopian and Scientific* (1882), "scientific socialism is indeed an essentially German product and could arise only in that nation whose classical philosophy had kept alive the tradition of conscious dialectics: in Germany." The reason for the general importance of German universities, and of the mimetic strategy of conversion, to our subject lies in social order. From their beginnings, universities in Germany had been regarded as expressions of princely grandeur. On the whole, they did not spring up (according to precedents in England and France) as loose associations of colleges founded at different times by religious orders in their corporate rivalries or by acts of private benefactors. Instead, princes established them full-blown as public institutions to declare the greatness and to safeguard the honor of prince and country. During the Reformation, universities, like principalities, followed the religion of the ruler.

The character of German universities as organs of state and repositories of theological doctrine proved to be decisive in the seventeenth and eighteenth centuries, especially in the Protestant states of western and northern Germany. Dispute raged incessantly. And yet the subjects at issue were deemed so crucial in explaining and adorning human affairs that princes not only maintained but made strenuous efforts to build up the faculties of theology and philosophy.

The distinctiveness of this social phenomena is emphasized by contrasting the Napoleonic reform of French education in 1808, which greatly reduced the place of speculative philosophy and theology, with the reforms crowned by the establishment of the University of Berlin, where those very subjects were given dominance by the appointments of Fichte, Schleiermacher, and Hegel to the faculties. Correspondingly, during the eighteenth and early nineteenth centuries, many of the major figures in German literature and philosophy held university positions, and all had studied at universities and formed their thinking in running academic controversies. The fact that Marx was among the greatest of these reminds us that we have tapped the role that German universities played as seed-beds of ideology and political action during the revolutions of the mid-nineteenth century.

In this extremely volatile atmosphere, the members of the two faculties of theology and philosophy constantly returned to the common tradition of their inquiries: that is, to the texts of classical and Christian antiquity.

Drawing on those ancient materials, they were able to conclude that culture was an organic whole and yet a contradictory structure of change and identity. They deduced that revolution had been the means of mediation between actual and ideal, art and nature, by which "the national character," "the general will," or any of the Romantic *Geister,* including "the spirit of Revolution," evolved, realized, and transcended its ideals. If the phenomenon of mediated asymmetry could be understood, its paradigms could be used, for example, in the construction of Prussia as a nation-state or in the broader regeneration of society.

One crucial fact was that these intensive debates took place in universities that were not only German but specifically Lutheran. For, though it had been transformed in many ways, Luther's concept of man's spiritual alienation from God continued to ferment in academic controversies. Another, equally important, element of Luther's theology also retained its force. From mystical texts of earlier centuries, Luther had accepted doctrines of radical unity through God's omnipresence. God's power, Luther had written, was present in all creatures, even in the smallest leaf of a tree, and in their creative processes. All men, good and evil, were masks of God. Even Satan and his demonic minions received their life and power from God and worked within the divine order. The spiritual alienation of man therefore belonged to the movements of God hidden within and impelling the discordant and contradictory events of history toward an ultimate resolution. Focused, incessantly recast, and institutionalized in Lutheran universities, these doctrines of alienation and wholeness exerted an extraordinarily powerful and diverse impact on pre-Romantic poets and philosophers, not least on Herder.

In German Lutheran universities, historical philosophers continued to interpret the past in terms of alienation that operated within and served a progressively unfolding mediated asymmetry. Theology remained a dominant area of speculation and debate. Thus, doctrines about the Trinity and about the person and work of Christ were pronounced features in intellectual life, and with them the redemptive acts of mediation and mimesis.

The strategy of mimesis by augmentation received its most vivid statement in Goethe's *Faust*. Before I come to Goethe's poetic vision, however, I shall describe three other views that had particularly strong repercussions in nineteenth-century thought. Their authors were luminaries in Berlin: the linguist Wilhelm von Humboldt (1767–1835), and two others on whom traditions of redemptive theology exerted powerful effects, the philosopher G.W.F. Hegel (1770–1831), and the theologian Friedrich Schleiermacher (1768–1834).

Humboldt, Hegel, and Schleiermacher

All three men were intellectual heirs of Herder; all had been imbued with classical learning from early childhood. But the simultaneous appearance of three extraordinarily powerful historical idealisms in early nineteenth-century Prussia had more immediate causes. These were rooted in the obsolescence of the Prussian monarchy at the end of the eighteenth century, the collapse of Prussia before Napoleon's armies, and the thorough reform of government at every level, of the army, of land-holding, of the Prussian Church, and of education that began immediately after the Peace of Tilsit. The decay of their own society and its deliberate nationalistic reconstruction according to ideologically developed programs of reform bore a double relation to the French Revolution. First, the Revolution, following Napoleon's eagles, had given reformers the chance that they long sought. Second, the Revolution itself was seen as a fundamental reform of society according to a system of order that addressed, not temporary or regional needs, but abstract and universal principles. The formation of liberal and conservative parties in Prussia according to carefully developed programs of action, and the continual strife between them, culminating in the Revolution of 1848, also predisposed men to consider human experience, past or present, in typological ways.

One aspect of this monumental, collective labor weighed especially on the three scholars under discussion: namely, the reform of the educational system. At its darkest moment, in 1808, Prussia entrusted that task to Humboldt, who had an established reputation in the diverse areas of diplomacy and aesthetic theory. During his short term as minister of public instruction (1808–1810), Humboldt instituted a thorough reorganization of primary and secondary instruction in Prussia, and he presided over the establishment of the University of Berlin. The structure of education was planned as a diversified, but coordinated system, crowned by the University, which Humboldt intended to be a center for original research and discovery, as well as instruction. Before he left office to resume his diplomatic career, Humboldt engaged Schleiermacher in this great enterprise. Humboldt abandoned his ministerial appointment, in part, because he lacked the administrative independence that he felt its responsibilities demanded. By the time Hegel joined the still inchoate University (1818), the nexus between education and bureaucracy, which Humboldt feared, had been solidified. Despite differences of mood and goal, however, all three men approached their scholarly work with a keen, pragmatic awareness of man's power to shape the future according to his ideals through deliberately created institutions such as schools and universities. They were all guided by the theoretical model of mimesis by augmentation, but they differed widely regarding the kind of movement through which ideals took shape in society.

Humboldt held that change occurred mainly through subversion. Each stage in the development subverted its predecessor. But subversion was not a single catastrophic act from outside. It was instead a subtle interaction of all the parts within a culture. Humboldt reached this concept of social movement through his study of language. His linguistic studies convinced him that language had a dual function; it represented the inner life of the speaker, and it also shaped the speaker's mentality. In both respects, it served ideality: in the first, by reflecting the subjective ideal and, in the second, by creating that ideal. Because a language was made up by the communications of all of its speakers, it was the objectification of all subjective ideals, the growing sum of its parts. Because each speaker had to follow the collective rules of syntax in order to be understood, his individual speech expressed a common synthesis. Humboldt also insisted that the collective synthesis could grow; for language was not something that was made once and for all, but an energy constantly moving and articulating itself as an instrument both of expression and of discovery. It was a kind of organism in growth, and the idealism that it expressed and shaped correspondingly had to be analyzed in stages of development and by empirical means.

Such was the interpretive model that Humboldt also applied to history. Here, too, the parts mediated unity and form to the whole. Humboldt's concept of historical idealism repeated the motifs of ideality that were both subjective and universal, and of empiricism, and his comments on the duties of the historian were couched in the same aesthetic terms of form, unity, and coherence that he used in describing syntax. He understood human events as being, like language, a genetic process in which, through the interchange of many parts, the idea continually struggled to express, and so to realize, itself.

For this reason, Humboldt utterly rejected the concept of imitation as an artistic technique. Any attempt to revive ancient norms was bound to fail. Modern poetry, he thought, existed under norms entirely different from those of the ancient world. The proverbial imitation of nature was hardly more than an empty figure of speech, since the artist's function was to raise man above his physical, or actual, existence by giving free reign to his creative imagination. Nature and art belonged to entirely different orders. The dialectic between form and matter was indeed a struggle, the outcome of which was not predetermined. Consequently, every event was a singular representation of ideal reality, and the sequence of such events, generated by the energy or force of the dialectical tension, established the course and form of history. Under Kant's influence, Humboldt was convinced that universals—such as nature and communities—were composed of individuals, and that, in turn, individuals had meaning only in the light of composite, universal categories that were constantly enlarging and ramifying as new constituents were added to the mass.

Thus, history itself had an ideal, which was not a fixed goal in time or even a stable and enduring character, but which endlessly redefined and redirected itself through the cumulative efforts and experiences of men. Each event contained, as a microcosm, the previous course and the future outcome of the whole. Each work of art also had its ideal unity and coherence; it could be judged on its own, without reference to the artist. Because the historian has only the event or the work on it before him, and not the idea that it both discloses and hides, the idea that is in the event without being part of it, he cannot detect the ultimate goal of history. And yet the historian has obligations that correspond with the mimetic energy of the entire process. His highest obligation, which Humboldt specifically describes as mimesis, is to represent not merely the external description of an event but also, as nearly as he can, its latent inner form, the form that binds what is new and finite to what is pre-existent and universal. Like the artist, the historian is bound to the particularity of his material, but, in the particular, he also discloses and enlarges the incremental, yet general, truth of form.[1]

By contrast with Humboldt, Hegel and Schleiermacher approached the strategy of mimesis from theology. Like Herder, they believed that history was the story of the world's redemption, and Christ its central figure. The narrative lines they read into the past hinged on Christology, but here they departed from patristic doctrines even further than Herder had done.

More sharply than Herder, they perceived the consequences for idealists of excluding supernaturalism and of redefining transcendence to mean historical transition. They realized that the eternal and the temporal must become identical; they found their solution in a formula that Nicholas of Cusa, Jacob Boehme, and many others before them had used: the coincidence of opposites. Thus, they continued to believe that mankind was a fallen race in quest of salvation; they continued to regard Christ as the manifestation of God through which the world was to be saved; they continued to teach that salvation came by acts of mediation and mimesis. But the crucial acts did not occur supernaturally, in the descent of God to man and man's answering ascent, beyond the human condition, to union with God. They occurred in the transition from one historical state to another, through powers that were immanent in history and in human nature.

When he wrote that the advent of Christ was the point to which and from which history moved, Hegel gave one indication of the conclusions to which the coincidence of opposites led him. Christ's advent was the hinge (*Angel*) on which the history of the world turned.[2] Yet, the tautology that Hegel had in mind was not that of a closed circle, but rather the open, lengthening path of a spiral.

[1] "Über die Aufgabe des Geschichtsschreibers," *Werke, Gesammelte Schriften*, vol. 4 (Berlin 1905).

[2] *Vorlesungen über die Philosophie der Geschichte* (*Sämtliche Werke* [*Jubiläumsausgabe*. Stuttgart, 1949] 11: 410).

One could think of Christ, Hegel wrote, as an estimable and long-dead teacher; but, if one regarded Him as "merely historical," one ignored the absolute truth that His life, death, and resurrection manifested. Hegel took up a tradition that went back to John Scotus Eriugena when he taught that God was ignorant of His own nature and learned about it from its manifestations or theophanies in the world, the chief of which occurred in Christ. Hegel taught that, in His death, and in His history generally, Christ presented the eternal history of the Spirit. He made it possible to recognize God as Spirit because He revealed a triune scenario of movement. When thought reflects upon itself, an antithesis is set up between subject and object. As knower, thought is subject; as the thing known it is object. When it recognizes itself in its objective reflection, thought moves back, by reflex, into its subjective existence, but at a higher level. The three prongs of movement are the two antitheses—thought as subject and thought as object—and the mediating reflex of thought back into its subjective life.

Hegel taught that the career of Christ manifested this recurrent pattern of antithesis and resolution as the informing strategy of history. Certainly, the long pre-history of the Gospel prepared for the axial manifestation. But the state of mind necessary for it arose among the Jews. The essential piece in the puzzle—the mediating reflex—had not yet been given them, but the prophets of the Old Testament perceived the antithetic condition of life. They recognized man's need to feel that he was the negation of himself, a need to merge his outer (objective) suffering with the inner (subjective) sorrow of the inner man. They felt a profound longing to free themselves from the pain of divided existence by transcending the fragmented state of mind. The life, crucifixion, and ascent of Christ into glory completed the pattern of which the prophets had known only the antitheses and the painful yearning to make them coincide.

Opposites coincided in Christ because He was a finite person embodying infinite and absolutely independent existence. But His mission was to demonstrate the strategy by which they were made to coincide. He revealed that there was a mediating link between the poles of man as subject and man as objective self-negation: the link of self-awareness through suffering. Christ was not Spirit from the beginning. He was Spirit only after His death and ascent into heaven. Consequently, His own experience disclosed that suffering was a necessary means for transforming man into Spirit by self-consciousness: that is, for the unity of man with God. Each man had to perform this act of mediation for himself in order to exist as Spirit or, in other words to exist as a moment of the divine Idea.[3]

Above all, the necessity of suffering in self-consciousness that distinguished men from animals, and the enactment of that mediating pain, composed the history of the world.

Thus, Hegel taught that mediation occurred through mimesis on several, interrelated levels. There was, first of all, the passage of the Spirit in its eternal history as "it came to absolute self-consciousness by mirroring itself in itself from the state of alienation, that is its division and pain." There was, second, the replication of this archetypal strategy in the life, crucifixion, and exaltation of Christ. Third, each man recapitulated the same movement in his spiritualization as he himself became, like Christ, the coincidence of opposites—finite when considered in himself but the Image of God and fountainhead of infinity when considered for himself.

Mimesis occurred on one other level; for the Church community "is the eternal repetition of the life, passion, and resurrection of Christ in the members of the Christ," and "this repetition is expressly completed in the sacrament of the Eucharist," that is, by the unity of the subject and the absolute object in "the eternal sacrifice."[4]

Here, again, the antithesis of objective and subjective came into play, and its mediation was the moving force in history. The organization of the institutional Church in the apostolic age showed that the freedom of the will existed abstractly (i.e., subjectively) but not in concrete fact. The entire course of history was the progressive realization of the abstract in the concrete or, as Hegel also wrote, the manifestation of religion as human reason. For long centuries, the Church remained subservient to the sensory world. The decisive moment came in the Reformation with Luther, who, Hegel argued, removed the discord between the subjective freedom of the soul and the objective freedom of the Church.[5] Like Christ, the Church advanced through the mediating pain of divided existence toward the manifest freedom of Spirit.

Let us now examine the wider conclusions that Hegel extracted from his ideas about salvation through mediation and imitation.

As his paradigm of mediated antithesis indicates, Hegel thought that

---

[3] Ibid., p. 416.

[4] Ibid., p. 412. *Vorlesungen über die Philosophie der Religion* (*Sämtliche Werke* [*Jubiläumsausgabe.* Stuttgart, 1928] 16: 338).

[5] *Vorlesungen über die Philosophie der Geschichte,* pp. 429, 523.

historical mimesis occurred through inversion not merely by a succession of stages, each overturning its predecessor, but more exactly by the transformation of each stage into its opposite. He began with intractable materials. Transcendence, Luther's theological paradoxes, and the Christian exaltation of poverty, self-abasement, suffering, and death were the core of what Hegel called the "moral ambiguity" of Christianity. Sin was the pre-condition of grace. The salvation of the world was advanced by crime. As in the garden of Eden, evil was a way to knowledge that made man as God. Through Hegel's appropriation of dense mystical doctrines, particularly those of Jacob Boehme, this ambiguity widened from the sphere of morals to every mode of thought or action. Just as revelation simultaneously discloses and hides in its totality, he held, every positive term implies and subsumes its negative. The entire course of history was a sequence of ideals realizing themselves and so being inverted from reality to unreality, from being into not-being. In a way clearly reminiscent of Eriugena's doctrine of the ignorance of God, Hegel conceived this grandiose pageant as a series of self-recognitions and self-negations by the Absolute Spirit. The "highest freedom" of the Spirit lies in the power to overreach its limits at a particular stage in time, to abandon itself, and to achieve a new level of consciousness. By reaching beyond its limits, the Spirit annihilates itself in self-sacrifice, its Golgotha. Only by this radical inversion can Spirit realize itself in the world of nature and climb to a higher level of self-knowledge. History, Hegel wrote is like a gallery of pictures displaying previous manifestations of the Spirit, a gallery in which existence is left behind and only recollection persists. "In its going into itself it has submerged itself in the night of its self-consciousness. Its vanished existence, however, is preserved in [that night], and this elevated existence—the previous one, but newly born out of consciousness—is the new existence, a new world and Spirit-form. In [that night of consciousness], it has to begin all over again, naively from the start, in its immediacy." True to tradition, Hegel considered this movement to be genetic as well as aesthetic. It was typified, he wrote, by the sexual opposition and union of man and woman, realized in their progeny. But more than typology was involved; for the "immediate permeation" of man and woman was the moment at which one generation changed into another, the life of a nation was affirmed, and Spirit realized and transcended itself.[6]

---

[6] *Phänomenologie des Geistes,* 394–403, 764 (*Sämtliche Werke,* ed. Otto Weiss [Leipzig, 1909] 2: 611.

Guided by his conceptions that reality was spiritual, and that progress advanced by spiritual death and rebirth, Hegel reached a characteristic view of the relation between art and physical nature. As he described it in his *Lectures on Aesthetics,* the purpose of art was to awaken man's knowledge of the universal in him, to penetrate to his inmost feelings and will by the use of sensuous means. In its purest form, art was self-alienation of the artist's thought, with which the viewer established contact in contemplating the real beauty hidden beneath the particular representation. Artistic beauty was higher than the beauty of nature because it sprang from mind and freedom. Hegel poured contempt on artists who struggled to represent things as they appeared to the eye.

Naturalism, Hegel wrote, was futile. The actual things already existed. Why try to replicate them at all, especially in a medium that would always fall short of nature? The result could only be a parody of life, a trick instead of a work of art. The fact was that the beauty of nature imperfectly reflected the beauty of the mind, and the excellence of art depended on the degree of its affinity to mind (and its distance from matter). Hegel considered poetry the universal art of the mind because, of all the arts, it was freest from physical media, and because it worked most immediately on the feelings. His devotion to the dominant values in Prussia enabled him to argue that, outside Europe, art had never achieved genuine beauty and that, even in Europe, art had become a thing of the past, having lost its truth and life—that is, its power to re-create genuine life and reality—to the philosophy or science of art. Sensuous art, he judged, had been superseded by philosophical reflections about art.

Despite its cultural and intellectual provincialism, Hegel's conception of art belonged to an ambitious total vision of human experience. In its constant strivings against itself, the Spirit "has world history as its scene, its possession, and the sphere of its realization." The fallen civilizations of the past are monuments of the Spirit's previous stages in the process of realizing, and so transcending, its ideal being.[7]

The Reformation and the French Revolution had especially privileged positions in this sequence of ideas recognized, realized, and transcended. "Finally, after the long, eventful, and dreadful night of the Middle Ages," the day of universality broke upon the world, a revolution that the German people drew from its "simple and unassuming heart." Luther defied the externalities of Christian belief. He affirmed

---

[7] *Vorlesungen über die Philosophie der Geschichte,* pp. 89f., 119.

faith, not in what was absent, over, and gone, but in what was present, the "subjective consciousness of the external, of the truth that is in and for itself, the truth of God."[8] Consequently, the old opposition between Church and state was resolved, and the integrity of human life in freedom was recognized. The state was seen as "the divine idea, as it is present on earth," "spiritual idea in the externality of the human will and its freedom."[9] Previous stages in world history had revealed, first, that one man, the ruler, was free and, later, that some men, the ruling class, were free. From his vantage point in Lutheran Prussia, Hegel saw a grander prospect. The Reformation had taught that all men were free. But the Reformation took root only in certain nations; its benefits were not universally dispersed.

They did not permeate the life of France, Hegel continued, because the French left the inner life aside as an alien and indifferent matter; they left their inmost being to the Church. But, in the free, conscientious obedience required by the Church, there remained the possibility for reason and freedom to develop. In the event, therefore, while the effects of the Reformation had been consolidated in Protestant countries, they were exceeded in France, where men passed immediately from theory to practice.[10] Hegel did not like France, but he rejoiced in the French Revolution. When he rhapsodically wrote about it, he qualified his celebrated Prusso-centric perspective on history, and he was able to say that France exemplified how the primacy of reason, the idea of freedom, and the idea of right could be immediately expressed in laws and institutions. Thereby, he added, France demonstrated before the other nations of Europe that "the history of the world is nothing other than the development of the idea of freedom." The Revolution had been a glorious moment irradiating all history, in which periods of happiness were blank pages, in which the leading actors ended their lives with disgrace and misery and the Spirit continually warred against itself—a history that was the work of God.[11]

Hegel's grimly inversionist idealism was vastly more mystical than Humboldt's doctrines. It derived much from the language and conceptions of Plotinus and Boehme, rivaling even their systems in impenetrable ambiguities. Like Humboldt's subversionist idealism, however, Hegel's doctrine taught an immanence of the idea in historical process that suppressed the finite moral values of individual persons and, indeed, that categorized individual lives as moments in the realization of

---

[8] Ibid., pp. 518, 519, 523f.   [9] Ibid., pp. 71, 80.   [10] Ibid., pp. 531, 557.
[11] Ibid., pp. 77, 81–85.

the idea. Deferring to that latent form, Hegel contemptuously discounted "the happiness, the periods in which peoples flowered, the beauty and grandeur of individuals, and the interest that their fate has, whether in pain or in joy. Philosophy has to do only with the splendor of the idea that mirrors itself in the history of the world."[12] As the lineage of ideas ramified, the somber results of this attitude continued well into the twentieth century.

Like Humboldt and Hegel, Schleiermacher found man's true nature in history, and he regarded history itself as the self-creation of the human mind. He adhered to the general concept of mimesis by augmentation. But, unlike Humboldt, who understood that self-creation was a process in which each stage subverted its predecessor, and Hegel, who described a movement that advanced by inversion (or self-negation), Schleiermacher detected yet a third pattern of augmentative change. The elegance, complexity, and appeal of his doctrine lay in the promise that mimesis occurred, not by an involuntary, quasi-genetic mutation, or by an etherial self-negation, but by conscious, deliberate reconstruction in which the individual had a dignified part to play.

Like Hegel and Herder before him, Schleiermacher began with the premise of a fallen world, and, through Christology, he concluded that redemption came by mediation and mimesis. However, his ambitious reconstruction of theology led him to a perspective that markedly differed from Hegel's. Hegel regarded Christ's life, death, and resurrection as the pivotal event of history. By contrast, Schleiermacher, a pastor and preacher, as well as a professor, considered the manifestation of humanity in Jesus, rounded out by the establishment of a new collective life in the Church, as the first complete creation of human nature.

Correspondingly, the distinctive features of Schleiermacher's teachings about mediation and mimesis were, first, his emphasis on Jesus as the archetype of humanity, and, second, his concept of mediation through the collective, and cumulative, life of the Church, as a spiritual community.

In exceptionally great detail, Schleiermacher analyzed the pre-history of Christianity. Hegel declared Christianity the absolute religion. Schleiermacher too placed it at the apex of a long development in which religion had advanced from polytheism through progressive stages of monotheism. Experience, not supernatural revelation, was

[12] Ibid., pp. 568f.

decisive at every stage. Each historical period constituted a distinctive whole, and each literary work expressed the way of thinking characteristic of the period, nation, and region to which its author belonged, always allowing for his individual point of view. Thus, even the Scriptures were artifacts of specific cultures and circumstances that were long past, and they had no literal application to the lives of men in other situations. Jesus of Nazareth Himself was a man of a finite age and society, and what was merely historical in His person and work had ephemeral meaning.

Drawing especially on the Gospel of John, as Herder had done, Schleiermacher argued that, however out-dated the text of Scripture and the life of Jesus may have been, there ran through them a thread of universal importance. The history of religion demonstrated that there was in man a persistent conflict between lower consciousness, tied to material aspects of this world, and higher consciousness, directed toward God. Schleiermacher equated lower consciousness with the life of sin. He understood that it permeated the whole network of human relationships, and that it was sheltered and conveyed by social traditions. However, the Scriptures depicted the higher consciousness expressed in the collective life and traditions of the ancient Hebrews. Through these collective institutions, the effects of sin were partially corrected, but the advent of Christ opened a fuller corrective program.

Like Kant, Schleiermacher considered Christ a coincidence of opposites; an exemplar that became fully historical. The Word-made-flesh was God-in-man, rather than a transcendent divine person. In Jesus, consciousness of God achieved perfection and He, consequently, became archetypal man, the exemplar of mankind's humble and utter dependence on God and of its future glory. Schleiermacher equated consciousness of God with immanence of God. Together with his theories of historical obsolescence, this emphasis on the naturally immanent consciousness of God led Schleiermacher to his distinctive teachings on mediation and mimesis.

Christ was the exemplar of human nature, but the establishment of the Church supplemented His work, and completed the creation of human nature. After the death of Jesus, His action was mediated through the Church, a community that, however imperfectly, displayed His image. By the imitation of Christ individuals entered the community and enlarged its attack upon the common life of sin. Indeed, through individual consciousness of God, Jesus was continually incarnated in the Church, and, through the community of life in Christ, representing, enlarging and fulfilling His work, the person of the Savior continued to work in the world from which He was physically absent. In this fashion, Schleiermacher regarded individual self-consciousness, the developing relationships that constituted world history, and God as parts of a whole, linked by the endlessly repeated but never redundant act of imitation.

Evidently Schleiermacher's version of mimesis combined mystical elements with empirical. It drew on exalted visions of man's unity with the creative processes of nature, which had entered German Romantic philosophy through the writings of Spinoza, Meister Eckhart, Plotinus, and, of course, Plato, whose works Schleiermacher translated into German. Schleiermacher did not yield, as did others, to one temptation embedded in these texts: he did not argue that the individual person was merely one expression of the universal spirit. Rather, he insisted on the uniqueness and the integrity of the individual, and at the same time he argued that, in himself, the individual was nothing. Whether a person or a fact, the individual had meaning because he (or it) was a transition point in a total nexus of relationships, located between and defined by its origin and its effects.[13] Schleiermacher's theory therefore hinged on a doctrine that the individual and the universal were both separate and in some measure identical. On the one hand, in yielding to the impulse to individuate himself, each person contributed a distinctive element toward forming the true universe, humanity, "the eternal community of spirits." On the other hand, the individual destroyed himself in so far as he isolated himself, resisting the impulse to be absorbed and determined in the whole.[14] For it was in submitting to this second impulse that the individual could feel his utter dependence resolved into identity with the soul of the infinite world, and himself accomplished as nature's inmost center and outermost circumference.[15]

This radical ambiguity meant that, by one and the same act, man communicated himself to others, and the world reacted upon and formed him. It also meant that inwardly every person acted freely in

[13] *Friedrich Schleiermachers Ästhetik,* ed. R. Odebrecht (Berlin, 1931. *Das Literatur-Archiv,* Bd IV), p. 79.

[14] *Reden über die Religion,* II (*Schleiermachers Werke* [Scientia Verlag reprint of the Leipzig, 1928 ed] 4: 264 [90]); *Monologen,* ch. 1 (*Werke* 4: 408 [15f.], 409 [16–18]). *Reden über die Religion,* I (*Werke,* 4: 214 [6f.]). Cf. Odebrecht, pp. 77, 121.

[15] *Reden über die Religion,* III (*Werke* 4: 314 [171f.]).

choosing and performing a work, but that in the world of external relations the work itself was governed by uniform, eternal laws.[16] Developing his argument, Schleiermacher was able to conclude that art was identical with nature and, indeed, that man was nature as well as its representer. He was also able to reverse Aristotle's maxim that art imitates nature. For, since a person acted as an artist in responding to a work of art, as well as in making one, nature imitated art: that is, man imitated himself.[17]

The method of imitation was central to Schleiermacher's celebrated hermeneutics. How could one apply to culture as a whole the rule that humanity was composed of men imitating men? How could imitation reach back beyond the present to remote times without falling into anachronisms or into self-delusions like those of the Neoclassicists? Schleiermacher's answer was that one could reconstruct the past. To do so, one had to be able to draw upon the collective memory of mankind. Schleiermacher assumed a spiritual universe, created as "a great historical picture" by eternal humanity.[18] Plato had seen no disjunction between nature and art. Schleiermacher, his devotée and translator, modified this position when he equated man with nature and art. He needed a method by which, through a work of art, he could pass through the determined, external expression and enter into the mind that freely created, a divinatory method by which, as he wrote, the scholar could transform himself "into the other person in order to grasp his individuality without mediation," a comparative method by which the individual and the general characteristics of a given work could be distinguished from each other.[19]

The hermeneutic supplied this twofold need, the male and female powers of human knowledge, as Schleiermacher called them. Schleiermacher's great concern was literary analysis. He sought to widen the practical usefulness of his theories by grounding them in psychology and in technical practices that could be employed in a number of disciplines. But throughout his goal remained the same: to establish the relations among the components of a particular artifact and thus to define the reciprocal interaction of the parts and the whole. In other words, it was to decompose an object and reconstruct it, to extrapolate a world of relationships from a fragment, just as one extrap-

---

[16] *Monologen,* ch. 1 (*Werke* 4: 409 [16–18]).   [17] Odebrecht, pp. 6–8.

[18] *Reden über die Religion,* II (*Werke* 4: 265 [92]).

[19] *Hermeneutik und Kritik,* ed. Manfred Frank (Frankfurt-a.-M, 1977) p. 169.

olated universal order from the world, the visible portion of a greater whole.[20] For thereby, one imitated the process by which the work was originally made and the meanings that, consciously and unconsciously, the author (or artist) put into it.

With the vagueness of a high Romantic philosopher, Schleiermacher wrote that the organ of perception was feeling, a divinatory power of love. Causality became elusive in this doctrine, with its emphasis on the totality of relationships, in the mind of an artist or in the world. No effect could be ascribed to a single cause; nor could the multiplicity of causes be sorted out by magnitude. Likewise, at the highest level of synthesis, historical facts ceased to be isolated. Vast changes occurred in human experience. Nineteenth-century Christianity was not the same as primitive Christianity. Through advances in technology, Schleiermacher wrote, modern man had freed himself from the bondage to physical nature under which all previous generations had toiled. And yet the heremeneutic method liquified differences of time and culture into Spirit. All religions were seen to be modulations of a universal religion; all nationalities, with their vernacular arts and institutions, were disclosed as parts of a great manifold.[21] All languages, texts, and actions were silent mimics of Spirit waiting for the enquirer to unlock the relative truths with which they testified to the expanding unity of things.[22]

The outer world of art reflected the inner world of spirit; the spirit reproduced all things.[23] By feelings, exercised in hermeneutics, the mind expressed and transcended the individuality of its own complex of thoughts. It entered the area of identity, the movement by which the Universal, as an artist, composed humanity. For through the act of reconstruction, interrelations in that great composition became apparent and mutually understandable. One interpreted the Artist, even as one explained "the later works from the earlier and the earlier from the later. Let past, present and future encircle us, an endless gallery of the noblest works of art, eternally multiplied by a thousand brilliant mirrors"[24]; that is, the minds of men.

---

[20] *Reden über die Religion,* II (*Werke* 4: 260 [83]).

[21] Cf. Odebrecht, pp. 88–90.

[22] *Reden über die Religion,* V (*Werke,* 4: 399 [312]).

[23] Ibid., III (*Werke,* 4: 314 [171f.]).

[24] Ibid., III (*Werke,* 4:314 [173]). On the use of related metaphors by Augustine, John Scotus Eriugena, Thomas Aquinas, and Meister Eckhart, see Chapter 3, note 18; Chapter 6, note 17; Chapter 8, note 44; Chapter 9, note 16.

Humboldt's genetic model of change by subversion was taken up and developed by Ranke; Hegel's model of change by inversion was recast by Marx; Schleiermacher's reconstructive model reappeared in Dilthey's doctrine of the social sciences. The movements initiated by these men carried their ideas into institutions and ways of thinking that spread far beyond Germany and that endured long after the end of the nineteenth century.

What did the three Prussians leave to their successors? Scholarship and science of the Enlightenment had forced them to re-examine the oldest problem in philosophy: the relation of the individual to the universal. Although the three men employed different methods in analyzing this problem, they agreed that it had to be resolved in terms of human experience: that is, history. They also agreed that the relation of the particular to the universal was a typological one and, consequently, that it had to be approached in terms of archetype and copy. By this route they came to mimesis. Hegel and Schleiermacher came to it additionally through Christology and their hopes for the redemption of the fallen world.

Mimesis as they conceived it betrayed the strains of combining empiricism with idealism. One of the most obvious strains resulted from the basic argument that man composed his own nature by imitating a primal, creative movement rather than static forms. This view militated against what were regarded as metaphysical illusions, but it also led to a complex proposition. Creativity was endless. How could one respond to its radical decomposition of the present leading to continually new forms?

The sense of decay that haunted humanistic thought in the nineteenth century was more than the feeling that the world had grown too old to survive, or that institutions had outlived their usefulness, or that they were confronted with difficulties beyond their resources. As the mimetic strategies set forth by Hegel and Schleiermacher for the recreation of the world indicate, it was also a sense of the eliding reality inherent in any historical situation, a dialectic of self-negation.

One characteristic of a great theory is that no single interpretation exhausts its possibilities. Such was the case with mimesis by augmentation. But I have not yet mentioned the most powerful revision of that concept, one framed not in Berlin but at another Lutheran court, Weimar. Appropriately, given the origins of the mimetic tradition, it came in poetry.

Goethe and Some Conclusions

I began by describing two currents in European thought, one negating idealist mimesis, the other affirming it. I asked how it was possible for a common culture to be formed out of such disparate elements, and I have now identified three grounds on which a synthesis was possible. (1) Philosophers who rejected idealist mimesis in some lines of inquiry retained it as an organizing principle in others, notably in historical thought. (2) Mimesis of ideals was worked into formulae of subversionist change within society, particularly by Herder. (3) Even prior to Herder, these efforts provided Kant the materials out of which he laid the philosophical bases of historical idealism, which was taken up in different modes by three powerful writers, Humboldt, Hegel, and Schleiermacher. I shall now illustrate Goethe's portrayal of the general synthesis that had taken place and shall indicate some lines along which it later developed.

Goethe's career expresses the ambiguous state of the mimetic tradition in the Enlightenment. He regarded himself as an advocate of classicism. He followed Winckelmann in idealizing ancient literature and art. To his consternation, Romantics claimed him as their inspiration and model, though he thought that they revived the worst excesses of *Sturm und Drang* and embodied what he considered the depravity of the French Revolution. The reason for this divergence was that Goethe used old materials in new and sometimes inconsistent ways. Despite his classicism, Goethe realized that culture must change to stay alive. Like others in his immediate circle, he applied to culture an axiom drawn from natural philosophy: "Change or perish." He formed his views partly under Herder's influence, and partly in dialogue with associates at the University of Jena, including Friedrich Schlegel. But he enlarged and confirmed them primarily by his own studies of morphology in plants and in human anatomy, studies that anticipated Darwin's theory of organic evolution. The analogy between morphologies of change in nature and in culture appealed to Romantic writers, and Goethe never applied it more effectively than in *Faust.*

The power of man to impose form—and, indeed, his duty to bring order out of confusion—was an enduring theme in the mimetic tradition. Goethe placed it at the center of his epic.

The event on which the narrative line turns is Faust's compact with

Mephistopheles. This occurs after Faust has expressed his discontent with the cumulative wisdom of every established branch of study, and in particular after he has anathematized high-mindedness, deluding appearances, cheating dreams, comforting wine, the highest charm of love, hope, belief, and, above all, patience. The chorus underscores the consequences of what Faust has done:

> Woe! Woe!
> You have destroyed
> The beautiful world
> With a mighty fist.
> It falls, it disintegrates!
> A demigod has smitten it!
> We bear
> The fragments into the Nothing,
> And lament
> The lost Beauty.
> Mightier,
> For the sons of earth,
> More splendid,
> Build it again,
> In your bosom, build it up!
> Begin
> The new course of life,
> With clear sense,
> And let new songs
> Resound on it! (1607–1626)

"Die schöne Welt"—understood as Plato's intelligible cosmos of forms in which changelessness characterized perfection—was untenable. Faust must rebuild it along new principles. What is the pattern for reconstruction? Earlier in the poem, Faust alludes to that model in an exegesis on John 1:1, a Scriptural verse that has frequently recurred in our account: "In the beginning was the Word," Goethe was thoroughly aware of the importance this text had had in Christian theology both for the doctrine of the Logos, the creative Word, and for the doctrine of the Trinity, especially in the character of the Word as the image of the invisible God.

However, the Word is not for Goethe an ageless archetype or the repository of such immobile patterns. It is indeed a model, but a fluid one. Speaking through Faust, Goethe can not take "Word" at face value. He decided that it does not mean "thought" (*Sinn*) or "power" (*Kraft*). It means "deed" (*Tat*). Action, not the transcendent person, the Word-made-flesh, was, for Goethe, the Word that was with God, and that was God. Christology was left aside. This emphasis on action as the creative principle recurs in the compact itself when Faust agrees to let Mephistopheles take his soul if he ever wishes that time stand still.

Goethe's novel use of mimetic metaphors indicates the direction of his thought. From theology, he took the conception of man as the image of God, and from classical philosophy, the metaphors of microcosm and macrocosm, of refracted light, and of the mirror itself. Other familiar components of the Neoplatonic tradition also appear: the Good and the Beautiful as principles outside of time; the conception of man as *homo duplex*, drawn on the one side to the things on earth and on the other to higher spheres (1110ff.), and of love (*Eros*) as the principle of all things (8479). The restless yearning of finite man for the infinite powers was a dynamic aspect of Neoplatonism, as was the view that this insatiability, the cause of man's misery and dignity, derived from the reason (285f., 3240).

In *Faust,* these ancient components are transformed by an ambiguity in which the historical is also the ideal. Man is described as the image of God, but Goethe also acknowledges that men represent the power of the gods in human form. Faust is not a microcosm because, as earlier writers had taught, his soul already replicates the spiritual structure of the world and his body, its elemental composition. Instead he aspires to become a microcosm by taking into his own heart all the pain imparted to man, by testing all bliss and sorrow, expanding his own self to include the selves of those feelings, only to perish with them at the end—perhaps falling short of the crown of humanity because he can be only what he is (1765ff.). What earlier writers had described as the uncreated and all-creating Light refracted through forms of life, but always the same in itself, becomes unsteady in Goethe's world. Mephistopheles describes the light as born of the primal darkness, struggling with its origin as it infuses into bodies and beautifies them, but also being impeded and imprisoned by them and tending toward extinction (1345ff.). Faust too uses the light metaphor in a wavering sense. Above the great rushing tumult of the world, the splendid rainbow arches with its changeful duration, now clearly outlined, now fleeing into thin air. The rainbow reflects human striving, the refracted color from which we have life (4721ff.).

Finally, the metaphor of the mirror illustrates the effort to combine the historical with the ideal. Familiar uses appear, such as the magic mirror that conjures up images of absent persons (2499ff., 2599f.). But, in these uses, or in the phantoms mirrored in fire or mist (10,418; 10,588), it is clear that the mirror represents illusion or at best a provisional reality. Early in the tragedy, Wagner remarks on the shortness of life and the length of art, arguing with Faust that work left incomplete by a sage may be taken up and accomplished by later generations, and that this collective achievement discloses a guiding spirit of the times (*der Geist der Zeiten*). Faust rejects this appeal to cumulative literary tradition. Wagner should look for refreshment, not to his dusty parchments, but to the springs of his own soul; for the past is like a book sealed with seven seals, and what Wagner calls the spirit of the times is in fact nothing but the reflection of the present looking at itself in artifacts of the past (566ff.).

The ironic subservience to, and isolation from, the past is naturally part of Goethe's view of the obsolescence of knowledge and of his argument that man must earn his freedom and existence by daily reconquering them. The mirror metaphor consequently appears under the aspect of change—the rainbow, refracting light, fire and mists reflecting conjured images, and water. Goethe frequently alluded to the glassy, reflective quality of water (6912, 7284, 9999), which was so crucial a symbol in Romantic painting, and, when he sought a metaphor for Faust himself, he hit upon water, not smooth and calm, but a cataract, the aimless, restless monster leaping maddened downward into the abyss (3350ff.), hurling upward into the air the mist that refracts light into a fugitive rainbow (4715ff.). The motif of water recurs at the end, in Faust's crowning achievement—the reclamation of land from the sea—and in the thousand rivulets flowing into the abyss of heaven, which represent the all-creating love of God (11,866ff.). Water, as the glassy sea or the maddened cataract, is the representation of ultimate reality, the ambiguous moment in which the enduring and the transitory are one. As Goethe makes Thales say, "Everything springs from Water. Everything is sustained by Water. . . . It is you who preserve the freshest life" (8435f., 8443). For Goethe keenly sensed the principle of flux in all things identified by the ancient philosopher, Thales, and expressed it in his mimetic metaphors.

In *Werther,* an early work, Goethe had written that the soul was "the mirror of the infinite God."[25] His neglect of that particular metaphor in *Faust* is significant of a change from static to transitive forms in Goethe's own thought and, as we have seen, in literature generally

---

[25] Entry of 10 May, 1771.

at the end of the eighteenth and the beginning of the nineteenth century.

By the time, late in life, when he prepared the final draft of *Faust,* Goethe recognized one logical escape from the search for universal form in the flux of events: that is, to give up wrestling with ironic illusions. At the beginning of the drama, Faust nearly abandoned the struggle through suicide. Toward the end, Faust does abandon it. He cannot see beyond this world; it is enough, he thinks, to gain what can here be understood, to stride onward, with insatiable mind, through torment and happiness (11,450f.). But this acceptance of the act, without an ideal content, precedes Faust's blinding by Care and the delusion that makes him breathe the fatal wish to retain the fleeting, happy moment, the wish by which he forfeits his soul.

Goethe's message is that skepticism, despair, and suicide arise from a failure to accept the ambiguity, and irony, at the heart of life as it really is. They reject change and, consequently, accept the alternative—to perish.

Plato had described how the soul, passing in the world of ideas, beheld the eternal and changeless forms. Faust made his way into the solitude of the Mothers, in the void apart from space, position, and time, the boundless realm of forms. He saw formation, transformation, eternal discourse of eternal thought (6287). In the ceaseless chaos, this "Nothing," Faust sought the All (6256). But, even here, there is ambiguity. For the chaos is the night from which, Mephistopheles said, the creative light was born; it was the chaos of which Mephistopheles himself was the son (1384, 8027). Mephistopheles is a part of the past that once was all, part of the darkness that gave birth to light (1346ff.).

Within this primal reality of change, man must strive, and err as long as he strives. *Die schöne Welt* is reconstituted by man endowed with the power of nature, even though nature be sin, and of mind, even though mind be devil (4898f.). He imposes upon the world the design formed in his mind (499ff.). This creative work belongs especially to the poet who, escaping the confused and distorted forms of the world, enters the solitude of his own heart, confiding in himself (5690ff.), drawing all the disharmonies of natural being into concord, distinguishing the ranks of creation, and composing the whole into majestic order. This is the supreme right, the right of humanity, given him by nature—the power of man revealed in the poet (Prologue, 134ff.). Still, the principle of creation is utility and its worth is transitory; for "he can use only what the moment produces" (685). The alternatives of suicide or frustration indicate why Goethe patterned the beginning of his tragedy on the book of Job.

The ironic ideality of the poetic act has a further aspect reminiscent of Platonism in its Christian form. Love is the origin of all things, and in human creativity it has two characteristics: the movement of the soul toward the beloved, and the union of the lover's soul with that of the beloved. Faust moves through progressively higher and more spiritualized forms of love until the soul of the human creator encounters the Love that is God. Rapt in the eternal self-discourse of primal chaos, overflowing into the world of time as its ground of being, it is that almighty Love that forms and raises all things (11,872f.). By his striving, Faust, the servant of the Lord (299) participated in that love and became a noble member of the spiritual world, capable of redemption despite his unholy alliance, or perhaps because of the works achieved through his league with that child of the all-creating light, the Devil, beholding the revelation of eternal Love that expands into beatitude (11,751f., 11,924ff.). Here, as in his use of the Easter interlude that averted Faust's suicide, Goethe used the language of Christian Platonism to convey his ideality of act, in which creation was not the discovery of timeless forms, reflected by creatures, but the ceaseless imposition of new forms upon them by man's poetic imagination. For, in this way, life renewed itself in the midst of works that, without poetic irony, could only be transitory and thus dead and illusory (8305). The direct antecedents of this conception lay in Christian mysticism, in Meister Eckhart and in Jacob Boehme. In *Faust,* Goethe summed up the synthesis of mimesis with counter-doctrines toward which European thought had moved since the Reformation, and he also anticipated directions that the reconstituted tradition would take.

It would be possible to accept the judgment of the *Encyclopédistes* that the microcosm-macrocosm analogies were a thing of the past and that the servile imitation of antiquity was a debasement of art. But scientific cosmology and style had never been central to the mimetic tradition. Thus, students of literary criticism may be perfectly right in determining that, toward the end of the eighteenth century, decades of attrition in rhetorical thought took their toll. "Form became a surface quality . . . and mimesis itself went the way of formalism and finally was largely rejected as a viable concept of art."[26] But such was not the answer of mystics and idealist philosophers, or aestheticians who wrote

---

[26] John D. Boyd, *The Function of Mimesis and Its Decline* (Cambridge, Mass., 1968), p. 99. On mimesis in the *Encyclopédie,* see above, Chapter 12.

under their influence, or even of empiricists in some areas of their work. Nor, indeed, was it the judgment of the *Encyclopédistes,* who cherished critical imitation as continual invention, a way to originality.

Could man find a formula in which his symbolic being made sense? Was there some universal scenario of being that he reenacted in giving form—and thus intelligibility, direction, and meaning—to his existence? It seemed likely that the concept of being, as ideal essence, had been driven from the field by the concept of historical existence, and, indeed, of life as a struggle for existence that ended only in death.

The new positions, however, did not extinguish mimetic thought of the idealist hue. While the attack on anthropomorphic symbolism advanced on most fronts, the mimetic literature continued to exert a profound influence, and the articles of the mimetic tradition of mediated asymmetry between nature and art were reinterpreted and transfigured into new formulas, even within schools of thought that were, on balance, anti-mimetic.

There is no need to look below the surface for obscure vestiges or scattered remnants of a lost system.

Thinkers of the age constantly went back to the texts of the mimetic tradition. For theologians, and some philosophers, the advent of Christ was the axial event of all human experience, and Christology, the key to pattern in history. Great writers of the seventeenth and eighteenth centuries embraced as kindred spirits, and so as contemporaries, St. Augustine and the German mystics culminating in Jacob Boehme, and the effects of this continual recourse appear in the school of Cambridge Platonists and the German pre-Romantic (or idealist) philosophers. Writers who ignored Christology still relied on literary foundations of the mimetic tradition. Shaftesbury's approach to religion by way of aesthetics leading to ethics was deeply Platonic. In fact, it drew in part on works of the Cambridge school. It preserved the theory of innate ideas, the uniformity of human nature, the identity of the beautiful, the good, and the true, and the need of emotion and intuition to perfect the reason. Through its vast influence on such thinkers as Diderot, and Herder, it introduced Platonism into extremely diverse systems of thought. The subversion of the Platonic world of Ideas that the works of Locke, Berkeley, Hume, and Kant collectively brought about—the destruction, as Berkeley observed, of the eternal truths—was counteracted by the "magic idealism" of Novalis, which was systematized and developed by Schlegel and Schelling. This reinforced the survivals of two worlds, the real and the reflective in the very diverse conceptions of Herder and Kant.

Finally, the mimetic allegory survived, though in this regard the effects of the attack upon theological anthropomorphism are most apparent. The Platonists and Neoplatonists of the period came to terms with the charge that man had made God and the world in his own image. They insisted, not that man was the expressive likeness of an immutable God, but that mankind, all history, was God realizing His inmost character and presenting Himself to His own sight. Jacob Boehme taught this solution to his followers: "As a man before a mirror beholds himself, since his image is there, in the mirror (but lifeless), just so we are to consider the image of God as also the whole creation, to be that of man from eternity, for thus God has seen all things from eternity in the mirror of his wisdom."[27] Schelling's reliance on Boehme made it possible for him to consider each individual thing a "mirror of the All," as a microcosm of the world soul, and man as the image of the cosmos. Hegel took up this view. For him, incessant creation of the world was the revelation of the Absolute Spirit to itself, the act of self-alienation that was the Spirit's own self-recognition.[28] Thomas Aquinas had written that God was the intelligible mirror in which man saw all things. Carlyle expressed the reversal that we have described: "Our works are the mirror wherein the Spirit first sees its natural lineaments."[29] For Aquinas, we need God, in whom only we can recognize and know what our humanity is. For Carlyle, God needs human works in His ceaseless process of self-recognition, self-alienation, and reconstruction.

Carlyle's was the idealism of the Young Hegelians that Marx attacked as a new form of old theology, and against which he taught an inverted mimesis: that visible institutions of society reflected invisible economic realities.

The tone and constitution of the new kinds of historical mimesis departed widely from their antecedents. The goal of mankind's collective movement had changed, as pluralism superseded uniformity. In the first place, there was no stable world of Ideas. The spheres of time and eternity are identical, and, for some writers, the ideas are not moral absolutes: there is no good-in-itself, no difference between what is and what ought to be. Realizing itself in time, the Spirit, or Idea, does not unfold itself from the highest form down through levels of decreasing perfection. Rather, it unfolds from the lowest forms up, in an organic evolution from the simplest to the more complex, as in Herder's con-

---

[27] *De Electione Gratiae*, chap. 5, sec. 12, ed. W.-E. Peukert, *Jacob Böhme, Sämtliche Schriften* (Stuttgart, 1957), 6: 53f.
[28] Above, Chapter 14, at note 6.   [29] *Sartor Resartus*, 2. 7.

cept that life first appeared in its vegetal, then its animal, and finally its human form, each germinating within the previous one and carrying it to a higher level. The individual was therefore subsumed in the general. Herder's concept of cultural (or traditional) advance followed the same evolutionary model and led to his attack upon "egoism" as the great enemy of humanity. In this subordination of the individual to the whole (though not in its spiritual ideals), his theory of culture as organism was like Burke's. The ideal could not be personified or crystallized once and for all; it was not transcendent; it changed in time.

From this blending of ideal and real followed a second departure from earlier mimesis: there was no stable world of intellectual nature. The eternal archetype of reason was no longer seen as the hub to which all intellectual beings pointed. Man was not moving toward his natural end. Instead, the natural end was expressing itself in man, enlarging and realizing itself incrementally. Further, the social determination of character by tradition, informed by a different spirit, or a different modulation of the Absolute Spirit, made intellectual nature an incessantly varying one, conforming with one absolute pattern neither in a given people at different epochs nor in diverse peoples at the same epoch. Different perceptions of beauty, of virtue, of truth, may lead to the same power or spirit, but not to the same Ideas.

The task of the seventeenth and eighteenth centuries was to counter the decomposition of the world of knowledge by creating a new unity. It was not clear what the principle of integration would be. As in many other cases, there was a lag between the work of reconstitution itself and the development of a vocabulary appropriate to describe it. The mirror metaphor survived in that lag, and I have used it to indicate the line by which a qualitative model was discarded and a quantitative one composed. The crucial difference was that eternity had come to be considered a duration, whenever it was retained at all, and that the interplay between exemplar and copy was given its *locus* in time.

The passage had begun from idealism to ideology, to the awareness that man can make not only culture, his second nature, but the models on which that nature is shaped. The use of an ancient metaphor to describe unprecedented circumstances was part of the process by which thought moved from fragmentary intuitions in many areas of inquiry to general abstraction. In this search for a model, and for meaning that ran throughout and unified human experience, the dramatic scenario of mimesis survived: the theme of a primal unity destroyed, an image estranged from its archetype, and an asymmetrical unity constituted through a medium in which the two became one by a vicarious ex-

change of idioms. Revolution—the word used to describe this tauto-
logical process—also came from the age before the flowering of empirical sciences and the building of great philosophical systems; and
with it came the tragic irony implicit in any idealism, in any permanent asymmetry between nature and art, or between ideal and actual.

Chapter 15

The Art of Revolution and the Nineteenth Century

Introduction

BY THE BEGINNING of the nineteenth century, numerous syntheses of mimetic and anti-mimetic doctrines had been proposed. It remained to be seen whether these learned theories would enter into the wider life of Europe. In fact, such an extension did occur through disputes within the Church, through the work of revolutionary associations, and through the inquiries of social scientists. It took place in a process of stimulus and response that earlier ages had also known. The clash of ideas continued. Again and again, conflict proved how fragile the reconciliations of contradictory elements had been. As theories were tested in practice and rethought, inconsistencies became obvious. Even writers committed to mimetic strategies had to wrestle continually with ideas that they accepted and taught but that challenged ideas of mimetic order.

There were chiefly five troublesome points. They had been bequeathed to the nineteenth century by the Enlightenment. All five posited discontinuity and disorder rather than enduring form in the nature of things.

1. Empirical psychologies isolated the individual in the unique and incommunicable world of his own perceptions. Surely this premise ran counter to the universals of mimesis. Was consensus a viable alternative to solipsism? Further, if the human mind were passive, and carried only the content that its society gave it, did not solipsism put the beautiful and the ugly, the analogue and the anomaly, on the same level? For if all forms, all mentalities, were the products of society, and all were equally and indifferently imposed, how could there be an ideal form, much less imitation of it?

2. Along another line of argument, awareness also grew that, through his works, man expressed more than he intended. In art or in history, he drew on the unconscious as well as on the rational. He first recognized his hidden and uncontrolled powers when they took material shape. How could occult and singular genius conform with universal forms?

3. If he plied his art critically, man broke his object down analytically before he chose the shape to give it, before he put his hand to the materials. Decomposition of the object was an essential part of composition. How could imitation figure in this effort to make something that did not previously exist and possibly—casting aside all rules and precedents—quite unlike anything that did?

4. The equation of nature with art meant the death of classicism. The ideal, bound to culture, time, and place, supplanted the timeless idea. Under the rule of duration, could any style escape from becoming anachronistic? Under the cognate rule that each art was autonomous, how could there be any room for the unities and analogues among arts that mimesis required?

5. Writers who rejected metaphysics also discarded the stable *a priori* of form and being. Reality was a manifold process, a complex movement, so intricate and full of chance that it vitiated any causal explanation. How could man imitate it in arts that had as their whole purpose to fix single, static images?

In fact, the Enlightenment itself had inherited these arguments from an earlier age. Pascal had anticipated most of these objections to mediated asymmetries between nature and art, and some had been recognized in the fifteenth century by Nicholas of Cusa. Both men pictured the world in terms of mathematical infinity, rather than in those of metaphysical hierarchy. The first sacrifice had been mimesis by diminution, the Neoplatonic concept of the world as a descending order of perfection, like a beam of light declining in likeness the further it passed from its source. This conception became meaningless when the source was described as the absolute maximum and minimum, the infinity that is universally and equally present in a numerical series, and a sphere whose circumference is nowhere and whose center is everywhere. A second casualty had been the associated Neoplatonic concept of mimesis by transposition. The ascent of the soul had no meaning in a world thus conceived. Instead, an entirely different set of problems emerged. One was the loss of originality. If every component in the universe—every soul—could be regarded as a cipher in a numerical series, it had meaning, not in itself, but by virtue of its place in the series. Functionally, every cipher was equal and equivalent with every other one. Another problem was radical ambiguity. In a series that mediated as a whole between maximum and minimum, a cipher was both plus and minus, positive and negative, both cause and effect, both mediate and immediate. Most devastatingly, the finite was annihilated in the presence of the infinite. More clearly than Nicholas, Pascal anticipated a further objection to mimesis that matured throughout the Enlightenment: what passed as universal principles of natural law were actually a majority judgment, customs invented by man and confined to particular times and places. Far from ageless, they were subject to perfection and, thus, destruction by progress. The unities provided by human custom were all founded on mutual deceit or on the prudent "noble lie" perpetuated on the community by its leaders.[1]

What was the natural model that men ought to imitate? Pascal did not know. The nature of man was not static form but movement, and yet, without metaphysical unities, that movement reduced the world to atomized, numerical components, each being its own nature and its own good, each isolated and canceled out in the presence of the infinite velocity that was God.[2] Nicholas of Cusa and Pascal had withdrawn from this chilling spectacle of disorder into intuitive convictions of unity and into the reassuring system of Christian theology.

Eighteenth-century idealism was to embrace the continued adaptation of mimetic strategies by appropriating anti-mimetic principles, especially those of mathematical quantity that had troubled Pascal.

Adapting tradition always required costs and paradoxes. In this case, the cost was the exclusion of natural sciences as studies that built up the unity of knowledge. Certainly, people agreed, the natural sciences should be included in an educational curriculum because they disciplined and enlarged the mind. Certainly, they held an honorable place in culture as a whole because they increasingly freed man from bondage to nature and, most of all, because they were collective achievements of human ingenuity, massive works of art. And yet, they fell outside the circle of unity described by studies that had social man and human utility as their subjects. How was this exclusion possible? A paradoxical re-interpretation of Aristotle bears on the explanation.

Not everyone went as far as John Henry Newman in exalting Aristotle as an "oracle of nature and truth."[3] But it is a measure of their

---

[1] *Pensées,* 92, 97, 100, 294.   [2] Ibid., 33, 129, 426, 231, 233.

[3] *The Idea of a University* (new ed., London, 1893), Discourse 5, "Liberal Knowledge Its Own End," p. 109.

intellectual separation from the natural sciences that such men as Karl Marx, Wilhelm Dilthey, and Émile Durkheim refashioned Aristotle's doctrines into their own, original theories.[4] From the sixteenth century—and, more remotely, from the fourteenth—onward, the expulsion of Aristotle from serious thought had been one major task of the natural sciences. Of course, he did not linger unchanged in the humanities and the social sciences.

Ancient principles and authorities persisted, but in fact all discussions of form took place against an unprecedented background. From classical antiquity onward, skepticism had warred against systems of thought that assumed inherent, rational pattern in the world and in human life. Before the late eighteenth century, skeptics had not used their acute methods of reduction to pass beyond criticism and to construct systems of their own. Empirical studies of social phenomena, however, gave them the materials needed for the task. In philosophy and religion, in historical and political thought, and in speculation about the arts, writers were able to embrace discontinuity as the natural state of affairs, and perhaps a desirable one. Previous discussions of mimesis had ebbed and flowed, but incoherence had been assumed to be an aberration, a ripple on the surface that left the deepest realities untroubled. In the nineteenth century, writers who tried to affirm the contours of enduring form in events could no longer rely on this as a common assumption. Instead, knowledge that aimless plasticity was a convincing alternative to their own theories imparted urgency to their hybridization of mimetic and anti-mimetic principles.

This subtle, anxious debate took place in three areas, in which writers used doctrines of asymmetry between nature and art mediated by strategies of mimesis to explain and justify social discontinuities. From late antiquity on, the Church had been a major institutional repository of mimetic theories, and through the sixteenth century transformations of those theories took place largely through theological study and conflict. Intramural controversy of this sort also marked the nineteenth century. Ecclesiastical disputes had always been governmental as well as intellectual; in the event, attempts to scrutinize ideological founda-

---

[4] It is worth noting explicitly that Dilthey studied Aristotle under Trendelenburg's direction at Berlin and that, apart from large doses received during his student days, Durkheim taught courses on Aristotle's *Politics* and *Nicomachean Ethics,* while at Bordeaux. On Dilthey's antecedents in Schleiermacher, Trendelenburg, and others, see M. Ermarth, *The Critique of Historical Reason* (Chicago, 1978), passim. On Durkheim's theories see E. Wallwork, *Durkheim. Morality and Milieu* (Cambridge, Mass., 1972), pp. vii, 5ff., and passim.

tions of administrative order were often repressed. Frequently, the challenging ideas survived repression, however, and, at another time, under changed circumstances, the institution adapted itself to them. The career of John Henry Newman illustrates an intramural episode of this sort. With regard to the Church, the other two areas are distinctly extramural. The first, revolutionary thought, was an obvious and impatient threat to all the ideas of mimesis bruited about in the ecclesiastical enclosure by Newman and his adversaries. The second, theories of sociology, presented a challenge that was capable of being more abstruse than revolutionary doctrines and perhaps, in the long run, at least as destructive as they were of presumed eternal verities.

Mimesis implies a circular movement—within the mediated asymmetry of an image to its archetype. This strategy might appear to contradict the idea that history moves in a straight line, and thus also the idea of progress. But as we first saw in the Church Fathers the course of history could be imagined as being made up of several kinds of movement. The Fathers taught that the circularity of mimesis was never exact. The tension between archetype and image remained. Instead of a closed, repetitive pattern, therefore, a progressive spiral movement emerged, driven on by that very tension toward greater and greater stages of perfection. As we have seen, this combination of circular and rectilinear movements persisted from the age of the Fathers onward. It was a strategy for the perfectibility of man rooted in Europe's cultural heritage; but the heritage itself, with its lessons of quasi-genetic mediation and mimesis, persisted through so many ages and societies because it addressed a deep and universal need for rebirth to wholeness. It began and remained a strategy embraced particularly by those who felt themselves an enlightened minority, bound to reform an imperfect world. This heritage, need, and the role assigned by tradition to militant minorities pervaded the three areas of conflict that I shall now consider.

Old Paradigms at War

The career of John Henry Newman (1801–1890) illustrates the centrality of mimesis to the running conflicts that shaped the nineteenth century. First, and least substantial, among the issues that we are to consider are the affinities that both he and Marx inherited from the long history of mimesis. Second are his own theories of history. Despite their relatively loose formulation, they marked him out as following the paradigm of mimesis by augmentation. How perilous it was to apply this eighteenth-century interpretive model to theology in Newman's day is indicated by the third point. For, finally, there was the vast panoply of papal doctrine, rooted in the reversionist and conversionist paradigms, which to his astonishment and grief Newman found arrayed against him.

The conviction was pervasive that historical reality and ideal reality were identical. Exactly how pervasive is shown by its importance to men who combined theory and action, to men as disparate as Marx and Newman. In fundamental respects, the two were polar opposites. If he had ever taken Newman seriously, Marx would have dismissed him in much the same way he dismissed Proudhon, arguing that he did not write "profane history—the history of men—but sacred history— history of Ideas. According to his viewpoint," Marx wrote of Proudhon, "man is simply the instrument that the Idea or the eternal reason uses for its development."[5] This diametrical opposition between "the history of men" and "sacred history" renders the parallels that exist in their biographies and thought particularly striking. The year 1844 was crucial for both men. Marx's political activism and philosophical reflections broke through to new levels of clarity, wholeness, and originality, which he expressed in his essay "Toward a Critique of the Hegelian Philosophy of Law." Newman's long quest for authenticity, gestating in *An Essay on the Development of Christian Doctrine,* led him to his dramatic withdrawal from the Church of England. The most crucial parallel was the search for laws of development attested by the facts of history. Historical development was the idea on which everything else hinged. Beyond question, Marx's dialectical materialism and Newman's dogmatic spirituality overlapped on few points other than the fundamental assumptions that history was the unfolding of basic principles; that human experience through time therefore had a meaning that united all events into a cumulative and progressive whole; and that, in the interplay of theory and practice, experience was prior to thought.

These normative assumptions are suggested in the way the two men wrote of the mind as a mirror reflecting the world around it and not eternal principles, a sense that Newman reinforced by using the metaphor of the stomach interchangeably with that of the mirror to indicate

[5] Letter to P. W. Annenkov, 28 Dec. 1846, in *Marx-Engels Werke* (Berlin, 1959), 4: 557.

the mind's digestive and incremental powers.[6] The priority of experience gave the mirror metaphor a novel twist, for, while it had formerly suggested the loss of a primordial image, Newman was able before his conversion to Rome to see the mirror as first shattered and then whole in Christ's incarnation: "The world was like some fair mirror, broken in pieces, and giving back no one uniform image of its Maker. But He came to combine what was dissipated, to re-cast what was shattered, in Himself."[7] Newman's emphasis on catholicity, rather than on antiquity in itself, as a test of true doctrine marks the sermons that he delivered just before he left the Church of England and particularly his decisive work, *An Essay on the Development of Christian Doctrine*. It is apparent even in the first sentences of that book, in which Newman declared that Christianity's home was in the world and that "to know what it is, we must seek it in the world, and hear the world's witness of it." Revelations and great ideas are not grasped all at once. They require years and centuries of reflection by many minds and of the cumulative judgment of public opinion to reach an "adequate representation." Experience in societies and governments was an essential part of this development, which made human existence, in principle, a "warfare of ideas," an endless struggle that imparted "to the history both of states and religions its specifically turbulent or polemical character."[8]

Newman illuminated his ideas about mimetic discontinuity with the subversionists' metaphors of larvae changing into butterflies, of eggs changing into birds, of mustard seeds germinating into plants. He could say, in the language of analogy, that in doctrine, too, old principles reappeared in new forms and changed with their forms to remain the same. Plato, the father of mimetic tradition, would have been astonished to read the argument that claimed to be idealism and yet taught that, so far as men could know perfection, its essence was change.[9] As his questioning friend, John Keble, reasoned, Newman's principle of development undercut the concept of tradition, of a de-

---

[6] Cf. Marx, afterword to the second German edition of *Capital,* and his use of the words *spiegeln* and *Spiegelung* in one form or another, as in "Zur Kritik der Hegelschen Rechtsphilosophie," *Marx-Engels Gesamtausgabe* (Frankfurt a.M., 1927), 1: 607, 612. On Newman's alternate use of metaphors in *The Idea of a University,* see A. D. Culler, *The Imperial Intellect* (New Haven, 1955), p. 206.

[7] "Sermon on the Three Offices of Christ," sect. 3 in *Sermons Bearing on Subjects of the Day* (2d ed., London, 1885), p. 61.

[8] New York and Philadelphia, 1845, pp. 12, 22.   [9] Ibid.

posit of belief conveyed intact from generation to generation. It also made it possible for Newman to see Christianity as forming itself in and of the world as revolutionary, contemptuous of private wealth, antagonistic to society, and subversive of government. This conception of Christianity's self-explication enabled Newman to argue that Christ continued and fulfilled the Law by destroying it, that the Apostle Paul kept the Law by eating unclean beasts, and that the establishment of the papacy according to social needs in the fifth century accomplished precepts of the first. These insights, which led Newman to Rome, also, by a curious irony, made him useful to the Modernist movement within the Roman communion. As early as 1860, they made him known to some anti-Modernists as "the most dangerous man in England."

Newman gained eminence through controversy, but it was also in conflict that he framed his doctrines. In 1854, he accepted the most grandiose task of his career. After great struggles among themselves, the Irish bishops had broken with a decades-old policy. Following the convictions of Pope Pius IX, they rejected the "mixed" system of education according to which Catholics had been authorized to be educated in the same schools as Protestants. They intended to establish an exclusively Catholic system of education, crowned by the university that Newman was invited to organize and to administer as its first rector. When he delivered his celebrated inaugural discourses, proclaiming his principles of instruction, Newman had no way of foreseeing that the entire project would fail, partly on his account.[10] Experience should have taught him, however, to guard his tongue on the subject that he knew best: literature. Greater sensitivity might have kept him from supposing that, like him, the Irish Catholics regarded Shakespeare and Milton as major figures in their national literature and from assuming that the Catholic literature that they hoped to evoke would ramify from an English trunk. A greater offence, however, lay in the concept of development with which Newman explained the unity of the curriculum that he intended to establish. It was this concept that had led Newman to embrace Catholicism nine years earlier, and that had made him profoundly suspect at Rome. Every word that

---

[10] On Newman's career in Ireland, beginning with his selection by Archbishop Cullen as rector of the Catholic University and ending with his resignation, see Emmet Larkin, *The Making of the Roman Catholic Church in Ireland, 1850–1860* (Chapel Hill, 1980), pp. 121–125, 233–240, 384–392, 431. Larkin describes the University as part of a far wider educational project that Cullen envisioned as a major tool in his reconstruction of the Irish Church.

he uttered on the subject reduced the Irish clergy's support for the university.

In fact, Newman used two ill-reconciled voices when he described his models of unity. He stated one model with the voice of a convert, and the other with that of a literary critic. Newman himself recognized that, in important ways, religious dogmatism ran counter to the system of disunity that his historical thought revealed. The disjunction between the two levels of his argument is indicated by the fact that mimesis appeared only in the dimension of history, as a tool of duration, chance, and material culture—that is, of discontinuity—and not in the higher dimension of divine order.

Newman, the convert, asked how men had "lost the idea of unity"? How could they envisage a university as a bazaar, with a separate stall for hawking each academic specialty?[11] He blamed the utilitarian insistence that universities introduce students to every kind of knowledge and, especially, prepare them for increasingly scientific and specialized professions.[12] He was consciously "re-iterating an old tradition" when he argued that the object of education was to form the mind, that is, to enlarge it, to cultivate the intellect, and to refine the feelings, and when he added that the study of literature, especially texts of classical antiquity, was, as it always had been, the best way to achieve that end.[13] His vision required more, for if knowledge—even knowledge of the classics—were pursued for its own sake, there could be no unity among the various lines of inquiry.[14] Newman's vision required the inclusion of theology, the science that, he argued, held the key to universal knowledge, that kept the various arts from wandering off into self-isolating autonomy, and that prevented the natural sciences from excluding, and literature from corrupting, the truth that they should serve.[15]

Therefore, Newman thought that the curriculum should consist of

---

[11] Culler, *Imperial Intellect,* p. 174. See also Culler's discussion of the contributions of Aristotle and Bacon toward Newman's conception of a "science of sciences" that gave an architectonic unity to learning.

[12] *The Scope and Nature of University Education* (N.Y., 1958), preface, pp. xxx f; Discourse 5, "Liberal Knowledge Its Own End," and Discourse 7, "Liberal Knowledge Viewed in Relation to Professional Skill," *Idea,* pp. 106ff., 117f., 158f.

[13] "Christianity and Letters," chs. 3, 5, in *Idea,* pp. 256, 263.

[14] Discourse 5, "Liberal Knowledge Its Own End," *Idea,* p. 103.

[15] *Scope,* pref., p. xxi; Discourse 2, "Theology a Branch of Knowledge"; Discourse 3, "Bearing of Theology on Other Branches of Knowledge"; Discourse 4, "Bearing of Other Branches of Knowledge on Theology"; Discourse 9, "Duties of the Church Towards Liberal Education," *Idea,* pp. 19f., 47, 61, 64f., 218f., 226.

three parts: the natural sciences, literature, and theology—the highest, unifying element. He conceived education in artistic terms as a process of formation determined by its object—to teach the art of social life.[16] The most complete education imparted to learning the interconnection of its parts, its wholeness and center; it perfected the intellect in knowledge of history and human nature, read under the light of "almost supernatural charity" and confirmed by its resemblance to "the beauty and harmony of heavenly contemplation."[17]

A priest and convert, Newman saw that this theological unity led (1) to the identification of European culture as "human society" and "civilization" to the exclusion of other cultures;[18] (2) to instruction in the sciences as subjects subordinate to literature in the order of learning, and, in a university setting, never primarily as areas of research and discovery;[19] (3) to an unsympathetic reading of literature, including philosophy that was hostile to Christian doctrine, that was "tainted with licentiousness or defaced by infidelity or scepticism";[20] and (4) perhaps to indices of permitted and forbidden books and to emendations of useful though blemished texts.[21]

Newman had every reason to know where such restrictions in the name of unity could lead. In 1851, three years before his debut in Ireland, he had delivered a series of agitated lectures on *The Present Position of Catholics in England*. His object was to impeach "the Protestant tradition." Pervading every aspect of their thought, speech, and action, Newman said, the Protestant tradition had convinced Englishmen that Catholics were "the veriest reptiles and vermin which belied the human form divine," that they were as repellent as "some hideous baboon, or sloth, or rattlesnake, or toad." Catholics, the tradition taught, were "brutishly deluded." Against them was arrayed rational humanity, entirely bent on destroying their impaired state of mind and the institutions to which it had given rise. Thus, Catholics were condemned by the established Church. Legal disabilities had been imposed, excluding them from Parliament, the universities, and

---

[16] Discourse 7, "Liberal Knowledge Viewed in Relation to Professional Skill," *Idea,* p. 177.

[17] Discourse 6, "Liberal Knowledge Viewed in Relation to Learning," *Idea,* pp. 134, 139.

[18] "Christianity and Letters," ch. 2, in *Idea,* pp. 251ff.

[19] *Scope,* pref., p. xxxii; "Christianity and Letters," ch. 5, in *Idea,* p. 263.

[20] "Catholic Literature in the English Tongue," sec. 3, chs. 4, 5, in *Idea,* pp. 315, 319.

[21] Ibid., sec. 3, ch. 2, p. 310.

schools. Approved texts written for the education of the young mis-represented their past by deliberate and calculated distortion of histor-ical fact. They were derided by conventions of literature. They had been, and might again be, subjected to bloody persecution, perhaps even to "wholesale massacre."

In 1851, Newman recognized that "the Protestant tradition" still constituted the entire English way of life, a "moral identity" so tightly woven together that no part of it could be altered without repercus-sions on the whole.[22] He also recognized that his accusations mirrored those that Protestants had made against the Roman Church. Curiously, but understandably, he did not ask how the pre-Reforma-tion Catholic tradition in England transformed itself into the post-Ref-ormation Protestant tradition. However, when he spoke in Ireland, three years later, he acknowledged that, in its assertion of unity, the Catholic tradition for which he argued might well have costs similar to those of the Protestant in denial and suppression.

Measured by the criteria of literary criticism—such as medium, style, and period—the subjects of instruction fell apart before New-man's eyes. It was well and good to argue that all together they formed "one large system, or complex fact . . . with countless interrelations of parts."[23] But Newman's critical faculties told him that even individual sciences harbored truths that were "irreconcilable with each other." Among themselves, he saw, the arts and sciences taught inconsistent and contrary truths and inspired mutually hostile actions. For exam-ple, social man collided with physical man when the useful arts re-quired by the social system turned out to be "destructive of health, en-joyment, and life."[24]

At this point in his inaugural lectures, the theory of development asserted itself. In his second voice, Newman, the literary critic, insisted that each national literature had a distinctive and unalterable integrity through its history, and that, despite its doctrinal faults, English litera-ture would act as a standard for him and his companions. He recog-nized that he had presented two arguments that were hard to reconcile; he assured his audience that he was not indulging in paradox. His ex-planation of the apparent contradiction, however, deepened the mis-trust of the Irish clergy.

He aroused misgivings, in the first place, because he regarded man's

[22] *The Present Position of Catholics in England* (Chicago, 1930), pp. 1, 11, 43, 221, 223, 229, 231, 274, 281, 309.
[23] Discourse 4, "Bearing of Theology on Other Branches of Knowledge," *Idea,* p. 45.
[24] "Christianity and Scientific Investigation," in *Idea,* pp. 464f.

moral nature (and literature, its reflection) as the result of collective experience. He was a moralist. Consequently, he placed greatest weight, not on the natural sciences, which ignored "the idea of moral evil," nor on theology, which, he believed, sprang from divine revelation, independent of man, but on literature, the expression of "the ideas, feelings, views, reasonings, and other operations of the human mind."[25] The fascination, and the importance, of man's moral and social nature as set down in literature was precisely its variability. For, unlike physical nature, which remained bound to fixed laws that it had not made, moral and social nature was self-governed, constantly moving exactly as it willed. The human mind acted in accordance with objective truth when it acted according to its own laws.[26]

Literature therefore represented collective man in the process of constituting his historical nature, and this autobiography of the natural man in all his beauty and fierceness could not be narrowly limited to orthodox Christian texts.[27] Voltaire and Rabelais contributed to the formation of French literature, and so too "there are great English authors, each breathing hatred to the Catholic Church in his own way, each a proud and rebellious creature of God, each gifted with incomparable gifts."[28]

Newman went on to describe the process of chance and mimesis by which literature unfolded. To bishops who disapproved the resistance of national churches to papal dominance and who were currently embroiled in the birth of Irish nationalism, it was ominous that Newman took national character as his point of departure. A shadow of Aristotle's argument for genetic (and functional) mimesis appears in his basic premise. "Every great people has a character of its own," Newman wrote, "which it manifests and perpetuates in a variety of ways." Among those ways he included political institutions, cities and public works, laws, traditions, and religion. The national language and literature was another element in this intricate bundle of distinguishing manifestations.[29] Each national character was unique; correspondingly, the language that expressed it had its own capacities. Generally,

[25] Discourse 9, "Duties of the Church Towards Liberal Knowledge," *Idea,* pp. 228, 224. "Literature," ch. 9, *Idea,* p. 291.

[26] Discourse 9, "Duties of the Church Towards Liberal Knowledge," *Idea,* p. 227. "Catholic Literature in the English Tongue," sec. 2, ch. 1, in *Idea,* p. 300.

[27] Discourse 9, "Duties of the Church Towards Liberal Knowledge," *Idea,* pp. 228, 231 (on the scope of Scripture). "Catholic Literature in the English Tongue," sec. 3, ch. 4, *Idea,* pp. 316f.

[28] "Catholic Literature in the English Tongue," sec. 3, ch. 2, *Idea,* pp. 309.

[29] Ibid., pp. 308ff.

it was no more possible to translate ideas from one language into another than it was to transfer the beauty of the original into a copy or to achieve in painting what could be done in sculpture.[30]

The unfolding of a national character through language also followed a distinctive and unpredictable course. Language passed through stages, as did the course of a man's life, from the least formed to the most complete. As its origin lay in likeness to the national character, its development advanced by imitation. Each period had its own style, which was authentic in the total setting of its culture but potentially destructive if, in some later age, it was anachronistically received. (Writing about the Gothic revival in architecture, with the robust anti-Catholicism of Pugin in mind, he observed, "Our rules and our rubrics have been altered now to meet the times, and hence an obsolete discipline may be a present heresy.")[31] Again like Aristotle, Newman gave a large place to the role of generic mimesis in the development of art. The growth of a language required "a succession of skillful artists," each imitating his predecessors and going beyond them "according to the circumstances of the times." It required the spread of their achievements in flexibility, force, vocabulary, or harmony through imitation by many writers and speakers until their adaptations and turns of phrase had become part of the living voice of their people. But language and style changed with the events of history as did thought.[32] The pace of growth differed in every area of expression, for it was a matter of chance when a great artist appeared and advanced language to a higher level, thereby helping to unite his people and to stabilize the national character.[33] Likewise, no one could foresee how far the process of advancement by generic imitation could go before it ended in saturation. At that moment, language "has ex-

[30] "Literature," chs. 7, 8, *Idea*, pp. 287ff.

[31] Discourse 4, "Bearing of Other Knowledge on Theology," ibid., *Idea*, pp. 82f. For Newman and his contemporaries, style expressed ideology. In England, Pugin and others deliberately promoted the Gothic revival as part of a wider campaign against Roman Catholicism, represented, in their minds, by Renaissance and Baroque architecture. Newman entered his caution against the hostility embedded in their anachronism. See F. Haskell, *Rediscoveries in Art: Some Aspects of Taste, Fashion, and Collecting in England and France* (Ithaca, 1976), pp. 68f. It is a measure of how much mimesis is in the mind of the beholder, rather than in the work, that Friedrich Schlegel, another celebrated convert to Roman Catholicism, was devoted to the Gothic style as an expression of authentic belief.

[32] "Catholic Literature in the English Tongue," sec. 3, ch. 3; sec. 4, ch. 1; sec. 3, ch. 2, *Idea*, pp. 314, 321, 310.

[33] "Literature," chs. 7, 8, 10. *Idea*, pp. 287f., 293.

panded to the loss of its elasticity and can expand no more," and innovation amounts to essays in novelty that offend the canons of taste or to adulterative borrowings from foreign tongues. Newman suggested that English might have reached this stage at which, on the whole, language became the repetition of stereotypes and, in the general leveling, all writers appeared to be anonymous.[34]

Newman's offense did not lie in teaching that the philosophy of education was "founded on truths in the natural order"; or in his premises that language (and culture) were made by man, and that they followed a pattern of genetic unity and growth; or in his argument that, like all men, great writers were submerged in social collectivity, that they were formed for and by society, the "creatures of their times," even while they also rose above the collectivity as "the creators of their language."[35] His offense did not even lie in his identification of man's moral nature with the chance unfolding of a national character through language, a process that was not Christian, that, indeed, was anti-Christian in its sinfulness. His great offense lay precisely where his conversion to Rome had begun. He applied these principles of disunity to theology, emphasizing a dangerous parallel to the career of language; namely, that religion, too, belonged among the man-made artifacts that expressed national character, and that, through historical experience, sacred doctrine had been altered.[36]

It is a peculiarity of great theories that they take on meanings in the public mind quite foreign to the minds of their originators. Toward the end of his life, Marx rejected new doctrines that appealed to his authority. He said, "I am not a Marxist." When Newman received the cardinalate (1879), after living for years under suspicion of heresy, he similarly felt obliged to clarify his stand: "For thirty, forty, fifty years, I have resisted to the best of my powers the spirit of Liberalism in religion."[37] Liberalism in religion, he said, was "the doctrine that there is no positive truth in religion," but that all beliefs are authentic as they strike the fancy of the individual. "It is inconsistent with any recognition of any religion as *true*. It teaches that all are to be tolerated, for all are matters of opinion." Newman went on to connect this tendency

[34] "Catholic Literature in the English Tongue," sec. 4, ch. 3, *Idea,* pp. 326–328. Cf. ibid., sec. 4, ch. 1, p. 320.

[35] Discourse 1, "Introductory," *Idea,* p. 5. Discourse 9, "Duties of the Church Towards Liberal Knowledge," *Idea,* p. 227. "Catholic Literature in the English Tongue," sec. 3, ch. 3, *Idea,* p. 312; cf. ibid., sec. 3, ch. 2, pp. 331f.

[36] Discourse 3, "Bearing of Theology on Other Knowledge," *Idea,* p. 52.

[37] W. Ward, *The Life of John Henry Cardinal Newman* (London, 1913) 2: 460.

with the exclusion of Christianity from the principles of government, social action, and public education. On receiving the red hat, Newman lamented these relativist aspects of contemporary life. He regarded them as devices of Satan, as instruments for the ruin of many souls, as threats to the revealed theology of the Church. Yet these were exactly the consequences that Newman's own system of mimetic discontinuity suggested both to very liberal and to very conservative readers, and the points on which they overlapped with revolutionary theories of social change.

Attacked on many fronts and stripped of its territorial sovereignty, the Papacy also made education a dominant concern. The struggle was not merely political and military. The Papacy would refurbish its most ancient skill: teaching. Indeed, it would intensify its effort to inform the minds of future generations, to fortify them against the perfidious doctrines of the day, to enlist them in the army of Christ. No general account of mimesis in the nineteenth century would be complete without mention of the doctrines that motivated the Papacy in this effort: namely, the older tradition of mimesis by reversion and conversion. This doctrine figured brilliantly in the controversies of the time, not least in those that flashed around Newman, whose fluid personal views ran athwart doctrines that had all the massive solidity, entanglements, and inertia that 1,800 years of institutional life could give. Newman, however, was a small figure in a great movement of institutional politics and doctrine that began before his day and continued long after it. Indeed, it is hard to determine whether ultimately it was his doctrines or his suitability as a political pawn that counted for more in that broad panorama as Rome saw it.

Steadfastly and powerfully, one voice was raised in the political arena against the new magistracy of revolution for which Newman sometimes appeared to speak: the voice of the papal magistracy. The popes of the nineteenth century recognized many of the new social doctrines as inverse formulations of Christian teaching. The two popes whose reigns extended through most of the nineteenth century contended in different ways with the doctrines of revolution, both those that had won and been institutionalized in the nation-state and those still seeking to rise through the destruction of the nation-state. Pius IX (1792–1878, reigned 1846–1878) began his pontificate as a liberal and appeared to cherish some sympathies toward political nationalism. The Revolution of 1848, which expelled him from Rome, markedly altered his views. His hostility toward the nation-state blazed with a special ferocity against the Kingdom of Italy, which, in time, suppressed the Papal States; it also led to the conflict with the Prussian government under Bismarck known as the *Kulturkampf*. Pius adamantly opposed revolutionary labor movements. During a long episcopate before he became pope, Leo XIII (1810–1903, reigned 1878–1903), revealed considerable sympathy for social reform and as pope followed a more accommodating policy toward the nation-state than had his predecessor. He came to terms with Germany and Belgium, and his effort to find some common ground with the anti-clerical government of the French Third Republic failed through no fault of his. In Italy, however, he remained, as Pius had been after 1870, the prisoner in the Vatican, staunchly denying the legitimacy of the Kingdom. This insistence on the lost temporal power of the popes had a doctrinal base applicable even outside Italy, where Leo could afford to be concessive; for he continued to teach that democracy, as institutionalized revolution, was incompatible with ecclesiastical authority. He had little spirit of accommodation towards advocates of revolution outside the governmental order of the nation-state. At his accession, Leo declared war on the general secularism of society, and especially on socialists, communists, and nihilists, whom he held responsible for impelling the human race to the point of final dissolution.[38] His attacks continued; they extended to the papacy's old enemy, Freemasonry, and all others whom the Pope considered to be working to destroy the Church and thus also to compound the "prevailing moral degeneracy."[39]

The great error conveyed in these doctrines, Leo wrote, was license in thought and action—license mistaken for freedom, which had undermined all sense of security in public and in private life. He inveighed against the doctrine that power depended on the will of the people and not on God. He thought that this concept was born when popular passions erupted in the Reformation; he traced its passage, as it scattered bloodshed and violence in its wake and issued in the ultimate horrors, "to wit, communism, socialism, and nihilism, hideous deformities of the civil society of man, and almost its ruin."[40] But one even more fundamental supposition was prior to the ascription of power to the people, a premise also rooted in the disaster of the sixteenth century: personal autonomy. Leo praised the stand taken by his predecessors, Gregory XVI and Pius IX, against unaccountable freedom of conscience[41]; for right liberty presupposed law—the law that

---

[38] *Quod Apostolici Muneris,* ch. 2, 28 Dec. 1878.
[39] *Humanum genus,* ch. 2, 20 April 1881; *Rerum Novarum,* ch. 1, 15 May 1891.
[40] *Diuturnum,* ch. 23, 29 June 1881.   [41] *Immortale Dei,* ch. 34, 1 Nov. 1885.

had its principle in God's transcendent reason, that was duplicated in man's soul as the image of God, that was revealed in the Scriptures, and, finally, that lay at the core of all rightful civil laws.

The Pope drew his concept of natural law from scholastic philosophy and particularly from the work of Thomas Aquinas, whose writings he made an obligatory part of seminary instruction and whose patronage he extended to all Catholic schools. Natural law affirmed the right of the family to exist, the right of man to move toward his final end (that is, God) in the way set for him by God, and the right to own and use private property. The entire structure of society stood on these pillars; and yet these were the principles that the new social doctrines undermined in their general onslaught against religion and thus against moral order and liberty. The Church was the perfect society, having the powers to teach, legislate, judge, and punish.[42] As the Body of Christ, the Church possessed the fullness of man's natural and supernatural freedom. To avert catastrophe, the world must return to the Church's doctrines. It must see that there was a natural order of law in man's soul and in human society, and that this order was derived from God. Every kind of power was derived from God; in a sense, all authority, and especially that of fathers, was stamped with the image and form of the authority that was in God.[43] Every man must be bound in love to God and to his neighbor, since all men participated in the infinite goodness of God and carried in their inmost hearts the impress of His image and likeness.[44] Beyond these lines of natural mimesis, linked with a cosmic and transcendent reason, the Church also revealed a supernatural mimesis. It proclaimed the ideal of sacrifice in Jesus, the "divine Model," who revealed that man's dignity lay in moral qualities, and who demonstrated how the pain and grief of this life could be transformed into motives of virtue. "No man can hope for eternal reward unless he follow in the bloodstained footsteps of the Savior."[45]

These declarations were intended to open the way for Catholics to engage in movements for social welfare without violating the limits of ecclesiastical tradition. The unlearned, or the enthusiast, found it difficult to recognize what those limits were, however, or perhaps to grasp how ancient rules should be applied to conduct in technologically advanced society. Leo's authority was invoked to support programs and

[42] *Libertas Praestantissimum,* 20 June 1888, especially ch. 40.

[43] *Diuturnum,* ch. 11, 29 June 1881.

[44] *Sapientiae Christianae,* ch. 40, 10 Jan. 1890.

[45] *Rerum Novarum,* chs. 21, 24, 15 May 1891.

actions far more radical than what he himself considered appropriate. Consequently, in 1901, he issued an encyclical to clarify his position.[46] To many readers, this pronouncement appeared a retreat from stances taken in *Quod apostolici muneris* and *Rerum novarum,* even though the Pope explicitly described it as an extension of their teachings.

Attempting to bring Christian social movements into line with ecclesiastical tradition, Leo repeated his defense of private property, the family, and man's right to move toward his universal end. But many, even within the Church, read retreat into his use of exemplarism when he defended the existing political order by saying that God impressed the character of justice on every human society (c. 6); when he taught submission to the existing order by pointing to the examples of St. Paul and Christ (cc. 9–11); and when he appeared to accept the oppressed status of workers by referring to the Holy Family of Nazareth as an example of sanctity shining in the midst of poverty and awaiting a reward in the life to come (c. 25).

Leo's successors continued to teach the perfectibility of man by reversionist mimesis, and two of them, whose pontificates fell in the twentieth century, gave this ancient doctrine exceptional force. This emphasis certainly grew out of the fabric of Church doctrine. It also owed something to the intellectual achievements of the individual popes. Leo, for example, was an eminent scholar, who had particular familiarity with classical antiquity. The two successors to whom I referred were also exceptionally accomplished students of the literature in which the mimetic tradition took shape and received its fullest exposition. Before his pontificate, Pius XI (1857–1939, reigned 1922–1939), served as director and prefect of the Ambrosian Library in Milan, and subsequently as sub-prefect and prefect of the Vatican Library. John XXIII (1881–1963, reigned 1958–63) was a profound student, and occasionally, a professor of Church history and patrology.

Pius XI encountered political disorders whose magnitudes differed from those met by Leo. His pontificate spanned the years of the Great Depression, the years in which the fascist governments of Italy and Germany established themselves. Yet the norms of his thought remained those which Leo had called the "ageless philosophy" (*philosophia perennis*), the teachings of Thomas Aquinas. The reversionist mimesis of natural reason and the *imitatio Christi* circumscribed his thought. In an extraordinarily powerful encyclical that he issued against the Hitlerian idealism, Pius denounced the argument that there

---

[46] *Graves de communi.*

was a peculiar German mode of being. Hitlerian teaching denied the supernatural realm of grace through which God raised man to inward participation of life with Himself; it denied the natural realm of reason in which the norms of morality had been written by the finger of the Creator on the hearts of men. To teach that power derived from the people and that whatever benefited the people was right, as the German government was doing, was to place moral teaching at the mercy of subjective human opinions, and thus to open the floodgates of destruction.[47] The purpose of human society was to reflect the everlasting perfection of God, and this mimetic function did not mean that the state engulfed the person. Rather, it was intended to instruct the individual person so that he could rightly praise and adore the Creator. The formation of good Christians was identical with the formation of good citizens.[48]

The Platonic theme of formation (*morphosis*) by imitating a primordial model was at the heart of Pius's thought. He gave it unusually sharp expression when he spoke on education. His encyclical *Divini illius Magistri* is an early warning against points of view that Pius had already met in the fascist government of Italy, and that he later saw come to fruition in Germany. He rebuked those who wished to cut education out of the religious sphere and subject it to what Pius called "naturalism." God created man in His image and likeness and destined man to move toward Him. God planted the need, the impulse, to move toward moral perfection—as perfect being—in man's rational nature. Error enters the picture when men try to draw principles of education out of human nature without any reference to God, the first principle and final end of man and of the entire universe. They tie themselves to transitory things instead of to what is permanent and real. Through Christ, God has revealed Himself as man's end. Therefore, "there can be no complete and perfect education that is not Christian education" (chaps. 4–6), and any scheme of education was vain if it left out of account the Decalogue, the Gospel, the law of nature stamped by God in the heart of man and proclaimed by right reason (chap. 53). The Church itself was a great school, through its formal instruction, through its missions in every part of the world, through the treasures of art, philosophy, and literature that it inspired, preserved, and transmitted from generation to generation.

This work supposed that God destined all men to the same super-

[47] *Mit brennender Sorge,* chs. 33–35, 14 March 1937.

[48] *Divini Redemptoris,* ch. 29, 19 March 1937; *Divini illius Magistri,* ch. 48, 31 Dec. 1929.

natural end (chaps. 23–24); it rested on "that same humanism whose highest development was reached in the schools of the Church" (chap. 76). All education was directed toward Christ as universal model, toward the formation in man of the supernatural virtue and life in Christ (chaps. 81, 88), toward the formation of a "supernatural man who thinks, judges, and acts constantly in accordance with right reason illumined by the supernatural light of the example and teaching of Christ" (chap. 82).

In another letter, Pius spoke of man as a "microcosm" through his God-given powers of body and soul,[49] but he was a microcosm whose capacities needed to be developed and given shape according to the lines of transcendent reason, and according to the supernatural imitation of Christ's life of prayer, sacrifice, and zeal.[50] Without these models, men wandered in the self-destructive blindness of their own hearts, violating their true nature and lacking the end for which they were made.

The thought that John XXIII expressed in his papal decrees actually took form in the late nineteenth century, during the last years of Leo XIII's pontificate. Indeed, John was educated according to the reformed curriculum that Leo instituted in seminaries. Entries of the diary that John began when he entered seminary disclose the effects of the mimetic tradition. He pledged to keep the "shining mirror" of his soul unblemished (1897); he repeated St. Augustine's concept of the trinity of the soul (memory, reason, and will) as the image of the divine Trinity in its actions, and as sharing in the beauty of God Himself (1900). He accepted the reason as the *locus* of the divine image. But likeness to God required grace. Inside the human being, there were many ravening beats—wolves, tigers, lions. Grace alone keeps them under control; without restraining grace, the soul falls victim to them (1940).

How was this humanizing grace to be achieved? In the first instance, by the gift of God, but secondarily by imitation. Imitation of the saints allowed the substance of their virtue to pour into the life-blood of their followers (1903), and participation by imitation also united the believer and Christ. Thomas à Kempis's *Imitation of Christ* was a normative book in John's youth; it remained so throughout his life (1895, 1898, 1943, 1950). The supernatural imitation of the Crucified, leading to participation in His sufferings and glory, correspondingly had a

---

[49] *Divini Redemptoris,* ch. 27, 19 March 1937.
[50] *Firmissimam constantiam,* chs. 10–12, 28 March 1937.

central place in John's spirituality. He longed "to suffer with Jesus who suffers" (1931); he embraced the mystical death through which he became detached from everything earthly and from himself, and indifferent to anything but God's will (1943). Christ was his model; and through imitation, he lived in Christ, and Christ in him.

It was not surprising that John took as his papal motto the Platonic verse from the Gospel of John: *"Ut unum sint."* Nor was it surprising that his papal writings conveyed the mimetic concept. He was convinced that the world was framed according to an objective moral order corresponding with God's transcendent reason; that man participated in the divine perfection through his natural reason; and that human affairs were just only if they conformed with the universal archetypes of righteousness. In his major proclamation concerning social problems, *Mater et Magistra* (1961), John condemned the modern industrial-economic system as "radically deranged" because it violated this order in favor of the law of the strongest (chap. 1). He appealed for a more just and equitable social structure corresponding with the eternal principles that underlay the changing conditions of this world. But the supernatural motivation was also present. John began the encyclical by urging the imitation of Christ, who fed the hungry. He closed it by describing the effects of the *imitatio Christi:* that men are called to live by Christ's very life and what they do, in union with Christ, becomes His own work, penetrated with His redemptive power. As was written in the Platonic Gospel from which John took his name and motto: "He that abideth in me, and I in him, the same bringeth forth much fruit (John 15:5).

Such were the doctrines against which Newman unwittingly offended. The view of history was important in the political conflicts between the Papacy and its antagonists. Here, if ever, politics was a symbolic form of ideas. On the level of theory, how greatly the old reversionist idealism of form contradicted the new one of mimesis by augmentation, to which it had given rise, is indicated by the papal attitude toward historical criticism, an attitude that was especially clear in the pontificate of Pius IX. From the time of his conversion, Newman's doctrines were considered doubtful by many and heretical by some. Among the latter was Mgr. Talbot, a close adviser of the Pope and the very person who called Newman "the most dangerous man in England." Orestes Brownson (1803–1876), who had passed by stages from Unitarianism to Transcendentalism to Roman Catholicism, vehemently condemned Newman as heretical, and, through *Brownson's*

Quarterly Review, he won a large following in the United States, especially among the bishops. The great projects that Newman attempted between 1850 and 1860 were all thwarted, in measure, by this suspicion and by the fear of association with him that it inspired. The Catholic University of Ireland failed because the Irish bishops, including Archbishop Cullen, of Dublin, who originated the project, would not support him, for reasons already indicated. The translation of the Bible, begun at Cardinal Wiseman's request, came to an early end because the English bishops gave no encouragement. Newman's project for a branch house of the Oratory, at Oxford, was approved by Rome, but on condition that he himself would not reside in it. His editorship of the *Rambler* ceased at the request of the Bishop of Birmingham, who was able to indicate to Newman that his editorial policies and his own articles had given rise to further questions at Rome about his orthodoxy, questions so grave that he might be summoned to defend himself before the papal Curia. The composition of the *Apologia* did much to rehabilitate Newman in British public opinion.

It did nothing, however, to alter Rome's opinion of his developmental theories. Indeed, the same year (1864) saw the appearance of the *Apologia* and the publication of Pius IX's *Syllabus of Errors,* in which the Pontiff specifically condemned the premises that divine revelation was progressive and cumulative and that its growth corresponded with that of human reason. As parts of the same declaration, Pius firmly condemned freedom of religion, freedom of the press, the exclusion of ecclesiastical doctrines and supervision from public education, and the argument that modern science had discredited principles of scholastic theology and rendered them inappropriate to the nineteenth century. "It is an error," he concluded, "to believe that the Roman Pontiff can and should reconcile himself to, and come to agreement with, progress, liberalism, and contemporary civilization."

Newman was fortunate. While he knew that Rome mistrusted him, and while his hopes suffered bitter reversals, he escaped formal condemnation such as Pius imposed upon Döllinger and others who held firm to historical criticism in opposing the temporal power or the infallibility of the popes. At the age of 78, when he was very infirm, Newman received the red hat from a new pope, Leo XIII. Within limits, Leo wished to come to terms with modern society, and, in his view, those limits were wide enough to comprehend two apparent incompatibles, both the revival of Thomistic theology and doctrines of the historical evolution of thought. Privately, Newman had argued against the extreme declarations of Pius IX. Newman was prepared to accept papal infallibility as an administrative principle of long standing. But his conviction of the force of tradition—including the progress of knowledge and the human weakness of individual popes—persuaded him that it was not a doctrine. Moreover, the principle frequently exceeded what consensus, expressed in the Church's actual practice, allowed. Yet even though he thought that the proclamations of the Vatican Council had shaken the Church off her ancient moorings, he shared these fears only with his closest friends. Outwardly, he preserved hierarchic obedience through what was perceived to be the power of silence. For Leo, Newman was a convenient symbol of the developmental view; he had not fallen into open disobedience toward Rome, as had Döllinger; he was celebrated; he was old. The Pope could count on a grateful Newman to rebuke, with the dignity of the cardinalate, the Christian liberals and socialists who had invoked his authority.

The attitudes expressed by Pius IX endured, however, and they returned to the level of papal policy under Pius X (1835–1914, reigned 1903–1914), who indicated, by his choice of a pontifical name, the great reverence for Pio Nono that marked his actions. In his decree, *Lamentabili sane exitu* (1907), which he deliberately cast as a second *Syllabus of Errors*, Pius prohibited the use of historical criticism in sacred theology. A few months later, in *Pascendi Dominici Gregis,* he condemned modernism and particularly its developmental theories. A series of severe decrees followed, including the *motu proprio, Sacrorum antistitum* (1910), in which Pius required, as a condition of office, an oath from clergy and Church officers against "the heretical fiction of the evolution of dogma." These policies were enforced by the use of excommunication, the establishment of an effective censorship (associated with the codification of canon law), an austere exercise of discipline over theology, and the reorganization of scholarly commissions so as to safeguard conservative theological teachings.

Since the pontificate of Pius X, the papacy has entirely accepted the methods of historical criticism. The Vatican has become a major center of research into the history of Christianity and of other religions. But the problem of reconciling historical development with the tradition that is always the same has remained elusive, and with it, the role of the Church, and of the values conveyed by its traditions, in political affairs.

The ancient mimetic ideality of reason and sacrifice survived; the ancient humanism survived, with its patterned continuities. But it lived on precisely in the institution that represented to critics of society and government all that was hostile to advances in science, political freedom, and social welfare. Now, the ancient idealities were opposed by other, fully developed ideals of humanity rooted in the discontinuities and the economic and social disorders of time.

Newman skirted the anti-mimetic propositions of the Enlightenment; the popes, on the whole, ignored them except by way of refutation. Neither stance was possible for those who wished to analyze the turbulent world in which they lived. Among scholars as well as revolutionaries, the French Revolution and its antecedents had become part of the myth by which Europeans explained their collective identity.[51] Leopold von Ranke, Hegel, and Marx explicitly understood themselves and their culture as coming late in a sequence of revolutions of which the Reformation was the first. Although Ranke held as a first principle that every age must be judged in its own terms, he also had in common with Hegel, Marx, and Newman the trait of reasoning backward from his own time. History was teleological, and it disclosed its true end, and continuity, in the nineteenth century. Insofar as they were of historical, and not merely antiquarian, significance, earlier events were read in the light of that goal, as antecedents or analogues. The traditions of culture were traditions of revolution. Historical idealisms constituted one family of answers to general issues that vexed the nineteenth century, issues of anxiety and unrest that deeply stained contemporary literature. There also appeared a range of responses to the malaise of transition, which was neither mimetic nor teleological, but which had a bearing on our theme.

Empirical and critical thought seemed to dispel erroneous pretensions and superstitions that debased human life and to emancipate man from terror and fanaticism. The application of scientific principles to man's collective life was therefore pursued with great vigor. Jeremy Bentham's resort to a calculus of social welfare was followed by other experiments, such as Auguste Comte's (1798–1857) adaptation of physical laws, Herbert Spencer's (1820–1903) of biological, Walter Bagehot's (1826–1877) of psychology, and of Marx's of political economy. Still, as the sciences of man took form, they ironically compounded the divisions that they were meant to close; for each parted company from the others in methodology and in purpose.

The consequences of many non-teleological analyses of human ex-

---

[51] See J. Joll, *The Anarchists* (New York, 1964), pp. 40ff.

perience nevertheless overlapped with historical idealisms in ways that reinforced the premises of revolutionary theorists. Perhaps the most arresting of these common points is that, in shifting the focus of interpretation from persons to relations between social functions, the center of attention shifted from man to the works of man. This was Carlyle's meaning when he said that God looked upon human works to see His own reflection, to know Himself. Similarly, the sciences of man took form, driven by the inspiration that man is a social function, not a rational or primarily a political being. Man is not born; he is made by what he does. Abstractly considered in this way, he is formed by the humanly made conditions in which he functions, and he can develop only in society, the necessary context and precondition of his work. Enlightened self-interest, or class interest, dictated by expedience or utility was the basis of conduct and of government.

Each historical context was regarded as distinct from all others, and, at the moment when many ancient civilizations and languages were being scientifically analyzed or actually discovered, historicism declared that civilizations had no exemplary character, and only such value as the present age assigned. For individual human beings painted their achievements in the fugitive colors given them by their nation, race, or age.

As Mircea Eliade has observed, such views allowed man to be swallowed up in time, tied to the ultimate extinction of his own social structure. In realizing this, the historians of the nineteenth century left man, collectively and individually, isolated before time: that is, before death and nothingness.[52] There was more. The age that first used the words "anachronistic" and "prehistoric" was also the first to grasp the possibility that, whatever institutions it might devise to guard its biological survival, the human race might evolve into extinction. In this torrent of change, perhaps running toward the abyss, the only reality was the labile equilibrium of experience itself, which was more real than the men who experienced it. But even torrents follow laws. Perhaps by knowing the principles governing change, one could modify or redirect the modeling of man's social character and destiny.

Such were the unlikely materials from which new strategies of mimesis were framed outside the walls of the Church to explain and justify social discontinuity. They were applied in revolution and intellectualized in the social sciences.

[52] *Myths, Dreams, and Mysteries* (London, 1972), pp. 236ff.

The Poetry and Tradition of Revolution

Revolutionary theorists denied the meaninglessness of change. In the vivid awareness that their world was coming to a close, that another had not appeared, and indeed that there might be no abiding world before them, they proclaimed the death of man as he had been defined by centuries of reflection, and the vanishing reality of man as he actually existed. The existence of man was contaminated by the very substance that composed it: change. Their apocalypses were negations of man, revelations of death, leading to new life; they were negations that cried out for community in existing relations where there was only deprivation of community. Whether they drew on the "national ideas" of Ranke, the "Absolute Spirit" of Hegel, or the social and economic forms of Marx, they added to theory zeal, fervor, and, above all, moral compulsion. They taught that it was the duty of those who rightly understood the idea to realize it in human affairs. Idealist historians had accepted revolution as a constitutive, though involuntary, part of European culture. Revolutionary theorists had the full commitment of men commanded to be not hearers only but doers of the word. They labored under the moral imperative of dispelling the reality in social structure that was passing into unreality and of building new social forms along the contours of the revolution in their minds. When he described "the Revolution as a work of art," Michelet captured the ancient rationale that made it possible to use mimetic doctrines to justify radical change.

As a theory about making, Marx's doctrines of history and revolution were aesthetic. He refused to accept the distinction between nature and human action that had given rise to the dichotomy of nature and art. Nature, he argued, was the history that man made according to the norms of order (or beauty) which were—like science, law, and social institutions—products of economic activity.

Marx frequently treated his own philosophical predecessors with the slight respect that he gave all "theologians." His insistence that the means of producing food and shelter were a social medium prior to religion, law, or government, and his explication of the theory of surplus value removed the confusion of the "I" with the "you" that Marx held against the Young Hegelians. But, in calling for a medium, his own structure of thought retained the familiar asymmetry of ideal and image, seeking reconciliation in a mediator. Consequently, it also retained the iconoclasm that had always been encased in mimetic theories of form. Marx was deeply conscious of his intellectual heritage, as well as of his originality. He recognized the ways by which past blueprints inform the minds of present workmen.

"Men make their own history," Marx wrote in 1852, adding: "They do not make it out of free elements, but rather under immediately antecedent, given, and traditional conditions. The tradition of all dead generations weighs like an incubus on the brain of the living." Surely, epochs of revolutionary crisis impress the ghosts of the past into their service. There was a "tradition of revolution." "The awakening of the dead in every revolution serves therefore to ennoble the new struggles, not to parody the old." Yet this retrospection had become pernicious. The revolution of the nineteenth century had to let the dead bury their dead in order to develop its own content and purpose; the social revolution of the nineteenth century had to create its poetry out of the future instead of the past. The proletarian revolution must set itself apart from its antecedents in the bourgeois revolution by self-criticism so severe and so repeated that it would not be possible to go back, to draw sustenance from the past. In 1852, whether that could or would be done remained to be seen.[53]

The creative effort had to be collective, just as the artist's hand was the organ and product of labor. Individuality and originality were subsumed in the whole system of labor, a unity of interlocking parts in which all kinds of labor were equal and equivalent insofar as they made up human labor in general.[54] Indeed, this equivalence would become apparent when historical processes reached their end. All art was class-art. With every other class, that of artists would disappear in the withering away of the state; every person would then be an artist.

"Men make their history," Engels (1820–1895) wrote, repeating Marx's phrase,[55] "as history always results in that each man pursues his own consciously willed objectives, and the results of these many wills acting in different directions and of their manifold effect upon the external world is precisely, history. It depends, therefore, upon what the great majority of individuals intend."[56] Marx and Engels were typ-

---

[53] Der 18ten Brumaire des Louis Napoleon, ch. 1, Marx-Engels Werke (Berlin, 1960) 8: 115ff.

[54] F. Engels, "Anteil der Arbeit an der Menschenwerdung des Affen," Marx-Engels Gesamtausgabe, Sonderausgabe (Moscow, 1935), p. 695. Marx, Capital, part I, ch. I, sec. 3. B. 3. ad fin.

[55] Der 18ten Brumaire, pp. 115f.

[56] Ludwig Feuerbach und der Ausgang der klassischen deutschen Philosophie, ch. 4 (Karl Marx-Friedrich Engels, Werke [Berlin, 1962] 21: 297).

ical of revolutionary theorists in appealing quite consciously to traditions that went back in philosophy through to the remotest periods of Western thought, and, in practice, through the Paris Commune, the French Revolution, and the Reformation.[57] In this one respect, their sense of revolution as a collective work transmitted through time corresponds oddly with the perceptions of the aristocratic Alexis de Tocqueville (1805–1859). He understood that the *ancien régime* itself had completed the revolutionary education of the masses, and that the masses indeed took from it "customs, conventions, and modes of thought," and "even those very ideas which inspired our revolutionaries to destroy it."[58] In this way, mimesis by inversion gathered up into itself elements of earlier varieties of mimesis.

At the same time as Newman, baffled and wounded, passed through his tribulations, Marx, who was living more obscurely than Newman in England, went about preparing the materials for *Das Kapital.* The same sense of historical development from one form to another quite different form, the same subversionist metaphors of gestation and germination that Newman knew and used were at work in Marx's mind. He was fully aware of the doctrines of form woven into the religious web from which he broke when he separated himself from the Young Hegelians, but which he still recognized as part of the incubus of dead generations weighing on the mind of the living. Marx applied the subversionist paradigm when he argued that historical criticism had moved by stages from religion to law, from theology to politics, carrying components of earlier generations in it. He also stood in harmony with earlier doctrines when he accepted the Reformation as the theoretical antecedent of the philosophy in the heart of the proletariat that was leading it to the ultimate stage of revolution, to its "resurrection."[59] Yet Marx's doctrines culminated in the relativism of mimesis by inversion that Engels concisely described in his essay on Feuerbach.

Although Engels published this essay in 1888, it referred to a crucial moment forty years earlier. After he met Marx in 1844, and both of them moved to Brussels, they entered into a ferocious debate with a

[57] See references below, n. 59; and Engels, introduction to the first edition of *Socialism, Utopian and Scientific.*

[58] *De l'ancien régime,* preface.

[59] "Zur Kritik der Hegelschen Rechtsphilosophie," *Marx-Engels Gesamtausgabe,* 1: 608, 615, 621. See also the partial genealogy of his ideas sketched by Marx in "Die Heilige Familie," sect. VI, *Marx-Engels Gesamtausgabe* (Berlin, 1958) 2: 132ff.

Feuerbachian branch of German socialism. While they repudiated the socialist position, they also recognized in Feuerbach's materialism something of crucial importance to their own position. The effects began to be apparent in their journalistic works and in the *Communist Manifesto* (1847). After Marx's trial for sedition in the *Neue Rheinische Zeitung* case, and Engels's failure in the Baden revolution, they moved to England, where they continued to domesticate Feuerbach. In 1888, Engels looked back over the position that they had achieved: "once and for all, the demand for final solutions and eternal truths stops; one is ever conscious of the necessary limitation of all acquired knowledge, of the qualifications placed on it by the conditions under which it has been acquired. One cannot be imposed upon any longer by the irreconcilable antitheses in the still customary old metaphysics of true and false; good and evil; identical and differentiated; necessary and accidental. One knows that these antitheses have only a relative validity, that what is now recognized as true, has a concealed false side that will appear later . . . just as what is now recognized as false has its true side, on account of which it could earlier pass for true."[60] The remote echoes of St. Augustine's exegesis on Jacob's lie became yet more distinct, as Engels continued. "So in the course of development all earlier reality becomes unreality, loses its necessity, its right to exist, its rationality, and into the place of the dying thing that was real steps a new vital reality, peaceable when the old is sufficiently sensible to go to its death without a struggle, forcible when it strives against this necessity."[61] Freedom, indeed, was the recognition of necessity.

Just as Hegel and Ranke envisioned the end of history in the complete realization of an idea in the actual world, Marx foresaw the apocalyptic end of the historical dialectic when class conflict ceased. In that moment, the proletariat, having subsumed all other classes and realized the socialist economic order, would itself cease to exist, as all other classes had done. That complete consciousness and realization, he wrote, would end the process of creation; it would conclude the prehistory of human culture and begin its history.

Revolutionary theorists came in many shades. Marx and the others with whom we have yet to deal were not only idealists but also conscious traditionalists. The appeal to tradition, with its accumulated diversity, was an important test of ideological orthodoxy among theorists who held that authentic social doctrine was an empirical science drawn from man's cumulative experience. Those denizens of the nine-

---

[60] *Feuerbach,* ch. 4, pp. 293f.   [61] *Ibid.,* ch. 1, p. 266.

teenth and twentieth centuries who had a mental picture of all revolutionaries as wishing to overturn inherited institutions and wisdom misread one part of the situation. For there was a powerful sense of continuity in doctrine and purpose among parties, labor unions, and families. By the 1920s, there were Russians who traced their descent through four generations of revolutionary forebears. The appeal to tradition was not strange to them. It evoked pride of lineage, even a sense of dynasty, among them, as it also did in France and Germany among those whose fathers, grandfathers, and great-grandfathers had participated in the organization of labor unions and in the strikes of the late nineteenth century, and who could trace their intellectual formation through unbroken lines of teachers back to the men who failed in 1848, including the founders of French socialism and Marx himself.

Even as they insisted on their traditions, however, theorists of revolution also insisted that their function was to overthrow what Emma Goldman called "truth grown false with age." They invoked the dialectical premise that any moment is both negative and positive, both the past vision falling into unreality and the future one becoming real.

The principles of historical dialectic characterize an enormous range and variety of literature. They are normative in works of Lassalle and Kropotkin, of Bakunin and Sorel. Because they were interpreted in many ways, they grew ever more sharply defined through theoretical disputes that set each branch of revolutionary thought apart and that split individual parties of thought. One concrete example of historical ideality refined through dispute was a series of articles written by a staunch follower of Marx, Rosa Luxemburg (1870–1919), against Eduard Bernstein's revisionist approach to Marxism. These articles have a particular bearing on our discussion; for in Luxemburg's eyes Bernstein had to be refuted because his revisionism denied the apocalypse to which she had given her passionate commitment and on which everything depended.

Luxemburg was born in Russian Poland, where she early joined the socialist movement. She fled from Poland to Germany and, for political reasons, acquired German citizenship by marriage. The Revolution of 1905 drew her back to Poland. On its failure, she returned to Berlin, where she joined others in founding the Spartacist League. After intermittent imprisonment from 1914 onward, she was arrested and killed while in police custody. The articles against Bernstein were written and published in 1898/99, shortly after Luxemburg reached Berlin, and, taken as a unit, they constitute one of her most enduring theoretical statements.

For Luxemburg, it was fundamental that Marx's thought was "the most colossal product of the human mind (*Geist*) in the [nineteenth] century"[62] and that his great discovery had been the conception of capitalist economy as a historical phenomenon that, as such, was transitory and led to its own inevitable collapse and the establishment of socialism in its place. This discovery was the magic key with which Marx opened the innermost secrets of capitalist phenomena and provided the socialist movement with a scientific base.[63]

Marx's inversion of mimesis reappears in Luxemburg's premise that theories are "the reflexes of the phenomena of the exterior world in the human brain,"[64] and in her insistence that the progress of socialism depended upon the education of the proletariat in theoretical knowledge that would make it conscious of its historic role.

Consequently, Bernstein's view that the class conflict was subsiding and that communism and capitalism were approximating one another was, to Luxemburg, a grave error of historical perspective. In her judgment, Bernstein had abandoned the correct class viewpoint and accepted the dominant (bourgeois) science, democracy, and morality. He stood for the reform of capitalism instead of for the realization of socialism, and he ended by renouncing the movement.

Bernstein's errors consisted in his eclectic reconstitution of theories that Marx and Engels had destroyed fifty years earlier. Two symptoms of his regression to a circular idealization of something that no longer existed were his treatment of democracy and his recourse to justice. Bernstein judged democracy to be the great fundamental law of historical development, whereas it had so exhausted its function as a prop of the existing order that not the bourgeoisie but the proletariat, in the international labor movement, was its main support. For, while democracy was dead for the bourgeois, it was only through the exercise of its democratic rights, in the struggle for democracy, that the proletariat could become aware of its class interests and its historic task. Only through the transitory phenomena of democracy could the conquest of political power by the proletariat become both possible and necessary. Bernstein's resort to justice, she wrote, was also erroneous. For this invocation of the idea of justice was remounting "the old warhorse on which all those who wanted to improve the earth have ridden for millennia, lacking surer, historical means of locomotion."[65] The quixotic search for justice was illusory and no substitute for the scien-

---

[62] *Sozialreform oder Revolution?* (Berlin, 1967, rpt. of Leipzig. 1899 ed.), p. 4.
[63] Ibid., p. 40.   [64] Ibid., p. 7.   [65] Ibid., p. 45.

tific theories of socialism, which were "the axis of intellectual crystallization around which individual facts group themselves as the organic whole of a consistent ideology (*Weltanschauung*)."[66]

In the historic development of socialism before his day, Bernstein's theories had played an important role. They had been effective theories of proletarian class struggle; they had been the children's boots by which the proletariat had learned to walk onto the stage of history.[67] Marx and Engels had superseded them.

Luxemburg's critique of Bernstein indicates the historical ideality of her own thought, in which the word "idea," laden with objectionable bourgeois connotations, has been replaced by the scientifically acceptable term, "theory." It is apparent that her theory was one of a dialectic in process, a process that through rectilinear movement avoided the tautologies of philosophical idealism. The dialectic originated in the contradictions of capitalism. It advanced first by experience, then by thought, and finally by action as the working class understood the transitory nature of its yoke to the oppressing class, then embraced revolution in the world of thought, and at last seized the apparatus of government and production.

The moment of recognition was crucial for the realization of socialism within the economic conditions of capitalism. It was this that changed socialism "from an 'ideal' that hovered before mankind for thousands of years into a historical necessity."[68] But it was also this that gave to socialism the provisional and ambiguous character of development.

The dialectic is not the simple one of oppressor and oppressed, capitalist and proletarian. For each new movement finds its support within the preceding one, even though they may contradict each other. It grows within the social form of the old order until it discards it, as the new grain bursts through the old husk.[69] There is more than an echo of Hegel's view that the owl of Minerva takes wing when dusk is falling—that philosophy performs its generalizing from social experience only when the life of a society is over—in Luxemburg's concept of the germination and succession of social forms. She insists that legislative reform and political revolution are not, as Bernstein held, different methods of historical development, but that they are different factors in the development of class society. Each legislative reform is the product of a society that came into being in the previous revolution, and it must occur within the framework of the social forms that that revolu-

---

[66] Ibid., p. 58.   [67] Ibid., p. 61.   [68] Ibid., p. 34.   [69] Ibid., p. 4.

tion established. Conversely, reforms such as those achieved by the proletariat through the institutions of democracy also could prepare for the passage of a historic period from one form of society to another. Indeed, the scientific theories of socialism, embodied in a program setting the limits for stage-by-stage action by the proletariat, gave all the assurance needed that the contradictions of capitalism would unavoidably be suppressed through a socialist transformation of society.

In this dialectical process, neither the individual nor organization mattered; for socialism was a movement of the generations, of the masses. Nor did the particular event matter. Every attempt of the proletariat to seize political power would be premature. The effort would not lead to a sudden victory; it would lead along a path through long and stubborn struggles, with many reverses. It was necessary that the proletariat be often repulsed, so that it would achieve, slowly and permanently, the political maturity required for the definitive victory of the revolution. In this way, the daily struggle was united with the transformation of the world in which the historical dialectic would be resolved. The series of developmental stages would exhaust its potentialities, the gap between exemplary models and actual existence would then be closed. The edifice described by the socialist blueprint, or program, would stand complete, and the intellectual crystallization of socialist theories, their coherent conceptions of the world, would become the principles on which the phenomena of the external world were actually organized.

How could a revolutionist like Marx or Luxemburg, who wanted to overturn the established order and bury the past, claim to speak out of the heritage of idealism?

Certainly, theories of revolution diverged from Platonic mimesis in some fundamental ways. The metaphysics of revolution deny that any forms are final, universal, or self-sufficient. The basis of this assumption is the conception of being described by Nietzsche: " 'being' is merely a continual 'has been,' a thing that lives by denying and destroying and contradicting itself."[70] The original effect of Reformation theology on the development of this concept of being that was for the time Being is surely one reason why Ranke, Hegel, and Marx considered the Reformation the first in the series of revolutions that constituted the modern world. For under the aspect of national ideas, the

[70] "Von Nutzen und Nachtheil der Historie für das Leben," ch. 1, in *Friedrich Nietzsche, Gesammelte Werke* (Munich, 1922) 6: 232–242. Cf. pp. 299, 203. On the mediative function of history, see ch. 9, p. 308, and "Was bedeuten asketische Ideale?" *Zur Geneologie der Moral,* chap. 26.

Idea of Freedom, or the atomization of social relationships, there appeared the conviction that historical existence and ideal being were two facets in the career of the same reality.

Unplatonic as it may be, the metaphysics of revolution is also an idealism. That is, it is an a prioristic system of deductions. It starts from the assumption of ideas, or theoretical premises, and proceeds by logically necessary steps through a series of propositions each of which has meaning by its position in the whole sequence. As idealism, the metaphysics of revolution is monistic. It traces all reality to one underlying principle, of which thought and the empirical world are two manifestations. Further, it is a self-justifying tautology in which the first principle is also the final goal. A change occurred in the conception of ideas that corresponded to the change in the way people understood being. The provisional, "as if," connotations of "transcendental" (instead of "transcendent") and "ideal" (instead of "idea") indicate the change from the idea as a form of absolute being to the ideal as a universal mode of transition.

The affinities of revolutionary metaphysics to mimesis are most apparent in its inversional, or dialectical, structure. Mimesis had taught that self-estrangement was part of self-knowledge, conflict part of harmony, and alienation part of community. Resolution of the contradictory terms came through a medium that was both ambiguous and ambivalent, since it combined qualities of the ideal and the actual. Dialectical opposition and resolution through a medium was part both of man's inner life and of his collective existence. We have seen an analogue to this in the metaphysics of revolution. The assumption that only the historical was real carried the prior assumption that the historical process became real by self-negation. Similarly, self-recognition through crisis required the mind to form itself by negating its previous form. Hegel's concept of the world as the medium in which the Absolute Spirit enacts its Golgotha, reconstituting itself by self-alienation, recognition, and negation, is an exact use of mimetic principles. So too is Marx's deliberate inversion of Hegelianism: that the historical world is the medium into which collective man projects and recognizes and alters his authentic self.

The culture of revolution indicated its religious and philosophical antecedents when it reduplicated the conflict and reconciliation at the heart of mimesis, the restless series of transformations that in Neoplatonism had marked the soul's progression toward an infinitely distant object of its love. A direct lineage takes the pedigree of this thought from Marx to Hegel, and thence to Spinoza and Boehme, and finally to Plotinus, who synthesized Platonic with Aristotelian mimesis. Even in the dialectical transference that occurred between the tradition of mimesis and the traditions of revolution, the distinction survived between man's primary, or biological, nature, and the second or artificial nature that he shaped by imitating his proper model. Christian theology had taken this distinction from ancient thought and woven it into the fabric of its doctrines on nature and grace. To limit the two natures to the dimension of time, setting aside the assumptions of eternal and final models, had the result that man-as-he-is was considered the primary nature and man-as-he-is-to-be, the secondary nature.

The relation between the formal structure of mimesis and that of revolutionary theory has another aspect. The mimetic world had been cast in terms of transcendent models that were outside the world and immanent need in the world. Aristotle departed from Plato in describing God as both transcendent to the world and immanent in it. When Aristotle's genetic doctrines began to re-enter Western thought, this coincidence of transcendent and immanent returned. At the moment when the culture of revolution took its full shape, the coincidence became identity, and so it passed into the culture of revolution by way of Hegel, Feuerbach, and Marx. Translated first into materialism and then into historical dialectic, the identity between external and internal was at the basis of seeing man as a surface or social function. It was natural, in view of this equation, that once man, or the social nexus, was seen as the reconciling medium, he was also burdened with the ambivalence of the theological mediator.

Thus transfigured through three stages after the twelfth century, the tradition of mimesis entered the thought of Rosa Luxemburg. It also enabled other revolutionary theorists to appeal to the idealist tradition and simultaneously proclaim the destruction of the old order and the appearance of a new humanity. Though he belonged to a wing of Marxism entirely opposite to Luxemburg's, Leon Trotski (1877–1840) was such a man. He understood the fusion of *mimesis* and *poesis* that Goethe had seen and had represented in *Faust,* the fusion by which idealism was compressed into the dimension of time. He quoted Goethe's inversion of the first verse from the Gospel of St. John. Others believe, he said, that " 'In the beginning was the word.' But we believe that in the beginning was the deed. The word followed, as its phonetic shadow."[71] Thus he could, at the same time, declare that the Bolshevik Revolution of 1917 had overthrown the social and economic

[71] *Literature and Revolution* (Ann Arbor, 1960), p. 183.

bases of earlier culture, rendering the aesthetic and literary, as well as the institutional, aspects of pre-Revolutionary society sterile and irrelevant to the new order, and invoke the revolutionary traditions of the 1905 Revolution, the French commune, the risings of 1848, the French Revolution, of Hegel, the English classical political economists, and the theories of scientific communism that Marx and Engels drew from the content of bourgeois culture. Even defeated and in prison, Trotski could appeal to the abstract principles of dialectical materialism, the algebra of Revolution, to explain the certainty of victory in the great social conversion that unfolded before him, and, at the same time, seek to understand the proletarian Revolution through poetry, "the process of feeling the world in images, and not with the process of knowing the world scientifically."[72]

I have been concerned to identify elements in the long history of Western experience that passed through the subversionist paradigm of transformation to the idealist philosophy of history and into the ideology of revolution. Trotski's references to Hegel as the first theorist of historical dialectic points to the religious, and even mystical, origins of mimesis by inversion that I have attempted to define. Trotski's text will help draw the strands together.

Trotski's insistence that ideas follow events, that poets and prophets reflect their epochs, that "mind limps after reality" points, through Hegel, to the conversionist doctrine of the fourteenth-century mystic Meister Eckhart—that God becomes as phenomena express Him— and to similar positions taken by Renaissance humanists. But the trail goes further back. The language and content of St. Paul's reversionist mimesis recurred in Trotski's description of the Revolution as a struggle "in the name of a new ideal to enrich man and to form a new man."[73] That ideal was the moral teleology without which there would be no Revolution, and other aspects of Trotski's discussion indicate how thoroughly centuries of reflection on St. Paul's new man, and on the new heaven and new earth of the Hebrew prophets, combining the structures of reversion and augmentation, had been secularized. He appealed to a twofold tradition of interpretive knowledge—in written texts and in cumulative, inherited experience—preserved and transmitted by a select and militant party, which required of its adherents asceticism, fidelity, "consecration," and self-denial. The perception of truth hidden in events and disclosed by that tradition enlarged through

[72] Ibid., p. 147. For Marx on the poetry of revolution, see above, Chapter 15, at note 53.

[73] Ibid., pp. 19, 98.

time. By their consciousness of the authentic knowledge, "the inner relation of historical events," men advanced toward the goal of all human experience. The unified process of historical development constituted a history of salvation impelled by a dialectic in which every stage was both old and new.

Even the proletariat, having grown up in the old society that it had overthrown, used the methods of the old society in class struggle, violence, and destruction. There was a parallel between this conception and the theological one of the Church as a pilgrim city, still bound to time and world, both sinful and holy, which was, in some sense, the sacrifice mediating between man and his final end. The parallel is the stronger for Trotski's doctrine of the universal applicability of the received tradition, of the duty to proclaim it, and hence of permanent revolution throughout the world. Trotski's teleology also had an eschatalogical component: the apocalyptic end when the dictatorship of the proletariat will cease and the last social class will end, introducing the perfect and enduring equality of mankind.

Trotski despised Christianity. The Church and its theology epitomized the ideology of the social order that he hated and did much to destroy. He poured contempt on revolutionaries who, to his mind, did nothing but carry their old theology with them from the old order to the new, who understood the spirit of the Revolution as "the spirit of Christ rampant."[74] His conscious antipathy both testifies to continuities that I have traced and renders particularly striking the survivals of different mimetic paradigms in his own thought.

Of course, the revolutionary's appeal to idealism, exemplified by Trotski, also drew on a pre-Christian conception. When Trotski described the teleological ideal in terms of abstract mathematical formulae that underlay and informed what the eye saw as the formlessness and boundlessness of phenomena, and when he said that the greatest poetry of the Revolution lay in its political geometry, the distant voice of Plato could be heard.

Analogy of Experience: Dilthey and Durkheim

Apart from theology and revolutionary theory, there was a third area of historical inquiry where the tradition of mimesis informed nineteenth-century thought: that is, in the developing social sciences.

[74] Ibid., p. 122.

Every branch of learning was altered by the propositions of disunity framed in the Enlightenment. The social sciences, however, originated in those very propositions. During the nineteenth century, they gained shape, organization, and power in the world of learning through the establishment of scientific facts, without regard for metaphysical speculation. Two eminent scholars, Wilhelm Dilthey (1833–1911) and Émile Durkheim (1858–1917) drew heavy fire, therefore, when they appeared to embrace metaphysics, using mimetic strategies to explain social discontinuities.

There was a distinct metaphysical strain in each man's intellectual genealogy. Dilthey established his antecedents in the German mystical tradition, as recast in German Romanticism, with his massive biographies of Schleiermacher and the young Hegel and by appropriating and adapting many features of Schleiermacher's thought into his own analytical methods. He also drew on Kantian and Neo-Kantian philosophy, and he never escaped the influence of the theologian, Trendelenburg, under whose direction he had studied Aristotle and medieval philosophy. Durkheim acknowledged his intellectual forebears among the positivists–Saint-Simon, Comte, and his own teacher, Fustel de Coulanges. Other debts to the theories of Montesquieu and Rousseau about collective mentalities coincided with the personal mysticism of Comte himself, with Kantian philosophy imbibed from Renouvier, and with the spiritualism of German Romantic philosophy taught by Victor Cousin and enshrined by him in the French educational system. Apart from collateral lines of intellectual descent, Dilthey and Durkheim had something else in common. Both men grew up in families that were intensely committed to religious traditions, and, for a time, each prepared himself for ordination.

Long after they abandoned ministerial careers, Dilthey and Durkheim, in their separate ways, surveyed the "anarchical atomization"[75] into which the world of learning had fallen and saw in it a reflection of prevailing social disunity. It was no wonder that they sought an unseen ground of unity in analogies of experience—in religious consciousness, in symbolism and ritual, even in the conduct of daily life. They extracted mimesis from their intellectual heritage. How did they rework it into the social theories that they implanted in the schools?

For my purposes, it is important that they framed their doctrines as advocates for the new science of pedagogy and that their teachings en-

---

[75] Durkheim, "Evolution and the Rôle of Secondary Education," in *Education and Sociology,* trans. S. D. Fox (Glencoe, 1956), p. 140.

tered the mainstream of educational theory and practice both through their lectures to classes of people who aspired to teach and through their voluminous writings.

Dilthey started with the fact of disunity. He understood that it had come about in a series of events, beginning with the disintegration of a unitary world-view in the Renaissance, and accelerated by the dramatic reconstitutions of society that followed the English Civil War and the French Revolution. A certain vision of unity, based on natural law and natural religion, persisted in the sciences until the eighteenth century, but that too had dissipated, leaving a vestige in the antiquated and destructive ideal of a universally valid program of education. Schleiermacher had encountered the atomization of intellectual life at an earlier stage, and, therefore, in a form rather different from the one that Dilthey encountered. Yet he had also affirmed that unity did exist among the various branches of human inquiry, and he advanced grounds of unity that Dilthey found cogent.

Schleiermacher's equation of art and nature recurs in Dilthey's laconic sentence, "The totality of man's nature is only history."[76] In following Schleiermacher's lead, Dilthey arrived at his celebrated division of natural sciences from the sciences of mind (*Geisteswissenschaften*). He had many reasons for this division. For example, he considered that the physical world was outside man and alien to him and that students of that world must know it indirectly by its external features, not immediately, as it really was. By contrast, he argued, the structure of the mind was common to all human beings, and one could participate directly in the creative efforts of other people, even those long dead, by reliving the experience preserved and revealed in their works of art, their literature, and their social order.

One explained physical nature, but one understood mental activity. From understanding, one reached the categories of value and meaning, both foreign to the natural sciences. Dilthey recognized that to exercise the art of living to the full man needed to know both the external causal connections described by the natural sciences and the meaning determined by the sciences of mind. But such unity as he could extract from the circumstances of his day was derived from and included only the latter. Even so, Dilthey left unclear the interrelationships among the sciences of mind. They formed no hierarchic order, as the natural sciences did. There was no overarching science of sciences (though,

---

[76] *Gesammelte Schriften* (hereafter cited as *G.S.*) 8: 166. See Ermarth, *Critique*, pp. 46f. Ermarth provides an excellent discussion of Dilthey's attitude toward his predecessors.

from time to time, Dilthey yielded to temptation and assigned psychology that place of honor, only to retract the judgment later on). The sciences of mind stood together as equals, and Dilthey acknowledged that some—even some in the limited field of Greek and Roman history—cared little for each other. The grounds for unity therefore lay elsewhere than in formal arrangement.

Schleiermacher had indicated the basis of unity and the method that recovered and expressed it. The basis was the humanity in which all men shared; the method was hermeneutics, an advanced form of the analytical decomposition of the object practiced in all criticism. By these means, Dilthey grappled with the anti-mimetic propositions framed during the Enlightenment and absorbed them into a mimetic system of thought.

For Dilthey, art, especially poetry, held the key to understanding all human creativity. It displayed, with the fullest historical documentation, how over centuries man the maker had evoked and changed representations of his inner life; thus it verged on other areas—scientific and practical—in which his imagination had also been applied, though with stricter limits than in the arts. When he responded to the Enlightenment's anti-mimetic propositions, Dilthey therefore couched much of what he had to say in terms of poetry and painting, and of history, which he also considered an art of imaginative composition, both in the making and in the writing. His use of mimetic strategies is especially interesting in that he conceived the Aristotelian doctrine of mimesis to have been a thing of the past, gradually discarded by poets from the Renaissance on, and rejected from philosophical doctrines of judgment by Descartes, the English empiricists, and definitively by Hegel.[77]

As I said at the beginning of this chapter, the first anti-mimetic proposition had three parts: (a) that thought was solipsistic; (b) that the mind passively received its character from external impressions; and (c) that the analogue and the anomaly, the beautiful and the ugly, were equivalent. Dilthey's response hinged on the propositions that there was a universal life from which all human life derived its unity. The whole existed in the individual.[78] While a person was possessed by his ideas, he was not confined to solipsism, therefore, because the universal in him was the means by which he could pass into and relive the experiences of other people. Dilthey answered the second point—the

[77] *G.S.* 6: 110ff., 115f., 118. Cf. Ermarth, *Critique*, pp. 133ff., 259.
[78] *G.S.* 1: 40. R. A. Makkreel, *Dilthey: Philosopher of the Human Studies* (Princeton, 1975), p. 72.

argument for passivity—with his concept of the radical interdependence between the individual and the whole. On the one hand, the ways a person thought and expressed himself were historically conditioned. What a person did bore the characteristic marks of his culture and his age. Furthermore, his work had value, not because it told something about him, but because of its place in a broad development of style and experience.[79] On the other hand, the individual made the world that he belonged to. Man exists, Dilthey wrote, not to be, but to act, and the efforts of the individual were precisely those innumerable manifestations of freedom in the context of objective necessity that constituted history.[80] For the depth of individuality was the inmost workshop of all historical life.[81] Dilthey's conception of the universal and of the interdependence of the universal and the individual indicated an answer to the third point. For, while it was true that style and taste were historically (or socially) conditioned, it was also true that human works, and art in particular, expressed and addressed the universal feelings of mankind. Mentalities were not equal and equivalent, any more than all works of art had the power of a classic to satisfy aesthetic needs in its own time and in other times and places.[82]

The second anti-mimetic proposition was that art sprang from the unconscious—especially that of a genius—rather than from rational order. Dilthey agreed that creativity sprang from feeling and that the entire structure of coherence out of which an artist or writer worked could never be brought to consciousness.[83] Dreams and madness were as much outer representations of inner states as speech and metaphysical concepts. Quite possibly a person first recognized the guiding principle of his thought and work when he saw it expressed in what he had made.[84] Even so, through the hermeneutic method, others could reconstruct his creative process, penetrate into his unconscious ideas (including the presuppositions of his language and time), and understand his work better than he himself.[85]

The essential fact for Dilthey was not that man worked out of his unconscious, but that the unconscious had a structure that appeared in art and social life, and that could be reconstructed and re-experienced by scholars. Consequently, the antithesis of conscious reason and unconscious will was false. The two interlaced and became identical in feeling. Feeling was not amorphous; it comprised a hierarchic order up

[79] *G.S.* 14/2: 722.   [80] *G.S.* 14/2: 722; 9: 203f.; 1: 6.   [81] *G.S.* 14/2: 721.
[82] *G.S.* 6: 236.   [83] *G.S.* 6: 140–143.
[84] H. A. Hodges, *Wilhelm Dilthey: An Introduction* (New York, 1944), p. 14.
[85] *G.S.* 14/2: 707.

which the mind advanced, through various representations, to assign value to its own existence.[86] Because he insisted that man created his structure of reality in terms of this hidden order of feeling, and that the poet exercised this normal integrative function to an extraordinary degree, Dilthey was able to argue against the ancient premise, refurbished by the Romantics, that the poet had no control over his richest insights, since they emerged from madness. "The genius," he wrote, "is not a pathological phenomenon, but the healthy, the complete, human being."[87]

The third anti-mimetic proposition freed the artist from all rules. Dilthey agreed. The loosening of bonds in the world of learning since the Renaissance, had brought with it understanding that style and technique were norms of specific historical periods. Prescripts drawn from ancient works were discarded, and the poet was therefore liberated from forms and rules of the past, freed to draw the law of the beautiful and the rules of poetry from human nature. By the same token, it was impossible to project the future of poetry out of its present.[88]

The fact remained, however, that man's nature was his history. Art was a mirror of its time precisely because it represented a contemporary structure of principles, values, and goals that worked in various media. The artist could be free of technical, academic rules; unlimited possibilities for experimentation in form might extend before him. But there were tacit perimeters about his freedom. They were set, in the first place, by the enduring structure of the human mind and, in the second, by the state of consciousness existing in his society. The character and goals of education were defined by an unspoken national ideal. Likewise, in the arts, creative freedom was confined by nationality and by its cognate, language, as a system of concepts.[89]

The fourth anti-mimetic proposition derived from the equating of nature with art. How could any human work avoid becoming anachronistic as man changed his nature through his works? If art—or, more atomistically, the individual arts—were autonomous, how could one posit the unities and analogues of mimesis? Dilthey answered both questions in the same way. The entire course of culture was a process by which reason endlessly grew into nature. The crucial fact was that every work created in the process reproduced the dual character of the person who made it: although its style and medium were time-bound,

---

[86] *G.S.* 14/2: 524; 6: 150.   [87] *G.S.* 6: 91, 94. Makkreel, *Dilthey*, pp. 153f.

[88] *G.S.* 6: 126, 238, 236.   [89] *G.S.* 6: 230–236, 157; 14/2: 706f.

its content included something universal. That essential or typical component was the means by which people in other places and times recognized their likeness to the artist. It gave the work a symbolic life immune to anachronism, though capable of extreme mutations.[90] Access to the symbolic content of a work came through feeling and, for the scholar, through hermeneutic analysis. In either case, the past was appropriated by the present. The scholar certainly disclosed the content of the work in its own terms, but he did more. Giving access to the process by which a work was made in the past, and to the structured view of human life that it expressed, hermeneutic analysis also enlarged the experience of the present. On this second level, symbolic content was more than a souvenir of a moment that was irretrievably over. Rather, its foreign origins faded away when it was reconstructed into the fiber of the present.

Finally, Dilthey considered the fifth anti-mimetic proposition: that reality was a complex and random process that could not be reproduced in fixed and single images. His entire concept of hermeneutic analysis responded to this objection. Processes, not things, were the subject expressed in human arts; for inner representations by which one moved from one circle of feeling to another and finally to external expression were processes. The complexity was there, and the process displayed not a causal series so much as a patterned system of inter-relationships.[91] Dilthey considered the work itself a convergence of experiences, instead of a single image. The object of hermeneutic analysis, therefore, was not to disclose the static formula by which an artist had solved his problem. It was to retrieve the empirical movement by which he reached the solution: in other words, to imitate the original process of construction by which the work took shape.[92]

Dilthey's escape from the single image (and from the model of causal series, in which the single image was one episode, isolated and frozen) also appears in his historical thought. The three-level hierarchy that he drew, passing upward from autobiography to biography and finally to historiography, outlines a passage from the multi-faceted self-representation to the collective portrait. His own vast biographies of

[90] *G.S.* 6: 186f. Cf. ibid., pp. 280f.

[91] *G.S.* 14/2: 701. On Dilthey's exclusion of causality from the mental sciences, and its effects in the anti-scientism of Heidegger and Gadamer, see R. E. Palmer, *Hermeneutics. Interpretation Theory in Schleiermacher, Dilthey, Heidegger, and Gadamer* (Evanston, 1969), pp. 102, 126.

[92] *G.S.* 14/2: 706f.

Schleiermacher and Hegel illustrate that his concern was not narrative unity. Instead, he stripped history of its narrative qualities and described how concepts of the world were refracted in the minds of a circle of men. To this end, for example, he prepared to write the biography of Schleiermacher by composing biographical sketches of German Romantic philosophers associated with him.

How was Dilthey able to review his own theories and to conclude that the principles of imitation had been expelled from poetry and philosophy? One reason was that he held firmly to a rhetorical tradition, continuous from the Renaissance, that defined mimesis exclusively in terms of a misunderstanding of Aristotle. Although Aristotle's conception was extremely varied and comprehensive, the rhetorical tradition deformed it in two ways. First, it extracted one strand of the Aristotelian fabric, the axiom that poetry imitated action. Second, it interpreted this axiom in the light of Plato's equation between copying and imitating,[93] though Aristotle plainly did not mean literal reproduction. Though he knew Aristotle's writings intimately, Dilthey was captive to this ingrained tradition. Reading the past through pseudo-Aristotelian glasses, he described the liberation of poetry during and after the Renaissance as coming when men realized that poetry need not imitate a pre-existent reality but that it was a creative effort to make something that exceeded, or recreated, reality—an organ, like science and religion, by which the world was understood.[94] In the same fashion, he wrote that the genius of the portraitist lay not in rendering the sort of uncreative, exact likeness that could be gotten in a photograph, but rather in leading to a deeper understanding of the reality that he represented. Every imitative art[95] expressed a bond that gave life its coherence, and it was only at a moment when art was exhausted that naturalism—the literal reproduction of seen reality—appeared. In Dilthey's own day, he wrote, naturalism came as a protest against styles left over from the fifteenth and sixteenth centuries, an unwitting effort to create a new inner form for art generally, and a new style and technique in the individual arts.[96]

Misled by this narrow definition of mimesis, Dilthey discounted the degree to which his theories continued Aristotelian doctrines of form as they had been taken up and elaborated through the ages. In fact there are particularly close parallels with Aristotle in Dilthey's teachings:

---

[93] *Republic* 3. [94] *G.S.* 6: 110ff., 155.
[95] Painting, sculpture, and poetry of the epic and dramatic genres, *G.S.* 6: 277.
[96] *G.S.* 6: 281ff.

1. regarding the problem of solipsism, that the universal existed in the individual, that the two were radically interdependent, and that, in the case of man, reason and nature were equivalent;

2. regarding the unconscious, that the work became in actuality what the artist was in potentiality;

3. regarding freedom from rules, that the artist created something that never existed before, but that, in composing the picture in his mind, he was guided by social canons of beauty and probability—the counterpart of Dilthey's "acquired mental coherence (or nexus)"—which habit and education had written in his mind, as on a blank slate;

4. regarding the timeless and the time-bound in art, that the mimetic rapport of a work depended on the viewer's recognition of a universal element in it, and on his ability to internalize or relive the beauty displayed in the statue, or the passions represented on the stage, before him;

5. regarding the representation of process in a single image: (a) that the work of art was an organic—and not necessarily a logical—unit in which the parts and the whole mutually illuminated each other; and (b) that the unit was constituted by the movement of the artist's mind, which repeated itself in the critic's analysis and the viewer's experience, and which thereby entered their own mental worlds under the rubric that the mind became identical with the objects of its thought.

Dilthey also had in common with Aristotle the view that responsive mimesis of the audience or viewer was an essential means of learning, and hence, of society's general advancement.

Dilthey's profound originality lay in reconciling ancient doctrines such as these with the anti-mimetic results of eighteenth-century thought. In achieving that task, he naturally departed from ancient formulae. One departure was greater than the others: mimesis as he reconstituted it was ateleological. The unity that he sought in education as in life had no metaphysical goal, nor even a historical object. "For, in the mysterious and unfathomable countenance of life, with the laughing mouth and the sadly gazing eyes, all races of thinking and composing men try to read, and that too has no goal." Dilthey could not always accept the resulting lack of closure. He observed that his age had experienced a total shattering of concepts such as mankind had not seen since the end of the Greco-Roman world, with a consequent disorientation of cultural norms.[97] He recognized a sign of this

---

[97] *G.S.* 9: 172f.; 6: 287, 242, 245f.

disorientation in the absence of ideals free from time and space, in the dearth of victorious heroes, and in crises without authentic reconciliations that characterized the literature of his day. In literature, as in society itself, everything was becoming, moving listlessly, toward the unknown.[98] He regretted this openness and diffuseness, without always acknowledging that he had given it a philosophical rationale.

For Durkheim, the problem of unity lacked the heavy aesthetic colors that Dilthey gave it. A pronounced difference in method also divided the two men, for Durkheim excluded psychology from his research. And yet, they perceived the nature of disunity in similar ways, and incorporated mimesis in their efforts to systematize disorder.

Durkheim held the common view of education as an institution that imitated, manifested, and perpetuated the character of a given society. It was guided by a collective ideal of man, a portrait reflecting all the characteristic features of society itself.[99] The present educational system expressed the character of the nation, as distinct from the city-state of classical antiquity. Its fragmentation into academic specialties was due, in part, to the destruction of a unified tradition by the Renaissance humanists and, in great measure, to the instability of transition into which Europe fell with the French Revolution, and from which it had not emerged. Durkheim was aware that profound flux was part of Western culture's evolutionary transition, but he was reluctant to follow his own theories to their logical conclusion and to accept radical instability as representing collective values.

Education, he argued, should convey to the young the wholeness of a collective mentality (or consciousness), the interrelatedness of all aspects of life and, thus, of all academic disciplines that studied them. In his day, Durkheim wrote, the task was not to present a uniform model (as had been done, he believed, by teaching the classical curriculum). The approach to art, or patterns of behavior, through a few masterpieces or exemplary heroes no longer held. The contemporary task was to represent the intricacy and variability with which man responds to incalculably varied conditions and thereby to prepare the child to play his role in an increasingly specialized society. Durkheim continued to regard the prevailing disorder as an aberration rather than as a symbolic form of the collective mind. Thus, he held, the educational system spectacularly failed to achieve full integration because it was in-

[98] *G.S.* 6: 241f. Ermarth, *Critique,* pp. 17f.
[99] "Pedagogy and Sociology," in *Education,* pp. 122f.

formed by no commonly held purpose. Reform was overdue. It would not come from the natural sciences, however significant they were as creations of the human mind, however powerful they were in educating men to think with logical rigor.

Reform would come, Durkheim argued, from the constellation of sciences that served sociology, providing it with materials both for detailed comparative analyses and for overarching syntheses. History was valuable, not for itself or for its integrative powers, but for what the present could draw out of it for its own uses. History was a tool, and its practitioners should take their guidelines from sociology, which had superior powers of comparison and synthesis. Indeed, in the sociologist's generalizing labors, the primary tools of historical discourse—including chronology—were discounted. Ultimately, all historical data existed in the same dimension: the sociologist's present. Data about remote periods in the European past were equivalent to ethnographic data about contemporary tribal life in Australia. And yet sociology, which should achieve the integration of knowledge, was a new science, on the frontiers of its existence. Durkheim acknowledged that, while it had undoubted powers, there was no way to predict how it might finally achieve its task of unification.

Durkheim reasoned, as Dilthey did, that society took shape according to a distinct pattern, which its institutions self-reflexively expressed. He also thought that the unity of the intellectual world could be pursued through historical studies, with marginal attention to the natural sciences. But this hardly distinguished either scholar from Cardinal Newman. There were deeper similarities between the two sociologists.

Durkheim dismissed the challenge of solipsism much as Dilthey had done. The interdependence of the individual and the general appears in his argument that each human being had two characters: an inborn, personal one and an acquired, social one. Plato had argued that the ideal political order was the "soul writ large"; but Durkheim considered the soul and the collective life to be of entirely different, if intersecting, orders. Each person, he held, contributed to the formation of society through his natural insights and efforts. Man was born egotistical and anti-social. Society was artificial, a collectively made world, independent of nature and opposed to its antinomian character. Institutions, language, and religion had little contact with the world perceived through the senses. All of them were built according to a hidden complex of ideals, a social conscience that collective man had made according to models that he had also constructed from the manifold of experience. Education, the means by which the individual entered society was, in fact, a process by which human nature was de-natured, and the social conscience internalized. The two structures co-existed. They could become conterminous, with the result that individuality was suppressed by identity.[100]

Departing from this basic principle of reproduction, Durkheim also engaged the problem of the unconscious. No one could have given heavier weight than he to the decisive role of instinct in man's personal and collective life. No one could have mistrusted more profoundly than he the artistic and political cults of irrationality that flourished in the late nineteenth century. His two attitudes were not contradictory. For Durkheim believed that the unconscious had a logic and coherence beneficial to the social order. His study of suicide and his argument that crime was a necessary and ameliorative element in collective life alarmed critics. They judged that he had raised the unconscious, as a passionate, uncontrollable, and disruptive force, over the rational and constructive powers of mind. In fact, they overlooked his distinction between the individual and the collective conscience, each of which had its own hidden depths, its own specifications for enactment. Personal and social norms might diverge. Crime might indeed be a personal evil, but a social benefit in strengthening the collective evaluation of law and, occasionally, in anticipating the direction of moral growth. Ultimately, the evaluation of crime, in religious or secular society, depended on a generally and tacitly accepted structure of credence. For the unconscious from which social order, religion, and art came was the coherent order of interrelated forms—a structure of "faith and cult"—which orchestrated both conformity and dissent in a wider process of self-definition.

Durkheim thought of society, and its ethos, as a man-made composition, but he also considered it a complex organism. Accordingly, he appraised the institutions, norms, and practices of society according to their functions, a point of view that inevitably evoked comparisons with mechanical engineering. Each component of the social complex had its place, as a constituent organ, in the whole, inseparable from all

---

[100] On Durkheim's debate with Tarde on the subject of cultural mimesis, see S. Lukes, *Émile Durkheim. His Life and Work: A Historical and Critical Study* (New York, 1972), pp. 306–310. On the "de-naturing" results of education, ibid., pp. 125–127. For a critique of this teaching, see Wallwork, *Durkheim*, pp. 72–74. The result was that the concept of the uniformity of human nature, which Durkheim attributed to Renaissance humanists, had to be replaced by a concept of its extreme malleability under social norms. Ibid., pp. 142f., 156.

the others and acting interdependently with them. This emphasis on function led Durkheim to pay special attention to the diversification of labor within societies and to anticipate the day when specialized occupational groupings would replace the family in prescribing the ethics and goals of productive labor.

Where did originality fit into this scheme of things? Could any individual—an artist, for example, or a sociologist—act freely of rules? Durkheim recognized the power of one person to alter the state of knowledge, or even to create an entirely new area of knowledge, as he himself did in sociology. But, like Dilthey, he also insisted that habitual or inherited patterns of thought and behavior limited originality. Each man was an organ in a large, complex organism that lived through the interaction of its parts. Furthermore, nothing could be created out of nothing. The most basic and constructive innovations had to come by recasting inherited materials in new forms. The present shaped the model that the man of the future would reproduce.[101]

These assumptions presupposed a means of communication that persisted through time, and a method by which it could be decoded. The means was symbolism; the method, reconstruction of the past. Durkheim's emphasis on the symbolic function of religion and of other social institutions increased toward the end of his career, and, with his researches in ethnography, it became yet more apparent than in Dilthey's studies that the comparative study of symbolic forms placed all evidence on the same level. The primary object of the exercise was not to restore the evidence in its original historical context, or to use it to cast light on the experience of a particular culture, though both might be achieved. The major purpose was to derive conscious and unconscious patterns from evidence of varied times and peoples, and, if possible, by collating them to identify abstract forms, undefined by time or culture.

Outside the comparative methods of sociology, decomposition and reconstruction was the ordinary method by which any people delved into its own past, recovered unconscious bonds of unity, and re-examined their symbolic representations. Durkheim did not teach, as Dilthey did, that by this process one should disclose and relive the creative process followed by earlier men. Rather, he considered it a process of self-discovery, in which the collective conscience renewed

---

[101] "Evolution and the Role of Secondary Education," in *Education,* pp. 145, 149. On the "cult of the individual" in Durkheim's thought, see Wallwork, *Durkheim,* pp. 81f.

the norms that it reproduced in the minds of its present members and created the model that its future members would realize. Moreover, it was a process in which Durkheim transcended the causal chain, with its sequence of single images (except as a figure of speech), and replaced it with an incomprehensibly manifold causality, grasped as the interacting sum of things in society.

At times, Durkheim came close to Henry James's position that freedom was an illusion, since all fundamental patterns of thought and action were socially conditioned.[102]

Critics of Dilthey and Durkheim were entirely correct in finding powerful traces of scholastic philosophy in them. For the two men applied their own doctrines as they went about reconstructing their theories out of traditional materials. Their theories combined apparent opposites: empiricism and the poetry of mimesis. The identity of nature and art had been grafted onto philosophical theology by Schleiermacher and Hegel. Dilthey and Durkheim explored two ways in which that identity could be upheld, without accepting what they considered the atomization of thought by pragmatists, the regressive theology of Catholicism, or the self-destructive doctrines of revolutionary ideologues. They also held fast to their idealist heritage when they judged that existing society was deformed by comparison with an ideal order that it faintly anticipated, and that enlightened men and women should reshape the actual along the contours of the ideal.

Drawing together similarities between Dilthey and Durkheim, we can notice that they worked within a mimetic structure of credence having five major characteristics:

1. both an interdependence and an identity between the whole and its parts, between society and its individual members;

2. the origin of visible representations in an unconscious order;

3. an analogy of experience linking to the past even those who considered themselves most free of established rules;

4. the shared language of abstract symbolic forms, decoded intuitively by feeling and methodically by a systematic deconstruction and recomposition of objects; and

5. the abandonment of an ordered causal series, with its single

---

[102] On the obligation to obey, and the liberty to challenge, society's moral standards, see Wallwork, *Durkheim,* pp. 170ff.

images, in favor of the manifold images of a random process unified in hindsight by self-reflection.

The distinctive aspect of mimesis in the teachings of Dilthey and Durkheim was that it lacked closure. To be sure, the heuristic circle of image and archetype persisted in their work. It figured in the metaphysical vestiges, the "social realism," which their critics belabored. But the universals—the metaphysical archetypes—changed, and there was no eschatology, no historical goal of things. This absence of closure set the theories of Dilthey and Durkheim apart from the other nineteenth-century positions that I have mentioned. It also exemplified stresses brought to bear upon historical idealism.

The name Charles Darwin will indicate why, unlike earlier theories, theirs lacked closure. Both Dilthey and Durkheim were profoundly influenced by Darwin through the medium of Herbert Spencer's application of the theory of evolution to moral life. They did not fully realize that Spencer had drawn on pre-Darwinian ideas of evolution that led back to J.-P. Lamarck's (1744–1829) studies of animal and vegetal forms (and hence, more remotely, to Lamarck's predecessors). Nor did they appreciate that Darwin himself had rejected some of the theories that Spencer revived in his theories of society. What did they find persuasive in Spencerian Darwinism?

First was "the general analogy of nature." Building on precedents that reached into the seventeenth century, Darwin rendered untenable Aristotle's theory of fixed species. He displayed another world, one in which old species changed or became extinct and new ones appeared. Over against the Aristotelian world, he arrayed one in which selectivity in the struggle for existence did not run parallel with selective procedures of human reason, caught in the circle of its self-verification. The contours of the Darwinian world changed as the evolution of species—and therefore of their interrelations—went endlessly on. Still, the Aristotelian problems remained: problems of relating the universal to the particular, of conceiving an ultimate unity achieved through the coordination of parts, and of explaining the perpetuation of likeness through genetic reproduction. As the arguments of Spencer and his admirers, Dilthey and Durkheim, indicated, it was possible to draw analogues between nature so conceived and human experience.

Two particular concepts, moreover, had a bearing on our account. The first was the interplay that, according to Darwin, united the individual to its species, and its species to others. Aristotle had insisted that the individual was the primary reality, and Darwin presented a counterpart in his doctrine that the mutation of a species occurred through the "accumulation of innumerable slight variations," each appearing first in one individual, and then passing through its offspring into the genetic pool. Every individual was both the point at which all previous experiments intersected and the initiator of future experiments. In a sense, the individual was the living, concrete form of evolutionary process. Darwin therefore drew a picture of change as a series of random experiments in individual form, leading to a slow, progressive and general development.

The second particular concept explained how these experiments were made, and led from one to another. Darwin thought that selectivity took place through competition, through a struggle for existence, against the environment, against other species, and, most severely, against other members of the same species. It could occur by design, as in man's domestication of animals and plants. But even there, the process of natural variation and selection did not cease. Either in planned mutation or in mutation by unconscious response to competition, two elements were in play: inheritance (through the reproduction of permanent characters) and variability (through reaction to conditions of life). However mutation went on, form (or structure) followed function. How did the acquired characteristics of an organic modification suit the individual to cope with his environment? What degree of change was needed for the species to cope with it most efficiently? Grades of modification in countless individuals, tested in the complex relations of life, would decide the issue. The beauty of nature, Darwin argued, was demonstrated in the laws of trial and error by which the fittest was proven and the unsuitable extinguished, processes that, as he wrote, favored the good and rejected the bad. Beauty, good, and bad were terms of form; but they were defined in terms of function. The decisive question, put to any form, was "Does it work?"

The strains on historical idealism in the theories of Dilthey and Durkheim came from views such as these concerning the empirical and accidental production of form. Some difficulties inevitably arose from the effort to combine Darwinian and pre-Darwinian ideas. One of these concerned how the mimetic archetype was defined. Like any historical idealist, Dilthey and Durkheim wished to transcend the limits of the historical situation, and especially to absorb the basic historical unity, the individual person, into metahistorical categories. Unlike other idealists, however, they did not assume that the ideal, the object of imitation, necessarily existed as anything more than a collective function, put together and elaborated over time. They did not claim for it the objective reality that Plato ascribed to the Forms, for example, or Christian theologians did to ideas in the mind of God, or Hegel, to the Absolute Spirit. If the object existed at all, it inhabited the regions of the unconscious, of feeling. Whether it existed or not was irrelevant, however. One was concerned only with phenomena that pretended to represent it, just as any cultural artifact—a statue, a painting, or a drama—could represent an object that never existed. What one can disclose through the phenomena and artifacts is the collective mentality, the context that makes the ideal thinkable. The value of an ideal was not its truth but its function. Durkheim and his followers represented this stance so fully that, in their designs of social structure, they seemed to go about their studies as though they were mechanics or engineers. As an artifact, or fiction—something made in response to perceived needs—does it solve the problems to which it is addressed? Within the common structure of credence, does it work?

Other stresses on historical idealism concern the process of imitation. Lacking a metaphysical or historical end, the process as a whole was directionless. It moved by chance or accident, rather than by a natural attraction of the finite to the infinite or a providential design. The important thing about imitation was precisely that it could not be described as a single movement. Even causality was inadequate to explain the complex interplay of multiple relationships involved. What an ideal, or a statue, expresses is the process by which it was created, an endless network of construction, decomposition, and reconstruction by countless minds. A work of art represents this manifold experience more than it does the spirit of its particular age, or the identity of its maker, and, through it, the viewer becomes a participant in the process of making.

Finally, the arguments of Dilthey and Durkheim indicated the perplexities of historical idealism by weakening the ties of narrative unity. Both men grounded their theories on history, and explained the existing state of culture—in art or pedagogy, for example—in terms of sequences that ran back from the nineteenth century to Charlemagne and, in some respects, to classical Greece. But to their minds, history was a matter of sequence, rather than of identity, of duration, rather than continuity. Their accounts of art or education record series of experiments without beginning, middle, or end, having only such meaning and coherence as lay in the mind of the beholder or in the collective self-appraisal of society. For historical depth as well as continuity was undercut by the argument that all works, of whatever age, co-existed in the labile present, as materials for the anonymous and collective labor of reconstruction.

These characteristics indicate the strangeness—and perhaps the breakdown—of historical idealism in the theories of Dilthey and Durkheim. They do not alter the fact that mimetic formulae gave coherence to those theories, and that, through the teachings of Dilthey and Durkheim, the formulae have persisted not only in the social sciences but also in theories of education, in philosophy (especially phenomenology), and in various areas of historical analysis, including classical philology. Indeed, they also may provide a clue to the persistent question of Cubism's place in the traditions of painting. For the rejection of the single image, irreality of the object, the multiplicity of relationships achieved and expressed through experiments in decomposition and reconstruction, the concept of the work as expressing a creative process that engages the participation of the viewer, the appraisal of a work in terms of its function (or its elegance as the solution to a problem), and the abandonment of narrative unities were pronounced features of Cubism, combined, as in these theories of society, with a limitless search for universal forms.

Chapter 16

Epilogue: On the *longue durée*
of Mimesis

"To recognize the bonds that unite patristic mediation to the most advanced elements of contemporary thought is to discover a paradoxical unity of Western thought beyond the superficial divergences of beliefs and ideologies."
—René Girard, *"To double business bound." Essays on Literature, Mimesis, and Anthropology* (Baltimore, 1978), p. 7.

THE WORDS "classical tradition" connote symmetry, balance, and harmony. Obviously, the tradition did include canons of form, but it could not have survived long without strategies for criticism, assimilation, and timely change. I have been concerned with one of those strategies. The career of mimesis illustrates how hostile the strategies of reform were to rigid formalism. The lifeless, redundant laws of academic "classicism" had nothing but an empty name in common with imitation as the tradition defined it: that is, as the nucleus of a program for perfection in art, morality, and social institutions.

Culture lives by two clocks—the one ticking away daily and hourly changes, and the other marking events of glacial slowness. The fleeting norms of an age—classicism, for example—are measured by the first clock. The programmatic level of culture synchronizes itself with the *longue durée* of the second, and it is there that we have found the strategy of mimesis.

Hardly anyone would question that societies and cultures unconsciously procreate and reform themselves by mimetic processes. Dilthey and Durkheim were authors who drew parallels between those modeling processes and the formative impulses in biological evolution, as did Bagehot, Spencer, and many others before and after them.

I have been concerned with an entirely self-conscious tradition that developed mimesis as a strategy of how to pass from an impaired existence to wholeness of life. I have argued that, from the earliest days of

Western civilization, the strategy, with its promise of wholeness, played a role in cognitive (and social) evolution analogous to unconscious mechanisms of genetic reproduction and mutation. Ancient philosophers defined three areas in which mimetic strategies operated. The first was in the involuntary processes of nature, where mimesis impelled the cycles of planetary motion, of the seasons, and of biological reproduction. The second was in the practical area of the arts, each of which was guided by a number of mimetic strategies, corresponding with the special function of that art. The third was in the speculative area where men—especially philosophers and theologians—deliberated on the asymmetry between nature and art and, by critical thought, mediated between those poles. The self-conscious and critical mediation between nature and art has been my theme. "Nature" has meant what man could or ought to be; "art," what he is. I have maintained that, throughout the long centuries from classical Athens on to the present day, the concept of mimesis was quite deliberately framed and reframed in the area between nature and art as a tool that man used to shape his individual and collective identities, and that the parallel to genetic change was explicitly drawn, never more explicitly than in Christian doctrines of rebirth by imitation.

Discontinuities and continuities have turned up in this account. How should they be weighed? Much depends on one's point of view. Discontinuities are most pronounced if mimesis is emphasized as a term of art or a matter of style; and continuities are accentuated if mimesis is regarded as a conscious program, or strategy, of mediation. I have followed the latter course.

Plato, the father of the mimetic tradition, foresaw that his idealist philosophy could be applied to actual society, but he also grasped the cost. If philosophers were given control of a community, he wrote, their first act would be to abolish all existing practices and institutions. Having wiped the slate clean, they would compose an entirely new constitution, patterned on the universal forms revealed to them, but hidden from the great mass of humanity (*Republic* VI. 497, 501). Centuries passed before Plato's vision of a militant minority revolutionizing the social order according to idealist principles came true in the Christianization of the Roman Empire. And then it became clear that the strategy of mimesis demanded reform, not as a single act, but as a continual process, since the asymmetry between ideal and actual could never be resolved into equivalence. The reformers had to be reformed. This slowly learned lesson continued into modern times.

In the philosophies of Plato and Aristotle, mimesis was a term of mediation in nature, in art, and in the area between them. The further distinction between art and particular works of art was primary. This distinction rendered mimesis something more than a term of style. Mimesis inhered, not in the thing made (a picture or a play), but in the process, or strategy, of making—or, to be exact, a process of modeling. Mimesis was above all an explanation of change, of how one thing could change, or be made to change, into something else. Asymmetry might not be resolved, but it could be mediated. True to antique norms of compositional unity, the explanation took account of a beginning, a middle, and an end. The middle term, mediating between exemplar and copy, or between potential and actual states of existence, had an essential role; it, or he, was the means of change. An effective mediator could be neither exemplar nor copy; it had to possess characteristics of each. This meant that it held the fullness of the exemplar and the neediness of the copy, and that, in its very being, it expressed the ambiguity of its function. Since change (in art or in growth) involves suffering, the mediator was also subject to the yearning that the copy had for the archetype and the pain that it experienced in being transformed by assimilation to it.

For Plato, love was the mediating term; for Aristotle, growth; for Christians, Christ. Indeed, Christology kept asymmetry, and the combination of mediation and mimesis, at the heart of Western culture from the apostolic age onward. The two natures of Christ—divine and human—served as foci for different mimetic strategies, relating man, as image, to God, his archetype, and writers employed them in various ways according to their particular theological convictions. The genetic model of rebirth through imitation followed from these doctrines.

Like Plato's love, Christ, as Logos, served one kind of mimesis: mimesis by reversion, through which the copy returned to a primordial archetype. It was part of the dramatic scenario of egress and return that passed from Platonic teachings about the soul into the Christian doctrine of man's creation, fall, and redemption. However, unlike Plato's love, Christ, as Logos, provided a model for historical progress through stages of perfection, in a strategy of growth that, before theologies of the Logos took shape, Aristotle located in the processes of nature. As head of the Church, the first-born of many brethren, Christ set a paradigm of mimesis by augmentation, manifesting in the ever-growing company of believers a mystery hidden from the beginning of the world.

Mimesis by augmentation on the cosmic level advanced by the complex act of individual conversion, which engaged mediation of another sort, and augmentation within the particular soul. In the cumulative process of its regeneration in conformity with Christ, the individual soul was seen to act as mediator to itself. Mimesis by reversion emphasized one aspect of the conversion process: assimilation to an archetype outside the soul through a mediator that also came from outside. By contrast, as it mediated to itself, the soul advanced through quasi-embryonic phases by building itself up from within. This second aspect of the conversion process took place through mimesis by augmentation on the personal, not the cosmic, level. Through augmentation, as St. Augustine wrote, the individual soul was changed "from form into form."[1]

The Fathers never forgot that people were not born, but reborn, as Christians. The soul was like a statue being carved, but it was also the sculptor. The artist was an integral part of the composition. Combining aesthetic and genetic metaphors, Gregory of Nyssa captured the point at which imitation and innovation became identical in the modeling process. "After a fashion, we are," he wrote, "fathers to ourselves, giving birth to ourselves as whatever we want to be, and, by our own decision, shaping ourselves into whatever form we choose."[2] Gregory also described the process of augmentation through which the soul was transformed into higher and higher modes of likeness to God. It advanced struggling against itself. Every stage of perfection through which it passed was subsumed in the next. Every stage was ambiguously both the end of previous stages and the means for later ones, won at the cost of self-negation. Every stage was a new beginning, and the entire process of mimetic transformation passed "from beginnings to beginnings through beginnings that have no end." As a modern scholar has commented, "the 'reality' of man [for Gregory] is not to *be* spiritual, but continuously to *become* so. In this sense, *Wandlung* is the very reality of man."[3] Such was the process of rebirth by which human beings fulfilled their vocation to be, not men, but "gods and children of the Most High."[4]

The strategies of mimesis by reversion and augmentation were

---

[1] *De Trinitate* 15. 8 (*Corp. Christ. ser. lat.* 50 A: 480).

[2] *Life of Moses,* Theoria II. 3–4, in *La Vie de Moïse ou Traité de la perfection en matière de vertu,* Jean Daniélou, ed. (2d ed. [Paris, 1956], pp. 32f.). As Daniélou points out, Gregory here drew on a Judaic tradition also employed by Philo and Origen.

[3] Jean Daniélou, "The Dove and the Darkness in Ancient Byzantine Mysticism," *Papers from the Eranos Yearbooks,* vol. 5: *Man and Transformation* (London, 1964), pp. 280, 284, 295.

[4] Above, Chapter 3, note 10.

therefore attached to Christ's divine nature and to the soul's regeneration through a quasi-genetic process. When the Fathers turned to Christ's human nature (that is, to the historical event of the Incarnation), they conceived strategies of inversion and subversion. These strategies enabled writers to explain how the Incarnation made it possible to understand the apparently contradictory shifts in moral standards (as between the Old and New Testaments) and the overthrow of one institution by another (as when the Church superseded the Synagogue) as episodes in a coherent process of advancement, in which each stage was both end and means, subsuming and completing all previous stages, and containing the seeds of the next.

By the ninth century, the strategies of inversion and subversion had lost their independent functions; they had been grafted onto the strategies of reversion and augmentation, notably onto the latter so as to elucidate the "concorporation" or "convisceration" of believers in the growing body of Christ, endlessly expanding in their own flesh the manifestations of His humanity. Through various permutations, the permanent asymmetries of image and archetype and potential and actual and the union of mediation and mimesis in Christology continued to inform historical interpretations during the entire period under review, and not least in nineteenth-century German philosophies of history.

A major element in this account has been the combination, by the Church Fathers, of circular and rectilinear movements in the same concept of historical progress. Mimesis established a circular relation between archetype and image (and potential and actual states of existence), but a basic dissimilarity, and thus a tension, remained. Asymmetry was permanent. The movement of the image to the archetype—of the soul to God, or of mankind toward the fulfillment of God's redemptive plan—was therefore never closed. It described a spiral, or helix, instead of a closed circle. Out of this abiding tension and circularity came the progressive rebirth of the soul and of the world. Thus, mimetic circulatory and rectilinear advance were combined in the same view of human experience.

A double conservatism—first, of literary culture in religion and philosophy and, second, of educational, civil, and ecclesiastical institutions—kept these ways of thinking about patterning change alive into modern times. I have held that some elements of the concept of conversion served as a paradigm, first, for theories about the historical transformation of the Church (Christ's *corpus mysticum*) and, later, for doctrines concerning the self-regeneration of secular society. This was particularly true of mimesis by augmentation, with its ambiguity of means and end. When strategies of mimesis entered their secular phases, society, state, and nation were portrayed as mediators between a defective present and an ideal future life; they shouldered the ambiguity and the suffering of mediators in earlier mimetic doctrines.

Education was a paramount concern of those who worked in the area between nature and art, both for the formation of a community and for the training of an enlightened élite to guide it. The Church Fathers consciously and deliberately built a system of methods for the spread, development, and enforcement of Christian doctrine, including the intellectual strategies considered here. The tactics of the liberal arts, philosophical reasoning, and coercion that they employed permanently marked the career of mimesis. Thus, the impetus of tradition lay behind not only the ideas of Hegel and his heirs but also the actions of governments and parties that embraced those ideas, and it characterized especially the educational reforms that they instituted.

Clearly, continuities with earlier methods of thought and tactics of coercion were to be expected in formal idealisms and in their political and educational incarnations. However, it must be emphasized that, while Hegelianism and its offshoots took root in the minds of individual scholars, they also drew on collective, inherited wisdom. For the earlier paradigms of mimesis had permeated the thinking of all orders of society, together with the assumption that the true pattern of change, and the duty of achieving it, had been entrusted to a militant minority. The extraordinary appeal that the writings of Boehme, a cobbler in a remote Silesian village, had for Issac Newton and the parallels between the doctrines of religious enthusiasts of the eighteenth century and quasi-pantheistic philosophies of the same time make this point. Long, pervasive, and universal experience, and the role conceded by tradition to militant minorities, set the stage for various socialist movements in the nineteenth century. The mutual resonances between academic and popular culture made possible the otherwise improbable effects of philosophy. Heine noted them when he wrote that, given Kant's impact on revolutionary thought, the people of Königsberg should have trembled before him as though he were their executioner. Engels alluded to one side of the mutual exchanges in his famous epigram, "The German workers' movement is the heir of German classical philosophy."[5]

---

[5] *Ludwig Feuerbach und der Ausgang der klassischen deutschen Philosophie,* ch. 4, Karl Marx-Friedrich Engels, *Werke* (Berlin, 1962) 21: 307.

As part of the classical tradition, the strategy of mimesis in a field of permanent asymmetry belonged not only to Hegel and his intellectual heirs but to many writers who were bound by entirely different commitments. The spectrum of mimetic theories includes the doctrines of Newman as well as those of Marx, those of Pope Pius IX as well as of Durkheim and Dilthey. The history of mimesis did not follow a single line of development, nor could this be expected of a concept that demanded progress by relentless self-criticism of every system of thought or belief, and that accepted conflict as a means of progress.

"New" and "old" can be homonyms, if not synonyms, in the language of tradition. Mimesis by reversion survived in nineteenth-century theology, and, through religious belief, it continued to be one determinant of the mental orientations and the private and collective acts of men. What applies to this, the earliest of our paradigms, can also be said of the others. New and old phases co-existed in the same age, and even in the same minds. Together, they gave tradition enormous flexibility in the work of adaptation, but they also multiplied the possibilities for personal anguish, sectarian dispute, and ideological warfare.

Any tradition exhibits the contemporaneity of past and present phases. But at the center of my theme, beyond the elaborate dogmas and forms and institutions that the mechanisms of tradition can convey, a simple need exists—a need for wholeness. Throughout his life, Marx delighted in classical literature, and, by intellectual alchemy, he transmuted some ancient doctrines into his own economic and social teachings. A crucial instance was a doctrine of Aristotle that proved to be the point of departure for Marx's theory of values. Marx was also spurred to work by his acute sense of man's estrangement from society and from himself. More than once, he referred to the progressive role that imitation had in the reflex between the classical tradition and the need for wholeness. In a text that he drafted for *A Contribution to the Critique of Political Economy,* he asked how it was possible that the art and poetry of ancient Greece could still give us aesthetic pleasure, and that they could still be considered, in some ways, as unattainable ideals. Gunpowder had made Achilles obsolete. The printing press had expelled the muse of epic poetry. Greek art presupposed mythology: that is, the imaginative representation of a particular people's natural and social conditions. Those conditions had irrevocably passed. Nevertheless, Marx concluded, the Greeks exert on us the sort of charm that children exercise on adults, who, although they can not become children again, try to reproduce a child's truthfulness on a higher level.

In the interplay between past and present that impels tradition to change, every generation grasps for the ideal as a child may thrust himself toward the image in a mirror. The stakes are high. If the reflector is opaque, one risks shattering the image. The wager is that the reflector will prove to be penetrable and that, seeing through the glass darkly, mankind can cease to be captivated by illusions about itself, as it was in its childhood, and possess the realities. This is a wager that, here and now, men reflect and need to conform inwardly with a great ideal. Those with mentalities that do not conform with the ideal may be either animals in human form or gods. This way of thinking began in Plato's stroke of poetic madness. In opposition to all human reason, it entered the cultural dynamics of Europe because man's life is unified, in part, by passions, including faith. And so, the generations have insatiably played a real and awesome game, staking humanity as it is against humanity as it ought to be, always knowing that, in this game, only the risks were certain.

Appendix

Thinking Mimetically About History: Some Bibliographical Orientations

I BEGAN the present essay to determine why historians had stood aloof from scholarly debate over mimesis and what they might contribute to general discourse if they did intervene. The enterprise has led me to reconsider the way in which mimesis has generally been discussed, primarily by students of the visual and literary arts. Two results, in particular, may be clarified by a wider bibliographical discussion than has been possible elsewhere in the essay. The first is the distinction between thinking mimetically and being mimetic, and my resulting argument that mimesis should be regarded primarily as a way of thinking, rather than as a technique of style. The second is the assumption that there was a mimetic tradition.

A Matter of Philosophical Commitment

A major contention of the present essay is that mimesis should be regarded, above all, as a strategy of change that runs through many styles. Indeed, as an abstract critical strategy, it was used for the radical correction of deficiencies of style, and even for the subversion of one style by another.[1] Operating between nature and art, it extended from practice, to method, to the yet higher intellectual level of theory. The distinction between thinking mimetically and being mimetic was obvious to Plato, who would have excluded imitative poets from his Republic of idealist philosophers.[2] Not long after Plato, the painter, Eupompus, struck the same distinction when he repudiated people

---

[1] See E. H. Gombrich, *The Ideas of Progress and Their Impact on Art* (New York, 1971), pp. 4, 14–18.
[2] R. G. Collingwood, *The Principles of Art* (New York, 1958), pp. 48–50.

who slavishly copied his works. "Nature is to be imitated," he said, "not the artist."[3]

I have been particularly concerned with the habit of thinking mimetically about history. From the preceding discussion, it should be apparent that this habit may have been gained, and was certainly internalized, by the discipline of philosophical commitment. Conversely, there are non-mimetic or anti-mimetic habits of thinking about history, and the first point that I must register here is that the place that mimetic theories of history played in the evolution of Western culture may well have been obscured in recent times by a widespread hostility to integrative theories of human experience.

Recently, the landscape of non-mimetic ways of understanding the past has become densely populated. No one would question that new cultural forms actually take shape within old ones, and reflect them, even as they subvert them.[4] But it takes more than this to constitute a theory of mimetic change. Awareness of the discontinuity and multiplicity of things has aroused mistrust of broad, integrative theories, especially those that—like mimesis—purport to explain change in terms of analogy. The danger of using analogies in interpreting the past was that facts could be obscured or falsified, by metaphor. Evidence could be substituted for proof and woven together with the reckless abandon of poetic license. If this occurred, history was "nothing but poetry without the wings."[5] Thus, many historians argue that

[3] Pliny *Hist. nat.* 34. 19.

[4] A particularly fine statement of this fact occurs in Louis Althusser, "On the Young Marx," in *For Marx* trans. B. Brewster (London, 1977), pp. 85f.: "And if we are prepared to stand back a little from Marx's discovery so that we can see that he founded a new scientific discipline and that this *emergence* itself was analogous to all the great *scientific discoveries* of history, we must also agree that no great discovery has ever been made without bringing to light a new object or a new domain, without a new horizon of meaning appearing, a new land in which the old images and myths have been abolished—but at the same time the inventor of this new world must of absolute necessity have prepared his intelligence *in the old forms* themselves, he must have learnt and practised them, and by criticizing them formed a taste for and learnt the art of manipulating abstract forms in general, without which familiarity he could never have conceived *new ones with which to think the new object.* In the general context of the human development which may be said to make urgent, if not inevitable, all great historical discoveries, the individual who makes himself the author of one of them is of necessity in the paradoxical situation of *having to learn the way of saying what he is going to discover in the very way he must forget.*"

[5] In late Roman antiquity, this view was expressed by Lucian of Samosata, *The Way to Write History,* ch. 8. Above, Chapter 3, note 7.

their legitimate task is to dismantle theories built up by analogical inference, prying individual facts loose from settings into which ideologies have wedged them, and then, if need be, to think again "about the patterns into which they might fall." Thus, historical study is reduced "into a kind of *pointillisme*," and "complex phenomena" are broken apart into their simplest components.[6]

The evidence is permitted to speak for itself; no architectonic theory of change is imposed upon it. Theory follows facts; but there is no great need for theory. Anti-mimetic results of this conviction become apparent when the evidence is so vast that no pattern emerges from the *pointillisme*. They become equally apparent when the evidence is fragmentary, as is the case, for example, in research based on medieval statistics. There, one may be able to recover a frozen image, a "snapshot," from a given moment, reflecting a limited aspect of collective life in a specific place. The connecting moments between snapshots and the processes of transformation are lost beyond recovery. With luck, one could accumulate a vast number of still photographs and incorporate them into a moving picture.[7] But, as Bergson observed long ago, one would have only an illusion of movement drawn from snapshots strung together on a continuous film and run through the projecting apparatus of one's own knowledge and presuppositions. The illusion would be external to the snapshots and, more to the point, external to the subjects that they portrayed; it would be projected upon them by the viewer.[8] One could not assume that an integrating theory of change imposed upon the evidence corresponded to reality; one would be left with an accumulation of still photographs that could be sorted into different sequences, chronological or not.

Pointillisme and the snapshot are, therefore, two metaphors for non-mimetic, and even anti-mimetic, historical study. There is a revealing contrast between the snapshot metaphor and Hegel's description of history as a gallery of pictures.[9] Like photographs, Hegel's pictures were frozen, isolated moments. The important thing for Hegel, however, was not the pictures themselves, but the process by which the entire series had been made. The important thing was the process of mi-

---

[6] E. g., Theodore Zeldin, *France, 1848–1945* (Oxford, 1977) 2: 1155–1156.

[7] David Herlihy and Christiane Klapisch-Zuber, *Les Toscans et leurs familles. Une étude du catasto florentin de 1427* (Paris, 1978), pp. 12, 165, 617. The metaphor of fitting snapshots into a continuous film occurs on p. 12.

[8] Henri Bergson, *Creative Evolution* trans. Arthur Mitchell (London, 1912), pp. 321–324.

[9] *Phänomenologie des Geistes,* 764. Above, Chapter 14, at note 6.

metic self-recognition and alienation by which the Spirit moved through time. The pictures were only remembrances of the Spirit's previous manifestations. Hegel's subject was the integrative process hidden within events, and mediating between them, not its fragmentary, visible results, the pictures.

A further word in this general subject may be helpful. Thinking mimetically is a discipline conveyed by the classical tradition. It was Neitzsche's insight that the tradition was motivated by two complementary impulses. Under the Apollinian impulse, an artist took his guidance from dreams, or inner visions; he expressed himself visually (as in sculpture); and, given the nature of his materials, he created a stable, particularized work—a statue or a painting, for example—that could be taken in at one instant. His aim was to convey the sense of beauty, calm, and moderation. By contrast, under the Dionysian impulse, an artist was spurred to act, not by inner vision, but by ecstasy that raised him beyond his own powers, and that worked upon him from the outside, making the artist himself a work of art. He expressed himself non-visually (as in music), and he created a fluid, ever-shifting work that was not formed so much as performed, a work that took shape over time and that required memory and reflection from its audience. Finally, instead of ideal serenity, he conveyed the passion and intoxication by which, in an act of creative imagination, he was able to reconcile isolated and hostile elements in a universal harmony.

Nietzsche argued that, in ancient Greece, an artist actually drew on both kinds of inspiration; and other writers have demonstrated how, throughout the long career of the classical tradition, the sweetness and light of the Apollinian impulse was twinned with the fire and strength of the Dionysian.

The two impulses correspond with our distinction between being mimetic and thinking mimetically. Expressed visually, in a stable, objective form, according to standards of clarity and proportion, the Apollinian corresponds with the representation of reality in works of art: that is, with being mimetic, as a statue or painting may be. Expressed non-visually, in an elusive intellectualized form, according to standards of universal harmony, the Dionysian corresponds with thinking mimetically. Thus, insofar as our subject is an abstract one—thinking mimetically—it belongs to the Dionysian strain in the classical tradition and, consequently, in humanistic disciplines. Insofar as the subject is particular—thinking mimetically about the past—the Dionysian idea that passion and ecstasy informed the creative imagination took root especially in systems that, like Christianity and Hegelianism, were at home with mystery.

However, the two strands have rarely combined in the work of the same author. The prevalence of non-mimetic ways of thinking about the past may be new; however, the failure of discourse between those who think mimetically about the past and those who do not is an old phenomenon. There have been distinguished examples of opposition—and even of non-comprehension—between writers who practiced this way of evaluating evidence and others who rejected or even failed to recognize it.

These disputes have not contributed as much as they should have done to the understanding the deep issues that they stirred up. They have passed with a flurry of articles and reviews, leaving behind little awareness of how perfectly able scholars could address one another with such a lack of mutual understanding. The further result—or non-result—is that the investigation of the historical career of mimesis has not advanced.

During and just after the Second World War, two scholarly disputes arose that elucidated the philosophical issues of thinking mimetically about the past. The first engaged two colleagues at the John Hopkins University, Leo Spitzer and Arthur O. Lovejoy. The second centered on Eric Auerbach's book, *Mimesis: The Representation of Reality in Western Literature,* and it consisted of a debate, running for some years, between Auerbach and his critics. It is possible to consider both controversies as episodes in a recurrent confrontation. Spitzer and Auerbach were philologists, experts in classical and modern European languages. They had been educated and had begun their academic careers in Germany. They fled from Nazism; found refuge in Istanbul; and eventually secured academic positions in the United States.

One interest of these controversies is precisely that they arose when Spitzer and Auerbach had just found themselves in the unfamiliar intellectual and social environment of the New World. Another is that the controversies arose among scholars who were fully conversant with mimetic themes and with the literatures that expressed them. One of Spitzer's major studies concerned the idea of the world as a great harmonious structure, an idea that persisted through the centuries, he argued, exactly because European culture nurtured faith in an underlying pattern, or order, that was reflected in the composition of the world. He challenged Arthur Lovejoy, a philosopher whose book, *The Great Chain of Being,* dealt with a primary metaphor and principle of

Platonic (or rather Neoplatonic) and therefore mimetic thought. Auerbach's treatise, *Mimesis,* treated different perceptions of reality at various stages of European history and the marks that those variations left at turning-points in the development of literature. A number of his critics were also entirely familiar with the fact and the idea of mimesis.

At first glance, the controversies might appear to have been squabbles among literary critics, all of them grounded in classical languages and literatures and prepared to find repercussions of antiquity in modern thought and expression. And yet there were profound differences.

Spitzer identified the differences in his challenge to Lovejoy. In his introduction to *The Great Chain of Being,* Lovejoy had compared the history of ideas with analytic chemistry. Like the chemist, the historian of ideas was to break individual systems of thought into their component elements, "unit ideas." Spitzer objected that this mode of analysis tore apart the fabric of thought; it left a student with an unintegrated plurality, and thus it could not "explain historical events." By contrast with the history of ideas, he continued, *Geistesgeschichte* did function synthetically, disclosing "the total system of ideas charged with emotion that explains an historical movement." Spitzer traced the clash of disciplines to the divergence of French and German scholarship. Lovejoy, he contended, derived principles for the history of ideas ultimately from the French Encyclopedists, while he himself, as an advocate of *Geistesgeschichte,* stood in a tradition that had roots in the revived Neoplatonism of German philosophy and that reached its full development in the nineteenth and early twentieth century, with Burckhardt, Dilthey, and Tröltsch.[10]

Lovejoy wrote from outside Neoplatonic traditions; Spitzer and Auerbach from inside them. Lovejoy concluded that the Great Chain of Being belonged to an outmoded system of thought, a philosophical depiction of nature that, certainly, had left a residue in various areas of culture, but that had been discredited by the rise of empirical sciences. Many of Auerbach's critics also expressed detachment from the subject of imitation, regarding it as a theme in science, or rhetoric, or aesthetics that belonged to a previous dispensation, one that had passed in the eighteenth century.

The argument could certainly be made that Spitzer did not do justice to Lovejoy's wide familiarity with German scholarship or to the depth of the sense of beauty that drew him, especially, to poetry. It

---

[10] Leo Spitzer, *"Geistesgeschichte* vs. History of Ideas as Applied to Hitlerism," *Journal of the History of Ideas* 5 (1944): esp. pp. 191, 201. Arthur O. Lovejoy, "Reply to Professor Spitzer," ibid., pp. 204–219.

could also be held that Lovejoy's analytical methods, acceptance of the demolition of old knowledge as necessary to progress, and recognition of confusion as a normal state in human affairs were all more appropriate to historical inquiry than Spitzer's contrary ideas.

However, my point is that mimesis was a living reality for Spitzer and Auerbach; it provided the sanction of long centuries for change within continuity. Spitzer believed that the mimetic idea of the world as a musical composition had been driven from culture as a whole between the Reformation and the Enlightenment; but he also continued to believe in the essential necessity of the idea. Its collapse was a prelude to the events that had destroyed his professional life and cast him into an alien world. But he could not write about it as something dead and meaningless. "We have in our republic of letters too many scholars whose abstract coolness is due largely to their lack of belief in what they have chosen to study, and I feel that the scholar cannot adequately portray what he does not love with all the fibers of his heart."[11] As Auerbach also surveyed the ruins of his world, he hoped that his study would find readers among his friends of former years "if they are still alive," as well as among others, and that it would "contribute to bringing together again those whose love for our western history has serenely persevered."[12]

In Spitzer's view, the history of ideas as practiced by Lovejoy atomized what had been integral structures of thought, feeling, and action in the past, while *Geistesgeschichte* was more true to life in seeking to recover organic wholes.

It is evident from his response that Lovejoy resented assertions that he had dismantled the integrity of an ethos, particularly by discounting emotional factors. However, his response to Spitzer, and his own writings, including the declaration of editorial policy with which he launched the *Journal of the History of Ideas,* indicates the core of truth in Spitzer's assessment. He stated the *Journal*'s objectives without specifically mentioning *Geistesgeschichte,* but he plainly had it in mind when he took his stand against "affective" and "sociological" explanations. Practitioners of *Geistesgeschichte,* and none more than Dilthey, had advanced exactly those kinds of explanations, resting them, moreover, on the ability of historians to build their explanations around an empathetic—indeed, an aesthetic—participation in the past through

---

[11] *Classical and Christian Ideas of World Harmony. Prolegomena to an Interpretation of the Word "Stimmung"* (Baltimore, 1963), p. 4.

[12] *Mimesis: The Representation of Reality in Western Literature* (Princeton, 1953), p. 557.

its surviving evidence. Lovejoy judged that the aesthetic address to evidence was illicit; it played on the insights and feelings of present people, saying nothing about the past. In Lovejoy's view, the historian had to approach his evidence objectively, as documents, rather than as stimuli of his own feelings.

Lovejoy went further. Without discounting the emotions altogether, he opposed emphasizing "non-rational motives for other men's reasonings." Logic was a major "operative factor in the history of thought." Indeed, throughout the course of European civilization, Lovejoy detected a persistent, deep-seated "aversion from manifest and admitted irrationality," and a corresponding appeal "to common rational principles." He exemplified this central and enduring appeal by referring to three great figures of the English Enlightenment, Locke, Berkeley, and Hume—philosophers who stressed the empirical and atomistic character of thought.[13]

Naturally, Lovejoy regarded Spitzer's challenge as obtuse, and there was no meeting of the minds between the two colleagues. Spitzer considered evidence as manifestations of *Geist;* Lovejoy thought they were historical documents. Spitzer sought out links and transitions, improbable survivals and permutations, while Lovejoy looked for inconsistencies and discontinuities. Spitzer admitted the impulses of feeling, particularly of aesthetic feeling, to the repertoire of human motivation and to the techniques of historical synthesis; but Lovejoy eschewed non-rational motives and gave first place to logic among human motives and historical methods. When he took up an essay by Spitzer, Lovejoy would not find the attention to logical, and chronological, distinctions that he regarded as paramount. He would find vast erudition, to be sure, but, over the space of two pages, he might also read about a large number of writers, ranging from classical antiquity to the twentieth century, mixed up without regard for chronological order or *genre* or historical context. Spitzer thought that he was "continuously rediscovering the same pattern of thought recurring . . . throughout the centuries," a pattern grounded in "the all-embracing ancient and Christian tradition which is at the bottom of all the main European languages."[14]

The general outline of their disagreement is clear. To Spitzer's mind, Lovejoy wrote history (*Geschichte*) analytically, without the unifying element of *Geist.* The nub of their mutual incomprehension was

---

[13] "Reflections on the History of Ideas," *Journal of the History of Ideas* 1 (1940): esp. pp. 20, 22.
[14] *Classical and Christian Ideas of World Harmony,* pp. 3, 7.

Spitzer's habit of thinking about the past mimetically: that is, in terms of a recurrent pattern of thought that had lost ground in European culture since the Enlightenment, but to which he himself gave his allegiance. This philosophically ingrained habit led him to methods of analysis and synthesis that Lovejoy found uncongenial.

Like Spitzer, Auerbach wrote under the conviction that the peoples of Europe had shared, until lately, "a common substrate of classical and Christian civilization." The implications of Auerbach's analysis were spelled out by his reviewers, and most acutely by those bred in the same institutional and intellectual traditions as himself.[15] They

---

[15] *Literary Language and its Public in Late Latin Antiquity and in the Middle Ages,* trans. Ralph Manheim (New York, 1965), p. 5.

One reviewer, Friedrich Gogarten, did consider the importance of Auerbach's book for students of historiography. See F. Gogarten, "Das abendländische Geschichtsdenken: Bemerkungen zu dem Buch von Erich Auerbach 'Mimesis,'" *Zeitschrift für Theologie und Kirche,* 51 (1954), pp. 270–360. The bulk of this article is one theologian's summary of Auerbach's book, with an emphasis on the concept of historicity, rather than on strategies for change at work in historical processes. In his concluding sections, Gogarten turned to two questions that Auerbach's interpretation raised for him. Did Auerbach's discussion of figuralism imply that a Christian understanding of history was possible only with the help of figural interpretation? Gogarten invoked the example of Luther to illustrate that other possibilities existed. Did its lack of figural interpretation mean that modern realism had detached itself both from Christian belief and from the concept of history? His inquiry into the idea of progress convinced Gogarten that neither conclusion accounted for possible syntheses of historicity and Christianity with the penumbra of modern realism.

The following reviews and essays have been especially helpful in establishing the position stated in the text above: E. Auerbach, "Epilegomena zu Mimesis," *Romanische Forschungen* 65 (1954): 1–18. R. R. Bezzola, review in *Zeitschrift für deutsches Altertum und deutsche Literatur—Anzeiger* 65 (1951): 77–85, with an addition by R. Gruenter, "Zu E. Auerbachs Begriff der mittelalterlichen Stilrevolution," ibid., 85–88. H. Dieckmann, review in *The Romanic Review* 39 (1948): 331–335. L. Edelstein, review in *Modern Language Notes* 65 (1950): 426–431. N. Fuerst, review in *Journal of English and Germanic Philology* 47 (1948): 289f. R. Mortier, review in *Revue belge de philologie et d'historie* 28[1] (1950): 189–192. C. Muscatine, review in *Romance Philology* 9 (1955/56): 448–457. W. Naumann, *Modern Philology* 45 (1947–48): 211f. A. Oras, review in *Journal of English and German Philology* 53 (1954): 444–448. F. Schalk, *Deutsche Vierteljahrschrift für Literaturwissenschaft und Geistesgeschichte* 24 (1950): 281–285. H. E. Wedeck, review in *Latomus* 13 (1954): 610–613. R. Wellek, review in *Kenyon Review* 16 (1954): 299–307. Difficulties in Auerbach's theory of style were also taken up by E. C. Witke, in his review of Auerbach's *Literatursprache und Publikum in der lateinischen Spätantike und in Mittelalter,* *Speculum* 34 (1950): 443. An article by C. Breslin, "Philosophy or Philology: Auerbach and Aesthetic Historicism," *Journal of the History of Ideas* 22

welcomed and praised his work as a literary *tour de force* of the first magnitude, and still they found that Auerbach had illustrated propositions without proving them. His own book was a representation of historical reality, but was it an accurate one?

Auerbach had written about perennial enigmatic relations between nature and art, but he did not intend to tell the story of mimesis from the historian's point of view. The scant attention that the work received from historians and in historical journals corresponds with nature and content. Certainly, *Mimesis* deals with texts of historical importance. Its argument is that, as a representational art, literature provides a measure for the ways in which cultures perceive reality and that Western literature displays two decisive changes in perception. The first came about through Christianity, which discarded classical levels of style. "It was," Auerbach wrote, "the story of Christ, with its ruthless mixture of everyday reality and the highest and most sublime tragedy, which had conquered the classical rule of styles."[16] The result was that actual events came to be regarded as having two kinds of reality, the one, concrete and temporal, the other figural and ageless. The second break, Auerbach argued, came in the nineteenth century, with another revolt against the classical levels of style. All that was doctrinaire in literary cannons was rejected; the banal, or ugly, facts of daily life were taken up as significant in and of themselves and worthy of *belles-lettres;* and, finally, by the mid-twentieth century, the concept of reality had dissolved "into multiple and multivalent reflections of consciousness," a stage of literature that, Auerbach argued, signaled the decline of the European world and even "hatred of culture and civilization."[17] This viewpoint was not unfamiliar in historical writing after Schopenhauer, nor was it surprising in a man who had escaped from Hitler, and who, among fellow refugees in Istanbul, was watching the horrific course of World War II. The difficulty was that the evidence did not match his pattern of history.

Auerbach claimed that he had deliberately avoided imposing *a priori* definitions on the materials, preferring to let definitions emerge gradually and naturally from discussion. But it was apparent that, perhaps against his own will, he had tailored his evidence according to "certain philosophical ideas which [were] far from being casual and

---

(1961): 367–381, is helpful in placing Auerbach in the context of nineteenth- and twentieth-century intellectual history.

[16] *Mimesis,* p. 555.   [17] Ibid., 551.

[could] not have been derived from the texts themselves."[18] The burden of objections concerned the method of stylistic analysis that Auerbach applied. The method, reviewers pointed out, was admirable for exposing the content of individual texts, but it left the way open to—indeed, it invited—subjective and presentist judgments by the author. Thus, they continued, Auerbach had dealt with his evidence in a one-sided and sometimes arbitrary fashion. He neglected the "value of traditional forces in style," disparaged or ignored conservative impulses and movements (as in modern German literature), and paid no attention at all to the cross-fertilization of opposite tendencies within Western culture, and even in the minds and works of individual authors. In short, like many others, he found what he went looking for. He cast his materials in his own aesthetic norms, and trimmed away the variety that actually existed and that gave no support to his guiding principles. Finally, it was observed that the method of stylistic analysis militated against any continuous narrative sequence, breaking it up into fragments that had remote, obscure connections, and rendering his book a collection of monographic essays on isolated texts that had little or nothing to do with each other.

As historiographical materials, these criticisms, and Auerbach's response, identify the source of Auerbach's philosophical stance. Though his commentators repeatedly berated Auerbach for the elusiveness of his definitions, they agreed that, on balance, he conceived of "reality" in a narrow sense, as "historical," "problematical," "existential," and "tragic." He thus excluded most of the six kinds of reality that one reviewer identified in medieval literature,[19] not to mention the Platonic concept of reality with which the mimetic tradition began, and modern conceptions of existence as something intensely personal, opposed to the "anonymous, collective forces of history."[20] But his restrictive definition and method of analysis locate Auerbach in the orbit of phenomenologists.

Accordingly, his definition and method give a relatively exact meaning to Auerbach's own statement that (like Spitzer) he wrote out of the tradition of *Geistesgeschichte*. The long friendship with the theo-

---

[18] H. Dieckmann, in *The Romanic Review* 39 (1948): 333. Dieckmann had some insight into Auerbach's cast of mind, since the men had been colleagues in the seminar of Romance Philology at Istanbul. See *Travaux du seminaire de philologie romane*, I (Istanbul: Istanbul State University, 1937).

[19] C. Muscatine, *Romance Philology* 9 (1955/56): 454.

[20] R. Wellek, in *Kenyon Review* 16 (1954): 305f.

logian, Rudolf Bultmann, of which Auerbach was justifiably proud,[21] had a strong intellectual content. To both men, *Geistesgeschichte* meant a comprehensive approach to cultural life. Auerbach traced it to Hegel and the German Romantic philosophers. But it centered, above all, on a hermeneutic method first developed by a colleague of Hegel at Berlin, Friedrich Schleiermacher, a method later recast and transmitted by Dilthey and his followers to the generation of Spitzer, Auerbach, and Bultmann.

The metaphoric vocabulary of mimesis, and its dialectical tension between archetype and copy, is a pronounced characteristic of this academic school. Auerbach trained to practice law before he decided upon a career in philology, and the hermeneutic method may well have struck resonances with the lawyer's analysis of cases. At any rate, it is striking to find in Schleiermacher some of the very traits reviewers considered impairments in the historical value of Auerbach's work: for example, the view that the task of scholarship was not to discover, but to reconstruct reality; the subjectivity—the divinatory intuition—by which a scholar can assume that he understands a text better than the man who wrote it;[22] the assurance with which the hermeneutic circle permits one to pare away a work to its essentials[23]; and the willingness to reconstruct an entire work of art from any random fragment,[24] a whole culture from a single text or even an excerpt of a text, or, in Spitzer's case, from the history of a single, telling word.

One thing divided Auerbach from Schleiermacher and Bultmann. He practiced *Geistesgeschichte,* one reviewer observed, but he had lost faith in *Geist.* Or, as another wrote, "He shows, indeed, the weakness of a purely aesthetic approach to something that is more than aesthetic, which has the power of resting on a belief." *Geistesgeschichte* was by nature conservative: conserving "idealism, spirituality, heroism, individualism. That, for most of European literature, these things were the very objects of *realism* is a truth assiduously concealed in all the pages of *Mimesis.* "[25]

As the commentators on Auerbach's book kept saying, there were realities and, thus, kinds of mimesis that, for no obvious reason, he left

[21] *Romanische Forschungen* 65 (1954): 10 n. 13.

[22] R. Mortier, in *Revue belge de philologie et d'histoire* 28[1] (1950): 192.

[23] R. Bezzola, *Zeitschrift für deutsches Altertum und deutsche Literatur—Anzeiger* 65 (1951): 82–84.

[24] H. E. Wedeck, *Latomus* 13 (1954): 612.

[25] N. Fuerst, *Journal of English and Germanic Philology* 47 (1948): 290; W. Naumann, *Modern Philology* 45 (1947–48): 212.

unmentioned, and of which a historian would have to treat. Auerbach attributed some shortcomings of his book to the fact that he wrote it in Istanbul, where library collections for the task were limited. But there were compensations. He took advantage of the fact that one of his fellow émigrées in the seminar for Romance philosophy at Istanbul State University was Spitzer. There were other Western Europeans who could have forewarned him of the criticisms that his work eventually received. Another colleague was Herbert Dieckmann, who later wrote an especially penetrating review of *Mimesis*.

Ironically, one person who could have best understood the intricacies of Auerbach's subject was also one who would have most argued with his silence regarding the enigmatic equivalences between nature and art. There was a double irony, for the man did substantially help Auerbach. As it happened, the papal representative in Istanbul at the time gave whatever solace he could to refugees from the holocaust. He was himself a historian. How could he assist Dr. Auerbach? The Dominican monastery of San Pietro di Galata owned a complete set of Migne's *Patrology,* that vast collection of texts indispensable for mediaevalists. Mgr. Roncalli granted Auerbach access to the attic room that housed the monastic library, and it was there that the research on *figura* and *passio,* crucial to the argument of *Mimesis* was done.[26]

We know from his journal, and from the encyclicals that he issued as Pope John XXIII, that Roncalli held a concept of mimesis as a modeling process that made room for enigma and paradox and that, consequently, differed powerfully from Auerbach's in context, historical dimension, and applicability.

As to content, Roncalli's mimesis was quite independent of style. In fact, it was opposed to style, since it taught the persistence of enduring forms (chiefly moral) throughout every age from the beginning of the world. It was also anti-stylistic because the reality that was represented could not be found in the world of existential being; it was immutable, inexhaustible, and, most important, ineffable. Finally, mimesis was detached from style because it was not a way that an artist had to produce illusions or to share his perception with others. Instead, to Roncalli's thinking, it was a way of participating in an ultimate unity. He could have argued, against Auerbach, that mimesis must be understood not as an independent category, but as a function of that unity.

As to the historical dimension, Roncalli thought of mimesis as belonging to a way of life, laid down in Christian antiquity, practiced by

---

[26] *Romanische Forschungen* 65 (1954): 10 n. 12.

philosophers and mystics, elaborated through the ages, lived by himself and many others, and extending into the future. Because his concept of reality was identical with that of unity, he did not think that the career of mimesis charted the disintegration of the collective mind and spirit. Of course, what Auerbach called figural reality was part of Roncalli's daily life. He lived it when he meditated on the *Imitation of Christ,* when he practiced Loyola's *Spiritual Exercises,* and when he preached on the Gospel of John. Working in the shadow of Haghia Sophia, he deeply felt the pressure of historical continuity, all the more, since as Apostolic Delegate over Greece and Turkey, he was immediately identified with the regions where the philosophical bases of the mimetic tradition were laid by Plato and Aristotle, elaborated by their followers, recast by St. Paul, and systematized by Christian writers in the patristic age. But it was his hope and expectation for the future that gave meaning to the remote past and to his own labors. He would have agreed with Auerbach that Christology greatly altered the concept of mimesis. But he would have insisted that this did not occur because the life of Christ pitched the sublime at the level of simple, everyday events. Instead, to Roncalli's way of thinking, it occurred because the imitation of Christ involved historical progression on two levels: the biographical, where the central act was individual conversion, and the collective, where, through many individual conversions, the Body of Christ was continually enlarged.

Finally, as to application, mimesis as Roncalli understood it established moral goals for collective and for personal life. It was more than the object of detached study that Auerbach wished to present. Doctrines of mimesis informed Roncalli's thought about Church government, and more broadly about the origins and functions of social order. Partly under their impetus, Roncalli as pope drew a caesura across the history of the Church in his century. Those doctrines also prescribed standards of personal conduct, such as Roncalli acted on, in a small way, when he opened the library of San Pietro di Galata to Auerbach. The mutual repulsion between the ways in which the two contemporaries used mimesis to resolve the enigma of nature and art is crucial.

Lovejoy hinted that Spitzer wrote *Geist* without *Geschichte.* Spitzer found that Lovejoy wrote *Geschichte* without *Geist.* To his critics, Auerbach appeared to write *Geistesgeschichte* neither with *Geist* nor with *Geschichte.* I have drawn out a number of points that any inquiry into the historical career of mimesis would have to take into account, especially the various kinds of theoretical unity—in philosophy and religion—to which mimetic mediation between opposites was pegged, and the functions of mimesis in the self-critical and regenerative mechanisms by which the Western tradition procreated itself.[27] Evolution requires variety, cross-breeding, selection, and conflict. These are also features of the story I have told. Our inquiry has taken us into an area called by many names in the course of Western civilization, a space where opposites coincide in believable paradoxes, where man verifies the substance of things hoped for and the evidence of things unseen, a common space where advocates of different mimetic paradoxes have often found themselves at daggers drawn.

It may be useful to conclude this section by emphasizing how Spitzer and Auerbach can be said to have thought mimetically about the past. They thought mimetically in two essential ways. Their commitment to *Geistesgeschichte* (which, to be sure, they practiced differently) led them to insist on an organic wholeness in the world of culture, a wholeness maintained by a vast network of similitudes. They believed that the individual artist expressed both conscious and unconscious values of his culture. In the first place, therefore, Spitzer and Auerbach thought mimetically because they believed that things were mimetic. They reasoned as follows: a work of art (or even a scholarly book) was mimetic. It represented the ideas, desires, and skills of the artist; it represented a subject; it represented the creative process by which the artist formed it; and, finally, it represented collective aesthetic values, the tradition of mind and feeling out of which the artist worked and within which his achievement could be judged beautiful or not.

The second way in which they thought mimetically concerned the historian's act of creative imagination. The rule of wholeness applied to historical scholarship. Spitzer and Auerbach held that the work of the historian was synthetic. Assuming that a work of art expressed the vital signs of a past culture, they believed that the philologist, or the "historical semanticist," ought to recover those vital signs, both conscious and stated criteria of judgment and unconscious and tacit emotional responses that were expressed, and ritualized in the arts. The principles of *Geistesgeschichte* taught that the historian performed this

---

[27] On relation between *mythos* and *mimesis,* see P. Ricoeur, *The Rule of Metaphor: Multi-disciplinary Studies of the Creation of Meaning in Language* trans. R. Czerny et al. (Toronto, 1977), 244–246. See the very helpful discussion of paradox as a way of divining a hidden coincidence of opposites in R. L. Colie, *Paradoxia Epidemica. The Renaissance Tradition of Paradox* (Princeton, 1966), "Introduction: Problems of Paradoxes," 3ff.

task by re-living the aesthetic reactions that he was studying; that is, by an emphatic recovery of, and participation in, the past. In this act of recapitulation, he could achieve a historical synthesis—a vision of what Spitzer called "the total system of ideas charged with emotion that explains an historical movement." This concept of the mimetic historian naturally excluded detachment, as Spitzer indicated when he described his own scholarly commitment as an intense and total love.[28] It also entailed other assumptions about method that no one could accept if he were committed to critical standards set forth by Locke, Hume, or the French *Encyclopédistes*. A scholar of Lovejoy's philosophical commitments would have found that some of those assumptions ran counter to the most elementary principles of logic in evaluating evidence, and that they even undercut the most obvious feature of narrative, the chronological sequence of events.

On the Trail of the Mimetic Tradition

How can one think about a mimetic tradition, extending from classical antiquity to the present day? A bibliographical survey will suggest the range of possibilities considered in writing this book. I have borrowed the term, "mimetic tradition," from H.D.G. Kitto. In his Sather Lectures, Kitto explored mimesis as a principle of ancient Greek literature. In Aristotle's view, he argued, it was a method of composition by which an author made himself invisible and, through supreme artistry, gave the impression that the characters in an epic poem or a play were actually speaking for themselves, rather than (as they obviously were) speaking the mind of the author. This device made poetry—in literature and drama—an artificially distilled imitation of life.

Kitto observed that mimesis so defined was not "peculiarly Hellenic; what [was] peculiarly Hellenic [was] the fact that it was used so consistently" (*Poiesis. Structure and Thought* [Berkeley, California, 1966] esp. 23 ff. 244 f.). Through this consistency, mimesis became a tradition employed by Plato in some of his dialogues, as well as by poets and tragedians. It was not Kitto's purpose to examine what that persistence in style may have indicated about deeper levels of reason and emotion, and the subject of his lectures certainly did not take him

---

[28] Above notes 10, 11.

away from classical texts into the whirlpools and eddies along the broad sweep of European thought.

Another distinguished critic has, perhaps inadvertently, suggested what a complex picture might emerge if one traced the "mimetic tradition" into the twentieth century. Darko Suvin also used that term to identify the strange persistence of Aristotelian norms in Brecht's drama. By contrast with Kitto, Suvin did intend to describe the *longue durée*. He maintained that, during the nineteenth century, "bourgeois aesthetics" attenuated the relation between art and nature, without which the Aristotelian doctrine of mimesis made no sense. Brecht defined himself in opposition to Aristotelian drama. But a denial always bears witness to what is denied, and retains some of its features. Therefore, Suvin held, although Brecht claimed to have created a non-Aristotelian drama, he actually "took up and refashioned the mimetic tradition which middle-class aesthetic practice and theory had interrupted." Suvin represented the old mimesis with the metaphor of the mirror, and Brecht's with that of a dynamo (enlarging, tacitly, Henry Adams's contrast between the Virgin and the Dynamo), and he provided a checklist of "illusionistic and individualistic aesthetic attitudes" that pertained to pre-Brechtian mimesis, and of "critical and dialectical aesthetic attitudes" that pertained to Brecht's. ("The Mirror and the Dynamo," in L. Baxandall ed., *Radical Perspectives in the Arts* [Baltimore, 1972], esp. 72–76. See also the important discussion of mimesis by S. Morawski, "What is a Work of Art?," in the same anthology, pp. 324–370.)

These studies portray mimesis as a technique of art, practiced differently during various periods. Their conclusions are important for my argument that mimesis was an age-old strategy, expressed in many styles through the centuries. However, I would emphasize the continuity of the classical tradition rather more than either Suvin or Morawski. And, in so doing, I take a line of argument different also from those who have maintained that classicism was a primary characteristic of the mimetic tradition. Valuable statements of this position, with regard to rhetoric, occur in A. Duhamel, "Mimesis and Persuasion from Aristotle through the Eighteenth Century: Some Recent Studies," *Medievalia et Humanistica,* n.s. 4 (1973), 195–202 (a review article), and K. Martin, "From 'Mimesis' to 'Fantasia': The Quattrocento Voculabury of Creation, Inspiration and Genius in the Visual Arts," *Viator,* 8 (1977), 347–398. I have been dealing with mimesis as a concept that demanded not the rigidities of classicism, but continual invention and rivalry, as part of imitation, and that extended to all the literary and visual arts, and ultimately to the great integrative enterprises of philosophy and theology.

This approach has suggested lines of inquiry rather different from those followed by Richard McKeon in "The Philosophic Bases of Art and Criticism," in R. S. Crane ed., *Critics and Criticism* (Chicago, 1957), pp. 191–273, a splendid monograph reviewing the idea of imitation as a tool of poetic criticism used by philosophers from Plato to John Dewey. McKeon returned to the subject, with the same rigor and scope in "Imitation and Poetry," in Richard McKeon, *Thought, Action, and Passion* (Chicago, 1954), pp. 102–227.

Our emphasis on rivalry in mimesis points toward other perspectives on the course of Western culture. With rare insight, René Girard had this emphasis in mind when he wrote: *"To double business bound:" Essays on Literature, Mimesis and Anthropology* [Baltimore, 1978], 7, 201, and *passim.*)

Mimetic rivalry is one aspect of the persistence of the classical tradition, the study of the literatures of ancient Athens and Rome that continued into the twentieth century to be a standard part of the educational curriculum. But the word "classicism" evokes connotations of tranquility, balance, and order. It is hard to believe that rivalry has a place in the classical tradition, a place that justified Blake in exclaiming "The classics! It is the classics, and not Goths nor Monks, that desolate Europe with wars!"[29] I have reached this unfamiliar position with much assistance, which should be acknowledged.

Any essay on the theme of mimesis naturally owes much to the magisterial works of Auerbach and Lovejoy. The material covered by the present work is more heterogeneous than that studied in either. In the text above, I have discussed Auerbach's book, *Mimesis: The Representation of Reality in Western Literature.* In it, he demonstrated ways in which literature, the works of individual artists, reflected cultural views of reality that changed from the Old Testament to Virginia Wolff. The models of reality changed and so, consequently, did testimonies to them. But Auerbach was concerned with the act of mimesis in the literary imagination, rather than with the history of the strategy, as in the central areas of cosmology, epistemology, and ethics. Consequently, the aspects of historical structure and function fell outside the scope of what he chose to do. The same is true of his illuminating discussion of mimesis in *Dante, Poet of the Secular World* (tr. R. Man-

---

[29] *Prophetic Writings* (Oxford, 1926) 1: 640.

heim [Chicago, 1961]), and his even more concise and penetrating analysis, "Figura," in *Scenes from the Drama of European Literature: Six Essays* (New York, 1959). Lovejoy portrayed a learned convention shared by cosmology and literature, one that disintegrated in early modern times as a result of discoveries in astronomy, botany, and biology. The account presented here differs both from his work and from Auerbach's, first, in dealing with a cultural tradition instead of a literary or scientific convention, and, second, in describing the persistence of a tradition, the first time after the Greco-Roman culture to which it was indigenous had died, and, again, after its content had changed through innovations in many branches of inquiry from the sixteenth century onward. As I have tried to show, it is important to realize that the mimetic concepts underlying the understanding of life that Lovejoy excellently described outlived the cosmology treated in his book and reappeared, flourishing, in historical idealism. The story that I have to tell, therefore, is not the decline and fall of a tradition, but its transformation.

I also owe a certain debt to the study of Herschel C. Baker, *The Dignity of Man: Studies in the Persistence of an Idea* (Cambridge, Mass., 1947. Reprinted as *The Image of Man,* N.Y., 1961). Unlike the other authors who were driven by the Second World War to consider the Western tradition bankrupt, Baker chose to reaffirm the tradition of humanism in this book. His major argument is that the ideal of man arose among the pre-Socratic philosophers, achieved a distinct—and as it turned out a permanent formulation—in Plato's philosophy and, enriched by Christian theology at various moments thereafter, continued until the Reformation. The ideal postulated a divine element in man that distinguished him from other creatures: reason, a capacity for knowledge that would elevate a man's inner life by reproducing in his private consciousness the permanent and unchanging order of things. Beginning at the latest in the sixteenth century, this ideal and the tradition that conveyed it were subjected to increasingly severe examination. They both survived, but as the center of running debate, rather than as commonly acknowledged linch-pin of culture. While I agree with Baker on many points, I suggest that his account omits, or discounts, three major elements: (1) the centrality of the pararational to the ideals of man, (2) discontinuities before the Reformation, (3) the degree to which, as Fanon put it, the humanities oppose humanity, in the sense of Rousseau or, more recently, in the very different contexts set by Fanon himself and Heidegger.

Of course, individual moments in the history of the tradition have been sharply defined. The insistence that life had shape issued from Platonism; it therefore dealt with the doctrine of ideas, especially that of Beauty. From this standpoint, three German scholars in the 1920s and 1930s examined the concept of mimesis. They had a common background in the theory of historical ideas developed by Humboldt and Ranke in the first half of the nineteenth century and perpetuated through educational institutions under the label *Ideengeschichte*. In meticulous detail, Ernst Cassirer examined human creativity as a philosophical problem in his essay, "Eidos und Eidolon: Das Problem des Schönen und der Kunst in Platos Dialogen," *Vorträge der Bibliothek Warburg*, 2 (1922/23) 1-27. This work crystallized Cassirer's own philosophical position that all the works of high culture (including language, myth, religion, political thought, institutions, and science, as well as art) reflect collective ideals. When he published this essay, Cassirer was in the process of writing a systematic and comprehensive exposition of that approach to human culture (*The Philosophy of Symbolic Forms*). The Neo-Kantian idealism that it expressed marked Cassirer's later studies of Renaissance and Enlightenment philosophy, of humanistic education in the nineteenth and twentieth centuries, and of the origin of totalitarian political ideology.

Cassirer's essay on the Platonic idea of Beauty inspired the second scholar, Erwin Panofsky, to compose a brief, but exemplary, account of idealism in the theory of art from Plato into the seventeenth century (*Idea: Ein Beitrag zur Begriffsgeschichte der älteren Kunsttheorie* [Leipzig, 1924]). This work, like Cassirer's essay, appeared under the auspices of the Warburg Institute, and, in dealing primarily with art theory rather than with actual works of art, it expressed the purpose of the Institute: to encourage the study of culture in its widest scope. Panofsky drew together poetic, philosophical, and theological materials. He was able in a concise and illuminating way to describe a change in the meaning of the word "idea" within a continuous literary tradition. His account had a particular value in that it demonstrated a mutation in art theory that corresponded with the change in the meaning of "idea" in philosophy, from Plato to Locke, and this coincidence was later reinforced in the area of literary criticism by Auerbach in his study of mimesis.

The third scholar of this group was Werner Jaeger. He wrote his magisterial study *Paideia* from a point of view much like Cassirer's. In that work, he considered the transformation of Greek (and specifically Athenian) culture from the archaic period to the mid-fourth century. Plato dominates his account and his analysis. For, like Cassirer, Jaeger considered branches of human creativity—such as epic poems, dramas, and philosophical treatises—to be expressions of cultural ideas. His theme was the growth of those ideals from elements already present in Homer through Athens' struggle against Persia, and their testing in the Peloponnesian War. Crisis produced moral uncertainty. Plato's theory of Ideas was the complete statement and definitive affirmation of the inherited values to which, through discipline, the individual soul and actual society were to be educated. In a later study, Jaeger described the persistence in Christian thought of this view that there were universal models with which individuals and societies had, by nature, to conform, and that conformity was achieved through established patterns of education by which the soul was shaped (*Early Christianity and Greek Paideia* [Cambridge, Mass., 1961]).

The present work has drawn extensively on *Ideengeschichte* as exemplified and practiced by Cassirer, Panofsky, and Jaeger. They defined the major issues: What is man's nature? How does his work express that nature? What relation is there between a man, singular, and man in the aggregate, as society? What does human creativity mean? What is it worth? They also set down answers to those questions, within Platonic categories, and illuminated changes in idealism in some areas of thought and in some specific societies.

The three scholars were concerned with the change of elements in a philosophical tradition that ramified into art and literature. Their work suggested that it was possible to inquire into a yet more fundamental problem: the transformation of the tradition itself. Two further works have been germane to that particular issue and hence to the substance of the present essay. The first of them is Gerhart B. Ladner's *The Idea of Reform: Its Impact on Christian Thought and Action in the Age of the Fathers* (Cambridge, Mass., 1959). The subject of this work is precisely innovations brought into the Platonic tradition by Christian doctrine. Mimesis is an important element in the distinction that Ladner draws between the doctrine of reform and other, pre-Christian concepts of change. In contrast with other theories, Christian reform doctrines consisted of three elements that authors differently emphasized: man's return to a lost paradise, the restoration of man's image-likeness to God, and the establishment, on earth, of a society representing the heavenly kingdom of God. Ladner devotes considerable attention to these doctrines as they were interpreted by the Greek Fathers, especially Origen and Gregory of Nyssa, and he describes the emergence of differences between the Eastern view of mimesis and the Western, as most completely enunciated by Augustine. These differences derived, in large part, from a special emphasis by Western authors not only on man's inherent likeness to God (or to Christ as the Word of God) but also as the new formation of his soul through a likeness to the crucified and glorified Christ. From this it followed that, in Western theology, mimesis gained practical, disciplinary aspects that it did not have in the East, even though Greek theologians framed doctrines of the Empire and the Church as copies of the heavenly kingdom. Those disciplinary aspects appeared in monastic institutions of penance, as recast by Augustine and disseminated by followers and adapters of his *Rule.* They taught institutional reform as a part of the total mimetic scheme of things. The development of a doctrine of Church reform as such did not occur until the eleventh century; it achieved full articulation in the thirteenth and fourteenth centuries. But, in the period reviewed by Ladner, there already existed elements that later theologians systematically worked out, and that hinged on a relation between personal rebirth (or renewal) and institutional reform, a relation that was, in some respects, analogy and, in others, identity. Ladner defined reform as characterized by a "belief in inerradicable terrestrial imperfection," and by a "relative perfectibility the extent of which is unforseeable" (p. 31). The great contributions of his book to the present study are that he established the relation of reform, so defined, to mimesis and that he also demonstrated the connection, in Western thought, between the teleology of personal renewal and that of institutional reform.

For my purposes, it is important to mention also the seminal contribution that Ladner made in his short, but rich, study, *Ad Imaginem Dei: The Image of Man In Mediaeval Art* [Latrobe, Pa., 1966], with a bibliography covers the patristic and early mediaeval periods. In the first sentence of this lecture, Ladner made the vital connection between Christian art and the fact that the keystone of Christian theology, the Incarnation, rendered visible the "Image of the invisible God." Subsequently, he related changes in the ways in which artists portrayed the human form with innovations in theology during the twelfth and thirteenth centuries.

Ladner's research took him into an area untouched by the other authors whom I have mentioned: an area not merely of political thought but also of government. One of his distinctions in that area has a bearing on my discussion. He distinguished sharply between the idea of reform and that of revolution. He had in mind some very broad discussions of the latter idea; he intended to correct what he took to be a distorted perspective that represented theories of fundamental and inevitably destructive change as primary in Western thought. And yet other authors have perceived that reform and revolution are not mutually exclusive and that, in fact, many reforms may cumulatively produce—and may be planned to produce—a radical change of social order.

The second book that deals with the metamorphosis of the mimetic tradition is Charles Trinkaus's study, *"In Our Image and Likeness": Humanity and Divinity in Italian Humanist Thought,* 2 vols. (Chicago, 1970). As this historical sketch has already indicated, the Renaissance was a pivotal moment in the transformation of the tradition. Trinkaus described the very ample and complex materials out of which that change came, a change that was essential to the development of revolution as an Idea in the Platonic sense. Though he was not precisely concerned with mimesis, as the imitation of absolute, abstract ideas, Trinkaus dealt with the content of the mimetic tradition and with the strategy of mimesis as considered by some leading Italian writers in the fourteenth and fifteenth centuries. The men he described were caught in tension between inherited convictions and the actual world, or rather between two components of their own knowledge, the secular and the ecclesiastical. In the sixteenth century, Protestants took one option, according to Trinkaus's interpretations, by breaking with inherited institutions and the ideologies that sustained them. Catholics strove for a resolution of incompatible elements, sometimes with daring and potentially destructive results.

In the period under review, Trinkaus described how some humanists attempted to resolve the tension between the old wisdom and new experience by going back to the fundamental tenet that man was made in the image and likeness of God. He was such, in his creativity, and, as they circled around the problem of change and continuity, they unfolded an approach to the totality of human achievement in which all events, good and evil, reproduced the divine creative act and, in some ways, continued that act and advanced it to higher and higher levels of perfection.

The humanists discussed by Trinkaus reaffirmed traditional theology in their emphasis on continuity and in their adherence to inherited wisdom. They repeated the ambiguity that man was exalted because of his inherent divinity and bestial in his depravity and in the misery of his life. They had recourse to the creation of man and to the Incarnation of God (as a second creation) in defining the problem of giving form. They scrutinized, quoted, and edited writings of the Church Fathers, and they practiced ingenious methods of allegory by which they could explain Christian doctrine and pagan mythology as testimonies to the same truth. All this was drawn from old convention, stretching back through the twelfth century. Even their principal emphasis on the will, and not the reason, as the creative faculty derived from Augustine and developed in conflicts between rationalist and voluntarist branches of scholastic philosophy. But the result of their efforts to reconcile incompatibles was new in that it combined the Platonic doctrine of transcendent form (or Ideas) with a doctrine of immanence in such a way as to identify God, not with changelessness, as Plato had done, but with historical transition.

One of the major effects of the present study is precisely to draw together the two moments of change described by Ladner and Trinkaus and to establish a connection between the pre-Christian philosophy of mimesis, the Christian theology of personal redemption and institutional reform, and the ideology of revolution forecast in the historical thought of the Renaissance.

I have argued that mimesis belonged to a self-critical strategy of thinking that persisted, in many forms, throughout the nineteenth century. Other writers have not defined mimesis in this way, and, consequently, they have read the later history of the concept differently.

For example, historians of literature agree that the late eighteenth and the early nineteenth centuries were a decisive moment for mimesis as an artistic conception. Here, Auerbach's study, *Mimesis,* must again take pride of place. Auerbach described that time as summing up a series of changes that began in the early modern period. In the late eighteenth century, he found, the concept of literature as reflecting timeless ideals was rejected. Instead, literature was seen as representing everyday events that expressed distinctive psychologies of individual persons, and this was followed, in the mid-nineteenth century, by a realism that portrayed man, including members of lower social orders, as situated in a total political and economic context. Finally, there occurred a change from mimesis of reality as the historical situation of man to that of reality as a stream of consciousness in the mind of the author. John Boyd held that the story had a more abrupt end. Mimesis, as a formal concept, ceased to be employed in the eighteenth century. Dr. Johnson attempted to translate mimesis of stable forms into mimesis of form in process, in imitation of life as it was lived. But, in Boyd's view, Johnson's experiment was neutralized by the Enlightenment's dehumanizing rationalism (John S. Boyd, *The Function of Mimesis and Its Decline* [Cambridge, Mass., 1968]). Finally, M. H. Abrams had described the gradual exclusion of mimesis—between art and nature—as a guiding conception in the arts during the eighteenth century, and the supplanting of the view of poetry as a representation of the world with that of it as one of the poet's own spirit or mood. He also described a change in the generation of Wordsworth and Coleridge by which metaphors describing artistic creation were transformed, and the artist's mind, instead of being compared with a passive mirror, was characterized as an active force, a lamp, fountain, or growing plant. Abrams regarded this shift from one set of images to another as "a convenient index to a comprehensive revolution in the theory of poetry and of all the arts" (*The Mirror and the Lamp: Romantic Theory and the Critical Tradition* [New York, 1953] esp. 53).

My own review of the evidence indicates that all these metaphors—mirror, lamp, plant, and so forth—were present in the mimetic tradition at least from Plotinus's day onward. Some of them were ascendant over others from time to time, and the meanings attached to them altered. Abrams recognized their remote antecedents, but came to an appraisal of the evidence different from mine. For reasons stated above, I suggest that the metaphorical innovations of the early nineteenth century did not amount to the death of a tradition or to its abrupt replacement by unprecedented figures of speech. Even the metaphor of the machine, which injects a tone of sparkling modernity into eighteenth-century understandings of man's place in the world, had a direct antecedent in the scholastic concept of the *machina mundi*.

For examples in the application of the analysis of metaphor to the history of culture, I have looked to works by Northrop Frye (especially, *Anatomy of Criticism* [Princeton, 1957]), *Fables of Identity: Studies in Poetic Mythology* (New York, 1963), to philosophical discussions like that of D. Berggren, "The Use and Abuse of Metaphors," *Review of Metaphysics*, 16 (1962/63), 237–258, 450–472, who emphasizes that metaphorical thought is inevitable in the natural sciences as well as in religion and metaphysics, and to rhetorical studies like those by Owen Barfield, *Poetic Diction: A Study in Meaning* (London, 1952); and *Speaker's Meaning* (Middletown, 1967).

On the rhetorical background of nineteenth-century historical thought and the varieties of analysis that it inspired, particularly with reference to metaphor, a work of unusual value is Hayden V. White's book, *Metahistory. The Historical Imagination in Nineteenth-Century Europe* (Baltimore, 1973). The point to be made is that while mimesis as a formal technique of rhetoric may have declined in the eighteenth and nineteenth centuries, ancient habits of metaphorical thinking persisted. They were deeply ingrained in the European cultural tradition and, along with them, there flourished the restless, self-critical strategy of mimesis.

A large number of other miscellaneous works illuminate particular moments, themes, and idioms of the mimetic tradition. A few examples will suffice.

With regard to political mimesis, the works of Ernst Kantorowicz are normative, and they have suggested a number of lines of inquiry followed in the present essay.

A specific instance in which the imitation of nature by art was invoked as a legal principle is discussed by Julius Kirshner, " '*Ars Imitatur Naturam*': A *Consilium* of Baldus on Naturalization in Florence," *Viator,* 5 (1974), pp. 289–331

On the Church Fathers, in addition to Ladner, with rich bibliographical references, see J. Heijke, "St. Augustine's Comments on 'Imago Dei,' " *Classical Folia,* Supplement 3 (1969). On the twelfth-century theology, consult R. Javelet, *Image et ressemblance au XIIe siècle, de saint Anselme à Alain de Lille,* 2 vols. (Paris, 1967); S. Otto, *Die Function des Bildbegriffes in der Philosophie und der Theologie des 12. Jahrhunderts* (*Beiträge zur Geschichte der Philosophie und der Theologie des Mittelalters,* XL, 1) (Münster, 1963). On Meister Eckhart, see the excellent essay by A. M. Haas, "Meister Eckharts mystische Bildung," in A. Zimmermann ed., *Der Begriff der Repraesentatio im Mittelalter. Stellvertretung, Symbol, Zeichen, Bild.* (Miscellanea Mediaevalia 13) Veröffentlichungen des Thomas-Instituts der Universität zu Köln (Berlin–New York, 1971), 113–138. Haas provides a most helpful bibliography on the mirror metaphor as employed by German mystical writers. Three other essays in the same collection are particularly germane to our discussion: R. Javelet, "La Réintroduction de la liberté dans les notions d'image et de ressemblance, conçues comme dynamisme," 1–34; M. Kurdzialek, "Der Mensch als Abbild des Kosmos," 36–76, esp. 57 ff, on the continuity of the Platonic structure of the soul in the Middle Ages; and J. Miethke, "Repräsentation und Delegation in den politischen Schriften Wilhelms von Ockham," 163–185. An illuminating discussion of mimesis in medieval literature is contained in F. Goldin, *The Mirror of Narcissus in the Courtly Love Lyric* (Ithaca, N.Y., 1967), with a helpful bibliographical review in the first chapter. In 1967, another excellent study on Narcissus appeared, with a wider chronological span than Goldin's work: L. Vinge, *The Narcissus Theme in Western European Literature up to the Early 19th Century* (Lund, 1967). Apart from the information that this work contains, the reader will discover much of interest in Vinge's methodological introduction, where the possibilities and the limits of *Stoffges-chichte* are considered.

Despite a general recognition of the mirror as a primary symbol in western thought, it has rarely been discussed iconographically, and even more rarely as a barometer of cultural change. There are very welcome exceptions. See, especially, H. Schwarz, "The Mirror in Art," *Art Quarterly,* 15 (1952), 96–118, and, also consult C. F. Hartlaub, *Zauber des Spiegels* (Munich: 1951); Elizabeth Lea and T. Frings, "Das Bild vom Spiegel und von Narziss," *Beiträge zur Geschichte der deutschen Sprache und Literatur,* 87 (1965), 40–200.

Index

idolatry, 37, 40, 71, 85, 101, 108, 139, 151, 153, 154, 173, 174
idols, 151, 241, 299
Image: of the Father, Christ as, 63, 68–70, 132, 165, 170, 172, 233, 248; of God, man as, 32, 35, 36, 40, 41, 59, 94, 99, 113, 162, 176, 179, 182, 189, 200, 208, 211, 217, 219, 233, 240, 242, 329, 353, 355, 393, 419, 420; of the One, 40. *See also* Christ; man
images, 59, 60, 62–65, 69, 72, 73, 81, 93, 99, 127n, 151, 159, 169, 173, 200, 226, 292, 297, 236, 238, 244, 245, 270, 271, 292, 338, 372, 379. *See also* epistemology
imitation, 8, 58, 70, 73, 100, 106, 111, 114, 127, 141, 155, 157, 165, 171, 172, 182, 189, 201, 270, 273–279, 281, 285, 286, 289, 290, 297, 298, 314, 317, 324, 333, 356, 380, 388, 389, 391–393, 404; bad, ix, xn, 8, 15, 59, 93, 101, 183, 189, 272, 277 (*see also* Satan); of Christ, 41, 42n, 45, 48, 54, 70, 71, 86, 89, 94, 110, 125, 127, 132, 154, 155, 165, 182, 184, 192, 202, 213, 217, 218, 223, 231, 234, 235, 301, 317, 322, 353, 354, 356, 357, 412; of Christ's humility, 189; of Christ's patience, 71; of the devil, 71, 86, 89, 189 (*see also* Satan); of the Divine, 28; of the divine creative act, 40; of faith, 157, 189 (*see also* Abraham); of the future, 41; of the Holy Spirit, 155; of malice, 183; of man, 94; of Moses, 38, 39, 40; of sin, 189; servile, ix, xi, xvi, 14, 266, 270, 276, 286. *See also* love
Incarnation, 46, 48, 80, 102, 122, 155, 156, 174, 180, 201, 207, 223, 234, 252, 322, 323, 395, 420. *See also* Christ
insanity, *see* madness
intellect, 33–35, 37, 141, 167, 170, 179, 185, 205, 220, 233, 240, 259, 290, 345. *See also* reason
Isaiah, 102, 104, 106, 110, 210

Jacob, 87, 365
James I (king of England), 295, 296
James Henry, 386
Jeremiah, 99, 102, 106, 110, 151
Jerome (monk of Bethlehem), 117
Jesus, *see* Christ
Jews, 33, 39, 40, 43, 52, 65, 80, 86, 88, 89, 91, 93, 101, 102, 109, 112, 124n, 127, 137, 153, 181, 316
Job, 71, 112, 332
John XXIII (pope), 354, 356, 357, 411, 412
John, Apostle, 56, 129, 186, 190, 298–300. *See also* John, Gospel of
John, the Baptist, 131, 154, 186
John, Gospel of, 66–75, 94, 185, 298–301, 322, 357, 371, 412
John of Damascus, xii
John of the Cross, 247
Johnson, Samuel, 272
Judah (son of Jacob), 63, 87n
Judas Iscariot, 72
Jupiter, 104
justice, 97, 106, 108, 205, 233, 236, 278, 290, 291, 292, 294, 295, 303, 354, 367

Kant, Immanuel, 258, 262, 281, 297, 304, 307–310, 314, 322, 327, 333, 396
Keble, John, 343
Kierkegaard, Sören, 260
kinesthesia, 57, 83. *See also* terror
Kleist, Ewald Christian von, 258
knowledge, *see* epistemology
Kropotkin, Peter Alekseevitch, 366

Lamarck, Chevalier de (Jean Baptiste Pierre Antoine de Monet), 387
La Rochefoucauld-Liancourt, Duc François Alexandre Frédéric de, 257
Lassalle, Ferdinand, 366
law, 157, 159, 171, 243, 257, 277, 280, 291, 299, 304, 308, 320, 324, 342, 348, 352, 361, 362, 384; of nature, 39, 241–243, 302, 305, 353, 355, 375. *See also* canons
Law, Mosaic, 37–39, 43, 44, 48, 86, 102–104, 197, 231, 344
Law, William, 253

Library of Congress Cataloging in Publication Data

Morrison, Karl Frederick.
   The mimetic tradition of reform in the West.
   Includes bibliographical references and index.
     1. Civilization, Occidental. 2. Europe—Intellectual
life. 3. Imitation. I. Title.
CB245.M64   909'.09821   81–47935
ISBN 0–691–05350–2   AACR2